D070009

THE IRELAND ANTHOLOGY

This book is published with the financial assistance of
An Chomhairle Ealaíon/The Arts Council, Ireland

NATIONAL UNIVERSITY
LIBRARY   SAN DIEGO

THE IRELAND ANTHOLOGY

Edited by Seán Dunne

Introduction and Notes by George O'Brien

St. Martin's Press ✹ New York

A THOMAS DUNNE BOOK.
An imprint of St. Martin's Press.

THE IRELAND ANTHOLOGY. All rights reserved. © Selection, the Estate of the late Seán Dunne, 1997. © Introduction and Notes, George O'Brien, 1997. Copyright in the selected writings is the property of the individual authors. Printed in Great Britain. No part of this book may be used or reproduced in any manner whatsoever without written permission except in the case of brief quotations embodied in critical articles or reviews. For information, address St. Martin's Press, 175 Fifth Avenue, New York, N.Y. 10010.

ISBN 0-312-18429-8

First published in Great Britain by Gill & Macmillan Ltd.

First edition

10 9 8 7 6 5 4 3 2 1

CONTENTS

Foreword   xi

Publishers' Note   xiii

Introduction   xv

Acknowledgments   xxix

Explanatory Notes   xxxi

Part I: The Place

Giraldus Cambrensis, *An island where human corpses exposed in the open do not putrefy*   1

Samuel Lewis, *Pre-Famine Parishes*   1

John Montague, 'Windharp'   4

Arthur Young, *Soil, Face of the Country and Climate*   5

Edmund Spenser, *A Dialogue of Irenius and Eudoxus*   7

Francis Stuart, 'Ireland'   11

Robert Lloyd Praeger, *Howth and Lambay*   11

E. Estyn Evans, *Soil and Blood*   14

Brendan McWilliams, *Valentia Observatory*   17

Daniel Corkery, *Quiet Desperation*   18

Deirdre Madden, *Dying of the Light*   20

Seamus Heaney, from 'Sweeney Praises the Trees'   21

E. Charles Nelson and Wendy Walsh, *Forest Clearance*   22

John Millington Synge, 'To the Oaks of Glencree'   24

Anonymous, 'The Blackbird by Belfast Lough', translated by Frank O'Connor   24

John Millington Synge, 'Winter'   25

Brendan Kennelly, 'Sea'   26

Richard Murphy, 'Pat Cloherty's Version of *The Maisie*'   27

Part II: Places Apart

Maurice Craig, *The Duke Returns*   33

Mr and Mrs S.C. Hall, *Dublin in the 1840s*   37

Chevalier de La Tocnaye, *Social Customs*   40

Dermot Bolger, *Moving to Finglas*   42

Anonymous, 'The Zoological Gardens'   44

Oliver St John Gogarty, 'An Offering of Swans'   44

Elizabeth Bowen, *Stephen's Green*   45

Brendan Behan, *Behan's Dublin*   48

Pettigrew and Oulton's Street Directory 1848, *Abbey-street, Lower*   50

William Trevor, *A Dream of Munster's Arcadia*   52

Richard Milliken, 'The Groves of Blarney'   55
Claud Cockburn, *Polio*   57
Sean O'Faolain, *Cork*   58
Francis Sylvester Mahony (Father Prout), 'The Bells of Shandon'   59
Irish Townlands: County Cork   61
Seán Dunne, *John's Park*   62
George O'Brien, *School Essay*   64
Dervla Murphy, *West Waterford*   67
Tomás Ó Criomhthain, *Our Houses*, translated by Robin Flower   70
William Makepeace Thackeray, *Killarney*   74
Desmond O'Grady, 'Tipperary'   76
Dennis O'Driscoll, 'Thurles'   78
Samuel Ferguson, 'Cashel of Munster'   80
Chevalier de La Tocnaye, *In County Limerick*   81
Kate O'Brien, *Summer with Charlie*   83
Anonymous, 'Garryowen'   85
Michael Coady, 'Stopping by a Clare Graveyard After Hours'   87
Micheál Ó Braonáin, 'The Shannon in Clare'   89
Derek Mahon, 'A Disused Shed in Co. Wexford'   90
Anonymous, 'The Streams of Bunclody'   93
Tony O'Malley, *Inscape — Life and Landscape in Callan and
    County Kilkenny*   94
Donal Foley, *Ferrybank*   98
Anonymous, 'The Curragh of Kildare'   102
John Millington Synge, *Glencree*   103
James Plunkett, *The Grand Canal*   105
Aidan Higgins, *Boyhood*   107
Oliver Goldsmith, 'Sweet was the sound . . .'   109
Frank O'Connor, *In County Meath*   111
Sir Jonah Barrington, *Duelling Extraordinary*   112
Thomas Moore, 'The harp that once through Tara's halls'   114
Dermot Healy, *Another Country*   115
David Thomson, *Twilight of the Big House*   118
Desmond Fennell, *Killala*   121
Tim Robinson, *Leviathan*   123
Reverend Alexander Synge, *Letter (1851)*   126
Richard Pococke, *Galway*   127
Somerville and Ross, *Connemara*   129
Liam O'Flaherty, *The Black Bullock*   132
Thomas Lavelle, 'The County of Mayo', translated by George Fox   135
Paul Durcan, 'Going Home to Mayo, Winter, 1949'   136
Francis A. Fahy, 'Galway Bay'   137

George Barker, 'Galway Bay'   138
William Makepeace Thackeray, *Clifden to Westport*   140
Michael Longley, 'On Mweelrea'   145
W.B. Yeats, 'The Wild Swans at Coole'   146
Lady Gregory, *From Her Journal*   147
John McGahern, *Why We're Here*   150
John Waters, *The Parable of the Fat Chieftain*   153
John Healy, *Emigration*   157
Colm Tóibín, *The Road to Darkley*   158
Patrick Kavanagh, 'Shancoduff'   162
Maurice Craig, 'Ballad to a Traditional Refrain'   163
Nell McCafferty, *A Welfare War*   164
Eamonn McCann, *The Provisional IRA*   166
Percy French, 'The Mountains of Mourne'   168
Art Mac Cumhaigh, 'Fair Churchyard of Cregan', translated by
    Seamus Deane   170
Sam McAughtry, *Funerals Have Lost Their Style*   172
George Sigerson, 'The Inniskillen Dragoon'   174
Polly Devlin, *Ardboe*   175
John Montague, 'Dancehall'   179
Nora Hopper Chesson, 'The Short Cut to Rosses'   180
Patrick MacGill, 'Going Home'   181
William Allingham, 'The Winding Banks of Erne'   182
Seamus Heaney, 'The Strand at Lough Beg'   185
John Hewitt, 'Ulster Names'; 'Postscript, 1984'   186

Part III: History
John Montague, 'The First Invasion of Ireland'   193
Geoffrey Keating, *The Origin of the Battle of Clontarf,* A.D. *1014* 194
Anonymous, 'The Viking Terror', translated by Frank O'Connor   196
Sean O'Faolain, *Terra Incognita*   196
Reverend E.A. D'Alton, *Battle of Kinsale*   199
Aodhaghán Ó Rathaille, 'Last Lines', translated by Frank O'Connor   201
Richard Murphy, from 'The Battle of Aughrim'   203
Jonathan Swift, *A Modest Proposal*   205
Eibhlín Dhubh Ní Chonaill, 'The Lament for Arthur O'Leary',
    translated by Eilís Dillon   207
Maria Edgeworth, *Sir Murtagh and His Lady*   214
John Philpot Curran, *August 15th, 1785*   218
Anonymous, 'The Wearing of the Green'   219
Anonymous, 'Rody McCorley'   220
P.J. McCall, 'Boolavogue'   222

John Keegan Casey, 'The Rising of the Moon'   223
Anonymous, 'The Sash Me Father Wore'   224
Anonymous, 'The Auld Orange Flute'   225
Robert Emmet, *Speech from the Dock*   227
Anthony Cronin, *The Bauld Robert Emmet*   230
Thomas Moore, 'She is far from the land'   235
Samuel Lewis, *Contents of a Village, 1837*   236
John Mitchel, *The Horrors of Famine*   237
N. Marshall Cummins, *The Great Irish Famine*   240
Eavan Boland, 'That the Science of Cartography is Limited'   251
Charles J. Kickham, *Burglary and Robbery*   253
Friedrich Engels, *Engels to Marx*   254
W.B. Yeats, 'Come Gather Round Me, Parnellites'   255
Elizabeth Bowen, *August 1914*   257
Jennifer Johnston, *Sailing to War*   260
T.M. Kettle, 'To My Daughter Betty, the Gift of God'   261
James Connolly, *Nationalism and Religion*   262
Proclamation of the Republic (1916)   264
Sean O'Casey, *Spirit and Flesh*   266
Hanna Sheehy Skeffington, *The First Raid*   268
Katherine Mansfield, *After the Rising*   269
W.B. Yeats, 'Easter 1916'   270
Ernie O'Malley, *Ambush and Aftermath*   272
J.J. Lee, *The Treaty*   275
Michael Collins, *Letter to Kitty Kiernan*   278
Eiléan Ní Chuilleanáin, from 'Site of Ambush'   280
P.F. Quinlan, *Remembering Seán*   281
Bernard Shaw, *Celt and Saxon*   283
Winston Churchill, *Dreary Steeples of Fermanagh and Tyrone*   285
Louis MacNeice, 'Neutrality'   285
Eamon de Valera, *From the Reply to Mr Churchill*   286
Andrée Sheehy Skeffington, *Censorship and Discreet Silence*   289
Noël Browne, *Levers of Power*   291
J.J. Lee, *Educational Revolution*   295
Nuala Ní Dhomhnaill, *The Corpse That Sits Up and Talks Back*   297
Paul Muldoon, 'Anseo'   300
Michael Hartnett, from 'A Farewell to English'   301
Michael Longley, 'The Linen Industry'   303
Tom Paulin, 'Of Difference Does it Make'   304
Vincent Buckley, 'Hunger-strike'   305
John Hume, *Reconciliation of the Irreconcilable*   309
Paul Muldoon, 'Ireland'   310

Benedict Kiely, *Afterword*   311
Frank McGuinness, *Enniskillen*   312
Mary Robinson, *A New Ireland*   315

Part IV: Religion
St Patrick, *Confessio*   319
Anonymous, 'The Deer's Cry', translated by Kuno Meyer   320
Lady Gregory, *Brigit, the Mary of the Gael*   323
Lady Gregory, *Columcille, Saint of the Gael*   323
Helen Waddell, *The Abbot Helenus and the Crocodile*   324
Anonymous, 'The Hermit's Song', translated by Kuno Meyer   325
Anonymous, 'The Trip To Rome', translated by Seán Dunne   326
Peter Fallon, 'The Rag-tree, Boherard'   327
Anonymous, 'To Christ the Seed', translated by Thomas Kinsella   328
Anonymous, 'A Charm for Love and Lasting Affection',
    translated by Thomas Kinsella   329
William Makepeace Thackeray, *The Pattern at Croaghpatrick*   330
Alexis de Tocqueville, *Interview with the Parish Priest at Tuam*   333
William Carleton, *Midnight Mass*   334
Mrs Cecil Frances Alexander, 'All Things Bright and Beautiful'   336
John Betjeman, 'Ireland with Emily'   337
Seán Dunne, *The Protestant Church*   339
Ian Paisley, *Open-air Preaching*   342
Frank Ormsby, 'At the Jaffé Memorial Fountain, Botanic Gardens'   344
Pope John Paul II, *Address in Dublin*   345
Paula Meehan, 'The Statue of the Virgin at Granard Speaks'   347
Patrick Kavanagh, from 'Lough Derg'   349
Seamus Heaney, 'In Gallarus Oratory'   351
Patrick Kavanagh, 'Having Confessed'   352

Part V: The Imagined Country
Anonymous, *The Fate of the Children of Lir*   357
Cúchulainn, from *The Táin*, translated by Thomas Kinsella   361
W.B. Yeats, 'Cuchulain Comforted'   363
Standish James O'Grady, *Fionn goes Hunting*   364
Anonymous, *The Pursuit of Diarmaid and Gráinne*, translated by
    Nessa Ní Sheaghdha   366
Michael Hartnett, 'The Hag of Beare (1969)'   369
St Brendan, *Jasconius*, translated by John J. O'Meara   372
Anonymous, 'Lament of Liadan', translated by Kuno Meyer   374
Anonymous, from 'The Land of Cockaygne'   375
Hubert Butler, from *The Eggman and the Fairies*   377

Flann O'Brien, *Casey and Sweeny*   381
Michael Hartnett, 'There Will Be A Talking'   382

Part VI: All Of Life Is There
Eamon Dunphy, *Italia '90*   387
P.D. Mehigan (Carbery), *Munster Final, 1944*   388
Bernard O'Donoghue, 'Munster Final'   391
Breandán Ó hEithir, *Footballers*   392
John Waters, *Lifting a Latch*   394
Anonymous, 'Two Fragments'   395
Laurence Whyte, 'Recitativo'   395
Chevalier de La Tocnaye, *Dublin Promenades*   400
Chevalier de La Tocnaye, *Drinking in Dublin*   401
Daibhí Ó Bruadair, 'A Glass of Beer', translated by James Stephens   402
Peter Somerville-Large, *The Anglo-Irish*   402
Molly Keane, *A Massive Statue*   405
Alice Taylor, *The Christmas Candle*   407
Jonathan Swift, 'O'Rourk's Noble Fare'   408
Myrtle Allen, *Ballymaloe Brown Bread*   409
Mrs Delany, *Caledon House*   411
Francis Ledwidge, 'June'   412
Brian Merriman, from 'The Midnight Court', translated by
    David Marcus   413
Anonymous, 'Love is Teasing'   417
Edna O'Brien, *I Brought It On Myself*   417
Samuel Beckett, *No Bone to Pick with Graveyards*   419
Anonymous, 'Keep Your Kiss To Yourself', translated by
    Lord Longford   420
Nuala Ní Dhomhnaill, 'Labasheeda (The Silken Bed)',
    translated by Michael Hartnett   421
W.B. Yeats, 'He wishes for the Cloths of Heaven'   423
Anonymous, 'I Am Stretched On Your Grave', translated by
    Frank O'Connor   423
Samuel Beckett, [I would like my love to die]   424
Geoffrey Keating, from *The Three Shafts of Death*, translated by
    Alan Harrison   425
John Banville, *A Murder*   426
Anonymous, 'A Father Keens His Drowned Child',
    translated by Patrick Pearse   429
John Millington Synge, *Keening*   430
St Columcille, 'The Sea-Blue Eye', translated by Seán Dunne   431
Shane MacGowan, 'The Body of an American'   432

Index of Contributors and Acknowledgments   435

FOREWORD

When Seán first developed the idea of a literary map of Ireland, he was clearly very excited about it. He wanted this anthology to be an informative journey into the archives of Ireland's cultural heritage. After much deliberation and discussion with me, he compiled the original list of contents. With his untimely death, it seemed unlikely that this book would be completed.

Some time after his death, Jonathan Williams approached me with the idea of seeing the publication through. We spent many hours going through the contents list and found that Seán, in his meticulous way of working, had earmarked clearly most of the pieces he wanted. There was no reason why this book should not go ahead; however we felt that an editor was needed for this type of book.

Seán had always admired George O'Brien's work and with this in mind, he was approached. From the very beginning George O'Brien acted with integrity and respect for Seán's ideas and for this I would like to thank him.

I would like to acknowledge assistance from the following: Cork Examiner, especially Dan Linehan; Cork City Library; Boole Library, University College Cork, especially Helen Davis.

Trish Edelstein

PUBLISHERS' NOTE

This anthology was to have contained three extracts from the work of James Joyce. They were the closing section of 'The Dead' from *Dubliners* and the opening pages of the Proteus and Aeolus episodes from *Ulysses*.

We are unable to reproduce these extracts because the James Joyce Estate has refused permission to do so. This refusal arises from the dispute between the Joyce Estate and Picador over the publication of the Reader's Edition of *Ulysses*, edited by Danis Rose, to which the Estate objects. Picador is an imprint of Macmillan London.

The Publishers of this anthology, Gill & Macmillan in Europe and St. Martin's Press in North America, are both part of the Macmillan group of companies. Gill & Macmillan is an independent associate company within the group; it has had no part in the publication of the disputed edition of *Ulysses*. St. Martin's Press is a subsidiary of Macmillan and controls the Picador imprint in North America. The Joyce Estate made it clear that it was unwilling to grant reproduction rights to any company associated with Macmillan.

We acknowledge that the Estate has the right to withhold permission; we equally regret that it has chosen to exercise this right. The dispute between the Estate and Picador is a specific matter which should not impinge on ordinary applications for reproduction of copyright material in other publications.

Literary estates have obligations as well as rights, not least a moral obligation to the wider literary community. It is difficult to discern what possible service is rendered by the refusal to permit quotation from the greatest of all Irish writers in an anthology such as this.

INTRODUCTION

i

On gloomy October afternoons and March evenings full of brittle light, the grown-ups of the house in which I grew up, in Lismore, Co. Waterford, sat with friends and neighbours around the big black range in the kitchen, smoking pipes and cigarettes, drinking tea and chatting without ceasing in subdued voices. I knelt on a chair at the table, bent over my long division homework, glad of the warmth and the company of the incomprehensible talk. Every so often, however, a phrase jumped out at me and I hankered for a moment after what had given rise to it. All the phrases that caught my ear had an air of finality (a grown-up speciality): so-and-so was 'the greatest thief unhung'; some other one was in for 'a rude awakening'; such-and-such act or statement had never been seen or heard in 'the length or breadth of Ireland'.

Banality though it was, this last phrase was the one which produced a complicated response. It wasn't only its finality that struck me, it was its obvious silliness. If length was a measurement of time, the phrase would pass muster, because the country did go back a long way. Not that how far it went back impressed me, particularly. After all, every country was old; it pretty much had to be. It wasn't time that was meant at all, however, but space, and as every schoolboy knew neither the length nor breadth of Ireland was anything to write home about. We were only four degrees of latitude (51° to 55° north) and five of longitude (5° to 10° west). Most Sundays we saw Texas ranches bigger than that on the screen of the Palladium. Any of the world's cities worth talking about had more people in them than there were in the whole of our little country. Think of the number of miles between places in France and Germany and even in England. There were no distances to speak of between our places, with the possible exception of Northern Ireland, which back then didn't count.

It was as if Ireland was an exception to everything. That made me squirm. And so did these grown-ups, who must have felt very small to think that Ireland was some sort of universe. At the same time, though, I couldn't help imagining how great it would be if the country had some sort of size or range or ampleness to it. Better yet — what if there was something other than miles and square miles, some unique and unsuspected extra dimension to give us stature? I kept wondering what this missing property might be. Or was it that I was missing something?

This was in the 1950s, when the discovery of Ireland was just getting under way.

As Ireland was first mapped by Ptolemy, the second-century astronomer, it doesn't make a lot of sense to say that it still awaited discovery eighteen hundred years later, especially since in the interval the country had more or less made its name by entertaining the designs of all sorts of people coming into it. Yet discovery of a sort was what appeared to be going on. Busloads of tourists made their stately way around our little roads, their cheery waves conveying that they were as happy as the day was long and not at all concerned about either length or breadth, most unlike us. And it was not surprising that they smiled down on us. They were being shown things that we saw only on calendars. They were being put in the picture about land and locale, history and myth, varieties of faith and the different manners of society, everything that every day surrounded us without our ever having quite got to know it. Like rajahs on elephants, they lumbered through our somnolent summers. We even got used to it over the years.

But when the big bus waddled round the corner out of sight, I felt jealous. It wasn't just that I wanted to go with them. That was part of it, of course. The thought of being a fellow-traveller and to 'ooh' in awe at some great slab of mountain or a remote and rambling ruin was just about irresistible. That was the done thing, it seemed, and from the modest smirks of uplift that I had observed in visitors to Lismore Castle, it would undoubtedly do me the world of good. There would be afternoon tea in a hotel, too. The ham sandwiches and fairy cakes would not go amiss. And it would be interesting to see if other hotels smelled of oxtail soup like ours did.

But there would be more to my getting on the bus than simply gawking. There would be knowing as well — travellers are always in the know. Fine as seeing things would be, learning about them would be even better. I would find out if the Devil's Bit — the piece that appeared to be missing from the shoulder of a mountain in Tipperary's Slieve Bloom range — had really been torn out by the teeth of a giant, who then had spat it southwards, where it came to earth as the Rock of Cashel. When I went to Kerry and roved among the Macgillycuddy's Reeks, not only would I see Carrauntoohill, the highest mountain in Ireland. I would discover who Macgillycuddy was, and the reason why he reeked.

There had to be something behind all those castles and churches, the dark groves of trees, the empty moorland, the two large houses that stuck out at either end of so many villages. Otherwise, we might as well have been living in a postcard, behind whose sunny front there was just a blank. So when one of the few interesting items of the day disappeared in a cloud of petrol-blue exhaust fumes, not only was I envious, I also had an obscure, generalised, unfocused feeling of resentment. I badly wanted to be able to say something, offer something. But it was as if there wasn't anything that I could call my own. What little I did know — Church and State were Big Mammy and Big Daddy; England was iffy, America spiffy; if I was 'good', I'd get on — was not what I saw with my own eyes. But what I saw I had no way of thinking about. I was more of an outsider than the outsiders themselves.

I was a child. And all this was a long time ago. But the urge to know is still there, not so as to best the tourists, but to acknowledge that they are correct in their assumption that there is something worth knowing. Without them, the country might still be not quite visible; its textures, idiosyncracies, ancient stories, holy sites and scenic places might just be looked on as part of the commonplace, instead of occasions of relish and wonder and pride, which is what they become when filtered through the eyes of the lively and informed beholder. The evidence of such eyes is what *The Ireland Anthology* contains. A treasury of perspectives, a harvest of particulars, a mosaic of localities, here is a vade-mecum to the unique complexities of the length, breadth, height, depth and all the other much more subtle dimensions of the Irish experience.

ii

First, there's the look of the land and the lie of the land.

'To this day I can see Italy as a leg with a shoe on the end of it, and a bone going down the middle', writes Donal Foley, recalling the magical geography lessons in his father's school in Ferrybank, Co. Waterford. So maybe the visual aid when Ireland was the geographical subject was a bowl or a saucer, representing the ring of mountains round the coast and the flat interior that they enclose. Pleasingly homely as the piece of crockery may be, however, its accuracy is more apparent than real. The image it gives is too uniform, too consistent, too general. Of course, the topography of Ireland does consist of coastal heights and an inland plain. But it is also true that the west coast, with its islands and indentations, is so different from the virtually straight line of the east coast as to seem a deliberate contradiction of it.

Or take the words 'Central Plain'. At face value they might be taken as the name for an expanse of pasture or tillage, our own little prairie. But one of the plain's main features is bogland, a state of nature that has existed from a time before there was even husbandry, never mind landlords, owner occupiers or Eurocrats, and which persists despite them all, functioning not only as the source of the cash crop of turf but as a kind of aspic in which are such diverse objects as sacred vessels from ancient Christian Ireland and the carcasses of elks. And a good deal of what isn't bogland is made up of lakes. In fact, the name Central Plain has, to borrow a phrase of Dervla Murphy's, an 'un-Irish prosaicness'. The name is too broad, too plain; it has no intimate sense of locale about it. It's a reminder that Ireland may readily be described in terms of the typicality of its terrain, but that it is difficult to see it, or experience it, in terms of that typicality.

Rather, what's experienced is a proliferating sequence of small, densely packed, distinctive localities — the Ring of Kerry, Connemara, Inishowen, the Ards peninsula, the Boyne valley . . . Every county is a kind of extended neighbourhood of such places, discrete but connected, each existing in the light of its difference from anywhere else. And county boundaries are by no means a reliable guide to the extent of these neighbourhoods. Mostly they follow the fall of land as dictated by the course of a river or the lie of a mountain. Some have lost their boundaries, like the Decies in the Kilkenny–Waterford area. Others have had their boundaries newly invented, like Fingal in County Dublin.

The sky changes. Great cliffs of cloud roll in from the Atlantic, letting through light that seems like muslin. Then the clouds break up, throw shadows on the hills, release a shower of rain, and off they drift. The weather changes. The weatherman says the outlook is changeable. The days are showery, and there can be 'sun showers', when it rains while the sun is shining. The days are 'soft' or 'close'; sometimes the wind can be 'a bit stiff'. Often it clears up around four in the afternoon. In the summer there is not quite a midnight sun; it just stays light until closing time.

The sea is responsible for all this protean weather-play. It brings the climate that makes all those shades of green. Thanks to the Gulf Stream, there are palm trees in West Cork. The sea is the playground of seals, who are hosts to the souls of the dead, and of shellfish and sharks, and of Fungi, the Dingle dolphin. There's a great store of oil and gas currently being piped ashore from the seabed. An endless welcome mat of sandy beaches greets the sea. Here the white horses, as the breakers are called, make their presence known and litter the strands with seaweed, some of which is edible (dilisk) and some of which used to be dried and burned for fertiliser (kelp). Bird-life on the shoreline is various and abundant. Thanks to the sea, there are those western islands whose way of life and natural conditions are so detached from those of the mainland that the tempo of the days there and their rocky starkness make them seem the offspring of the ocean, anchored to the mainland only by their difference.

And then there's the landscape. Since Ireland has commonly been thought of as rural, a place where nature is in the ascendant and people are present largely as nature's caretakers and dependants, it is easy to overlook how the hand of man has continually shaped and changed the look of the land. This restless hand has been at work not merely in clearing the land for cultivation but in adapting it for other than agricultural purposes. The great neolithic mound at Newgrange, Co. Meath is a site of European significance. But other prehistoric peoples undoubtedly had their earthworks too, shaped hills to be smooth and round because curves were important to them, made humps and excavated hollows, moved rocks, created vistas and vantage points from which to view the stars in their courses and the equinoctial sun.

The motte-and-bailey enclaves built by the Normans moved the earth as well. Somebody made those irregular-shaped fields that stagger up the sides of those hills one sees when coming in to land at Shannon. Others contrived the quilt of fields that cling to the short, sharp slopes of County Monaghan drumlins. Ditches and double ditches have been laboriously banked up everywhere as boundaries. Granite and limestone were quarried to build the Big Houses of the gentry, and some of the quarries were worked out, abandoned, overgrown, but are part of the story of the landscape nevertheless. 'Bunmahon must be pierced with shafts!' declared the nineteenth-century patriot Thomas Davis, who was very much in favour of developing the country's natural resources along proper industrial-revolution lines. And in days gone by, the cliffs near the County Waterford village of Bunmahon were pierced with shafts and copper was extracted. The sites of the bore-holes are still visible and the cliffs are closed to walkers. Thirty miles or so to the west is the village of Tallow, whose name in Irish is Tullach an Iarainn, which means Hill of Iron, though nothing of iron remains. Peeking over the trees in the noted beauty spot of the Vale of Avoca, in County Wicklow, are the chimneys of smelters dating from when the area was the centre of Irish mining.

All these makers of the landscape are reminders of how what appears to be missing can be still extant in the Irish world, like the Famine road in Eavan Boland's poem 'That the Science of Cartography is Limited', like the declivities in certain fields that are Famine graves. Somebody made these too, as they did the disused canals and the now abandoned, overgrown paths of railways; as they planted the parklands of defunct estates; as they made the little lake behind Lismore Castle where South American water lilies, larger in circumference than tractor tyres, were introduced in the nineteenth century by the Duke of Devonshire.

Looking over the bridge in Lismore at the water-meadows in the shadow of the castle, it is possible to make out ridged lines of ground, forming a large square. In winter a hundred years ago, water from the river was let into that square to freeze and make a skating rink for the people of the town. Nobody remembers that now. Land and people are growing further apart in Ireland, because of urban drift and social mobility and television and all the other virtualities of modern life. But landscape, repository of transience, remembers.

iii

Land begets landscape; landscape begets place. The image of Ireland as a rural country undoubtedly runs deep in popular sentiment and cultural expression. But the reality one encounters when travelling any given ten-mile stretch of winding country road consists of not only white-washed farmhouses and the wind among the barley, red barns and blue hills on the horizon, but an equally eye-catching and much more intriguing abundance of very different types of human settlement. One bend of the road reveals where a once-great monastery stood, the next the remains of a Norman keep. The pub and filling-station at a crossroads is a place, and so is the Big House of a former landlord, glimpsed among the trees. There are barely visible remnants of Famine villages, deserted for reasons Goldsmith would have been unable to envisage. And there are places which are plainly visible but impossible to identify — townlands and parishes, lapsed but still remembered administrative districts like the barony of Muskerry in County Cork, ancient kingdoms such as Thomond of which the city of Limerick is the centre, tribal territories such as Breffni O'Rourke in County Cavan, old-fashioned but still functioning divisions of counties like the North and South Ridings of Tipperary. All coexist as though naturally, like so many wild-flowers in a hedgerow, without regard for, much less awareness of, each other, without even signposts.

Of all these divisions and subdivisions, each a unity in itself, distinct from but contributing to larger unities, the most fundamental is the one that also happens to be the least visible: the townland. The Ballinaspic, Macollop and Araglen that Dervla Murphy views in County Waterford are townlands. 'The name of our townland . . . is Muinterevlin', writes Polly Devlin, 'one of the thirty townlands that make up the Parish of Ardboe' in County Tyrone. But unless you are in the know within that parish, and have some business connected with the land there, it is very difficult to discover what the shapes and sizes of these townlands might be. There may be deep divisions between them. People on the high ground may not see the world in the same way as people on the bottom land. Access to woods and water can cause differences. Townlands are places with intricate borders. In them, custom and usage can be more powerful than law. Right-of-way goes back generations. Country roads are full of twists and turns because townlands aren't neat and tidy. An informal formality, better known in the minds of the people than in the realm of cartographers, as difficult for the outsider to define as to overlook, the townland is the peculiarly vague yet strikingly intimate essence of the local.

Then there are the towns, and these are also different in their own way, with a variety peculiar to themselves. There are Viking towns — Dublin, of course, is the main one — whose original main streets ran like a spine along the water by which the Vikings entered, with side-streets branching off like limbs, as though the old town-planners' inspiration was a skeleton. Armagh was an ecclesiastical powerhouse a thousand years ago, and is still the country's ecclesiastical capital. Landlords needed towns to service their operations, and marked their places by imposing the word 'town' and the family name on them, or by renaming whatever was there before as Castle- or Mount-. They redeveloped communities — 'improved' was the accepted term — by installing broad squares and wide thoroughfares as reminders of what they had seen abroad while on the Grand Tour. In the nineteenth century, model towns developed around factories; one of them, Portlaw, Co. Waterford, is laid out like a hand and its fingers.

And no matter what else they may be, they are all towns, with the exception of cities. Are there no villages in Ireland? Of course there are, and hamlets too, and a number of them are in Dublin, Cork, Galway, and especially Belfast. But nobody refers to them as that. The meanest single-street cluster of colourless houses belongs to the same general class of place as the thriving provincial centre. And to locals, the gradations of difference between even one huddle of grey and another are myriad and subtle. These differences, too, often arise out of invisible elements, such as which way a certain town voted or votes, whether its history is nationalist or otherwise, or even, as Tony O'Malley recalls, what brand of nationalism was favoured. The phrase 'a good town' is used to identify a place that has a tradition of enterprise and steady work, a tradition in which by no means all towns are able to share. Irish towns may seem quiet and self-contained, but that doesn't mean there is nothing going on in them. There are towns noted for their civility, and towns with reputations for rough-housing and bitterness and inferior porter. Many towns have two sections in them, one of which is an 'Irishtown', a place often on a hillside where people live in dwellings very different from those of the solid burghers of the main streets.

Even if there isn't anything going on, and all they reveal are plastic fascia and litter in the streets and the fact that the finest house on Main Street is the bank, the towns of Ireland can command an intense loyalty from their natives, a kind of committed intimacy which says that, be it ever so humble, there's no place like it. They are all special events, exclamation points amid the diffident fields. Many local songs express as much. So do the poets, Yeats and Kavanagh, Heaney and Hewitt. It is a fidelity that assumes the status of a cult and a fetish in the fiction of Joyce. The very names of places can organise a rhythm of experience, as Paul Durcan shows in his poem 'Going Home to Mayo, Winter, 1949': 'Kilcock, Kinnegad, Strokestown, Elphin . . .' (the stress falls on the last syllable in all cases but the third). Sequence without pattern, names punctuating the road to the west, 'passwords into eternity', says the poet, recalling his childish delight at the drive.

Not that it's a mere matter of the names themselves. There's no such thing as just the names on their own, it being impossible to divorce names from their invisible freight of feelings and associations, that savour of the story, event, character, turn of phrase that makes a place its distinctive, talismanic self. The trainloads of emigrants from John Healy's Charlestown, also in Mayo, travelling in the opposite direction to young Paul Durcan, may well have felt the names of places they passed through to be passwords of a different kind. But they would have known, too, what the poet meant, the tug of place, the homing instinct, the invisible power of memory and attachment, the understated yet overwhelming allure of the local.

iv

One strand in the skein of connotations that a place evinces is its own distinctive history. Another strand is the story of how a particular place participated in the history of Ireland. These two strands are so fundamentally implicated in each other that it may seem destructive to unravel them. Yet in the case of many places, local history does not parallel the national story. History, meaning events that marked a permanent change in the fate of the country, often washed over even the very places it selected for its sites. Kinsale had its battle, and the bridge of Toome saw the execution of Rody McCorley. But it would not be enough to say that this is all that ever happened in those places. The shade of William Penn might stir uneasily if it were forgotten that the father of the founder of Pennsylvania worked in the Kinsale custom house. It is not being suggested that these two Kinsale events are comparable. They obviously are not. But the fact that they are both true helps to give a more prismatic sense of what history contains.

History, in the sense of *la longue durée*, or the long run — which tends to be the history of the local, with its less emphatic rhythms of development and its focus on the physical materials and mental strategies of social survival — is also very much part of the Irish story, though one that receives less attention. Local history may ultimately be compatible with the national one, but that does not deprive it of its own warp and woof. It would be fascinating to see how the whole story might be enriched if there were less focus on history from, so to speak, the top down and more on it from the bottom up; if instead of knowing so much about what was done to us we knew more about what we did for ourselves. Arms to fight England were concealed in the thatched roofs of farmhouses. This means, among other things, that thatchers were earning a living. In 1798, Wexford and Antrim rebelled, but not the neighbouring counties of Waterford and Derry. Local history both assists and resists the idea of the big picture.

And maybe the tangled web of relationships between local event and national narrative is a miniature version of the complex patterns of infiltration, accommodation, adaptation and resistance that emerge from Ireland in the context of the Atlantic world, Europe and the various manifestations of the British presence. Supposing 'The First Invasion of Ireland' is true, and that Ireland was peopled by what might be called — to stretch a point beyond breaking, perhaps — Palestinian refugees fleeing the Flood. One point to emerge from such a supposition is that it establishes Ireland as having from the beginning a foot in world events. Whether or not that particular point is tenable, there is no doubt that the history of the country has been shaped by world systems which it found irresistible and with which to some extent it found itself, not altogether unwillingly, identified.

It has often been observed that Ireland escaped the brunt of the powerful forces that shaped European history and culture. And sometimes that observation has been used as evidence of the exclusive nature of Irish experience, that circumstances saw to it that from an early date we were 'ourselves alone'. But the history of Irish Christianity does not support such a view. Neither do many of the remains of the towers, monasteries and houses, which, though obviously built with Irish labour, echo English and Continental designs. Ireland's being an island did not cut it off from the variety of two-way traffic that passed through, and shaped, other places.

Nor can many of the country's leading historical figures be described in terms of their singularity. Our patron saint was a Roman citizen. The sixteenth-century chieftain Hugh O'Neill, whose career is often thought of as the last line of resistance to Elizabethan ambition, was also Earl of Tyrone and spent his youth in England among the great families of the day. Down the ages, a large number of Ireland's favourite sons departed from the tradition into which they were born. Membership of the established church and education at Trinity College Dublin were as much a qualification as they were an inhibition to calling for freedom for the diverse and illustrious roll-call of Irish patriots that includes Henry Grattan, Theobald Wolfe Tone, Robert Emmet, Thomas Davis, John Mitchel and Charles Stewart Parnell. Not that what they accomplished constitutes the whole of the national story, but the varieties of Irish freedom that they and many others of their background invented are a basis for appreciating the many different energies at play in the panorama of Irish history.

There was a time when Irish history was considered to be mainly a chronicle of dispossessions and defeats, armed struggles and crushing blows. To see beyond that simple and repetitive story is a challenge. But it is a challenge well worth taking up, particularly since doing so clarifies rather than erases the obvious calamities. To feel entitled to explore the varieties and complexities of their history should be the aspiration of a free people, if only because acknowledgment of the many different strands of the historical fabric will make the overall pattern that much more lifelike.

v

It is tempting to think that if history for the Irish consists of disruption, dispossession and demoralisation, religion for them is the signature of continuity and security. Such a thought obviously presumes that there is such a discrete entity called the Irish, and that it has preserved itself intact from the coming of St Patrick, fundamentally untouched by the presence of others in its midst — an obvious racial fantasy. On the other hand, however, it can hardly be denied that Christianity has been a persistent presence in the Irish world. But here again, the nature of that presence has been as fluid and variegated as that of any other aspect of the country's experience.

For one thing, Christianity in Ireland is by no means synonymous with Irish Catholicism. And it is also misleading to think of Protestantism as exclusively identified with the Church of Ireland. Other Protestant churches are also very much part of the Irish religious picture, and either have not shared or were not allowed to share in the established church's privileged status as the official crown religion. Once upon a time, Presbyterians were discriminated against as if they were as much a threat to the crown as were Catholics, although the penalties against them were not as severe or as long-lasting. And, as is well known, Presbyterian insistence on its right to its own thought and its own forms of association and governance had a radical influence on the origins of Irish republicanism.

There are at least two home-grown Irish Protestant sects: the Plymouth Brethren and the Cooneyites. The work of Quakers in the Famine was acknowledged during its one-hundred-and-fiftieth anniversary, though their efforts were neither inspired by nor confined to that dire time. Nor were they Ireland's only charitable Protestants. It belittles all concerned to think that they acted mainly to save souls from Rome. Even if they were motivated by their mission, they can hardly have converted everyone they helped. In any event, their presence is a fact of Irish religious life, to be admitted in the spirit of William Trevor's mention of walking by the Methodist church in Skibbereen, Co. Cork. He makes nothing of it. The church stands where it is and has as much a right to do so as anything else has. But he doesn't overlook it either. To do so would be to subscribe to a version of the view of Mr Deasy in *Ulysses* about Ireland and the Jews (richly ironic considering the origins of the book's hero, Leopold Bloom): 'We never let them in.'

A thousand years ago, when Ireland was an island of saints, there were simply Christians rather than Catholics and Protestants. Perhaps the existence of saints has made early Christianity appear in retrospect more Catholic than Protestant, sainthood being a Catholic benefaction. But what a saint was then is not necessarily the same as what a saint is now, and the line that connects today's church with that of the eighth century has more than a few noteworthy kinks in it. The number of Irish placenames beginning with 'kill' — meaning church (although some of them may derive from 'coill', meaning woodland) — shows the degree of penetration attained by the early Irish church throughout the country. Yet, the comprehensive nature of that penetration required a great deal of physical labour, with presumably commanding personalities to oversee it. The standard picture of early Christian Ireland as a land of devotional organic communities, secure and at peace, at one with nature and with God, has a compensatory tinge to it, a product of the cultural interests of later times. Monastic settlements as large as St Kevin's in Glendalough and St Kieran's in Clonmacnoise neither came down from heaven nor grew on trees.

The adaptation of Ireland to Christianity also entailed the adaptation of Christianity to Ireland. This success, together with the achievements of Irish missionaries in Britain and Europe, made the Irish church one of the most powerful components of early Christendom. Irish church fathers were aware of this power and used it to challenge papal authority on doctrinal and administrative positions that ran counter to Irish practices. In the seventh century there was a major controversy between the Pope and the Irish hierarchy about the dating of Easter. Other controversies followed. Such independent-mindedness may or may not be the same spirit that animated clerical resistance to persecution during the dreadful seventeenth and eighteenth centuries, when Catholicism became identified with the fate of the common people; it may or may not be the same spirit that fortified the defensive and socially dogmatic character of Irish Catholicism after the Famine.

But regardless of the complexities of the church's ecclesiastical history, one of the hallmarks of Irish Catholicism has been the loyalty of its adherents. A very large number of Irish Catholics remain *croyant et pratiquant*, and take pride in being so. That pride finds expression not only in the regularity with which they carry out their weekly and monthly confessional duties, but in the number of additional religious observances in which they participate — pilgrimages, retreats and the like. Some of these confessional practices have a noticeable strain of folk culture in them, for which Catholicism has paradoxically acted as a preservative. The bacchanalian Christmas Eve so vividly depicted in William Carleton's 'Midnight Mass', with not only its Breughelesque peasantry but culturally evocative torches lighting the faithful's way, has passed into history. But rag trees, such as those depicted in Peter Fallon's poem 'The Rag-tree, Boherard', may still be seen, as may other sites and practices which, while they have been assimilated within the ambit of orthodoxy, do not necessarily owe their origins to it. Here again, the idiosyncracies of the local — enshrined in wells and patron saints and what, for want of a more sophisticated term, are referred to as superstitions — complement, enlarge and run counter to easy assumptions about Irish life.

vi

In 1814, workmen at Lismore Castle excavated a number of ancient treasures, among them the Lismore crozier (its ornate gold work a reminder of the riches and the refined taste of the early Irish church) and the Book of Lismore. Among the contents of this book are the lives of saints, the rules of monasteries — many of the major monasteries had their own rule, another instance of their founders' power and independence — and a selection of ancient sagas. Other books contain, in addition or as alternatives, prayers and other types of devotional texts, anecdotal material, romances of the type represented by *Buile Suibhne* (*Sweeney Astray*, in Seamus Heaney's translation) and accounts of fantastic voyages, among them journeys to the other world. They were, in fact, anthologies of a kind. It is because of the great variety, as well as the intrinsic interest, of their contents that these books are the principal cultural legacy of early Irish Christianity, surpassing even the exquisite sacred vessels of the period, themselves a powerful expression of the material wealth and aesthetic sophistication of the period. The books ratify the cliché that during the monastic era Ireland was an island of saints and scholars.

By the standards of the books that have survived, the Book of Lismore is of relatively minor importance. It can hardly compare to the world-renowned manuscript of the gospels, the Book of Kells, whose lettering and colouring are marvels of the scrivener's art. But because of its contents, the Book of Lismore is also much more typical than the Book of Kells of the compilations of material that have come down. The motivation of clerics to produce a copy of the gospels that seems almost superhumanly painstaking and elaborate is self-evident. The Book of Kells exists as a monumental act of homage and devotion, and as such has earned a proud place in the cultural annals of Europe. What prompted monks to write down the sagas, poems, tales and a great deal of other material of a distinctly secular character is more difficult to determine. But although a good deal of the material is now missing, as gaps in the manuscripts show, there is no mystery about the monks' commitment to documenting and preserving this material.

Whatever the motivation, the outcome shows a fascinating compatibility between worlds. It is difficult to imagine stories further removed from the gospels than the sagas and legends that the holy men recorded. The main body of material consists of four cycles, or rough sequences, of tales — the Ulster cycle, the Fenian cycle, the cycle of the Kings and the Mythological cycle. Fionn, Maeve, Cúchulainn, Deirdre, Conchubar (pronounced Conor) and the rest of the sagas' heroic *dramatis personae* clearly had never heard of the Ten Commandments, much less the Sermon on the Mount. Sexy, arrogant, guileful, violent, they seem to exist by virtue of no other authority than the energy of their own natures. And while it is impossible to state definitively what degree of sanitising took place, it seems to have been minor at most, since the texts as we now have them are quite candid about the characters' physical attributes and functions. Another intriguing aspect of the material is the directness and buoyancy with which the stories are related, unimpeded by either the moral judgments or scholastic quibbles that might perhaps be expected to arise from the non-pagan outlook of those who took the tales into their keeping. Perhaps some of the material's qualities — its daring and self-confidence, for instance, or its complicated belief in the power of the word — influenced the monks. In any case, it is unlikely that such qualities died out overnight.

The sagas themselves did not die out. In book form, they became a fount of learning and a reservoir of imaginative adornment for generations of Irish poets, particularly those like Ó Rathaille and Ó Bruadair who felt the cultural ground being cut from under them. Translated into English, they returned to Irish life by being understood as sources of cultural self-respect and independence after the Act of Union 1800 removed the social and political bases for those values. This rediscovery culminated in the poetry of W.B. Yeats, who found in Standish James O'Grady's translations the ingredients of a vision which he imagined would rehabilitate the Irish spirit.

The appeal of the cadre of aristocratic, non-Christian, pre-English exemplars that Yeats retrieved from the ancient literature is easy to see. For these creatures of epic, thought and action are one. Brazen, energetic, resourceful, they are in tune with both their natural surroundings and the power of their own temperaments, and are at home in a world of their own making. These resurrected presences nourished not only Yeats's imagination. By various direct and indirect means, they percolated into the mind-set that brought modern Ireland into being, blending past and present, myth and history, origins and future into the fusion of tendencies and nuances, shadows and substances, evolving tradition and accomplished fact that typifies the palimpsest of Irish reality.

vii

Many attempts have been made to represent Ireland as the land of 'either/or'. In that country, the native is fundamentally opposed to the invader, Catholic makes Protestant see red and vice versa, and the writ of the tribe has it in for the rights of the individual. It is even to some extent understandable how such a version of Ireland came about. The constant traffic in difference that the island has seen has inevitably produced a reaction against it, a desire to override complexity, and a need to live in a world of one's own. Yet understandable and perhaps commonplace as such an idea of the country is, there is an alternative view which sees how Ireland persists in being a 'both/and' kind of place. This more inclusive perspective regards borders as membranes, looks at the stony space created by differences and detects seams of valuable ore in them, recognises that there are many versions of the story of Ireland and, rather than prize one above another, accepts that they are all significant.

To discover Ireland, then, is to find that here is a place that both is and is not what is said about it. Its topography shapes one sense of it, its history another. Religion offers a third approach. And the contents of these categories both modify and complement each other, as do the contents of any other categories that might be applied. Such a conclusion to the explorer's efforts may seem puzzlingly intangible. It isn't a pot of gold at the end of a rainbow. But the aim of exploration is not definition and finality. Instead, it is a less demanding, more provisional excursion into openness, a venture behind and beyond the familiar story and the simple picture.

Seán Dunne had a name for the outcome of such a venture. He called it 'inner geography'. As well as the physical kind, he said:

'There is a second type of geography which is harder to define. Each place contains its own version. It is an inner geography which is formed over a long period. It is a map shaped by memory, culture and experience. This geography varies from person to person and evolves over generations. It includes songs, stories, jokes, poems, politics, works of art, sporting events, local loyalties, parochial enthusiasm — the entire paraphernalia of a particular place. It is more than that vague thing, the spirit of place. It is a sense of life lived in a particular area, and of the way that life is expressed.

If we map attentively and comprehensively and lovingly enough, we map not only where we are but who we are. In *The Ireland Anthology* we have Seán's act of homage and commitment to such mapping, showing it to be as much principle as practice, and more ethos than editing.

Alas, Seán Dunne did not live to see his work in its final form. Let this book stand, then, to the clarity of his vision, his keen insight, his sound ear, his love of language, the breadth of his interests and the sensitivity of his poetic spirit.

> Before leaving, I climb the mountain.
> High among sheep and bladed winds,
> I add my stone to the peak's cairn
> And another for you: a summit reached.

> (Seán Dunne, 'The Healing Island')

George O'Brien
August 1997

Acknowledgments

George O'Brien gratefully acknowledges the assistance of the following in the preparation of *The Ireland Anthology*: Aimée Cooper, Professor Patricia Coughlan, John F. Deane, Aidan Dunne, Peter Fallon, Professor Leona Fisher, Michael Foley, Professor Kevin Hart, Stephen Hawthorne, Lynne Hirschfeld, Professor Christina Hunt Mahoney, David Marcus, Professor James McKillop, Professor Joseph O'Connor, Professor Jason Rosenblatt, Carina Rourke, Professor Joseph Sendry, Eddie Stack, Peter Steele SJ, Anne Walsh, and the Reference Desk staff of the Joseph Mark Lauinger Library, Georgetown University (especially Carolyn Colwell and Carolyn DeLuca). A special word of thanks to my infinitely obliging friends, Vincent Hurley and Máire Kennedy. Jonathan Williams's help was also invaluable.

EXPLANATORY NOTES

Some of the extracts in this book carry explanatory notes or references. In some cases these are taken from the source of the extract, while in others they were compiled by George O'Brien. Notes or references which are indicated by superscript numbers in the text and which *precede* the source of the extract are taken from that source. Notes which are in the form of glosses and which *follow* the source of the extract were supplied by George O'Brien.

THE PLACE

GIRALDUS CAMBRENSIS

The Normans who invaded Ireland in 1169 came from Pembrokeshire, as did Giraldus. In fact, he was related to the Fitzgeralds, or Geraldines, the most powerful of the invader families. His Topography is based on two trips to Ireland, the first in 1183 and the second two years later, when he travelled as a member of Prince John's entourage. Both visits were extended, amounting to about two years in all, though Giraldus's first-hand experience of the country appears to have been limited to the Norman-held south-east.

Considered controversial and overstated even in its own day, the Topography has long been viewed as less a traveller's tale than a traveller's travesty. But while Giraldus does indeed have the colonist's arrogant outlook, he is also very much alive to 'the many good points of the island and the natural qualities of the country'.

An island where human corpses exposed in the open do not putrefy

There is an island in the sea west of Connacht which is said to have been consecrated by Saint Brendan. In this island human corpses are not buried and do not putrefy, but are placed in the open and remain without corruption. Here men see with some wonder and recognise their grandfathers, great-grandfathers and great-great-grandfathers and a long line of ancestors.

There is another remarkable thing about this island: while the whole of Ireland is infested with mice, there is not a single mouse here. For no mouse is bred here nor does one live if it be brought in. If by chance it is brought in, it makes straight for the nearest point of the sea and throws itself in; and if it be prevented, it dies on the spot.

from *Topographia Hiberniae* (1220)

SAMUEL LEWIS

The passage of the Act of Union in 1800, whereby Ireland lost its own parliament and became directly subject to Westminster, coincided with the dawn of the imperial civil service's heyday. The sound of officialdom consolidating its presence is audible in the full title of Lewis's opus: A Topographical Dictionary of Ireland, Comprising the Several Counties, Cities, Boroughs, Corporate, Market, and Post Towns, Parishes, and Villages, With Historical and Statistical Descriptions; Embellished with Engravings of the Arms of the Cities, Bishopricks, Corporate Towns, and

Boroughs; and of the Seals of the Several Municipal Corporations: With an Appendix, Describing the Electoral Boundaries of the Several Boroughs, as Defined by the Act of the 2d & 3d of William IV.

The two-volume Dictionary was published in 1837 when the Ordnance Survey, which anglicised the names and standardised the measurements of modern Ireland, was in full swing.

Pre-Famine Parishes

DUNGOURNEY, a parish, partly in the barony of IMOKILLY, but chiefly in that of BARRYMORE, county of CORK, and province of MUNSTER, 4½ miles (N.) from Castlemartyr, on the road from Cork to Youghal; containing 2640 inhabitants. This parish comprises 8991 statute acres, of which 5925 are applotted under the tithe act, and valued at £4529 per annum; about 70 acres are woodland, nearly one-fourth of the land is waste, and the remainder is arable and pasture. The soil is generally good, but the system of agriculture is in an unimproved state; there are some quarries of common red stone, which is worked for various purposes, and there is a moderate supply of turf for fuel. The Dungourney river rises in the neighbouring hills of Clonmult, and flows through a deep glen in the parish, assuming near the church a very romantic appearance, and towards the southern boundary adding much beauty to the highly cultivated and richly wooded demesne of Brookdale, the seat of A. Ormsby, Esq. The other seats are Ballynona, that of R. Wigmore, Esq.; Ballynona Cottage, of H. Wigmore, Esq.; and Young Grove, of C. Foulke, Esq. An agricultural school, in connection with the Protestant Agricultural Society of Cork, has been established at Brookdale, under the patronage of Mr Ormsby, for the instruction of 30 boys in the practical knowledge of agriculture, combined with a useful and religious education, and including board and clothing; the institution is maintained by a payment of £5 per annum from each of the scholars, and the produce of the farm, aided by donations and subscriptions; when qualified to become useful, the scholars are provided with situations by the Committee, and receive a gratuity of £5. There is also a female school on the same principle, in which 35 girls are boarded, clothed, and educated, under the personal superintendence of Mrs Ormsby; on leaving the institution they are provided with situations. The buildings for both these establishments have cost more than £1000. The living is a rectory, in the diocese of Cloyne, and in the patronage of Major Fitzgerald: the tithes amount to £664. 12. 3½. The glebe-house is a good residence, and the glebe comprises 12 acres. The church, a plain building with a shingled spire, was erected by a gift of £500 from the late Board of First Fruits, in 1800, and the Ecclesiastical Commissioners have recently granted £119 for its repair. Attached to Brookdale House is a private chapel, in which a clergyman of the Established Church officiates. In the R. C. divisions the parish forms part of the union of Imogealy, or Castlemartyr. There is a private school, in which are about 170 children.

DUNHILL, or DON ISLE, anciently called DONDRONE, a parish, in the barony of MIDDLETHIRD, county of WATERFORD, and province of MUNSTER, 8 miles (S. E.) from Kilmacthomas; containing 2128 inhabitants. It is situated on St George's channel, and comprises 6115 statute acres, as applotted under the tithe act. The high lands are principally composed of pudding-stone and clay-slate, with large masses of jasper, some of which is very beautiful. The village of Annestown has a few lodging-houses for the accommodation of visitors in the bathing season. The living is a vicarage, in the diocese of Lismore, united to the vicarages of Guilcagh and Newcastle, and in the gift of the Corporation of Waterford, in which the rectory is impropriate. The tithes amount to £210, of which £110 is payable to the impropriators, and £100 to the vicar; and the vicarial tithes of the union are £194. The glebe comprises above 6 acres. The church at Annestown was rebuilt in 1822, by aid of a gift of £900 from the late Board of First Fruits; and there is a chapel of ease at Guilcagh. In the R. C. divisions the parish is the head of a union or district, and has a commodious chapel. The most remarkable ruin is Don Isle or Donhill castle, which was a principal seat of a branch of the La Poers, and was taken by Cromwell's army, after an obstinate defence made by a female proprietor, who was called Countess of Don Isle. Near it are the ruins of the church, against one of the walls of which stood a statue with a coronet, which has lately been placed in front of the R. C. chapel. In its vicinity is a cromlech of silicious slate.

DUNISKY, a parish, in the barony of WEST MUSKERRY, county of CORK, and province of MUNSTER, 4 miles (S. S. E.) from Macroom; containing 479 inhabitants. This is a very small parish, comprising only one ploughland, situated on the south bank of the river Lee, near Warrens-court. The land is good, and the substratum consists entirely of clay-slate. It is a rectory, in the diocese of Cork, being part of the union of St Peter's, Cork, and of the corps of the archdeaconry: the tithes amount to £107. There being no church, the parishioners attend divine service at Canaway. The ruins of the old church are a mile and a half north of Warrens-court, on rising ground, and show it to have been a small building. In the R. C. divisions the parish is part of the union or district of Kilmichael.

DUNKANELY, a village, in the parish of KILLAGHTEE, barony of BANNAGH, county of DONEGAL, and province of ULSTER, 9 miles (W.) from Donegal, near Inver bay, and on the road from Killybegs to Donegal: the population is returned with the parish. In 1618 this place was a settlement of ten British families, having a territory of 1500 acres, a bawn of lime and stone, and a castle, and able to muster 50 men at arms. It consists of one street, has a penny post to Donegal, a dispensary, a place of worship for Methodists, and a public school. Twelve fairs are held in the course of the year for farming stock, and a manor court monthly for the recovery of debts under £3. In the village are the ruins of the old parish church, and in the immediate vicinity is the present church. Half a mile to the west are the ruins of Castle Mac-Swine, occupying a point of land little broader than its foundation, which projects some yards into the sea at the head of Mac-Swine's bay. — See KILLAGHTEE.

from A *Topographical Dictionary of Ireland* (1837)

applotted . . . apportioned

Board of First Fruits . . . Ecclesiastically speaking, first fruits referred to a payment, usually amounting to the first year's income, made by the new holder of a benefice to his superior. The board was established in 1711.

R. C. divisions . . . Roman Catholic parishes. Existing parishes became Church of Ireland parishes at the Reformation, and also the basic unit in land surveys, tax assessment and so on.

union . . . a number of parishes amalgamated to facilitate administration of the Poor Law

pudding-stone . . . a rock made of fused pebbles

impropriate . . . to appropriate benefices

population is returned with the parish . . . a reference either to census returns or to the collection of tithes

bawn . . . a cattle-fold, or the fortified enclosure of a castle

JOHN MONTAGUE

As well as noting 'the prevailing north-west wind that bends the trees', Giraldus Cambrensis's Topography records how prevalent the harp is in Ireland. Such longevity underlies the instrument's complex history as a heraldic symbol, as part of the United Kingdom's iconography, as the national symbol of independent Ireland, and as slang for an Irish-American.

Another harp also seems relevant. This is the Aeolian Harp, an invention of English Romantic poets, which likens poetry's effects to those of a breeze on an open, sensitive, stringed instrument. The strains of its music may be heard throughout, for instance, W.B. Yeats's The Wind Among the Reeds (1899).

The poem is dedicated to the Irish painter Patrick Collins (1910–94).

Windharp

for Patrick Collins

The sounds of Ireland,
that restless whispering
you never get away
from, seeping out of
low bushes and grass,
heatherbells and fern,
wrinkling bog pools,
scraping tree branches,
light hunting cloud,
sound hounding sight,
a hand ceaselessly
combing and stroking
the landscape, till
the valley gleams
like the pile upon
a mountain pony's coat.

from *Collected Poems* (1995)

ARTHUR YOUNG

Edmund Spenser, in A View of the Present State of Ireland *(1596), reports the soil of Ireland to be 'goodly and commodious'. Young was well able to appreciate good land, being the 'Apostle of the Agricultural Revolution'. His theories greatly influenced the modernisation of farming along scientific lines, though he also held that 'the magic of property turns sand into gold'. One Irish landlord to whom the scientific approach appealed was the Enlightenment-oriented Richard Lovell Edgeworth, Maria's father. He considered 'Mr Young's picture of Ireland . . . the first faithful portrait of its inhabitants'.*

Young landed in Ireland on 20 June 1776 and toured the country until the end of the following year. The following two years he spent as agent of Lord Kingsborough's Mitchelstown, Co. Cork, estate.

Soil, Face of the Country and Climate

To judge of Ireland by the conversation one sometimes hears in England, it would be supposed that one half of it was covered with bogs, and the other with mountains filled with Irish ready to fly at the sight of a civilised being. There are people who will smile when they hear that, in proportion to the size of the two countries, Ireland is more cultivated than England, having much less waste land of all sorts. Of uncultivated mountains there are no such tracts as are found in our four northern counties, and the North Riding of Yorkshire, with the eastern line of Lancaster, nearly down to the Peak of Derby, which form an extent of above an hundred miles of waste. The most considerable of this sort in Ireland are in Kerry, Galway and Mayo, and some in Sligo and Donegal. But all these together will not make the quantity we have in the four northern counties; the valleys in the Irish mountains are also more inhabited, I think, than those of England, except where there are mines, and consequently some sort of cultivation creeping up the sides. Natural fertility, acre for acre, over the two kingdoms, is certainly in favour of Ireland; of this I believe there can scarcely be a doubt entertained, when it is considered that some of the more beautiful, and even best cultivated counties in England, owe almost everything to the capital art and industry of the inhabitants.

The circumstance which strikes me as the greatest singularity of Ireland is the rockiness of the soil, which should seem at first sight against that degree of fertility; but the contrary is the fact. Stone is so general, that I have great reason to believe the whole island is one vast rock of different strata and kinds rising out of the sea. I have rarely heard of any great depths being sunk without meeting with it. In general it appears on the surface in every part of the kingdom; the flattest and most fertile parts, as Limerick, Tipperary, and Meath, have it at no great depth, almost as much as the more barren ones. May we not recognise in this the hand of bounteous Providence, which has given perhaps the most stony soil in Europe to the moistest climate in it? If as much rain fell upon the clays of England (a soil very rarely met with in Ireland, and never without much stone) as falls upon the rocks of her sister island, those lands could not be cultivated. But the rocks here are clothed with verdure; those of limestone, with only a thin covering of mould, have the softest and most beautiful turf imaginable.

The rockiness of the soil in Ireland is so universal that it predominates in every sort. One cannot use with propriety the terms clay, loam, sand, etc., it must be a *stony* clay, a *stony* loam, a *gravelly* sand. Clay, especially the yellow, is much talked of in Ireland, but it is for want of proper discrimination. I have once or twice seen almost a pure clay upon the surface, but it is extremely rare. The true yellow clay is usually found in a thin stratum under the surface mould and over a rock; harsh, tenacious, stony, strong loams, difficult to work, are not uncommon, but they are quite different from English clays.

Friable sandy loams, dry but fertile, are very common, and they form the best soils in the kingdom for tillage and sheep. Tipperary and Roscommon abound particularly in them. The most fertile of all are the bullock pastures of Limerick, and the banks of the Shannon in Clare, called the *Corcasses*. These are a mellow, putrid, friable loam.

Sand which is so common in England is nowhere met with in Ireland, except for narrow slips of hillocks, upon the sea coast. Nor did I ever meet with or hear of a chalky soil.

The bogs, of which foreigners have heard so much, are very extensive in Ireland; that of Allen extends eighty miles, and is computed to contain 300,000 acres. There are others also, very extensive, and smaller ones scattered over the whole kingdom; but these are not in general more than are wanted for fuel.

Few countries can be better watered by large and beautiful rivers; and it is remarkable that by much the finest parts of the kingdom are on the banks of these rivers. Witness the Suir, Blackwater, the Liffey, the Boyne, the Nore, the Barrow, and part of the Shannon; they wash a scenery that can hardly be exceeded. From the rockiness of the country, however, there are few of them that have not obstructions, which are great impediments to inland navigation.

The mountains of Ireland give to travelling that interesting variety which a flat country can never abound with. And at the same time, they are not in such number as to confer the usual character of poverty which attends them. I was either upon or very near the most considerable in the kingdom. Mangerton and the Reeks in Kerry; the Galtees in Cork; those of Mourne in Down; Croagh Patrick and Nephin in Mayo; these are the principal in Ireland, and they are of a character, in height and sublimity, which should render them the objects of every traveller's attention.

from *A Tour in Ireland* (1780)

EDMUND SPENSER

Spenser was nearing the end of his twenty-year career in Ireland when he wrote his View in 1596. These were years of rebellion and uncertainty. Dire military methods dealt with rebellion, and Spenser, holder of a succession of crown appointments, witnessed them. Officials found him 'a man endowed with good knowledge of lerneing, and not unskillfull or without experience in the service of the warrs' when making him Sheriff of Cork.

As for uncertainty — what Spenser called 'mutabilitie' — it was debated in policy papers circulated at court. The View is an elaborate one of these in the form of a dialogue between Irenius (literally 'man of peace') and Eudoxus ('the good teacher'). But Spenser was also a poet, who saw Ireland as 'a most beautiful and sweete countrie'. The landscape around Kilcolman Castle, Spenser's property near Doneraile, Co. Cork, looms large in his epic poem The Faerie Queen. So do the Glen of Aherlow in County Tipperary, and nearby Galtymore, where the gods convene to ponder mutabilitie.

A Dialogue of Irenius and Eudoxus

Iren: They have another custom from the Scythians, that is the wearing of mantles and long glibs, which is a thick curled bush of hair hanging down over their eyes, and monstrously disguising them, which are both very bad and hurtful.

Eudox: Do ye think that the mantle cometh from the Scythians? I would surely think otherwise, for by that which I have read it appeareth that most nations in the world anciently used the mantle, for the Jews used it as ye may read of Elias' mantle of —. The Caldees also used it, as ye may read in Diodorus, the Egyptians likewise used it, as ye may read in Herodotus and may be gathered by the description of Berenice in the Greek commentaries upon Callimachus. The Greeks also used it anciently, as appeareth by Venus' mantle lined with stars, though afterwards they changed the form thereof into their cloaks called *pallia*, as some of the Irish also use. And the ancient Latins and Romans also used it, as ye may read in Virgil who was a very great antiquary, that Evander, when Aeneas came to him at his feast, did entertain and feast him sitting on the ground, and lying on mantles. Insomuch as he useth the very word *mantile* for a mantle, *mentilia humi sternunt*, so that it seemeth that the mantle was a general habit to most nations, and not proper to the Scythians only as ye suppose.

Iren: I cannot deny but anciently it was common to most, and yet Sithence disused and laid away. But in this latter age of the world since the decay of the Roman Empire, it was renewed and brought in again by those northern nations, when breaking out of their cold caves and frozen habitation into the sweet soil of Europe, they brought with them their usual weeds, fit to shield the cold and that continual frost to which they had at home been enured; the which yet they left not off, by reason that they were in perpetual wars with the nations where they had invaded, but still removing from place to place carried always with them that weed as their house, their bed and their garment, and coming lastly into Ireland they found there more special use thereof, by reason of the raw cold climate, from whom it is now grown into that general use in which that people now have it; afterward the Africans succeeding, yet finding the like necessity of that garment, continued the like use thereof.

Eudox: Since then the necessity thereof is so commodious as ye allege, that it is instead of housing, bedding, and clothing, what reason have you then to wish so necessary a thing cast off?

Iren: Because the commodity doth not countervail the discommodity. For the inconveniences which thereby do arise are much more many, for it is a fit house for an outlaw, a meet bed for a rebel, and an apt cloak for a thief. First the outlaw being for his many crimes and villanies banished from the towns and houses of honest men, and wandering in waste places far from danger of law, maketh his mantle his house, and under it covereth himself from the wrath of heaven, from the offence of the earth, and from the sight of men; when it raineth it is his pentice, when it bloweth it is his tent, when it freezeth it is his tabernacle; in summer he can wear it loose, in winter he can wrap it close; at all times he can use it, never heavy, never cumbersome. Likewise for a rebel it is as serviceable: for in his war that he maketh (if at least it deserve the name of war) when he still flyeth from his foe and lurketh in the thick woods and straight passages waiting for advantages, it is his bed, yea and almost all his household stuff. For the wood is his house against all weathers, and his mantle is his cave to sleep in. There he wrappeth his self round and ensconceth himself strongly against the gnats, which in the country do more annoy the naked rebels whilst they keep the woods, and do more sharply wound them than all their enemies' swords or spears which can seldom come nigh them; yea and oftentimes their mantle serveth them when they are near driven, being wrapped about their left arm instead of a target, for it is hard to cut through it with a sword; besides, it is light to bear, light to throw away, and being as they then commonly are naked, it is to them all in all, Lastly, for a thief it is so handsome, as it may seem it was first invented for him, for under it he can cleanly convey any fit pillage that cometh handsomely in his way, and when he goeth abroad in the night on freebooting it is his best and surest friend, for lying as they often do, two or three nights together abroad to watch for their booty, with that they can prettily shroud themselves under a bush or a bankside till they may conveniently do their errand. And when all is done he can, in his mantle, pass through any town or company, being close hooded over his head as he useth from knowledge of any to whom he is endangered. Besides all this he or any man else that is disposed to mischief or villainy may, under his mantle, go privily, armed without suspicion of any, carry his headpiece, his skene or pistol, if he please to be always in a readiness. Thus necessary and fitting is a mantle for a bad man. And surely for a bad housewife it is no less convenient. For some of them that be these wandering women, called of them *Monashut*, it is half a wardrobe, for in summer ye shall find her arrayed commonly but in her smock and mantle to be more ready for her light services; in winter and in her travel it is her cloak and safeguard, and also a coverlet for her lewd exercise, and when she hath filled her vessel, under it she can hide both her burden and her blame; yea, and when her bastard is born it serves instead of all her swaddling clothes, her mantles, her cradles with which others are vainly cumbered, and as for all other good women which love to do but little work, how handsome it is to lie in and sleep, or to louse themselves in the sunshine, they that have been but a while in Ireland can well witness. Sure I am that ye will think it very unfit for good housewives to stir in or to busy herself about her housewifery in sort as they should. These be some of the abuses for which I would think it meet to forbid all mantles.

Eudox: O evil minded man, that having reckoned up so many uses of mantles, will yet wish it to be abandoned. Sure I think Diogenes' dish did never serve his master more turns, notwithstanding that he made his dish his cup, his measure, his waterpot, than a mantle doth an Irishman, but I see they be all to bad intents, and therefore I will join with you in abolishing it. But what blame lay you to then glib? Take heed, I pray you, that you be not too busy therewith, for fear of your own blame, seeing our Englishmen take it up in such a general fashion, to wear their hair so unmeasurably long that some of them exceed the longest Irish glibs.

Iren: I fear not the blame of any undeserved mislikes, but for the Irish glibs I say that besides their savage brutishness and loathly filthiness, which is not to be named, they are fit masks as a mantle is for a thief, for whensoever he hath run himself into that peril of law that he will not be known, he either cutteth off his glib quite, by which he becometh nothing like himself, or pulleth it so low down over his eyes that it is very hard to discern his thievish countenance, and therefore fit to be trussed up with the mantle.

from *A View of the Present State of Ireland* (1596)

Scythians . . . Nomadic people of the Black Sea region, with whom the Irish were frequently compared because of their alleged wildness and because of a mistaken connection between the origins of their name and those of *Scotiae*, one of the names for the people on the margins of the Roman Empire. Recent archaeological discoveries show the Scythians to have been as gifted artists in metal as the Celts.

glib . . . forelock

Diodorus . . . *Herodotus* . . . The modern editor of the *View*, W.L. Renwick, has professed himself unable to locate a number of Spenser's classical references.

sithence . . . since; seeing that

weeds . . . clothes

pentice . . . penthouse

skene . . . Now the Irish word for knife, in Spenser's day it referred to the dagger carried by the Irish in arms.

Monashut . . . corruption of the Irish *mná shiúil*, literally 'walking women'; 'prostitutes'

Diogenes . . . Lived from c. 412 to 323 B.C. To practise what he preached about the virtues of a simple life, he lived in a tub. It is said that he threw away his drinking vessel when he saw somebody cup his hands to drink.

FRANCIS STUART

There are many poems of exile in Irish literature, enough to suggest that they constitute a distinctive branch of Irish writing. But none has been composed in the notorious circumstances in which Francis Stuart wrote 'Ireland'.

His career in the 1920s and 30s included a period in jail for republican activities, a time as a chicken farmer, and a career as an admired and prolific novelist. In 1940, however, Stuart took up a university position in Berlin, and between 1942 and 1944 made weekly radio broadcasts to Ireland. As 'Ireland' suggests, Stuart did not exactly feel at home in the Berlin of 1944. He was imprisoned briefly after the war, and returned to Ireland in 1958.

As a young man, Stuart married Iseult Gonne, daughter of Maud. That relationship is commemorated by Yeats in 'Why Should Not Old Men Be Mad' — 'A girl that knew all Dante once/Live to bear children to a dunce'.

Ireland

Over you falls the sea light, festive yet pale
As though from the trees hung candles alight in a gale
To fill with shadows your days, as the distant beat
Of waves fill the lonely width of many a western street.
Bare and grey and hung with berries of mountain ash,
Drifting through ages with tilted fields awash,
Steeped with your few lost lights in the long Atlantic dark,
Sea-birds' shelter, our shelter and ark.

Berlin 1944

from We Have Kept the Faith (1982)

ROBERT LLOYD PRAEGER

In 1935, at the age of seventy, Robert Lloyd Praeger toured Ireland, applying to the country the trained eye and undimmed enthusiasm that had made him an eminent botanist, a distinguished geologist, and one of the country's leading scientific figures. The result is The Way That I Went, a distinctive blend of observation and anecdote and, as the author said, 'a kind of thank-offering' for a lifetime of delighting in and learning from the Irish landscape.

If hearing about the distinctive flora of Lambay and of Dublin generally takes today's reader unawares, it may be because Praeger's fears concerning 'the greed of land-owners' have been realised. Lambay remains in private hands. Ireland's Eye is a bird sanctuary. Sir Edwin Lutyens (1869–1944) was a prominent English architect and artist.

Howth and Lambay

Howth was still an island within early human history; the sand-spit that joins it to the mainland at Sutton is a sea-beach raised above wave-level in Neolithic times. As I first knew Howth, half a century ago, it was a delightful old-world place. Even round its rock-bound margin houses were few, and one could wander at will along its grassy slopes and over its broad heathery top. Now houses and bungalows, most of them inartistic eyesores quite out of keeping with their setting, encroach more and more on the open spaces; along the southern shore, with its superb view across Dublin bay, the greed of land-owners confines the visitor to a narrow muddy track between high barbed-wire fences. But much of the plateau-like top, where in late summer the Heather and Gorse form one of the loveliest sights in Ireland, is mercifully still unspoiled, and free to the weary town-dweller — how long will it remain so? Howth is full of varied interest — ancient churches and prehistoric monuments, rare flowers (it has the largest flora for its size of any area in Ireland), shelly gravels plastered by the ice of the Glacial Period against the steep seaward slopes, nesting gulls, obscure fossils in the ancient rocks (the oldest fossils in the country) and prospects both to north and south that are unsurpassed in Ireland. Would that so unique a national inheritance — what remains unspoiled of it — might yet be saved as a breathing-place for the increasing thousands of Dublin's population.

The island called Ireland's Eye, on the north side of Howth, furnishes a curious case of name-corruption. Its old name was *Inis Éreann*, island of Eire or Eira, who was a woman. The Danes substituted the termination *öe*, island, for the Irish *inis*: subsequently *Éreann* (of Eire) was mistaken for *Éireann* (of Ireland) and Eire's island became Ireland's Eye. This islet is very picturesque, with high cliffs on one side, and rocks and sand elsewhere around its Bracken-covered surface. An ancient church, and a granite martello tower erected to repel Napoleonic landings, are emblematic of the monuments found all over Ireland, representing piety and war.

Looking north from Howth, the eye is caught by the dark rocky profile of Lambay (*not* Lambay Island, for the last syllable already signifies 'island', being the Danish *öe*, variously mutilated as in Dalkey, Saltee, Anglesea and Ireland's Eye). Lambay is a delightful island, especially interesting on account of its origin, for it is the stump of a little ancient volcano. It was away back in Ordovician times that lavas, of the type called andesitic, broke through the crust and poured out over an area which may have been considerably larger than they occupy now (the island is only about a square mile in extent). Probably the far-reaching Carboniferous sea afterwards engulfed it, and spread over it the limestones that are so extensively developed in Ireland; but if so all trace of them is now worn off, and except for a small patch of Old Red Sandstone of the familiar conglomeratic type the whole island represents the product of the volcanic phase. Like Howth, it is scraped round three sides by the sea, with picturesque cliffs and stacks, and only in the east does it slope down to a beach. And as on Howth, the central part is high (to 418 feet) and covered with Heather and Bracken.

I got to know Lambay very well during the years 1904–10. Cecil Baring, as he was then, came to the National Library seeking information concerning his new possession. He told me how in Munich in 1903 (I think) he and his wife saw in *The Field* an advertisement 'Irish Island for Sale', and how they promptly bought it and set about making habitable its old castle, which was probably the fortress recorded as being there in 1467, already modified to suit more modern requirements. Under the guiding hand of Sir Edward Lutyens, it was eventually converted into a very delightful medieval-modern residence. A couple of cottages upon the hill were also set in order, and there or in the castle my wife and I spent many a delightful holiday. I think the Barings would willingly have spent their lives on the island, for they became intensely interested in everything it contained: but continuous sojourn did not last long. After a few years business affairs in London intervened. Then Mrs Baring died, and was interred on the island she loved so much; and more recently her husband has been buried beside her. Shortly after he took possession of Lambay, I suggested to him that a detailed study of its natural productions — animal, vegetable and mineral — would be interesting, and might have important scientific results. He accepted the suggestion at once. Workers in various branches of natural science were enlisted, and during 1905 and 1906 twenty naturalists in all stayed on Lambay, some of them several times, as the guests of Mr and Mrs Baring, and ransacked the island from end to end. Considering its small size and the uniformity of prevailing conditions, the results were rather surprising. Five of the smaller animals found — three worms, a mite and a bristletail — proved to be new to science; twelve other animals were new to the Britannic fauna; and between eighty and ninety animals and plants were hitherto unrecorded from Ireland.[1] It was the unexpected success of this intensive study of a limited area that led to the carrying out a few years later of a similar undertaking on a much larger scale — the Clare Island Survey, which added very largely to our knowledge of the fauna and flora of Ireland.

Lambay fortunately remains in possession of the Baring family, and the present Lord Revelstoke continues his father's policy of preserving the island as a sanctuary for animal and plant inhabitants. Under protection, the great colonies of breeding sea-birds have increased, and in many cases spread from the cliffs to the grassy slopes, where you have to pick your steps among innumerable nests. Rarer birds like the Peregrine and Raven are unmolested there, and the Fulmar Petrel is a recent arrival; the Great Grey Seals, always a fascinating feature of Lambay life, bask on the rocks and breed in the caves. Once I stalked a group of them there on a flat tidal rock until I lay among them, and could count every bristle and hair on their mastiff-like faces; they watched me closely, but never stirred. And we had delightful adventures with white baby seals, quite devoid of fear, which bumped against the boat and let us stroke them, while a watchful mother swam continuously and silently round.

The flora of the county of Dublin is attractive, and is large in view of the small size of the area. This is due mainly to the varied nature of the materials of which it is built up — sea sands, clays, limestones, slates, granites, the last rising to 2473 feet on the Wicklow boundary. Of the various habitats for plants, lowland bog and lake alone are missing in Dublin, and the absence of the latter is compensated by flower-fringed canals. In addition to a large native flora, Dublin is exceptionally rich in alien plants which have established themselves there; some, like the silver-leaved Cineraria of the Dalkey cliffs, to the enhancement of natural beauty. That knowledge of Dublin plants is so complete and so accessible is due to the work of Nathaniel Colgan (1851–1919). The home county had always been a playground of Dublin botanists, but Colgan systematised and greatly enlarged our knowledge, and his *Flora of the County Dublin*, published in 1904, will long remain the final court of appeal on matters relating to local plants.

1. 'Contributions to the Natural History of Lambay', *Irish Naturalist*, Vol. xvi (1907), pp. 1–112, plates 1–25.

from *The Way That I Went* (1937)

E. ESTYN EVANS

According to ancient Irish history, there were seven invasions of Ireland. Then in the early Christian period Danes and Vikings landed and settled. They were followed by Normans, English and Scots. Later contributors to the gene-pool include Germans, who settled in County Limerick, and Huguenots, who made their mark in Dublin. And like every other nationality, Irish includes foreign trades people — Italian plasterers and, later, church decorators; Spanish sailors washed ashore from the wreck of the Armada; soldiers who deserted. There is a Jewish cemetery dating from the seventeenth century in the back yard of a house in Fairview, Dublin.

Nevertheless, signs of a hankering for pure Irishness can also be detected. Nazism had some Irish adherents.

Robin Flower (1891–1946) was a renowned scholar of Irish closely associated with the Blasket Islands, translator of Tomás Ó Criomhthain, An tOileánach *(The Islandman, 1934), and author of, among other works,* The Irish Tradition *(1947).*

Soil and Blood

I t seems that the ideas which a nationalistic society, on the European model, has about its past are not only most dangerous when they are erroneous, but also most powerful. The concept of pure races has long been rejected by anthropologists, who think of human types as conveyors of bundles of heritages which are recombined in every generation. We should abandon, as Robin Flower suggested, the vain search for the pure uncontaminated Celt. If it were possible to sort out the genes of the Irish people I would hazard a guess that those coming from English settlers would exceed those deriving from 'the Celts', and that those coming from older stocks would constitute the largest proportion.[1] The popular conception of race as an ideal quality which has somehow lost its purity seems to spring from the biblical story of the garden of Eden, and finds analogies in the grammarian's concept of an original 'common Celtic' and in the theories of the Grimm brothers on the origin of folk tales in a pure Indo-European cradle. The extension of these notions into the idealisation of Nordic man in Nazi Germany should be a warning.

It is more to the point to notice that, among the physical heritages which are strong in the people of Ireland, are large and moderately long heads and, particularly in the west and north, a relatively high proportion of blood group O, a feature which is characteristic also of Scotland, Iceland, the Basque country and the western Mediterranean region, that is its distribution is markedly peripheral in Europe — which generally has a relatively high A frequency, as has south-east England — and in a larger view is also peripheral in the Old World. Certain other distinctive regional characteristics, though as variations in the human species they may not be as long established as the blood group heritage, have been observed in Ireland; for example, the lightly pigmented eye occurs in over 80 per cent of the population, but, while this feature has been thought to be an adaptation to the cloudy skies of north-western Europe, in Ireland it is commonly combined with hair which shows no corresponding reduction of pigmentation. According to the findings of one anthropometric survey, the combination of very dark hair and blue eyes is most common in County Wexford, and stranger still, the Aran Islanders, popularly regarded as the purest of Gaels, have relatively high frequencies of blood group

A, thanks, it is suggested, to Cromwell's garrison of Fensmen. It is less surprising that there are relatively high A frequencies in the population of eastern Ireland.[2] In summary, it can be said that anthropometric research gives us a picture of the Irish population which is far removed from the stereotypes of blonde invaders and black-a-vised natives. In particular it points to very considerable heritages from Neolithic farmers and from Mesolithic fisherfolk, the latter being strongest in the western peninsulas. But I do not wish to pursue the problem of race. Whatever virtue there may be in physical character seems to spring from cross-breeding rather than from any supposed purity of race, but this is not to deny that racial or facial forms may, for instance, have a bearing on pronunciation and therefore have cultural significance. We get a very restricted view of the Irish people by thinking of them as 'Celts', overlooking not only the productive mingling of many varieties of historic settlers but also the substantial contribution of older stocks who had peopled the land in pre-Celtic times and absorbed its nature. It is not only writers of popular history and political propaganda who pursue the Celtic myth. Some Celtic scholars have been guilty of the very crime with which they reproach English historians of medieval Ireland, of treating the country as though nothing of significance had happened there before. The history of early Celtic Ireland has been written in much the same imperialist spirit as that in which the history of Roman Britain used to be written, as though the natives were conscious of their inferiority and anxious to receive the benefits of civilisation. Prehistorians, however, are steadily revealing and re-evaluating the cultural variety and vitality of an older Ireland.

1.   C.S. Coon, *The Races of Europe* (New York: 1939): 376–84, considers that at least half the genetic ancestry of the composite modern Irishman is to be referred to the survival of strains from the oldest (Mesolithic) settlers. A.E. Hooton and C.W. Dupertuis, *The Physical Anthropology of Ireland* (Cambridge, Mass: 1955) are more cautious. They searched, however, for the supposed 'Celtic' type and found it uncommon among native Gaelic speakers and best represented down the east coast.

2.   E. Hackett and M.E. Folan, 'ABO and RH Blood Groups of the Aran Islands', *Irish Journal of Medical Science* 390 (1958): 247–61. The A frequency for the Aran Islands is given as 40 per cent, the O, 50. These figures resemble those for eastern Ireland. Averages for western Ireland are A, 26.5; O, 60. The available figures for Northern Ireland are A, 33; O, 55.

from *The Personality of Ireland* (1973, revised edn 1981)

BRENDAN McWILLIAMS

Valentia is well-placed as Ireland's weather-eye partly because of the Gulf Stream, the most decisive influence on the country's climate. It flows north from Florida, turns north-east off the coast of North Carolina, and hits Ireland in the south-west, where it leaves its calling card in the form of exotic plants and lashings of rain.

Valentia's readings are remembered not only for their scientific and practical interest but also for helping to make possible the shipping forecast. The recitation on the radio of the names of far-off sea areas — Rockall, Malin, Finisterre — was a familiar, evocative ritual for many youngsters in the 1950s.

Robert Fitzroy (1805–65), noted for his meteorological innovations, was captain of the Beagle when Charles Darwin made his famous voyage. He also was secretary of the Lifeboat Association, a service to the annals of which the Valentia boat has made many outstanding contributions.

Valentia Observatory

At eight o'clock in the morning on 8 October 1860 the very first Irish 'real time' weather observation was transmitted from Valentia Island in Co. Kerry. Weather reports have been coming in a continuous stream from that part of the country ever since, albeit not from precisely the same spot.

The historic message was sent on the electric telegraph to Fitzroy in London for use in his newly organised system of storm warnings. The observation was performed by Mr R.J. Lecky, who at the time was manager of the telegraphic station on Valentia Island. Lecky continued with this valuable service on a daily basis for many years; he was made redundant only by the establishment of an official Observatory on the island on 15 June 1868.

The new Observatory was at first a very modest undertaking. It occupied a rented house on the narrow strait which separates Valentia Island from the rest of Kerry, and from there the routine flow of observations continued until March of 1892. It was in that year that Valentia Observatory moved across the sound to its present site on the mainland near the town of Cahirciveen, retaining for *auld lang syne* its traditional name — the name by which, somewhat confusingly, it is still known.

Its new home was Westwood House, theretofore the residence of one Captain Needham, the local agent of Trinity College which was at that time a very prominent landowner in the locality. Westwood was purchased for the not inconsiderable sum of £1,400, and in the succeeding years was decked out with the impressive array of scientific instruments which was in due course to make Valentia Observatory one of the most important meteorological and geophysical observatories in all of Western Europe.

Valentia Observatory is today one of the Irish weather-observing stations whose hourly reports of current weather conditions are circulated around the globe; it performs upper-air measurements, using a *radio-sonde* attached to a hydrogen-filled balloon to obtain values of pressure, temperature and humidity many miles above the earth; it monitors variations in the earth's magnetic field, and carries out precise measurements of radiation coming from the sun; the Observatory also operates a seismograph, which detects and records tiny vibrations which may have their origins thousands of miles away in earthquakes half-way around the world.

from *Weather Eye* (1994)

DANIEL CORKERY

The place is Cork city; the time, the early years of the century; the atmosphere not just rainy but watery — stifling and clinging. How to keep one's head above it is the subject of Corkery's novel. Frank Bresnan is suffocated by it and drowns himself. His brother Finnbarr goes to sea. Lily, their sister, becomes a nun. It is left to characters like Martin Cloyne to travel the narrow channel of the ordinary, treading water as best he can. The epigraph to The Threshold of Quiet *comes from Henry David Thoreau's* Walden: *'The mass of men lead lives of quiet desperation.'*

Most of Corkery's fiction consists of short stories about the soul and soil of West Cork, a very different part of the world from his native Cork city. It was two protégés of his, Frank O'Connor and Sean O'Faolain, who put Cork on the literary map.

Quiet Desperation

Mercifully, as it seemed, the rain splashed, sharply, violently, against his window; he heard the wind begin to rush along the ground. What he was waiting for seemed to have come: listening to the driving by of wind and rain it was easier to deny audience to past and future; the present had assumed being, had now an existence of its own, an objective existence. He remembered that the flame of his candle had been tortured by draughts while he undressed; now the wind was strong, rising to a storm; when had it begun? It was a south-west gale; but was there not something of the north-west in this fitful violence? Ah, now it was gone, that fitfulness; a steady, solid, onward-driving hurricane this was, impossible to think of as without purpose.

He remembered how, passing over South Gate Bridge that day, he had noticed the river in spate, foamy, and brown with the earth of torn banks, full of field debris, making a great noise as it rushed through the narrow arches; and how, where the foam ceased just beyond the arches, the brown-green water looked like a seal's snout as it rose up now here, now there, to look over the quay wall. Tomorrow there would be floods in the centre of the city. How long was it since the big flood came down the Blackpool valley and people had to be rescued in boats? It was a Christmas Day, he remembered, and Frank and Lily . . . Ah, there was the past seeking to make good its entrance! How obliquely it had stolen up to the doors of his consciousness! To listen to the pelting rain, ever beginning anew, as it seemed; to listen to the wind, ever growing stronger, on this must he concentrate. Luckily the storm was insistent; it sounded like a never-ending column of artillery prancing, galloping, jolting, rolling, rushing, flying across bridge after bridge, through gorge after gorge, from destruction or towards destruction.

Was this the Lough he heard? Could its water make such a seascape sound? Were the water-birds screaming? Tomorrow there would be great flocks of seagulls and gannet on the shores; the water-hens would come out to catch the shining worms; around the shores would be a belt of lake-wrack, water-plants and broken reeds.

He forced his brain into a barren activity; he had become afraid of sleep: as with fiery swords, its gates were perilous with dreams. Quite still he lay, with his brows drawn down, determined to keep his thoughts in the narrow path his decree had marked out for them. Sometimes he moved his lips: he tried to recall bits of sea-poems, bits of storm lyrics; then again he made calculations as to the speed of great gales, telling himself that their speed is not nearly what people imagine. And each operation, in its turn, seemed the one thing needed.

Yet in spite of all his care, of the constant spurring of his jaded brain, his whole being, craving sleep and forgetfulness, would crawl, softly at first, in mere playfulness, as it were, towards the gates of sleep; would have almost passed them — the air within was all balm — when once again a fiery sword, all light and pain, would flash from a concealed scabbard and 'Oh God' would again tell of his soul's latest adventure to the howling winds.

It could not endure for ever. After a long stare at the darkness — he had almost ceased to hear the storm — his lids fell, lifted, fell . . . suddenly he sprang almost from the bed, 'God! God! God!' he said, all in a breath, like a man being flayed. And he sat up, with his hands against his face, and the tears ran through his fingers.

On the north side of the city is a railway cutting, spanned by a stone bridge, along the parapet of which runs a chamfered coping; to walk along this coping, the rails thirty feet below, was one of the tests of heroism among the boys of the district. Though he knew he was not made for daring deeds, Martin Cloyne *would* do it, had his feet on the coping, was hanging on with his finger-tips to the parapet above him, when a voice called: 'You mustn't, Martin, Frank says you mustn't.' In the dream Martin Cloyne was neither boy nor man, he was simply Martin Cloyne; but Frank Bresnan was a beautiful boy, a hero, who had just performed the deed, and Lily Bresnan was a little girl. He saw the little girl's face, it stared at him, the eyes wide with earnestness; and her voice was in his very ears! The voice seemed infinitely nearer than the staring eyes. It was the sound of it that had caused his very body to curl up like a spring.

from *The Threshold of Quiet* (1917)

DEIRDRE MADDEN

Claire is a painter, one of three women in Nothing is Black *who have retreated to rural County Donegal while they go through important transitions in their lives. One of Claire's preoccupations is the haunting presence of her dead friend, Alice, herself a superbly talented and self-confident artist.*

The novel's title is taken from the diary of the Mexican painter Frida Kahlo, who sees colour as follows: 'Cobalt Blue: electricity and purity. Love. Black: nothing is black, really nothing.'

Dying of the Light

As they walked back down the valley to the house where they were staying, dusk was falling, and she had never seen the valley look so beautiful. After the sun went down, the colours of the trees and the grass suddenly became more vivid than when the sun shone full upon them. They watched the grey clouds cover the peaks of the mountains, and the clustered villages became crowns of light in the dimness. As they rounded a curve in the path they startled some deer, which ran away and hid, shy and light, running in the dusk. And all the time she was thinking of Alice, of her having to leave life. The full moon shone that night, too. It had been there, blank white during the day, and they watched it fill with silver light as the dusk fell.

Shortly after they got back to the house, Tommy rang to say that Alice had died some hours earlier.

from *Nothing is Black* (1994)

SEAMUS HEANEY

Sweeney was a king who was cursed by a cleric and as a result lost his wits in battle. He then went on to spend long years wandering the country, naked and miserable, living in trees, lamenting his fate and praising the natural world in verse of piercing simplicity and beauty. At length he ends up at the monastery of Moling — St Mullins, Co. Carlow — where he attains a kind of stability.

Modern Irish writers, foremost among them Flann O'Brien and Seamus Heaney, have found the legend's tensions suggestive and emblematic. In the introduction to his version, Seamus Heaney notes that 'insofar as Sweeney is also a figure of the artist, displaced, guilty, assuaging himself by his utterance, it is possible to read the work as an aspect of the quarrel between free creative imagination and the constraints of religious, political, and domestic obligation'. The title of Seamus Heaney's essay on early Irish nature poetry is 'The God in the Tree'.

The original text of The Madness of Sweeney — *in Irish,* Buile Suibhne — *is thought to date from the twelfth century, though the events themselves apparently belong to an earlier age.*

from *Sweeney Praises the Trees*

The blackthorn is a jaggy creel
stippled with dark sloes;
green watercress in thatch on wells
where the drinking blackbird goes.

Sweetest of the leafy stalks,
the vetches strew the pathway;
the oyster-grass is my delight,
and the wild strawberry.

Low-set clumps of apple trees
drum down fruit when shaken;
scarlet berries clot like blood
on mountain rowan.

Briars curl in sideways,
arch a stickle back,
draw blood and curl up innocent
to sneak the next attack.

The yew tree in each churchyard
wraps night in its dark hood.

Ivy is a shadowy
genius of the wood.

Holly rears its windbreak,
a door in winter's face;
life-blood on a spear-shaft
darkens the grain of ash.

Birch tree, smooth and blessed,
delicious to the breeze,
high twigs plait and crown it
the queen of trees.

from *Sweeney Astray* (1983)

E. CHARLES NELSON AND WENDY WALSH

The elimination of trees from the Irish landscape began in earnest in Elizabethan times and went on into the eighteenth century, by which time, according to Arthur Young, 'the greatest part of the Kingdom exhibits a naked, bleak, dreary view for want of trees'. Agriculture was only one of the reasons why the land was cleared; another reason was that Irish forests supplied English shipyards. A third reason, unlikely as it may seem now, was the development of Irish ironworks. In addition, woods gave sanctuary to those resisting English settlement, so the military wanted them axed. And selling woodland became a way of settling debt.

All this interference in the look of the land and in the economy underlying it registered its cultural and symbolic significance in verse. Not so very long ago, every Irish schoolboy knew the opening lines of 'Kilcash', which in translation read: 'What will we do now for timber?/The woodlands all over are down.'

Forest Clearance

The first farmers had to create patches of open ground in which to sow seeds of grains. They felled and burnt small areas of woodland, grew several crops and after a few years abandoned each patch when the soil was exhausted, moving to another piece of woodland and repeating the process. Herbs and shrubs recolonised the abandoned plots, and tree saplings eventually were established, leading to the possibility of a regeneration of woodland. This type of temporary forest clearance, termed landnam, prevails today in some tropical regions, but has not been practised in Ireland for many millennia.

Slowly, forest clearance and agriculture altered the vegetation of lowland Ireland. The composition of the woodlands changed in response to human activities and the gradual shifts in climate, which became cooler and drier about 5500 years ago. Hazel became more abundant again, oak declined but ash increased. Scots pine was soon eliminated in many parts of Ireland. But the abundance of the different trees fluctuated as areas were exploited and then abandoned by the farming communities, and as new farming techniques were introduced.

The arrival of the plough in Ireland about 2600 years ago was followed by a substantial decline in elm and hazel, suggesting that woodland and scrub were cleared to make way for small fields.

Professor Frank Mitchell has argued that the advent of the ard-type plough marks the beginning of the period of wholesale forest clearance in Ireland.[1] The arrival about a millennium later, c. AD 300, of a more efficient plough with a coulter, capable of slicing through mats of roots and thus making tillage on a large scale much easier, further hastened the decline of natural woodlands.

Forests, perhaps substantially altered by human activities, still covered about one-sixth of Ireland 400 years ago — folk could then have told about the squirrel that walked from here to there through the tops of the trees. The final phase of felling of the native woodland began in the seventeenth century:

> The rape of the Irish forest took no more than one hundred years. The operation started in earnest about 1600 AD, and in 1698 AD, before one hundred years has passed, Parliament had enacted the first of a long series of acts (nearly all quite ineffective) to conserve stocks and encourage replanting.[2]

By 1800 less than 2 per cent of the land-surface of Ireland was cloaked by woodland. In the twentieth century the forest acreage is three times that, but only a small fraction is composed of native trees.

1.   G.F. Mitchell, *The Irish Landscape* (1976).
2.   G.F. Mitchell, 'The Influence of Man on Vegetation in Ireland . . .', *Journal of Life Sciences* (Royal Dublin Society), 3:7–14.

from *The Trees of Ireland* (1994)

JOHN MILLINGTON SYNGE

Less than twenty miles from Dublin, Glencree is a community, a river and one of the many valleys that make this northern stretch of the Wicklow mountains so spectacularly scenic. As can be imagined from his plays, Synge was a great walker and this part of Ireland was among his favourite haunts. Its isolation and its straight, stark roads were temperamentally appealing to him — as they were later to Samuel Beckett. When Belacqua Shua, protagonist of Beckett's short story 'Love and Lethe', finds himself in this part of the world, 'he thought of Synge and recovered his spirits'. The roads date from the 1798 Rebellion, when they were built to facilitate troop movements.

Another account of the spectral allure Glencree had for Synge is in his prose book In Wicklow, West Kerry and Connemara. *Little or nothing remains of the stands of old-growth oak that were once a striking feature of this landscape.*

Synge is buried at Mount Jerome cemetery, Dublin.

To the Oaks of Glencree

My arms are round you, and I lean
Against you, while the lark
Sings over us, and golden lights, and green
Shadows are on your bark.

There'll come a season when you'll stretch
Black boards to cover me:
Then in Mount Jerome I will lie, poor wretch,
With worms eternally.

from *Poems and Translations* (1909)

ANONYMOUS

Pre-Christian, Early Christian, Norman . . . Mention of just three of the phases of Irish civilisation shows how very different from each other those phases can be. Yet there is also a sense in modern Ireland that the Irish language, despite the many complex changes that it went through, maintains a thread of continuity from the earliest times. A large number of modern Irish writers have been intrigued by this cultural conceit, and have been inspired by it to approach Early Christian verse, in particular, in a spirit of homage and preservation. One reason for these approaches may be that this is poetry that, in Frank O'Connor's words, 'glows in its own light, the literature of a people full of confidence in itself'. But another reason may be that in this poetry was heard, in words attributed to the ancient Irish hero Finn McCool, 'the best music in the world . . . the music of what happens'.

The Blackbird by Belfast Lough

What little throat
Has framed that note?
What gold beak shot
    It far away?
A blackbird on
His leafy throne
Tossed it alone
    Across the bay.

translated by Frank O'Connor, from Brendan Kennelly (ed.),
The Penguin Book of Irish Verse (1970)

JOHN MILLINGTON SYNGE

The first version of 'Winter' was written in 1896 but, like all Synge's work, it was later subjected to extensive revisions. Synge spent the winter of that year in Paris where he met W.B. Yeats, who advised him to 'Give up Paris . . . Go to the Arran [sic] Islands. Live there as if you were one of the people themselves; express a life that has never found expression.'

This advice changed Synge's life. In 1898 he visited Aran for the first time. A revolution in Irish drama followed.

Winter

With little money in a great city

There's snow in every street
Where I go up and down,
And there's no woman, man, or dog
That knows me in the town.

I know each shop, and all
These Jews, and Russian Poles,
For I go walking night and noon
To spare my sack of coals.

from *Poems and Translations* (1909)

BRENDAN KENNELLY

Sea power is largely a mythological matter in Irish tradition. The sea is host to the otherworld — 'tír fé tonn', the land under the waves. Manannán, the legendary Celtic shape-changer, is so closely associated with the sea as to have the surname Mac Lir, son of the sea. Aran Islands fishermen never learned to swim, acknowledging the futility of struggling against the ocean. Age-old notions of the sea's divinity have perhaps obscured an appreciation of Ireland's maritime tradition, awareness and commemoration of which seem less prominent than might be expected of people living on an island. And modern Irish literature includes relatively little in the way of sea stories. Even its epic, Ulysses, is landlocked.

Brendan Kennelly grew up on the shore of the powerfully tidal Shannon estuary.

Sea

I am patient, repetitive, multi-voiced,
Yet few hear me
And fewer still trouble to understand

Why, for example, I caress
And hammer the land.
I do not brag of my depths

Or my currents, I do not
Boast of my moods or my colours
Or my breath in your thought.

In time I surrender my drowned,
My appetite speaks for itself,
I could swallow all you have found

And open for more,
My green tongues licking the shores
Of the world

Like starved beasts reaching for men
Who will not understand
When I rage and roar

When I bellow and threaten
I am obeying a law
Observing a discipline.

This is the rhythm
I live.
This is the reason I move

In hunger and skill
To give you the pick of my creatures.
This is why I am willing to kill,

Chill every created nerve.
You have made me a savage master
Because I know how to serve.

from *Selected Poems* (1990)

RICHARD MURPHY

In 1960–67, Richard Murphy ran a boating business between Cleggan and Inishbofin, on the coast of Connemara. Pat Cloherty had been the Bofin mailboat's helmsman in the days of sail. This poem is based on what Cloherty recalled hearing about the sinking of The Maisie, *which went down in 1900 off the coast of Mayo.*

*   The Maisie was a hooker, a gaff-rigged cutter peculiar to the west coast of Ireland, a cart-horse of the sea.*

Pat Cloherty's Version of The Maisie

I've no tooth to sing you the song
    Tierney made at the time
        but I'll tell the truth

It happened on St John's Day
    sixty-eight years ago
        last June the twenty-fourth

The Maisie sailed from Westport Quay
    homeward on a Sunday
        missing Mass to catch the tide

John Kerrigan sat at her helm
    Michael Barrett stood at her mast
        and Kerrigan's wife lay down below

The men were two stepbrothers
   drownings in the family
      and all through the family

Barrett kept a shop in the island
   Kerrigan plied the hooker
      now deeply laden with flour

She passed Clare and she came to Cahir
   two reefs tied in the mainsail
      she bore a foresail but no jib

South-east wind with strong ebb-tide
   still she rode   this way   that way
      hugging it   hugging it   O my dear

And it blew and blew hard and blew hard
   but Kerrigan kept her to it
      as long as he was there he kept her to it

Rain fell in a cloudburst
   hailstones hit her deck
      there was no return for him once he'd put out

At Inishturk when the people saw
   The Maisie smothered up in darkness
      they lit candles in the church

What more could Kerrigan do?
   he put her jaw into the hurricane
      and the sea claimed him

Barrett was not a sailor
   to take a man from the water
      yet the sea claimed him too

At noon the storm ceased
   and we heard *The Maisie*'d foundered
      high upon a Mayo strand

The woman came up from the forecastle
   she came up alone on deck
      and a great heave cast her out on shore

And another heave came while she drowned
   and put her on her knees
      like a person'd be in prayer

That's the way the people found her
   and the sea never came in
      near that mark no more

John Kerrigan was found
   far down at Achill Sound
      he's buried there

Michael Barrett was taken
   off Murrisk Pier
      he's buried there

Kerrigan's wife was brought from Cross
   home to Inishbofin
      and she's buried there

from *New Selected Poems* (1989)

PLACES APART

MAURICE CRAIG

James Butler (1610–88), first Duke of Ormond, was a member of a family that had been a power in Ireland since Norman times. He had already played an important role in Irish affairs during the turbulent 1640s, with Owen Roe O'Neill (1590–1649) as an ally, before his triumphant return. Among the changes he made to the city are the Phoenix Park, the Royal Hospital Kilmainham and the quays — Ormond Quay is immediately east of the Four Courts. He also saw to it that the seal of legal approval was put on Cromwell's confiscations of land. When James II came to the throne in 1685, Ormond retired, just before the onset of further 'unsettled times'.

In recent years, the area between Christ Church and St Patrick's Cathedrals in particular, and old Dublin generally, have been rationalised into office buildings and roadways.

James Ussher (1581–1656), Archbishop of Armagh, played an active part in the complicated events of the 1640s. The building of the Four Courts began in 1786; its bombardment by Free State forces in June 1922 started the Civil War.

The Duke Returns

On the 29th of May, 1453, the city of Constantinople fell to the troops of Mahomet II. With a dull explosion the Byzantine polity disintegrated, and the roads to Western Europe were, if the verdict of history is to be trusted, packed thick with refugee scholars, each clutching a precious codex, some now and again casting a backward glance to where, above the smoke of the fallen city, the shallow dome of Hagia Sophia, with monumental buttresses like the paws of a lion or a sphinx, still stood in its tenth century of power. A solemn scene, and one from which the academic mind is prone to date the beginning of modern history.

In due course the smoke dispersed; Constantinople settled down to its long Ottoman repose; the scholars, hospitably received at Western courts, left their manuscripts in the libraries of Rome and Milan. Like a seismic ripple or the last reverberation of a tidal wave, this great Levantine catastrophe spread its rings until, two hundred years later, a little wave washed up the sands of a remote western shore, and James Duke of Ormonde stepped out of his pinnace on to the sands of Dublin Bay. The Renaissance, in a word, had arrived in Ireland. It was July the 27th in the year 1662. The peasantry welcomed him on the shore, dancing and strewing flowers in his path. They sang, in Irish, 'Thugamar féin an samhra linn': 'We brought the summer with us.'[1] The Duke's reception in Dublin 'was, for the splendour thereof, a kind of epitome of what had lately been seen at London upon His Majesty's happy restoration'. The Middle Ages were at last at an end.

The Duke of Ormonde was now fifty-two, the ninth member of the house of Butler to hold viceregal office, and himself an ex-viceroy. He brought back with him memories of his last departure from Dublin twelve years earlier, involved in the defeat of his royal master. He had more recent memories of the opulent grandeur of Louis XIV's Paris, and of his own poverty and humiliation in the lean years of exile. He had seen in France the happy effects of the toleration of Huguenots, and had learnt the lesson which the French King was so soon to forget. He himself had a family background which was partly Catholic, partly Protestant, matching to a nicety the country he was now to rule. Above all, he had absorbed on his travels the conception of the centralised state and the ceremonial capital.

Ormonde's ideal, then, was an Ireland of Protestant and (if possible) Catholic, whose greatest need was peace, and the noblest outward sign of peace, public works. And as charity begins at home, so improvements were best placed where they would make the best showing, in the capital itself. Any measure which would emphasise Dublin's position as the head and front of Ireland was in tune with the new policy. For it must be remembered that only now did Dublin become the capital in any modern sense. It was less than a century since Drogheda had been abandoned as a venue for Parliament. Even more recently, a large quasi-parliament had sat in Kilkenny.[2] The Dublin Parliament of 1613, only fifty years before, was the first to be in any sense representative of the whole country; and it was also the first, by a natural consequence, in which any serious anti-English opposition was encountered. The ecclesiastical capital was, and still is, Armagh. For many a long year after 1660 there were whole tracts of the country which held little or no communication with Dublin.

But Ormonde's policy, half-consciously inspired by the Parisian example, was permanently successful in this sense: that Dublin became and remained an object of first interest for all important movements from now on. In the recent past, native Irish leaders such as Owen Roe O'Neill had conducted their strategy almost without reference to the capital as such. But even the Gaelic mind was now to learn the urban habit. Dublin, from being merely the chief garrison of the English Pale, was to become an object of pride and of contention to Irishmen of whatever race or creed.

As it stood in 1660, it was hardly an object of pride to anybody. In area it was about one-sixth of the area of mediæval London, being nearly half as long, nearly half as wide, and roughly the same shape.[3] The area of mediæval London was about two-thirds of a square mile, that of Dublin about one-ninth of a square mile. Like London it was a rectangle with one of the longer sides bordering the river. In the south-west corner the Castle corresponded to the Tower of London. But, as Dublin lay south of the Liffey instead of north of the Thames, the Castle stood on a landward corner, with the miserable trickle of the Poddle river serving as a ditch round two of its sides. The Castle was fairly enough described by one of Ormonde's relatives in 1684 as 'the worst castle in the worst situation in Christendom'.

Round the walls there stood, besides the castle, some seventeen towers and gate-towers, mostly in poor repair. In the centre of the city stood Christchurch Cathedral, also in a semi-ruinous condition, and within the walls there were six or seven parish churches of the Establishment,[4] as well as an even more indefinite (though probably smaller) number of Catholic churches. The population, by a census of 1659, was under nine thousand;[5] and this included six parishes without the walls. We may therefore infer that a large proportion of the houses were derelict. Few of them, in any case, can have been more than single-storey cabins, and the unsettled times must have discouraged adequate repairs, to say nothing of new building. A handful of three- and four-storey houses dating from Elizabeth's reign and even earlier survived into the mid-eighteenth century, and the one of which a drawing . . . survives shows that in parts, at least, this earlier Dublin was not unlike the London which perished in the Great Fire.

Hardly anything now remains of the Dublin of 1660. The mediæval street-plan, both within and without the walls, is still almost as obvious on the ground as it is on the map. Some of the old street-names have disappeared: though Copper Alley still survives, the famous Smock Alley close by has become Essex Street West; the Blind Quay has been barbarously re-named Exchange Street Lower; Giglots' Hill has become, more excusably, St Michael's Hill. But Fishamble Street, Winetavern Street, Ship Street ('Sheep' Street), survive in both name and fact. Bull Alley and Golden Lane are there in name but in little more; and little but the name survives of Hoey's Court where in 1668 Jonathan Swift was born.

Of the actual buildings still less is to be seen. So little indeed that an attempt at a complete catalogue will hardly be out of place. The remains consist, with only one exception, of the military and ecclesiastical structures, stone-built and of mediæval date. There are the Cathedrals, much-restored in the nineteenth century, of St Patrick's and Christchurch. The Archbishop's Palace of St Sepulchre, long converted into a police-barracks. It contains a mediæval vault and a sixteenth-century window. The mediæval church of St Audoen's, three-quarters ruined and the remaining quarter botched. The chapter-house of St Mary's Abbey of Oxmantown, half underground. A long stretch of early mediæval wall, marking the line before the city had even reached the banks of the Liffey, much remodelled but containing a gate — St Audoen's Gate — which is not quite so much of a fake as it appears to be. Another stretch of wall, from New Gate (the western gate) in a south-easterly direction towards the vanished Hanging Tower. Until a few years ago the Corporation carefully protected with a railing a fragment of New Gate itself; but without warning the same agency abolished it overnight. In the Castle itself there remain the stumps or cores of three towers and other walls, either invisible or heavily overlaid with later work. Of the original Trinity College hardly a vestige remains except a recumbent effigy of an early Fellow, of alabaster hideously eroded by damp, and kept (by the dramatic inspiration of some bygone Clerk of Works) in a gloomy triangular yard which sets off its macabre luminosity to perfection. It would be a fitting place in which to take our leave of the mediæval city, picturesque from a distance, with water-meadows and a still unsullied river flowing past the walls, but at close quarters squalid and constricted. (The effigy has now been taken indoors.)

If we wish to revisit it, the simplest course is to go at night to Castle Street or Fishamble Street, St Michael's Hill . . . Bride Street or Back Lane. The darkness will obscure the fact that the houses have been rebuilt, and the streets will appear narrower and more tortuous than ever. The derelict tenements might, for all we can discern, have been knocked about by Cromwell's Colonels. In the occupied buildings candle-lighting is still usual, and out of the high windows lean Skeltonian women with wispy hair, gossiping with neighbours in other houses. Even the tall blocks of improving flats built by the Iveagh Trust forty years ago remind one at night of the Old Town at Edinburgh. There have been public-houses on some of these sites since long before Ormonde's time, and in their narrow back rooms sit pensive men with hats on, raising from time to time long black pints of porter to long dark faces. The towers and spires of the Protestant churches, chilly, empty and very firmly shut, cluster together to blot the skyline. Darkness softens the elements of restoration and modernity, and is even merciful enough to hide the French Gothic of the Augustinian Church.

History does not record the antiquity of the festivities on New Year's Eve in Christchurch Place, when crowds gather, young and old, drunk and sober, letting off fireworks and dancing in eddying rings as far as O'Connell Bridge, while the Christchurch peal rings out the old. Few, on these occasions, give a thought to the dank vaults of St Werburgh's where Sir James Ware and Lord Edward Fitzgerald sleep, or to those of the roofless and derelict St Nicholas Within, where nobody sleeps at all. Few even noticed that a year or two ago the tall house[6] bearing the arms of Archbishop Ussher, which had long surveyed the scene, had gone. A few yards down Werburgh Street, at the entrance to Hoey's Court, a bust of Jonathan Swift faces us from a niche in the wall of a public-house. The associations of the place are unending, and to follow up the most notable would lead us well into the nineteenth century.

We may turn instead into St John's Lane, so narrow that the bells are almost inaudible, deadened by the weight of stone above us. But as we emerge into Winetavern Street . . . the sound drowns thought again, the clanging waves hitting the windows of the old houses in the Crescent and reverberating back upon us. We descend the steep street, lined with tottering tenements shored up with great baulks of wood. The street-lighting is meagre. We have passed through the King's Gate, long extinct, and looking back we realise how forcibly the Cathedral, small in itself but perched on a high and peaty hillock, dominates the walled city. As we reach the river the sound of the bells is reduplicated, struck back again from the housefronts along the Quays. The lamps are reflected in the water, but the shadows are black under the graceful arches of the bridge. Beyond, stretching almost to the next bridge, is the river-front of the Four Courts, and rising out of it, dim above the glare of the lamps, the gigantic drum and dome. We have come to 1786: we have come, indeed, to 1922.

1.   Donal O'Sullivan, *The Bunting Collection* (Irish Folk-Song Society) III, 58 (1930). See also *JRSAI* [*Journal of the Royal Society of Antiquaries of Ireland*], LXXIX, 93 (1949).

2.   The Confederation Parliament of 1649.

3.   The areas given are those within the walls. By 1660, of course, both cities had spread outside their walls.

4.   i.e. the Anglican Church of Ireland.

5.   *CARD* [Sir John Gilbert, *Calendars of Ancient Records of Dublin*] IV, 560.

6.   No. 3 Fishamble Street, in which, also, James Clarence Mangan [1803–49; the best-known Irish poet of the nineteenth century] was born.

from *Dublin 1660–1860* (1952)

MR AND MRS S.C. HALL

Sackville and Carlisle are now both O'Connell. The name of the square behind the Rotunda has been changed from Rutland to Parnell. Kingstown went back to being Dún Laoghaire in 1920. On the other hand, the majority of Dublin's main thoroughfares retain the names of bygone landlords and viceroys, foreign now to 'the stranger' and the local alike. The Halls' interest in making the visitor feel at home is more than simple geniality. In the preface to their Ireland, Its Scenery, Character, &c, *written at the height of the campaign to repeal the Act of Union, they hope 'to make Ireland more advantageously known to England — that the tie which unites them may be more closely knit, and that the people of both countries may think, feel, and act as* ONE PEOPLE'.

*   The gallant wretch who allegedly designed the Bank of Ireland is evidently a figment of the authors' imagination — an early example of the urban folk-tale, perhaps. The best authorities credit the building to the architect Sir Edward Lovett Pearce (1699–1733).*

Dublin in the 1840s

Returning to the bay, we leave the pretty island of Dalky and enter the channel between two huge sandbanks which are called — from the perpetual roaring of the sea over them — 'the Bulls', north and south. But the place of ordinary debarkation is Kingstown formerly called Dunleary, but which received its modern name in honour of His Majesty George IV who took shipboard there on leaving Ireland in 1821. To commemorate the event of the king's visit, an obelisk was erected on the spot where he last stood with an inscription setting forth the fact.

The harbour of Kingstown is safe, commodious and exceedingly picturesque. From the quay — the first stone of which was laid in 1817 by Lord Whitworth, the Viceroy of Ireland — the railway carriages start, and convey passengers a distance of seven miles in about twenty minutes to the terminus within a few hundred yards of the centre of the city. This is the Dublin and Kingstown Railway which was opened for the public on 17 December 1834, but the entire distance was not finished until the year 1837.

The stranger cannot fail to receive a most agreeable impression of Dublin, for its principal streets and leading attractions lie within a comparatively narrow compass, and his attention is sure to be fixed upon some object worthy of observation — to be succeeded, almost immediately, by some other of equal note.

If he arrives sea-ward he will have fully established the magnificence of the approach, and there is scarcely one road that conducts to it on which he will not have journeyed through beautiful scenery and obtained a fine view of the city as he nears it.

But we must place him at once nearly in the centre of the city upon Carlisle Bridge, and perhaps from no single spot can the eye command so great a number of interesting points.

He turns to the north, and looks upon a noble street — Sackville Street. Midway is Nelson's Pillar, a fine Ionic column surmounted by a statue of the hero. Directly opposite this is the Post Office, a modern structure built in pure taste. Beyond is the Lying-In hospital and the Rotunda and, ascending a steep hill, one of the many fine squares.

To the south he has within his ken the far-famed Bank of Ireland and the University.

To the west the Four Courts — the courts of law — and the several bridges.

To the east the Custom House, a superb, though lonesome building, and the quays.

Towering above all, and within his ken wherever he is directed, are numerous steeples, of which no city, except the metropolis of England, can boast so many. In fact, nearly all the great attractions of Dublin may be seen from this bridge.

These buildings we shall proceed to describe, but we must do so briefly. First, the College:

The Dublin University differs from the universities of Oxford and Cambridge in being limited to a single college, but the distinction between the university and the college is very rarely noticed, and in common parlance they are confounded together.

The College was founded in 1591 by Elizabeth; its charter was confirmed and extended by James I who conferred upon it the privilege of returning two members to the Irish Parliament. Additional privileges were granted by Charles I, George IV and Queen Victoria. The fellows are indebted to the present queen for the liberty to marry without being deprived of their fellowships, and the advantage taken of the boon proves how earnestly it was desired.

The front of the College faces Dame Street, and by its architectural beauty it is harmonised with the magnificent structure formerly occupied by the Irish Parliament.

Trinity College was honoured by the inspection of Her Majesty and Prince Albert on the occasion of the royal visit to Dublin in 1849. The august party were received by the provost and senior fellows and conducted to the magnificent library, which excited their admiration by its extent and excellent adaptation to the purpose to which it is applied. The number of volumes is about 150,000. The present librarian has zealously exerted himself to render the collection complete, especially in foreign literature. In the eastern pavilion there is another collection of books called the Fagel Library which amounts to 20,000 volumes. It was the property of the Fagel family and was removed to London from Holland in 1784, upon the invasion of that country by the French. The Manuscript Room contains many valuable manuscripts.

The Bank of Ireland — which was the Parliament House before the Union — is universally classed among the most perfect examples of British architecture in the kingdom, and indeed it is perhaps unsurpassed in Europe. Yet, strange to say, little or nothing is known of the architect, and the history of this graceful and beautiful structure is wrapped in obscurity almost approaching mystery.

The historians of Dublin are singularly unsatisfactory upon this head. We learn from them only that the 'Parliament House was begun to be built during the administration of John, Lord Carteret, in the year 1729, and was executed under the inspection of Sir Edward Lovel Pearce, engineer and surveyor-general, but completed by Arthur Dobbs, Esq., his successor, about the year 1729.' Dr Walsh, the historian, who is usually so searching in his inquiries and so minute as to facts, tells us no more than Harris, the historian who preceded him, and who makes no mention of Mr Cassell or Castell, the architect to whom the building is usually attributed, but of whom very little is known. Mr Brewer states, but does not give upon authority, that Mr Cassell did not visit Ireland until the year 1773, nearly fifty years after the structure was commenced.

However, whomever it was, it is clear that he was content with supplying the design and instructions without superintending the work in its progress. Perhaps it was some needy man who, oppressed by poverty, was tempted to remain in the background and sell both his genius and his glory to the engineer and surveyor-general.

from *Ireland: Its Scenery, Character &c,* 3 vols. (1st edn, 1841–3)

CHEVALIER DE LA TOCNAYE

The Duke of Ormond's idea of Dublin as not just a capital but a metropolitan showplace reached full flower in the eighteenth century. Beginning with the Wide Streets Commission in 1757, the city centre began to realise itself in space and light. Squares were created, the North and South Circular Roads were laid down, and a glittering theatrical and musical life came into being.

By the time the Chevalier de La Tocnaye made his visit in 1796, something had happened to the enlightened energy of those developments. As he noted, 'the splendid carriages and the apparent wealth of the principal houses' were still in evidence. But social life strikes him as chaotic, and manners unseemly, if not actually eccentric. De La Tocnaye makes a complicated pun: déroutes means routed like a defeated army. Elsewhere, the country is arming.

This is the same year that Wolfe Tone, who founded the republican United Irishmen five years earlier, went to France in search of support for the Irish cause. It was French republicanism that caused the royalist de La Tocnaye to be in Ireland.

Social Customs

From seeing Irishmen abroad one would imagine them to be most gallant and incapable of living without society. The very same men who appear to find so much pleasure in dancing attendance on our ladies allow cavaliers to flirt with their own. When an Irishman presents himself at the door of a Jacques Roastbeef in England, the latter fears immediately an attack on his purse, his wife, his daughter, or his wine. In revenge Dublin is shy in receiving the foreigner. One would say that the Dubliners remember their own faults of youth.

There are few social functions except those that are called *routs*. With reason I might describe them as *déroutes*. Where a house might comfortably entertain twenty persons, sixty are invited, and so in proportion. I have seen routs where, from vestibule to garret, the rooms were filled with fine ladies beautifully dressed, but so crushed against each other that it was hardly possible to move. A foreigner has cause for embarrassment in these too brilliant assemblies, for he may here see really charming women in greater number than in most cities, and he thinks it a pity to see them lose on a stairway the time which might be passed much more agreeably with a small number of appreciative friends.

Nearly all the rich, I am told, spend more than their incomes, and so are obliged to resort to ruinous expedients in order to keep up style. In most European countries such prodigality is not so injurious to society, in that the expense goes to encourage art and talents, which serve to make life agreeable. Here in Ireland there is no such redeeming result, for the things on which the money is spent are not products of the country, and those who practise the fine arts, being without encouragement, and being, indeed, despised, seek other lands where their work is more highly appreciated. To nobles who are bent on ruining themselves, I counsel the spending of their means on Irish-made goods. That would be real patriotism.

When it was known that I intended to write the trifles which occupy the attention of the reader at the moment, several people exerted themselves to procure for me entry to various establishments where never before had foreigner been admitted.

I was warned by the case of a certain Mr Twiss to be careful as to what I should put on paper. This Twiss was an Englishman, not wanting in wit, but still an Englishman of a commonly-seen type, full of prejudice in favour of his own country and considering all peoples of other lands as very inferior species. After having travelled over the greater part of Europe he came to Ireland, and had the imprudence to express discontent when several persons for whom he had letters of recommendation did not invite him to their houses. He should have remembered that the usage had been copied from England, where people will sometimes pay you the compliment of inviting you to an inn and leave you to pay your own charges. Such treatment was, perhaps, responsible for some dry responses at which he was much mortified. Thereupon he proceeded on his travels, and found in the towns what I myself have experienced — that is to say, a too ceremonious hospitality, the person to whom you have presented your letter paying you a visit of ceremony and then sending you on the day following an invitation for three or four days ahead. Surely it is a curious compliment to oblige a traveller to remain so long in a little town, where he has neither friend nor acquaintance, in order that he may, at last, have the pleasure to see much beautiful silver shining beautifully on the sideboard, servants in livery, and a huge piece of beef on the end of the table with hungry executioners round it. But it is the custom, and those who practise it think they are acting with great politeness in not asking you on the first day.

from *A Frenchman's Walk Through Ireland* (1797)

DERMOT BOLGER

The 1960s saw a major change in the life and atmosphere of Dublin, with the evacuation of the greater part of its inner-city population to new housing estates on the city's northern fringes. One of these was built in the semi-rural village of Finglas. The road to Finglas crosses the Royal Canal by Mountjoy Jail, turns right at Doyle's Corner and continues on past Glasnevin Cemetery. The funeral of Paddy Dignam in Ulysses travelled this road. But the funeral only went as far as the cemetery. The story of The Woman's Daughter moves beyond Glasnevin into a different kind of terra incognita where alienation, neglect and emotional underdevelopment contribute to the making of the daughter in question.

The countryside beyond Finglas was once called Fingal — the land of the foreigner. Partly with that in mind, Samuel Beckett wrote an unnerving short story entitled 'Fingal'. In 1994, a new local government jurisdiction was established to administer the northern part of County Dublin. It is called Fingal.

Moving to Finglas

D on't stare at me like that, you frighten me with those eyes. They've gone now, I tell you, they'll never harm you. I've always looked after you, you know I always will. Don't move away from me again, come back daughter, come here like you used to, do you remember? Take down your dress and rock in my arms the way you loved to when you were small. And I'll tell you a story; I'll tell you how we came here, me and Johnny and Mammy and Daddy.

We were all up on top of a huge open lorry and Daddy was cursing because he couldn't get the rope to fit around it. There was a crowd of neighbours from Rutland Street gathered around the lorry and he'd bought a bag of Lemon's boiled sweets for all my friends even though it wasn't Saturday. They kept jumping up and waving at me until I felt like a film star, and then Daddy climbed in beside the driver and with a big black puff of smoke we moved off with the children running behind and old Mrs O'Byrne from the same landing leaning out of her window and calling to my mother who was sitting on one of the new chairs.

We drove away up the North Circular Road with Johnny and myself clasping our hands under the chairs to keep from falling off, past Doyle's Corner until we came over Cross Guns Bridge and saw the big flashing lock of the canal at the flour mill where that woman was murdered, and then out past the orphanage where all the boys in short trousers with their hair cropped like convicts raced over to the tall railings to stare at us and shout at Johnny, and then along by the grey stone wall with the towers till we reached the railings of the cemetery. That scared me when I saw it first, with those carved out tombs of priests and bishops just within the walls covering the bones of figures stretched out in stone, and the big crowd of sombre mourners waiting for some hearse. And then we reached the countryside with the big houses set in their own grounds across from the graveyard and the road sweeping down towards the stone bridge with a pub where the wood began.

We swung left there and up that hill where there was a little row of small cottages and a country lane leading down to the back of the dairy. It felt like we were out in Meath or Wicklow. And then the truck swung left again into an uneven road and we had to grip the chairs tight to cling on. And as I swung my head round to see this street with muck and stones from the builders all over the road and every second house still empty, I got so excited I almost cried out with so much space everywhere.

Another crowd gathered when the lorry pulled up, but this time nobody waved to us. Instead the children stared silently from the doorways or called backwards to their parents inside. My father got out and I could see he was angry. He stood looking up at the furniture as if he wanted to bundle it all up under his coat and run inside.

'We should have waited for darkness,' he said, 'to get the stuff into the house.' He carefully avoided the watching eyes as he hauled at the ropes only intent on trying to save his pride.

My mother was different. She climbed down from the truck and stood there brushing her hands as if every detail of the street was to be savoured like a prize. A neighbouring woman approached her and with a careless wave of her hair she was gone off to drink tea in a kitchen. Some of the children came closer and craned their necks to gaze up.

'Oi, headtheball, where'd ya get the sister?' one boy shouted and they all laughed. Johnny sat with his feet swinging over the edge of the lorry talking to them. He jumped down to join the crowd as they moved off and called to me over his shoulder. But even though I wanted to follow, I stayed there expecting him to turn again or stop and call for me, but he never bothered and they all just ran on with their feet scrambling for a kick at a small plastic ball.

My father and the driver were working without ever exchanging a word, shifting piece after piece of furniture in through the hall door. After a while, the driver stopped as if asserting his independence and offered Daddy a cigarette. They stood in the doorway silently smoking. The winter twilight was coming in, dragging a cold mist down with it.

from *The Woman's Daughter* (1987, revised edn 1992)

ANONYMOUS

Dublin Zoo is in the Phoenix Park, the westernmost gate to which is at Castleknock. Founded in 1830, it is the third oldest public zoo in the world. Over the years, one of its specialities has been the breeding of lions. It is doubtful if any other zoo has had its popularity attested to quite like this by swain and maid — 'mot', in Dublin slang. The Lough might be the Salmon Pool at Islandbridge.

The Zoological Gardens

Oh thunder and lightening it's no lark,
When Dublin city is in the dark.
If you've any money go up to the park,
And view the Zoological gardens.

Last Sunday night we had no dough,
So I took the mot up to see the Zoo,
We saw the lions and the kangaroos
Inside the Zoological gardens.

Well we went out there by Castleknock,
Said the mot to me 'Sure we'll court by the Lough.'
And I knew she was one of the rare old stock,
Inside the Zoological gardens.

Said the mot to me 'My dear friend Jack
Would like a ride on the elephant's back.'
'If you don't get ou'a that, I'll give you such a crack
Inside the Zoological gardens.'

Now we went out there on our honeymoon,
Said the mot to me 'If you don't come soon,
I'll have to sleep with the hairy baboon
Inside the Zoological gardens!'

OLIVER ST JOHN GOGARTY

In January 1923, at the height of the Civil War, Gogarty, who supported the Free State, was kidnapped from his home at gunpoint and, in his own words, 'held as a hostage in an empty house near the Salmon Pool by the Islandbridge'. Assuming that he was about to be shot, he pleaded a call of nature, threw the fur coat which was all he was wearing over the heads of his captors, and jumped into the river. Swimming for his life, he swore that, if he survived, he would present two swans to the river in thanksgiving.

A pair of swans was ceremonially donated a little more than a year later. Legend has it that all Liffey swans are descended from these.

The personage mentioned in the opening verse is Fionnuala, daughter of Lir, whom a wicked stepmother turned into a swan. The 'Twin Sportsmen' are Castor and Pollux, offspring of Zeus's encounter with Leda.

An Offering of Swans

Keep you these calm and lovely things,
And float them on your clearest water;
For one would not disgrace a King's
Transformed beloved and buoyant daughter.

And with her goes this sprightly swan,
A bird of more than royal feather
With alban beauty clothed upon:
O keep them fair and well together!

As fair as was that doubled Bird
By love of Leda so besotten,
That she was all with wonder stirred:
And the Twin Sportsmen were begotten!

from *Collected Poems* (1951)

ELIZABETH BOWEN

St Stephen's Green had existed for many centuries as common land before it was taken over and improved in the late seventeenth century. At that time, houses began to be built around it, and the green became a place for residents to enjoy — residents only. It was not until 1880 that one of the residents, Lord Ardilaun, a member of the Guinness family, had the green made into a public amenity, paying for the landscaping himself.

Elizabeth Bowen's closest Irish associations are with her father's family home of Bowen's Court, near Mitchelstown, Co. Cork; here she spent her summers. But she was born in Dublin, at 15 Herbert Place, on the banks of the Grand Canal, from where the water in the lake at St Stephen's Green comes. Her mother was a Dubliner, Florence Colley, of Mount Temple, Clontarf. When Elizabeth Bowen was seven, her father had a nervous breakdown and she and her mother went to live in England where her mother died in 1912.

Stephen's Green

Yes, for quiet walking we crossed the canal. But Dublin, the city behind Herbert Place, was magnetic. Miss Baird liked centres of life; she liked Grafton Street; she liked Stephen's Green with its patterns of lawns and lake, its peopled footbridge, its mounds and its boskage that was romantic even in winter-time. Though English, she was a born Continental; the most nearly foreign governess that I had. She could divine (in the water-divining sense) any possible scene of fashion. Often, and not really I think from kindness, we went out to feed the ducks in Stephen's Green. I carried the bag of crusts; she carried a muff. Towards the point where we took up our station, on the kerb of the lake, the water-fowl converged with a darting smoothness, their ripples making spokes of a fan.

Among the floating and bloating crusts the reflections were broken up. The birds jabbed brutally with their beaks. I tried to insist on justice: there was always a slow duck or a wistful duck that did not get anything. Round me and the lake the rock-stuck mounds and the arbour-work against the evergreens sometimes glittered or glistened in sunshine that was frosty or damp, but were sometimes haunted or derelict under a brown veil. The lake's polish varied with our days. Under my nostrils the smell of sopping bread filled the air. The trams running round us, outside the trees and railings, according to weather sounded distant or near. The throbbing tune of a barrel-organ underran the hum and rumble of traffic: for minutes together a tune took command of the City. Everyone seemed to listen; it seemed to suspend the world.

At one of these minutes I remember my mother standing on the bridge over the lake, looking for us. She sometimes came here on an impulse to join Miss Baird and me. Her hat was perched on the hair piled over her pointed face; I could have known her only by the turn of her head as she looked along the lake for my scarlet coat. I was as easy to see as a pillar-box. She started towards us through the strolling and standing people as though through a garden that was her own.

My mother's feeling for Stephen's Green was native, subtle, nostalgic, unlike Miss Baird's. As a young girl between classes at Alexandra College she had walked and sat here — sometimes in love with a person, always in love with an idea. The most intense moments of her existence all through her life had been solitary. She often moved some way away from things and people she loved, as though to convince herself that they did exist. Perhaps she never did quite convince herself, for about her caresses and ways with me I remember a sort of rapture of incredulity. Her only child had been born after nine years of waiting — and even I was able to understand that she did not take me or her motherhood for granted. She was so much desolated that she unnerved me when anything went wrong between her and me. If my mother was a perfectionist, she had the kind of wisdom that goes with that make-up. She explained to me candidly that she kept a governess because she did not want to scold me herself. To have had to keep saying 'Do this,' 'Don't do that,' and 'No,' to me would have been, as she saw it, a peril to everything. So, to interpose between my mother and me, to prevent our spending the best part of our days together, was the curious function of every governess. It was not that there were more pressing claims on my mother's time: she was not a worldly woman (though she did like pleasure) and my father was out the greater part of the day. When she was not with me she thought of me constantly, and planned ways in which we could meet and could be alone.

I know now the feeling with which she stood on the bridge, looked along the lake till she came to my scarlet coat, then thought, 'That *is* my child!'

When I had been born my mother was thirty-four — so that in these winters I write about she was approaching the end of her thirties. I do not remember her clothes distinctly; I only see the fluid outline of her. I believe that she had a sealskin jacket and that her skirts swept barely clear of the ground. One of my father's brothers sent back from South Africa grey ostrich feathers for her and white for me. She possessed an ermine wrap and a string of pearls, and diamond and other rings that she wore on her blue-veined hands. Her style of dressing was personal; a touch of haughtiness set her against fashion. Susceptible to her charm, the glow of her face and being, I could feel its action on people around us — of this she was never conscious herself. She could withdraw into such a complete abstraction that she appeared to enter another world. Her beauty — for I know now it *was* beauty — was too elusive and fine for a child to appreciate: I thought I only thought she was lovely because I loved her.

She wore her bronze-coloured hair (which was threaded with silver early) in a pompadour over her forehead; at the back the hair was brushed up from the nape of her neck, then coiled on the top of her head. She shored up the weight of it with curved tortoiseshell combs. Her eyes, alternately pensive and quizzical, were triangular, with arched upper lids; they were of a grey-blue that deepened, and she had large pupils. Her dark eyebrows were expressive. When she smiled her nose turned down at the tip, and the smile sent her cheeks up in subtle curves. In her cheeks showed the blue-pink of a sweet-pea. She flushed easily, when she was startled or angry, drank red wine or sat too near a fire — for this last reason there were hand-screens, of stretched silk painted with flowers, all over the drawing-room at Herbert Place. Her complexion had the downy bloom of a peach, and she dusted this over with fuller's earth. She used *Peau d'Espagne* scent. Her name, Florence, suited her.

from *Seven Winters: Memories of a Dublin Childhood* (1942)

BRENDAN BEHAN

Communal experience and its ironic solidarities are an underlying interest in a lot of Brendan Behan's writings. Perhaps that interest originated not merely in the fact that he was born into the working class but that he acknowledged the distinctive view of the world his origins gave him. He worked in the family trade of house-painting and identified with the needs of organised labour and with the political implications of those needs. These aspects of his background tend to be masked by his more dramatic republicanism.

When Brendan Behan died, Heinrich Böll wrote: 'Had he been born in Germany, the clichés prefabricated by centuries of misconceptions would already have been to hand: Leftist Catholic, worker-poet, anarchist. Not one of those clichés would have covered even a portion of the man.'

The 'skyscraper' is the current Liberty Hall. Behan's uncle, Peadar Kearney (1883–1942), took part in the Easter Rising. He also wrote the words to the Irish national anthem.

Behan's Dublin

I t's the working class that binds me to this town; they're the only real people here. The middle classes put years on me. If they didn't see my name in the *Sunday Times* and the *Observer*, they wouldn't want to know me; and that goes for Catholics as well as Protestants, lawyers as well as doctors. Not that I'm idealising the working class — far from it. They don't pretend to care. Their attitude is, well, they know me a long time, they've seen me around for as long as they can remember and they don't give a damn what I'm doing or think I'm doing. They've a great spirit and good neighbourly hearts — if they couldn't do you a good turn, well, they wouldn't do you a bad one.

You find the people I like on both sides of the river but, mainly, they live more or less along a line that you might draw between the Custom House and Glasnevin Cemetery — between birth and death, come to think of it. The Custom House is a remarkable building — though, to tell you the truth, I'm not particularly knowledgeable about architecture, Georgian or otherwise, possibly due to an architect friend solemnly informing me at some stage in a very austere voice: 'Good architecture is invisible.' The Custom House, as far as I'm concerned, is notable mainly for the fact that it was there I used to get false birth certificates in order to get false passports when I was in the IRA. It was burned by the Volunteers in 1921 and that's what brought British administration in Ireland finally to a standstill, for all local government records were housed there. Across the way from it stood Liberty Hall, the headquarters of the Irish Transport and General Workers' Union, where the Irish Citizen

Army had its headquarters in 1916. It has been knocked down now and they're building a skyscraper block on the site.

Not far away is the General Post Office which was the headquarters of the 1916 Rising. The story of the Rising is too well known to go into it all again, but during that week an aunt of mine went down to the GPO to look for her husband who was in there fighting. Shells from a gunboat on the Liffey were falling all around the place and my aunt was asked with some urgency to go away. (She had a baby son in her arms who was afterwards killed in France while fighting with the British Army in 1944.) She refused to get away and kept demanding to see her husband who finally came to a sandbagged window and roared: 'Go away, Maggie,' and she shouted back: 'I only wanted to know if you were going to your work in the morning.'

Turning down Bachelor's Walk at the Liffey by O'Connell Bridge where British troops fired on the people of Dublin in 1914, you come to the Metal Bridge or, as it is sometimes called, the Ha'penny Bridge. It's known as the Metal Bridge for the very obvious and unIrish reason that it's made of metal, but in my father's day it was better known as the Ha'penny Bridge because you had to pay a halfpenny toll to cross it. Further along there is the Four Courts where the Anti-Treaty forces dug in in 1922. I remember the man that was more or less second-in-command there told me that during the attack on the building, a young IRA man from the country — a boy of seventeen or eighteen — was going up the stairs carrying the Chancellor's large wig. 'Hey, where are you going with that?' he called and the boy answered: 'I'm only going to take the kettle off the fire.'

Near by is O'Meara's pub — the 'Irish House', though why it should be called that in Ireland, I don't know. I used to know the man that owned it — it has changed hands since; and I remember him principally for a few lines of poetry that he recited to me:

'Then Hoolihan hit Hannaghan and Hannaghan hit McGilligan
And everyone hit anyone of whom he had a spite,
And Larry Dwyer, the cripple, who was sitting doing nothing
Got a kick that broke his jawbone for not indulging in the fight.'

A friend of mine painted that pub one time — Dinny Bowles, a very famous man — a signwriter he was and a very good one at that.

from *Brendan Behan's Island* (1962)

PETTIGREW AND OULTON'S STREET DIRECTORY 1848

Victorian Dublin is a phrase that has nothing of the resonance of Georgian Dublin, but it might reasonably be claimed that the later period did more to shape the city. It was then that the bureaucracy of Dublin Castle was extended, the service sector of commercial life was consolidated, areas like Rathmines and Ballsbridge were developed, and street names began to have contemporary imperial echoes. Rows of railwaymen's and other artisans' dwellings were built. Slums became more prevalent in the inner city. Street directories map this world of goods and chattels, lending it a stability of sorts, as Joyce realised when he made Thom's Official Directory of the United Kingdom of Great Britain and Ireland *a mainstay of* Ulysses.

Elsewhere in Ireland in 1848, the Famine was still going on and there was an abortive uprising. Notable trials for sedition were held in Dublin. The following year there was a cholera epidemic in the city.

Abbey-street, Lower

The lines between parenthesis, denote the breaks and intersections of the different Streets, &c., by which all corner houses in the City can be readily distinguished; and the figures at the end of each line the valuation of the House and Premises.

From Lr Sackville st. to Beresford pl.
Parish St Thomas. City.
1   Elizabeth Moore, vintner, 46*l*.
2   Samuel M'Comas, importer of woollens & merch. tailor, 60*l*.
3   Wm White, tobacconist, 50*l*.
4   Digby Fredk Foulkes, house painter and glazier, 50*l*.
5   Edw. Shelley, hotel & tav. 50*l*.
6   *Dublin Mechanics Institute,* 50*l*.
    Union Chapel
7   Office of the *Irish Railway Gazette,* Durham Dunlop, esq. editor, 50*l*.
8   Thos Le Messurier (late Tegg and Co.) wholesale bookseller and stationer, 50*l*.
    Wesleyan Methodist Chapel
9   Frs Graham & Co. grocrs, 50*l*.
    (Marlborough street)
10   Patrick Kavanagh, shell-fish tavern, 16*l*.
11   Jas Fitzpatrick, vintner, 12*l*.
12   Vacant, 12*l*.
    Music Hall, 120*l*.
    National Savings Bank, 100*l*.

Baptist Church
(Northumberland square)
13   Vacant, 40*l*.
14, 15 & 16 Timber yard of Messrs Charles Robinson, and John Carolin, builders, 115*l*.
17   Thomas Finn, vintner, 35*l*.
"   Wm Cairnes' Drogheda ale stores, 20*l*.
18   Edmund Egginton, Royal Victoria comml & family hotel, and 12 Beresford place, 40*l*.
(Beresford place)
18   Patrick O'Brien, fruiterer
19 & 20 *Northumberland Baths*
21   Michael M'Weeny, metal sash & stained glass manufactr
22   Andw Geraghty, green grocer
23   William St Clair, dealer in curiosities, 40*l*.
24   Jas Meares, prov. dealr 35*l*.
(Ferrall's arch)
25   Patk Moran, fruiterer, & 23 Anglesea fruit market, 30*l*.
26   Peter Ryan, grocer and spirit merchant, 30*l*.
27   Tenements, 25*l*.
Theatre 80*l*.
(Marlborough street)
28   Samuel M'William, Belfast hotel and tavern, 60*l*.
29   Jn Queely, agency office, 52*l*.
30   Miss Mary Beith, 63*l*.
31   William Cumming, esq. 63*l*.
"   Joshua Beatty, esq.
32   Offices of Charitable Socs 63*l*.
"   William Henry Porter, esq.
33   David B. Bell, professor of elocution, 63*l*.
"   Mrs Bell, ladies' seminary
34   Jn Parker & Co. wine mers, 80*l*.
Royal Hibernian Academy
Geo. F. Mulvany, esq. 100*l*.
35   Phœbe Wynn, commercial lodging house, 70*l*.
36   Chas Mulvaney and Co. flint glass manufacturers — F.M. Kinnier, agent, 70*l*.
37   Joseph Smyth & Co. Balbriggan hosiery warehouse, 70*l*.
"   Miss Atkinson, artist
(Harbour court)
38   Alex. M'Crea, umbrella and parasol manufacturer, 35*l*.
39   Wm Valentine, Italian wh. 35*l*.

WILLIAM TREVOR

In the country, and in the countryside, of William Trevor's 1930s' childhood, the bicycle and the old-time waltz were more the vogue than motor-cars and Ronald Colman. As for metropolitan excursions, the high rate of emigration in those years made many people more familiar with London and Birmingham than with urban centres nearer home. Trips to Cork tended to be a rush for train or bus, and were less likely to be for pleasure than for some unavoidable purpose — to see a specialist, to visit a friend or neighbour in the Bon Secours or Mercy hospitals, to buy a First Communion dress or Confirmation suit.

Once there, though, it was impossible to resist the city's allure. Public transport did not allow time for the cinema, and eating out consisted of a cup of tea and a bun from Thompson's. But a round of the shops was obligatory. The Munster Arcade, of course, and Cash's, and the Queen's Old Castle too.

William Trevor's father was a bank official, in the 1930s a profession as peripatetic as a policeman's. The Mitchelstown 'martyrs' refers to events of 1887, when police shot dead three demonstrators for land reform.

A Dream of Munster's Arcadia

All memory is grist to the fiction-writer's mill. The pleasure and the pain experienced by any storyteller's characters, the euphoria of happiness, the ache of grief, must of course be the storyteller's own. It cannot be otherwise, and in that sense all fiction has its autobiographical roots, spreading through — in my case — a provincial world, limited and claustrophobic.

I grew up in what John Betjeman called 'the small towns of Ireland' — in my case, Mitchelstown, cut down to size by the towering Galtee mountains and the Knockmealdowns, Youghal by the sea, Skibbereen lost somewhere in the back of beyond.

There were others besides, but to these three in County Cork I return most frequently. Mitchelstown is still famous for its martyrs and its processed cheese, a squat little town, looking as though someone has sat on it. A good business town, my father used to say.

Youghal, smartly elegant in my memory, is tatty on a wet afternoon. A carful of German tourists crawls along the seafront, the misty beach is empty. Once, people pointed here and remarked: I listened and my eavesdroppings told of an afternoon love affair conducted on that brief promenade, he a married doctor, she a lady in disgrace. I see them now as I made them in my fascination: she is thin, and dressed in red, laughing, with pale long hair; he is Ronald Colman with a greyer moustache. They smile at one another; defiantly he touches her hand. They are breathtaking in their sinning, and all their conversation is beautiful; they are the world's most exciting people.

I walk away from their romance, not wanting to tell myself that they were not like that. On the sands where old seaside artists sprinkled garish colours the rain is chilly. Pierrots performed here, and the man and woman who rode the Wall of Death sunned themselves at midday. From the Loreto Convent we trooped down here to run the end-of-term races, Sister Therese in charge. The sands haven't changed, nor have the concrete façades of the holiday boarding-houses, nor the Protestant church with its holes for lepers to peer through. But Horgan's Picture House is not at all as it was. It has two screens now and a different name, and there are sexual fantasies instead of Jack Hulbert in Round the Washtub.

In Youghal there was a man who shot himself in a henhouse. Life had been hell for this man, the voices whispered, and the henhouse, quite near the back of our garden, developed an eeriness that the chatter of birds made even more sinister. The henhouse isn't there any more, but even so as I stand where it was I shudder, and remember other deaths.

Youghal itself died in a way, for yellow furniture vans — Nat Ross of Cork — carted our possessions off, through Cork itself, westward through the town that people call Clonakilty God Help Us, to Skibbereen, at the back of beyond.

Memory focuses here, the images are clearer. Horses and carts in the narrow streets, with milk churns for the creamery. On fair-days farmers with sticks standing by their animals, their shirts clean for the occasion, without collar or tie. A smell of whiskey, and sawdust and stout and dung. Pots of geraniums among chops and ribs in the small windows of butchers' shops. A sun-burnt poster advertising the arrival of Duffy's Circus a year ago.

It was a mile and a half, the journey to school through the town, past Driscoll's sweetshop and Murphy's Medical Hall and Power's drapery, where you could buy oilcloth as well as dresses. In Shannon's grocery there was a man who bred smooth-haired fox-terriers. He gave us one once, a strange animal, infatuated by our cat.

In the town's approximate centre, where four streets meet, a grey woman still stands, a statue of the Maid of Erin. E. O'Donovan, undertaker, still sells ice-cream and chocolate. The brass plate of Redmond O'Regan, solicitor, once awkwardly high, is now below eye-level. In the grocers' shops the big-jawed West Cork women buy bread and sausages and tins of plums, but no longer wear the heavy black cloaks that made them seem like figures from another century. They still speak in the same West Cork lisp, a swift voice, difficult for strangers. I ask one if she could tell me the way to a house I half remember. 'Ah, I could tell you grand,' she replies. 'It's dead and buried, sir.'

The door beside the Methodist church, once green, is purple. The church, small and red-brick, stands behind high iron railings and gates, with gravel in front of it. Beyond the door that used to be green is the dank passage that leads to Miss Willoughby's schoolroom, where first I learnt that the world is not an easy-going place. Miss Willoughby was stern and young, in love with the cashier from the Provincial Bank.

On the gravel in front of the red-brick church I vividly recall Miss Willoughby. Terribly, she appears. Severe and beautiful, she pedals against the wind on her huge black bicycle. 'Someone laughed during prayers,' she accuses, and you feel at once that it was you although you know it wasn't. 'V poor' she writes in your headline book when you've done your best to reproduce, four times, perfectly, 'Pride goeth before destruction.'

As I stand on the gravel, her evangelical eyes seem again to dart over me without pleasure. Once I took the valves out of the tyres of her bicycle. Once I looked in her answer book.

I am late, I am stupid. I cannot write 20 sentences on A Day in the Life of an Old Shoe. I cannot do simple arithmetic or geography. I am always fighting with Jasper Swanton. I move swiftly on the gravel, out on to the street and into the bar of the Eldon Hotel: in spectral form or otherwise, Miss Willoughby will not be there.

Illusions fall fast in the narrow streets of Skibbereen, as elsewhere they have fallen. Yet for me, once there was something more enduring, nicest thing of all. Going to Cork it was called, 52 miles in the old Renault, 30 miles an hour because my mother wouldn't permit speed. On St Stephen's Day to the pantomime in the Opera House, and on some other occasion to see the White Horse Inn, which my father had heard was good. In Cork my appendix was removed because Cork's surgical skill was second to none. In Cork my tongue was cut to rid me of my incoherent manner of speaking. *To* Cork, every day of my childhood, I planned to run away.

Twice a year perhaps, on Saturday afternoons, there was going to Cork to the pictures. Clark Gable and Myrna Loy in Too Hot to Handle. Mr Deeds Goes to Town. No experience in my whole childhood, and no memory, has remained as deeply etched as these escapes to the paradise that was Cork. Nothing was more lovely or more wondrous than Cork itself, with its magnificent array of cinemas, the Pavilion, the Savoy, the Palace, the Ritz, the Lee, and the Hadji Bey's Turkish Delight factory. Tea in the Pavilion or the Savoy, the waitresses with silver-plated tea-pots and buttered bread and cakes, and other people eating fried eggs with rashers and chipped potatoes at half-past four in the afternoon. The sheer sophistication of the Pavilion or the Savoy could never be adequately conveyed to a friend in Skibbereen who had not had the good fortune to experience it. The gentleman's lavatory in the Victoria Hotel had to be seen to be believed, the Munster Arcade left you gasping. For ever and for ever you could sit in the middle stalls of the Pavilion watching Claudette Colbert, or Spencer Tracy as a priest, and the earthquake in San Fransisco. And for ever afterwards you could sit while a green-clad waitress carried the silver-plated tea-pot to you, with cakes and buttered bread. All around you was the clatter of life and of the city, and men of the world conversing and girls' laughter tinkling. Happiness was everywhere.

from *Excursions in the Real World* (1993)

RICHARD MILLIKEN

There has been a castle at Blarney since at least the fourteenth century. It was some time after Cromwell, at the end of the Williamite wars that brought the seventeenth century to a close in Ireland, that the castle became the property of the Jeffreys family. Lord Donoughmore was John Hely-Hutchinson, a prominent politician at the time of the Union, which was when Milliken wrote his poem. According to the editor of Milliken's Poetic Fragments, his lordship 'thanked the author for his mention . . . the Murphys, Clearys, and Healys . . . who . . . had ventured life and limb in support of the Hutchinson cause, and had thus made their blood relationship with him unquestionable.'

The same source reports that Milliken's poetic intention 'was to ridicule the songs which ignorant Irish village bards — with a vast fondness for rhyme, and imperfect knowledge of the English language, and a pedantic ambition to display the full extent of their classical knowledge — were . . . in the habit of composing'.

In the event, he out-Blarneyed Blarney, and without having kissed the famous stone. This practice dates from the nineteenth century. In 1838 Mrs Hall had a smash hit on the London stage with her play The Groves of Blarney.

The Groves of Blarney

The groves of Blarney they are so charming,
　　All by the purling of sweet silent streams;
Being banked with posies that spontaneous grow there,
　　Planted in order by the sweet rock close.
'Tis there's the daisy and the sweet carnation,
　　The blooming pink, and the rose so fair;
The daffodowndilly, besides the lily —
　　Flowers that scent the sweet fragrant air.
　　　　　　　　　　　Oh, ullagoane, etc.

'Tis Lady Jeffreys that owns this station,
　　Like Alexander or Queen Helen fair;
There's no commander throughout the nation
　　For emulation can with her compare.
She has castles round her, that no nine-pounder
　　Could dare to plunder her place of strength;
But Oliver Cromwell did her pummel,
　　And made a breach in her battlement.
　　　　　　　　　　　Oh, ullagoane, etc.

There's gravel walks there for speculation,
　　And conversation in sweet solitude;
'Tis there the lover may hear the dove, or
　　The gentle plover, in the afternoon.

And if a young lady should be so engaging
    As to walk alone in those shady bowers,
'Tis there her courtier he may transport her,
    In some dark fort, or under ground.
                      Oh, ullagoane, etc.

For 'tis there's the cave where no daylight enters,
    But bats and badgers are for ever bred;
Being moss'd by natur', that makes it sweeter
    Than a coach and six or a feather bed.
'Tis there's the lake that is stored with perches,
    And comely eels in the verdant mud;
Besides the leeches and the groves of beeches,
    All standing in order for to guard the flood.
                      Oh, ullagoane, etc.

'Tis there's the kitchen hangs many a flitch in,
    With the maids a stitching upon the stair;
The bread and biske', the beer and whisky,
    Would make you frisky if you were there.
'Tis there you'd see Peg Murphy's daughter
    A washing *praties* forenent the door.
With Roger Cleary and Father Healy,
    All blood relations to my Lord Donoughmore.
                      Oh, ullagoane, etc.

There's statues gracing this noble place in,
    All heathen goddesses so fair —
Bold Neptune, Plutarch, and Nicodemus,
    All standing naked in the open air.[1]
So now to finish this brave narration,
    Which my poor geni' could not entwine;
But were I Homer, or Nebuchadnezzar,
    'Tis in every feature I would make it shine.
                      Oh, ullagoane, etc.

1.   Alas! These statues were knocked down by the magical touch of the auctioneer's hammer to Sir Thomas Deane —

        'Who bought the castle, furniture, and fixtures, O!
        And took off in a cart
        ('Twas enough to break one's heart)
        All the statues made of lead, and the pictures, O!'

Vide extracts from *Reliques of Father Prout* [1836], page 230.

from *Poetical Fragments of the late Richard Alfred Milliken* (1823)

CLAUD COCKBURN

Not very long after Claud Cockburn and his family settled in Ireland at the end of World War II, a polio epidemic broke out. This happened before a vaccine for the disease had been discovered. Fear of the disease was understandably widespread, all the more so since many households then needed the income of children leaving school at the age of fourteen to work in the labouring or service sectors.

Although Cockburn's wife, Patricia, came from the Youghal area, the family home was eastward down the coast at Ardmore, Co. Waterford. The author's novel, Beat the Devil, *later filmed by John Huston and starring Humphrey Bogart, was first published under the name James Helvick. Helvick Head is the imposing headland at the eastern end of Ardmore Bay.*

This part of Claud Cockburn's memoirs is leading up to the discovery that his youngest son had contracted polio.

Polio

We Cork people found ourselves, without the slightest word being said — and perhaps with not much of a conscious thought being thought — sitting at one end of the bar and buffet car, with the Dubliners at the other.

As the situation deteriorated in Cork, the Cork people defensively spread terrifying stories about what was happening elsewhere. It was said, and absolutely believed by very many people, that in Dublin the epidemic was worse still than in Cork. People were dying like flies in every fever hospital in the city. But, due to the savage wiles and intrigues of the Dubliners, the newspapers had been, as the Irish saying goes, 'brought to see' that it would not be in their interests to report the state of affairs in Dublin. Instead they should concentrate on ruining poor Cork.

And in Cork itself the owners of some of the biggest stores in the city made a *démarche*. In deputation to the newspapers they threatened to withdraw advertising from such newspapers as might continue to report regularly and in detail on the polio epidemic there. They were intent on bringing the newspapers to see the justice of their viewpoint. As always, too, in the sordid backwaters of panic, there were people made to suffer by the frights of others. Some nearly bedridden people nearly died in various parts of the city because it was thought that all bedridden people must be polio victims, and in consequence nobody would go to their houses to deliver the milk and meat and vegetables they needed. The Gardai had to be called in to make the deliveries to those houses which were supposedly so dangerous but in reality — not that the delivery men had any means of knowing that — were no more dangerous than the air you breathed at the railway station or the General Post Office. And that was dangerous indeed.

from *I Claud* (1967)

SEAN O'FAOLAIN

'I cannot be objective about Cork', O'Faolain says at the beginning of his account of the city in An Irish Journey. *And he was insufficiently objective about the then Bishop of Galway as well in the book. The bishop's threat of legal action caused the book's Irish edition to be withdrawn.*

Roughly translated, Statio Bene Fida Carinis — *'The first Latin I loved to mouth', says O'Faolain — means, 'A place favourable to ships'.*

During the prolonged infancy and adolescence of the Irish Free State, many Irish writers travelled around it. Their resulting accounts combine journeys of discovery, reports on the state of the nation, oblique and restless autobiographies, frank critiques, and outbursts of bad temper. The work of people who more often than not felt like strangers in their own country, these books are, to say the least, very interesting contributions to Irish travel literature.

Cork

As for the pocket of the town itself, what the natives call 'the flat of the city', or, really, in their own flat accent, 'the flaat o' deh city', having lived in it all through my youth I know that there must be many corners in it that my homesick ghost will haunt. There is the whole length of the quays, especially the pleasant bits where there are a few trees, such as the North Mall, or the Sand Quay, or the bit near the Opera House, though there only at particular hours, such as at about five o'clock on a summer afternoon, or perhaps a little later than that, when the fishermen are drying their nets, or tarring their nets, and the angelus will soon be ringing in various tones and at various speeds all over the city, whose humming then slowly drops away into silence as the day ends. At such an hour Cork becomes without pretension the Lilliput it is. It offers no obstacle to the quiet tasting of quiet love. One season above all will haunt me, I know, and that for any corner of Cork — the time of the equinoctial gales: reminding us that Cork is a seaport and the sea at our door. Then the floods rise, the streets are sometimes submerged, and the winds from the ocean tear into the cup of the valley of the town. Then the age of the place, so well hidden under its rouge of paint (like a French seaport), is shamelessly exposed in the rattling and shaking and shivering and banging of all its poor decrepit parts. In these gales it flies in slivers through the air and, on mornings after gales, the streets where there are such houses are likely to be strewn with slates. The winters are hard here, and lashing rains, gutters spilling, pavements rippled with flood-water, hoardings flapping, and the news, passing from mouth to mouth like the gossip in a Dutch town, that the river is rising, all give a great sense of nearness to the elements. Cork, in its old meaning of *marsh*, is never far from its origins in that way — sleepy in summer, wet in winter. So that you soon find out that the city is not merely built on a marsh but on islands in the marsh, and that the streets are, often, covered canals or rivers. Patrick Street is winding merely because the river under it winds — one winter the river burst the wood-paving and we saw it underneath; and if you lean over the parapet near Patrick's Bridge you will (or used to) see it emerge there into the Lee. The South Mall was water — hence the name Morrison's Island behind it. Drawbridge Street indicates that water was near; it came up as a quay into Emmet Place. The Coal Quay is not a quay now, but it was. Oh, but any winter evening, stand on Montenotte, in the bay of some cosy bourgeois house, and look down through the battered, wind-rattling window at the rain-washed town, and the spars of the ships on the quay shining in arc-light, and you can recapture easily the maritime quality of Cork. My father-in-law who lived away at the farthest, western end of the city, in Sunday's Well, an old sailor, used to hurl it all back on me when, as he lay bedridden in the heel of his days, he would suddenly cock an ear and say — 'There's a ship coming up the river.' And I would lift my head, and ever so faint and far away, out of the little, poky, stuffy sick-room, down the valley of the city, down the river between its mudflats or on its first loch, I would hear the gentle hoot of a siren, a cock-crow of triumph for safe entry from the sea. The arms of Cork record that endless adventure — a ship entering between two castles. *Statio Bene Fida Carinis.*

from *An Irish Journey* (1940)

FRANCIS SYLVESTER MAHONY (FATHER PROUT)

The bells of Shandon are in the Protestant parish church of St Anne. Its spire, as Mahony noted, 'is a prominent object, from whatever side the traveller approaches our beautiful city. In a vault at its foot sleep some generations of the writer's kith and kin.' So does the writer himself.

Legend has it that Mahony wrote the poem on the wall of his room when he was a lonely clerical student in Rome. 'Adrian's Mole' is a nickname for the mausoleum of the Roman Emperor Hadrian (76–138); also known as the Castel Sant' Angelo, it is connected by a secret passage to the Vatican. 'Kiosko' or kiosk originally meant an open pavilion with a balustrade. Prout envisages it as the platform on the mosque from which the Islamic faithful are called to prayer.

The church dates from the early eighteenth century and stands in one of the poorer parts of the city.

The Bells of Shandon

With deep affection and recollection,
    I often think of those Shandon bells,
Whose sounds so wild would, in days of childhood,
    Fling round my cradle their magic spells.
On this I ponder, where'er I wander,
    And thus grow fonder, sweet Cork, of thee;
        With thy bells of Shandon,
        That sound so grand on
The pleasant waters of the river Lee.

I have heard bells chiming full many a clime in,
    Tolling sublime in cathedral shrine;
While at a glib rate brass tongues would vibrate,
    But all their music spoke nought like thine;
For memory dwelling on each proud swelling
    Of thy belfry knelling its bold notes free,
        Make the bells of Shandon
        Sound far more grand on
The pleasant waters of the river Lee.

I have heard bells tolling, 'old Adrian's Mole' in,
    Their thunder rolling from the Vatican,
With cymbals glorious, swinging uproarious,
    In the gorgeous turrets of Notre Dame;
But thy sounds were sweeter than the dome of Peter,
    Flings o'er the Tiber, pealing solemnly,
        Oh! the bells of Shandon,
        Sound far more grand on
The pleasant waters of the river Lee.

There's a bell in Moscow, while on tower and Kiosko
    In St Sophia the Turkman gets,
And loud in air calls men to prayer,
    From the tapering summit of tall minarets.
Such empty phantom I freely grant them,
    But there's an anthem more dear to me,
        It's the bells of Shandon,
        That sound so grand on
The pleasant waters of the river Lee.

from *The Reliques of Father Prout* (1836)

IRISH TOWNLANDS

Irish placenames often have the words 'Bally' or 'Castle' or 'Town' attached to them. But though such names are plentiful, they are in the minority overall. They tend to be the names of population centres, but the majority of Irish placenames are those of townlands. The part of a name they are most likely to share with more prominent places is 'Kil', from the Irish for church.

But what is a townland? It is, 'In Ireland, a division of land of varying extent . . .' says the Oxford English Dictionary. Such vagueness is yet one more sign of how intensely local the Irish landscape can be. With every few acres of it, the name changes. Sometimes even the fields themselves have names — and not merely names like 'the south meadow' or 'the back twenty' but ones in which some nugget of area or family history is lodged, or a joke, or an idiosyncratic twist of some word in Irish. If these names could be read accurately and understood, a whole new way of looking at the countryside would emerge. As things are, it is difficult to know how to pronounce them.

Two prominent words here — 'inch' and 'illaun' — both mean 'island' in Irish. But the second of them can also mean an isolated place, while the first can also mean both to tell a story and the banks of a river.

Townlands of County Cork

Horsemount North	Imogane
Horsemount South	Imokishy
Huggartsland (C)	Imphrick
Ightermurragh	Inane
Illane	Inch
Illaunacullin Island	Inch East
Illaunagart Island	Inch West
Illauncreagh	Inch, Killeagh
Illauneana Island	Inchafune
Illaungawna Island	Inchakevin
Illauninagh East	Inchaleagh
Illauninagh West	Inchamay North
Illaunkearagh Island	Inchamay South
Illaunknocknanagh	Inchamore
Illaunmore Island	Inchanadreen
Illaunnacaheragh Island	Inchanapisha
Illaunranhee Island	Inchantotane
Illaunricmonia Island	Inchera
Illaunroe-More Island	Inches

Inchibeg	Inchileigh
Inchimore	Inchinagotagh
Inchibrackane	Inchinagoum
Inchiclogh	Inchinahoury
Inchidaly	Inchinanagh
Inchideraille	Inchinaneave
Inchigaggin Pt	Inchinapallas
Inchigeelagh	Inchinarihen
Inchigrady	Inchinashingane

from *Irish Townlands A–Z: Alphabetical Index to the Townlands of Co. Cork*

SEÁN DUNNE

In 1958, a report on the Irish economy was issued entitled Economic Development. *This became the blueprint for the reinvigoration of Irish social life that took place during the 1960s, when people started buying cars, television sets and double glazing, and higher education became more widely available. Irish traditional music began to be very popular then too.*

The glass factory in Waterford, home of the world-renowned crystal, dates from the late eighteenth century. But in 1851 it closed for a hundred years. Its successful entry into international markets upon reopening was one of the confidence-builders of the day.

Although the thought of there being an Irish working class outside of Dublin and Belfast and, perhaps, Cork may take a little getting used to, Waterford city has a strong and historically complex working-class tradition. In a sense, these John's Park homes, with their shin of beef and neck of lamb for dinner, seem not so far away from, say, industrial Lancashire and its much sought-after tripe.

John's Park

Like my father, many others in John's Park had arrived there from backgrounds different to the world in which they now lived. Some had come from the city or small towns, but many came from the Waterford and Kilkenny countryside and from coastal villages. Now they were all part of a working-class community. In this way, John's Park became a melting-pot, but some of those who lived there upheld an order which showed itself in small ways that might remain invisible to an outsider.

Our parents mostly had grown up in an impoverished Ireland. Now, as people stayed at home and factories seemed to be opening everywhere, there was a desire to get on in life. It was no longer the case that children would leave school, like my father, at the age of thirteen; neither would they walk barefoot through the streets and lanes with nothing before them only the boat to England or America.

Above us, there was the middle-class. They lived in other parts of Waterford like Grange Park and Newtown. Their streets had mature trees and their houses had large windows. Above them, in some realm that had as much meaning for me as a fairy castle, lived others with whom we never came into contact. These included filmstars and people like the Aga Khan or the McGrath family, who made a lot of money from an involvement in the Irish Sweepstakes and in Waterford Glass. They were names in a newspaper and touched our lives only in freakish, transient ways such as when Jacqueline Kennedy came on holidays to a house near Woodstown Strand, or Stanley Kubrick made a film in County Waterford which featured many people from John's Park as extras.

One day, Kubrick offered five pounds extra to anyone who brought a dog onto the set of *Barry Lyndon* the next morning. A man told me of how he had gone around John's Park in a van at dawn, gathering all the stray dogs he could find.

I saw the social order reflected in a way that was related to the amount of money my father brought into the house. He was paid on Friday and there was usually no money left by the following Wednesday at the latest. Thursday was a poor day and by tea-time there was little to eat besides the sliced pan which the breadman left on the windowsill. The breadman, who worked for the Gold Crust bakery, was paid on Saturday for the bread he left every day. It was the same with the milk and so we were never without these two staple foods. We sometimes bought food on credit in Doyle's shop. 'Tell him to put it on the book,' my father would say.

Friday was pay-day for most of the families around us. Since days of the week have a character of their own, Thursdays generally had a feeling of want, while Friday held an air of plenitude and surprise. The two local shops sold cheap meat on Thursdays, their windows boasting stacks of pigs' tails and offal. There were large bones we called chucks and thin bones we called handles, which were used to make stews. On Thursdays in summer, when many of the doors along our road were open, I could get the smell of these stews filling the street, some of them carrying the faint tang of boiled kidney.

Those families whose men worked in the glass factory were by far the best off. The wages in the glass factory were legendary and money was especially plentiful for these families at holiday-time when the workers were paid hefty bonuses. They and their families were among the first to go on foreign holidays. They went to resorts in Spain, where many of them booked into the same hotels. Up to then, people went mostly to Tramore, or to England to see relatives, or to Butlin's holiday camp at Mosney in County Meath. My parents went to Mosney on their honeymoon and I have a photograph of my mother there, sitting in front of a fountain in a cardigan and dress, the sleeves of the cardigan rolled up.

From one house to the next, small signs indicated social and local status. Some families seemed especially interested in status while others, because they felt secure or indifferent, or had simply despaired, had no interest in it at all. When the estate was finished, all the houses looked the same but small changes were made with time. All the front doors had letterboxes and metal knockers. In time, some families got doorbells and this, to me, seemed a sign of social mobility. Even within the range of doorbells, there was a kind of pecking order: older, broken or cheap bells gave a deep, growling noise when pressed. Sometimes it was necessary to press the button very hard to get any sound at all. In the same way, new, with-it doorbells worked the minute you pressed them and gave a clear, deliberate ring. One or two gave off loud ornate chimes similar to those heard at the entrances to big houses in American television series.

The metal knocker fell from some letterboxes and was not replaced. Then you had to knock by pressing in the metal flap of the letterbox a few times. Some of these metal flaps were stiff; others seemed as loose as gold-leaf paper and they rattled limply in the wind.

The number of each house was screwed into the front door above the letterbox. On some doors, these original numbers had been taken off and replaced by wooden or cheap plastic digits. A lamp was added to some porches. A few windows had net curtains; others had Venetian blinds or, like ours, plain curtains. Neither the houses nor the streets had official names. We called the streets by simple names: the Main Road, the Square, the Back Road. An older street outside John's Park was called Pearse Park while the road past the Ursuline Convent was known as the Ursuline Road. Later, an effort was made to introduce official names. One road was then called Cherry Blossom Avenue, but that never really caught on.

from *In My Father's House* (1991)

GEORGE O'BRIEN

Even though a good deal of Lismore Castle is a nineteenth-century imitation, built by the architect of the Crystal Palace, Joseph Paxton, the site has been continuously occupied by people of rank and power for well over a thousand years. Who knows what happened before then? The name of the town in Irish is Lios Mór Mochuda. A 'lios' is a fairy fort. About a mile east of the town on the south bank of the Blackwater is a spot called the Round Hill, which is in fact a round hill. It may be the site of a castle, or it may be a much older site. Mochuda is one of the names for the local saint. So the town's name can be taken to mean something like the large fairy fort to which a saint has been attached.

In any case, there is no denying Lismore's ancient ecclesiastical significance. When work was being done on the castle in the early nineteenth century, a very fine crozier was unearthed. And like many holy places of the early Irish church, Lismore has lent its name to a book, though the volume in question happened to have ended up in Lismore, rather than being written there.

The author grew up in Lismore during the 1950s, reared by his grandmother, 'Mam', his Aunt Chrissy, and his Uncle George. Lismore is now an official Heritage Town.

School Essay

'Picturesquely pitched on the banks of the Blackwater —' Pat Lyons read, and there Brother Blake interrupted him: "'Picturesquely *pitched* . . . ." Well, sure that sounds like someone threw it there. You should say "picturesquely situated".'

Unabashed, Pat resumed. He was reading out his composition on Lismore Castle to the whole class. Blakey had asked him to. It had come first. I listened dully, alert only when the interruption came, though it was nowhere near admonishing enough to please me. I was mortified and cross. My effort had only come third.

I was upset because family, as well as personal, pride had been offended. The assignment excited me because it was so different from the usual 'A Wet Day' or 'A Bicycle Wheel Tells Its Own Story': it was a much more agreeable challenge to write about something substantial, familiar and famous. But I hadn't expected the grown-ups at home to join in. Usually they left me severely alone with my homework. Now, however, the novel opportunity arose to say something about the most dominant physical feature of their world. The Castle — Irish seat of the Duke of Devonshire — was the structure which denoted that the village belonged to a context larger than its own. Yet much as that belonging was cherished, the manner of it was hopelessly beyond the village's control. Everything connected with the Castle, besides the emotions it evinced, was pre-ordained, possessed, arbitrated over by 'others': nobles, superiors, employers. The Duke's dominion was a perfect and apparently indestructible embodiment of the soul of ownership: the dispossessed admiring the proprietor's fortress, the fleeced kissing the shears. I admired, too, not feeling particularly dispossessed. And so did Chrissy. With an air of authority which clearly pleased her, she dictated, 'Built by King John in 1185 . . .' and I bowed my head over the spotless copybook.

Assured by Chrissy's enthusiasm that this was going to be my finest literary hour to date, I was extremely concerned that the composition be a masterpiece of penmanship as well. Of all the attainments of primary school, the one I took most pride in was 'light writing'; script faint to the point of virtual illegibility, barely more prominent than the blankness of the paper it rested on, a film of whose perspiration it might be imagined to be: testament, in its fastidiousness, to superb nib control and delicacy of finger pressure! No easy accomplishment, given the equipment: the coarse, absorbent texture of the off-white, brown-flecked jotters, the wooden-shafted pen with a nib the size of a cockroach, and just as resistant to being toilet-trained, and school ink which came in powder form and had to be mixed; it evaporated leaving a sticky sludge at the bottom of the ceramic inkwells. Against such odds I pitted myself, anxious to acquire a skill which had, I perceived, overtones of decorum, care and ceremonial attention, a translation of colouring-book *politesse*.

There was a further not unimportant consideration. Over and above the satisfaction of calligraphic heroics for their own sake, a blot-free copybook could mean a slap-free start to the school day. At the very least it would spare me Blakey's jibes about how we shouldn't be trying to plant a row of turnips with our pens, though God knows maybe some of us'd be better off trucking in mud and dirt, because we just weren't able to tell A from B, and never would. 'So come out here.' Then would follow a list of names, a scraping of reluctant hobnailed boots as the victims advanced, the production of the length of seasoned ash. And *swish, swish*: four blows apiece. The tension, the moaning, the lads with their incompetent hands thrust under armpits and between knees, faces gargoyled to ward off tears, every ounce of their presence bent in wringing out the detestable ashen sting, the exposure, the affront.

'Third!' exclaimed Chrissy and Mam together, taken mightily aback. 'Who came first?' and when I told them, 'Humph!' ironically, as though detecting a design, 'Who got second?'

'John O'Connor.'

'Oh my God!' This surprised them so much that they had to turn to insults. 'John Butch, h'mm? Oul Mallet-skull . . . ?' Then, this attack of bile subsiding, 'What did he say?' (Blake, about mine.)

'Too much history. He said I got it all out of a book.'

'Blasted cheek: does he take us for a parcel of know-nothings? What was Pat Lyons's like?'

I mentioned his alliterative indiscretion.

'Ha, picturesquely pitched, I'm sure. Where did he get that kind of language? Don't mind, boy; you're better than the whole lot of them put together.'

By this time I hardly minded at all, certainly not half as much as my elders and betters, with their mutterings about favouritism and mumbled explanations of how this blatant slight had come about. But Mam and Chrissy wouldn't rest until they'd arrived at a plausible salve for wounded self-respect. To do so was a sophisticated exercise in the hermeneutics of community attachments, requiring considerable imaginative and forensic skill, allowing intuition free play, invoking precedent and provenance and eking every last ounce of potential significance from the commonplace, until at length, slaked and satisfied by their thoroughness, they had nothing more to say but, 'That's it, surely.'

'Oh, that's it now.'

Secure interpretation of the everyday was a must, so little else tolerated or responded to interpretation.

Perhaps one reason that Chrissy and Mam vented their frustration so vehemently was that they'd never expected an opportunity to express themselves formally about the Castle. To be sure, the form was adventitious, unforeseen, but at least they knew they were equal to its demands (more than equal, indeed, as Brother Blake's criticism pointed out). Maybe they thought my failure to come first a judgment on what they expressed. Or was it simply that, irrespective of the approach, the Castle maintained its distance from common life and thereby, passively and inscrutably, upheld its identity as an enigma — impenetrable, unapproachable, remote? It simply stood in our midst as an irreproachable monument to land, money, grandeur, supremacy and all the other trappings of Mammon, which were not for the likes of us (whose kingdom was not of this world). And yet, for all its difference, we thought that there was something of 'our own' about it, we extended to it a secret sympathy, an illicit intimacy, as though in spite of all appearances, we understood it. Tacitly, though without embarrassment, we gave the symbol psychic houseroom (How could we not? Wasn't it a fact of life?); we domesticated the enigma, thereby making it enigmatic indeed — teasing, taunting, ticklesome. If Waterford City was known as *urbs intacta* (never penetrated by siege), what variety of virginity might describe our situation? Certainly some loftier, purer classification: perhaps we were the Holy Innocents, sanctified by our elimination from history, limbo's founding dynasty.

from *The Village of Longing* (1987)

DERVLA MURPHY

Dervla Murphy earned the right to speak about the Himalayas the hard way. In 1963 she rode a bicycle named Rozinante all the way from Lismore to see them. In fact, she went as far as Delhi, fulfilling an ambition conceived over twenty years earlier, when she was ten. 'I've never forgotten the exact spot on a hill near my home at Lismore, Co. Waterford, where the decision was made . . .'

The scenes around Lismore are the subject of a local song, and include spectacular mountain scenery — the Vee is a 'V' on its side actually — and restful river country. Dromana Castle is even more 'picturesquely pitched' on the Blackwater than is Lismore Castle. A Villiers-Stuart, a Protestant, stood for election locally in the 1820s as the Catholic Emancipation candidate, and won.

Seán Dunne recalled, in The Road to Silence, *that it was at Mount Melleray that he 'understood what the old Celtic monks meant when they spoke of two landscapes, one physical with its rocks and mountains; the other sacral and intensely connected with spirituality'.*

Dervla Murphy's father, a Dubliner, was the county librarian of Waterford for many years.

West Waterford

Two miles south of Lismore a wooded ridge — Ballinaspic — forms the watershed between the Bride and the Blackwater valleys. Standing on a certain gatepost on Ballinaspic's crest one can survey the whole sweep of West Waterford, and always I feel an intoxication of joy as my eye travels from the coast near Dungarvan to the Cork border near Macollop. There are profound differences between one's responses to familiar and unfamiliar landscapes. The incomparable grandeur of the Himalayas fills me with a mixture of exaltation and humility. But the beauty of the Blackwater valley is so much a part of me that it inspires an absurd pride — almost as though I helped to make it, instead of the other way round.

Looking across that fertile valley from Ballinaspic one sees three mountain ranges. The Comeraghs, above the sea to the north-east, seem like the long, casual strokes of some dreamy painter's brush. The Knockmealdowns, directly overlooking Lismore, are gently curved and oddly symmetrical and display as many shades of blue-brown-purple as there are days in the year. And the Galtees — more distant, to the north-west — rise angular and stern above the lonely moors of Araglen. Opposite Ballinaspic, another long, heavily wooded ridge separates the lower slopes of the Knockmealdowns from the lushness at river-level and is marked by several deep glens, each contributing a noisy stream to the quiet width of the Blackwater. And south-east of Ballinaspic, amidst a calm glory of ancient woods and irregular little fields, one can glimpse the marriage of the Bride and the Blackwater — after the latter has abruptly turned south at Cappoquin.

Due north of Lismore a mountain pass forms the letter V against the sky and is known, with un-Irish prosaicness, as the Vee. Less than three hundred years ago wolves were hunted hereabouts and not much more than one hundred years ago evicted peasants were forced to settle on the barren uplands of Ballysaggart. More fortunate settlers arrived in 1832, a group of Cistercian monks who were presented with a mountain-side by Sir Richard Keane of Cappoquin. Ten years later Thackeray observed that 'the brethren have cultivated their barren mountain most successfully', and now the grey Abbey of Mount Mellery stands solitary and conspicuous against its background of blue hills — an echo of those ancient monasteries which once made known, throughout civilised Europe, the name of Lismore.

In the seventh century St Carthage founded a cathedral and college in Lismore and by the eighth century the place had become a university city where in time both King Alfred the Great and King John (while still Earl of Morton) were to study. In 1173 the 'famous and holy city' was ransacked by Raymond le Gros; and when King John replaced the razed college with a castle it, too, was destroyed. Soon, however, the local bishops had built another castle, which Sir Walter Raleigh eventually acquired. But Sir Walter was not a very competent landowner and in 1602 he gladly sold his castle, surrounded by a little property of 42,000 acres, to Richard Boyle, First Earl of Cork. Some two hundred years later an heiress of the Earl of Cork married a Cavendish and Lismore Castle is still owned by the Devonshire family. Thackeray observed: 'You hear praises of the Duke of Devonshire as a landlord wherever you go among his vast estates: it is a pity that, with such a noble residence as this, and with such a wonderful country round about it, his Grace should not inhabit it more.'

Between the sixteenth and twentieth centuries West Waterford had to endure less than its share of Ireland's woes. The Villiers-Stuarts of Dromana and the Keanes of Cappoquin always lived on their estates and generally were compassionate landlords — while the Devonshires, though absentees, were not more than usually unscrupulous. Moreover, a local historian, Canon Power, noted that the region 'seems to have been largely cleared of its original Celtic stock on the conclusion of the Desmond wars and . . . the first earl of Cork was able to boast that he had "no Irishe tenant on his land"'.

This successful mini-plantation may partly explain a scarcity of Republicans in the area. Many local families had not been settled in West Waterford for as long as the main land-owning clans; and in the absence of inherited resentments — based on racial memories of conquest and land confiscation — unusually harmonious relations developed between landlords and tenants. But one has to grow up in a place to be aware of these nuances. My parents, looking in from outside, recognised none of the benefits that for centuries had been made available to both sides by West Waterford's feudal system. Judging the rural social scene by urban standards, they saw only arrogance and profiteering on the one side and spineless servility on the other. And nowhere a slot for themselves.

What sort of person would I now be had I grown up a typical Dubliner, regarding the countryside as something to be enjoyed in literature and avoided in life? But I simply cannot imagine myself as an urban animal. To me, city-dwellers are The Dispossessed, unfortunates who have been deprived of every creature's right to territory. There is a sense in which country folk, however impoverished, own their birthplace and all the land around it that can be covered in a long day's tramp — the natural, immemorial limit to the territory of a human being. Or perhaps it is that each region owns its people, exacting a special, subtle loyalty, a primitive devotion that antedates by tens of thousands of years the more contrived emotion of nationalism. Either way, there exists an element of *belonging* such as surely cannot be replaced or imitated by any relationship, however intense, between the city-dweller and his man-made surroundings.

from *Wheels within Wheels* (1979)

TOMÁS Ó CRIOMHTHAIN

The Blaskets — often referred to as 'the last parish before America' — are a group of small islands off the coast of the Dingle peninsula in County Kerry. The largest island, the Great Blasket, measures one mile by three, and is where the action of the book is set.

The first edition of The Islandman *appeared in Irish in 1929, when the author was seventy-three years of age. His aim, he said, was 'to set down the character of the people about me so that some record of us might live after us, for the like of us will never be again'. This aim has, by common assent, been reached. Relying on the patterns and pleasures of an oral tradition in which he was well versed, Ó Criomhthain gave a picture of daily life that has become a byword for economy and unassuming verve.*

Administration of the islands was the responsibility of the Congested Districts Board. Largely confined to the western seaboard, congested districts were areas deemed by Victorian officialdom to be in a chronic state of impoverishment. Despite a treacherous three-mile stretch of sea, traffic between islands and mainland was frequent and regular, though probably not that many islanders made it as far as Killorglin. This is where Puck Fair is held, a riotous August festival that culminates in the crowning of a puck goat.

The Blaskets have been uninhabited since 1953.

Our Houses

I may as well give some brief account here of the way we managed things in this Island when I was young, more particularly since the fashion of that world has passed away and nobody now living remembers it except a few old people.

As for the houses that we had in my youth, and for some time after, they differed among themselves, just as in other places. Some of them had a handsomer appearance than the rest, and others were pretty wretched. A number of them were only ten feet by eight. Others were larger — from that size to fifteen or twenty feet long. To divide the house into two a dresser stood out from the wall in the middle of the floor, and a partition met it from the other side. There were two beds in the lower portion, where people slept. Potatoes would be stored under these beds. A great chest was kept between the two beds up against the gable end. On the other side of the partition — the kitchen side — the family used to spend the whole day, or part of the day, ten of them perhaps. There was a coop against the partition with hens in it, and a broody hen just by it in an old cooking pot. At night-time there would be a cow or two, calf or two, the ass, the dog on a chain by the wall or running about the house. In a house with a large family you would find a post-bed, or maybe a bed on the floor. The old people used to spend the night in that beside the fire, with an old stump of a clay pipe going, or two pipes if there were two of them living, and smoking away; they would have a wisp of straw for a pipe-lighter. A good fire of fine turf smouldered away till morning; every time they woke they took a light from the fire and puffed at the pipe. If the old woman was alive, the old man would stretch across to give her a light from the wisp; then the smoke from the two old pipes would drift up the chimney, and you could imagine that the couple's bed was a steamship as they puffed away in full blast.

Two or three dogs would stretch out at the foot of the bed, the cow or the cows below them, head to the wall, and there would be a calf or two with the run of the kitchen, or lying muzzle to the fire. The ass would be tied up on the other side of the house opposite the cows, and a cat with a couple of kittens, maybe, in the chimney niche. The rest of the trumpery in the house was stuffed under the post-bed for the night. This bed was more than a couple of feet from the ground, and it was made of wood or iron. Some of the houses had no division to make a room, but there was a post-bed in one corner and a bed on the floor in the other. The dresser was up against the wall or the gable end. Every kind of house had two or three barrels of fish. And, besides all the other animals, you would find a pet lamb or two running about the house.

Those houses were made of stones mortared with clay, and most of them were very roughly finished, for their building was always hurried through, and everybody took a hand in it. Rushes or reeds were the thatch, over a layer of thick and stout scraws. The thatch would have been all right if the hens would only have let it alone, but they wouldn't. As soon as the rushes began to decay, and worms could be found in them, a man with a gun couldn't have kept the hens away from scratching and nesting there. Then the drips would begin, and a dirty drip it was too, for there was too much soot mixed with it. The hens nested so deep in the thatch that the women often lost them, for a hen wouldn't even answer the call to food when she was broody. The little lasses very often brought a hatful or a capful of eggs down from the houses. The children made a mess of the thatch, too, always hunting for eggs. It was as good as a day at Puck Fair to listen to two of the women whose houses adjoined, quarrelling with one another about the ownership of the eggs.

The good houses were from ten to twelve feet wide, and from twenty to twenty-five feet long. They had a cupboard and a dresser arranged crosswise to make a room of the lower half of the house, and two high post-beds below them. They were thatched in the same way as the little houses, though the hens had an easier job with the little houses, because they were built lower. I remember, however, a funny thing that happened in one of the big houses, the like of which never occurred in one of the little ones, in this very matter of hens. The family of this house were gathered, every one of them, round the table at supper, with plenty of potatoes, fish, and milk before them, and all their jaws keen set to grind them and send them on down. The man of the house was sitting at the head of the table, with a wooden mug full of milk beside him. He'd just put his hand to his plate, to take out a piece of fish, when he saw some object fall into the mug. He looked down, and there was a lump of something drowning in the milk. They had to fetch the tongs to get it out, and not one of them had the faintest idea what it was.

'It's a young chicken,' said the woman of the house, 'whatever the dickens brought it there?'

'It doesn't matter a damn to you what it is,' said the man of the house. 'It has sent you out of your wits soon enough,' said he, 'for where on earth do you imagine a thing of that kind could come in your way from?'

All at the table were getting madder, and Heaven knows how the evening would have ended if another chicken hadn't fallen on the potatoes, alive and kicking.

'For God's sake, where are they coming from?' said the woman of the house.

'Can't you see that they're not coming from hell, anyhow,' said the man of the house. 'It's some consolation that they're falling from above.'

A lad at the lower end of the table glanced up at the timbers of the roof and saw the wind and the sun coming through.

'Devil take it! There's a hole in the house,' says he to his father. 'Come here and you'll see it.'

When the man of the house saw the hole, 'Wisha,' said he, 'may Satan sweep all the hens and eggs and chickens out to sea.'

'God turn a deaf ear to you,' said the wife.

When they went to the hole to close it, they found ten other chickens and the hen.

I was cradled in one of the medium-sized houses. It was a little cramped house, but what there was of it was kept neat, for my father was a very handy man and my mother never knew what it was to be idle. She had a spinning-wheel for wool and another for flax, and combs for carding, and she used to have the job of spinning threads ready for the tailor with the distaff from her own wheel. Often enough she would spin it for the other clumsy women who couldn't put themselves in shape to do it, and were too lazy, anyhow, even if they knew the trick.

Some ten years after my marriage I built a new house. Nobody handed so much as a stone or a lump of mortar to me all the time I was at work on it, and I roofed it myself. It isn't a large house, but, all the same, if King George were to spend a month's holiday in it, it isn't from the ugliness of the house that he would take his death. It is roofed with felt, as every other house and shed in the village was until the Board put up six slate-roofed houses. When the new house was finished, a hen fluttered up on to the roof. My uncle Diarmid was just going by. He stopped to watch the hen and the desperate struggle she was making to maintain herself on the roof, but the slippery felt shot her off.

'Devil mend you,' said my uncle, 'that the day has come upon you when the roof shot you over the cliff!'

In my young days Patrick Keane, and some time before him, Patrick Guiheen, were the two chief men in the Island. I remember when this Patrick Keane — the grandfather of the King we have now — had four or five milch cows. I never saw the other, Guiheen; his grandchildren were alive in my day. I've often heard that he had eight or ten milch cows, a mare, and a wooden plough. A red mare she was. She helped to draw the gravel for the old tower on the Island, whenever that was built, and he was in attendance on her when he was sixteen years old. John Dunlevy, the poet, was a baby in the cradle at that time. That makes the poet sixteen years younger than the King's grandfather. The men of their standing had some half-dozen houses that were pretty good.

The tables used in the little houses were rather like a kneading trough — a board with a raised frame round it to keep in the potatoes or anything else they put on them, and a stand of tripod shape that could be folded up so that the stand and the kneading trough could be hung up on the wall till they were needed.

One day my uncle Liam came back from the strand with a fierce hunger on him. The tripod frame was standing ready, with the kneading trough on it, full of potatoes and whatever 'kitchen' went with them. A good-sized potato fell from the trough. Off went the dog after it. He carried the stand away with him, and the trough and all its contents rolled every way through the house. His wife fell to gathering up the potatoes. 'Holy Mary! little woman, it's as good as a fair day with you,' says Liam.

from *The Islandman* (*An tOileánach*), translated by Robin Flower (1951)

WILLIAM MAKEPEACE THACKERAY

The three lakes of Killarney and the mountains surrounding need no introduction, being pretty much a synonym for the picturesqueness of the Irish landscape, if not indeed a cliché. If there is one place in Ireland the tourist is encouraged to go, it is here. But when Thackeray visited, he found that 'the town is crowded with company for the races and other sports, and all the world is bent to see the stag-hunt on the lake'.

The most celebrated house near the lakes is Kenmare House, owned by the Browne family. And the cascade is now known by the more ornamental name of Torc. Thackeray travelled through Ireland in 1842, when popular demand for repeal of the Union was in full swing, led by Daniel O'Connell, the Liberator, whose home at Derrynane is not very far from Killarney. Irish readers of all kinds did not take kindly to The Irish Sketch Book *when it first appeared. Many of them were offended by Thackeray's belittling sketch of O'Connell, which shows him as a stereotypically puckish Paddy.*

Killarney

The morning had been bright enough; but for fear of accidents we took our mackintoshes, and at about a mile from the town found it necessary to assume those garments and wear them for the greater part of the day. Passing by the 'Victoria', with its beautiful walks, park, and lodge, we came to a little creek where the boats were moored; and there was the wonderful lake before us, with its mountains, and islands, and trees. Unluckily, however, the mountains happened to be invisible; the islands looked like grey masses in the fog, and all that we could see for some time was the grey silhouette of the boat ahead of us, in which a passenger was engaged in a witty conversation with some boat still further in the mist.

Drumming and trumpeting was heard at a little distance, and presently we found ourselves in the midst of a fleet of boats upon the rocky shores of the beautiful little Innisfallen.

Here we landed for a while, and the weather clearing up allowed us to see this charming spot: rocks, shrubs, and little abrupt rises and falls of ground, covered with the brightest emerald grass; a beautiful little ruin of a Saxon chapel, lying gentle, delicate, and plaintive on the shore; some noble trees round about it, and beyond, presently, the tower of Ross Castle: island after island appearing in the clearing sunshine, and the huge hills throwing their misty veils off, and wearing their noble robes of purple. The boats' crews were grouped about the place, and one large barge especially had landed some sixty people, being the Temperance band, with its drums, trumpets, and wives. They were marshalled by a grave old gentleman with a white waistcoat and queue, a silver medal decorating one side of his coat, and a brass heart reposing on the other flap. The horns performed some Irish airs prettily; and at length, at the instigation of a fellow who went swaggering about with a pair of whirling drumsticks, all formed together and played Garryowen — the active drum of course most dreadfully out of time.

Having strolled about the island for a quarter of an hour, it became time to take to the boats again, and we were rowed over to the wood opposite Sullivan's cascade, where the hounds had been laid in in the morning, and the stag was expected to take water. Fifty or sixty men are employed on the mountain to drive the stag lakewards, should he be inclined to break away: and the sport generally ends by the stag — a wild one — making for the water with the pack swimming afterwards; and here he is taken and disposed of: how I know not. It is rather a parade than a stag-hunt; but, with all the boats around and the noble view, must be a fine thing to see.

Presently, steering his barge, the 'Erin', with twelve oars and a green flag sweeping the water, came by the president of the sports, Mr John O'Connell, a gentleman who appears to be liked by rich and poor here, and by the latter especially is adored. 'Sure we'd dhrown ourselves for him,' one man told me; and proceeded to speak eagerly in his praise, and to tell numberless acts of his generosity and justice. The justice is rather rude in this wild country sometimes, and occasionally the judges not only deliver the sentence but execute it; nor does any one think of appealing to any more regular jurisdiction. The likeness of Mr O'Connell to his brother is very striking: one might have declared it was the Liberator sitting at the stern of the boat.

Some scores more boats were there, darting up and down in the pretty, busy waters. Here came a Cambridge boat; and where, indeed, will not the gentlemen of that renowned university be found? Yonder were the dandy dragoons, stiff, silent, slim, faultlessly appointed, solemnly puffing cigars. Every now and then a hound would be heard in the wood, whereon numbers of voices, right and left, would begin to yell in chorus — 'Hurroo! Hoop! Yow — yow — yow!' in accents the most shrill or the most melancholious. Meanwhile the sun had had enough of the sport, the mountains put on their veils again, the islands retreated into the mist, the word went through the fleet to spread all umbrellas, and ladies took shares of mackintoshes and disappeared under the flaps of silk cloaks.

from *The Irish Sketch Book* (1843)

DESMOND O'GRADY

Whether or not World War I soldiers knew the whereabouts of Tipperary, they knew what they meant by it. This anthem of a generation concludes 'For my heart lies there'. The song was written in 1912. One of the first to popularise it was Al Jolson. Among the countless recordings of it is one by John McCormack. Wandering, tramping, going on a pilgrimage: a complex of motifs related to such activities has recurred in Irish writing since Buile Suibhne. In the modern period, particularly, Irish writers great and small have made extensive use of one form or another of peregrination.

The epigraph for Tipperary, the book in which the poem appears, quotes the modern Greek poet George Seferis: 'beacons in this temporary archipelago/where we live'. The town of Tipperary lies at the head of the Golden Vale, one of the most fertile areas of Ireland. Limerick Junction is a noted railway station near Tipperary town; it is extensively used as a place to change trains — one line to Limerick, the other to Cork. Its name has a particular resonance for generations of emigrants to England.

Tipperary

Tipperary: from the Irish Tiobraidarann: the fountain of perception or enlightenment, intelligence.

It's a long way to Tipperary,
it's a long way to go — and various.
It's a torture of twists, about-turns,
disillusions, disappointments.
The way to Tipperary appears
perennially dark with only
occasional twilights.

If you decide to go to Tipperary
set out while you're young, plucky;
at that age when you're bright-eyed with visions
of radiant horizons of revelation and achievement
and you know nothing of twilights or the dark;
that age when all creation, all life shines clear
as spring sunlight, bright as light-catching gold.

When you set out you must go alone.
There are no maps of the way to Tipperary.
Your only compass is your own heart. Trust that!

Some see their Tipperary clearly from the start;
see it's a long road, full of daily pitfalls;
a labyrinth of curious sidestreets, inviting
guesthouses; giddy with the temptations
of those bogey people's trinket stalls'
hokeypokey — daily thieves of eternal energy —
easy come, easy go, you've sold your soul,
you've no more choice. They sell bedlam!

Explore all those sidestreets,
enjoy your chosen resthouses,
fool with a few trinkets to learn
something of the way to Tipperary.

The way to Tipperary darkened
with the shadows of all those
who never got there anyway;
those who settled for some resthouse,
some casual trinket thief of time.
Don't let those shadows,
mumbling in their own gloom,
deter or deviate you.
Hold to your main road. Keep going!

Once you've decided to go to Tipperary
you'll realise you no longer belong to yourself
but must keep Tipperary in your sights daily —
although you can't see it. Purpose is all.
Without your Tipperary you too are a mere shadow
at those Limerick Junctions of daily resolution.

On the way to Tipperary keep your eye open
for signals of direction, encouragement:
that nod of understanding, comradeship,
a cherishing arm on your pillow. You'll see
beautiful sights on the way to Tipperary:
man's mirage tales, imagination's monuments.
You'll behold the endless vistas, panoramas
of vision. Be curious about them all
for the gracious gifts they will afford you.
Without them you'd live that much the poorer.

It's a long way to Tipperary
and when you get there
nothing awaits you. You'll find no roadsign,
no brassband and welcoming committee
with a banner proclaiming you're in Tipperary
and a medallion to hang around your neck.
You'll find only what you brought with you
in your heart.

Then, what you must do
is make and leave some record
of what your Tipperary means to you —
as witness for all those behind you
on their ways to their own Tipperaries.

It's a long way to Tipperary
but all our hearts lie there.

from *Tipperary* (1991)

DENNIS O'DRISCOLL

*Thurles's main claim to fame is that the Gaelic Athletic Association was founded there
in 1884. This is the powerful body that regulates, supervises and organises competition
at all levels in Ireland's national games. Hayes's Hotel, in which the association's
inaugural meeting was held, is still going strong. In at the foundation was Archbishop
Croke, Thurles being the diocesan seat of the diocese of Cashel and Emly. It is in his
honour that the national headquarters of the GAA in Dublin, Croke Park, is named.
Tipperary is one of the elite hurling counties, and Thurles Sarsfields is among its
legendary clubs, even if, 'it was . . . the peripheral excitement rather than the sport that
would entice me from our back garden', as Dennis O'Driscoll has written elsewhere. He
has also said, 'one can experience immortality anywhere. My childhood intimations in
Thurles were as strong as Wordsworth's in Cumbria, the same unshakeable sense of
being among eternal things that I would enjoy eternally. It is because such certainties
are irrecoverable that things associated with childhood become imbued with a wonder
that is more than mere nostalgia.'*

Zbigniew Herbert (b. 1924) is an internationally acclaimed Polish poet.

Thurles

after Zbigniew Herbert

A childhood too boring for words
is lost without a fragment in that town.
And, so, I have held my tongue about its gutturals;
its sky slated consistently with cloud;
its mossy roofs restraining excesses of rain.

One house watches out for me, though.
I know where its cabbage colander is kept
and the special knack required to use its tin-opener
and the exact key in which the kitchen door,
scuffed by a ring-board, creaks:

things I cannot depict in dictionary terms,
through heartless words that fail to resonate.
Others are suppressed in embarrassment or pain
(all families have passed their own equivalents
to the Official Secrets Act).

Yet everything there translates into feeling:
the plates the dead have eaten from before us,
the layers of wallpaper that still pattern memory,
the hairline crack in marble that was my fault,
the rose-arched garden explored down to its last stone.

Back in the city, I resort to standard words again.
Unable to identify possessions by their first names,
I call them only by their surnames
— by their brand names —
and will never discover their real names.

from *Hidden Extras* (1987)

S AMUEL F ERGUSON

Thomas Moore's successful Melodies coincided with a broadening interest in Irish music and song. Abroad, composers such as Beethoven were setting Irish airs to music for voice. In Ireland, the collection and publication of music, song, folklore and antiquarian data developed rapidly. Anglo-Irish literature grew, in part, out of these developments. Samuel Ferguson was among the most prominent and seriously interested of those involved. Much of his prolific output of translations appeared in the influential Dublin University Magazine, *founded in 1832. His antiquarian learning and metrical skill led Yeats to praise Ferguson as a precursor who 'sought to lay the foundation of a literature for Ireland that should be in every way characteristic and national'.*

As in the literature of every country, there is a strong tradition of love poetry in Irish. Cashel, Co. Tipperary is an ancient political and ecclesiastical centre, the rich remains of which may be seen on its celebrated rock. Tyrone, in Northern Ireland, was once ruled by the powerful O'Neill clan.

It is not known who composed the original poem.

Cashel of Munster

I'd wed you without herds, without money, or rich array,
And I'd wed you on a dewy morning at day-dawn gray;
My bitter woe it is, love, that we are not far away
In Cashel town, though the bare deal board were our marriage-bed this day.

Oh, fair maid, remember the green hill side,
Remember how I hunted about the valleys wide;
Time now has worn me; my locks are turned to grey,
The year is scarce and I am poor, but send me not, love, away!

Oh, deem not my birth is of base strain, my girl,
Oh, deem not my birth was as the birth of a churl;
Marry me, and prove me, and say soon you will,
That noble blood is written on my right side still!

My purse holds no red gold, no coin of the silver white,
No herds are mine to drive through the long twilight!
But the pretty girl that would take me, all bare though I be and lone,
Oh, I'd take her with me kindly to the county Tyrone.

Oh, my girl, I can see 'tis in trouble you are,
And, oh, my girl, I see 'tis your people's reproach you bear;
'I am a girl in trouble for his sake with whom I fly,
And, oh, may no other maiden know such reproach as I!'

from Padraic Colum (ed.), *The Poems of Samuel Ferguson* (1963)

CHEVALIER DE LA TOCNAYE

Adare's present-day 'model village look' dates from the nineteenth century and the taste of the third Earl of Dunraven. He also saw to the upkeep of the medieval buildings: Desmond's Castle, the Franciscan Friary, the Augustinian Priory (today the Church of Ireland church), and the Trinitarian Abbey (now the Catholic church). This earl was the direct descendant of de La Tocnaye's host, the family name being originally Quin, subsequently becoming Wyndham-Quin.

It was a nobleman of another family, Thomas, first Baron Southwell, who created the Palatine. In 1709, as a result of French success in Swabia and the Rhenish Palatinate during the War of the Spanish Succession, over eight hundred refugees were resettled here and in County Kerry. Most of them did not stay very long, but to those who did the cliché about the Normans — that they became more Irish than the Irish themselves — applies. Their surnames are still to be found — Switzer, for example.

The established religion is the Church of Ireland. It was disestablished in 1869.

In County Limerick

From Newcastle to Limerick the country is superb. This is, without contradiction, the most fertile stretch of land in Ireland. Near Rathkeale I had occasion to visit three or four villages inhabited by the descendants of a German colony from the Palatinate, established by the owner of the soil nearly eighty years ago. Until now they have always married among themselves, and have preserved the customs of their country. At the time of my visit there was only one man living of the original members of the colony. There is no doubt that they were received on very advantageous conditions, each family receiving, in perpetuity, ground for house and garden, as well as several acres of farm land at a very moderate rate. The rich and fertile country on which they were established was uncultivated before their arrival. Their industry is still very remarkable. Their farms are certainly better cultivated than others near, and their houses, built after the fashion of their former country, are of a comfortable character, and so clean that they look like palaces in comparison with the poor cabins of the Irish. The women still wear the large straw hat and short petticoat as worn in the Palatinate. The natives hated them cordially at the beginning, and do not love them much better now, as they are very jealous of their successes, and such feelings do not tend to make them attempt to imitate the foreigners with intention to equal or even surpass them in results. Naturally, I suppose, the Palatines will finish by becoming Irish like their neighbours.

Passing through the long town of Rathkeale I directed my steps to Adare, where I was received by Sir Richard Quin. This town was formerly full of colleges and ecclesiastical establishments. The ruins of several well-preserved buildings are still to be seen, and four or five miles away, at Skelton, are ruins of abbeys, which are perhaps the largest I have seen in this country.

The ruins in the west of Ireland are of a style of architecture absolutely different from that in the east, where they are commonly rather small, while here they are somewhat of the grandeur and style of the Gothic churches of the Continent.

In reflecting on the prodigious number of ruins of churches and abbeys, and on the immense riches which still remain in the hands of the clergy of the established religion, one is tempted to believe that at one time the whole island belonged to priests, for if the Anglican clergyman could make the most of his estates himself, I imagine that his part would still be not very far away from the half of it. The manner in which these lands are let or farmed out is a hindrance. No beneficiary can let his land for longer than twenty-one years, but this time is pretty long for a man who is advanced in his years, and who is pressed to make some provision for his family. To rectify the trouble as much as possible, the Bishop or other beneficiary renews his leases every year with his tenant, on condition that he will be given what we call *un pot de vin*, which puts a certain sum into his pocket and makes him patient. Every clergyman who takes possession of a benefice is sure by this custom to find a tenancy renewed from the year before, and is obliged himself in some fashion to follow the same practice. I am convinced that there are certain bishoprics which are not let at the tenth part of their value, and which would produce in case of renewal of holding, sums of fifty, sixty, or even one hundred thousand pounds sterling per annum, instead of five, eight, or ten thousand. The Lord is mindful of his own.

I took the road to Limerick, and saw on the way a 'wake' in the house of a dead man. It was Sunday, and the women do not cry so loudly on that day, but the scene was, nevertheless, a rather singular one. The dead lay on a table, and the house was so full of women sitting on their heels that a bullet dropped among them would not have touched ground. The men were outside on the road, to the number of about two hundred, on foot or on horseback, and a great number prudently waiting at a neighbouring inn until it would please the dead to move.

It was the time of the horse races at Limerick, and also it was the duelling season. The confusion everywhere was extreme. The town was full of people coming and going. The workers were doing nothing. Everything had given way to the desire to see some breakneck performances on horseback; there were on the course more than twenty thousand persons. What made the people anxious to see was that three of the jockeys were peers; or was it that three of the peers were jockeys? You can take it whichever way you wish. The one is as bad as the other.

There came to the races some bullies from Cork and Youghal, with the laudable intention of putting lead into the brains of the Limerick folk. They went about saying to anyone they met, 'Do you want powder and ball? for we can give it.' During the eight days of the races there were ten or twelve duels

— an officer of the Irish brigade was killed. Then it occurred to the Chancellor to put an end to these quarrels by proceedings for criminal acts, and the warlike gentlemen took their departure.

The races finished at last, and happily for the country, for had they lasted three weeks longer, the inhabitants were so given over to sport that the harvest would have lain in the fields ungathered.

from *A Frenchman's Walk Through Ireland* (1797)

KATE O'BRIEN

In 1929, the Irish government passed the Censorship of Publications Act. More than any other single piece of legislation perhaps, this law stamped the new state as timid, narrow-minded, hostile to fresh thought, new ideas and free speech. Or perhaps it was not merely the law itself, but its implementation. Almost every Irish author of note had works banned. A case in point is The Land of Spices. It was the second of Kate O'Brien's novels to be banned; Mary Lavelle (1936) was the first.

The action of The Land of Spices is largely set in a convent, and deals with a nun's emotional and psychological conflicts. The title is from George Herbert's 'Prayer':
'Church-bells beyond the stars heard, the soul's blood/The land of spices; something understood.'

Kate O'Brien, daughter of a comfortable middle-class Limerick family, spent her childhood summers at a lodge in the seaside resort of Kilkee, Co. Clare.

Summer with Charlie

Doon Point was a village in the west where the Murphys always spent the months of July and August — a holiday plan ranging back into the childhood of Grandfather Murphy. A furnished house, called a 'lodge', was rented, and the family, with Delia and Mrs Rorke — indeed everyone who mattered at Castle Tory except Joe — was transported by a long train journey to the Atlantic coast. Daddy usually spent only the first month at Doon Point, returning perhaps for one or two week-ends of August. The arrangement in its entirety was a beloved tradition of summer.

One of the first real shadows flung on childhood for Anna was when this tradition seemed insecure, when she became aware of doubt as to its continuance. She was very much shocked when in the summer of 1912 the lodge was taken only for July. And during the summer term of 1913, when she went home for Sunday afternoons, she and Charlie listened anxiously for the customary promises and hints about Doon Point — but they did not come. She was fifteen now and Charlie was thirteen, and both knew better than to precipitate trouble with their elders by direct questioning. Perhaps also they feared the reply they might be given. Indeed, so passionate was their desire for summer at Doon Point that, though each saw, at every meeting in May and June, the fixed anxiety in the other's eyes, and knew its cause, they had not the heart to speak of it together. And Anna developed a superstitious hope that if no doubt were uttered custom would somehow unfold the expected pattern.

And it did, though not quite perfectly.

When the Murphy children, Harry, Tom and Anna, returned from school at the end of term they were told that they were going to Doon Point for August, to the usual lodge — but that this time they were Granny's guests, that business was bad just now for Daddy, and that they must all write and thank Granny very politely for being so kind as to give them this lovely summer holiday.

Anna did not care for Granny, who, although she seemed rich and was free with presents, exacted from children large measures of docility, piety, and reverence for herself. However, she wrote as directed; and indeed she *was* grateful, as she would have been to anyone who secured her Doon Point in August. But she perceived complications of sadness and anger behind such an arrangement; she felt it as a slur on the Murphys, a sign that the family was going downhill.

And one evening she was present during a crude piece of argument between her father and her mother.

'In any case,' Daddy was saying, 'we'll be well quit of each other in August. Because don't think I'm going next or near Doon Point this time, my girl! I've stood my share from that mother of yours, but I'm not going to stay in any house she pays for — by Christ I'm not!'

'Well really, Harry, I don't think she had meant to invite you. I believe her idea partly is to give me a rest from you.'

'Indeed? And do you mean to tell me that one doesn't know that your whole life is one long, sweet rest from me — an unbroken, chaste, devotional retreat, by God!'

'Are you aware that your daughter is in the room?'

'Is she? Poor child. Poor Anna!'

Anna left the room.

Nevertheless, summer at Doon Point was summer multiplied, rendered imaginatively indestructible. And this time Anna held its days like a miser or a lover. For the fluke of Granny's kindness, and the crude airs of sadness and rancour at home made her accept uncertainty at last, and look ahead at facts sometimes with wider-opened, adolescent eyes.

And when she beheld Doon Point again on August 1st, when after the day's hot journey she stood by the sea-wall and smelt and heard and beheld again all of this unchanging, unforgotten Paradise; when, astonished in joy as she had known she would be, she gathered in the welcome of its brilliant, evening innocence, she felt, in excess of her usual delight, a sharp bright pain which reminded her not of former arrivals like this, but of mornings of departure. For the first time she felt that Doon Point too was subject to sadness — not the brief disappointments and hurts of everyday which, she knew, were everywhere — but the undefined yet increasingly perceptible sadnesses of life beyond childhood, the changes and shadows that darkened older faces, and made so much uncertain that once was sure. She realised with a shock in that first minute of arrival, and for no special reason other than that she was now fifteen, and was more hurt than she knew by the flight of childhood, that even all this joy and beauty — so impervious-seeming from afar in winter and spring, so wrapped apart in an isolation like that of dreams, and of stories told and read — was a reality like other things, and, as she had witnessed, as much a source of trouble and anger.

from *The Land of Spices* (1941)

ANONYMOUS

'The little ruined outlet, which gives its name to one of the most popular national songs of Erin, is situate on the acclivity of a hill near the city of Limerick . . . Tradition has preserved the occasion of its celebrity, and the origin of its name, which appears to be compounded of two Irish words signifying "Owen's garden" . . . Owen's garden was the general rendezvous for those who sought for simple amusement or for dissipation . . . The festivities of our fathers, however, were frequently distinguished by so fierce a character of mirth, that, for any difference in the result of their convivial meetings, they might as well have been pitched encounters. Owen's garden was soon as famous for scenes of strife, as it was for mirth and humour; and broken heads became a staple article of manufacture in the neighbourhood.'

So begins Gerald Griffin's The Collegians (1829), the novel that put Garryowen on the literary map. The novel was adapted as a melodrama, The Colleen Bawn (1860), by Dion Boucicault, which then became the basis of an opera, The Lily of Killarney.

Garryowen is the name of the Citizen's dog in Ulysses; and it is the name of a Limerick rugby club, as well as a tactic in rugby from which much rough-and-tumble results.

The song itself — composer unknown — dates from the 1770s.

Garryowen

Let Bacchus's sons be not dismayed,
But join with me each jovial blade;
Come booze and sing, and lend your aid
To help me with the chorus: —

Instead of Spa we'll drink brown ale,
And pay the reckoning on the nail;
No man for debt shall go to gaol
From Garryowen in glory!

We are the boys that take delight in
Smashing the Limerick lamps when lighting,
Through the streets like sporters fighting,
And tearing all before us.
Instead, &c.

We'll break windows, we'll break doors,
The watch knock down by threes and fours;
Then let the doctors work their cures,
And tinker up our bruises.
Instead, &c.

We'll beat the bailiffs, out of fun,
We'll make the mayor and sheriffs run;
We are the boys no man dares dun,
If he regards a whole skin.
Instead, &c.

Our hearts, so stout, have got us fame,
For soon 'tis known from whence we came;
Where'er we go they dread the name
Of Garryowen in glory.
Instead, &c.

Johnny Connell's tall and straight,
And in his limbs he is complete;
He'll pitch a bar of any weight,
From Garryowen to Thomond Gate.
Instead, &c.

Garryowen is gone to wrack
Since Johnny Connell went to Cork,
Though Darby O'Brien leapt over the dock
In spite of all the soldiers.
Instead, &c.

from *The Lyrics of Ireland* (1858)

MICHAEL COADY

Together with his brothers Miko and Gussie, the poem's dedicatee, Pakie Russell, was a legendary traditional musician. Not only was he a native of the county which has become synonymous with traditional music, he came from the area around the village of Doolin, epicentre of the musical tradition in Clare. And along with the music comes certain social amenities — long nights with neighbours that pass in a twinkling, pub sessions for which closing time can be a pretty remote concept. The scene and the music in Doolin have made the village a place of pilgrimage, especially for the music's many German fans.

The spectacular cliffs of Moher rise to a sheer height of over six hundred feet out of the Atlantic, four miles from Doolin. The author's own translation of the closing line is: 'O friend of my heart, lie merry and lewd in your clay.'

Pakie played the concertina. He is buried in Doolin.

Stopping by a Clare Graveyard After Hours

for Pakie Russell, 1920–1977

I've walked up two miles from the pub
   through a mystical moonscape
And it could have been three what with taking
   both sides of the road,
I lean on the wall and my breathing
   is heavy and laboured
As I give you a greeting and offer you
   talk of the world.

Below in the village the men
   and the women are sleeping,

The lights are all out and the children
    away in their dreams,
The music and talk of tonight
    are gone to wherever
The tunes and the talk of all nights
    slip away on the air.

From shore to horizon the sea
    is a ravishing silver,
Awesome and innocent, untouched
    by joy or dismay;
The grass of the summer is gathered
    and tied in the haggards,
The dark brow of Moher is dreaming
    over the bay.

I'm not here to grieve for your bones
    or the earth where they're lying,
You've company round you of neighbours
    and friends from this place;
The men and the women who danced
    to your music are with you,
United you lie in the intimate
    rhythm of clay.

I know you were always a man
    with a heart for the true thing,
For a child or a saying, a woman,
    a flower or a song,
Life that came dancing through fingers
    was most of your praying
And your darkness redeemed in the shape
    and surprise of the word.

Out of all of the years and the laughter
    just let me remember
One moment of kissing I stood
    by the sea with a girl
While you were enthroned on the hill
    with the dawn at your shoulder
Gracing your music with wakening
    song of the birds.

The tiding old sea is still taking
    and giving and shaping,
Gentians and violets break
    in the spring from the stone,
The world and its mother go reeling
    and jigging forever
In answer to something that troubles
    the blood and the bone.

So I have to report there's no end
    to the song and the story,
With enough music in it to send us all
    drunk on our way;
As I go to my sleep I ask
    for a smile and a blessing:
'S a chara mo chléibh, bí meidhreach
    is gáirsiúil id' chré.

from *Oven Lane* (1987)

MICHEÁL Ó BRAONÁIN

The Irish for the Shannon is 'Sionainn' meaning 'elder', as in, say, elder of the tribe. And for most of its 240-mile length it meanders along in the manner of a stately elder. But once out of Lough Derg, which is where these verses begin, it starts its race to the sea, dropping a hundred feet in the twenty miles between Killaloe and Limerick. This fall is harnessed by the Ardnacrusha power station, built in the late 1920s, a landmark initiative by the fledgling Irish Free State.

On the eastern side the Nenagh river flows into Lough Derg near Dromineer. On the opposite side, near Scarriff, the river Bow joins Lough Derg.

The Shannon in Clare

The beautiful river of the land of Lough Graney
in the County Clare, in the length of her course
she is pleasant, fishful, much-watered,
and her stream is neither swift nor lazy.

Some distance east of Scariff her store goes in hidden
places augmenting strength with little noise,
in a course like all others in the edge
of the Shannon.

A strong river leads from the hip of a hill east from
Nenagh of Ormond and her full swift stream serves
many functions in her ordinary journey
to that same town.

From the pleasant districts of Nenagh she flows,
between hills and river-meadow marshes
without rest or stop until she goes into the
Shannon in Johnstown of the boats and the barks.

That is a short account of the choicest of the rivers
which pay high rent to the Shannon, from the land
of Lough Derg to the breast of the eel-weirs
of Killaloe of the current.

In approaching the protected eel-weirs of Killaloe
of the clerics without difficulty the powerful Shannon
draws her banks towards each other in the
form of a stream.

Although it is the understanding of many people in the
distant districts of the country that it is in Killaloe
of the barks that the fall or the rock is which
is a blemish on the Shannon,

but let everybody take notice definitely that the
fall or ridged rock is the space of four miles
distance up beyond Killaloe
of the monks.

from *Príomhshruth Éireann* (1994)

DEREK MAHON

The Majestic Hotel has burned to the ground. 'Here and there among the foundations one might still find evidence of the Majestic's former splendour: the great number of cast-iron bathtubs, for instance . . . twisted bed-frames also, some of them not yet

*altogether rusted away; and a simply prodigious number of basins and lavatory bowls.
At intervals along the outer walls . . . one can disinter small pools of crystal formed in
layers like the drips of wax from a candle, which gathered there, of course, from melting
of the windows. Pick them up and they separate in your hand into the cloudy drops that
formed them.'*

The Majestic, in imaginary Kilnalough, Co. Wexford, was a favourite haunt of
aging Anglo-Irish types at the turn of the century. It is the focal point of Troubles
(1970) by Derek Mahon's friend J.G. Farrell (1935–79).

A Disused Shed in Co. Wexford

*Let them not forget us, the weak souls among
the asphodels.* — Seferis, Mythistorema

for J.G. Farrell

Even now there are places where a thought might grow —
Peruvian mines, worked out and abandoned
To a slow clock of condensation,
An echo trapped for ever, and a flutter
Of wildflowers in the lift-shaft,
Indian compounds where the wind dances
And a door bangs with diminished confidence,
Lime crevices behind rippling rainbarrels,
Dog corners for bone burials;
And in a disused shed in Co. Wexford,

Deep in the grounds of a burnt-out hotel,
Among the bathtubs and the washbasins
A thousand mushrooms crowd to a keyhole.
This is the one star in their firmament
Or frames a star within a star.
What should they do there but desire?
So many days beyond the rhododendrons
With the world waltzing in its bowl of cloud,
They have learnt patience and silence
Listening to the rooks querulous in the high wood.

They have been waiting for us in a foetor
Of vegetable sweat since civil war days,
Since the gravel-crunching, interminable departure
Of the expropriated mycologist.

He never came back, and light since then
Is a keyhole rusting gently after rain.
Spiders have spun, flies dusted to mildew
And once a day, perhaps, they have heard something —
A trickle of masonry, a shout from the blue
Or a lorry changing gear at the end of the lane.

There have been deaths, the pale flesh flaking
Into the earth that nourished it;
And nightmares, born of these and the grim
Dominion of stale air and rank moisture.
Those nearest the door grow strong —
'Elbow room! Elbow room!'
The rest, dim in a twilight of crumbling
Utensils and broken flower-pots, groaning
For their deliverance, have been so long
Expectant that there is left only the posture.

A half century, without visitors, in the dark —
Poor preparation for the cracking lock
And creak of hinges. Magi, moonmen,
Powdery prisoners of the old regime,
Web-throated, stalked like triffids, racked by drought
And insomnia, only the ghost of a scream
At the flash-bulb firing squad we wake them with
Shows there is life yet in their feverish forms.
Grown beyond nature now, soft food for worms,
They lift frail heads in gravity and good faith.

They are begging us, you see, in their wordless way,
To do something, to speak on their behalf
Or at least not to close the door again.
Lost people of Treblinka and Pompeii!
'Save us, save us,' they seem to say,
'Let the god not abandon us
Who have come so far in darkness and in pain.
We too had our lives to live.
You with your light meter and relaxed itinerary,
Let not our naive labours have been in vain!'

from *Selected Poems* (1991)

ANONYMOUS

Bunclody is a town in north-west County Wexford. It was founded in the sixteenth century by James Barry, Sheriff of Dublin, and for many years was known as Newtownbarry. The town stands in the shadows of the Blackstairs mountains, of which Mount Leinster is the main peak. These mountains are where one of the streams in the song rises. This is the Clody, which runs in a narrow, tree-lined channel down the centre of Bunclody's broad main street. The other stream is County Wexford's main river, the Slaney.

Thomas Moore's song 'The Meeting of the Waters', set not very far from Bunclody in the Vale of Avoca, Co. Wicklow, uses the same idea of mingling as a metaphor of loving, though Moore does not factor in those social divisions which in 'The Streams of Bunclody' prevent nature taking its course. To be a freeholder is to possess a degree of security that is generally considered atypical of life on the land in Ireland long ago, especially the life of women.

The Streams of Bunclody

O was I at the mosshouse where the birds do increase,
At the foot of Mount Leinster or some silent place,
Near the streams of Bunclody, where all pleasures do meet,
And all I'd require is one kiss from you sweet.

If I was in Bunclody I would think myself at home,
'Tis there I would have a sweetheart, but here I have none.
Drinking strong liquor is the height of my cheer —
Here's a health to Bunclody and the lass I love dear.

The cuckoo is a pretty bird, it sings as it flies,
It brings us good tidings and tells us no lies,
It sucks the young bird's eggs to make its voice clear,
And it never cries, 'cuckoo' till the summer is near.

If I was a clerk and could write a good hand,
I would write to my true love that she might understand,
I am a young fellow that is wounded in love,
That lived by Bunclody, but now must remove.

If I was a lark and had wings, I then could fly,
I would go to yon arbour where my love she does lie,
I'd proceed to yon arbour where my love does lie,
And on her fond bosom contented I would die.

The reason my love slights me, as you may understand,
Because she has a freehold, and I have no land,
She has a great store of riches and a large sum of gold,
And everything fitting a house to uphold.

So adieu, my dear father, adieu, my dear mother,
Farewell to my sister, farewell to my brother;
I'm going to America, my fortune for to try;
When I think upon Bunclody, I'm ready to die!

from James N. Healy, *Irish Ballads and Songs of the Sea* (1983)

TONY O'MALLEY

'I started drawing while still a teenager, purely for myself. I had no idea of art — the Christian Brothers in Callan didn't have art classes!' From those beginnings, Tony O'Malley has become one of the foremost Irish painters of his generation. And his persistence, dedication, isolation and risk-taking are an exemplary expression of the possibility of self-realisation — to quote him again: 'When I started painting, the nature of it was improvisation.'

O'Malley's paintings draw not only on his Irish experiences but on his years in Cornwall and trips to the Caribbean. 'I have never regarded myself as the Irishman abroad who needed to go back', he has said. 'I had left Ireland but I brought it with me . . . I'm very much a person of the people, a small-town person.'

Inscape — Life and Landscape in Callan and County Kilkenny

My grandmother was a Marnell from outside Callan. Marnell's Cross was called after that family. She was born around 1840 and was married to Mattie Ryan, a gardener in the convent. There are photographs of my grandmother and Dan Ryan (his main companion, although they were not related) standing beside an ass and cart, holding a load of manure. My grandmother's (Margaret Marnell) brothers were active Fenians in the 1860s and they went out to America. Jack and Ned Marnell got away to America and remained there, but came back at different times to visit Callan. Ned was a bit of a scapegrace, consorting with disturbed elements, while Jack was a more orthodox kind of man. Their heroes were John Locke and Coyne of Bridge Street (which was Coyne Street originally) both leading Fenians in Callan — 'The ould Feneens' they were called. James Cody of Callan mill was also one.

My mother was Maggie Ryan, daughter of Mattie Ryan and Margaret Marnell. They were much knitted into the people of the countryside. The Ryans were a big clan of people. They were part of the Kilkenny/Tipperary texture. My grandmother used to say that her family was evicted from the Raheen down near Tullamaine. Tullamaine is an ancient place — one of the great early Christian bell shrines was made there. Because of the eviction, the Raheen became a kind of sanctified place which you went down to and pondered. I was conscious of it, not in terms of terrible violence or vengeance but in terms of stories told and memories. My grandmother was very fair: in a way, she was a socialist. She would not pre-judge a planter or a farmer, only ask whether he was a good man. She admired and was very interested in the Quakers and spoke highly of them. People like the Armitages and the Whites were very fair and distributed the meal during the Famine. One of her close friends was a Protestant, Linda Cherry, who worked in Gregory's of Westcourt. She was a confidante of my mother.

My father, Patrick O'Malley, was a Clare Island man. He was one of a large family, the children of Anthony O'Malley who was drowned during the time of the land war. After leaving the island, my father worked for the Congested Districts Board and then came to Kilkenny city as a representative for Singer Sewing Machine Company. He met my mother who was living in Callan and they married and settled down. My Clare Island inheritance which is more psychic and sea orientated is mixed therefore with the more introverted and land based Norman Celtic heritage of county Kilkenny.

My grandmother had Slievenamon Irish; around here is part of the decies, which overflowed into Kilkenny. She would say, if you asked her 'how are you?, 'achspleach' not 'neamhspleach'. My mother's sister was the same — she also had many words that were pure Irish. My grandmother talked of the Caravats and Shanavests, who were the factions then. Callan and Ballingarry were laid waste by the big faction fights. The Caravats were related in a way to the Ribbonmen and the lower class of people. The Shanavests were stronger socially. I never knew whether my grandmother was a Caravat or Shanavest but I think she was a Caravat. They were the labouring people. Somebody said one time in a pub in Callan — 'play up the Caravat jig' and there were immediate ructions. Amhlaoibh Ó Súilleabháin was known in Callan amongst old men when I was growing up — he was spoken of as 'Old Humphrey'. People knew where he lived in Green Street. He wrote about the factions. He was the authority, the Kerryman, the scholar: that acknowledgement was given to him. He took the trouble to learn all about Callan, walked about it, met the parish priest and the protestant clergyman. He was a great man of his time.

The schism was the next big thing in Callan, the reds and schismatics. The name 'schismatic' was applied to the bishop's men, the established authority of the church. The 'reds' were the people who supported Fr O'Keeffe, who was a social reformer. Callan was a poor town after the Famine. The bishop and the business people were regarded as 'schismatics'. My family were 'reds'. The word 'red' came into the language after the Paris commune. During the ructions, a picture and notice about Fr O'Keeffe were being nailed up in Callan. An old woman shouted up, as the men drove in the second nail, 'put another nail down there and you'll have him crucified'. I inherited sympathy for O'Keeffe from my mother and grandmother, who regarded him as a Champion of the people, against elites, clerical and otherwise — a distant echo of the influence of the French Revolution.

In our young years, we went to the convent up to the age of seven until we made our communion and then we were trained for the sacrament. We were taken up to the church and the two shilling pieces were put on our tongues. We were terrified; we could not make head or tail out of this. We would be marched up and taught by a monitor or monitoress. Then we were ready for our first communion. We were dressed up in clean shirts, which were a big outlay for people at that time. The girls had wreaths. You presented a candle at the altar rails. There was a fellow below me whose candle was decorated with flowers. It would be lit (we did not understand the full ritual at the time) and the server came along and took the candle and this fellow above me held onto the candle. 'I want me candle', he said. He did not like the fellow who was taking it from him either — the fellow who was in the soutane — so he held onto it.

When I was at school our great rendezvous was Pollard's stables — a place of oats and straw, and the smell of horse manure — a bastion under the edge of the town walls, where a carpenter worked, so there was coffins everywhere. When we wanted our homework done, we would go there, bringing Willie Walsh, a farmer's son, with us, who was good at maths. There would be a bottle of puce ink on the stable window and we would compel him to confront the conundrums, while we circled him, watching him working. We would be clever enough not to be too right, starting right and then going wrong towards the end. Brother Gleeson, a serious faced Nenagh man who knew everything, was our teacher — he was like a detective. One evening, six of us were lined up around Willie Walsh, forcing him to do the work. Suddenly, Brother Gleeson's voice erupted behind us 'I see I have the honour of being in Pollard's Academy — the university of West Street.' Another day, a fellow mitcher was in Pollard's when he heard his father coming up the yard after him — his father lifted the lids of the coffins and found his son lying face down in one of them. One legacy of the Christian Brothers is that, even still, I always see the man over my shoulder, correcting me.

When I went to the Christian Brothers, it was a big step in education at the time. The Christian Brothers' reputation was real terror — they 'bet' it into you. You had to be tough. Hurling was very strong with them, hurling and nationalism. This was 1922, the time of the civil war. One night Dinny Lacey's flying column of the IRA took Callan and blew up the middle arch of the bridge during the night. Somebody put planks across it and my mother said to me 'now look, go across the Friar's Bridge down to the Abbey meadow' (the Friars had opened their bridge to accommodate the people). Myself and three or four others, nothing would do us but to go across the planks. I slipped in the middle of the bloody planks, fell into the river and broke my arm. An old man on the bridge smoking a pipe came in and rescued me. He took me up and pulled me out and we all went up to school together. This will tell you what the terror of authority was at the time. I was drenched, with my arm limp, and I stood in the schoolroom above and it had to be explained to the Christian Brother what had happened to me. I was like a defaulter of some kind. I was taken up to Dr Phelan and he bandaged me up and sent me home. I had to go back by the Friary. Then there was great wailing from my mother about doing the wrong thing and going across on the plank — recriminations and character assaults.

My father was away from home at the time. The treaty had been signed and the civil war was on. The IRA at that time were called the irregulars and we knew many of them in Dinny Lacey's flying column. When my father came back, he said, 'there's nothing for it but to take this fellow up to Lanigan of Kilbroughan' (around Kilmanagh).

The Lanigans were great bonesetters; both the men and the women were naturally gifted — cattle or human it did not matter. So my father said to me 'I'll take you up on the bicycle.' The bike was the great mode of transport then. There were a few old Tin Lizzies around but they all had been commandeered by either the IRA or the Free Staters.

Just as we were setting out, news came that Michael Collins had been shot in Béal na mBláth. My father had supported the treaty; he was a pro-treaty man and he started crying and, as he pushed the bike all the way up to Kilmanagh, he cried. He was a very emotional west of Ireland man. He loved Collins and thought that he was the greatest — he saw him as one of his own people who had taken on the British and shown them. De Valera had no appeal for him. He had time for Dev intellectually but Collins was the man in the gap. We went up to Kilbroughan — it's a long, long journey — and we went into Lanigan's farm, a lovely, comfortable farm. Lanigan was overcome by Collins's death as well. After talking about it to each other, Lanigan decided to set my arm. While I was waiting there, he brought me out to the orchard for apples. Then Lanigan bound me and fixed me up. That was my memory of the civil war and I was only a few days in the Christian Brothers when that happened. It was an emotional time.

We held the Christian Brothers in profound respect but we were not foreign to them. They were the same kind of people as us. After all, Ignatius Rice was a Callan man. They understood us only too well and we understood them. We might have a fellow from Kerry who was a walking terror but we understood each other. They were practical educationalists who taught the poor when nobody else bothered. I always stand up for the Christian Brothers, knowing what they had done socially for the people after the Famine. With the Christian Brothers, we did learn. Children were never pampered at that time and we worked at home as well. I helped my mother in the shop when I was a young lad, carrying messages and weighing things like spuds. We were imbued with a fierce nationalism from the Christian Brothers. There is an objective historical side to me but I would also understand the emotional history and political difficulties of the time.

from William Nolan and Kevin Whelan (eds.), *Kilkenny: History and Society* (1990)

the decies . . . The Decies is a pre-Christian kingdom, in modern times usually associated with eastern County Waterford, an area rich in prehistoric burial chambers and similar sites.

'neamhspleach' . . . literally means independence

Amhlaoibh Ó Súilleabháin . . . Humphrey O'Sullivan (1780–1838) wrote the first diary in Irish.

the schism . . . The events mentioned are the basis of a novel, *The Big Chapel* (1971), by another Callan native, Thomas Kilroy.

Ignatius Rice . . . Edmund Ignatius Rice (1762–1844) founded the Christian Brothers in 1803. He was beatified in 1996.

DONAL FOLEY

One of Waterford city's greatest claims to national fame is that Ignatius Rice founded his first Christian Brothers' school there. The name of the school is Mount Sion. In time the name also became that of a successful hurling team. Quite probably many of the author's playmates in the 1920s and 30s eventually wore the Mount Sion colours, even if they were never educated at the school. The school they did attend in Ferrybank was run along much different lines from any connected with the Christian Brothers. The other prominent Waterford city hurling team is Erin's Own. It numbered young Seán Dunne and his father among its staunch supporters.

Donal Foley's three villages are Ferrybank, Dublin and London.

Ferrybank

S chooldays in Ferrybank were always a mixture of excitement and strange satisfaction and every day seemed to be an adventure in itself. The school had two rooms, a big room where two teachers taught the junior classes, and the gallery, a smaller room with steps right up to the back, where the principal teacher taught. All three teachers were close friends and they always seemed to have a great deal to talk about, particularly on Monday morning when they usually left us to our own devices for about half an hour before they began lessons.

Ferrybank was then a tiny village of one street with the little houses in a row together. The top part of the street was known as the Upper Slip and the lower part, which was closer to the river, was called the Lower Slip. The people were a mixture of dockers, sailors, railway men, factory workers and many unemployed. It was a tightly-knit community of less than 600, proud and fiercely tribal with the wives even closer than the husbands. There were no secrets. Both joys and sorrows were shared, and the comradeship which poverty often engenders was strong.

The school presented a fairly accurate reflection of the conditions of the people in that part of Ireland in those years. About a fifth of the boys came to school bare footed, even in the hardest winters, boys with pale little faces, dressed in tattered clothes handed down from their brothers. They came from that part of the village where the dockers lived by casual labour.

On arrival at school they were always given special places close to the fire and on wet days their clothes would be steaming. The rest of us in the school were also poorly shod and clothed, as the hand-me-downs were common to us all.

As so many of the fathers in Ferrybank were dockers the river was always watched carefully for the arrival of ships, or the sound of the hooter which signalled their coming. These same ships meant work and porter flowing in Ferrybank's half dozen pubs. When the siren of the coal boats blew in the river all the classroom would be joyful. Next day boys would come with the ritual note seeking permission to take down their father's dinner to the docks. It was something that, as a child, I always wanted to do. The meal was usually a stew made from the offal that could be purchased cheaply from Clover Meats, the factory in Ferrybank. It was carried down in an old sweet gallon tin and I am sure must have tasted great on the docks.

Looking back on it, that same Waterford river, the Suir, played a very big role in our childhood lives. We learned to swim in it and every summer the river landmarks, the Pier Head, the Ferry Slip and the Ballast Quay became our resorts. It was there, in the early days of June we had our first swim and experienced the exquisite joy of lying naked on the river bank, basking in the early summer sun.

It was the river Suir that gave Ferrybank its separate identity as a kind of native reservation opposite Waterford city, which we tended to look upon as alien. We thought of ourselves as part of Kilkenny and of the great hurling men of that county. It was the river which divided us. It was a kind of protection and, although we often crossed the bridge or took the Ferry to go to Waterford, we never really felt at home until we were back over the river again.

The fierce tribalism was recognised in the city and in some neighbouring villages, and the saying went 'You could walk through Ireland, but you run through the slip (Ferrybank).' We took it as a just tribute to our tribal abilities.

We were a kind of big family. It was the way the head teacher looked upon us. He was an unusual teacher, determined that school should be an exciting place. Geography, for instance, was taught by making huge sand maps on the school table. We all did it together, and we decided what would represent the rivers, the lakes. We used bits of glass, twine, pieces of chalk and a lump of coal to show where the mines were. To this day I can see Italy as a leg with a shoe on the end of it, and a bone going down the middle.

We learned about all the European countries and Ireland itself in this intimate physical way, but the Inspector never cared that we knew the shape and feel of Europe. If we couldn't rattle off the towns in County Kildare for him, he would tut tut in disapproval. He was shocked when we couldn't tell him where Maynooth was.

The history lessons were taught by linking every townsland in the Parish with a particular period, and we were encouraged to know as much as we could about every area. The Parish of Slievrue and Ferrybank was particularly rich in evocative place names — Rathculliheen, Kilculliheen, Ballinamona, Killaspy, Kimurry, Attymore, Ballinacrea, Knockane and Newrath. All were pure Irish names with strong historical association with the Pagan and Christian eras, with events and people like John O'Donovan for instance, who translated the Annals of the Four Masters and was born in Attymore.

As well as giving us a strong identity with the area it also gave us deep pride that we were born in such a great little place. Frank Heylin, another of the teachers, did a map of the Parish which was illustrated with his own drawings, showing all the associations, historical and cultural. In years gone by the Parish had been part of the Deise, the old tribal Waterford area, a fact that our Irish language loving teachers would not allow us to forget.

Among other subjects taught with great care in Ferrybank School was the gentle art of hurling. Hurling was taught through Irish on the grounds that the language had to be associated with pleasure always. We were shown how to hold a hurley properly, left hand below right; taught how to block an opponent and warned to stand close to an opponent so as to avoid injury. The Teacher's face would glow with pleasure as he demonstrated how to take a seventy. Even then, in his 40s, he had a mighty puck.

Hurling was an important part of the school life in Ferrybank and a hurley was an essential part of the pupil's equipment. We cut down young ash trees, often in the dead of night, and made our own hurleys.

The trees were cut into slabs by workers in Graves' Timber Yard. Each lunch-time we played a match in Pender's field behind the school. Sometimes the farmer who owned it, who was a cattle dealer from Waterford, would arrive on the scene in the middle of a match and drive us unceremoniously off his land.

Sometimes there would be a shouting match between him and the teacher who took the view that we had a communal right to play on the field anyway. It has since been bought by the local hurling club. Sometimes the teachers would take part in these matches which were played with the ferocity of a championship tie. Many of the same young players went on to become famous Waterford/Kilkenny hurlers.

Timetables and the usual rules of curriculum were never a strong point in the school. This did not please the Inspector who seemed to take more than a passing interest in Ferrybank's educational matters. He had a habit of bursting in the door and going straight to the timetable to see that we were working to rule. It was rare when we were working to any kind of plan because our Teacher usually became so engrossed in a subject that he forgot time. To devote just half an hour to a subject was to him unthinkable. He gave many lectures full of his own philosophy, often straying into politics, religion and even industrial relations in the neighbouring city.

There were always harsh words between the teacher and the Inspector. One day the Inspector was approaching the school at his usual trotting pace and the Teacher locked the door, explaining to him afterwards that we were close to a lunatic asylum and that when he saw a man running towards the school he thought it safer to lock the school.

The Inspector pushed past him and fell down a hole inside the school door which had been there for some months. The school manager had not attended to this matter despite many warnings. The Inspector was caught in the hole, his arms flapping like wings, his face a red glow while we all watched in hysteria, a mixture of fear and elation. The Inspector behaved better after that.

In those days mathematics in the National Schools were not as simple as now. We, for example, did three books of Euclid before we left at 14 and we learned algebra as far as simultaneous equations. We were not a particularly bright bunch, and one of the problems was that working class children could not see these subjects as of practical value. And some of us in today's terms would be classed as slow learners.

The task of the head teacher was how to show us that what we were learning was practical, and at the same time keep it simple. He consulted the local carpenter, and the wood was cut out in sections we could feel in our hands. For instance, to illustrate an equation like $(x + 3)(x + 4) = x^2 + 7x + 12$ the carpenter cut it all out for us, and we made up the equation on the school table. When theorems were beyond us they were constantly drawn on the black board until eventually we understood. Then we got the same joy from it as we got from our sand maps. I never learned maths afterwards, but those lessons stuck.

Simple interest was taught not by talk of investing money in the banks. We were told to imagine we were going to the local pawnshop, an institution in Waterford well-known to us all. To boys who pawned their fathers' suits every Monday morning until the following Saturday, simple interest became an absorbing reality. So this was how the old kindhearted pawnbroker made his money, we thought.

One Mother, whose sons were discussing these teaching methods at home, came up to complain. She was sensitive about the fact that they were constant visitors to this same institution. She was met by the teacher at the school door who gave her a hug and told her to go away and have sense. She went down the village saying 'You couldn't have a row with that man.'

It was a just tribute to him. He was an extraordinary teacher. He was also my Father.

from *Three Villages* (1977)

ANONYMOUS

Curragh means 'plain' in Irish and occurs in many placenames, particularly rural ones. But there is only one Curragh, and that is the 5,000-acre spread of flat pasture immediately to the north of the town of Kildare. If there is one specific place where the country consummates its romance with the horse, it is here. The National Stud is in the neighbourhood, and there are studs galore all around. Breeding, racing and selling combine to form a highly evolved modern industry, which, of course, requires large stakes to be involved. And race day now is more often than not a top event in the social calendar, for which outfits of 'velvet so green' would hardly do at all. But the Curragh has long associations with horse racing — a place to go to try one's luck.

There is also an army training centre at the Curragh. During the Civil War, and also during the Emergency, as the World War II years were known in Ireland, the Curragh Camp, as it was called, was used to intern republicans. Among those held there during the Civil War were writers Francis Stuart and Frank O'Connor.

The Curragh of Kildare

The winter it is past, and the summer's come at last,
And the small birds they sing on every tree,
Their little hearts are glad,
But mine is very sad, since my true love is absent from me.
Their little hearts are glad,
But mine is very sad, since my true love is absent from me.

The rose upon the bier
By the water running clear
Gives joy to the linnet and the bee;
Their little hearts are blest, but mine is not at rest,
Since my true love is absent from me.
Their little hearts are blest, but mine is not at rest,
Since my true love is absent from me.

A livery I'll wear
And I'll comb down my hair
And in velvet so green I'll appear;
And straight I will repair to the Curragh of Kildare,
For it's there I'll get tidings of my dear,
And straight I will repair to the Curragh of Kildare,
For it's there I'll get tidings of my dear.

JOHN MILLINGTON SYNGE

It is somewhat surprising that Lough Tay and Lough Dan, Sally Gap and The Scalp, and the numerous other beauty spots of the Dublin and Wicklow mountains are so accessible. But still there are a number of those 'white empty roads' that Synge tramped — white, in his day, because unpaved. These were originally military roads. This locality is the country of the O'Byrnes and was just outside the British enclave of the Pale, which the O'Byrnes frequently raided. The temporary success of the 1798 Rebellion also made the capital vulnerable. The roads are straighter than the typical Irish country road, and are carefully contoured along the shoulders of the hills. Synge's ancestors settled in County Wicklow in the eighteenth century, at Glanmore Castle.

It is recalled in Ulysses that Molly Bloom sang at one of the annual fund-raising dinners held at St Kevin's Reformatory, Glencree, now the Glencree Reconciliation Centre.

In 1907, when this piece was written, Synge's local landladies were a Mrs Dunne and a Mrs McGuirk. Some of his plays are set around here.

Glencree

This morning the air is clear, and there is a trace of summer again. I am sitting in a nook beside the stream from the Upper Lake, close down among the heather and bracken and rushes. I have seen the people going up to Mass in the Reformatory, and the valley seems empty of life.

I have gone on, mile after mile, of the road to Sally Gap, between brown dykes and chasms in the turf, with broken foot-bridges across them, or between sheets of sickly moss and bog-cotton that is unable to thrive. The road is caked with moss that breaks like pie-crust under my feet, and in corners where there is shelter there are sheep loitering, or a few straggling grouse. . . . The fog has come down in places; I am meeting multitudes of hares that run round me at a little distance — looking enormous in the mists — or sit up on their ends against the sky line to watch me going by. When I sit down for a moment the sense of loneliness has no equal. I can hear nothing but the slow running of water and the grouse crowing and chuckling underneath the band of cloud. Then the fog lifts and shows the white empty roads winding everywhere, with the added sense of desolation one gets passing an empty house on the side of a road.

When I turn back again the air has got stuffy and heavy and calm, with a cloud still down upon the glen; there is a dead heat in the air that is not natural so high up, and the silence is so great three or four wrens that are singing near the lake seem to fill the valley with sound. In most places I can see the straight ending of the cloud, but above the lake grey fingers are coming up and down, like a hand that is clasping and opening again. One longs for rain or wind or thunder. The very ewes and lambs have stopped bleating, and are slinking round among the stacks of turf.

I have come out again on the mountain road the third day of the fog. At first it was misty only, and then a cloud crept up the water gullies from the valley of the Liffey, and in a moment I am cut off in a white silent cloud. The little turfy ridges on each side of the road have the look of glens to me, and every block of stone has the size of a house. The cobwebs on the furze are like a silvery net, and the silence is so great and queer, even weazels run squealing past me on the side of the road. . . . An east wind is rising. Once in every minute I see the little mounds in their natural shapes that have been mountains for a week. I see wet cottages on the other side of the glen that I had forgotten. Then, as I walk on, I see out over a cloud to the tops of real mountains standing up into the sky.

There is a dense white fog around the cottage, and we seem to be shut away from any habitation. All round behind the hills there is a moan and rumble of thunder coming nearer, at times with a fierce and sudden crash. The bracken has a nearly painful green in the strangeness of the light. Enormous sheep are passing in and out of the skyline.

There is a strange depression about the cottage to-night. The woman of the house is taken ill and has got into bed beside her mother-in-law, who is over ninety, and is wandering in her mind. The man of the house has gone away ten miles for medicine, and I am left with the two children, who are playing silently about the door.

The larches in the haggard are dripping heavily with damp, and the hens and geese, bewildered with the noise and gloom, are cackling with uneasy dread. All one's senses are disturbed. As I walk backwards and forwards, a few yards above and below the door, the little stream I do not see seems to roar out of the cloud.

Every leaf and twig is heavy with drops, and a dog that has passed with a sad-eyed herd looked wet and draggled and afraid.

I remember lying in the heather one clear Sunday morning in the early autumn when the bracken had just turned. All the people of the district were at Mass in a chapel a few miles away, so the valleys were empty, and there was nothing to be heard but the buzzing of a few late bees and the autumn song of thrushes. The sky was covered with white radiant clouds, with soft outlines, broken in a few places by lines of blue sky of wonderful delicacy and clearness. In a little while I heard a step on a path beneath me, and a tramp came wandering round the bottom of the hill. There was a spring below where I was lying, and when he reached it he looked round to see if anyone was watching him. I was hidden by the ferns, so he knelt down beside the water, where there was a pool among the stones, pulled his shirt over his head, and began washing it in the spring. After a little he seemed satisfied, and began wringing the water out of it; then he put it on, dripping as it was, buttoned his old coat over it, and wandered on towards the village, picking blackberries from the hedge.

from *In Wicklow and West Kerry* (1912)

JAMES PLUNKETT

The Grand Canal was begun in 1756. It has two branches. One heads south as far as Athy, Co. Kildare, where it joins the river Barrow; the other, longer branch, goes as far west as the Shannon. It took the builders until 1791 to reach Athy. The Shannon connection was completed in 1804. Unlike its companion to the north, the Royal, the Grand Canal is a popular recreational resource. It is still navigable, making it possible, for example, to sail from Dublin inland to the sea at Waterford.

The canal banks in the vicinity of Baggot Street Bridge — Wilton Terrace, Herbert Place, where Elizabeth Bowen was born — are islands of ease in a bustling city. Here the poet Patrick Kavanagh famously found peace by stopping and staring at the 'leafy-with-love banks and the green waters'. But the volume of road traffic nowadays makes peace and ease rather more difficult to come by.

In his early days in Dublin, Frank O'Connor was a librarian at the Pembroke branch of Dublin Public Libraries in Ballsbridge.

The Grand Canal

A t Leeson Street bridge, just up the road, we watched the barges on the Grand Canal which were still, in many cases, drawn by horses. The keeper opened the lock gates, the barge entered. Then the gates were closed and the waters rose until the barge was level with the bank again. The spume blew against our faces, the air smelled of decaying vegetation. The Grand Canal is another legacy of the eighteenth century, when it was built to provide easy transport to the midlands and the south-east. It connects Dublin with the rivers Shannon and Barrow, and carried passengers as well as cargo. The canal route opens up countryside which is sequestered and quiet, cut through by narrow roads of great charm, which are well worth the trouble of finding on the Ordnance map. The hotels which served the travellers are still to be seen, deserted now, in little canal villages which were once the focal point of bustle and excitement. The fare for travellers was cheap (twopence a mile as against threepence by road) and the accommodation, by eighteenth century standards of travel, commodious, but the pace only averaged two miles an hour. Robertstown in County Kildare, less than 20 miles from Dublin, is a canal village which still retains the atmosphere of the period. Each year, when they hold their Canal Fiesta, the river front is thronged with boats, and in the evening the hotel windows welcome travellers with a blaze of candlelight. Some time ago people who can put up with anything provided it isn't beautiful, came up with a scheme to drain the canal and lay a sewer along the bottom before filling it in for a roadway. It took a public campaign to save the Grand Canal. To-day it is being developed as a boating amenity.

The stretch of water from Leeson Street to Baggot Street Bridge has the quality of canal peace about it, a greenness, an ineffable pensiveness. Old trees line either side. Dogs nose along the grassy banks or bob out suddenly with sticks between their teeth; children on the narrow planks of the lock gates offer their bright young lives hourly to the raging whirlpools below; old men, by repetition reassured, I suppose, smoke their pipes and look on placidly; goats used to graze here too — whoever owned them. And yet it was always quiet and timeless, as though the children and the dogs, the old men and the goats and the crashing waters existed only on canvas. I associate it with Frank O'Connor the writer, who, I think, fell in love with it too. He was born in Cork but came to Dublin as a young man and he had memories of it from the time he lived on Pembroke Road, existing on a diet of coffee and buns which he got in Bewley's restaurant, because he was as yet too shy to venture into places more formal and sophisticated. When he died he was living in a flat at the Baggot Street end, where his study window provided him with a frame which allowed him, as it were, to hang the canal masterpiece on the wall. I had travelled monastic Ireland with him the previous summer and that was where I last spoke with him. I left him seated at his desk, the view in front of him, a script before him, his thoughts already bending inwards, the sunlight falling on the abstracted face with its high forehead and silver hair. He had the air of someone who had found where he belonged, not an easy thing for a writer to achieve in the Ireland of his time.

from *The Gems She Wore* (1972)

AIDAN HIGGINS

Aidan Higgins grew up with his father, Dado, and mother, Mumu, and his three brothers in Springfield House, near Celbridge, Co. Kildare, a house dating from the middle of the eighteenth century. Another noted building in a part of the country known for its fine houses — Castletown House, Carton — is Celbridge Abbey; its main claim to fame is that it was the home of Dean Swift's 'Vanessa', Esther Vanhomrigh (1690–1723).

It is thought that the story of Judge Lynch is the origin of the term 'lynching'. That supposedly apocryphal story goes as follows. James Fitzstephen Lynch was Mayor of Galway at the end of the fifteenth century; as chief magistrate, he had found his son guilty of murdering a Spanish seaman. Since nobody was prepared to act as hangman, the father executed his son himself. Lynch's Castle, the best preserved medieval house in Ireland, remains intact on Shop Street, Galway's main thoroughfare.

Boyhood

I n freezing weather the Keegan boys came out at dusk with jugs and basins of cold water which they threw down on the already icy road between the two lodges, to let it freeze solid overnight, and next morning they had a slide a good hundred yards long and were already using it in their hobnail boots reinforced with brads at the toes.

In those days few cars went by, cyclists kept to the footpath and the turf carts remained at home as Neddy took a long run, jumped onto the slide and went sailing down, calling out, 'Wheeeeee!'

He had a splendid repertoire of styles invented on the spot, which Patsy attempted to elaborate on: arms outstretched as if crucified, arms akimbo, hands in pockets or turning to face the way he came, gliding down backwards, twirling or hands clasped behind the back as if figure-skating, crouched down on his hunkers and then slowly rising up again, and then down again — this was 'The Postman's Knock'.

My young brother and I took many tosses, cutting hands and knees but it was great gas all the same. The Keegans spent as much time as they could between chores. Neddy had to saw wood, pile some of it and bring some of it in, Patsy had to cycle to Celbridge on messages for his ma (half a stone of flour, a Boland's loaf, a dozen rashers), and John Joe, bleeding like a stuck pig, had homework.

Otherwise we crept through the plantation, did our business, and had fine times in a yew tree with John Joe who never blew his nose, never had a handkerchief, but always had crusty nostrils or runny snot which he licked up, or rather in, blowing his nose between thumb and first finger like his da, old Ned.

Neddy was a fearless tree-climber and thought nothing of ascending any of the tall pines until he was out of sight and we had to run into the meadow to see him; we saw only his cap come twirling down and heard the harmonica play 'Mairzy Doates' with all the glottal stops out. And there he was eighty feet up, a fore-topman in the shrouds, swaying and hallooing.

The big wooden door of the Abbey stableyard had a lich-gate let into it, but both were closed and rarely opened and the outer frame of the big door closely aligned to the wall, flush with it, so that the inquisitive (i.e., myself) could not see in. Such a fortress-like granite bulk with its sham-Gothic windows permanently sealed up just below the battlemented skyline that looked so hostile and forbidding in the setting sun was suggestive of Rafael Sabatini or Baroness Orczy castle-keep-and-moat costume-drama and Ronald Colman and Douglas Fairbanks in acrobatic swordfights along the lines of *The Prisoner of Zenda*, which we had seen at the Metropole, or *Captain Blood* with Errol Flynn and Basil Rathbone, who was wickedness personified, at swordplay on the sands.

Swordplay would take place on these battlements and punitive acts be carried out secretly within the keep and hanged men with tongues lolling out be suspended from windows as dire warnings, like the dead rats I had seen strung up on palings by a farmer, and shrivelled away to skin and bone.

Dado had told me some such story involving a Judge Lynch of Galway town and how he had come to sentence his own son to death and stayed up with him all night preparing his (the son's) immortal soul for the hereafter following breakfast and the noose next morning; how the father hung the son 'with his own hands' from one of the windows overlooking the meandering main street that changed its name three times before it finished, ran out of names; topping him at daybreak. But there again I may have got the details all wrong and all that stayed with me was a dead man suspended from an arched window, swinging in the breeze, gaped at by passers-by.

The small barred Judas set high up in the narrow arched front door of the Abbey suggested a deterrent against importunate charity-seekers. I had seen one such desperate and very determined shawled beggarwoman with babe hidden in smelly folds of the shawl, persistently begging charity as her right; revealing just the crown of the babe's head, she asked charity only for the child. And then waiting by the closed door until it opened again, just wide enough for the nun's hands to reach out with the stale bread and the high meat and the closed door receive the most profuse and insistent thanks of Godblessandkeepyou and invocations to the Holy Mother and all the saints.

And sure enough, by 1952, some years after we had quit Springfield for pastures new, the Abbey and grounds had again reverted to Church hands and the charitable-minded Hospitaller Brothers of St John of God were using it as a community house for the overflow of mentally retarded and physically handicapped inmates from Oakley Park, renamed again and now St Raphael's; later again I scaled the battlements and dropped down to walk by a recently scuffled path, going on the edge, leaving no footprints. Shovels and rakes were as they had been thrown down at the summons of the bell or the whistle for teabreak and the Brother and his mentally defective charges had hurried off for scoff, and were out of sight in the stableyard with a half-wit scullion pouring out generous dollops of strong tea from an outsize taypot before handing around thick wedges of bread and butter.

from *Donkey's Years* (1995)

OLIVER GOLDSMITH

There is an Auburn in Alabama and an Auburn in upper New York State and an Auburn Hills in Michigan. But there is no 'Sweet Auburn, loveliest of the plain'. This is the deserted village of Goldsmith's poem, a place now cleared by a modernising landlord which the poet's imagination reconstructs. Goldsmith draws on memories of growing up in Lissoy, Co. Westmeath, where his father — fondly remembered in this poem — was a Church of Ireland clergyman.

Published in 1770, the poem was written to pay off Goldsmith's debts, though it still took two years to complete. As one of the poet's contemporaries put it, The Deserted Village *'was received with universal admiration, as one of the most fascinating and beautiful effusions of British genius'.*

Sweet was the sound . . .

Sweet was the sound, when oft at evening's close
Up yonder hill the village murmur rose,
There, as I passed with careless steps and slow,
The mingling notes came softened from below;
The swain responsive as the milk-maid sung,
The sober herd that lowed to meet their young,

The noisy geese that gabbled o'er the pool,
The playful children just let loose from school,
The watch-dog's voice that bayed the whispering wind,
And the loud laugh that spoke the vacant mind —
These all in sweet confusion sought the shade,
And filled each pause the nightingale had made.
But now the sounds of population fail,
No cheerful murmurs fluctuate in the gale,
No busy steps the grass-grown foot-way tread,
For all the bloomy flush of life is fled.
All but yon widowed, solitary thing,
That feebly bends beside the plashy spring:
She, wretched matron, forced in age, for bread,
To strip the brook with mantling cresses spread,
To pick her wintry faggot from the thorn,
To seek her nightly shed, and weep till morn;
She only left of all the harmless train,
The sad historian of the pensive plain.

Near yonder copse, where once the garden smiled,
And still where many a garden-flower grows wild;
There, where a few torn shrubs the place disclose,
The village preacher's modest mansion rose.
A man he was to all the country dear,
And passing rich with forty pounds a year;
Remote from towns he ran his godly race,
Nor e'er had changed, nor wished to change, his place;
Unpractised he to fawn, or seek for power,
By doctrines fashioned to the varying hour;
Far other aims his heart had learned to prize,
More skilled to raise the wretched than to rise.
His house was known to all the vagrant train;
He chid their wanderings, but relieved their pain:
The long-remember'd beggar was his guest,
Whose beard descending swept his aged breast;
The ruined spendthrift, now no longer proud,
Claimed kindred there, and had his claims allowed;
The broken soldier, kindly bade to stay,
Sat by his fire, and talked the night away,
Wept o'er his wounds or tales of sorrow done,
Shouldered his crutch, and showed how fields were won.
Pleased with his guests, the good men learned to glow,

And quite forgot their vices in their woe;
Careless their merits or their faults to scan,
His pity gave ere charity began.

from *The Deserted Village* (1770)

FRANK O'CONNOR

During the 1940s, Frank O'Connor cycled many miles over narrow roads and 'between the western wind and the small rain', making inventories of the countryside for his two travel books. Strangely depopulated journeys some of these can seem.

Dean Swift was rector at Laracor. Stella, one of the central figures in his private life (Vanessa is the other), was Esther Johnson (1681–1728). Swift's Journal to Stella is a series of letters written to her from London. He also addressed a number of poems to her.

Richard Cassells (c. 1690–1751), a German architect, came to Ireland in the late 1720s. His best-known houses are Leinster House, seat of the Irish parliament, and Carton, Co. Kildare.

Nowadays, of course, cycling out of Dublin to the west or north-west could be hard going, because these areas have been developed almost beyond recognition.

In County Meath

After Carlow and Kilkenny my favourite counties are, I think, Meath and Louth, adjoining Dublin on the north, and when I say adjoining I mean adjoining, because if you set out to cycle through Phoenix Park you find yourself at the farther gate in County Meath and in the very heart of the Irish countryside. For some reason Dublin has never had any western or north-western development.

Meath is the high kings' county, actually a province in itself, and full, not only of history, but of prehistory. If you share my mania for Swift, you may well aim at Laracor, in which case you are likely to find yourself beside the very interesting ruins of Summerhill, a mansion of Cassell burned during 'the Troubles'. It is, for Cassell, a most ornate house, and for once he throws aside his usual tight Teutonic style and lets himself go.

Laracor is a disappointment. It contains no memories at all of the great dean, of Stella and Dingley, of Joe Beaumont and the other characters who grow upon you from the pages of the Journal to Stella. 'The willows by the river's side my heart is set upon', but you are not likely to find them. Trim is also very vivid in the Journal, but there isn't much left there either, except bits of the Castle and Priory and the shattered sides of the Yellow Tower, which you see for miles around. The best way to see it is as I saw it once in the dusk cycling home from Kells, when Castle and Tower seemed complete and one could imagine what it appeared like to some tired fifteenth-century traveller from the North.

Beyond it is Kells, where the famous Irish manuscript of the Gospels, now at Trinity College, was written, but little remains of its famous monastery except the remarkable collection of pictorial crosses for which Kells seems to have been a centre. One, which tradition says was used as a gallows by the English, fills the mouth of the painted, decorous Georgian street, with which it forms a striking and mysterious contrast. A number of others, complete, broken and even unfinished, are to be found in the churchyard, and all are well worth study, particularly the beautiful broken shaft near the round tower.

The Boyne road from Trim to Navan is enchanting. All this area to the sea is to Ireland what the country north of Salisbury to Swindon is to England. It has the same sense of having been populated from the remotest times and of having gathered together whatever was most striking in all.

from *Irish Miles* (1947)

SIR JONAH BARRINGTON

If, during his tour of Ireland, Arthur Young found the social life of the country largely consisting of 'hunting by day, getting drunk in the evenings, and fighting the next morning', the chief memorialist of these activities is Sir Jonah Barrington. In the three volumes of his Personal Sketches of His Own Times *are to be found prototypes of the Rakes of Mallow, the Monks of the Screw, the Hellfire Club and similar manifestations of roistering male energy. This is the raffish and irresponsible bad old eighteenth century when many a duellist was made a riddle, or sieve, of. For this, the satire of* Castle Rackrent *was meant to be an epitaph.*

Queen's County is now County Laois, and Maryborough is Portlaoise.

Duelling Extraordinary

Our elections were more prolific in duels than any other public meetings: they very seldom originated at a horse-race, cock-fight, hunt, or at any place of amusement: folks then had pleasure in view, and 'something else to do' than to quarrel: but at all elections, or at assizes, or, in fact, at any place of business, almost every man, without any very particular or assignable reason, immediately became a violent partisan, and frequently a furious enemy to somebody else; and gentlemen often got themselves shot before they could tell what they were fighting about.

At an election for Queen's County between General Walsh and Mr Warburton, of Garryhinch, about the year 1783, took place the most curious duel of any which have occurred within my recollection. A Mr Frank Skelton, one of the half-mounted gentlemen described [earlier], — a boisterous, joking, fat young fellow, — was prevailed on, much against his grain, to challenge the exciseman of the town for running the butt-end of a horse-whip down his throat the night before, whilst he lay drunk and sleeping with his mouth open. The exciseman insisted that snoring at a dinner-table was a personal offence to every gentleman in company, and would therefore make no apology.

Frank, though he had been nearly choaked, was very reluctant to fight; he said 'he was sure to die if he did, as the exciseman could snuff a candle with his pistol-ball; and as he himself was as big as a hundred dozen of candles, what chance could he have?' We told him jocosely to give the exciseman no time to take aim at him by which means, he might perhaps hit his adversary first, and thus survive the contest. He seemed somewhat encouraged and consoled by the hint, and most strictly did he adhere to it.

Hundreds of the towns-people went to see the fight on the green of Maryborough. The ground was regularly measured; and the friends of each party pitched a ragged tent on the green, where whiskey and salt beef were consumed in abundance. Skelton having taken his ground, and at the same time two heavy drams from a bottle his foster-brother had brought, appeared quite stout till he saw the balls entering the mouths of the exciseman's pistols, which shone as bright as silver, and were nearly as long as fusils. This vision made a palpable alteration in Skelton's sentiments: he changed colour, and looked about him as if he wanted some assistance. However, their seconds, who were of the same rank and description, handed to each party his case of pistols, and half-bellowed to them — 'blaze away, boys!'

Skelton now recollected his instructions, and *lost no time*: he cocked *both* his pistols at once; and as the exciseman was deliberately and most scientifically coming to his 'dead level', as he called it, Skelton let fly.

'Holloa!' said the exciseman, dropping his level, 'I'm battered, by Jasus!'

'The devil's cure to you!' said Skelton, instantly firing his second pistol.

One of the exciseman's legs then gave way, and down he came on his knee, exclaiming 'Holloa! holloa! you blood-thirsty villain! do you want to take my life?'

'Why, to be sure I do!' said Skelton. 'Ha! ha! have I *stiffened* you my lad?' Wisely judging, however, that if he staid till the exciseman recovered his legs, he might have a couple of shots to stand, he wheeled about, took to his heels, and got away as fast as possible. The crowd shouted; but Skelton, like a hare when started, ran the faster for the shouting.

Jemmy Moffit, his own second, followed, overtook, tripped up his heels, and cursing him for a disgraceful rascal, asked 'why he ran away from the exciseman?'

'Ough thunther!' said Skelton, with his chastest brogue, 'how many holes did the villain want to have drilled into his carcase? Would you have me stop to make a *riddle* of him, Jemmy?'

The second insisted that Skelton should return to the field, to be shot at. He resisted, affirming that he had done *all* that *honour* required. The second called him '*a coward!*'

'By my sowl,' returned he, 'my dear Jemmy Moffit, may be so! you may call me a coward, if you please; but I did it all for *the best.*'

'The *best!* you blackguard?'

'Yes,' said Frank: 'sure it's *better* to be a *coward* than a *corpse!* and I must have been either *one* or *t'other* of them.'

However, he was dragged up to the ground by his second, after agreeing to fight again, if he had another pistol given him. But, luckily for Frank, the last bullet had struck so fast between the bones of the exciseman's leg that he could not stand. The friends of the latter then proposed to strap him to a tree, that he might be able to shoot Skelton; but this being positively objected to by Frank, the exciseman was carried home: his first wound was on the side of his thigh, and the second in his right leg; but neither proved at all dangerous.

from Hugh B. Stapes (ed.), *The Ireland of Sir Jonah Barrington* (1968)

THOMAS MOORE

The Hill of Tara rises less than six hundred feet above the plain of Meath, but its lack of physical grandeur is more than made up for by the richness of its associations with Celtic and pre-Norman Ireland. Everyone who was anyone in those days has a Tara connection. Among other claims to fame, Tara was the seat of the high kings of Ireland and the capital of the now vanished fifth province of Meath.

Moore's invocation of a regal Irish past follows almost directly the passage of the Act of Union. Irish Melodies was first published in 1807. Paradoxically, the end of Irish legislative independence coincided with the rise of Ireland as an independent cultural entity. Matters Irish became the vogue. By the time the last batch appeared in 1834, the Melodies had earned Moore well over £10,000.

In another poem, 'The Origin of the Harp', Moore writes: ''Tis believed that this Harp, which I now wake for thee,/Was a siren of old who sung under the sea.'

The harp that once through Tara's halls

The harp that once through Tara's halls
    The soul of music shed,
Now hangs as mute on Tara's walls,
    As if that soul were fled. —
So sleeps the pride of former days,
    So glory's thrill is o'er,
And hearts, that once beat high for praise,
    Now feel that pulse no more.

No more to chiefs and ladies bright
    The harp of Tara swells;
The chord alone, that breaks at night,
    Its tale of ruin tells.
Thus Freedom now so seldom wakes,
    The only throb she gives,
Is when some heart indignant breaks,
    To show that still she lives.

from *Irish Melodies* (1807)

DERMOT HEALY

The year is 1968. The day before his family visits this arm of land in north-west Mayo — arguably the remotest part of Ireland — Sergeant Jonathan Adams had been policing a Derry civil rights march. He was brought in from Fermanagh 'not only because of a shortfall in numbers but also because outsiders would not be recognised'.

The novel goes on to show what happens when the Adamses move to the Mullet and one of Jonathan's daughters takes up with a local playwright — and playboy — Jack Ferris. Problems of adjustment, compatibility, integration and reconciliation abound. As in Synge's The Playboy of the Western World, *having one's nature revealed and accepting it for what it is also looms large. In point of pedantic fact, however, Christy Mahon, the Playboy, comes not from here, but from a more settled and fertile part of the country. The Mullet is Christy's place of revelation.*

Another Country

They drove at break of day into the west through Ballyshannon. With a sense of pride Jonathan Adams flashed his identity card as they entered the Republic. The guard, with a knowing nod, leaned in and said: 'That was a bad doing, yesterday.' 'What did he mean?' asked Maisie as they drove through the uplifted barrier. 'I don't know. Every last man of them is a Republican,' said the Sergeant, 'but they don't frighten me.' Then the family was undecided as to what to do. Because the girls wanted to see Yeats' grave they turned south and drove along the coast to Sligo. From Sligo, they drove out west to Achill Island. They stopped there for the night in the Valley House Hotel.

'What's thon island I can see from here?' Sergeant Adams asked.

'What's that you're saying?' asked the man.

'What is that island over there?'

'That's Mullet peninsula,' the manager told him. 'It's where the Playboy of the Western World came from.'

The intention was to spend the next night somewhere in Galway, but Jonathan Adams was drawn to explore the isolated peninsula to the north, and so at noon the following day they entered Belmullet town after a long drive through the unpopulated bogland of Erris. The Nephin Beg range of mountains, which had been shrouded the day before in mist, now rose clear and pure.

An old Fair Day was in progress in the town. Cattle and sheep and chickens were being bartered. Gypsies sold socks, gates and radios. A man swallowed lit cigarettes and brought them back up again still burning. Dogs fought. Goats butted the sideboards of carts. Men sat on steps eating sandwiches. Cows shat on pavements. Men sat on tractors licking ice-cream cones. It was like watching some medieval pageant. They drove from Erris Head in Broad Haven Bay down to Blacksod in the south, amazed at the isolation, the white sandy roads that ran by the sea; the Inishkea Islands, holy, absolute; the wind-glazed violent cliffs; the meteorological station; the endless bogs, the rips and cracks through the huge dunes; the black curraghs; the lighthouse that sat perched on Eagle Island like a castle in a fairy story; the piers, the harbour, the sea.

'What's the island beyant?' asked Jonathan Adams of a man who was oiling his Honda 50. He straightened up with a grimace.

'They are a great bike,' said the man, 'if you look after them.' He wiped his hands on his trousers, looked at the Honda and then looked at the island. 'That'd be Inishglora,' he said, and felt his wet nose with his thumb and forefinger. 'The Isle of Purity.'

'Oh.'

'That's right. Yes indeed.' He grimaced again. 'It's where Brendan landed.'

He saw that this remark did not signify anything to the Adams family.

'Brendan the navigator,' he explained, 'the lad who discovered America —

like the rest of us. Except that he was the first. Though of course that may not be true.' The family and himself stood looking out, with the Honda up on its stand, and the car engine running. 'And it's where the Children of Lir are buried, God bless them.' He felt his nose again. 'And there you have it.'

'Thanking you,' said the Sergeant, humbly.

'And what part of the world do ye hail from?'

'Fermanagh,' said Jonathan.

'Oh, but they're giving you a hard time,' said the man, and he shook his head sadly. 'The sooner you drive them to feck out of there the better.'

Sheepishly, they got into the car, the man slapped the roof and they drove on. And the man stood there, his hands on the grips of the Honda, looking out on Inishglora as if he were seeing it for the first time.

They booked into a bed-and-breakfast a few mile out the road in Corrloch. From her window there Maisie Adams saw that a large cut-stone house opposite was for sale. She was intrigued to hear from their landlady that the price of the property was only £1,200. Next morning, despite her husband's entreaties, Maisie arranged a viewing of the house with the auctioneer.

'The lighthouse men lived here,' he explained, 'They're known locally as The Dwellings.'

'Such huge rooms,' said Maisie.

'This one is mine,' said Sara.

But Jonathan Adams, treating the whole affair as foolishness, kept up only a desultory conversation with the auctioneer. And as the man pointed out what came with the property the Sergeant merely nodded, not wanting to enter into any false dealings. Yes, it was a fine house, he agreed, indeed it had a wonderful view. This being as far as manners and prudence would allow.

Afterwards, Jonathan Adams went down to the hotel in Belmullet for a coffee. They served him in the bar where he sat uncomfortably among the drinkers. First the Angelus rang out, then came the news from RTE on the black-and-white TV. The Sergeant took no notice till he heard sounds and names that gradually grew familiar. He looked up with terror and saw they were re-running an account of the march. This came as a shock to Jonathan Adams. He had seen no TV men there, nor was he used to them. It showed the Catholics gathering in Duke Street. Then the chaotic start of the march. The shouts for the police to give way were raised. With great religious zeal the Catholics called to the policemen. Within seconds a protester was being batoned. What happened next was seen by Jonathan Adams with blinding clarity. To the left of the picture could be seen a grey-haired policeman, hatless, chasing after a youth. When he lost him among the other marchers, he turned and batoned a middle-aged man who was already pouring blood.

The crowd in the bar shouted 'bastards'.

On the TV the old policeman had found his hat. As he put it on, he looked round for someone else to hit. Seeing no one he turned back and hit the screaming man again. A woman crouched low as she pulled her man away. The old policeman charged past the camera. Then, wild-eyed and wielding a baton, he stared remorselessly straight at the lens. Jonathan Adams had become a witness to himself. He saw the mad look of fury in his own eye. He looked round the bar but no one was taking any notice of him. His chin began shaking. Then he shook uncontrollably.

'Bastards,' said someone.

Jonathan Adams slipped away.

Next morning at six they left Mayo without breakfast. They were on the road in the dark. He brooked no complaints. And this time he kept his head down as they crossed the border lest anyone might recognise him. Everywhere this RTE film of the confrontation was being viewed. He was terrified. He could not wait to get back to the safety of his own home. He drove furiously, in his mind's eye watching himself right his hat and turn back to strike the man who was down and screaming.

from *A Goat's Song* (1990)

―――――

DAVID THOMSON

'I was eighteen when I first saw Woodbrook' is the opening sentence of David Thomson's Big House memoir. He is an Oxford undergraduate, reading history, and has come to the Kirkwood home to tutor the major's two daughters, Phoebe and Tony — Antoinette. It is 1932. Without realising it, he is just in time to see the twilight hours of the Anglo-Irish gentry dwindle towards darkness.

His connection with the house lasted ten years in all, a time made all the more memorable because the author fell for Phoebe. Then, in 1945, Phoebe died. After the war Woodbrook was bought by the Maxwell brothers. The house is three miles from Carrick-on-Shannon on the Boyle road.

Twilight of the Big House

Beside the girls stood Willie Maxwell, the oldest of the servants of the farm, a grave and solid man about thirty years of age, with a square impassive face, reserved and dignified, who looked calmly at us in turn and smiled only when he was spoken to. His smile, when it came, crinkled up his face, transformed him in a second and vanished. I came to know later that his smile showed more of himself than the self-protective look which covered him on that peculiar occasion. He belonged to the old Ireland of his father and grandfathers, and was nearer to them than to his younger brothers. He did not show his mobility of mind until you got to know him well. He was not a bit like his young brother Johnny who was by him. Johnny was light and small with a thin boyish face and eyes that never stayed still. He was the herd and could run after cattle and leap walls like a boy. Almost everything he saw and heard amused him and he could respond to solemn talk or a carelessly trite remark with intelligent wit or a glance that was disconcerting. His style of dress was unusual too and unsuited to the rough, hard-weather work of a herd. He always wore a formal blue suit, too faded and tattered for Mass, and sometimes he put on a tie.

Jimmy Maxwell, a good bit taller than Johnny and some years older — there was a sister, in between them, at home — came forward to help with the suitcases. I thought old James Currid reproved him for this in an undertone, but am not sure. Jimmy always helped other people unobtrusively and if he resented the old horseman's possessive grip on the family he did not show it as his brothers did.

All these people greeted us separately, as we struggled out of the car, with the words, 'Welcome home'. They addressed Mrs Kirkwood as 'Mistress' and when they spoke about her they always said 'The Mistress'. She had been living in London for the past six months and they were pleased to see her. They greeted me warmly too and called me 'Master David' from the start. They said 'Welcome home, Master David', as though I were one of the family and Woodbrook my home, which later it became. I felt happy and flattered like a dog that is patted by an agreeable stranger. I could not think how they even knew my name, but of course Major Kirkwood had met me often during his visits to London and must have told them about me.

The men straggled off and we went into the house led by Winnie and followed by the girls who stepped shyly through the carpeted hall and ran giggling with echoey footfalls into the darkness of a stone-flagged corridor which led, curved and windowless, towards the kitchen. Winnie, who was speaking rapidly to Mrs Kirkwood, broke off with a deprecating glance, apologising for them, and then began to say even more quickly, pointing out this and that, that this had got broken in the spring cleaning by Peter and that had been moved over there. The children put down their puppies, one of which immediately made a puddle on the carpet, and went to explore their old familiar house.

The hall was a large square room with white walls and dark furniture, black leather armchairs which had once been green, some upright chairs with seats the same, a round mahogany table and a smaller, oblong one on which stood a china vase of marigolds and daisies. It seemed dark and unlived in on that first day. Indeed the whole house except the servants' quarters and Major Kirkwood's bedroom had been unlived in for six months; when his family was in London he spent most of his time in the kitchen or out of doors. But a faded Indian carpet, Persian rugs torn in places and the brass rail of a fender by the empty fireplace were light.

The front door opened into the hall, not in the middle but at its right-hand side, so that the first thing I saw amid the confusion of people was the little vase of flowers which stood on the table before us. To the right of the front door before you came to this table was a room which they called the office where Major Kirkwood used to store a vast heap of bills and letters that were dealt with, if his creditors were lucky, on one or two winter evenings every year. The room was also a repository for shoes, boots, fishing rods and a seldom used gun, tennis rackets, most of them with broken strings, golf clubs and old coats, croquet hoops and mallets, riding-crops and walking-sticks and several kinds of balls. I remember with nostalgia the faded colours of the croquet balls, blue, yellow, green and black, and the feel of them, although I cannot remember any of us ever playing croquet.

Across the hall, opposite the office, a door opened into the drawing-room. It was spacious and beautiful, with three large sash windows, two looking out from the front of the house across the lawn and the sunken meadow called 'The Bottoms', and across the 'Canal' which was really a brook, to the road and Hughestown Hill, the other looking out on a huge copper beech, whose leaves with the sun shining through them were luminous that day like dragon-flies' wings or bits of stained-glass window. From here, at the side of the house, you could see part of the drive up which we had come curving away beneath a high bushy bank until it went out of sight and gave place to a piece of the long, low meadow, which stretched from the bottom of Hughestown Hill as far as the gate lodge to the west. By the time I looked out through this window the ground mist had gone and I saw deep grass in flower almost ready to be mown.

The old part of the house had two storeys, but the drawing-room and dining-room had no bedrooms above them; they had been built later of the same grey blocks of stone, forming low wings of beautiful proportion with flat roofs. One of the windows of the dining-room opened on to a rough sloping garden with more shrubs in it than flowers, beyond which lay a tennis court and paddock, and beyond those the lake with the Leitrim mountains blue in the distance to the east. On the way from the station I had seen neither mountains nor lake and this view from the window as we went in to dinner was a shock of delight; but a moment later, hovering round the long dining table which was laid for five, I was beset by anxiety.

from *Woodbrook* (1974)

DESMOND FENNELL

In August 1798, a French expeditionary force under General Humbert landed at Killala, Co. Mayo. With the aid of local support, it made headway towards Dublin, but was brutally stopped at Ballinamuck, Co. Longford, not very far from Edgeworthstown. These events are featured in Thomas Flanagan's historical novel, The Year of the French *(1979), and are also recorded in Bishop Stock's* Narrative of what Passed at Killala in the County of Mayo and the Parts Adjacent in the Summer of 1798. *There is also, now, a Humbert Summer School.*

'To Hell or to Connaught' is traditionally believed to have been the choice offered dispossessed Catholics by Oliver Cromwell. And Connaught has been known as the poorest Irish province. Even now, plants like the Asahi one in Killala are the exception rather than the rule. Asahi makes synthetic fibres. The Killala factory opened in 1977. Desmond Fennell writes: 'the practical reason for choosing this particular site was the availability of water to draw from, and of other water for the discharge of effluent'. The factory closed in July 1997.

Killala

Cycling on in the direction of Killala, I thought I might look at another antiquity marked on my Ireland West map, and I asked a man coming out of a lane where it was. 'I've no idea,' he said, 'never heard of it. I just know there's old things around here but I know nothing about them.' Killala appeared ahead, clustered around its fine round tower that had a church beside it. Having heard so much in recent years of the big Asahi factory at Killala, I expected to find the town transformed and booming. But it looked stunted and unhappy with itself, a mixture of dilapidation and tawdry newness. One of the first sights that met my eyes was two electricity poles, complete with fittings, lying in nettles near a gaunt, ruined store with rows of gaping windows. The poles with fittings amazed me until I remembered hearing that the town had had all its poles and wires removed from the streets for the filming of *The Year of the French* some years back. It is the only town in Ireland with all its wiring concealed. Not far away I came on a freshly-painted pub called The Village Inn, with a bright-red cartwheel standing on one side of the door and a palm-tree on the other. Inside, a bellows and a horse-shoe, which looked as if they had never been used, hung on a panel on the wall, and a saddle and some harnessing were displayed. I supposed all of this was meant to give a 'country atmosphere'. But the coffee was only 25p and the Corkwoman behind the counter was most obliging with information. Attached to the Inn was a premises called The Fiddler's Green. It advertised a Monster Disco for Saturday night 'with Top DJs'. On the footpath beside the Inn were two rusted petrol pumps that had long ceased functioning. The houses and shops of the town maintained the 'country colours' I had noticed in Ballycastle.

I walked around to have a look at the round tower. The small church beside it turned out to be the old Church of Ireland cathedral. Two German tourists were trying to get into the round tower which was about twenty yards away behind a locked gate. 'To gain admittance to Round Tower, contact caretaker next door', said a notice. The next door was the red sliding door of a workshop; it had 'Ireland Needs Fascism' chalked on it. In response to my knock an old man emerged and explained that you could only walk around the tower. 'You can't get in. There used to be wooden floors and stairs but they've fallen.' The Germans still wanted through the gate. 'Well,' he said, 'the second thing is you have to pay 20p.' 'Why?' I asked. 'Isn't it a national monument?' He began to tell a long story about how the key used to be in the Garda station because they couldn't get anyone to look after it, and then he had taken it. 'What need is there of a key?' I asked. He said there was a right of way to the tower which he claimed.

Leaving the Germans to do as they pleased, I walked across the street to an old Georgian house with a view of the harbour, which I took to be the house where Bishop Stock had been made a house prisoner by the French in 1798, and where he had kept a diary of those events. I could see eight fishing boats at the pier, and nearer, just below the house's well-kept garden, eight attractive holiday cottages. I climbed the steps to the open door, and a woman who appeared in the hall told me the house no longer belonged to the Church, and was not the house where Bishop Stock had lived, but the old deanery. Killala had long since ceased to be a Church of Ireland diocese, it had been incorporated into Tuam; and since the last dean died five years ago, it was no longer a deanery either, but was looked after by Dean Graham in Crossmolina. But the house had a connection with '98: it was being built when the French ships arrived, and workmen on the roof who saw them thought they were English.

Before leaving Killala I called into P.J. Carey's second Sizzler's in the hope of tasting some of those chips made from his own potatoes which he was so proud of. But the girl said only the Bangor Erris shop had them; they used frozen ones. I had some cod which I'd say had been frozen too. But with its small restaurant next door it was a stylish premises. On the way out of the town I was amazed, as so often in the West, by the sheer size of some of the new houses I passed.

from *A Connacht Journey* (1987)

TIM ROBINSON

Thirty miles off the coast of Galway are the three Aran islands — Inishmore, the big island; Inishmaan, the middle island; and Inisheer, the eastern island. Together they occupy a special place in Irish minds. For one thing, they contain amounts of evidence of pre-Christian settlement that are surprisingly large for so remote a place. Also, they are a place where a traditional way of life has persisted, despite an inhospitable landscape and exposure to what Tim Robinson has called 'the manic depressive regime of the Atlantic'. To some, this persistence has been interpreted as a metaphor for Irishness. Most, however, find such aspects of local colour as the clothing, the skill of the fishermen in the lath-and-canvas boats called currachs, and the Irish language, still very much alive here, to be sufficiently interesting in their own right.

The islands have had great appeal for writers and scholars, notably J.M. Synge, whose The Aran Islands *(1907) records his numerous visits to the islands. His celebrated play on island life,* Riders to the Sea *(1904), is set on Inishmaan. Robert Flaherty's evocative documentary,* Man of Aran, *was filmed in 1934 on Inishmore, which is also the landscape of this extract.*

Leviathan

The north-western coast of Árainn, from the wind-shadow of the Brannock Islands to the point where it turns east and faces Connemara, is open to the Atlantic, and rises in cliffs to stand against the gales and look out onto the ocean beyond Slyne Head. A fault parallel to the one at An Grióir breaks this mile of cliffs into two ranges, the western one lower than the eastern. One can walk around the coast from Port an Choma under the lower cliffs on a wide terrace of green-fringed rock-pools. If the weather is blowy one may have to time a dash between a rock-pool and the foam leaping up over the edge of the terrace at one point, but unless the tide is very high one can usually pick one's way around a jutting angle of the cliff called An Coirnéal, the corner, to the loveliest seclusion of this rarely visited facet of the island. There is an odd rakishness, a mettlesome spirit, running through the cubism of the rocks of this natural esplanade, which must be the combined effect of its undulant surface, the general twist the nearby fault has given to the vicinity, and the carefree poise of a square-faced block — I am sure it must measure forty feet each way — that has detached itself from the cliff against which it leans one elbow, and stands on two fat little legs looking as if it were about to skip into the sea with the ponderous charm of one of Picasso's surreal beach-girls. Just beyond it a boulder-filled creek marks the fault, and by comparing thicknesses of rock one can see that the terrace one is standing on here matches up with a level thirty feet higher in the cliffs on its east. This is quite insignificant compared to the faults geologists can trace in other parts of the world, with vertical 'throws' of thousands of feet or horizontal displacements of many miles, but this disruption is on an exhilarating, only-just-superhuman scale, like the Picasso bather; the gloss of its slanting fault-face on the other side of the creek makes its energy palpable, and yet by scrambling up the wave-worn cleft of the fault-line to the clifftop beyond it one can surmount the little cataclysm in a couple of minutes.

From these higher cliffs, one fine Easter Sunday, I watched a basking shark rolling lazily in the sun-filled water below. I remember the date because the visitor with me had just discovered a few dusty shards of chocolate-egg in the bottom of his knapsack, and I associate the unexpected taste unfolding as we rested there with the materialisation of the strange shape in our idle view. Its black dorsal fin arose first and its long snout with a little bow-wave, and then we saw its submerged bulk vaguely embodied in a slowly gliding net of ripple-shadow and sun-spangles. As its mouth gaped, its gills opened like five huge ruffs. I could not say how big it was — basking sharks of over forty feet in length and weighing more than three tons have been recorded, but I think our specimen was not quite in that class. By an irresistible paradox this, the world's biggest fish, eats only the smallest specks of life, and when it comes to the surface to yawn and loll about like this it is straining plankton out of the copious floods of water (up to twenty tons a minute) pouring in at its mouth and out by its fringed gills. In Irish it is called *An Liamhán Mór* or *An Liamhán Gréine*, the great *liamhán* (is this word derived from the biblical Leviathan, I wonder?) or the *liamhán* of the sun, and in English it used to be known in these regions as the sunfish too, because of its appearing inshore in the spring, to browse off the billions of copepods and other small fry multiplying in the sun-warmed surface waters. Not much is known of the rest of its life, except that after a winter of fasting and torpor out in the deeps it seems to make its way slowly northwards up the Atlantic coasts of Europe, and disappears again.

The commercial value of the basking shark, which lies in the oil from its gigantic liver, used to be so high that in the eighteenth and nineteenth centuries the shark fishery was second only to the herring in importance for the Galway Bay fleet. The men of Aran, Connemara and the Claddagh, Galway's fishing quarter, used to hunt the monsters from small open boats with hand-held harpoons. There is an account in Tom O'Flaherty's *Aranmen All*, given in suitably gargantuan terms, of how his grandfather organised the man of Gort na gCapall to the hunt when after many years of absence the sharks were once more spotted from the clifftops. All available tackle — 'spears, gaffs, bocáns, pocáns, buoys, bireógs, straimpíns, long knives and poles and chains taken from a ship wrecked at the Big Cleft' — was assembled and carried down to Port Bhéal an Dúin; a spear was attached by a rope and a cable to a chain wound around a big boulder in a deep pot-hole of the shore; five three-man currachs were launched, a shark was eventually speared, and when it had run itself to exhaustion another team of fifteen men hauled it ashore. The livers used to be boiled in iron cauldrons to extract the oil, which was sent to the mainland in barrels. Some of it was used in Aran for burning in the little lights called *muiríní*, consisting of a piece of rush as a wick lying in a scallop-shell of oil; shark oil was preferred to dogfish oil when it could be got, as it was less smelly and smoky. But when paraffin became available the oil lost its value, and the fishery was abandoned.

It seems the shark was absent again for years around the turn of the century, but it had reappeared a few seasons before Robert Flaherty arrived to make *Man of Aran*, and the shark-hunt was revived to give him a climactic episode for the film. Flaherty even had ideas of interesting buyers in the oil from the sharks caught on that occasion, and so restoring the industry to the islands, but the price at that time was too low for profit. Since then nobody in Aran had troubled about the fish, until the day described above on which we watched one from the cliffs and at the same time an idea was occurring to an Aran man on the hilltop behind us. We met him on our way home — a Cill Rónáin trawlerman who, when on land, spends as much time as possible looking at the sea, and on Sundays likes to put the family in the car and drive to some vantage point from which he can use his binoculars while they drowse and squabble and read the newspapers. This time he was watching a small trawler out in the North Sound which he told us was a Norwegian poacher making a big killing in a shoal of basking shark. Every few minutes we could see splashing as a shark was hauled on board and its carcass flung off again as soon as the liver had been cut out. At that time such plunderers had little to fear from the sparse patrols and mild penalties that guarded Irish fisheries, and in any case this massacre was not one to which the local fishermen objected, as they preferred the risk of catching one of the drifting corpses in their salmon-nets to that of a live shark entangling itself and destroying the net entirely. The Norwegians' example interested our Aran friend considerably and it prompted him to make enquiries of a firm in Achill Island, where the shark is still caught in fixed nets off the headlands. He found that there is a market for the oil, which has engineering applications as a fine lubricant — we were even told that a few drops of it went to the moon with the Apollo missions — and for the fins, which end up in Chinese shark's fin soup. So two or three owners of half-deckers entered into agreements with the Achill concern, and hired and mounted harpoon guns, and in the following year, 1980, the ancient fishery was briefly resurrected. Ever since *Man of Aran* the basking-shark hunt has been part of the romantic myth of Aran, and such was the interest in its revival that more boatloads of journalists than trawlers set forth, and many more photographs than sharks were taken. In fact sharks were few that year, and a vast amount of costly diesel fuel was burned in criss-crossing the seas from the Cliffs of Moher to far out beyond the Earragh lighthouse looking for them, and then in creeping up on them close enough for an inexpert harpooner to take a shot. The fishermen eventually tired of hearing from ambivalent shore-loafers like myself that a shark had been spotted, off the other end of the island the day before yesterday; then the salmon season took precedence and the harpoon guns were dismantled. The experiment was tried again with similar results in 1982, so one hopes that from now on the sun-loving basking shark will be able to take its vast and mysterious stroll, at least through Aran waters, in peace and safety.

from *Stones of Aran* (1986)

REVEREND ALEXANDER SYNGE

During the middle years of the nineteenth century, a good deal of energy was expended in Ireland in trying to convert the rural Catholic population. Direction of these efforts was in the hands of various societies, such as the Hibernian Bible Society, the Irish Evangelical Society, the Irish Church Missions. The Kildare Place Society was the best known of these.

Reverend Synge, the playwright's uncle, was the first Protestant clergyman to minister on Aran. In an effort to maintain his standard of living, he acquired a boat with the idea of fishing commercially for the Galway market. This, understandably, got the locals' backs up. At this time, Galway was a transatlantic port.

Letter (1851)

Thursday, July 17th 1851, to his brother Edward

My Dear Edward,

I am just setting out in a boat laden with 'fish and potatoes' for Galway 30 miles East — 'en route' for Tuam to be Priested on Sunday next — here I am Lord of all I survey — surrounded with dirt + ignorance — we have not got our Schoolmaster yet but we expect him shortly. it is a very wretched Island. the soil very scanty almost all a barren rock — we have a little church — 20 & 25 make our congregation mostly of the families of the coastguard I have 2 services each Sunday — I am at present living in a very small inn but intend next week DV to move into a 'private' Lodging a house with a kitchen and two small rooms overhead. I shall have one dirty little chap for my man Friday — who I expect will always be where I don't want him to be + never to be had when he is wanted however we must not be nice — it is very hard to make off a living here some times fresh meat we never think of I have it once in 5 weeks — and the chickens are scarce. it blew a little the last few days so we have no fresh fish and must do with salt ones or half saved bacon — we have no market nearer than Galway & no good boat to get there the hookers are all open & the passengers & things often get wet thro' — nice service for flour, groceries, etc. They stay away for a week at a time & we may do as we can until they choose to come back. I want a vessel for my self woefully. I am a regular prisoner — I get on with the people so far very well but how it will be when we begin to attack their bad ways & religion etc. I don't know. The proprietors of the Island are fitting up a house for me wh[ich] will be a very g[rea]t comfort when it is done. the noise and dirt of my present situation is very bad indeed — we have not a wheel machine cart or wheelbarrow on the Island the women carry everything on their backs — or else asses — Have you been to the Exhibition yet? do you think you will come over here? if you do I will run over and see it — but I have no one to take my place when I am absent they have no service — I will try to get over in Sept. if possible I [? would] like to see it very much — I have a good deal of time for reading and writing sermons — we have no good walks on the Island, the rocks are very sharp & no sandy beach either — shoes last no time — & as to black coats you can't have them — I came down in one but it soon ceased to be black. I never saw any thing turn brown faster —

May the Lord bless you and keep you and lift up the light of his countenance upon you — filling you with peace & joy in the Holy Spirit — which is the continual prayer on yr behalf from yr affte brother

Alex H. Synge

from 'Letters of the Reverend Alexander Synge, June 1851–December 1852', TCD MS 6200

RICHARD POCOCKE

Galway is 'The City of the Tribes'. These are the families of Norman and English extraction which supplanted the O'Hallorans and O'Flaherties. The latter, at least, did not go gently: a sixteenth-century inscription over the city's West Gate says: 'This gate was erected to protect us from the ferocious O'Flaherties'. By the time of Pococke's tour in 1752, however, the tribes had turned Galway into a prominent commercial centre and port.

Pococke names thirteen of the tribes. There were fourteen in all: Athy, Blake, Bodkin, Browne, Darcy, Deane, Font, French, Joyce, Kirwan, Lynch, Martin, Morris and Skerret. Legend has it that they were so successful that fortune even smiled on their inherited characteristics — for instance, the Joyces had the name of being joyous.

In early 1652, the city surrendered to Cromwell's forces after a land and sea blockade that had lasted nine months.

Galway

Galway is pleasantly Situated on a fine bay, which is a very good harbor, & on the river which comes out of Lough Chorrib, which spreading here to the east, they call it the Lough, the river runs on a rocky bed, & dividing into three parts it forms two Islands to the west of the Town, on one of which there is a Nunnery. This town was inhabited by the Hollerns Fishermen till one Lynch in 1280 got a grant of the lands of it, from Edward II, & as tradition saies built two Castles, both called Reinville, one against the Hollerns the other against the Flakerts of Cunnehmarrah. This was anciently in the Diocese of Anadown, which place I saw on the right on the Lough coming to Galway, it is now absorpt in Tuam. The people of the town got an exemption of this & Several other parishes from the Pope, on account as they pretended of the ill behaviour of the Clergy the Bishop sent to them: Some say this was when Anadown was united to Tuam. This exemption they got Confirmed to them by Charter from Edward the 6th, who gave them a power to elect, a guardian & three Vicars of the Church exempt from all jurisdiction whatsoever; the Guardian & senior Vicar preach alternately in the morning, the other two in the afternoon, & the three Vicars take their turns weekly to read prayers and visit the sick. The Corporation also have a power of punishing or even removing them within the year. This town was formerly of great trade, to which they apply'd themselves when the other parts of Ireland were very unquiet: they had a great trade in Spanish wines, which were formerly drank; but above all to America, till the act pass'd which obliged all ships from America to touch in England, from which time the trade of this town began to decay. When the town was in this flourishing Condition, there were many large houses built in it of hewn Stone, after the Spanish manner, most of which remain & one sees a great number of fine carved windows, Doorcases, Chimney pieces, & bow windows in these houses. The trade is now mostly carried on to France & Spain by the Roman Catholicks, who have correspondents there, & are jealous of others coming into any Share with them. When the town was in this flourishing Condition, the merchants here purchased almost all the Lands in this Country which doe not belong to the Church & the Earl of Clanrickard: The descendents of which merchants are now possessed to the value of £100,000 a year, & others have forfeited or sold to a much greater value. They were of the name of Blake, Darcy, French, Linche, Kirwan, Joyce, Martin, Brown, Bodkin, Terrets, Athy, Funt, Penrice, the three last are extinct or near it. If they had Submitted to Oliver Cromwell, it would probably have been much better for the town. The remains of the forts he built to attack the town & defend the passes between the Loughs & the Sea, are still to be seen. Lord Mountjoy built the Citadell at the South east part of the town. They have a large Church adjoining it, the Lynches have a Chapel in which they bury: In the Vestry on three large Stones are cut as big as human life, Our Saviour, the Virgin Mary to the right, & to the right of that God the Father & over his head the Dove, they were dug up some where about the Church: To the north of the town are the remains of a Franciscan Convent, & the face of an altar or tomb with some reliefs of Saints on it. Both ye Franciscans & Dominicans have Convents here, & there is a Nunnery which serves also for a Boarding School: Just without the gate is a mineral water of a Strong taste, which they use for purging, & when drank plentifully, it is said, they answer the end of Scarborough waters. About two miles to the north east in the way I came is a rivlet, which comes out of the river that falls from Lough Chorrib, it is call'd Pool Hurley, it goes under ground there & comes out into the bay of the sea which extends to the east. From a hill about a Mile above the town by the Canal, is a very fine prospect of the sea, of the Country on the other side of the bay, of the isles of Arran, Of Eyre Connaught, the Joyces Country & Lough Chorrib. They have in Galway three barracks, which hold two Regiments & a half of the present Compliment: for it is a garrison town with a Governor who has a salary of £300 a year, but he does not Commonly reside, & then the Commanding Officer acts as Governor.

from John McVeigh (ed.), *Richard Pococke's Irish Tours* (1995)

SOMERVILLE AND ROSS

Edith Somerville lived in a Big House called Drishane, in Castletownshend, near Skibbereen, on the coast of West Cork. Ross — Martin Ross, which was the pen-name of Violet Martin — lived in a Big House called Ross House, near Oughterard, Co. Galway. Their mothers were first cousins. They met for the first time in 1886, became fast friends, then literary partners, and by 1893 had published two novels and a travel book, Through Connemara in a Governess Cart.

Their tour of Connemara in a jennet and trap was made in 1890. The plan was to write up their experiences and sell the result to support themselves as novelists. The material appeared as articles in the Lady's Pictorial *before being published in book form in 1893. Although the Land War which had raged intermittently during the 1880s was not particularly virulent at the time of the tour, it is interesting that the cousins had a gun handy. Perhaps the gun might be there just to spice up the narrative!*

Connemara

We left the main road at the end of the lake, and turned into one running in another direction. It was, like every Connemara road, good and level, and in perfect order. Like all the others, too, it disdained fence or protection of any kind, unless an occasional deep ditch or lake on each side can be called a reassurance to the driver. Here and there on the road the little black demon cattle were standing disgustedly about, declining to eat the wet grass among the wetter heather, and concentrating all their attention on us in a manner that, taken in connection with the most villainous expression of countenance, and horns like Malay Krisses, made it advisable to throw stones at them while there was yet time. They at once withdrew, recognising the fact that is early implanted in the mind of every known Irish animal, that sermons in stones are unanswerable. We had got on to a long stretch of bog road, bounded only by the vaguely suggestive mist, and we were beginning to feel the ardour for a long walk awakening in us, when we heard a strange yelping on the road behind us, and looking back, saw a large brindled bulldog advancing out of the mist at a lumbering trot. No one was with him; a short piece of rope hung round his collar, and his aspect altogether was so terrific that my cousin and I again provided ourselves with the national weapon, and stood discreetly aside to let him pass. He instantly stopped and stared at us in what seemed a very threatening manner.

'Perhaps he's mad!' I suggested. 'Where's the gun?'

'In my pocket,' returned my cousin in a low voice 'and I can't get it out. It's stuck.'

'Well you'd better hurry,' I said, 'for he's coming.'

The bulldog was moving slowly towards us, uttering strange grunts, and looking excitedly round at the cattle, who were beginning to close in on us and him. My cousin with one strenuous effort ripped the pocket off her mackintosh.

'I've got it at last!' she panted, putting in a cartridge with trembling fingers and cocking the pistol. 'It's awfully stiff, and I know it throws high, but anyhow, it will frighten him — I don't really want to hit him.'

'For goodness' sake wait till I get behind you,' I replied. 'Now!'

There was a report like a cannon, and I saw my cousin's hand jerk heavenwards, as if hailing a cab. The next moment the cattle were flying to the four winds of heaven, and the bulldog, far from being alarmed or hurt, was streaking through the heather in hot pursuit of the largest cow of the herd.

This was a more appalling result than we could possibly have anticipated. Not only had we failed to intimidate, but we had positively instigated him to crime.

'He's used to guns,' I said. 'He thinks we are cow-shooting.'

'He's gone to retrieve the game,' replied my cousin in a hollow voice.

In another instant the bulldog had overtaken his prey, and the next, our knees tottering under us with horror, we saw him swinging from her nose by his teeth, while her bellowings rent the skies. Back she came down the hill, flinging her head from side to side, while the bulldog adhered with limpet tenacity to her nose, and, jumping the bog-ditch like a hunter, she set off down the road, followed by a trumpeting host of friends and sympathisers who had re-gathered from the mountain-side on hearing her cries. The whole adventure had been forced upon us so suddenly and unexpectedly that we had no time to argue away the illogical feeling that we were responsible for the bulldog's iniquities. I see now that the sensible thing would have been to have gone and hid about among the rocks till it was all over. But that course did not occur to us till afterwards. As a matter of fact, my cousin crammed the pistol into her uninjured pocket, I filled my hands with stones, and we pursued at our best speed, seeing from time to time above the heaving backs and brandished tails of the galloping cattle the dark body of the bulldog as he was swung into the air over his victim's head. Suddenly the whole *cortège* wheeled, and flourished up a bohireen that led to a cottage, and in the quick turn the cow fell on her knees, and lay there exhausted, with the bulldog prone beside her, exhausted too, but still holding on. The presumable owner of the cow arrived on the scene at the same instant that we did.

'Call off yer dog!' he roared, in a fearful voice.

'He's not ours!' we panted; 'but come on, and we'll beat him off!' the bulldog's evident state of collapse encouraging us to this gallantry.

The man's only reply was to pick up a large stone, and heave it at the dog. It struck his brindled ribs a resounding blow, but he was too much blown to bear malice satisfactorily; to our deep relief he crawled to his feet, slunk away past us on to the main road, and, setting off at a limping trot in the direction from which he had come, presently vanished into the mist.

The man stooped down and examined the poor cow's torn and bleeding nose, and she lay, wild-eyed, with heaving sides, at our feet.

'That the divil may blisther the man that owns him!' he said; 'and if he isn't your dog, what call have you taking him out to be running my cows?'

'We met him on the road,' we protested. 'We couldn't help his following us.'

'Aha! thin it's one of them dirty little fellows of officers that has the fishing lodge below that he belongs to!' said the man. 'I heard a shot awhile ago, and ye may b'lieve me I'll have the law o' them.'

We exchanged guilty glances.

'Yes; I heard a shot, too,' I said nervously.

'Well, I — a — I think we must be getting on now. It's getting late, and — a — I hope the cow isn't very bad. Anyhow' — my voice sinking into the indistinct mumble that usually accompanies the benefaction — 'here's something to get soft food for her till her nose gets well'.

The ambition for the long walk was dead. With more hurried good wishes and regrets we wished the man good evening, and so home, much shattered.

P.S. — We should like to meet the owner of that bulldog.

from *Through Connemara in a Governess Cart* (1893)

LIAM O'FLAHERTY

First published in the author's first short story collection, Spring Sowing *(1924), 'The Black Bullock' is set on the author's native Inishmore, Aran. Coillnamhan is O'Flaherty's name for Dun Aengus, the famous prehistoric fort on the island. Originally in ancient Irish mythology, Crom Dugh, 'the pagan god', was like an Antichrist, in particular a figure in opposition to St Patrick. Literally translated, his name means 'black stoop', suggesting a hunchback or crouched figure, giving him satanic connotations. But according to another story, St Patrick intervened on his behalf at the time of his death when demons came to spirit him off. The saint did this in recognition of Crom's annual gift to the poor of a bullock. In addition, tradition says that the encounter between Crom and St Patrick took place at the harvest festival of Lughnasa, celebrated on the Sunday nearest the first day of August — though obviously this is not the 'autumn' of the story.*

In The Aran Islands, *Synge noticed that the people 'have no feelings for the sufferings of animals'. This attitude is by no means confined to Aran.*

The Black Bullock

He was two years old when he came to Inverara. But he had been hungry all his life and he was no bigger than a donkey. His owner was a boatman on the mainland opposite Inverara and he had bought the black bullock for ten shillings when the bullock was a week old. Its mother had died of the colic or something (the poor widow who owned her said it was the Evil Eye). But the boatman had no land and the bullock grew up about the cabin, more accustomed to potato skins and nettles than to hay or clover or plain grass. By day he wandered around the little fishing hamlet, rambling on the roadside, chased by dogs and pelted by children, and by night he was tethered in his owner's kitchen to an iron hook in the wall by the back door. There was a deep groove around his neck where the rope rested, and the groove was deepest under his chin. For the lads of the village who visited his owner's cabin often amused themselves at night when the boatman was not looking by holding a potato in front of the bullock's mouth and retreating with it as the bullock strained after it moaning with hunger. Little boys amused themselves by riding him and sticking thistle heads in the end of his tail that only reached halfway down his legs. Yet he was by nature so healthy that his temper never soured under this ill-treatment and, in spite of hunger, his black hide was glossy and curly. He had no horns, and the tip of his skull where bullocks have horns was always caked with dried mud, for he was in the habit of playfully butting his head into the bog and wallowing like a wild one.

Then on the festival of the pagan god Crom Dugh in autumn his owner brought him to the island of Inverara to graze for the winter, in the hope that he would get fat, and be fit for sale in the following May. He gave him to a peasant named Jimmy Hernon of Coillnamhan. 'Feed him well, Jimmy,' he said, 'and I'll bring you the best boatload of turf that was ever cut in a bog when I am taking him away next May Day.' Hernon took off his hat, spat on both hands and swore by all the saints that he would keep the bullock's belly full if his own had to go empty. In the presence of the boatman he put the little black bullock to graze in a clover field with his own cow. 'There you are,' he said. 'There isn't a man in Inverara would treat your bullock so well.' And the boatman went away to the mainland highly pleased with the bargain he had made.

As soon as the little bullock found himself loose in the luscious clover he began to eat ravenously, wagging his tail, shaking his head and snorting. When he began to eat his belly was so thin that one could transfix it with a knitting needle, but it rapidly filled out so that he looked like a little cask. He soon made friends with the cow, although at first she horned him away when he sniffed at her flanks, and they wandered up and down the field all night side by side, their coarse tongues making a noise like tearing silk as they chopped the clover. Then in the morning when the cow leaned over the gap chewing her cud and lowed now and again wanting to be milked, the little black bullock stood by, chewing his cud with his eyes half shut, perfectly content.

But Hernon came with his wife to milk the cow and began to swear ferociously when he saw the black bullock's rotund stomach. 'I'll declare,' he said with an oath, 'that he'll eat three times as much as my cow, the miserable little wretch. Out he goes to the crag this very minute.' And he drove the bullock from the clover field up a rocky lane to the cliff top, hammering him with a big stick, so that the bullock ran and stumbled and bellowed, wondering what was happening to him. Then Hernon put him to graze in a broad barren crag overlooking the sea and went away.

The bullock roamed about the crag for a long time, scarcely able to make his way over the jagged rocks and pointed loose stones. Several times he tried to nibble at the stunted grass that grew in the tiny valleys, but the grass tasted too salt and sour. And the sea roared near him. And the crag was so high and exposed that it caught every breeze and gust of wind, so that he felt very miserable and was struck with terror. For he had always been used to living among people and within sight of houses and shelter. All day he never ate anything, even of the stunted grass that grew there, but spent most of the time circling the crag trying to find a way out. The fence was not very high and he might easily jump it or knock it down by thrusting his breast against it, but his terror was so acute that he was unable to muster up courage to do so. When he passed along the brink of the cliff overlooking the sea, where there was no fence, he was continually snorting and jumping sideways with fright.

Then night came and he had nowhere to take shelter from the bitter autumn wind that rose from the sea. Next morning his hide was wet with dew and sea froth and his belly was as empty as it had been when he landed in Inverara. As day advanced the sun shone brightly, warming him, so he capered about nibbling and felt fairly comfortable, though his hoofs were sore from treading the sharp rocks. The best grass grew in the deep crevices in the rocks and he had to scramble over the most difficult ground to reach it, sometimes even going on his knees and straining his neck down into the holes. When he had eaten sufficient he wanted to drink, and that too was difficult, for the little pools were almost dry and it was only after visiting six of them, scattered at long intervals, that he was satisfied.

He spent a week that way without seeing a soul, and every day he became hungrier, more thirsty and miserable. Then three wandering goats came on to his crag and stayed the day prancing about the cliff top. He tried to make friends with them, but when he came near them and stretched out his head and sniffed, they stamped and snorted and ran away. And in the evening they departed eastwards, jumping a low part of the fence quite easily. He stood looking over the fence where they had leaped a long time, lowing after them until they disappeared. Then, seized with fury, he pushed against the fence, knocked off a few stones and scrambled through the gap in a heap to the other side.

With his tail in the air he ran along in the direction the goats had gone until he came to a lane. There he met a donkey with a young foal. He nestled up to the donkey, but the donkey kicked him in the belly and then bared her teeth and tried to bite him. So he wandered on, until he saw a village ahead of him.

When he saw the houses and the people he thought he was home again. He began to low with joy and, tossing his head, he trotted along snorting playfully. But straying round the village smelling at gates and dunghills he was chased by dogs, and peasant women ran out and threw stones at him, so that he retired miserably to a waste plot at the back of a barn and lay down, very weary of life. For these people regarded him as a wild beast and would not let him come near them.

Then two stray dogs discovered him and chased him down to the village cross-roads where a number of young men were loafing. The young men, bored for want of amusement, herded him into a corner and tied a tin kettle to his short tail. Then they beat him and shouted 'Fe-och, fe-och' and turned him out into the road again. The tin kettle just tipped the ground, and at every step the bullock took it clattered against his heels.

He began to trot in order to get away from it. But the more he trotted the greater was the noise it made, and it hit his heels all the harder. Then he got mad, lashed out with his hind legs and broke into a gallop. The dogs barked and ran alongside him, biting at his mouth and his flanks. The men yelled and urged on the dogs. The bullock ran on and on frothing at the mouth until he reached a gap in the road fence that led into a crag. He rushed through the gap and on to the crag. But the kettle made a greater noise on the limestone crag and the dogs were better able to bite him, since he had to go slower. So he began to bellow and jumped headlong down into a little glen. It was but ten feet of a fall, but his hind hoof caught in a crevice as he jumped, and he fell on his back.

When Hernon found him his spine was broken, so he had to slaughter him.

from *The Short Stories of Liam O'Flaherty* (1937)

THOMAS LAVELLE

It seems painfully fitting that nobody is quite sure of even the name of the man who composed one of the best known of all Irish poems of exile. According to some, he was Thomas Lavelle. Others say that the poem used to have the alternative title of 'The Lament of Thomas Flavell'. His name in Irish is given as Tomás Ó Flannghail, which could be Thomas Flannelly. This translation dates from the 1830s, and the man who made it, George Fox (b. 1809), himself ended up in America. In the original, the reason for emigration is given as drink and cards, on the one hand, and on the other, that the law is too strong.

The emigrant's destination is unclear. At the time the poem was written, there was only one city of Santa Cruz, and that was in Bolivia. Perhaps Veracruz in Mexico is meant. Wherever it is, it does not have the same associations as Spanish ale. Patrick Lynch's boat suggests that he sailed from Galway.

A hair-bag was a small pouch into which back-hair was tidied; it is in English in the original.

The County of Mayo

On the deck of Patrick Lynch's boat I sit in woeful plight,
Through my sighing all the weary day, and weeping all the night,
Were it not that full of sorrow from my people forth I go,
By the blessed sun! 'tis royally I'd sing thy praise, Mayo!

When I dwelt at home in plenty, and my gold did much abound,
In the company of fair young maids the Spanish ale went round —
'Tis a bitter change from those gay days that now I'm forced to go,
And must leave my bones in Santa Cruz, far from my own Mayo.

They are altered girls in Irrul now; 'tis proud they're grown and high,
With their hair-bags and their top-knots — for I pass their buckles by;
But it's little now I heed their airs, for God will have it so,
That I must depart for foreign lands, and leave my sweet Mayo.

'Tis my grief that Patrick Loughlin is not Earl in Irrul still,
And that Brian Duff no longer rules as lord upon the hill,
And that Colonel Hugh MacGrady should be lying cold and low,
And I sailing, sailing swiftly, from the County of Mayo.

translated by George Fox, from *Irish Penny Journal* (1840)

PAUL DURCAN

Both the poet's parents came from Mayo, but the poet himself was born and reared in Dublin. Because of his parents, both places are home, and because of his parents neither place is home. But most Irish people of Paul Durcan's generation have experienced in a somewhat bewildered and only half-realised way erratic oscillations in the transition between capital and country, country and capital. The opposing tempo and ethos of these different worlds is one of the many sources of the anxiety of identity which is such a feature of present-day Irish culture. The social and political roots of the modern Irish state are rural and provincial, and have only superficially adapted to urban realities.

Geographically speaking, a turlough is a lakelike hollow that is sometimes filled with water but which at other times is dry.

Going Home to Mayo, Winter, 1949

Leaving behind us the alien, foreign city of Dublin,
My father drove through the night in an old Ford Anglia,
His five-year-old son in the seat beside him,
The rexine seat of red leatherette,
And a yellow moon peered in through the windscreen.
'Daddy, Daddy,' I cried, 'pass out the moon,'
But no matter how hard he drove he could not pass out the moon.
Each town we passed through was another milestone

And their names were magic passwords into eternity:
Kilcock, Kinnegad, Strokestown, Elphin,
Tarmonbarry, Tulsk, Ballaghaderreen, Ballavarry;
Now we were in Mayo and the next stop was Turlough,
The village of Turlough in the heartland of Mayo,
And my father's mother's house, all oil-lamps and women,
And my bedroom over the public bar below,
And in the morning cattle-cries and cock-crows:
Life's seemingly seamless garment gorgeously rent
By their screeches and bellowings. And in the evenings
I walked with my father in the high grass down by the river
Talking with him — an unheard-of thing in the city.

But home was not home and the moon could be no more outflanked
Than the daylight nightmare of Dublin City:
Back down along the canal we chugged into the city
And each lock-gate tolled our mutual doom;
And railings and palings and asphalt and traffic lights,
And blocks after blocks of so-called 'new' tenements —
Thousands of crosses of loneliness planted
In the narrowing grave of the life of the father;
In the wide, wide cemetery of the boy's childhood.

from *A Snail in My Prime* (1993)

FRANCIS A. FAHY

Second only to the lakes of Killarney as an inspiration of songs in praise of its scenic beauty, Galway Bay is also strongly associated with emigration to North America. This is partly because Galway was an embarkation point for emigrants, and partly because the broad expanse of the bay kept land in sight much longer than at other major emigration ports — Cobh, for example. Also, it was from the West that most Irish emigrants to America came, so much so that they came to be seen as the archetypal emigrant. Success in the New World and some strong memory of home consolidated the archetype.

This song — written by somebody who spent most of his adult life as an Irish emigrant in London — predates, and to some extent anticipates, the 'Galway Bay' popularised by the well-known Irish-American Bing Crosby.

Galway Bay

'Tis far away I am today from scenes I roamed a boy,
And long ago the hour I know I first saw Illinois;
But time nor tide nor waters wide can wean my heart away,
For ever true, it flies to you, my own dear Galway Bay.

My chosen bride is by my side, her brown hair silver-grey,
Her daughter Rose, as like her grows as April dawn to day;
Our eldest boy, his mother's joy, his father's pride and stay —
With gifts like these I'd live at ease were I near Galway Bay.

A prouder man I'd walk the land in health and peace of mind
If I might toil and strive and moil, nor cast one thought behind;
But what would be the world to me, its rank and rich array,
If memory I lost of thee, my poor old Galway Bay.

Oh, grey and bleak, by shore and creek, the rugged rocks abound,
But sweeter green the grass between than grows on Irish ground,
So friendship fond, all wealth beyond, and love that lives always,
Bless each poor home beside your foam, my dear old Galway Bay.

Had I youth's blood and hopeful mood and heart of fire once more,
For all the gold the earth might hold I'd never quit your shore;
I'd live content whate'er God sent, with neighbours old and grey,
And lay my bones 'neath churchyard stones beside you, Galway Bay.

The blessings of a poor old man be with you night and day,
The blessings of a lonely man whose heart will soon be clay;
'Tis all the Heaven I'd ask of God upon my dying day —
My soul to soar for evermore above you, Galway Bay.

from *Irish Songs and Poems* (1887)

GEORGE BARKER

Because it is the capital city of the West of Ireland, and the West is where the survival of the Irish language and ancient Irish folkways and beliefs was most extensively codified by Lady Gregory, W.B. Yeats and many others, Galway has often had its name mentioned in the same breath as vision, myth and Gaelic mystique. Even the fact that it looks to the west, where the Isle of the Blest is supposed to be, contributes to this view, making the city and the region fair game for otherworldly sightings and soundings.

Barker's mother was Irish, but Ireland was of little importance in his life or work.

Galway Bay

With the gulls' hysteria above me
I walked near these breakneck seas
This morning of mists, and saw them,
Tall the mysterious queens
Waltzing in on the broad
Ballroom of the Atlantic.

All veils and waterfalls and
Wailings of the distraught,
These effigies of grief moved
Like refugees over the water;
The icy empresses of the Atlantic
Rising to bring me omen.

These women woven of ocean
And sorrows, these far sea figures,
With the fish and skull in their
Vapour of faces, the icicles
Salting down from their eyelashes,
As I walked by the foreshore

Moved towards me, ululating:
O dragnet of the sweet heart
Bind us no longer! The cage
Bursts with passions and bones,
And every highspirited fish
Lives off our scuttled love!

I stood on a stone, the gulls
Crossed my vision with wings
And my hearing with caterwauling;
The hurdling wave, backbroken,
Died at my feet. Taller
Than the towering hour above me

The booming empresses of the sea
Came among me. And, shivering,
I felt death nuzzling in the nest
Of the diurnally shipwrecked
Drowned nocturnally breast.

from *Selected Poems* (1995)

WILLIAM MAKEPEACE THACKERAY

Thackeray considered that around Ballynahinch 'there are views of the lakes and the surrounding country which the best parts of Killarney do not surpass'. Ballynahinch House was once the seat of the Martin family. They lost it after the Famine. In the 1920s, the famous cricketer Ranjitsinjhi owned it. It is now Ballynahinch House Hotel.

One of the peaks to be seen as the road nears Westport is Mweelrea, and of course the so-called 'Reek' is Croagh Patrick. Lord Sligo's Delphi is actually a fishing lodge.

The crowded road underlines the fact that Thackeray is writing about pre-Famine Ireland.

Clifden to Westport

On leaving Ballinahinch (with sincere regret, as any lonely tourist may imagine, who is called upon to quit the hospitable friendliness of such a place and society), my way lay back to Clifden again, and thence through the Joyce country, by the Killery mountains, to Westport in Mayo. The road, amounting in all to four-and-forty Irish miles, is performed in cars, in different periods of time, according to your horse and your luck. Sometimes, both being bad, the traveller is two days on the road; sometimes a dozen hours will suffice for the journey — which was the case with me, though I confess to having found the twelve hours long enough. After leaving Clifden, the friendly look of the country seemed to vanish; and though picturesque enough, was a thought too wild and dismal for eyes accustomed to admire a hop-garden in Kent, or a view of rich meadows in Surrey, with a clump of trees and a comfortable village spire. 'Inglis,' the Guide-book says, 'compares the scenes to the Norwegian Fiords.' Well, the Norwegian Fiords must, in this case, be very dismal sights! and I own that the wildness of Hampstead Heath (with the imposing walls of 'Jack Straw's Castle' rising sternly in the midst of the green wilderness) is more to my taste than the general views of yesterday.

We skirted by lake after lake, lying lonely in the midst of lonely boglands, or bathing the sides of mountains robed in sombre rifle green. Two or three men, and as many huts, you see in the course of each mile perhaps, as toiling up the bleak hills, or jingling more rapidly down them, you pass through this sad region. In the midst of the wilderness a chapel stands here and there, solitary, on the hill-side; or a ruinous, useless school-house, its pale walls contrasting with the general surrounding hue of sombre purple and green. But though the country looks more dismal than Connemara, it is clearly more fertile: we passed miles of ground that evidently wanted but little cultivation to make them profitable; and along the mountain-sides, in many places, and over a great extent of Mr Blake's country especially, the hills were covered with a thick natural plantation that may yield a little brushwood now, but might in fifty years' time bring thousands of pounds of revenue to the descendants of the Blakes. This spectacle of a country going to waste is enough to make the cheerfullest landscape look dismal: it gives this wild district a woful look indeed. The names of the lakes by which we came I noted down in a pocket-book as we passed along; but the names were Irish, the car was rattling, and the only name readable in the catalogue is Letterfrack.

The little hamlet of Leenane is at twenty miles' distance from Clifden; and to arrive at it, you skirt the mountain along one side of a vast pass, through which the ocean runs from Killery Bay, separating the mountains of Mayo from the mountains of Galway. Nothing can be more grand and gloomy than this pass; and as for the character of the scenery, it must, as the Guide-book says, 'be seen to be understood'. Meanwhile, let the reader imagine huge dark mountains in their accustomed livery of purple and green, a dull grey sky above them, an estuary silver-bright below; in the water lies a fisherman's boat or two; a pair of sea-gulls undulating with the little waves of the water; a pair of curlews wheeling overhead and piping on the wing; and on the hill-side a jingling car, with a cockney in it, oppressed by and yet admiring all these things. Many a sketcher and tourist, as I found, has visited this picturesque spot: for the hostess of the inn had stories of English and American painters, and of illustrious book-writers too, travelling in the service of our Lords of Paternoster Row.

The landlord's son of Clifden, a very intelligent young fellow, was here exchanged for a new carman, in the person of a raw Irisher of twenty years of age, 'having' little English, and dressed in that very pair of pantaloons which Humphrey Clinker was compelled to cast off some years since on account of the offence which they gave to Mrs Tabitha Bramble. This fellow, emerging from among the boats, went off to a field to seek for the black horse, which the landlady assured me was quite fresh and had not been out all day, and would carry me to Westport in three hours. Meanwhile I was lodged in a neat little parlour, surveying the Mayo side of the water, with some cultivated fields and a show of a village at the spot where the estuary ends, and above them lodges and fine dark plantations climbing over the dark hills that lead to Lord Sligo's seat of Delphi. Presently, with a curtsey, came a young woman who sold worsted socks at a shilling a pair . . . .

It required no small pains to entice this rustic beauty to stand while a sketch should be made of her. Nor did any compliments or cajolements, on my part or the landlady's, bring about the matter: it was not until money was offered that the lovely creature consented. I offered (such is the ardour of the real artist) either to give her sixpence, or to purchase two pairs of her socks, if she would stand still for five minutes. On which she said she would prefer selling the socks. Then she stood still for a moment in the corner of the room; then she turned her face towards the corner and the other part of her person towards the artist, and exclaimed in that attitude, 'I must have a shilling more.' Then I told her to go to the deuce. Then she made a proposition, involving the stockings and sixpence, which was similarly rejected; and, finally, this splendid design was completed at the price first stated.

However, as we went off, this timid little dove barred the door for a moment, and said that 'I ought to give her another shilling; that a gentleman would give her another shilling,' and so on. She might have trod the London streets for ten years and not have been more impudent and more greedy.

By this time the famous fresh horse was produced, and the driver, by means of a wraprascal, had covered a great part of the rags of his lower garment. He carried a whip and a stick, the former lying across his knees ornamentally, the latter being for service; and as his feet were directly under the horse's tail, he had full command of the brute's back, and belaboured it for six hours without ceasing.

What little English the fellow knew he uttered with a howl, roaring into my ear answers — which, for the most part, were wrong — to various questions put to him. The lad's voice was so hideous, that I asked him if he could sing; on which forthwith he began yelling a most horrible Irish ditty — of which he told me the title, that I have forgotten. He sang three stanzas, certainly keeping a kind of tune, and the latter lines of each verse were in rhyme; but when I asked him the meaning of the song, he only roared out its Irish title.

On questioning the driver further, it turned out that the horse, warranted fresh, had already performed a journey of eighteen miles that morning, and the consequence was that I had full leisure to survey the country through which we passed. There were more lakes, more mountains, more bog, and an excellent road through this lonely district, though few only of the human race enlivened it. At ten miles from Leenane, we stopped at a roadside hut, where the driver pulled out a bag of oats, and borrowing an iron pot from the good people, half filled it with corn, which the poor tired, galled, bewhipped black horse began eagerly to devour. The young charioteer himself hinted very broadly his desire for a glass of whisky, which was the only kind of refreshment that this remote house of entertainment supplied.

In the various cabins I have entered, I have found talking a vain matter: the people are suspicious of the stranger within their wretched gates, and are shy, sly, and silent. I have, commonly, only been able to get half-answers in reply to my questions, given in a manner that seemed plainly to intimate that the visit was unwelcome. In this rude hostel, however, the landlord was a little less reserved, offered a seat at the turf-fire, where a painter might have had a good subject for his skill. There was no chimney, but a hole in the roof, up which a small portion of the smoke ascended (the rest preferring an egress by the door, or else to remain in the apartment altogether); and this light from above lighted up as rude a set of figures as ever were seen. There were two brown women with black eyes and locks, the one knitting stockings on the floor, the other 'racking' (with that natural comb which five horny fingers supply) the elf-locks of a dirty urchin between her knees. An idle fellow was smoking his pipe by the fire; and by his side sat a stranger, who had been made welcome to the shelter of the place — a sickly, well-looking man, whom I mistook for a deserter at first, for he had evidently been a soldier.

But there was nothing so romantic as desertion in his history. He had been in the Dragoons, but his mother had purchased his discharge: he was married, and had lived comfortably in Cork for some time, in the glass-blowing business. Trade failing at Cork, he had gone to Belfast to seek for work. There was no work at Belfast and he was so far on his road home again: sick, without a penny in the world, a hundred and fifty miles to travel, and a starving wife and children to receive him at his journey's end. He had been thrown off a caravan that day, and had almost broken his back in the fall. Here was a cheering story! I wonder where he is now: how far has the poor starving lonely man advanced over that weary desolate road, that in good health, with a horse to carry me, I thought it a penalty to cross? What would one do under such circumstances, with solitude and hunger for present company, despair and starvation at the end of the vista? There are a score of lonely lakes along the road which he has to pass; would it be well to stop at one of them and fling into it the wretched load of cares which that poor broken back has to carry? Would the world he would light on *then* be worse for him than that he is pining in now? Heaven help us! and on this very day, throughout the three kingdoms, there are a million such stories to be told! Who dare doubt of heaven after that? of a place where there is at last a welcome to the heart-stricken prodigal and a happy home to the wretched?

The crumbs of oats which fell from the mouth of the feasting Dives of a horse were battled for outside the door by a dozen Lazaruses in the shape of fowls; and a lanky young pig, who had been grunting in an old chest in the cabin, or in a miserable recess of huddled rags and straw which formed the couch of the family, presently came out and drove the poultry away, picking up, with great accuracy, the solitary grains lying about, and more than once trying to shove his snout into the corn-pot, and share with the wretched old galled horse. Whether it was that he was refreshed by his meal, or that the car-boy was invigorated by his glass of whisky, or inflamed by the sight of eighteenpence — which munificent sum was tendered to the soldier — I don't know; but the remaining eight miles of the journey were got over in much quicker time, although the road was exceedingly bad and hilly for the greatest part of the way to Westport. However, by running up the hills at the pony's side, the animal, fired with emulation, trotted up them too — descending them with the proverbial surefootedness of his race, the car and he bouncing over the rocks and stones at the rate of at least four Irish miles an hour.

At about five miles from Westport the cultivation became more frequent. There were plantations upon the hills, yellow corn and potatoes in plenty in the fields, and houses thickly scattered. We had the satisfaction, too, of knowing that future tourists will have an excellent road to travel over in this district: for by the side of the old road, which runs up and down a hundred little rocky steeps, according to the ancient plan, you see a new one running for several miles, — the latter way being conducted, not over the hills, but around them, and, considering the circumstances of the country, extremely broad and even. The car-boy presently yelled out 'REEK, REEK!' with a shriek perfectly appalling. This howl was to signify that we were in sight of that famous conical mountain so named, and from which St Patrick, after inveigling thither all the venomous reptiles in Ireland, precipitated the whole noisome race into Clew Bay. The road also for several miles was covered with people, who were flocking in hundreds from Westport market, in cars and carts, on horseback single and double, and on foot.

And presently, from an eminence, I caught sight not only of a fine view, but of the most beautiful view I ever saw in the world, I think; and to enjoy the splendour of which I would travel a hundred miles in that car with that very horse and driver. The sun was just about to set, and the country round about and to the east was almost in twilight. The mountains were tumbled about in a thousand fantastic ways, and swarming with people. Trees, corn-fields, cottages, made the scene indescribably cheerful; noble woods stretched towards the sea, and abutting on them, between two highlands, lay the smoking town. Hard by was a large Gothic building — it is but a poor-house; but it looked like a grand castle in the grey evening. But the Bay — and the Reek which sweeps down to the sea — and a hundred islands in it, were dressed up in gold and purple and crimson, with the whole cloudy west in a flame. Wonderful, wonderful! . . . The valleys in the road to Leenane have lost all glimpses of the sun ere this; and I suppose there is not a soul to be seen in the black landscape, or by the shores of the ghastly lakes, where the poor glass-blower from the whisky-shop is faintly travelling now.

from *The Irish Sketch Book* (1843)

Inglis . . . Henry Inglis, author of *A Journey Through Ireland* (2 vols., 1834)

Humphrey Clinker . . . hero of Tobias Smollett's novel, *The Expedition of Humphry Clinker* (1771)

wraprascal . . . a loose overcoat common in the eighteenth century

MICHAEL LONGLEY

A self-confessed native of 'darkest South Belfast', for twenty-five years or so Michael Longley has been visiting the Louisburgh area in south-west County Mayo — his 'home from home', as he has called it. The landscape of seashore and mountain of these remote parts constitutes a kind of spiritual ecology in his poetry.

Mweelrea rises to a height of 2,688 feet — high for an Irish mountain.

On Mweelrea

1

I was lowering my body on to yours
When I put my ear to the mountain's side
And eavesdropped on water washing itself
In the locked bath-house of the underground.

When I dipped my hand among hidden sounds
It was the water's pulse at wrist and groin,
It was the water that reminded me
To leave all of my jugs and cups behind.

2

The slopes of the mountain were commonage
For me clambering over the low walls
To look for the rings of autumn mushrooms
That ripple out across the centuries.

I had made myself the worried shepherd
Of snipe twisting the grasses into curls
And tiny thatches where they hid away,
Of the sheep that grazed your maidenhair.

3

September grew to shadows on Mweelrea
Once the lambs had descended from the ridge
With their fleeces dyed, tinges of sunset,
Rowan berries, and the bracken rusting.

Behind my eyelids I could just make out
In a wash of blood and light and water
Your body colouring the mountainside
Like uncut poppies in the stubbly fields.

from *The Echo Gate* (1979)

W. B. Yeats

Coole Park, near Gort, Co. Galway, was the home of Lady Gregory, Yeats's great friend and benefactor. The poem draws on the lake, woods and walks with which the poet was very familiar. Yeats made his first visit there in 1896, though his first extended stay was in the autumn of the following year. At that time he was consumed by his love for Maud Gonne; she is still on his mind at the time the poem was written in the autumn of 1916. Yeats was unmarried, while Maud Gonne had been widowed through the execution of her husband, Major John MacBride, a participant in the 1916 Rising. Swans are said to mate for life.

Yeats married Georgie Hyde-Lees in October 1917.

The Wild Swans at Coole

The trees are in their autumn beauty,
The woodland paths are dry,
Under the October twilight the water
Mirrors a still sky;
Upon the brimming water among the stones
Are nine and fifty swans.

The nineteenth Autumn has come upon me
Since I first made my count;
I saw, before I had well finished,
All suddenly mount
And scatter wheeling in great broken rings
Upon their clamorous wings.

I have looked upon those brilliant creatures,
And now my heart is sore.
All's changed since I, hearing at twilight,
The first time on this shore,
The bell-beat of their wings above my head,
Trod with a lighter tread.

Unwearied still, lover by lover,
They paddle in the cold,
Companionable streams or climb the air;
Their hearts have not grown old;
Passion or conquest, wander where they will,
Attend upon them still.

But now they drift on the still water
Mysterious, beautiful;
Among what rushes will they build,
By what lake's edge or pool
Delight men's eyes when I awake some day
To find they have flown away?

from *The Wild Swans at Coole* (1917)

LADY GREGORY

Coole Park was the property of Sir William Gregory, whom Isabella Augusta Persse, from nearby Roxborough, married in 1880. From him, in part, she learned about Egyptian politics. Widowed in 1892, Lady Gregory gradually involved herself with the Irish Literary Revival, in particular the Abbey Theatre, while Coole Park became a salon-cum-artists' retreat. W.B. Yeats had a special attachment to the house and to Lady Gregory — 'mother, friend, sister and brother', as he called her. In 1927, Coole Park was sold by her daughter-in-law Margaret, though Lady Gregory continued to live there with her grandchildren, Richard, Anne and Catherine, 'the chicks', until her death five years later. The house was pulled down in 1941.

The year is 1928. The O'Casey play is The Silver Tassie, *whose rejection caused a rift between O'Casey and the Abbey which hurt both. Lady Gregory's nephew was Hugh Lane, drowned in the sinking of the* Lusitania. *The fate of his modern art collection caused great controversy. 'Mr Blunt' is Wilfrid Scawen Blunt, with whom Lady Gregory had a brief affair. 'L.R.' is Lennox Robinson. Yeats was appointed chairman of the commission for the design of a new Irish coinage in 1926.*

From Her Journal

12 APRIL. A letter from May yesterday saying Frank was very ill, bronchitis. And then a telegram that he was gradually sinking. And another today, that he is gone.

He was the brother nearest to me in age and in affection. I stood by him in his unfortunate marriage and his wild days, and W. gave him his first chance of recovery, making him agent here. Then he did so well for a long time. And to the last he was helpful with advice, so practical and kind. Two years my junior. I trust I may pass as peacefully away.

My darlings here happy and gay — this week they have Ennis Point to Point races; and we all stayed a night at Lough Cutra, and they picnicked at Burren with Guy and Scott Kerr. Yesterday they went through a good part of

Connemara. Today Richard and Anne are to motor to Dublin with Quatermain in the Lough Cutra car for the night. Riding also, and all so cheery and content.

I am still typing and typing, the last day or two my 'First efforts to regain the pictures' — all sad, disheartening reading. How can we be expected to trust the honour of England?

SUNDAY, 18 APRIL. Yesterday I motored in the rain to Craughwell, to the poor graveyard where Frank's body was being laid. Only a few there, some old men from Lough Cutra who had worked under him and loved him; his daughters and sons-in-law — very few others, the time and place had by accident not been put in the papers. I joined the procession but did not go into the graveyard, for reasons besides the pouring rain. Somehow he was in my mind as I remembered him riding along one of those very roads in his early youth, on his horse, Twilight. He had lost his hat in the run, his fair hair was shining; as they passed the M.F.H., Burton Persse called out 'tell your mother I'm prouder of Frank than if he wrote the Bible!' The dancing light in his eyes had never gone out, was, like his kindness, still unquenched.

His two daughters, with the husband of one, the widowed husband of another came on here for tea, I was glad to have them and welcome them. This is the one house left open of all our family owned. Michael Shawe-Taylor and his mother were here, she stayed the night.

19 APRIL. Mrs Gough here yesterday. . . .

I've been reading Sir William Butler's *Autobiography*,[1] lent me by Sergeant Breen, very interesting. I wish I had known him, could have done so probably had I heard more about him and his sympathies, especially in the Egyptian matter. He says of Arabi that his 'putting to death under the shelter of Khedival authority was an idea prefectly agreeable to persons in very high ministerial positions in England', and gives credit for saving his life to 'the devoted efforts made by Mr Blunt and a few other friends of justice at the time in London'. I may surely count myself among these. His account of the death of the Prince Imperial justifies that in the *Kiltartan History Book*, and it brings to mind Mrs Martin Harvey telling me that her father, a Spaniard, had been sent to break the terrible news to the Empress. She said 'when he went to her his hair was black. When he came home next day it had turned white in that terrible night.'

He tells of Froude[2] also who he had met at dinner at Wolseley's, and that Sir H. Brackenbury had said of that meeting 'Butler got more into his confidence and intimacy in a day than I had done in six months; in the woes of Ireland they had a subject of deep common interest to both', and Butler said 'His heart was set on Kerry.' (And that is why, when I sat next to Froude at dinner at the Ricardos and he was glum and said, I don't know in connection with what — 'people are so uninteresting nowadays', and I said 'Not where I come from.' And when he knew it was the West of Ireland he waked up and talked to me all the evening and he wrote next day 'it was a joy to meet you'; though I did not belong to Kerry, only to Galway.)

Typing my diaries still — now at last year. Not very cheerful for the Gallery matter seems to have gone back if anything since then.

22 APRIL. I have had a kind letter from Sean O'Casey, chiefly of sympathy and suggestions about Hugh's pictures, even proposing a protest made to the League of Nations — 'Wasn't France made to give back things taken during the Napoleonic wars? And Germany recently.' But I am a little sad because he supposes (rightly) that I have read his play sent to L.R. by now — : 'I think it is by far the best work I have done. It is I think very different to my previous work, I am correcting proofs now and it will be published in a few months' time. You must take from me the first copy sent to anyone.' And L.R. is abroad, and I don't know if Yeats has read it yet, and I can't write until all — Starkie also — give their opinion, and don't like to think he may print it without their criticism — and without seeing it on the stage.

26 APRIL. A telegram from M. yesterday saying the chicks are to have their photographs taken in Galway for passports and go over next Tuesday or Wednesday to Boulogne. They have been happy here and well, gaining health and strength, but I'm glad they should go to learn, at least French.

Yeats wrote yesterday 'I have had Metcalfe (the designer of the new coins) for a couple of days staying with me, gentle, sincere, and able, and overwhelmed with shyness. He was inarticulate until at breakfast alone with George he burst out about his twins and about a dreadful hour he spent with one when it was two months old, trying to make it drink out of a bottle — "She won; it was dreadful to be defeated like that." From that on he was comparatively eloquent on all topics. I am being given vaccine injections once a week, and that is to go on for three months.'

SATURDAY, 28 APRIL. Yesterday Yeats' letter came with his criticisms of Sean O'C.'s play. I've made a copy of it. It shows him in full (mental) health again. I have now, having made a copy to keep, sent it on to Sean. Of course it must be a severe blow, but I believe he will feel its force, its 'integrity' and be grateful in the end. I have sent him also L.R.'s less forcible out-cries, and my own few words, all I had a copy of. I had to send them on at once because he had written that he was 'Correcting proofs' for publication. And I have sent a fourth letter, from Yeats today, with suggestions as to what words to use if he does publish it. But I had a bad night, or early morning, thinking of the disappointment and shock he will feel.

Typing my old diaries, about the Civil war and the threatened break-up of the home — sad enough memories. Yet I was perhaps nearer to Heaven in those anxious troubled times than now when there are not the same strong emotions breaking the clods of everyday life.

I had written that two or three days ago, before this necessary rejection of S.O.'C's play had shattered the mind's content.[3]

1. *Sir William Butler, an autobiography*, ed. by his daughter Eileen Butler (London, 1911). [Sir William Butler (1838–1910), a British army general who saw action in South Africa and the Sudan, was born and died in County Tipperary.]

2. James Anthony Froude (1818–94), the noted historian. [His works include *The English in Ireland in the Eighteenth Century* (1872–4) and a novel, *The Two Chiefs of Dunboy* (1889), set in eighteenth-century Kerry.]

3. The Abbey's rejection of *The Silver Tassie* provoked a bitter quarrel between Yeats and O'Casey, who published all the correspondence in *The Observer* and in *The Irish Statesman*, together with his step by step rebuttal of Yeats's rejection of the play. Lady Gregory supplied him with copies of some of the correspondence. While they continued to write to each other, O'Casey refused to see Lady Gregory again in spite of her requests, a decision he deeply regretted after her death.

from Daniel J. Murphy (ed.), *The Journals*, Vol. 2 (1987)

JOHN McGAHERN

John McGahern grew up in the very rural counties of Roscommon and Leitrim, where not only the train to Sligo runs but also the upper reaches of the Shannon with its loughs, fish and water meadows. This is a place where social life seems not to have made much of an impression. Yet now and then on either bank there are those dark stands of trees that signify Big Houses. This is also the country of Woodbrook — in fact, characters called Kirkwood feature in other McGahern stories.

Many properties like Woodbrook changed hands during McGahern's boyhood in the 1940s, as he probably noted on his way by bicycle to school in Carrick-on-Shannon. No doubt he also took in the emptiness, the bleak lives and the small minds that in those days passed for society and civility. And there must have been a lot of timber knocking around then, one way and another.

Beecher's Brook is a notoriously difficult jump in the Aintree Grand National steeplechase. The first transatlantic telegraph cable was laid from Valentia Island, off the coast of Kerry, in 1857.

Why We're Here

Gillespie tested the secondhand McCullagh chainsaw as soon as he came from the auction, sawing some blown-down branches stacked against the wall of the house into lengths for firewood. The saw ran perfectly. 'Now to get rid of the evidence. For it'll not be long till he's up with his nose smelling unless I'm far out,' he said to the sheepdog when he'd finished. He carried the saw and sawn lengths into the shed, scattering the white sawdust wide into the grass with his boot. Then he farted. 'A great release that into the evening, thank God,' he sighed, as he waited for the aroma of the decomposing porter he'd drunk in Henry's after the auction to lift to his nostrils, his eyes going over the ground beside the stack of blown-down branches again. 'Not much evidence left that I can see. Nothing to do now but wait for him to arrive up.'

He was waiting at the gate when Boles came on the road, the slow tapping of the cattle cane keeping time to the drag of the old feet in slippers, sharply calling 'Heel' to his dog as a car approached from Carrick, shine of ointment over the eczema on his face as he drew close.

'Taking a bit of a constitutional, Mr Boles?'

'The usual forty steps before the night,' Boles laughed.

The two dogs had started to circle, nosing each other, disturbing the brown droppings of the yew. They stood in its shade, where it leaned above the gateway.

'Lepping out of your skin you are, Mr Boles. No holding the young ones in these days.'

'Can't put the clock back. The old works winding down, you know.'

'No future in that way of thinking. You're good for ten Beechers yet, if you ask me.'

They watched the dogs trying to mount each other, circling on the dead droppings of the yew, their flutes erect, the pink flesh unsheathed, and far off a donkey braying filled the evening with a huge contentment.

'At much, this weather?' Boles asked.

'The usual foolin' around. Went to the auction.'

'See anything there?'

'No, the usual junk, the Ferguson went for a hundred. Not fit to pull you out of bed.'

'Secondhand stuff is not the thing, a risk, no guarantee,' Boles said, and then changed to ask: 'Did I hear an engine running up this way an hour ago?'

'None that I know of.'

'I'd swear I heard an engine between the orchard and the house an hour ago.'

'Country's full of engines these days, Mr Boles. Can't believe your ears where they come from.'

'Strange.' Boles was dissatisfied, but he changed again to ask: 'Any word of Sinclair this weather?'

'The crowd up for Croke Park saw him outside Amiens Street with an empty shopping bag. They said he looked shook. Booked close enough to the jump.'

'Never looked healthy.'

'*The ignorance and boredom of the people of this part of the country is appalling, simply appalling,*' Boles mimicked an English accent quietly. 'That's the speech he'll make to Peter at the gate. A strange person.'

'Touched, that's all. I got to know his form well, the summer I bought this place from him and was waiting for him to shunt off. Especially when I was close to the house, mowing with the scythe there between the apple trees, he used to come and spout to the end of the world. The ignorance and the boredom but nothing about his own, bad, manners and the rain, speaking as one intelligent man if you don't mind to another, O Saecula Saeculorum world without end Amen the Lord deliver us. He even tried to show me how to put an edge on a scythe.'

'I knew him fifteen years here.'

'Fifteen too long, I'd say.'

'No, he was a strange person. He suffered from the melancholy.'

'But he had a pension, hadn't he, from that cable in Valentia?'

'No, it wasn't money troubled him.'

'*No reason why we exist, Mr Boles. Why we were born. What do we know? Nothing, Mr Boles. Simply nothing. Scratching our arses, refining our ignorance. Try to see some make or shape on the nothing we know,*' Boles mimicked again.

'That was his style, no mistaking, nature of the beast. The way he used to treat that wife of his was nobody's business.'

'In Valentia he met her, a girl in the post office. He used to cut firewood in the plantation, I remember, and he'd blow a whistle he had when he'd enough cut. She'd come running with a rope the minute she'd heard the whistle. It was a fair sight to see her come staggering up the meadow with a backload of timber, and him strolling behind, golfin' at the daisies with the saw, shouting *fore.*'

'Poor soft bitch. I knew a few'd give him fore, and the size of him in those plus fours. He should have stayed where he belonged.'

'*I am reduced to the final ambition of wanting to go back to look on the green of the billiard table in the Prince of Wales on Edward Road. They may have taken it away though. Sign of a misspent youth, proficiency at billiards,*' Boles mimicked again.

'On the same tack to me in the orchard. A strange coot. Luther's idea about women. The bed and the sink. *As good to engage a pig in serious conversation as a woman. All candles were made to burn before the high altar of their cunts. It was no rush of faith, let me tell you good sir, that led to my conversion. I was dragged into your Holy Roman Catholic Apostolic Church by my male member.* I'll not forget in a hurry how he came out with that spiff.'

'He had a curious blend of language sometimes,' Boles said.

'And he ends up after all his guff with an empty shopping bag outside Amiens Street Station.'

'A lesson, but I liked him. Great smell of apples in the evening.'

'Rotting on the ground. Wouldn't pay you to gather. Except a few hundredweight for Breffni Blossom. They don't mind the bruises.'

'Better than wastin' in the grass.'

The passing cars had their headlamps on now. A mile away, over fields of stone walks, the lighted windows of the nine-twenty diesel rattled past.

'Train to Sligo.'

'Empty, I suppose.'

'I suppose . . . Time to be moving in the general direction of the bed.'

'No hurry, long enough lying down in the finish. How is the eczema?'

'Stays quiet long as I don't go near timber. I've got this stuff on to keep the midges off.' He brushed his finger lightly along his cheek.

'If everything was right we'd appreciate nothing.'

'Still, I'd have sworn I heard a chainsaw up this way today,' Boles said as he turned to the road.

'Must have been from elsewhere,' Gillespie contradicted. 'What the wind can do with sounds is no joke.'

'There was hardly a puff of wind today.'

'Surprising what even a little can do, as the woman said when she pissed in the sea,' Gillespie laughed aggressively.

'I was certain, but time to go,' Boles said and called his dog.

'No use detaining you if you have, though it's young, the night, yet.'

'Goodnight then.'

'"Night, Mr Boles.'

He watched him go, the light tapping of the cattle cane in time to the drag of feet in slippers, calling 'Heel' to the dog as headlamps flooded the road from Boyle.

'That's what'll give him something to think about,' Gillespie muttered as he called his own dog back and turned towards the house.

from *The Collected Stories* (1992)

JOHN WATERS

From the late 1960s to his retirement from politics in 1992, Charles J. Haughey was Ireland's most successful and controversial politician. His success was considered all the more remarkable in the light of his having been tried on a charge of importing arms. This was in 1970, when Haughey was Minister for Finance. He was acquitted.

The words for which the acronym GUBU stand — 'grotesque, unbelievable, bizarre, unprecedented' — were uttered by Haughey himself, though the acronym, which for a time became a byword for the political scene, was coined by Conor Cruise O'Brien. The words arose in connection with the arrest of a murder suspect in the flat of the Attorney General in 1982.

Seán Doherty was held to be an emblem and omen of the political culture of Fianna Fáil in the 1980s. The Irish-American politician Tip O'Neill's celebrated dictum that 'all politics are local' has a distinctive resonance within the geographically, economically and psychologically limited confines of Irish parliamentary constituencies.

The Parable of the Fat Chieftain

During the seventies, when Charlie Haughey and his friend P.J. Mara drove around Ireland on what was known as the chicken and chips circuit, it is likely that they regularly crisscrossed my father's mailcar run. This is what democracy does to politicians: drags them down to earth, makes it harder for them to lose the run of themselves. For how can someone who has had to endure such indignity to get elected ever lose sight of the source of his power?

The two vehicles might never have met, but their occupants were of one mind. They all had decided that the destiny of their country depended on the accession to power of Charles J. Haughey.

Haughey's belief in this inevitability was perhaps understandably transparent, though far more complex than is commonly understood. My father's was part idealism and part perversity. He really did believe that Haughey offered the best chance the country had, but was altogether more attracted by the fact that almost all the people he least identified with in Irish public life — people like Conor Cruise O'Brien and Garret FitzGerald — had decided that Haughey would return more or less over their dead bodies. The positive aspects of his faith in Haughey's reascent to high office, therefore, were inextricably bound up with anticipatory glee at what consternation such an eventuality would bring down on the people whose dislike for Haughey was perhaps matched only by my father's suspicion of them.

Haughey chewed chicken and chips by night, and my father proselytised on his behalf by day. He never called him 'Charles Haughey', or 'C.J.', but simply 'Haughey' or 'Charlie', depending on the demeanour of the person he was talking to at the time.

From time to time, someone would attempt to stir the sediment of latent passions, as the argument swung back and forth over the ropes in the Thames 800.

'Sure, what has that fellow in common with the likes of us, and he with a big mansion above there in Dublin? Not to mention boats and helicopters to beat the band?'

'Arrah, what about it? Sure if he made himself rich, mightn't he make us rich as well?'

My father would let the argument rage on, sometimes pulling his handkerchief out to wipe the tears of laughter from his eyes. I had never known a subject to entertain him so much. In the end, he would invariably make the same declaration: 'In parts of Africa, where people don't have half enough to eat, people always like to have a fat chief. They think: if he is well-fed, at least he is a man who knows how to feed himself. And if he can feed himself, sure mightn't he be able to feed a few more of us as well. So the first thing you do if you want to be chief is fatten yourself up.'

'Of course,' he would add after a pause, 'there'll always be someone to say that if he's as fat as he is, then it must be because he left some other poor devil with only half enough to eat.'

As I grew into my twenties, in the same way as I communicated with my friends through talking about rock music, politics became perhaps the only language of proper communication between myself and my father. By 'politics', I mean politics as we had been born to them. My own 'politics' were different: I considered myself a sort of socialist, though I knew little about the theory of Marxism and as little as most other Irish socialists about the reality of its practice.

My 'socialism' was as much a reaction to what I perceived to be the betrayed promise of my generation, to the lack of opportunity in my life and surroundings, as my father's championing of Haughey was a reaction to the attitude of the chanters of the 'flawed pedigree' smear.

But politics, as talked about in the van, in the pubs, or in the streets of the town, was a different animal to the politics we heard discussed on the radio. The measure of a politician was his ability to get things done on behalf of not just his supporters but his constituents in general. A politician was a fixer of last resort: when you did not know what else to do about a problem, you consulted your TD. For some people, the line of last resort occurred at a much earlier stage than for others, but it was not the politician's function, nor in his interest, to comment on this. The sure sign of a successful politician was to hear someone say that, even though they had never voted for him, he had delivered some assistance that had not been obtained from other sources. If someone had already tried his own party's TD, without success, and had gone over to the other side and been helped, there was a very high likelihood that the vote, too, would change sides in the next election. Throughout the early years of the nineteen eighties, I heard this comment made about one politician with far more frequency than about any other local politician. That politician was Sean Doherty.

If you listened to the radio, of course, you would know that such activity was frowned upon. It was known as 'clientalism', and if you paid careful attention, you realised that even the politicians who most objected to it had become very adept at its practice. They resented having to do it, and they resented those who were better at it than they were.

Cryptic Jim understood clientalism, and approved of it thoroughly, but I myself, being a 'socialist', did not. I agreed with the voices on the radio. It seemed natural, therefore, that I should be opposed to everything for which Sean Doherty stood.

When there was trouble with the mailrun — the van needed a new engine and we could not afford it — my father and I would discuss the problem in calm and measured terms, and then would have a fight about Sean Doherty. My father liked and admired Doherty; he believed he was a decent man and a good politician. The fact that he was also on the Haughey wing of Fianna Fáil, and a loyal spear-carrier, was icing on the cake. But he never defended Doherty as passionately as when others — and particularly outsiders — were attacking him.

Throughout the period of the 1983–87 coalition, Doherty would be the subject of much discussion, though little debate. In a large part of the public imagination, he had come to personify all those characteristics in a politician which were to be avoided at all costs. His name had become shorthand for a particular political condition: he was the archetypal rural redneck who had been corrupted by a couple of whiffs of real power. Words seemed to cling to him and then to swell up into malign tumours of suggested improbity, menace and political malodorousness. Dowra, for example, was the name of a small village in County Cavan in which, one morning in September 1982, a man was due to appear in court as a witness in an assault case in which the defendant was Sean Doherty's brother-in-law. But on the morning of the court case, the witness was arrested by the RUC at the home of a friend across the border and so was prevented from giving evidence. Doherty's intervention was suspected, though never proved.

Dowra came to be imagined in the public mind as a place of perpetual darkness, a place where strange and improbable things occurred. Even for people who did not know where the village was, or precisely what significance it possessed in the Doherty legend, the word 'Dowra' somehow came to encapsulate all the sins that were to be laid at Sean Doherty's door: how he had tapped the telephones of two leading political journalists, Bruce Arnold of the *Irish Independent* and Geraldine Kennedy of the *Sunday Tribune*, because he believed them to be involved in a conspiracy with anti-Haughey members of Fianna Fáil to remove Haughey as leader of the party, and therefore also as Taoiseach; how he had assisted a fellow minister, Ray MacSharry, in bugging a conversation between MacSharry and one of the anti-Haughey wing, Martin O'Donoghue, in which MacSharry suspected that he might be offered a bribe to withdraw his support from Haughey. 'Bugging': there was another word, a word for people to roll around on their tongues, a word that seemed to embody all the sinister undercurrents which swirled around the depths of the GUBU year of 1982.

from *Jiving at the Crossroads* (1991)

JOHN HEALY

One of the people to whom John Healy dedicated Nobody Shouted Stop! *was Douglas Gageby, editor of* The Irish Times, *where Healy worked and where most of the book first appeared in a series of articles. It was Gageby who gave the material its focus by asking, as Healy recounted the sight of trains filled with tear-stained emigrants, why nobody stopped them. The author recalls, 'I said "there was no one — no one shouted stop".'*

Originally published in 1968 with the title Death of an Irish Town, *this book became instrumental in focusing attention on the social and economic neglect of the West of Ireland and on the possibilities of renewal offered by the European Union's regional policies. As John Hume states in his foreword to the book's second edition, Healy succeeded in getting the point across that 'indeed a further border existed; Ireland was two nations divided east and west, by the Rivers Bann and Shannon. To the east of the rivers the region prospered; to the west the second Ireland languished.'*

These words were written in 1988. The West still feels isolated.

Emigration

So many millions of words have been spoken and written these past thirty years about emigration that you are inclined to vomit at the mere mention of the word.

Politicians, good, rank bad, and totally different, have come to spurious power and survived for years on the promise to end it. Others refused to recognise it: social economists, recognising the word's bad odour and fatalistic connotation of political defeat, have abandoned the word and substituted the euphemism of 'outward social mobility' for emigration.

To the people in our town, it doesn't matter anymore what they call it.

The game is lost: it was over and finished before they knew it had started. Today a few leave Charlestown every year but it is merely the muscular spasms of a corpse: it is as nothing to the wartime exodus when they went out in train loads to send back hated John Bull's lovely pounds by wire and money order and in hard cash. The spawning beds are empty in the hill homes of the small farms in the Moy valley and the men who once came home with the Winter spawning salmon and stayed to fertilise the land and their women come no more. No more are the women content with a two-month-of-the-year-marriage and the loneliness of life without a husband and father: if they marry and mate it is to have a marriage for real in London or Birmingham or Wigan.

Today whole villages around Charlestown — for centuries the spawning streams of the people of Mayo and Sligo — are silted by depopulation and where in my memory there were shoals of children, more populous than the salmon parr in the town's rich river, no child plays and there is no promise of a child.

In less than twenty-five years, these villages have been emptied and the sociologists and economists and politicians and priests and bishops and Government Ministers will all give you differing reasons why.

All from their own remove and not without a defensive attitude which disclaims a major share in any blame you might feel like apportioning to their profession.

But do they really know?

What makes an emigrant? What are the pressures which drive a young man or a woman from the townland of his birth and his family, pathetically equipped mentally, to try and make a living in an alien milieu?

Every man has his own story; every girl her own reason. Not all are literate and where literacy is present it is not emigrants but the statements are conditioned by their knowledge that Healy is a newspaperman and he'll be writing about us and the people at home might read it, so be careful.

And what man, with a wife and three young children in another country, is going to talk about marital fidelity or tell you that to ease the sexual longing for that wife he will merely go home to a drab digs in Camden Town and to bed and there turn to the wall to commit the sin of loneliness? That, or get rip-roaring drunk.

No: you may imagine it, you may observe outward manifestations of the social phenomenon but unless you have been through the mill, you remain a recording outsider.

from *Nobody Shouted Stop!* (1988)

COLM TÓIBÍN

The Government of Ireland Act of 1920 provided for the setting up of two parliaments, in Belfast and Dublin. The border was a result of the polity of Northern Ireland thereby established. It runs for the best part of three hundred miles from Derry to Newry, snaking around the countryside in a highly unpredictable manner. To some it is an absurdity, to others a snake in the grass, but to most it is essentially a nuisance; and in all but a cartographic sense, the border is unmappable. One of its main effects has been to create a field day for smugglers.

British troops were introduced to Northern Ireland civil strife in 1969. The first US troops to be stationed there in World War II arrived in 1942.

This particular stretch of the walk is very near the home ground of William Carleton and John Montague.

The Road to Darkley

I went back to Monaghan and the next day hitched a lift to Roslea, having checked the map and made up my mind to walk northwards to Fivemiletown and the Clogher Valley.

It was only when the British soldier was going through my bags in the village of Roslea, that I understood why I had chosen this route; it was remote. I was unlikely to meet anyone, I was unlikely to hear any stories of killing, revenge, or grief. I now possessed an Ordnance Survey map, which was even more useless than the Michelin map I had been using previously. This map had too many roads, the other one had too few. In the face of such a plethora of roads it was hard to know where to go, so I followed my nose and went in the direction I thought was north. One thing was sure: the little river Finn had made another appearance, innocent-looking, brown, apparently directionless, it had come back to haunt me, and I crossed over it warily. I was in the South now, having walked along a track from the North. The road was uphill all the way.

There were two new houses being built as I passed, one exactly on the site of an old house, the gable wall of the old house still standing. The second house had an excellent view of the countryside around, but the main windows were looking out on to the road. I came to a T-junction and once more in front of me, as though I were a spiked stick being led in search of water, was the lazy Finn, doing another casual twist and turn. I checked the map to ensure that this was the last time I would see it.

A man on a tractor passed me; he kept looking behind at me, as though I were a ghost, as if to make sure I was still there. The fields were full of rushes; the further uphill I went, the bleaker it became. A big mongrel dog came running out after me barking and yelping. Soon its owner emerged, a man in his fifties who called the dog off. He was puzzled at my presence; not many people came along this way, he said. I told him I was walking to Fivemiletown. It was a long way, he said. The border was closed, but I could probably get across by foot, he told me. There was another crossing, but the road had been cratered in several places and it was now almost completely impassable.

The road narrowed further as a light mist started to come down. There was a pine forest now on either side of the road. I passed over the white 'X' painted on the road for helicopters to see that this was where the United Kingdom of Great Britain and Northern Ireland began. Soon the road petered out, and the old familiar spikes came into sight, my old friends, sticking up towards the sky from an ugly misshapen mass of concrete in a metal casing. Several abandoned cars lay around, rusting. There was, for a good distance, unrelieved muck. After the first spikes came a huge crater followed by more concrete and more spikes.

On the other side of these impediments stood an abandoned house. I had to walk on to the verge to try and remove the muck from my shoes. I met two forestry workers who told me that there was a turn ahead which led back into the South, the road blocked by more spikes, craters and concrete. Fivemiletown was a good walk still, but I had no choice but to persevere, as there were a number of hotels there where I could rest my feet and get shelter from the mist which was coming down harder. As the afternoon went on it grew cold, with hints of winter. There was no traffic on the road.

I went to bed as soon as I checked into the hotel in Fivemiletown, and slept for several hours. When I woke up I had a meal, a few drinks, a walk up and down the dreary main street, whose hidden secrets I left dark and unearthed, and then I went back to bed where I slept soundly until morning.

After breakfast the next morning I looked at the map once more, discovered that the mountain I had walked over was Slieve Beagh, and determined to walk over it again, but this time in an easterly direction towards Emyvale, Glaslough and Armagh. The main road was busy; cars went by at high speed, and I wanted to get on to a by-road as soon as I could. It was a cloudy day, but the clouds were soft, and it was warm.

The Union Jack flew over the Clogher Valley Free Presbyterian Church, part of Ian Paisley's empire. I turned right and began to climb once more, unsure of my route, the Michelin and the Ordnance Survey map contradicted each other, and neither seemed to correspond with the actual terrain. I passed three men who were standing in a barn looking intently at a cow's behind, one of them holding the tail up to give them a better view.

I came to Kell Methodist Church, and I asked the man who was painting the outside if he knew the way to the border. I told him I was walking. He said he hadn't been near the border for years, but he thought if I kept climbing I would find a crossing I could pass on foot. The sun began to shine. A woman watched me from a window, and moved to another window, and then another window in her new bungalow, looking out all the time, observing me. I could see the concern and fear in her face.

The forest then began again. There was a sign, announcing Fardross Forest and a river walk, which was a relief after the hard asphalt of the road. I crossed a wooden bridge and lay down on a bench for some time, before continuing on my way. There was nobody around. I emerged from the forest walk on to another road. When I went up a bit higher I could see the whole Augher-Clogher Valley down below. There was a watchtower on one of the adjacent hills.

I asked the first man I met about the watchtower. He told me there was an old landlord buried there, who had ordered the tower to be built as his tomb, the view was so spectacular, with so many different mountains on the horizon. It was a good place for your bones to rest, the man said. However, the landlord had been dug up, and the bones scattered by people hunting for treasure. Rumour had it that the lead coffin contained whiskey and a gold watch. Were the treasure hunters local people, I asked. No, it was the American army. Did he mean the

British army, I asked. No, he said, the American army, billeted here during the war, the Second World War, known as the Emergency in the South. Local people had fooled them into thinking that there was treasure in the landlord's tomb, and after a few drinks one night they had gone up the hill and opened the coffin.

He pointed out a couple making hay in a field below where we were standing. They seemed to be working hard. 'Strange what some people have to do to get by,' he said. The man was eighty-five and the woman was in her seventies, he said. They had one son who was married, but he had left the area.

It was a Catholic area, he said, but still no one went South. The South was expensive. The life here was hard in the winter, he said, especially when there was snow. Sometimes it didn't melt for weeks, and houses would be cut off. Cars couldn't come up, and he remembered that years ago in the winter, if someone died the coffin would have to be carried down the mountain to the valley. The land was bad, and the grants for drainage, which had been as high as ninety-five per cent, were now as low as twenty per cent. The army, he said, never came by road. They flew by helicopter. 'I'd say they'd give a fellow like you a good drilling,' he said, smiling at the thought of it. He warned me that he had been told that the army was about the place today. I should watch out for them.

The land moved from bogland to land where nothing grew. Signs that this was a game sanctuary appeared at regular intervals. Gorse appeared, and then heather. There were no houses or signs of habitation. The day became fine, the sun hot, the white clouds hovered on the horizon. Sometimes over the next few miles the land improved, and once I met a farmer and his son working in a field, saving hay. The border, they said, was just a mile away.

There was a light sound from the wind, a few hills and bare fields, patches of purple heather. I kept feeling that I was near the sea, that beyond the hill were sand dunes and the ocean. Then I saw the soldiers straight ahead, the first one lying flat on his belly pointing a rifle at some target in the nearest hill. He turned towards me, asking me for identification. I showed him my press card, and he told me to walk ahead to where the next soldier would want to talk to me.

The next soldier was friendly. I told him I was walking into the South, and he seemed interested in this, as though he would like to come as well. It was lovely here, he said, he liked this part of the world. It resembled the Falklands, he said, these colours, the bleak landscape, the heather, the quietness. In the Falklands, however, there were no trees at all, he said. He had liked it there as well; one day he went windsurfing in the South Atlantic, and that was really exciting; it was beautiful — he was followed by dolphins.

I could tell from the accent that he was Welsh. He had been away from his wife and kids for three months now, he said; he missed them, but would be home in a few weeks. Then he would be back for a longer stretch; he would be able to bring them with him, and they would have their own accommodation here in the North. He showed me his map, making sure that none of his comrades could see what he was doing. The map was incredibly detailed, every house, every field, every road, carefully denoted and described. It would be impossible to go wrong with such a map. Different colours made everything clear. He laughed when I explained my plight with maps. I showed him my Michelin and my Ordnance Survey, and he shook his head in wonder at how out-of-date they were. His was the map I should have, he said.

from *Walking Along the Border* (1987)

PATRICK KAVANAGH

Patrick Kavanagh grew up in rural County Monaghan, a fact that he never forgot and that he made a keystone not only of his poetry but of his artistic outlook. In doing so, he brought a new tone to Irish poetry, the sound of which continues to resonate. It is a tone of realism and harshness and coming to terms, very much the opposite of the picturesque and sentimental poetic lens through which the Irish countryside had usually been seen.

Kavanagh called his outlook 'parochial', by which he meant that its basis was a faithful reproduction of life as distinctively experienced by an author in his native place. Therefore, Ulysses, for example, would be a parochial work, and Kavanagh praised it as such. But this view's main influence was that it emboldened other poets — Seamus Heaney, for one — to put on the cultural map parts of the country which did not have obvious historical associations or other claims to fame.

In the first line of 'Shancoduff' there seems to be an echo of a sort of Shakespeare's 'My mistress' eyes are nothing like the sun' (Sonnet 130).

Shancoduff

My black hills have never seen the sun rising,
Eternally they look north towards Armagh.
Lot's wife would not be salt if she had been
Incurious as my black hills that are happy
When dawn whitens Glassdrummond chapel.

My hills hoard the bright shillings of March
While the sun searches in every pocket.
They are my Alps and I have climbed the Matterhorn
With a sheaf of hay for three perishing calves
In the field under the Big Forth of Rocksavage.

The sleety winds fondle the rushy beards of Shancoduff
While the cattle-drovers sheltering in the Featherna Bush
Look up and say: 'Who owns them hungry hills
That the water-hen and snipe must have forsaken?
A poet? Then by heavens he must be poor.'
I hear and is my heart not badly shaken?

from *Collected Poems* (1991)

MAURICE CRAIG

Belfast as it is today is a recent phenomenon as these things go in Ireland. Originally a settlement named for the mouth of the river Farset — which now runs underground — its present character and social makeup are largely products of the nineteenth century. Renowned for its heavy engineering plants and linen mills, it is also where the United Irishmen began in 1791, and from them, Irish republicanism. Belfast officially became a city in 1888, thanks to Queen Victoria. Its City Hall dates from 1906. Murals of King Billy — William of Orange — on his white horse are commonplace in certain neighbourhoods.

Maurice Craig was born and raised in Belfast, though he has written: 'I am a Dubliner of many years' standing and by my own choice, and if I belong anywhere Dublin is where I belong.'

The poem was written about 1940.

Ballad to a Traditional Refrain

Red brick in the suburbs, white horse on the wall,
Eyetalian marbles in the City Hall:
O stranger from England, why stand so aghast?
May the Lord in His mercy be kind to Belfast.

This jewel that houses our hopes and our fears
Was knocked up from the swamp in the last hundred years;
But the last shall be first and the first shall be last;
May the Lord in His mercy be kind to Belfast.

We swore by King William there'd never be seen
An all-Irish Parliament at College Green,
So at Stormont we're nailing the flag to the mast:
May the Lord in His mercy be kind to Belfast.

O the bricks they will bleed and the rain it will weep,
And the damp Lagan fog lull the city to sleep;
It's to hell with the future and live in the past:
May the Lord in His mercy be kind to Belfast.

NELL MCCAFFERTY

Peggy Deery may not be Mother Courage exactly, but, as Nell McCafferty sees her, she crystallises the challenges, hardships and vulnerabilities of being a working-class member of the minority population in Northern Ireland. In Derry, however, this minority is in the majority. But notorious gerrymandering prevented this numerical superiority from being appropriately represented.

Left with fourteen children when her husband died in 1971, Peggy is presented as having no alternative but civil disobedience. 'Only one of Peggy Deery's . . . children has ever held a steady permanent job.' Two of her sons were killed within weeks of each other shortly before Peggy's own death in 1988, aged fifty-four.

'When Peggy died . . . she was still in debt. Her electricity bill showed that she was in arrears to the tune of £972.89; the outstanding rent on her house amounted to £512.63. It is perfectly normal for Derry people living on welfare to die in such debt today.'

A Welfare War

D erry has become known as 'pothole city', an appellation as cynical as it is accurate. It is widely accepted that not all who claim damages have sustained injury from falling into potholes. It is difficult for the British Government to refute the claims, since police do not patrol the streets, the army is in too much of a hurry to notice, property is regularly damaged by the security forces in smash-and-grab raids for weapons, and barricades spring up regularly. Also, the people of Derry have learned to show as much disregard for the awesome obligations of truth under British oath as have the guardians of law and order. The testimony of the Bloody Sunday regiment, which was not rejected by the Court of Inquiry, set the standard. Commenting on the outcome of the inquiry, the leader of the Nationalist Party, Eddie McAteer, said, 'At least the judge didn't find the dead guilty of committing suicide.'

The corrosion of morality is captured in an apocryphal story about pothole city. One man says to another man on crutches, 'Have you been to see your solicitor?' The cripple replies: 'I saw him before I fell.'

There was no government challenge to Peggy's claim of falling. The injuries sustained on Bloody Sunday had left her with a shortened leg and a foot without feeling. The shortest journey resulted in chafed and bleeding skin around a hole in her heel that never healed. She fell constantly. The British Army called her 'chicken-leg'.

Soldiers cheerfully signed chits for damages to her home after each ransack. The Emergency Provisions Act, also exclusive to the North, allows them to wreck doors, windows, floorboards and furniture at will. Refurbishment by government is slow, the tardiness excused on grounds of cost and cut-backs in public expenditure, and the increasing expense of maintaining a standing army in the North.

The British Army was the direct cause of Peggy Deery's acquisition of what was, in welfare terms, a fortune. The government paid her £14,000 compensation for her Bloody Sunday injuries. She lavished a great portion of that on her son Paddy. Money was also spent on family travel to the various prisons where some of her children were lodged as they reaped the bitter harvest of involvement after Bloody Sunday; each prison visit also meant the expense of a food parcel, and money lodged for cigarettes for the prisoner. Peggy supported also out of her fortune those of her children who fled across the border, seeking refuge or escape.

It did not last, but while it lasted she was generous, distributing cash gifts on the birthdays of her children and grandchildren and of her sisters and brothers, and at Christmas. As the fortune dwindled, she was obliged to cut the sums in half. A seasonal note to her sister Nellie caught her mood exactly as she faced a return to poverty:

Dear Nellie,

Here is a fiver. I'm sorry Nellie, it's all I can give you. Between children and grandchildren I'm effed off.
Love,
Peggy.

She never relinquished the most obvious status of wealth. The telephone which was at first an indulgence became a necessity as Peggy Deery kept urgent track of her fourteen children's whereabouts. The calls at dawn came invariably from police stations or hospitals or priests or solicitors. She learned because of the phone that one of the most enduring myths about the wartime North was untrue. This was that people who ran up telephone bills would never be cut off if they had an IRA relative in the family. Despite Paddy's involvement, and army interest in him, Peggy's phone was cut off in 1986 when he spent a short period in jail.

The family had a collection and the bill was paid. The government-run company accepted the money and sent her a letter which left her furious:

You are required to pay a further amount of £150 by way of security for payment in respect of further service. Deposit will be retained for a minimum of one year. The rate of interest is 6 per cent per annum.

Peggy wrote this off as a bad investment and had a new line installed in the married name of one of her daughters. The government's computer intelligence was unable to cope with such a ruse. The cost of the new installation was minimal, and of course the new client had a credit-worthy reputation which would ensure years of debt-in-good-faith.

from *Peggy Deery* (1989)

EAMONN McCANN

The city of Derry resonates with the historical background to the present civil conflict in Northern Ireland much more than Belfast does. The fact that it had its name changed to Londonderry in 1613 as a result of plantation is one feature of that background. Another is the famous seven-month siege in 1688–9, a powerful symbol of resistance to unwanted outsiders. The city walls are still in a sufficient state of repair and visibility to lend such symbolism support. Even the very names of the city's neighbourhoods — Bogside, Waterside — identify not merely communities but strictly demarcated territories.

Derry has seen some pivotal events in the current disturbances. Among these are police violence at a 1968 civil rights march — quite possibly the one in Dermot Healy's A Goat's Song; the 'explosion' of August 1969 — the 'Battle of the Bogside' — when the Royal Ulster Constabulary lay siege to that neighbourhood; the creation of so-called 'no-go areas' in the Bogside and Creggan Estate, where for a sustained period the writ of the security forces did not run; and the events of Bloody Sunday, 30 January 1972.

The Provisional IRA

Much has been written about the emergence of the Provos, almost all of it silly moralising. The Provisional IRA was not created by a section of the Fianna Fáil Party, although some money from Fianna Fáil sources did ensure that it was better financed at the outset than would otherwise have been the case. Nor was it the creation of a few blood-lusting Catholic Nationalists in the North. Nor, despite the paranoiac ramblings of churchmen and contributors to the *Daily Telegraph*, is it part of an international terrorist conspiracy to destroy civilisation as we know it.

The machinery of government could not operate democratically. It was not designed for the job. So the fight for a democratic Northern Ireland was always likely to become a fight against the state itself. The 'national issue' was going to be posed. The only question left open was: by whom and in what form?

When, in January 1969, Johnnie McMenamin saw a crowd of men in his street in the middle of the night smashing up houses and beating up his neighbours and rushed to the telephone to dial 999 he was reacting as any working-class person in an 'ordinary' society would to such a spectacle. But what does one do when it is the police themselves who are doing the marauding? Who then does one call in?

A few months later that question would have been answered in the Bogside with: 'the British Army'. And when the army begins to behave exactly as the police had done, what then?

One turns to oneself, there being no one else, and tries to put together an organisation as capable as possible of repelling the assaults. In the short term the politics of the defence group is irrelevant. It is irrelevant whether it has any politics at all. The long term is different. On a day-to-day basis defence groups can prevent random arrests, assaults and worse in an area simply by refusing admission to forces so intentioned. But tiny enclaves cannot exist in isolation for ever.

In 1970 the poster most frequently to be seen in windows and on gable walls in the Bogside and the Falls depicted a clenched fist and the words: 'Never Again!' Never again were mobs, whether in uniform or not, going to be allowed to rampage through the streets shooting and petrol bombing. The logic of that demanded that an offensive military campaign be launched against the state. When it is the state itself which threatens to destroy you it is necessary to attack the state, not just to defend oneself against *its* attacks, to try to ensure that there will be no repetition.

The trajectory of events led inevitably to a military campaign against the existence of Northern Ireland. The responsibility for the launching of the campaign rests entirely with those who created the situation which made that inevitable; that is, with the British ruling class and its agents in Ireland. That said, one can analyse why the campaign took the form that it did, how the politics of the activists involved developed and what, in the light of that, ought now to be done.

In 1968 and 1969 the left and the right, the 'militants' and the 'moderates' in the civil rights movement, were united on one point: that partition was irrelevant. No meeting was complete without at least one speaker declaring that we wished to make it clear that we were not setting out to unite Ireland, rather to achieve change within Northern Ireland — the extent of the change desired varying according to the tendency to which the speaker adhered. This was in line with the general drift of Catholic politics for the previous decade.

The left was, if anything, even more determined than other anti-Unionist groups to 'keep partition out of it'; and for reasons which were not ignoble. The partition issue had for so long been the 'property' of what we regarded as contending Tory factions that the mere mention of it smacked of jingoism. The result was that when, in 1969–70, Catholics in Belfast and Derry were, in the literal sense of the word, forced to raise partition there was no existing organisation for them to turn to naturally. So they created one. The Provisional IRA — notwithstanding allegations to the contrary from various 'leftists' in Ireland and Britain — did not 'bring partition into it'. The Provisional IRA exists because partition was going to come into it whether or not the right, the left, or anyone else thought this advisable.

from *War and an Irish Town* (1974)

PERCY FRENCH

Although set in London, rather than Boston or New York, 'The Mountains of Mourne' is perhaps the best-known Irish popular song about emigration and emigrants. It also shows to good effect the common touch and eye for detail that have ensured a permanent place for Percy French's numbers in the repertoire of Irish popular music. The songs and the popularity French attained in performing them make him an important figure in the history of stage-Irishness.

His early years as an engineer in rural Ireland — mainly in County Cavan — undoubtedly gave French a more varied acquaintance with provincial life than, as a son of the Big House, he might otherwise have had. But the charm of his work is also partly due to how it allows his own disarming view of himself to come through: 'I was born a boy and have remained one ever since.'

The music for most of Percy French's songs was written by his friend Houston Collison. And the mountains of Mourne, in south-eastern County Down, are certainly a sight to behold. They really do sweep down to the sea.

The Mountains of Mourne

Oh Mary this London's a wonderful sight
With people here working by day and by night.
They don't sow potatoes nor barley nor wheat
But there's gangs of them digging for gold on the streets.
At least when I axed [asked] them that's what I was told,
So I just took a hand at this digging for gold.
But for all that I found there I might as well be,
Where the Mountains of Mourne sweep down to the sea.

I believe that when writin' a wish you expressed
As to how the fine ladies in London were dressed
Well if you believe me, when asked to a ball
Faith they don't wear a top to their dresses at all
Oh, I've seen them myself and you could not in truth
Say if they were bound for a ball or a bath,
Don't be startin' them fashions now, Mary macree
Where the Mountains of Mourne sweep down to the sea.

I've seen England's king from the top of a bus
I've never known him, tho' he means to know us
And tho' by the Saxon we once were oppressed
Still I cheered, God forgive me, I cheered with the rest
And now that he's visited Erin's green shore
We'll be much better friends than we've been heretofore
When we've got all we want we're as quiet as can be
Where the Mountains of Mourne sweep down to the sea.

You remember young Peter O'Loughlin of course
Well now he is here at the head of the Force
I met him today, I was crossing the Strand
And he stopped the whole street with one wave of his hand
And there we stood talkin' of days that are gone
While the whole population of London looked on
But for all these great powers he's wishful, like me
To be back where the dark Mourne sweeps down to the sea.

There's beautiful girls here — oh never you mind
With beautiful shapes Nature never designed
And lovely complexions all roses and cream
But O'Loughlin remarked with regard to the same
That if at those roses you venture to sip
The colours might all come away on your lip
So I'll wait for the wild rose that's waitin' for me
Where the Mountains of Mourne sweep down to the sea.

from Mrs de Burgh Daly (ed.), *Prose, Poems and Parodies of Percy French*
(1929)

ART MAC CUMHAIGH

After the Battle of the Boyne (1690) and the Battle of Aughrim, followed by the Treaty of Limerick, the following year — all unhappy defeats — the aristocratic Catholic polity of Ireland lay in ruins. Rapid social and cultural deterioration followed as victorious English interests consolidated their control of the country.

The immediate literary response in Irish was a body of poetry consisting for the most part of bitter elegies for the passing of the ancien régime. *As the eighteenth century wore on, a modified form of these laments emerged. This form is known as* aisling, *or dream poem. Typically, the poet is discovered in a depressed state by a beautiful, spectral woman, who usually identifies herself as Ireland. She kindles the poet's imagination and lifts him out of his dispirited condition. The* aisling *tends to be very accomplished technically and verbally felicitous.*

Grainneog is in County Westmeath. The Fews is an area of County Armagh. Niall Frasach was High King of Ireland in the eighth century. Nell McCafferty has reported the pleasure of Sunday strolls in Creggan graveyard, Derry, with its 'sense of beauty, freedom and reward'.

Fair Churchyard of Cregan

At Cregan churchyard last night
I slept in grief.
And out of the dawnlight
That crimsoned her cheek
A maiden, gold fibre in her hair,
Came to kiss me. Just to stare
On that princess lifted the blight
From the world and gave it relief.

'Good-hearted man, don't be depressed,
Lighten that sorrowful glance;
Rise and come with me to the west
Where the land's not under the trance
Of the stranger; it's honey-sweet there,
And in the high halls the fair
Strains of the music will bless
Your ear and enchant.'

'I would not refuse you, not for the gold
Hoarded by all the kings
That lived since the days of old.
But the thought that stings

Is deserting my friends, for I care
For all that remain and more for my fair
Wife to whom in her youth I told
Promises to which her heart clings.'

'You have none left alive,
No family nor friends,
Not a jot or a jive
Do you own. You can't fend
For yourself, you are bare,
Hopeless, with nothing to share.
Instead of my filigree love, you'd abide
By your verses that all here deride?'

'O princess, of royal line,
Are you the Helen that brought
Armies to ruin? Or one of the nine
From Parnassus, so sweetly wrought
In their beauty? Star in clear air,
In what land, by what or where
Did you find nurture? And why is mine
The voice you want, as we go west, in your thought?'

'Don't question me; I do not sleep
On this side of the Boyne.
I'm a changeling; on the steep
Side of Grainneog, from the loin
Of fairy race I'm sprung; all aver
It is I who stir music where
There are true poets — in Tara by deep
Night, by morning on the plains of Tyrone.'

'It stabs me to know
The Gaels of Tyrone are gone,
The heirs of the Fews are low
Under the slabbed stone;
Niall Frasach's noble heirs
Who would not forsake verse
And at Christmas would bestow
Robes on those whose tribute was their song.'

'Since the tribes were torn apart
At Aughrim and, alas, the Boyne,
The Irish, who always gave support

To the learned, cannot again conjoin.
Wouldn't it be better, then, to be there
With us in the magic mounds where,
Instead of Orange arrows in your heart,
Each midday you'll have me, closely joined?'

'If it is foretold,
Princess, you are to be my love.
I would have to hold
You to an oath before we move
West on the road. Swear
That when I die, no matter where,
By the Shannon, the Isle of Man, in Egypt old,
I will be laid under in Cregan, its sweet soil above.'

translated by Seamus Deane, from his *Selected Poems* (1988)

SAM McAUGHTRY

'*A good funeral*' *used to be a common phrase meaning that there was a large turnout at the chapel and the graveyard. This was in the days before motorised hearses, morticians and so on. But these were funerals that took place where traffic jams were unlikely to arise. It is intriguing to picture mourners, neighbours and general hangers-on sauntering together towards a city cemetery. Such an image gives a flavour of a Belfast that still seems not very well known — an intimate, folksy sort of place. No such Belfast enters the thoughts of people in the South, who — if they think of the city at all — tend to see it as the home of the bitter word, the virtually foreign accent, dark, satanic mills, and televised funerals over which helicopters hover.*

Sam McAughtry would well appreciate going to Cheltenham race week, having for many years written a column for The Irish Field.

Funerals Have Lost Their Style

The working classes are in the grip of very severe changes. Take funerals. There's no great distance walked nowadays. Two or three yards for the sake of appearances, then pull in to the side and everybody into the motors.

Of course, some people say that you can't very well have a whole parade of family and friends walking along and causing traffic jams. I maintain that we never should have given way on that one. Flute bands didn't. There's no limit to the number of flute bands that you see out collecting for new instruments or uniforms, and they're not one bit worried about causing traffic jams. The cars can stretch behind them from Carrickfergus to Cork and it's all one to the fluters, and surely if it's good enough for them it's good enough for funerals.

There was something very special about dandering along the road with your hands behind your back, picking away at the man beside you, to see how much you could find out about the ones in front of you. It's not every day you get the chance of a nice leisurely conversation walking along behind the hearse. This goes particularly for family funerals. That second cousin who went away to Birmingham thirty years ago, why has he turned up for this one? Is he sounding the family out, to see who's going to be mug enough to put him up, now that he's ready for the pension? Oh yes, it's how are ye, and many a time I thought about ye, but there's some of us had to bunch up to get the fare for Birmingham for him in nineteen and forty nine, and we're waiting for our money back yet.

There used to be a time when the transport was only needed to bring the men back from the graveyard — you walked the whole road there, and apart from taking your turn with the lift, the journey was hardly noticed, the conversation was that good. Mind you, it was generally slow enough to start with, but once the pace had been established, and you were settled in with your chosen company, away you went, talking and listening, chewing the gossipy bits, remarking on the weather, comparing notes on the horse results with relations from across the water. 'Did you manage to get Monksfield in the Champion Hurdle?' you ask. 'Did I get it?' he'll say, 'sure I was at Cheltenham and saw the race.' 'Get away now,' you reply, 'isn't that great. Actually going to Cheltenham, eh?' And then whenever it's your man's turn for a lift, you say to the one beside you: 'His old fellow was a bit of a blow, and I see where it runs clear down the line.'

Oh aye, there was a great spice about funerals at one time. But what have you now? Walk the length of yourself and you're bundled into a big car, and with my luck, put beside the clergyman more than likely. You'll not hear much inside a motor car; by the time you've finished passing the smokes round you're turning into the cemetery and your chance is over.

And even after you get back it's not the same. If you say you're not staying long everybody looks relieved. I remember the time when you were considered an ignorant plug if you didn't stay between the house and the pub till the small hours of the morning, after a funeral.

I was at a funeral a while ago there. A far out friend. Do you know this? From start to finish of the whole performance there wasn't the slightest indication of trouble in the family. All pals together; christian names and letting on they were the best of friends, when I happen to know that the same crowd were eating each other. In fact, a while back solicitors' letters were on the go.

A funeral was always the time when the like of that came to the surface. Hints and dirty digs all night; references to breeding; remarks like Thank God there's nobody'll be able to say a word about me or my debts when my time comes. Some woman jumping to her feet and saying to her man: 'Get me my coat, for I'll have to go home out of this!' And then, after she's left, everybody saying: 'Sure that one never had any skin on her face. What would you expect from a spinner in the mill?'

It's all gone, the atmosphere. The whole life's away out of funerals. Even if I was to get my way, and I was to walk it the whole road to the cemetery, I would be the only one doing it, for everybody has their own cars now anyway. At this funeral I was at recently, the last remaining relic of family strife was the way a woman would clearly gloat when her man's motor car was better than somebody else's. But of course that's no good. The only one to get any pleasure out of a situation like that's the car owners. Nobody else can join in, the way we did in the old days.

But mind you, you think you're bad till you hear of somebody worse. Last week old Davy Brady was complaining about the unseemly haste at funerals too. 'I mind the time I could have joined the mourners walking along the street, and didn't even know if the departed was a man or woman. But during the long walk,' says he, 'it was easy to find out, listening to the others around me.' He shook his head. 'Twice a week I could have touched for a drink from people who thought I was a friend of the family. But sure you've no chance now,' he said, 'funerals go a mile a minute. There's no style left in them any more.'

from *Belfast Stories* (1981)

GEORGE SIGERSON

Enniskillen is included with other famous victories — 'Derry, Aughrim and the Boyne' — in 'The Sash', the anthem of unionist Ulster, for having withstood the Jacobites in the siege of 1689. And the town is associated with two regiments. The Enniskillen, Enniskilling, or Inniskilling Dragoons date almost from the town's prominence as the westernmost outpost of the Elizabethan empire in Ulster. That regiment, present in the modern British army as both the Inniskillings (6th Dragoons) and the 5th Royal Inniskilling Dragoon Guards, was initially formed during the reign of James I. Its regimental badge is Enniskillen Castle. The other regiment is the Royal Inniskilling Fusiliers, the 'Skins'. This was raised initially in 1689 as Tiffin's Regiment of Foot. Its regimental badge is a grenade surmounting Enniskillen Castle. Both regiments have certainly won 'fame in the war'.

'The Inniskillen Dragoon' is a staple both of folksingers, where it is done slowly, and in the repertory of British army bands, where it is a brisk, if not downright brazen, march.

The Inniskillen Dragoon

Farewell, Inniskillen! farewell for awhile,
To all your fair waters and ev'ry green isle!
Oh your green isles will flourish, your fair waters flow,
While I from old Ireland an exile must go.

Her hair is as brown as the young raven's wing,
Her eyes are as clear as the bluebells of spring;
And light was her laugh, like the sun on the sea —
Till the weight of the world came between her and me.

Oh, what can man do when the world is his foe —
And the looks of her people fall on him like snow,
But bend the brow boldly, and fare away far
To follow good fortune and get fame in the war?

If the worst comes to worst, sure 'tis only to die,
And the true lass that loves me can hold her head high;
Can hold her head high, though the fond heart may break,
For her lover loved bravely, and died for her sake.

from *Songs and Poems* (1927)

POLLY DEVLIN

Ardboe, or sometimes Arboe, is in County Tyrone, on the western shore of Lough Neagh. The High Cross was once a place of pilgrimage, and the waters where the youngsters swim were considered therapeutic. As well as the subjects mentioned, the cross depicts some twenty scenes from the Old and New Testaments, including Adam and Eve, the Sacrifice of Isaac, the Adoration of the Magi, and Cain and Abel.

High crosses date from the ninth and tenth centuries, and together with their height — the one at Ardboe is eighteen feet tall — and ornamentation are recognisable from the circle that seems to pass through the actual crosses' arms and shaft. The finest examples are those at Ahenny, Co. Tipperary, Monasterboice, Co. Louth, and Clonmacnoise, Co. Offaly.

It is piquant to think that while young Polly Devlin was keeping her ear to the ground, twenty-odd miles to the north, her future brother-in-law, Seamus Heaney, was also attuning himself to the pulse of things.

Ardboe

Our cohesion is not just a matter of a close family feeling or material connections. An outside influence or presence joins us together too, holds us literally in place — Muinterevlin, that ragged, low-lying place in which we were born — and, however we move, the place runs in on us as though to hold us tighter. We still converge on it as often as possible and, as we journey down the Moor Hill Road, we listen intently for the first distant sound of the water. As soon as we can hear it we know we are home, however permanent the place we have come from appears to be. For all of us the lough defines that place on the interior map which makes home uniquely home, so that any other place can always only be somewhere else: a simulacrum of the real place and outside our imaginative grasp.

The name of our townland, one of the thirty that makes up the Parish of Ardboe, is Muinterevlin, meaning in Gaelic 'the country of the Devlins', and the land over which we roam is composed of a body-mould of our forbears, dug and turned into the earth, fertilising it, flavouring it, and the very soil steeped in us, the surface exuding an aura and an odour of us. The old and heavy earth there seems to be as alive as we are, powered by a different kind of life motion, one that is infinitely slower, each heartbeat lasting decades, but to which we are connected. I sometimes think that if I could put my ear to it at the right time I might catch the throb, just as one glittering day I will see the flower on Lizzie's peony that only blooms every seven years, or find the apocryphal piece of wood petrified into stone by the lough water that I buried each year so long ago.

Muinterevlin reaches further into the lough than any other of the small fingers of land along the shore, all of which tentatively dip in to the water as though not sure of the welcome or depth and then dissolve gently into sedgy watery swamp before giving into the water. The edges are held down by boulders, tussocks, osiers and rushes. Just where Muinterevlin reaches the water it suddenly rears up, into Ardboe Point. It is the only hill on the long side of the lough shore and on its very tip stands the Cross reputed to have been built by St Colman and his monks in the seventh century. Behind it, a small graveyard surrounds the ruins of the monks' small church and almost vanished abbey. The graveyard is our magic playground and the Cross pins it to the ground.

The word Ardboe means 'high cow' in Gaelic, and the most romantic and most often repeated explanation for the name is that the mortar used for building the Cross and church was mixed with the milk of a magic cow, which gave it its staying power. Whatever the source of the liquid used to build the Cross and church, cow milk or lough water, it has been standing there, on the only eminence within ten miles, for over thirteen hundred years. The position of the small primitive group of holy buildings silhouetted against water and sky affects us, and most visitors, to initial stillness and silence. The crumbling arched windows frame the perpetual movement of the small crested waves of the lough, and more often than not the two white swans who nest on the Rock Shore, further round from the Cross Point, swim within the serene arched frame.

The Celtic Cross is an extraordinary monument, towering twenty feet and more above us. It is made of massive stone blocks, and each of the four sides of each great block are carved into panels illustrating episodes from the Bible and the Apocrypha. These carvings were once sharp and detailed but are now blurred into indentations and soft shapelessness by the rain and wind of a millennium. Like many Celtic crosses, the High Cross is ringed by four stone arcs at the junction of the shaft and arms, but two of these arcs have fallen away and lie in fragments at the base of the Cross. For years emigrants leaving for England, Scotland and the Americas have taken a small piece of these sacred stones with them as mementoes of what they have had to leave behind. With the advent of cars and a consequent increase in the number of visitors who also took a piece of the old stone as a souvenir, the Cross began to show signs of damage and the Ancient Buildings Authority have had high railings erected around it to prevent further depredations. At the same time, in the 1930s an official caretaker was appointed to look after the Cross, the graveyard and the abbey. The job was given to an old great-uncle (everyone in the district is inter-related) who is known for some lost reason as the Needle. He knows the arcane meanings and allegories illustrated in each panel of the Cross, and expounds them in a version handed down orally over the centuries. He is sensible to a fault of his official position and the standing it gives him — or he thinks ought to give him — in the community. He is the official expounder of the meaning of the Cross: its reading.

Returned emigrants, amateur archaeologists, strangers out for a day's jaunt, historians or scholars can easily prevail on him to read it, but it would not occur to him to read it to us, nor to us to ask him. We know he would think it a conceit, a waste of time, so what we learn is what we overhear. Since the Needle speaks our strong local dialect, few listeners from outside the parish can understand more than a few words, but no one's enjoyment seems to be lessened by this lack of comprehension.

The Needle is usually either leaning on his gate watching his small world, meander or cycle by, or is sitting on one of the tombstones surveying the lough and keeping an eye out for the water bailiff. Whenever anyone deemed worthy of having the Cross read arrives at its base, he leaves his vantage point and hurries to the Cross. Getting the keys from about his person is a business: he plunges about the waist and pockets of his ancient trousers and coats, scrabbling among pieces of fishing-line, impaling his fingers on eel-hooks, invoking the Holy Family under his breath and asking St Anthony to help him — this kind of search is called 'hoking'. Finally he finds the keys, opens the padlocked iron gate set into the rails with considerable flourish, steps in, closes the gate and looks out grandly at those left outside the barricade. Favoured visitors are occasionally allowed in with him to look more closely at the carvings. We are permanently banished and lurk outside, derisive but fascinated. There is an anticipatory silence.

The Needle hawks at his throat, spits on the ground, stabs at the Cross with his blackthorn stick, glares at the visitors and begins. He always begins on the East panels. 'The East panels. Here's Solomon, the wise man, axed to judge which of the two women's ba it is; both of them say it's theirs. He has a houldt of the ba by its two legs, here's the two legs.' (He jabs at two faint indentations.) 'And here's the sword he's lifting to cleave the child in two. That's to see who's the rightful mother. Whichever mother didn't want the child's head split, she would be the mother.' He looks around as though he has passed the judgement of Solomon himself. Those of his audience who understand some of what he has said murmur in admiration, the others, whispering, ask what he has said. He waits until the murmurs have ceased and stabs this time at the panel above. 'This here's Solomon with all couped round him. Above that Abraham has a lamb by the lugs.'

We love the Solomon story, that ancient marvellous test of mother-love, and savour the dreadful end of Samson and listen half in respect, half in derision, while the Needle, between expositions, beetles at us, trying by facial ferocity to make us go away. He resents our presence deeply, since he isn't explaining the panels for us and has, as he often says only loud enough for us to hear, 'a dale more to do nor talking to childer'; but he knows if he bids us more overtly to depart, his foolish and foreign audience might intervene on our behalf.

One memorable day I found the padlocked gate open and crept in, thrilled and fearful. The great Cross loomed high above me. The road past Treanor's towards our house looked different viewed through bars. I put my hand on the warm stone of the Cross for the first time and suddenly the Needle stepped out from behind it. I leapt with guilt. 'Get out,' he said, 'and away up the road with you, you skitter. You're like a musheroon. You couldn't be watched. You're not there one time, but the next time you look you were there all the while.'

We spend a great deal of our time — as much as we can get away from school — by the Old Cross and down by the lough shore. To reach it is a matter of walking four hundred yards along the road edged with a prodigal quantity of wild grasses, fruits and flowers. Hawthorn tumbles over bramble and wild roses, and below these bushes, sedges and wild strawberries grow profusely as well as sorrel, which we eat as part of our daily diet, examining each leaf with deep suspicion for the foamy sign of cuckoo sally. Odium attaches to eating this. We think the foam harbours worms, or rather that it breeds them, that they spring from the foam itself.

from *All of Us There* (1983)

JOHN MONTAGUE

John Montague is from County Tyrone, which, he has said, 'a Belfast poet [John Hewitt] once called "the heart land of Ulster"'. The townland where Montague grew up is called Garvaghey, which roughly translated means 'rough field'. He recalls that going back there 'in the early sixties . . . I had a kind of vision, in the medieval sense, of my home area, the unhappiness of its historical destiny. And of all such remote areas where the presence of the past was compounded with a bleak economic future, whether in Ulster, Brittany or the Highlands of Scotland . . .' Out of that vision, the long poem The Rough Field *grew.*

Dancehalls have also been landmarks in the career of a former leader of the Fianna Fáil party and Taoiseach, Albert Reynolds. In fact, one of the halls in his chain was a Roseland, though not the one mentioned here.

The early 1960s were the heyday of purpose-built dancehalls and the showbands that filled them. One of the pioneering and most popular bands at the time were effectively neighbours of Montague's, the Clipper Carlton, from Strabane.

Dancehall

And there, on a ravaged hillock
    overlooking the road,
the raw inheritor of this place,
    an unfinished hall.
Stung to soberness in the dawn
    I sway and stare.
Its blank eyes — gaps in concrete —
    stare blindly back.

Seemsh no escape. Poet and object
    must conshumate.
No lyric memory softens the fact —
    this stone idol
could house more hopes than any
    verse of mine.
I eye its girdered skeleton
    with brute respect.

Three miles away, a gutted castle
    stands; Sir John's
which my father helped to burn.
    Its elegant remains
still dominate the district, as

now this Roseland
shall, a concrete prow cargoed
    with vague dreams.

The shiny roofs of cars, shoals
    of minnows, may
swim around it, pairs stumble from
    the wide light
of the door to the narrow privacy
    of plastic seats.
A sigh, a kiss, hands wander
    near thin skirts

as music shakes & pounds.
    An industry built
on loneliness, setting the young
    to clamber over
each other, brief as mayflies
    in their hunger
for novelty, for flashing
    energy & change . . .

from *Collected Poems* (1995)

NORA HOPPER CHESSON

'The Rosses is on the west coast of County Donegal, Ireland. There are one hundred and nine townlands in the Rosses.' So begins My Story (1939) by Paddy the Cope Gallagher. The Irish-speaking Rosses was a definitive congested district, with most of its population engaged in migrant labour in Scotland or in 'the Lagan', as they called better-off parts of Ulster. Paddy the Cope changed that by introducing agricultural reforms and organising the Templecrone Co-operative Society — hence his nickname: 'cope', co-op.

Many exponents of the Celtic Twilight school of literature, such as Nora Hopper Chesson, seemed to believe that the emptier and more deprived an area of rural Ireland was, the more plausible 'fairies piping' and the like became — particularly if you were to cross their path on 1 May, the feast of Bealtaine, which began the old Irish summer. An alternative view of The Rosses is given in Flann O'Brien's An Béal Bocht (1941; trans. The Poor Mouth (1973)).

The Short Cut to Rosses

By the short cut to Rosses a fairy girl I met;
I was taken in her beauty as a fish is in a net.
The fern uncurled to look at her, so very fair was she,
With her hair as bright as seaweed new-drawn from out the sea.

By the short cut to Rosses ('twas on the first of May)
I heard the fairies piping, and they piped my heart away;
They piped till I was mad with joy, but when I was alone
I found my heart was piped away and in my breast a stone.

By the short cut to Rosses 't is I'll go never more,
Lest I be robbed of soul by her that stole my heart before,
Lest she take my soul and crush it like a dead leaf in her hand,
For the short cut to Rosses is the way to Fairyland.

from *Under Quicken Boughs* (1896)

PATRICK MACGILL

Patrick MacGill grew up in Glenties, Co. Donegal, but he was unable to live there very long. While not yet a teenager, he went on the Lagan — that is, worked for a farmer who hired him at Strabane hiring fair. At the age of fourteen, like many Donegal people, he took up 'tatie howking' — potato picking — in Scotland, and from that went on to general labouring on the railway and building sites. In 1909, aged eighteen, he was within a year of being a published writer. Eventually he turned all those early experiences to literary account in prose and verse, becoming known in the process as 'the navvy poet'.

And he did manage to go home, in a sense. In 1981, eighteen years after his death, the first meeting of the annual Patrick MacGill Summer School took place in Glenties.

The dedication of Brian Friel's play, Dancing at Lughnasa, *reads, 'In memory of those five brave Glenties women', the aunts with whom he spent childhood summers.*

Going Home

(Doherty's shack, 1909)

I'm going back to Glenties when the harvest fields are brown,
And the Autumn sunset lingers on my little Irish town,
When the gossamer is shining where the moorland blossoms blow
I'll take the road across the hills I tramped so long ago —
'T is far I am beyond the seas, but yearning voices call,
'Will you not come back to Glenties, and your wave-washed Donegal!'

I've seen the hopes of childhood stifled by the hand of time,
I've seen the smile of innocence become the frown of crime,
I've seen the wrong rise high and strong, I've seen the fair betrayed,
Until the faltering heart fell low, the brave became afraid —
But still the cry comes out to me, the homely voices call,
From the Glen among the highlands of my ancient Donegal.

Sure, I think I see them often, when the night is on the town,
The Braes of old Strasala, and the homes of Carrigdoun —
There's a light in Jimmy Lynch's house, a shadow on the blind,
I often watched the shadow, for 't was Mary in behind,
And often in the darkness, 't is myself that sees it all,
For I cannot help but dreaming of the folk in Donegal.

So I'll hie me back to Glenties when the harvest comes again,
And the kine are in the pasture and the berries in the lane,
Then they'll give me such a handshake that my heart will leap with joy,
When a father and a mother welcome back their wayward boy.
So I'm going back to Glenties when the autumn showers fall,
And the harvest home is cheery in my dear old Donegal.

from *Songs of the Dead End* (1912)

WILLIAM ALLINGHAM

'The Church stood on the highest ground, and commanded a wide prospect . . . Eastward you saw the river rushing down its rocky dell, and behind this some of the hill tops that guard the unseen great Lake out of which it flows. To the south, at a distance of some ten miles, a long range of blue mountains takes wonderful colours from the changing skies, and in their foldings run up shadowy valleys into a mystical inner region.'

This view from the Protestant church in Ballyshannon recorded in Allingham's Diary is what the poem details — down the coast of Donegal Bay via Bundoran to Mullaghmore, Co. Sligo, and inland to the Dartry mountains (very much Yeats country) and Belleek, Co. Fermanagh, where the Erne leaves Lower Lough Erne, 'the great Lake'.

Yeats called Allingham 'the poet of Ballyshannon', meaning that he wasn't anything more. But this poem, with its 'shanachus' (ancient stories), local lore and 'rath' (an earthen enclosure), shows him drawing on some of the same territory as the local ballads and folk poetry, of which he was such a keen collector.

The Winding Banks of Erne

(Or, The Emigrant's Adieu to Ballyshannon)

Adieu to Ballyshannon! where I was bred and born;
Go where I may, I'll think of you, as sure as night and morn,
The kindly spot, the friendly town, where everyone is known,
And not a face in all the place but partly seems my own;
There's not a house or window, there's not a field or hill,
But, east or west, in foreign lands, I'll recollect them still.
I leave my warm heart with you, though my back I'm forced to turn —
So adieu to Ballyshannon, and the winding banks of Erne!

No more on pleasant evenings we'll saunter down the Mall,
When the trout is rising to the fly, the salmon to the fall.
The boat comes straining on her net, and heavily she creeps,
Cast off, cast off! — she feels the oars, and to her berth she sweeps;
Now fore and aft keep hauling, and gathering up the clue,
Till a silver wave of salmon rolls in among the crew.
Then they may sit, with pipes a-lit, and many a joke and 'yarn'; —
Adieu to Ballyshannon, and the winding banks of Erne!

The music of the waterfall, the mirror of the tide,
When all the green-hill'd harbour is full from side to side —
From Portnasun to Bulliebawns, and round the Abbey Bay,
From rocky Inis Saimer to Coolnargit sandhills grey;
While far upon the southern line, to guard it like a wall,
The Leitrim mountains, clothed in blue, gaze calmly over all,
And watch the ship sail up or down, the red flag at her stern; —
Adieu to these, adieu to all the winding banks of Erne!

Farewell to you, Kildoney lads, and them that pull an oar,
A lug-sail set, or haul a net, from the Point to Mullaghmore;

From Killybegs to bold Slieve-League, that ocean-mountain steep,
Six hundred yards in air aloft, six hundred in the deep;
From Dooran to the Fairy Bridge, and round by Tullen strand,
Level and long, and white with waves, where gull and curlew stand; —
Head out to sea when on your lee the breakers you discern! —
Adieu to all the billowy coast, and winding banks of Erne!

Farewell Coolmore, — Bundoran! and your summer crowds that run
From inland homes to see with joy th' Atlantic-setting sun;
To breathe the buoyant salted air, and sport among the waves;
To gather shells on sandy beach, and tempt the gloomy caves;
To watch the flowing, ebbing tide, the boats, the crabs, the fish;
Young men and maids to meet and smile, and form a tender wish;
The sick and old in search of health, for all things have their turn —
And I must quit my native shore, and the winding banks of Erne!

Farewell to every white cascade from the Harbour to Belleek,
And every pool where fins may rest, and ivy-shaded creek;
The sloping fields, the lofty rocks, where ash and holly grow,
The one split yew-tree gazing on the curving flood below;
The Lough, that winds through islands under Turaw mountain green;
And Castle Caldwell's stretching woods, with tranquil bays between;
And Breesie Hill, and many a pond among the heath and fern, —
For I must say adieu — adieu to the winding banks of Erne!

The thrush will call through Camlin groves the live-long summer day;
The waters run by mossy cliff, and bank with wild flowers gay;
The girls will bring their work and sing beneath a twisted thorn,
Or stray with sweethearts down the path among the growing corn;
Along the river side they go, where I have often been, —
O, never shall I see again the days that I have seen!
A thousand chances are to one I never may return, —
Adieu to Ballyshannon, and the winding banks of Erne!

Adieu to evening dances, when merry neighbours meet,
And the fiddle says to boys and girls, 'Get up and shake your feet!'
To 'shanachus' and wise old talk of Erin's days gone by —
Who trench'd the rath on such a hill, and where the bones may lie
Of saint, or king, or warrior chief; with tales of fairy power,
And tender ditties sweetly sung to pass the twilight hour.
The mournful song of exile is now for me to learn —
Adieu, my dear companions on the winding banks of Erne!

from *Songs, Ballads and Stories* (1877)

SEAMUS HEANEY

A cousin of the poet, Colum McCartney was killed travelling north through southern County Armagh, which is where Newtownhamilton and the Fews are. In his banishment, King Sweeney of Buile Suibhne — Sweeney Astray, *in Heaney's translation — spent some time in the Fews Forest.*

Lough Beg, 'little lake', abuts the north shore of Lough Neagh, close to the Heaney family farm at Bellaghy, Co. Derry. Church Island, actually a peninsula in Lough Beg, contains the ruins of a medieval place of pilgrimage. The spire is an eighteenth-century addition. Scapulars are a devotional article consisting of two small rectangles of cloth joined by a pair of tapes that pass over the shoulders.

The context of the quotation from The Divine Comedy *is Cato's instructions on how Dante should be prepared before entering Purgatory. These instructions are evoked in the closing lines of 'The Strand at Lough Beg'. A different view of these lines is given in Section VIII of the title poem of Heaney's* Station Island *(1984).*

The Strand at Lough Beg

In memory of Colum McCartney

> All round this little island, on the strand
> Far down below there, where the breakers strive,
> Grow the tall rushes from the oozy sand.
> Dante, *Purgatorio*, I, 100–103

Leaving the white glow of filling stations
And a few lonely streetlamps among fields
You climbed the hills towards Newtownhamilton
Past the Fews Forest, out beneath the stars —
Along that road, a high, bare pilgrim's track
Where Sweeney fled before the bloodied heads,
Goat-beards and dogs' eyes in a demon pack
Blazing out of the ground, snapping and squealing.
What blazed ahead of you? A faked road block?
The red lamp swung, the sudden brakes and stalling
Engine, voices, heads hooded and the cold-nosed gun?
Or in your driving mirror, tailing headlights
That pulled out suddenly and flagged you down
Where you weren't known and far from what you knew:
The lowland clays and waters of Lough Beg,
Church Island's spire, its soft treeline of yew.

There you used hear guns fired behind the house
Long before rising time, when duck shooters
Haunted the marigolds and bulrushes,
But still were scared to find spent cartridges,
Acrid, brassy, genital, ejected,
On your way across the strand to fetch the cows.
For you and yours and yours and mine fought shy,
Spoke an old language of conspirators
And could not crack the whip or seize the day:
Big-voiced scullions, herders, feelers round
Haycocks and hindquarters, talkers in byres,
Slow arbitrators of the burial ground.

Across that strand of yours the cattle graze
Up to their bellies in an early mist
And now they turn their unbewildered gaze
To where we work our way through squeaking sedge
Drowning in dew. Like a dull blade with its edge
Honed bright, Lough Beg half shines under the haze.
I turn because the sweeping of your feet
Has stopped behind me, to find you on your knees
With blood and roadside muck in your hair and eyes,
Then kneel in front of you in brimming grass
And gather up cold handfuls of the dew
To wash you, cousin. I dab you clean with moss
Fine as the drizzle out of a low cloud.
I lift you under the arms and lay you flat.
With rushes that shoot green again, I plait
Green scapulars to wear over your shroud.

from *Field Work* (1979)

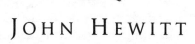

JOHN HEWITT

'In my experience,' Hewitt has written, 'people of Planter stock often suffer from some crisis of identity, of not knowing where they belong. Among us you will find some who call themselves British, some Irish, some Ulstermen, usually with a degree of hesitation or mental fumbling.' To overcome such tentativeness and to establish through his poetry the ground for an Ulster identity was one of Hewitt's main imaginative ambitions. He was an avowed regionalist. Larger than clan and smaller than nation, the region is, he said, 'an area which possesses geographical and economic coherence, which has had some sort of traditional and historical identity and which still, in some measure, demonstrates cultural and linguistic individuality'. It is interesting to compare this line of thinking with that of Hewitt's contemporary, Patrick Kavanagh.

In many respects, Hewitt was a Belfast man. But the places with whose names he identifies here are in the Glens of Antrim, in the highlands above Cushendall. It is hereabouts that he is buried. Down the road, at Garron Tower, an annual John Hewitt Summer School is held.

Ulster Names

I take my stand by the Ulster names,
each clean hard name like a weathered stone;
Tyrella, Rostrevor, are flickering flames:
the names I mean are the Moy, Malone,
Strabane, Slieve Gullion and Portglenone.

Even suppose that each name were freed
from legend's ivy and history's moss,
there'd be music still in, say, Carrick-a-rede,
though men forget it's the rock across
the track of the salmon from Islay and Ross.

The names of a land show the heart of the race;
they move on the tongue like the lilt of a song.
You say the name and I see the place —
Drumbo, Dungannon, Annalong.
Barony, townland, we cannot go wrong.

You say Armagh, and I see the hill
with the two tall spires or the square low tower;
the faith of Patrick is with us still;
his blessing falls in a moonlit hour,
when the apple orchards are all in flower.

You whisper Derry. Beyond the walls
and the crashing boom and the coiling smoke,
I follow that freedom which beckons and calls
to Colmcille, tall in his grove of oak,
raising his voice for the rhyming folk.

County by county you number them over;
Tyrone, Fermanagh . . . I stand by a lake,
and the bubbling curlew, the whistling plover

call over the whins in the chill daybreak
as the hills and the waters the first light take.

Let Down be famous for care-tilled earth,
for the little green hills and the harsh grey peaks,
the rocky bed of the Lagan's birth,
the white farm fat in the August weeks.
There's one more county my pride still seeks.

You give it the name and my quick thoughts run
through the narrow towns with their wheels of trade,
to Glenballyemon, Glenaan, Glendun,
from Trostan down to the braes of Layde,
for there is the place where the pact was made.

But you have as good a right as I
to praise the place where your face is known,
for over us all is the selfsame sky;
the limestone's locked in the strength of the bone,
and who shall mock at the steadfast stone?

So it's Ballinamallard, it's Crossmaglen,
it's Aughnacloy, it's Donaghadee,
it's Magherafelt breeds the best of men,
I'll not deny it. But look for me
on the moss between Orra and Slievenanee.

Postscript, 1984

Those verses surfaced thirty years ago
when time seemed edging to a better time,
most public voices tamed, those loud untamed
as seasonal as tawdry pantomime,
and over my companionable land
placenames still lilted like a childhood rime.

The years deceived; our unforgiving hearts,
by myth and old antipathies betrayed,
flared into sudden acts of violence
in daily shocking bulletins relayed,
and through our dark dream-clotted consciousness
hosted like banners in some black parade.

Now with compulsive resonance they toll:
Banbridge, Ballykelly, Darkley, Crossmaglen,

summoning pity, anger and despair,
by grief of kin, by hate of murderous men
till the whole tarnished map is stained and torn,
not to be read as pastoral again.

from Frank Ormsby (ed.), *The Collected Poems of John Hewitt* (1991)

HISTORY

JOHN MONTAGUE

Tradition has it that there were seven invasions of Ireland. The best-known are those by the Parthalonians, the Milesians, the Fir Bolgs, the Tuatha Dé Danann, and of course the Celts. The first signs of human life in Ireland date from 6000 B.C.

Of the group mentioned here, Ladhra was the navigator, Bith was Noah's son and the father of Cessair, and Fintan was Cessair's husband. Cessair died of a broken heart, and the other women died as well. The flood came forty days after their arrival. Fintan alone survived the flood. He seems to have been the holy man of the group because his subsequent history makes him out to have been a visionary and a man of knowledge. He lived for over five thousand years, sometimes under the guise of a salmon, at other times as a hawk. He survived until the coming of Christianity.

The First Invasion of Ireland

According to Leabhar Gabhála, The Book of Invasions, *the first invasion of Ireland was by relatives of Noah, just before the Flood. Refused entry into the Ark, they consulted an idol which told them to flee to Ireland. There were three men and fifty-one women in the party and they may have landed where the Barrow, Nore and Suir meet.*

Fleeing from threatened flood, they sailed,
Seeking the fair island, without serpent or claw;
From the deck of their hasty barque watched
The soft edge of Ireland nearward draw.

A sweet confluence of waters, a trinity of rivers,
Was their first resting place:
They unloaded the women and the sensual idol,
Guiding image of their disgrace.

Division of damsels they did there,
The slender, the tender, the dimpled, the round,
It was the last just bargain in Ireland,
There was enough to go round.

Lightly they lay and pleasured
In the green grass of that guileless place.
Ladhra was the first to die;
He perished of an embrace.

Bith was buried in a stone heap,
Riot of mind, all passion spent.
Fintan fled from the ferocious women
Lest he, too, by love be rent.

Great primitive princes of our line
They were the first, with stately freedom,
To sleep with women in Ireland;
Soft the eternal bed they lie upon.

On a lonely headland the women assembled,
Chill as worshippers in a nave,
And watched the eastern waters gather
Into a great virile flooding wave.

from *Collected Poems* (1995)

GEOFFREY KEATING

Brian Boru (941–1014) is the most famous of the Irish high kings. A native of County Clare, he began as king of Munster, with Kincora, Co. Clare as his seat. But it was not long before he succeeded by force of arms and political skill to become High King of Ireland, or even, as he put it, 'Emperor of the Irish'. One of his other claims to fame is that he introduced taxation to Ireland. Boru is a nickname whose root is 'bó', the Irish for cow. Brian's form of taxation was a levy on his subjects' cows.

The events described here were followed by a campaign by Brian against Leinster, the formation of an alliance between Leinster and the Vikings of Dublin, and a subsequent alliance between Dublin and other Viking strongholds, such as the Isle of Man. Hostilities culminated at the Battle of Clontarf, on the north shore of Dublin Bay, on Good Friday 1014. The Vikings were routed, but Brian — on his knees in his hut giving thanks for the victory — was cut to pieces by the fleeing enemy.

The Origin of the Battle of Clontarf
A.D. *1014*

When Brian Boru was living in Kincora, without war or dissension, he asked the King of Leinster — Maol Mórdha son of Murrough, to send him three masts of fine wood from Feegile. The King of Leinster cut the masts, and went with them to Kincora where Brian then was, and ordered the Ui Failghe to carry one mast, the Ui Faolain to carry another and the Ui Muireadhaigh the third; and they squabbled going up Sliabh an Bhogaigh. Then the King of Leinster himself gave a hand with the Ui Faolain's mast while he was wearing a satin tunic Brian had given him previously with a gold fringe around it and a silver button, and with the effort he made under the mast, the button broke. And when they reached Kincora, the King of Leinster took off his tunic, and gave it to his sister, Gormley daughter of Murrough, Brian's wife, to sew a button in. The queen took the tunic and tossed it into the fire before her and began abusing her brother for being in subjection or slavery to anyone in the world. 'The thing,' she said, 'your father or grandfather never agreed to.' And she said Brian's son would demand the same thing from Maol Mórdha's son.

Maol Mórdha remembered the queen's words. And it happened next day that Murrough son of Brian and Conaing son of Donn Chuan were playing chess next day—or according to some, it was the Abbot of Glendalough who was playing with Murrough. Maol Mórdha began to advise Murrough in his play and advised one move that lost him the game.

'You gave the Danes the advice that defeated them in the battle of Glen Mama,' said Murrough.

'If I gave them advice that defeated them then,' said Maol Mórdha, 'I shall give them other advice that will make them defeat you another day.'

'I should like to see them,' said Murrough.

That made Maol Mórdha furious, and he went to his quarters, and couldn't be induced to go to the drinking house that night, and left early next morning without taking leave of Brian.

When Brian heard that the King of Leinster had left the fort without taking leave of him, he sent a favourite serving man to detain him till he received wages and gifts. The serving man caught up on him at the end of the plank bridge of Killaloe on the eastern bank of the Shannon, while he was mounting his horse, and the serving man revealed his message from Brian. Maol Mórdha turned on the serving man and struck him three blows with the yew-stick he carried in his hand, and broke the bones of his skull, so that he had to be carried back to Brian. Cogaran was the man's name, and it is from him the Ui Chogarain of Munster are descended. Some of the Kincora household wished to follow the King of Leinster and not let him back to Leinster till he submitted to Brian. But Brian said he would not permit treachery against him in his own house. 'All the same,' he said, 'it is from the doorpost of his own house that satisfaction will be asked of him.'

from David Comyn and Patrick Dineen (eds), *Foras Feasa na hÉireann*, (1902–8)

ANONYMOUS

Vikings is the generic name given to sea-borne Scandinavian raiders who began their depredations on the coastal communities of Ireland late in the eighth century. Many of those communities developed into thriving Viking settlements. The suffix in the names Strangford, Wexford, Waterford, for instance, is the word fjord. 'From the fury of the Norsemen, Good Lord deliver us!' was the prayer of a ninth-century French monk. And no wonder. Monasteries, well-stocked with food and precious articles, were well worth plundering.

The tall slender buildings known as round towers are closely associated with these attacks. Already in use as belfries — bells were rung from the top of them — they also became lookouts. Their doorways were well off the ground; when the alarm sounded, the monks gathered themselves and their valuables inside, pulling in the ladder after them. But the round towers could be death-traps if they were set on fire, as many were, behaving in effect as chimneys.

Many round towers remain. There are particularly eye-catching ones at Glendalough, Co. Wicklow and Ardmore, Co. Waterford.

The Viking Terror

Since tonight the wind is high,
The sea's white mane a fury.
I need not fear the hordes of Hell
Coursing the Irish Channel.

translated by Frank O'Connor, from *Kings, Lords & Commons* (1959)

SEAN O'FAOLAIN

'There' in this extract's opening sentence is Ulster. This is where the conflict between the Gaelic chiefdom's way of life and the Elizabethan imperium's outlook found its most acute expression. O'Faolain's biography of Hugh O'Neill (1550–1616) is an imaginative reconstruction of the policies and mentalities at issue.

An additional aspect of what O'Faolain calls the 'labyrinthine perplexity' of the collision between the two countries and the two cultures is suggested by the fact that O'Neill was raised and educated in England — at, among other places, Penshurst, the family home of the noted soldier and poet Sir Philip Sidney — and held the titles third Baron of Dungannon and second Earl of Tyrone. His attempts to be an O'Neill while maintaining the trappings of a lord of the realm have been considered emblematic of the tensions and confusions of, to use O'Faolain's phrase, 'the process of absorption'.

Present-day Irish writers continue to find O'Neill an intriguing figure. Brian Friel has written a play about him, Making History *(1988), as has Thomas Kilroy,* The O'Neill *(1969).*

Terra Incognita

The sixteenth-century wars of conquest there mingled what was by nature immiscible. It is the same forced juncture of modernity and antiquity that comes with every imperial conquest, whether it is the conquest of Mexico by the Spaniards, or the colonisation of India by the Hanoverians, or the plantation of Ireland by the Tudors. For out of it emerges a kind of Siamese duality of mind just as indissoluble, and just as incoherent, producing at first, on the side of the conquistadors, extremes of idealism, loyalty, persistence, stubbornness, folly, by which all first puzzlements or stirrings of conscience are smothered up or brushed aside; and then, on both sides, when the confusion rises, mountains of treachery, an otherwise unimaginable brutality, indescribable savageries, recantations, selfishness, contempt, every known weapon of human ingenuity and bestiality to obliterate the enemy and justify his obliteration. In such a clash there is no simple story because there is no clear mind. In the final stage of all nothing remains but the oversimplified story of the victor and the oversimplified memories of the defeated, both of them unfaithful to the always confused and occasionally troubled split-mindedness of the time.

The truth is that Englishmen were fantastically ignorant about those countries which they assailed so blithely in the flush of their passion for adventurous conquest, and that the assailed were just as ignorant as to the nature of the forces and the order of life that assailed them.

For English contemporaries the entry into sixteenth-century Ireland was an entry into a world as strange as the Indies were to Columbus, nine-tenths of it an uncharted Thibet, and the O'Neills and O'Donnells and all its chief princes as remote and as unimaginable as the great Khan. So that had some English traveller reported that there lived deep in Ireland tribes who wore their heads, like the anthropophagi, beneath their shoulders, London would have believed him; and in fact, well after the Tudors, men were still picking up books from the counters of the booksellers under St Paul's that made report of things just as fantastic. One has but to look at the old map-books. Thus Speed's map of 1610 could repeat from Giraldus Cambrensis such tales as that there exist in Ireland islands 'some full of angels, some full of devils, some for male only, some for female, some where none may live, some where none can die'. Just as it also repeated the legend that the map-maker wrote on the map of Ortelius (1574), that there was no Lough Erne until the people who once farmed the solid earth there committed 'filthy abominable acts with beasts' and the waters rose and smothered them. In that same treacherous map of Ortelius which smoothened away vast headlands of rock to doom the pilots of the Armada, the Aran Islands are helpfully marked in Latin as places where no corpses can putrefy; and students of the fate of the Armada conning the Map of the Westerne Oceane (1609) found it as seriously enlivened at Sligo by the legend that here lie 'the high hills of Ben Bulben where yearly limbereth a falcon esteemed the hardiest in Ireland', as at Derenishe that here 'three Spanish shipps were caste awaye'. The usual sea-monsters are doubtless a convention, but other things are conventional in a different way: thus the farther islands are suggested much as modern maps suggest the unexplored Arctic with incomplete guess-work outlines; and the general position of lakes and rivers is indicated with an imaginative abandon. In Norden's map of 1609, when our story is well-nigh over, small lochs like Carra spread to the size of the widest waters of the Shannon: scores of others, including one entire Shannon lake, Allen, have vanished completely; or a lake like Lough Conn can appear two counties away from where it should be. A modern, searching the maze of rivers for a familiar clue, is lost among streams that have neither beginning nor end, but devour their own tails like the impossible beasts in the intricate medieval designs of the Book of Kells, and the whole river-system looks less untracked than the upper waters of the Amazon a hundred years ago. In Ortelius all Tirconnell is as blank as the Sahara. In the best of these maps, Speed's of 1610, forests and mountains lie haphazard and there is not one road. In others the picture is like a film which has melted away, hither and thither, into distortion. There is no really effective map until the *Hiberniae Delineatio* by Sir William Petty in 1685, almost at the threshold of the eighteenth century, and if one goes back behind those I have mentioned — behind Speed, and Camden's *Britannia* of 1607, and Peter van den Keere's of 1599, to the first map of the British Isles ever engraved, at Rome in 1546 — not, of course, the first map drawn — only fifteen places in all Ireland are marked, and all we see in Ulster is Lough Foyle (*Lacus Foilus*), Armagh (*Armacana Metrop*), and one great black entry into the bowels of the earth, like the entry into Hell, marked *Purgatorium Sancti Patricii*. The rest is a waste land.

That wonderment existed, apparently without discomfort, side by side with the staid facts of constant contact by trade, on the periphery of a wholly commonplace commercial communication between London and coastal towns like Dublin and Wexford and Drogheda and Dundalk, and the stories came back undiminished of their wonder by rubbing with the beef, salmon, suet, butter, lard, hawks and horses, linen, wool, and leather exported from the Irish ports in exchange for the coal and cloth of England, or the guns and ammunition smuggled back for the Gaelic captains fighting the same England in the hinterland. All the varied trade from the Continent into Ireland, wine from Canary and the Levant, spices for Irish *uisgebaugh* from Italy, Spanish wine, salts and dyes from Toulouse and Picardy (one could build it up without trouble into an impressively solid record as well as a prettily sonorous litany from such studious books as Alice Stopford Green's *Making of Ireland* or Ada Longfield's *Anglo-Irish Trade in the Sixteenth Century*) did nothing to diminish the basic feeling that Ireland was behind it all a lost land. And this is natural, because all this communication was on the fringe of the hinterland, and these ports and towns — barring one or two like Donegal — were Norman rather than Gaelic, Anglo-Irish rather than Irish, and the core of the life of the country was that of people who never developed any kind of town-life, being satisfied, rather, to develop rural life to the point where, normally, it should have spilled over into urbanity — and most obstinately would not. The island, accordingly, was to its neighbour ringed with entries, familiar lighthouses, behind which lay a great deal that was quite unknown.

Indeed that may be seen also by reference to the maps, in so far as none of them shows any real focus or centre. The city of Dublin appears as a castle no more impressive than any other castle along the coast, such as Knockfergus, Carlingford, Dundalk, Wexford, Youghal, Kinsale; and every inland centre of any size promises us as fair as the next to develop into a city as Kilkenny did or to decline like Cashel into a ruin. Clearly each centre is the centre only of its own *locus*. No hierarchy or predominance has been established. History is still a complete gamble. To the stranger the past of this island is darkness and its future can only be written in blood. There are not even these firm local centres in Ulster, unless we count the Cathedral of Armagh in the east or the Monastery of Donegal in the farthest west. The fort of Portmore on the Blackwater River, so jealously watched by both colonist and native, its capture repeatedly claimed as a victory, proves to be a small wooden blockhouse on a little mound about forty feet in diameter.

from *The Great O'Neill, A Biography of Hugh O'Neill, Earl of Tyrone* (1942)

REVEREND E.A. D'ALTON

Part of Hugh O'Neill's strategic manoeuvrings entailed contact with the great English enemy of the age, Spain. From that connection came a force of some 3,500 men, under the command of Don Juan del Águila. The force should have landed in Ulster, but it put in on the south coast instead. The date was September 1601.

The actual Battle of Kinsale was fought in December of that year. O'Neill signed the Treaty of Mellifont in 1603, but peace did not restore him to power. In September 1607 he and the remaining Ulster chiefs sailed for the Continent from Lough Swilly,

Co. Donegal. This event is known as the Flight of the Earls. It effectively ended the prospects for an Irish polity serving indigenous interests.

An extensive contemporary account of these events is contained in Pacata Hibernia: Ireland Appeased and Reduced *(1633), based on the papers of Sir George Carew.*

Battle of Kinsale

The intended destination of the Spaniards was Cork; and they first arrived there, borne in 45 vessels; but the wind suddenly changed, and, unable to land, they put in at Kinsale. The English garrison there evacuated the place on their approach, and when the Spaniards landed they were well received, and were billeted through the town more readily, says Carew, than if they were the Queen's troops. Daguilla published a proclamation that none would be molested, and that whoever wished to leave might do so, taking their goods with them.[1] Carew and Mountjoy were then at Kilkenny. They had been warned from England that the Spaniards were coming, and had gone to Kilkenny to take counsel. Mountjoy proposed returning to Dublin to make his preparations; Carew's advice was that all their forces be at once sent to Munster, his object being to overawe the natives, lest they might join the Spaniards. This advice was taken, and from all quarters the English and their allies flocked to the south. From England 2,000 soldiers came; the Earl of Thomond arrived with 1,000 more; Clanricarde came from Connaught, and Ormond from Kilkenny; the garrisons were withdrawn from Ulster; and by the middle of October, Mountjoy and Carew were in front of Kinsale in command of 12,000 men.[2] In these circumstances Daguilla sent urgent letters to the Ulster chiefs, begging them to come to his assistance; and O'Donnell, leaving his brother Rory to watch Nial Garve and the English, set out for Munster, with nearly 2,000 men. The force of 2,000 men which Carew took from Kinsale was at least twice that number when he arrived at Cashel, for further reinforcements had been sent. Yet he was in no hurry to fight; and O'Donnell wished to reserve his strength, and taking advantage of a frost which had made even the bogs passable for troops, he turned west, and passed over the mountains of Slieve Felim; and within 24 hours had reached Croom, a distance of 40 English miles, the greatest march with carriage that Carew had ever heard of before.[3] Passing through Duhallow and Muskerry, O'Donnell arrived at Kinsale, about the middle of November.

The narrow channel which connects Kinsale with the open sea was guarded on each side by two strong castles, Rincorran on the east, and Castle ny Park on the west, in both of which Spanish garrisons had been put, and thus was the town protected on the sea side. On the land side, it was more difficult to protect. The position of the town itself, on the slope of Compass Hill, laid it open to be swept by an enemy's batteries placed on the ascending side. But Daguilla had done the best he could; had built up the crumbling walls; and from the bastions his cannon were pointed to deal death on an advancing foe. On the 16th of October, Mountjoy encamped 5 miles from Kinsale. He had not yet a sufficient supply of artillery; but, on the 23rd, his wants in this respect were supplied, and three days later he crossed Oyster Haven and pitched his camp on the Spittle, and on the 29th attacked Rincorran Castle. Daguilla endeavoured to relieve it from the sea, but was unable, and after a heroic defence the garrison capitulated, on condition that their lives were spared. On the 10th of November, Daguilla published a proclamation that any of his soldiers who quitted his post, without directions from his officers, should be punished with death. Yet in spite of all this the besiegers gained ground. The capture of Rincorran allowed the English admiral, Levison, to enter the harbour with his ships, and the town was soon invested completely both by sea and land. Castle ny Park was then assailed, and as the Spaniards in the town could lend no assistance, the garrison was compelled to surrender; and such was the progress made by the English, that, on the 28th, they summoned the town to surrender. Their messenger was not allowed to enter, but was informed at the gate that the Spaniards held the town for Christ and for the King of Spain, and were ready to defend it against anyone and everyone who might assail it.[4]

1. *Pacata Hibernia*, pp. 277–80.

2. ibid., pp. 287–93.

3. ibid., Vol. II, pp. 8–12.

4. *Carew Papers*, pp. 170–88; [Fynes] Moryson [*Itinerary* (1617)], pp. 127–51; *Pacata Hibernia*, Vol. I, pp. 275–302.

from *History of Ireland from Earliest Times to Present Day*, Vol. III (1890)

AODHAGHÁN Ó RATHAILLE

The long dying of Gaeldom commenced after the Flight of the Earls. It went on in various forms throughout the dreadful seventeenth century. A bloody uprising in Ulster in 1641 was followed by the eclipse of the Anglo-Catholic aristocracy, which in turn was followed by Cromwell's campaign; the culmination was the Jacobite wars at the end of the century, the last act of which was another flight, this time of the Wild Geese, those of title and land who had fought for James II. The best known of these is Patrick Sarsfield, Earl of Lucan. This final collapse of any pretence to political power by those with the property and position to be entitled to it produced the extreme of isolation and vulnerability which is the burden of the poet's lament.

It was Ó Rathaille's misfortune to experience the social and cultural rupture resulting from the Jacobite defeat. His name is not only associated with misfortune, but with the achievement of wringing poetry from it.

'Last Lines' continues for another three verses and concludes with a pledge of allegiance to his Gaelic chieftains, the McCarthys. Ó Rathaille is buried in their grave in Muckross Abbey, Killarney, Co. Kerry.

Last Lines

I shall not call for help until they coffin me —
    What good for me to call when hope of help is gone?
Princes of Munster that would have heard my cry
    Will not rise from the dead because I am alone.

Mind shudders like a wave in this tempestuous mood,
    My bowels and my heart are pierced and filled with pain
To see our lands, our hills, our gentle neighbourhood,
    A plot where any English upstart stakes his claim.

The Shannon and the Liffey and the tuneful Lee,
    The Boyne and the Blackwater a sad music sing,
The waters of the west run red into the sea —
    No matter what be trumps their knave will beat our king.

And I can never cease weeping these useless tears;
    I am a man oppressed, afflicted and undone,
Who where he wanders mourning no companion hears
    Only some waterfall that has no cause to mourn.

Now I shall cease, death comes, and I must not delay
    By Laune and Laine and Lee, diminished of their pride,
I shall go after the heroes, ay, into the clay —
    My fathers followed theirs before Christ was crucified.

translated by Frank O'Connor, from *Kings, Lords & Commons* (1959)

RICHARD MURPHY

Aughrim is in east County Galway, and the battle fought there on 12 July 1691 effectively concluded the Williamite war in Ireland. The forces of James II, funded by Louis XIV, were commanded by an insufferable French general, St Ruth. William of Orange's army was under a Dutchman, Baron Ginkel. The Jacobite army seemed to have won the day, but a cannon ball decapitated St Ruth, leading to disarray and flight. Moreover, as was often the case, there was treason in the Irish ranks.

'Planters' were those English settlers whom the various 'plantations', particularly seventeenth-century ones, had brought to Ireland. 'Rapparees', on the other hand, were dispossessed former landholders who preyed on those who supplanted them. An Irish word for pike is 'rapaire'.

Sefauchi's Farewell is a piece for harpsichord by the English composer Henry Purcell (c. 1659–95). Red-mouthed O'Donnell is Hugh Balldearg O'Donnell, a descendant of Red Hugh O'Donnell, the original Earl of Tyrconnell. 'Balldearg' means red spot (whereas 'red-mouthed' would be 'béaldearg'), and leads to 'a wine-blotted birth-mark', which according to popular belief at the time the true Earl of Tyrconnell would have.

from *The Battle of Aughrim*

Planter

Seven candles in silver sticks,
Water on an oval table,
The painted warts of Cromwell
Framed in a sullen gold.
There was ice on the axe
When it hacked the king's head.
Moths drown in the dripping wax.

Slow sigh of the garden yews
Forty years planted.
May the God of battle
Give us this day our land
And the papists be trampled.
Softly my daughter plays
Sefauchi's Farewell.

Dark night with no moon to guard
Roads from the rapparees,
Food at a famine price,
Cattle raided, corn trod,
And the servants against us
With our own guns and swords.
Stress a hymn to peace.

Quiet music and claret cups,
Forty acres of green crops
Keep far from battle
My guest, with a thousand troops
Following his clan-call,
Red-mouthed O'Donnell.
I bought him: the traitor sleeps.

To whom will the land belong
This time tomorrow night?
I am loyal to fields I have sown
And the king reason elected:
Not to a wine-blotted birth-mark
Of prophecy, but hard work
Deepening the soil for seed.

Rapparees

Out of the earth, out of the air, out of the water
And slinking nearer the fire, in groups they gather:
Once he looked like a bird, but now a beggar.

This fish rainbows out of a pool: 'Give me bread!'
He fins along the lake-shore with the starved.
Green eyes glow in the night from clumps of weed.

The water is still. A rock, or the nose of an otter
Jars the surface. Whistle of rushes or bird?
It steers to the bank, it lands as a pikeman armed.

With flint and bundles of straw a limestone hall
Is gutted, a noble family charred in its sleep,
And they gloat by moonlight on a mound of rubble.

The highway trees are gibbets where seventeen rot
Who were caught last week in a cattle-raid.
The beasts are lowing. 'Listen!' 'Stifle the guard!'

In a pinewood thickness an earthed-over charcoal fire
Forges them guns. They melt lead stripped from a steeple
For ball. At the whirr of a snipe each can disappear

Terrified as a bird in a gorse-bush fire,
To delve like a mole, or mingle like a nightjar
Into the earth, into the air, into the water.

from *The Battle of Aughrim* (1968)

JONATHAN SWIFT

Swift was appointed dean of St Patrick's Cathedral, Dublin, in 1713. He considered it a step down after the three years of political engagement and literary camaraderie which he had just spent in London. But in 1720 he began to lend his brilliant pamphleteering skills to conditions in Ireland, the highlight of which were his Drapier's Letters (1724–5). In these he wrote as a Dublin draper opposing the imposition on the Irish economy of a debased coinage, Wood's ha'pence, so called because the brass coins were made by an English ironmonger named William Wood. The opposition was successful, making Swift's name a household one in Ireland.

This extract is from the last and most famous of Swift's Irish pamphlets, the full title of which is A Modest Proposal *for preventing the children of poor people from being a burthen to their parents or country, and for making them beneficial to the public. Written in 1729, it not only excoriates the neglected state of the country, but also addresses an undoubted fear of people of Swift's class — that of being overrun by the sheer numbers of those unsettled and dispossessed as a result of the Cromwellian and Williamite wars. As vicar of Laracor, Co. Meath in 1700, Swift would have seen those unable to serve in the armies of Catholic Europe. And presumably they were still visible at Markethill, Co. Armagh, where* A Modest Proposal *was written.*

There was a traffic in servants from Ireland to Barbados from at least the 1630s. Swift's friend Thomas Sheridan (1687–1738), grandfather of Richard Brinsley Sheridan the playwright, was from County Cavan.

A Modest Proposal

It is a melancholy object to those who walk through this great town, or travel in the country, when they see the streets, the roads, and cabin-doors crowded with beggars of the female sex, followed by three, four, or six children, *all in rags*, and importuning every passenger for an alms. These mothers, instead of being able to work for their honest livelihood, are forced to employ all their time in strolling, to beg sustenance for their helpless infants, who, as they grow up, either turn thieves for want of work, or leave their dear Native Country to fight for the Pretender in Spain, or sell themselves to the Barbadoes.

I think it is agreed by all parties that this prodigious number of children, in the arms, or on the backs, or at the heels of their mothers, and frequently of their fathers, is in the present deplorable state of the Kingdom a very great additional grievance; and therefore whoever could find out a fair, cheap, and easy method of making these children sound useful members of the commonwealth would deserve so well of the public as to have his statue set up for a preserver of the nation.

But my intention is very far from being confined to provide only for the children of professed beggars; it is of a much greater extent, and shall take in the whole number of infants at a certain age who are born of parents in effect as little able to support them as those who demand our charity in the streets.

As to my own part, having turned my thoughts, for many years, upon this important subject, and maturely weighed the several schemes of other projectors, I have always found them grossly mistaken in their computation. It is true a child, just dropped from its dam, may be supported by her milk for a solar year with little other nourishment, at most not above the value of two shillings, which the mother may certainly get, or the value in scraps, by her lawful occupation of begging, and it is exactly at one year old that I propose to provide for them, in such a manner as, instead of being a charge upon their parents, or the parish, or wanting food and raiment for the rest of their lives, they shall, on the contrary, contribute to the feeding and partly to the clothing of many thousands.

There is likewise another great advantage in my scheme, that it will prevent those voluntary abortions, and that horrid practice of women murdering their bastard children, alas, too frequent among us, sacrificing the poor innocent babes, I doubt, more to avoid the expense than the shame, which would move tears and pity in the most savage and inhuman breast.

The number of souls in this kingdom being usually reckoned one million and a half, of these I calculate there may be about two hundred thousand couple whose wives are breeders, from which number I subtract thirty thousand couples who are able to maintain their own children, although I apprehend there cannot be so many under the present distresses of the kingdom, but this being granted, there will remain an hundred and seventy thousand breeders. I again subtract fifty thousand for those women who miscarry, or whose children die by accident or disease within the year. There only remain an hundred and twenty thousand children of poor parents annually born: The question therefore is, how this number shall be reared, and provided for, which, as I have already said, under the present situation of affairs, is utterly impossible by all the methods hitherto proposed, for we can neither employ them in handicraft, or agriculture; we neither build houses (I mean in the country), nor cultivate land: they can very seldom pick up a livelihood by stealing till they arrive at six years old, except where they are of towardly parts, although, I confess they learn the rudiments much earlier, during which time they can however be properly looked upon only as *probationers*, as I have been informed by a principal gentleman in the County of Cavan, who protested to me that he never knew above one or two instances under the age of six, even in a part of the kingdom so renowned for the quickest proficiency in that art.

I am assured by our merchants that a boy or a girl, before twelve years old, is no saleable commodity, and even when they come to this age, they will not yield above three pounds, or three pounds and half-a-crown at most on the Exchange, which cannot turn to account either to the parents or the kingdom, the charge of nutriment and rags having been at least four times that value.

I shall now therefore humbly propose my own thoughts, which I hope will not be liable to the least objection.

I have been assured by a very knowing American of my acquaintance in London, that a young healthy child well nursed is at a year old a most delicious, nourishing, and wholesome food, whether stewed, roasted, baked, or boiled, and I make no doubt that it will equally serve in a fricassee, or a ragout.

I do therefore humbly offer it to public consideration, that of the hundred and twenty thousand children already computed, twenty thousand may be reserved for breed, whereof only one fourth part to be males, which is more than we allow to sheep, black-cattle, or swine, and my reason is that these children are seldom the fruits of marriage, a circumstance not much regarded by our savages, therefore one male will be sufficient to serve four females. That the remaining hundred thousand may at a year old be offered in sale to the persons of quality, and fortune, through the kingdom, always advising the mother to let them suck plentifully in the last month, so as to render them plump, and fat for a good table. A child will make two dishes at an entertainment for friends, and when the family dines alone, the fore or hind quarter will make a reasonable dish, and seasoned with a little pepper or salt will be very good boiled on the fourth day, especially in winter.

from *A Modest Proposal* (1729)

EIBHLÍN DHUBH NÍ CHONAILL

Swift speaks of Irishmen fighting in Spain. They also served in France, and many like Arthur O'Leary were officers in the army of Marie-Thérèse of Austria. This could be why his widow can picture him expensively dressed, and it may have added to the bravado of his behaviour. He refused to sell his horse to Abraham Morris, High Sheriff of Cork, after it had beaten Morris's in a race, and there was already bad blood between the two men. O'Leary seems to have survived being on the run well enough. It was his decision to have it out once and for all with Morris that led to his death.

Eileen O'Connell was the aunt of Daniel O'Connell, the great nineteenth-century politician. Her family had disapproved of her marriage to O'Leary. Oral tradition carried her lament into the nineteenth century, which is when it was transcribed. Scholars think of the poem as a 'keen', a traditional form of lamentation in Irish performed by women over the bodies of dead men. The poem is one of the best-known testaments to the Irish voice in print.

The Lament for Arthur Cleary (1989), a prize-winning play by Dermot Bolger, adapts the poem's narrative to contemporary Irish experience. The play was originally a Bolger poem.

The Lament for Arthur O'Leary

Lo! Arthur Leary, generous, handsome, brave,
Slain in his bloom, lies in this humble grave.

I

Eileen speaks:
My love forever!
The day I first saw you
At the end of the market-house,
My eye observed you,
My heart approved you,
I fled from my father with you,
Far from my home with you.

II

I never repented it:
You whitened a parlour for me,
Painted rooms for me,
Reddened ovens for me,
Baked fine bread for me,
Basted meat for me,
Slaughtered beasts for me;
I slept in ducks' feathers
Till midday milking-time,
Or more if it pleased me.

III

My friend forever!
My mind remembers
That fine spring day
How well your hat suited you,
Bright gold-banded,
Sword silver-hilted —
Right hand steady —
Threatening aspect —
Trembling terror
On treacherous enemy —
You poised for a canter
On your slender bay horse.
The Saxons bowed to you,
Down to the ground to you,
Not for love of you
But for deadly fear of you,

Though you lost your life to them,
Oh my soul's darling.

IV

Oh white-handed rider!
How fine your brooch was
Fastened in cambric,
And your hat with laces.
When you crossed the sea to us,
They would clear the street for you,
And not for love of you
But for deadly hatred.

V

My friend you were forever!
When they will come home to me,
Gentle little Conor
And Farr O'Leary, the baby,
They will question me so quickly,
Where did I leave their father.
I'll answer in my anguish
That I left him in Killnamartyr.
They will call out to their father;
And he won't be there to answer.

VI

My friend and my love!
Of the blood of Lord Antrim,
And of Barry of Allchoill,
How well your sword suited you,
Hat gold-banded,
Boots of fine leather,
Coat of broadcloth,
Spun overseas for you.

VII

My friend you were forever!
I knew nothing of your murder
Till your horse came to the stable
With the reins beneath her trailing,

And your heart's blood on her shoulders
Staining the tooled saddle
Where you used to sit and stand.
My first leap reached the threshold,
My second reached the gateway,
My third leap reached the saddle.

VIII

I struck my hands together
And I made the bay horse gallop
As fast as I was able,
Till I found you dead before me
Beside a little furze-bush.
Without Pope or bishop,
Without priest or cleric
To read the death-psalms for you,
But a spent old woman only
Who spread her cloak to shroud you —
Your heart's blood was still flowing;
I did not stay to wipe it
But filled my hands and drank it.

IX

My love you'll be forever!
Rise up from where you're lying
And we'll be going homewards.
We'll have a bullock slaughtered,
We'll call our friends together,
We'll get the music going.
I'll make a fine bed ready
With sheets of snow-white linen,
And fine embroidered covers
That will bring the sweat out through you
Instead of the cold that's on you!

X

Arthur O'Leary's sister speaks:
My friend and my treasure!
There's many a handsome woman
From Cork of the sails
To the bridge of Toames
With a great herd of cattle
And gold for her dowry,

That would not have slept soundly
On the night we were waking you.

XI

Eileen speaks:
My friend and my lamb;
You must never believe it,
Nor the whisper that reached you,
Nor the venomous stories
That said I was sleeping.
It was not sleep was on me,
But your children were weeping,
And they needed me with them
To bring their sleep to them.

XII

Now judge, my people,
What woman in Ireland
That at every nightfall
Lay down beside him,
That bore his three children,
Would not lose her reason
After Art O'Leary
That's here with me vanquished
Since yesterday morning?

XIII

Arthur O'Leary's father speaks:
Bad luck to you, Morris! —
May your heart's blood poison you!
With your squint eyes gaping!
And your knock-knees breaking! —
That murdered my darling,
And no man in Ireland
To fill you with bullets.

XIV

My friend and my heart!
Rise up again now, Art,
Leap up on your horse,
Make straight for Macroom town,
Then to Inchigeela back,
A bottle of wine in your fist,
The same as you drank with your dad.

XV

Eileen speaks:
My bitter, long torment
That I was not with you
When the bullet came towards you,
My right side would have taken it
Or a fold of my tunic,
And I would have saved you
Oh smooth-handed rider.

XVI

Arthur O'Leary's sister speaks:
My sore sharp sorrow
That I was not behind you
When the gun-powder blazed at you,
My right side would have taken it,
Or a fold of my gown,
And you would have gone free then
Oh grey-eyed rider,
Since you were a match for them.

XVII

Eileen speaks:
My friend and my treasure!
It's bad treatment for a hero
To lie hooded in a coffin,
The warm-hearted rider
That fished in bright rivers,
That drank in great houses
With white-breasted women.
My thousand sorrows
That I've lost my companion.

XVIII

Bad luck and misfortune
Come down on you, Morris!
That snatched my protector,
My unborn child's father:
Two of them walking
And the third still within me,
And not likely I'll bear it.

XIX

My friend and my pleasure!
When you went out through the
    gateway
You turned and came back quickly,
You kissed your two children,
You kissed me on the forehead,
You said: 'Eileen, rise up quickly,
Put your affairs in order
With speed and with decision.
I am leaving home now
And there's no telling if I'll return.'
I mocked this way of talking,
He had said it to me so often.

XX

My friend and my dear!
Oh bright-sworded rider,
Rise up this moment,
Put on your fine suit
Of clean, noble cloth,
Put on your black beaver,
Pull on your gauntlets.
Up with your whip;
Outside your mare is waiting.
Take the narrow road east,
Where the trees thin before you,
Where streams narrow before you,
Where men and women will bow
    before you,
If they keep their old manners —
But I fear they have lost them.

XXI

My love and my treasure!
Not my dead ancestors,
Nor the deaths of my three children,
Nor Domhnall Mór O'Connell,
Nor Connall that drowned at sea,
Nor the twenty-six years woman
Who went across the water
And held kings in conversation —
It's not on all of them I'm calling

But on Art who was slain last night
At the inch of Carriganima! —
The brown mare's rider
That's here with me only —
With no living soul near him
But the dark little women of the mill,
And my thousand sorrows worsened
That their eyes were dry of tears.

XXII

My friend and my lamb!
Arthur O'Leary,
Of Connor, of Keady,
Of Louis O'Leary,
From west in Geeragh
And from east in Caolchnoc,
Where berries grow freely
And gold nuts on branches
And great floods of apples
All in their seasons.
Would it be a wonder
If Ive Leary were blazing
Besides Ballingeary
And Guagán of the saint
For the firm-handed rider
That hunted the stag down,
All out from Grenagh
When slim hounds fell behind?
And Oh clear-sighted rider,
What happened last night?
For I thought to myself
That nothing could kill you
Though I bought your habit.

XXIII

Arthur O'Leary's sister speaks:
My friend and my love!
Of the country's best blood,
That kept eighteen wet-nurses at work,
And each received her pay —
A heifer and a mare,
A sow and her litter,
A mill at the ford,
Yellow gold and white silver,

Silks and fine velvets,
A holding of land —
To give her milk freely
To the flower of fair manhood.

XXIV

My love and my treasure
And my love, my white dove!
Though I did not come to you,
Nor bring my troops with me,
That was no shame to me
For they were all enclosed
In shut-up rooms,
In narrow coffins,
In sleep without waking.

XXV

Were it not for the small-pox
And the black death
And the spotted fever,
That powerful army
Would be shaking their harness
And making a clatter
On their way to your funeral,
Oh white-breasted Art.

XXVI

My love you were and my joy!
Of the blood of those rough horsemen
That hunted in the valley,
Till you turned them homewards
And brought them to your hall,
Where knives were being sharpened,
Pork laid out for carving
And countless ribs of mutton,
The red-brown oats were flowing
To make the horses gallop —
Slender, powerful horses
And stable-boys to care them
Who would not think of sleeping
Nor of deserting their horses
If their owners stayed a week,
Oh brother of many friends.

XXVII

My friend and my lamb!
A cloudy vision
Came last night to me
In Cork at midnight
Alone in my bed:
That our white court fell,
That the Geeragh withered,
That your slim hounds were still
And the birds without sweetness
When you were found vanquished
On the side of the mountain,
Without priest or cleric
But an old shrivelled woman
That spread her cloak over you,
Arthur O'Leary,
While your blood flowed freely
On the breast of your shirt.

XXVIII

My love and my treasure!
And well they suited you,
Five-ply stockings,
Boots to your knees,
A three-cornered Caroline,
A lively whip,
On a frisky horse —
Many a modest, mannerly maiden
Would turn to gaze after you.

XXIX

Eileen speaks:
My love forever!
And when you went in cities,
Strong and powerful,
The wives of the merchants
All bowed down to you
For they knew in their hearts
What a fine man in bed you were,
And what a fine horseman
And father for children.

XXX

Jesus Christ knows
I'll have no cap on my head,
Nor a shift on my back,
Nor shoes on my feet,
Nor goods in my house,
Nor the brown mare's harness
That I won't spend on lawyers;
That I'll cross the seas
And talk to the king,
And if no one listens
That I'll come back
To the black-blooded clown
That took my treasure from me.

XXXI

My love and my darling!
If my cry were heard westwards
To great Derrynane
And to gold-appled Capling,
Many swift, hearty riders
And white-kerchiefed women
Would be coming here quickly
To weep at your waking,
Beloved Art O'Leary.

XXXII

My heart is warming
To the fine women of the mill
For their goodness in lamenting
The brown mare's rider.

XXXIII

May your black heart fail you,
Oh false John Cooney!
If you wanted a bribe,
You should have asked me.
I'd have given you plenty:
A powerful horse
That would carry you safely
Through the mob
When the hunt is out for you,
Or a fine herd of cattle,

Or ewes to bear lambs for you,
Or the suit of a gentleman
With spurs and top-boots —
Though it's sorry I'd be
To see you done up in them,
For I've always heard
You're a piddling lout.

XXXIV

Oh white-handed rider,
Since you are struck down,
Rise and go after Baldwin,
The ugly wretch
With the spindle shanks,
And take your revenge
For the loss of your mare —
May he never enjoy her.
May his six children wither!
But no bad wish to Máire
Though I have no love for her,
But that my own mother
Gave space in her womb to her
For three long seasons.

XXXV

My love and my dear!
Your stooks are standing,
Your yellow cows milking;
On my heart is such sorrow
That all Munster could not cure it,
Nor the wisdom of the sages.
Till Art O'Leary returns
There will be no end to the grief
That presses down on my heart,
Closed up tight and firm
Like a trunk that is locked
And the key is mislaid.

XXXVI

All women out there weeping,
Wait a little longer;
We'll drink to Art son of Connor
And the souls of all the dead,
Before he enters the school —
Not learning wisdom or music
But weighted down by earth and
    stones.

translated by Eilís Dillon, from Seán Dunne (ed.), *The Cork Anthology* (1993)

MARIA EDGEWORTH

'What's the secret of Castle Rackrent?' asks a character in The Great Gatsby, evidently thinking of a gothic shocker. But Castle Rackrent is a different kind of horror story. Subtitled An Hibernian Tale taken from facts and from the manners of the Irish squires before the year 1782, it is an exposé of feckless, squandering landlords, and of the extortionate — rack — rents that paid for their lifestyle. Instead of rack and ruin, Edgeworth recommends a greater sense of responsibility and self-respect, as exemplified in her time by the landed gentry of the Patriot Parliament of 1782.

Castle Rackrent was published in 1800, the same year as the Act of Union was passed. Sir Murtagh is Sir Murtagh Rackrent; the novel deals with several generations of Rackrents. Its narrator is the family's loyal retainer, Thady Quill, who is based on the steward of the Edgeworth estate, John Langan. The novelty of Thady's speech, and of the material generally, is such that the novel was equipped with a glossary, edited excerpts from which are given in the notes. The Linen Board was established in Dublin in 1711 to supervise the rapidly expanding linen trade.

Sir Murtagh and His Lady

I t's a long time ago, there's no saying how it was, but this for certain, the new man did not take at all after the old gentleman — The cellars were never filled after his death — and no open house, or any thing as it used to be — the tenants even were sent away without their whiskey[1] — I was ashamed myself, and knew not what to say for the honour of the family — But I made the best of a bad case, and laid it all at my lady's door, for I did not like her any how, nor any body else — she was of the family of the Skinflints, and a widow — It was a strange match for Sir Murtagh; the people in the country thought he demeaned himself greatly — but I said nothing — I knew how it was — Sir Murtagh was a great lawyer, and looked to the great Skinflint estate; there, however, he overshot himself; for though one of the co-heiresses, he was never the better for her, for she outlived him many's the long day — he could not foresee that, to be sure, when he married her. I must say for her, she made him the best of wives, being a very notable stirring woman, and looking close to every thing. But I always suspected she had Scotch blood in her veins, any thing else I could have looked over in her from a regard to the family. She was a strict observer for self and servants of Lent, and all Fast days, but not holidays. One of the maids having fainted three times the last day of Lent, to keep soul and body together we put a morsel of roast beef into her mouth, which came from Sir Murtagh's dinner, who never fasted, not he; but somehow or other it unfortunately reached my lady's ears, and the priest of the parish had a complaint made of it the next day, and the poor girl was forced as soon as she could walk to do penance for it, before she could get any peace or absolution in the house or out of it. However, my lady was very charitable in her own way. She had a charity school for poor children, where they were taught to read and write gratis, and where they were kept well to spinning gratis for my lady in return; for she had always heaps of duty yarn from the tenants, and got all her household linen out of the estate from first to last; for after the spinning, the weavers on the estate took it in hand for nothing, because of the looms my lady's interest could get from the Linen Board to distribute gratis. Then there was a bleach yard near us, and the tenant dare refuse my lady nothing, for fear of a law-suit Sir Murtagh kept hanging over him about the water course. With these ways of managing, 'tis surprising how cheap my lady got things done, and how proud she was of it. Her table the same way — kept for next to nothing — duty fowls, and duty turkeys, and duty geese,[2] came as fast as we could eat 'em, for my lady kept a sharp look out, and knew to a tub of butter every thing the tenants had, all round. They knew her way, and what with fear of driving for rent and Sir Murtagh's law-suits, they were kept in such good order, they never thought of coming near Castle Stopgap without a present of something or other — nothing too much or too little for my lady — eggs — honey — butter — meal — fish — game, growse, and herrings, fresh or salt — all went for something. As for their young pigs, we had them, and the best bacon and hams they could make up, with all young chickens in spring; but they were a set of poor wretches, and we had nothing but misfortunes with them, always breaking and running away — This, Sir Murtagh and my lady said, was all their former landlord Sir Patrick's fault, who let 'em all get the half year's rent into arrear — there was something in that, to be sure — But Sir Murtagh was as much the contrary way — For let alone making English tenants[3] of them, every soul — he was always driving and driving, and pounding and pounding, and canting and canting,[4] and replevying and replevying, and he made a good living of trespassing cattle — there was always some tenant's pig, or horse, or cow, or calf, or goose, trespassing, which was so great a gain to Sir Murtagh, that he did not like to hear me talk of repairing fences. Then his herriots and duty work[5] brought him in something — his turf was cut — his potatoes set and dug — his hay brought home, and in short all the work about his house done for nothing; for in all our leases there were strict clauses with heavy penalties, which Sir Murtagh knew well how to enforce — so many days duty work of man and horse, from every tenant, he was to have, and had, every year; and when a man vexed him, why the finest day he could pitch on, when the cratur was getting in his own harvest, or thatching his cabin, Sir Murtagh made it a principle to call upon him and his horse — so he taught 'em all, as he said, to know the law of landlord and tenant. As for law, I believe no man, dead or alive, ever loved it so well as Sir Murtagh. He had once sixteen suits pending at a time, and I never saw him so much himself — roads — lanes — bogs — wells — ponds — eel-wires — orchards — trees — tythes — vagrants — gravel-pits — sandpits — dung-hills and nuisances — every thing upon the face of the earth furnished him good matter for a suit. He used to boast that he had a law-suit for every letter in the alphabet. How I used to wonder to see Sir Murtagh in the midst of the papers in his office — why he could hardly turn about for them. I made bold to shrug my shoulders once in his presence, and thanked my stars I was not born a gentleman to so much toil and trouble — but Sir Murtagh took me up short with his old proverb, 'learning is better than house or land'. Out of forty-nine suits which he had, he never lost one but seventeen;[6] the rest he gained with costs, double costs, treble costs sometimes — but even that did not pay. He was a very learned man in the law, and had the character of it; but how it was I can't tell, these suits that he carried cost him a power of money — in the end he sold some hundreds a year of the family estate — but he was a very learned man in the law, and I know nothing of the matter except having a great regard for the family. I could not help grieving when he sent me to post up notices of the sale of the fee simple of the lands and appurtenances of Timoleague. — 'I know, honest Thady,' says he to comfort me, 'what I'm about better than you do; I'm only selling to get the ready money wanting, to carry on my suit with spirit with the Nugents of Carrickashaughlin.'

He was very sanguine about that suit with the Nugents of Carrickashaughlin. He would have gained it, they say, for certain, had it pleased Heaven to have spared him to us, and it would have been at the least a plump two thousand a year in his way; but things were ordered otherwise, for the best to be sure. He dug up a fairy-mount[7] against my advice, and had no luck afterwards. Though a learned man in the law, he was a little too incredulous in other matters. I warned him that I heard the very Banshee that my grandfather heard, before I was born long, under Sir Patrick's window a few days before his death. But Sir Murtagh thought nothing of the Banshee, nor of his cough with a spitting of blood, brought on, I understand, by catching cold in attending the courts, and overstraining his chest with making himself heard in one of his favourite causes. He was a great speaker, with a powerful voice; but his last speech was not in the courts at all. He and my lady, though both of the same way of thinking in some things, and though she was as good a wife and great economist as you could see, and he the best of husbands, as to looking into his affairs, and making money for his family; yet I don't know how it was, they had a great deal of sparring and jarring between them. — My lady had her privy purse — and she had her weed ashes,[8] and her sealing money[9] upon the signing of all the leases, with something to buy gloves besides; and besides again often took money from the tenants, if offered properly, to speak for them to Sir Murtagh about abatements and renewals. Now the weed ashes and the glove money he allowed her clear perquisites; though once when he saw her in a new gown saved out of the weed ashes, he told her to my face, (for he could say a sharp thing) that she should not put on her weeds before her husband's death. But it grew more serious when they came to the renewal businesses. At last, in a dispute about an abatement, my lady would have the last word, and Sir Murtagh grew mad; I was within hearing of the door, and now wish I had made bold to step in. He spoke so loud, the whole kitchen was out on the stairs — All on a sudden he stopped, and my lady too. Something has surely happened, thought I — and so it was, for Sir Murtagh in his passion broke a blood-vessel, and all the law in the land could do nothing in that case. My lady sent for five physicians, but Sir Murtagh died, and was buried. She had a fine jointure settled upon her, and took herself away to the great joy of the tenantry. I never said any thing, one way or the other, whilst she was part of the family, but got up to see her go at three o'clock in the morning — 'It's a fine morning, honest Thady, says she; good bye to ye' — and into the carriage she stept, without a word more, good or bad, or even half-a-crown; but I made my bow, and stood to see her safe out of sight for the sake of the family.

1. It is usual with some landlords to give their inferior tenants a glass of whiskey when they pay their rents. Thady calls it *their* whiskey; not that the whiskey is actually the property of the tenants, but that it becomes their *right* after it has been often given to them. In this general mode of reasoning respecting *rights*, the lower Irish are not singular, but they are peculiarly quick and tenacious in claiming these rights.

2. In many leases in Ireland, tenants were formerly bound to supply an inordinate quantity of poultry to their landlords.

3. An English tenant does not mean a tenant who is an Englishman, but a tenant who pays his rent on the day that it is due. It is a common prejudice in Ireland, amongst the poorer classes of people, to believe that all tenants in England pay their rents on the very day when they become due. An Irishman, when he goes to take a farm, if he wants to prove to his landlord that he is a substantial man, offers to become an *English tenant*.

4. Selling substantially by auction.

5. It was formerly common in Ireland to insert clauses in leases, binding tenants to furnish their landlords with labourers and horses for several days in the year. Much petty tyranny and oppression have resulted from this feudal custom.

6. Thady's language in this instance is a specimen of a mode of rhetoric common in Ireland. An astonishing assertion is made in the beginning of a sentence, which ceases to be in the least surprising when you hear the qualifying explanation that follows.

7. Barrows. It is said that these high mounts were of great service to the natives of Ireland when Ireland was invaded by the Danes. Watch was always kept on them, and upon the approach of an enemy a fire was lighted to give notice to the next watch, and thus the intelligence was quickly communicated through the country. Some years ago, the common people believed that these barrows were inhabited by fairies . . .

8. By ancient usage in Ireland, all the weeds on a farm belonged to the farmer's wife, or to the wife of the squire who holds the ground in his own hands. The great demand for alkaline salts in bleaching rendered these ashes no inconsiderable perquisite.

9. Formerly it was the custom in Ireland for tenants to give the squire's lady from two to fifty guineas as a perquisite upon the sealing of their leases.

from *Castle Rackrent* (1800)

JOHN PHILPOT CURRAN

One of the reasons for the rise of the Irish Volunteers and the Patriot Parliament of the 1780s was discriminatory economic policies against Ireland by England. Thomas Orde (1745–1804), the Chief Secretary, twice introduced bills to address this issue, but both were substantially undermined by the English parliament, which had the last word on legislation introduced in Dublin. As a result, both bills were rejected by the Irish parliament.

Among other members of the Patriot Parliament were Henry Flood (1732–91), who was also a noted orator, and Thomas Conolly (1738–1803), who later supported passage of the Act of Union. Among the provisions of 'The Sixth of George I', or the Declaratory Act, was one declaring that the English House of Lords could overrule the legal decisions of the Irish House of Lords. This Act was in force from 1720 to 1782.

Curran was better known as a lawyer than as a legislator. His many celebrated legal cases included the defence of Theobald Wolfe Tone after the 1798 Rebellion.

August 15th, 1785

Mr Orde, on presenting the bill, abandoned it for the session, and for ever. Thereon Flood moved the following resolution: —

'Resolved — That we hold ourselves bound not to enter into any engagement to give up the sole and exclusive right of the parliament of Ireland to legislate for Ireland in all cases whatsoever, as well externally as commercially and internally'

Curran supported him: —

I shall support the resolution proposed by the honourable member, because I think it necessary to declare to the people, that their rights have not been solely supported by one hundred and ten independent gentlemen, but that, if eight or ten of them had been absent, those who had countenanced the measure, would have abandoned every idea of prosecuting it further.

It has ever been the custom of our ancestors, when the constitution has been attacked, to take some spirited step for its support. Why was Magna Charta passed? It was passed not to give freedom to the people, but because the people were already free. Why was the repeal of the 6th of George I.? Not to give independence to the men of Ireland, but because Ireland was in itself an independent nation. This resolution does not go to give rights, but to declare that we will preserve our rights. We are told to be cautious how we commit ourselves with the parliament of Great Britain; whether this threat carry with it more of prudence or timidity, I leave gentlemen to determine. I rejoice that the cloud which had loured over us has passed away. I have no intention to wound the feelings of the minister, by triumphing in his defeat; on the contrary, I may be said to rise with some degree of self-denial, when I give to others an opportunity of exulting in the victory.

The opposition in England has thrown many impediments in the way, but I shall remember, with gratitude, that the opposition there has supported the liberties of Ireland. When I see them reprobating the attacks made upon the trial by jury, when I see them supporting the legislative rights of Ireland, I cannot refrain from giving them my applause. They well know that an invasion of the liberty of Ireland would tend to an attack upon their own.

The principle of liberty, thank heaven! still continues in those countries: that principle which stained the fields of Marathon, stood in the pass of Thermopylæ, and gave to America independence. Happy it is for Ireland, that she has recovered her rights by a victory unstained by blood — not a victory bathed in the tears of a mother, a sister, or a wife — not a victory hanging over the grave of a Warren or a Montgomery, and uncertain whether to triumph in what she had gained, or to mourn over what she had lost!

from *The Speeches of The Right Honorable John Philpot Curran* (1865)

ANONYMOUS

The widespread revival of interest in Irish traditional music of all sorts which has continued unabated since the 1960s has enabled audiences to see beyond ballads worn out by familiarity such as 'The Wearing of the Green'. Yet this ballad contains many of the ingredients that give such songs their appeal and their place in the scheme of things cultural. It lends authoritative voice to the anonymous. It carries news — bad news generally — and it raises to the level of song matters such as loss and exile which otherwise might be difficult to contemplate.

Ballads became an important means of communication in Ireland during the eighteenth century, when the publication of broadside ballads became prevalent. In them, the evolution of English as it came to be spoken in Ireland can be glimpsed, though 'The Wearing of the Green' is not a good case in point; it is a bit polished, and there is a written feel to it. But singing it could quite possibly end in trouble, green being a highly charged political colour at the time of the United Irishmen, which James Napper Tandy (1740–1803) helped to found in 1791 in Belfast. He died in France.

Frank O'Connor called this song 'our Marseillaise'.

The Wearing of the Green

O, Paddy dear, and did you hear the news that's going round?
The shamrock is forbid by law to grow on Irish ground;
St Patrick's Day no more we'll keep, his colours can't be seen,

For there's a bloody law agin the wearing of the green.
I met with Napper Tandy, and he took me by the hand,
And he said, 'How's poor old Ireland, and how does she stand?'
'She's the most distressful country that ever yet was seen,
They are hanging men and women for the wearing of the green.'

Then if the colour we must wear be England's cruel red,
Let it remind us of the blood poor Ireland has shed.
You may take the shamrock from your hat and cast it on the sod,
But 'twill take root and flourish there, though under foot 'tis trod.
When laws can stop the blades of grass from growing as they grow,
And when the leaves in summer-time their verdure dare not show,
Then I will change the colour that I wear in my caubeen,
But till that day, please God, I'll stick to wearing of the green.

But if at last our colour should be torn from Ireland's heart,
Her sons with shame and sorrow from the dear old isle will part;
I've heard a whisper of a land that lies beyond the sea,
Where rich and poor stand equal in the light of freedom's day.
O Erin, must we leave you, driven by a tyrant's hand?
Must we ask a mother's blessing from a strange and distant land?
Where the cruel cross of England shall nevermore be seen,
And where, please God, we'll live and die still wearing of the green.

ANONYMOUS

Ballads seem to have come into their own in Ireland with the 1798 Rebellion. The United Irishmen were firm believers in the power of the ballad. They published a collection of ballads entitled Paddy's Resource *in Belfast in 1795 and it quickly went through a number of editions. Later, the events of the rebellion inspired such well-known ballads as 'The Boys of Wexford' and John Kells Ingrams's 'The Memory of the Dead', the fame of the first line of which — 'Who fears to speak of Ninety-Eight?' — is such that the only answer is, 'Nobody'.*

The two parts of the country in which the 1798 Rebellion was most serious are County Wexford and an area within a twenty-mile radius of Belfast where many of the leaders were Presbyterians. The bridge of Toome is near Randalstown, Co. Antrim. In fact insurgents tore it down.

There is undoubtedly a historical basis for the recurring presence of 'the clever tall young youth' in ballads about every Irish rebellion, though this figure embodies not just historical accuracy but also complicated rhetorical overtures.

Rody McCorley

Come tender hearted Christians all, attention pay to me,
'Till I relate these verses great, these verses two or three,
Concerning of a clever youth who was cut off in his bloom,
And died upon the gallows tree near to the bridge of Toome.

The hero now I speak of, he was proper tall and straight,
Like to the lofty poplar tree his body was complete,
His growth was like the tufted fir that does ascend the air,
And waving o'er his shoulders broad the locks of yellow hair.

In sweet Duneane this youth was born and reared up tenderly,
His parents educated him, all by their industry,
Both day and night they sorely toiled for all their family,
Till desolation it came on by cursèd perjury.

'Twas first the father's life they took and secondly the son,
The mother tore her old grey locks, she says 'I am undone
They took from me my property, my houses and my land,
And in the parish where I was born I dare not tread upon.'

'Farewell unto you sweet Drumaul, if in you I had stayed,
Among the Presbyterians I wouldn't have been betrayed,
The gallows tree I'd ne'er have seen had I remainèd there
For Dufferin you betrayed me, McErlean you set the snare.

'In Ballyscullion I was betrayed, woe be unto the man,
Who swore me a defender and a foe unto the crown,
Which causes Rody for to lie beneath the spreading thorn,
He'll sigh and say "Alas the day that ever I was born".'

Soon young Rody was conveyed to Ballymena town,
He was loaded there with irons strong, his bed was the cold ground,
And there young Rody he must wait until the hour has come,
When a court-martial does arrive for to contrive his doom.

They called upon an armèd band, an armèd band came soon,
To guard the clever tall young youth down to the Bridge of Toome,
And when young Rody he came up the scaffold to ascend,
He looked at east and looked at west to view his loving friends.

And turning round unto the north he cried 'O faithless friend,
'Twas you who proved my overthrow and brought me to this end.
Since 'tis upon Good Friday that I'll executed be,
Convenient to the Bridge of Toome upon a Gallows Tree.'

They called on Father Devlin, his reverence came with speed,
'Here's one of Christ's own flock,' he said, 'ye shepherds for to feed.'
He gave to him the Heavenly food, that nourishes the soul,
That it may rest eternally while his body is in the mould.

And looking up unto the Lord he says, 'O Lord receive,
Here is my soul, I do bestow my body unto the grave,
That it may rest in peace and joy without the least surprise,
Till Michael sounds his trumpet loud, and says "Ye dead arise".'

P.J. McCALL

There were two Father Murphys active in 1798 in Wexford, Father Michael and Father John. The latter is the one famously commemorated in 'Boolavogue', a townland outside Enniscorthy where he was curate. The burning of his chapel by the yeomanry on 26 May 1798, after a day of unrest which cost Lieutenant Bookey his life, marked the beginning of hostilities in County Wexford. As the song indicates, rebellion spread from top to bottom of the eastern part of the county. The rebellion in Wexford effectively came to an end less than a month later at the Battle of Vinegar Hill, overlooking Enniscorthy. British forces were a mixture of Irish-manned yeomanry and militia, regular British army, and Hessian mercenaries.

'Boolavogue' was written by P.J. McCall (1861–1919) to coincide with the centenary of the 1798 Rebellion. According to a ballad called 'Father Murphy', dating from much closer to the actual events, 'He was brought to Tullow and used severely,/This blessed priest they burned him sore'.

Boolavogue

At Boolavogue as the sun was setting; O'er the bright May meadows of Shelmalier
A rebel hand set the heather blazing; And brought the neighbours from far
and near
Then Father Murphy from old Kilcormac; Spurred up the rock with a warning
cry
'Arm, arm' he cried 'for I've come to lead you; For Ireland's freedom we'll fight
or die.'

He led us 'gainst the coming soldiers; And the cowardly yeomen we put to flight
'Twas at the Harrow the boys of Wexford; Showed Bookey's regiment how men
could fight

Look out for hirelings, King George of England; Search every kingdom where
    breathes a slave
For Father Murphy of County Wexford; Sweeps o'er the land like a mighty wave.

We took Camolin and Enniscorthy; and Wexford storming drove out our foes
'Twas at Slieve Coilte our pikes were reeking; With the crimson blood of the
    beaten Yeos
At Tubberneery and Ballyellis; Full many a Hessian lay in his gore
Ah! Father Murphy had aid come over; The Green Flag floated from shore to
    shore!

At Vinegar Hill o'er the pleasant Slaney; Our heroes vainly stood back to back
And the Yeos of Tullow took Father Murphy; And burnt his body upon the rack
God grant you glory brave Father Murphy; And open heaven to all your men
The cause that called you may call to-morrow; In another fight for the Green
    again.

JOHN KEEGAN CASEY

The dominant image that has come down from the rebellion in Wexford in 1798 is the pike, though it was by no means the only weapon the rebels used. Pre-industrial in origin, made without difficulty by the local smith from materials readily to hand, easily concealed in rural settings, it can be seen to memorialise the sense of populist, agrarian, humble and in a sense militarily disadvantaged struggle which is one of the ways the events of the summer of 1798 have filtered down through tradition. 'The Rising of the Moon', a ballad written by John Keegan Casey to the air of 'The Wearing of the Green' and often associated with the abortive Fenian rebellion in 1867, seems keen to evoke the pike's symbolic, talismanic power.

The power of the ballad itself is dramatised by Lady Gregory in a one-act play, The Rising of the Moon (1907), in which a Fenian on the run and disguised as a ballad-seller makes common cause with a policeman who is a member of his search-party. He escapes unscathed to the tune of 'The Rising of the Moon'.

The Rising of the Moon

'Tell me, tell me Sean O'Farrell, tell me why you hurry so.'
'Hush, a bhuachaill hush and listen', and his cheeks were all aglow.
'I bear orders from the Captain, get you ready quick and soon,
For the pikes must be together at the rising of the moon.'

'Oh! then tell me, Sean O'Farrell, where the gatherin' is to be?'
'In the old spot by the river, right well known to you and me.
One word more, for signal token whistle up the marchin' tune,
With your pike upon your shoulder at the rising of the moon.'

Out from many a mud-wall cabin eyes were watching thro' the night.
Many a manly heart was throbbing for that blessed warning light;
Murmurs passed along the valley, like the banshee's lonesome croon,
And a thousand blades were flashing at the rising of the moon.

There beside the singing river that dark mass of men was seen,
High above their shining weapons flew their own beloved green,
'Death to every foe and traitor! Forward! Strike the marchin' tune!
And Hurra! my boys, for freedom; 'tis the rising of the moon!'

Well they fought for poor old Ireland, and full bitter was their fate;
Oh! What glorious pride and sorrow fill the name of 'ninety-eight.
But, thank God, there still are beating strong young hearts in manhood's
    bloom,
Who will follow in their footsteps at the rising of the moon.

ANONYMOUS

The Twelfth of July is the date on which the Battle of the Boyne was fought in 1690, the victor of which was William of Orange. The actual Orange Society, or Order, as it became, was founded in 1795, following the so-called 'Battle of the Diamond' in County Armagh between two agrarian secret societies, the Protestant Peep o' Day Boys and the Catholic Defenders. The issues between the sides were local and agrarian, though, as history shows, it did not take long for them to become tribal and territorial.

The Twelfth is marked with great pomp and circumstance, the most public display of which are ceremonial marches with bands playing 'The Sash' and other stirring airs in the Orange tradition. Members of the order parade in these in full regalia. The chief article of their outfits is the sash, its orange facing decorated with insigniae and similar esoterica proper to a secret, oath-bound society, which the Orange Order still is.

It is also an international organisation, Glasgow being only one of its main overseas centres. The words below are not the only lyrics of 'The Sash'.

The Sash Me Father Wore

Sure I'm an Ulster Orangeman from Erin's Isle I came
To see my Glasgow Brethren all of honour and of fame
And to tell them of my fore-fathers who fought in days of yore
All on the twelfth day of July in the sash me father wore.

Chorus
It's ould but it's beautiful it's the best you ever seen
Been worn for more nor ninety years in that little Isle of Green
From my Orange and Purple Fore-father it descended with galore
It's a terror to them paypish boys the sash me father wore.

So here I am in Glasgow Town youse boys and girls to see
And I hope that in good Orange style you all will welcome me
A true-blue blade that's just arrived from that dear Ulster shore
All on the twelfth day of July in the sash me father wore.

Chorus
It's ould but it's beautiful, etc.

And when I'm going to leave yeeze all 'Good luck' till youse I'll say
And as I cross the raging sea my orange flute I'll play
Returning to my native town, to ould Belfast once more,
To be welcomed back by Orangemen in the sash me father wore.

Chorus
It's ould but it's beautiful, etc.

ANONYMOUS

Sam McAughtry's portrait of the decline of the Belfast funeral notes in passing how commonplace 'flute bands' are in that part of the world. These are the bands to which Orange parades march, though it tends to be the rattling rhythm of the drums that comes to mind in connection with those bands, rather than flutes or melodies.

The Orange credentials of the flute in this particular song are suggested by its being the musical expression of the watchword, 'No Surrender!' The tunes it plays are all classics from the Orange repertoire: 'The Protestant Boys' is also known as 'Lillibullero', and 'Croppies, Lie Down!' draws on the events of 1798, when hair cropped short was an expression of support for the French Revolution.

Much of interest has been written about the cultural richness and sociological complexity of the Orange Order. It also remains a formidable political influence on the politics of unionism.

The Auld Orange Flute

In the County Tyrone near the town of Dungannon
There were many a ruction meself had a hand in,
Bob Williams who lived there a weaver by trade
And all of us thought him a stout Orange blade.
On the twelfth of July as the yearly did come,
Bob played on his flute to the sound of the drum,
You may talk of your harp, your piano or lute,
But nothing could sound like the auld Orange flute.

But this treacherous scoundrel, he took us all in,
For he married a Papish called Bridget McGinn.
Turned Papish himself, and forsook the old cause
That gave us our freedom, religion and laws.
Now the boys in the townland made noise upon it
And Bob had to fly to the province of Connaught
He flew with his wife and fixings to boot,
And along with the others, his auld Orange flute.

At chapel on Sundays, to atone for past deeds,
He'd say Pater and Aves, and counted his beads,
'Till after some time, at the priest's own desire,
He went with that auld flute to play in the choir.
He went with that auld flute to play in the loft,
But the instrument shivered and sighed and then coughed,
When he blew it and fingered it, it made a strange noise,
For the flute would play only '*The Protestant Boys*'!

Bob jumped up and started and got in a flutter,
And he put the auld flute in the bless'd holy water.
He thought that it might now make some other sound,
When he blew it again it played '*Croppies, Lie Down!*'
And all he did whistle and finger and blow,
To play Papish music he found it 'no go!'
'*Kick the Pope*', '*The Boyne Water*', and such like 'twould sound,
But one Papish squeak in it could not be found.

ROBERT EMMET

'Bold Robert Emmet, the darling of Erin!' Of all the young Irishmen who lost their lives because of political involvement, the most romanticised and even idolised is Robert Emmet. In the course of the nineteenth century, particularly, his became an indispensable presence in the pictures and music of Irish nationalist culture as it burgeoned at home and abroad.

Emmet was the leader of an abortive rebellion in Dublin in 1803. The outbreak lasted only a few hours. Emmet's followers murdered out of hand the Lord Chief Justice, Lord Kilwarden, and his nephew. But his fame rests largely on his speech from the dock, and the statement: 'Let my character and my motives repose in obscurity and peace, till other times and other men can do them justice. Then shall my character be vindicated. — Then may my epitaph be written.' The phrase 'Let no man write my epitaph' occurs slightly before the end.

One of Emmet's friends in student days was Thomas Moore, who shared his republican enthusiasm. A number of Moore's Irish Melodies are haunted by Emmet and those days, particularly one entitled, 'Oh! breathe not his name'.

Speech from the Dock

Why the sentence of the law should not be passed upon me, I have nothing to say — why the sentence which in the public mind is usually attached to that of the law, ought to be reversed, I have much to say. — I stand here a conspirator — as one engaged in a conspiracy for the overthrow of the *British* Government in *Ireland*; — for the fact of which I am to suffer by the law; — for the motives of which I am to answer before God. — I am ready to do both. — Was it only the fact of treason — was it that naked fact alone with which I stood charged — Was I to suffer to other punishment, than the death of the body, I would not obtrude on your attention, but having received the sentence, I would bow my neck in silence to the stroke. But, my Lords, I well know, that when a man enters into a conspiracy, he has not only to combat against the difficulties of fortune, but to contend with the still more insurmountable obstacles of prejudice: — and that if, in the end, fortune abandons him and delivers him over bound into the hands of the law, his character is previously loaded with calumny and misrepresentation. For what purpose, I know not, except, that the Prisoner, thus weighed down both in mind and body, may be delivered over a more unresisting victim to condemnation. — It is well: — But the victim being once obtained and firmly in your power, let him now unmanacle his reputation. — Not, my Lords, that I have much to demand from you, — it is a claim on your memory, rather than on your candour, that I am making. I do not ask you to believe implicitly what I say. I do not hope that you will let my vindication ride at anchor in your breasts; — I only ask you, to let it float upon the surface of your recollection, till it comes to some more friendly port to receive it, and give it shelter against the heavy storms with which it is buffetted.

I am charged with being an emissary of *France*, for the purpose of inciting insurrection in the country and then delivering it over to a foreign enemy. — It is false! — I did not wish to join this country with *France*. — I did join — I did not create the rebellion — not for *France*; but for its liberty. It is true, there were communications between the *United Irishmen* and *France*; — it is true, that by that, the war was no surprise upon us. There is a new agent at *Paris*, at this moment, negotiating with the *French Government* to obtain from them an aid sufficient to accomplish the separation of *Ireland* from *England*, and before any expedition sails, it is intended to have a treaty signed, as a guarantee, similar to that which *Franklin* obtained for *America*. Whether they will do that now, *England*, you may judge. But the only question with the members of The Provisional Government was: Whether *France* should come to this country, as an enemy? — Whether she should have any pretext for so doing? — Whether the people should look to *France*, as their only deliverer, or through the medium and control of the Provisional Government attain their object? It is not now, that I discovered, or that the rest of the Provisional Government of *Ireland* feel what it is that binds states together. They well know, my Lords, that such a disposition exists only in proportion to its mutuality of interest; and wherever that mutuality does not exist, no written articles can secure the inferior state, nor supply the means of protecting its independence.

In this view, it never was the intention of the Provisional Government of *Ireland* to form a permanent alliance with *France*; well knowing, that if there is between states a permanent mutual interest, more or less, though treaties may be made, yet for the most part, it is not the treaty which binds them together, but a sense of common interest, and where that interest does not exist, treaties are soon represented as unjust — they are qualified and interpreted at pleasure, and violated under any pretext. Under these views, it never was the intention to form a permanent treaty with *France*, and in the treaty which they did make, they had the same guarantee which *America* had, that an Independent Government should be established in the country, before the *French* should come. — God forbid! that I should see my country under the hands of a foreign power. On the contrary, it is evident from the introductory paragraph of the address of the *Provisional Government* of *Ireland*, that every hazard attending an independent effort was deemed preferable to the more fatal risk of introducing a *French* army into the country. For what? when it has liberty to maintain and independence to keep, may no consideration induce it to submit. If the *French* come as a foreign enemy, Oh, my Countrymen! meet them on the shore with a torch in one hand — a sword in the other — receive them with all the destruction of war — immolate them in their boats before our native soil shall be polluted by a foreign foe. If they succeed in landing, fight them on the strand, burn every blade of grass before them, as they advance; raze every house; and if you are driven to the centre of your country, collect your provisions, your property, your wives and your daughters, form a circle around them — fight while two men are left, and when but one remains, let that man set fire to the pile, and release himself and the families of his fallen countrymen from the tyranny of *France*.

Deliver my country into the hands of *France!* — Look at the Proclamation. — Where is it stated? — Is it in that part where the people of *Ireland* are called upon to shew the world, that they are competent to take their place among nations? — that they have a right to claim acknowledgment as an *Independent* country, by the satisfactory proof of their capability of maintaining their independence? — by wresting it from *England*, with *their own* hands? Is it in that part, where it is stated, that the system has been organised within the last eight months, *without the hope of foreign assistance*, and which the renewal of hostilities has not accelerated? — Is it in that part, which desires *England* not to create a deadly national antipathy between the two countries? — Look then to another part of the Proclamation — look at the military regulations: — is there a word introduced from the *French* nomenclature? — Are not all the terms *English* — all the appellations of the intended constituted authorities — *English*? — Why then say, the system was from *France*? — Yes, there was one argument urged; one quotation from the Proclamation relied upon, to prove, that we must have meant to resort to *France*. 'You are to shew to us, that you have something in reserve wherewith to crush hereafter, not only a greater exertion on the part of the people; but a greater exertion, rendered still greater by *foreign assistance*.' From which an inference is drawn, that foreign assistance is the support of the present system. Because you are called upon to shew, that your strength is such, that you can put down the present attempt without bringing out all your force — to shew, that you have something in *reserve*, wherewith to crush *hereafter*. Therefore, the conclusion drawn is, because a *future* exertion *may be* rendered greater by foreign assistance, that foreign assistance *is* the foundation of the present exertion.

But it is said, we must have had it in view to deliver up the country to *France*, and this is not attempted to be proved upon any ground, but that of assertion. — It is not proved from our declarations or actions; because every circumstance attending the attempt which took place, shews, that our object was to anticipate *France*. — How could we speak of freedom to our countrymen — how assume such an exalted motive and meditate the introduction of a power, which has been the enemy of freedom wherever she appears. — See how she has behaved to other countries. How has she behaved to *Switzerland*, to *Holland*, and to *Italy*? Could we expect better conduct towards us? No! Let not then any man calumniate my memory, by believing that I could have hoped for freedom from the government of *France*, or that I would have betrayed the sacred cause of the liberty of this country, by committing it to the power of her most determined foe.

With regard to this, I have one observation to make: — It has been stated that I came from abroad: — If I had been in *Switzerland*, I would have fought against the *French*; for I believe the Swiss are hostile to the French. — In the dignity of freedom, I would have expired on the frontiers of that country, and they should have it entered only by passing over my lifeless corse.[1] — But if I thought the people were favourable to the *French*. — I have seen so much what the consequence of the failure of revolutions are — the oppressions of the higher upon the lower orders of the people. — I say, if I saw them disposed to admit the *French*, I would not join them, but I would put myself between the *French* and the people, not as a victim — but to protect them from subjugation, and endeavour to gain their confidence, by sharing in their danger.

So would I have done with the people of *Ireland*, and so would I do, if I was called upon tomorrow. — Our object was to effect a separation from *England* —.

1.   An archaic word for 'corpse'.

from *Field Day Anthology of Irish Writing* (1991)

ANTHONY CRONIN

'Our object', said Emmet in his speech from the dock, 'was to effect a separation from England.' And, like other republicans, he had been in France to secure assistance, meeting Napoleon and Talleyrand in 1802. But he also made clear at his trial, 'I did not come from France', meaning that he was not acting under French orders. Emmet seems to have financed his uprising himself. This may be another reason why he used to occupy such a high place in the pantheon of Irish patriots. A further reason possibly is that, like Father Murphy of 1798 fame, he maintained direct contact with the people — not necessarily an explicit feature of the command structures of Irish revolutionary activity.

Emmet was hanged outside St Catherine's Church, Thomas Street, Dublin, not far from where most of his supporters lived and also near where Lord Kilwarden and his nephew had been murdered. 'Tom' is Emmet's older brother, Thomas Addis Emmet (1764–1827), also prominent in the United Irishmen. Emmet's defence team consisted of Peter Burrowes and Leonard McNally. The latter was an informer. Luke White (d. 1824) made his name and fortune securing funds for the government with which to bribe opponents of the Union. Robert Kee's book The Green Flag was published in 1972.

The Bauld Robert Emmet

There isn't going to be much fuss about the bi-centenary of the birth of Robert Emmet; and the reasons are not far to seek. Republicanism, nationalism, separatism of all sorts, shades and descriptions, are, in spite of the Giant Electoral Victory of the Republican Party, still at a pretty low ebb. Heroism, pure and undefiled, at a low rate of discount; romanticism, shining and bright, at an even lower; martyrdom, a joke in poor taste: and a hero, a martyr who died with a smile is, as we all know too well, what the bould Robert Emmet is supposed to have been.

But he was also a revolutionary conspirator; and even supposing such people were approved of in these parts nowadays — which they most certainly are not — he would not be regarded as any sort of advertisement for the breed. For Emmet, in that department, was the arch bungler. The figure he presents to the world is one of quite astonishing ineptitude and carelessness. The fate of Lord Kilwarden, the 'remarkably humane' Lord Chief Justice whom 'the mob' (aided by the seldom-referred-to agents provocateurs) pulled from his carriage and piked in the street rivals his own in its fame.

The cruelly dismissive chapter in Mr Robert Kee's widely circulated *The Green Flag* just about sums up the current attitudes, as doubtless it is meant to, for my old friend Mr Kee's work is, sad to say, a deliberate job of de-bunking right through; and as such it is, on the whole, just about as a-historical as the old bunking jobs on which we were brought up. Mr Kee insists that as the would-be head of a revolutionary mass movement, Emmet was a presumptuous, elitist bore, ready to drag a cowed and anxious people into a calamity of his own creating; while as a conspirator, with his drunken messengers, his premature explosions, his mixed-up fuses, his bolting cab-horses and his signal rockets that were never fired, he cuts a totally ridiculous figure.

It is a far, far cry from the days when he hung in his green cut-away coat and white pantaloons on every cottage wall. In spite of Mr George Colley's visit to Kilmainham, Emmet, in the popular estimation nowadays, was a bit of an eejit, and the less said about him the better.

Interestingly enough, all the efforts of the Administration at the time were directed towards making Emmet a ridiculous figure with elitist notions also. He had in the words Norbury used in the candle-lit courtroom, 'the honour to be a gentleman by birth' whose father 'filled a respectable situation' under the Crown; but, the prisoner was told, 'you have conspired with hostlers, bakers, butchers, and such persons, whom you invited to council when you erected your provisional government'. The prosecuting lawyer could barely contain his amusement at the contrast in social station between Emmet and his associates, Dowdall the clerk, Quigley the bricklayer, Stafford the baker, 'illiterate victims of the ambition of this young man'. In all the Administration's unctuous pronouncements, in the editorials of its bought newspapers and the orations of its doubtless more-easily-convinced lawyers, the point is hammered home. Emmet was a dilettante and his followers were 'miserable victims' who had been 'misled by phantoms of revolutionary delusion'.

At the same time, of course, there had to have been horrors committed and further horrors untold in the prospect of success. The young gentleman from Trinity College, Mr William Conyngham Plunket told the jury, 'would doubtless have been immolated by his followers if he had succeeded'. A Jacobin terror was a clear possibility, as the fate of Lord Kilwarden should remind everybody. And when it was all over the *Dublin Evening Post* (whose editor, incidentally, was drawing a secret service allowance of one hundred pounds a quarter) hammered the points thus far made home. Emmet's associates were 'an outlawed bricklayer, and such contemptible creatures, as an outlawed clerk, hodmen, hostlers, old clothes men, etc.'

The conspiracy therefore 'was contemptible and inefficient, and stood isolated and detached from popular sympathy and co-operation'. Yet at the same time 'it was one of those efforts of mob-like riot and licentiousness to which mad enthusiasm can almost at any time, with the aid of a little money, rouse the desperate profligacy of a great capital'.

In other words, the prosecution's case was much the same as Mr Kee's; the only difference being the unspoken admission, reflecting an unspoken fear, that Emmet had nearly succeeded in getting out of the web of conspiracy and making himself the leader of a mass movement which included a very large number of honest working-class people. But being the same as Mr Kee's, it is the same as the general opinion which Mr Kee has helped to form: Emmet was the creator of unnecessary bloodshed, brutal, inefficient and hopeless all at the same time, and as such little better than a murderer.

And opposed to this stupid, sordid and unnecessary invocation of violence, with its degrading means and its impossible object, stood, according to Mr Conyngham Plunket, the ordinary processes of politics and the law:

> What does it avow itself to be? A plan — not to correct the excesses or reform the abuses of the government of the country; not to remove any specks of imperfection which might have grown upon the surface of this constitution, or to restrain the overgrown power of the Crown, or to restore any privilege of parliament, or to throw any new security round the liberty of the subject. No. But it plainly and boldly avows itself to be a plan to separate Great Britain from Ireland; to dissolve the Union and put 'a free and independent republic in Ireland' in its place. To sever the connection between Great Britain and Ireland!
>
> Gentlemen, I should feel it a waste of words and public time were I addressing you or any person within the limits of my voice to talk of the

frantic desperation of the plan of any man, who speculates upon the dissolution of that empire, whose glory and happiness depend upon its indissoluble connection. But were it practicable to sever that connection, to untie the links that bind us to the British constitution, and to turn us adrift upon the turbulent ocean of revolution, who could answer for the existence of this country, as an independent power, for a year? God and nature have made the two countries essential to each other. Let them cling to each other. Let them cling to each other to the end of time, and their united affection and loyalty will be proof against the machinations of the world.

Mr Plunket, of course, could not see into the future. The Act of Union was only three years old; and he could no more at that stage have foreseen the cynical lack of any attempt to make it work as it was supposed to work than he could have prognosticated the 'glory and happiness' of the death-toll which the system under which Ireland then laboured was to bring about four decades later. Nor, we may be mildly assured, did Mr Plunket much care. He had spoken, in company with the egregiously obnoxious Curran and Tom Emmet's old friend the part-time informer Peter Burrowes, against the Union, and he was at this moment most anxious to work his passage home. But nothing in the records of the time is more striking than the contrast between the idealism of Robert Emmet and the self-seeking, the brief-hunting, the placemanship, the cool run-of-the-mill chicanery and corruption of everybody who surrounded him with the exception of his own hostlers, butchers and brickmakers.

It may be said — as indeed the prosecution and the propagandists said in effect — that Emmet's 'idealism' was merely the sublimation and the guise of a different kind of ambition, which might have included martyrdom but nevertheless involved the ruin and death of a great many other people. We know a good deal now, we think, about the psychology of heroism, and perhaps of romanticism also, which is not to its credit. But nevertheless the contrast remains, and in viewing the picture — the smooth-talking, bought lawyers with their assurances that the law had the answer to every complaint, the careerist politicians with their reasonable belief in progress, the dissolute editors with their clever echoes of the middle-class man in the street, the enormous network of spies and secret agents with their eye to the main chance on one side; and the youthful, pathetic figure with its pleading voice and its belief in human idealism on the other — a lot will depend on the respondent's most instinctual and fundamental reactions.

Yet again, we would be falling into a trap carefully enough set in most times and places if we allow ourselves to be on the side of mere 'idealism'. For in what way, we should really ask ourselves, were Emmet's ideas less worthy of respect than his opponents'? The thirty decrees attached to the Proclamation of the Provisional Government which was read by the light of smoky candles to the hostlers and hod-carriers in the depot in Thomas Street (and met with their approval) abolished tithes; made Church lands the property of the nation; suspended all dealings in land and securities until the formation of a national government; and instituted a sovereign assembly elected by universal suffrage and secret ballot.

The Proclamation itself declared that: 'We war not against property, we war against no religious sect, we war not against past opinions or prejudices, we war against English dominion.' Not very original-sounding now, perhaps, and if impracticable only because it was, as they say, 'far in advance of its time'. But the validity of Emmet's ideas was and is somehow held to be affected by the fact that he was still sending out to buy blunderbusses a few minutes before he led out his pikemen; while the practicality of his opponents' was amply endorsed when, the day after his trial, the banker Luke White called at the Castle and said he would immediately take £500,000 in Exchequer-bills at par.

But the final and most cruel of all the ironies contained in Emmet's and Ireland's situation is perhaps revealed by a clearer look at his actual character and abilities than the romanticism of subsequent generations, the sordidity of his failure and the subtle calumnies of his opponents have perhaps ever permitted. He was only twenty-four years of age when he returned from Paris, reaffirmed his connection with the United Irishmen and entered on his disastrous, conspiratorial course. A year later his charm, ability and attractions (including, of course, his class-attractions) had placed him at the head of what in hard fact did very nearly become a mass movement of daunting proportions, with a fair chance of success.

There are questions still unanswered about its failure; but the ability and the eloquence of the boy leader are surely undeniable. He made his famous speech from the dock unrefreshed, late at night and in the face of hostile and effective interruption, after standing in the courtroom for more than twelve hours. If Ireland had been a free country, or Irish society had been a free society in which a man of honour could have cared to rise, there is absolutely no doubt whatever that Emmet would have distinguished himself as a politician of humane instincts and near-to-dazzling genius. But the situation in which his country found itself forced him, as it has done so many others, to turn his talents in a particular direction for which he was totally unfitted. He was perhaps the most inept conspirator on record; and on that alone, he is apparently, by current consensus, to be judged.

from *An Irish Eye* (1985)

Thomas Moore

His rebellion a failure, Emmet fled the city and spent some time in the Dublin mountains. But he returned to the city in order to be near Sarah Curran, the daughter of John Philpot Curran, to whom he was secretly engaged. This led to his discovery by the authorities.

John Philpot Curran took such a dim view of his daughter's attachment that she left the family home. Two years after Emmet's execution, she married a British officer. She died in England in 1808.

Emmet's go-between while he was in the mountains was Anne Devlin (1778–1851), Sarah Curran's servant. She suffered arrest and imprisonment, but never said a word. Her story is the subject of a prize-winning film, Anne Devlin *(1984), written and directed by Pat Murphy.*

She is far from the land

She is far from the land where her young hero sleeps,
    And lovers are round her sighing,
But coldly she turns from their gaze and weeps,
    For her heart in his grave is lying.

She sings the wild song of her dear native plains,
    Ev'ry note which he lov'd awaking,
Ah! Little they think who delight in her strains,
    How the heart of the minstrel is breaking.

He had liv'd for his love, for his country he died,
    They were all that to life had entwin'd him;
Nor soon shall the tears of his country be dried,
    Nor long will his love stay behind him.

Oh! Make her a grave where the sunbeams rest,
    When they promise a glorious morrow;
They'll shine o'er her sleep, like a smile from the West,
    From her own lov'd island of sorrow.

SAMUEL LEWIS

Nowadays, the focus on this part of the world is reversed, with Piltown getting what little attention there is and Fiddown very much playing second fiddle. Much of Lewis's inventory remains, including a great variety of pre-Christian and early Christian sites. The Ponsonby mausoleum is still there. According to another source, Bessborough House, the Ponsonby family seat, was built in 1751 by Francis Bindon. Burned down in 1922, it was subsequently restored as a monastery. Fiddown church is on the site of the sixth-century monastery of St Mo-Mhoedhóg — which sounds like the Welsh name, Madoc. The land is still productive and the river-views are fetching, though this stretch of the Suir has little traffic now. The city of Kilkenny is known as 'The Marble City' on account of the black marble to be seen there. This material in its raw — 'grey' — state is what Lewis has seen. It becomes black through polishing.

Contents of a Village, 1837

FIDDOWN, a parish and village, in the barony of IVERK, county of KILKENNY, and province of LEINSTER, on the high road from Kilkenny to Carrick; containing, with the post-town of Pilltown (which is separately described), 4296 inhabitants, of which number, 193 are in the village. This parish, the name of which is said to be derived from *Fiodh*, 'a wood', and *Doon*, a 'rath' or 'fort', is bounded on the west by the river Lingawn, which is crossed by a good stone bridge, and on the south by the river Suir; it comprises 10,485 statute acres, as applotted under the tithe act, and valued at £8145 per annum. The soil in some parts is of astonishing fertility, and there is no waste land; the system of agriculture has much improved within the last seven years, through the exertions of the Irish Farming Society. There are numerous limestone and sandstone quarries; and near Pilltown is a quarry of variegated grey marble, susceptible of a high polish. The village of Fiddown consists of 36 houses, and has fairs on April 25th, June 10th, Sept. 29th, and Nov. 30th. It is situated on the bank of the river Suir, which is navigable throughout the extent of the parish for vessels of large burden, and abounds with excellent salmon and trout. Besborough, the fine old mansion of the Earl of Besborough, and from which his lordship takes his title, is situated in a well-wooded park of more than 500 acres. The house, which is built of hewn blue limestone, is 100 feet in front by 80 in depth; the great hall is supported by four Ionic columns of Kilkenny marble, each of a single stone $10\frac{1}{2}$ feet high; it was erected in 1744 from a design of David Bindon, Esq., and contains a fine collection of pictures. The other seats are Belline, the elegant residence of W.W. Currey, Esq., surrounded by a beautiful demesne; Fanningstown of J. Walsh, Esq.; Tyburoughny Castle, of M. Rivers, Esq.; Willmount, of G. Briscoe, Esq.; Cookestown, of J. Burnett, Esq.; Garrynarca, of N. Higinbotham, Esq.; and the glebe-house, of the Rev. W. Gregory. The living is a rectory and vicarage, in the diocese of Ossory, united by act of council, in 1689, to the rectories of Owning or Bewley, and Tubrid, and the rectories and vicarages of Castlane and Tipperaghney, and in the patronage of the Bishop: the tithes of the parish amount to £687, and of the benefice to £1228. The glebe-house was built by aid of a gift of £100 and a loan of £1500 from the late Board of First Fruits, in 1817; the glebe comprises 48 acres. The church is situated in the village, on the site of an abbey, of which St Maidoc or Momoedoc is said to have been abbot in 590: it is an ancient structure, handsomely fitted up by the late Earl of Besborough, and contains several monuments to the Ponsonby family, among which is one to Brabazon, first Earl of Besborough, who died in 1758, consisting of half-length figures of the earl and his countess, on a sarcophagus of Egyptian marble, under a pediment supported by four Corinthian columns and four pilasters of Sienna marble. In the R. C. divisions the parish forms part of the union or district of Templeorum; the chapel, a neat building, is at Pilltown. In the schools at Pilltown, an infants' school, and a national school at Tubbernabrona about 300 children are instructed: there are also a private school, in which are about 40 children, and two Sunday schools. Throughout the parish are ruins of several ancient churches, Danish forts, and druidical altars or cromlechs. Several vestiges of antiquity have been found at Belline, and many are still to be seen in its immediate neighbourhood. The horns, with a great part of the skeleton, of a moose deer were found in a bed of soft marl, and are preserved at Besborough House.

from *A Topographical Dictionary of Ireland* (1837)

JOHN MITCHEL

The 1840s were a time of great political and ideological turbulence in Ireland. Daniel O'Connell's campaign for repeal of the Union reached its unproductive climax. The Young Irelanders, a group of journalists and intellectuals, founded The Nation *newspaper and broke with O'Connell over matters of policy and strategy. Mitchel, the most militant of the Young Irelanders, broke with them and founded his own newspaper, the* United Irishman. *In 1848, there was a minor rebellion. And over all these events hangs the frightful shadow of the Famine.*

Also in 1848, Mitchel was sentenced to fourteen years' transportation to Van Diemen's Land (now Tasmania). This extract is from his Jail Journal, an account of his experiences and a justification of his cause. He escaped in 1853 and made his way to the United States, where he became an outspoken defender of the Confederacy during the Civil War. Mitchel's American journalism also did much to form the conscience of Irish-American nationalism. Jail Journal first appeared in his New York newspaper, The Citizen, *in 1854.*

The Horrors of Famine

I n 1846 came the Famine, and the 'Relief Acts' advancing money from the Treasury, to be repaid by local assessment; and of course there was an aggravated and intolerable Poor-rate to meet this claim. Of which Relief Acts, only one fact needs to be recorded here — that the Public Works done under them were strictly ordered to be of an unproductive sort — that is, such as would create no fund to repay their own expenses.[1] Accordingly, many hundreds of thousands of feeble and starving men were kept digging holes, and breaking up roads — doing not only no service, but much harm. Well, then, to meet these Parliamentary advances there was nothing but *rates*: and, *therefore*, there was the higher premium to landlords on the extermination, that is the slaughter, of their tenantry. If the clearing business had been active before, now there was a rage and passion for it; and as if the Cheap Ejectment Acts were not a speedy enough machinery, there was a new Poor-law enacted containing amongst other clauses, the 'Quarter Acre clause', which provided that if a farmer, having sold all his produce to pay the rent duties, rates and taxes, should be reduced, as many thousands of men were, to apply for public out-door relief, he should not get it until he had first delivered up all his land to the landlord.[2] Under that law it is the able-bodied idler only who is to be fed — if he attempt to till but one rood of ground, he dies. This simple method of ejectment was called 'passing paupers through the workhouse' — a man went in, a pauper came out.

Under these various Poor-laws and Relief Acts, there were at least 10,000 government offices, small and great; looking and canvassing for these were 100,000 men; a great army in the interest of England.

At the end of six years, I can set down these things calmly; but to see them might have driven a wise man mad. There is no need to recount how the Assistant Barristers and Sheriffs, aided by the Police, tore down the roof-trees and ploughed up the hearths of village after village — how the Quarter Acre clause laid waste the parishes, how the farmers and their wives and little ones in wild dismay, trooped along the highways — how in some hamlets by the seaside, most of the inhabitants being already dead, an adventurous traveller would come upon some family eating a famished ass — how maniac mothers stowed away their dead children to be devoured at midnight — how Mr Darcy of Clifden, describes a humane gentleman going to a village near that place with some crackers, and standing at the door of a house; 'and when he threw the crackers to the children (for he was afraid to enter), the mother attempted to take them from them' — how husband and wife fought like wolves for the last morsel of food in the house; how families, when all was eaten and no hope left, took their last look at the Sun, built up their cottage doors, that none might see them die nor hear their groans, and were found weeks afterwards, skeletons on their own hearth; how the 'law' was vindicated all this while; how the Arms Bills were diligently put in force, and many examples were made; how starving wretches were transported for stealing vegetables by night;[3] how overworked coroners declared they would hold no more inquests; how Americans sent corn, and the very Turks, yea, negro slaves, sent money for alms; which the British Government was not ashamed to administer to the 'sister country'; and how, in every one of these years, '46, '47 and '48, Ireland was exporting to England, food to the value of fifteen million pounds sterling, and had on her own soil at each harvest, good and ample provision for double her own population, notwithstanding the potato blight.

To this condition had forty years of 'moral and peaceful agitation' brought Ireland. The high aspirations after a national Senate and a national flag had sunk to a mere craving for food. And for food Ireland craved in vain. She was to be taught that the Nation which parts with her nationhood, or suffers it to be wrestled or swindled from her, thereby loses all. O'Connell died heart-broken in 1847 — heart-broken not by a mean vexation at seeing the power departing from him; the man was too great for that; but by the sight of his People sinking every day into death under their inevitable, inexorable doom. His physicians ordered him to a warmer climate: in vain: amidst the reverent acclamations of Paris, through the sunny valleys of France, as he journeyed southward, that *Banshee* wail followed him and found him, and rung in his dying ear. At Genoa he died: ordering that the heart should be taken out of his dead body, and sent, not to Ireland, but to *Rome*; a disposition which proves how miserably broken and debilitated was that once potent nature.

Politics, by this time, was a chaos in Ireland. 'Conciliation Hall'[4] was sending forth weekly an abject howl for *food! food!* The 'Irish Confederation'[5] (of which the present writer was a member) had no much clearer view through the gloom; though it had more energy and honesty. Two or three vain efforts were made by its leaders to put a good man into the representation (Meagher at Waterford),[6] or to keep a bad man out (Monahan at Galway)[7] — both efforts in vain. The representation and the franchise were too cunningly calculated for British interests.

Every week was deepening the desolation and despair throughout the country; until at last the French Revolution of February, '48, burst upon Europe. Ireland, it is true, did not then possess the physical resources or the high spirit which had 'threatened the integrity of the Empire' in '43; but even as she was, depopulated, starved, cowed and corrupted, it seemed better that she should attempt resistance, however heavy the odds against success, than lie prostrate and moaning as she was. Better that men should perish by the bayonets of the enemy than by their laws.

1.   Peel introduced relief schemes in 1846 to provide work and money with which to buy food. These included various improvements to piers and harbours and, chiefly, to

roads. The Whig government under Lord John Russell reorganised the works scheme and laid itself open to the charge that the work to be done was of a largely unproductive nature. It was the Whig administration too that imposed the cost of the schemes on property owners in the distressed areas. The relief works were phased out midway through 1847 and were replaced by a direct relief programme.

2.   A Poor Law Amendment Act was passed in 1846 to reorganise the administration of the workhouse system. Part of its aim was to make the Irish landlords, rather than the treasury, pay the cost of relief. It was in the financial interest of the landlords to evict smallholders; this led to the 'Famine clearances'. The act also contained a clause, known as the 'Gregory' or 'Quarter-Acre Clause', which excluded from relief anyone with a holding of more than a quarter of an acre. As a consequence, many smallholders were forced to sell and emigrate or to take workhouse relief.

3.   In a footnote, Mitchel cites a case at Bantry Sessions in which a couple was transported for seven years for stealing turnips and parsnips.

4.   Conciliation Hall, on Burgh Quay, Dublin, was the home of O'Connell's Repeal Association. The Young Irelanders were scornful of O'Connell's plea for food to the Whig government with which he had been in alliance.

5.   Mitchel was a founding member of the Irish Confederation, formed in 1847 after Young Ireland's split with O'Connell's Repeal Association. Mitchel resigned from the Confederation in 1848 after a disagreement on the issues of passive resistance and guerilla warfare — both advocated by Mitchel himself.

6.   Thomas Francis Meagher, one of the most charismatic of the Confederates, was defeated in a by-election in Waterford in early 1848. Mitchel had opposed Gavan Duffy's attempt to get Meagher elected on the grounds that it was a concession to the constitutional politics by which Ireland had been ruined.

7.   In February 1847, the Confederates combined with the Repeal Association in a by-election in Galway against James Monaghan, the solicitor general. Monaghan won by four votes. A petition against personation for Monaghan failed. This was another moment in Mitchel's increasing disgust with the constitutional methods advocated by his Confederate friends.

from *Field Day Anthology of Irish Writing* (1991)

N. MARSHALL CUMMINS

The Great Famine of 1845–9 is so called to distinguish it from the other famines that took place in Ireland in the eighteenth and nineteenth centuries. Not only was it greater than these in magnitude and in historical consequences, the response to it differed in various important ways from earlier and later responses. Much more is known about the failings of the authorities' reaction to the disaster than about the efforts of the citizenry to counteract it.

Certain parts of the country were hit so hard that they became synonymous with hardship and suffering — the workhouse at Kilrush, Co. Clare; the enforced emigration from Strokestown, Co. Roscommon, where the Famine Museum is now; the coastal area of West Cork, in particular the towns of Schull and Skibbereen.

The one-hundred-and-fiftieth anniversary of the Famine has been marked by the publication of much new material on which a more comprehensive and sophisticated view of events may be based. Many other local and more intimate marks of respect to the dead have also been made. Altogether, there is something of an air of a silence being broken in this anniversary.

Father Mathew is Fr Theobald Mathew (1790–1856), who in 1838 began the temperance crusade for which he is renowned.

The Great Irish Famine

The great Irish Famine of 1845–47 was perhaps the greatest calamity that ever afflicted the Irish race, not only because of the many thousands who died, but also from the far-reaching consequences this dreadful visitation caused. It is impossible to mention here more than a fraction of what happened in the South of Ireland, as every town and hamlet had its own particular horror. I can only record some of the more dramatic episodes that occurred and a few of the leading figures who filled the stages of Irish life in those terrible years.

The first signs of the famine, due to the failure of the potato crop, were dramatically portrayed by Father Mathew, writing to Mr Trevelyan, Secretary of the Treasury: 'On the 27th July, 1846, I passed from Cork to Dublin and this doomed plant bloomed in all the luxuriance of an abundant harvest. Returning on the 3rd August I beheld one wide waste of putrefying vegetation. In one week the chief support of the masses was utterly lost. The famine had an immediate and devastating effect on the Irish people. The destitute rushed to the workhouses, which soon became crowded to excess by those who had been able-bodied men and women, whilst the aged, the sickly and the children were left to starve. Over-powered by hunger they lay down helpless, the ready victims of the pestilence that followed close upon the footsteps of famine, and died in thousands.'

The following heart-rending letter[1] sums up all the horrors of the famine in a few short words. It was published by Mr M.T. Moriarty, of Ventry Cottage, Dingle, who saw the whole pitiful drama enacted before his eyes: 'Near my house there lately lived a house of eight persons. One by one did one of the daughters, alone and unassisted, carry her father and sisters to their long home, merely covered in the rags they died in, and then, worn out and unable to reach her wretched house where the last member of the family was at the moment expiring, she laid down her weary limbs and aching head beside a ditch and there her tired spirit obtained the wished for release.'

On the 4th February, 1847, Fr Mathew wrote to Mr Trevelyan: 'We are in a deplorable state in Cork from the influx into the city of more than 10,000 foodless, homeless people, young and old. The Workhouse has been closed and there is no refuge for these miserable creatures.' Mr J.F. Maguire, MP, writes of 1847: 'The famine was raging in every part of the afflicted country, and starving multitudes crowded the thoroughfares of the large towns. Death was everywhere — in the cabin, on the high seas, in the garret, in the cellar, and even on the flags of the most public streets of the city. In the Workhouse the carnage was frightful and it was increasing at a prodigious rate. More than 100 Workhouse officers fell victims during this fateful year to the famine fever. For three months in 1847 the number of human beings that died in the Cork Workhouse was 2,130. In Father Mathew's cemetery alone, within nine months, 10,000 bodies were buried. At the Church of St Ann Shandon, under a kind of shed attached to a guard house, lay huddled in their filthy, foetid rags, about forty-two human creatures — men, women and children, and infants of the tenderest age — starving and fever stricken, most of them in a dying state, some dead, and all gaunt, yellow, hideous from the combined effects of famine and disease. Under this open shed they had remained during the night until about 10 o'clock in the morning, when the funeral processions were passing by, and their indescribable misery was beheld by the leading citizens of Cork, including the Mayor. The odour which proceeded from that huddled-up heap of human beings was of itself enough to generate a plague. As the procession reached the Church of St Ann Shandon a cry of horror was raised at the spectacle which was there beheld.'

A correspondent writes:[2] 'I would wish to direct the attention of the city to the danger they are in from those who have died, and who are interred in the open vaults under our city churches, particularly St Finbarr's and St Ann Shandon. There is no danger at the present time of the doctors wanting subjects for dissection, but the congregations attending these churches are exposed to danger by the offensive smells, especially at the Cathedral, by the great numbers interred there.'

Cork City and County suffered more severely than most places in Ireland. Dr Callanan reports: 'From the commencement of 1847, fate opened her book in good earnest here, and the full tide of death flowed on everywhere around us. During the first six months of that dark period, one-third of the daily population of our streets consisted of shadows and spectres, the impersonation of disease and famine, and crowding in from the rural districts and stalking along to the general doom — the grave — which appeared to await them, but at the distance of a few steps or a few short hours. And so in sad truth it was, for the obituary of our Workhouse here for 1847 gives the appalling return of

3,329 deaths. Within the month of March, 757 inmates of that dismal abode perished from famine and fever.'

In the workhouse, the inmates were put 3, 4 and 5 in a bed, and in the convalescent ward there were 45 beds for 120 patients.

J.T. Collins writes:[3] 'Fr Augustine Maguire, a young priest, had as his first mission to aid the chaplain in ministering to the sick in the Cork Workhouse in the famine. In later years he acted as chaplain at Scutari Hospital during the Crimean War. Looking back upon the 50 years of his priesthood, he said then that what stood most vividly in his memory were his early experiences in the Cork Workhouse. As compared with them his experiences in the Crimean War were but trivial. The smoke of battle, the blood, the sight of maimed and dying, never affected him like the sight of his fellow countrymen dropping dead by the roadside, carried off by the starvation and the fever that came on suddenly and gave them no chance to fight against it. "I remember one day," continued Monsignor Maguire, "when no less than 80 people were brought up to the Workhouse in a body. They filled a long line of cars, and as rapidly as I could I gave Absolution and anointed these poor creatures before they died."'

In a population of 80,000 in Cork in 1847 there were seven to eight hundred patients under daily treatment for fever. In the three years — 1845, 1846 and 1847 — there were 12,805 cases of fever, with 583 deaths in the Cork Fever Hospital.

The following temporary fever hospitals were opened in 1847:

The Cat Fort Hospital treated 1,477 patients, with 99 deaths.

The Barrack Street Hospital treated 2,529 patients, with 444 deaths, and of these, 214 deaths were due to cholera.

The North Fever Sheds admitted 839 patients, with 48 deaths.

The North Infirmary was taken over as a fever hospital. Fever cases kept coming in until the very lobbies were filled with beds; 1,602 fever patients were admitted, with 156 deaths.

Dr W. Beamish reported[4] that: 'Even the Cork County Jail, which was built for 240 inmates, at one time held 959 persons, chiefly fever cases.'

The Cove Fever Hospital: In the two years, 1847 and 1848, Dr Cronin reported 1,239 cases of fever, with 75 deaths.

In all these hospitals, each physician was responsible for over 125 patients and was paid the princely salary of 5/- a day.

The south-western coastal districts of County Cork suffered terribly severely. 'In the middle of December, 1846', Mr W. O'Brien writes, 'a visit of inquiry was undertaken to near Skibbereen by Mr Nicholas Marshall Cummins, J.P., a well-known and leading Cork merchant. Strongly moved by what he had himself seen, he lost no time in communicating to the British public the results of his visit. This he did in the shape of an urgent and most impressive appeal addressed by him in a published letter to the Duke of

244 N. MARSHALL CUMMINS

Wellington, which I can distinctly recall, produced everywhere an immediate and most powerful effect in attracting general attention and much munificent relief to this remote and, then, sorely stricken region.'

To His Grace, Field Marshal, the Duke of Wellington: My Lord Duke,

Without apology or preface I presume so far to trespass on Your Grace as to state to you and, by the use of your illustrious name, to present to the British public the following statement of what I have myself seen within the last three days:

Having for many years been intimately connected with the western portion of the County of Cork, and possessing some small property there, I thought it right personally to investigate the truth of the several lamentable accounts which had reached me of the appalling state of misery to which that part of the country was reduced. I accordingly went on the 15th instant to Skibbereen and, to give the instance of one townland which I visited as an example of the state of the entire coast district, I shall state simply what I saw there.

It is situated on the eastern side of Castlehaven Harbour and is named South Reen, in the parish of Moyross. Being aware that I should have to witness scenes of frightful hunger, I provided myself with as much bread as five men could carry, and on reaching the spot I was surprised to find the wretched hamlet deserted. I entered some of the hovels to ascertain the cause, and the scenes that presented themselves were such as no tongue or no pen can convey the slightest idea of. In the first, six famished and ghastly skeletons, to all appearance dead, were huddled in a corner on some filthy straw, their sole covering what seemed to be a ragged horse-cloth and their wretched legs hanging about, naked above the knees. I approached with horror and found by a low moaning they were alive; they were in fever — four children, a woman, and what once had been a man. It is impossible to go through the details, suffice it to say that in a few minutes I was surrounded by at least 200 of such phantoms, such frightful spectres as no words can describe. By far the greater number were delirious, either from famine or from fever. Their demoniac yells are still ringing in my ears, and their horrible images are fixed upon my brain. My heart sickens at the recital, but I must go on. In another case — decency would forbid what follows, but it must be told — my clothes were nearly torn off in my endeavours to escape from the throng of pestilence around when my neckcloth was seized from behind by a grip which compelled me to turn. I found myself grasped by a woman with an infant, *just born*, in her arms and the remains of a filthy sack across her loins — the sole covering of herself and babe. The same morning the police opened a house on the adjoining lands, which was observed shut for many days, and two frozen corpses were found lying upon the mud floor, *half devoured by the rats.*

A mother, herself in fever, was seen the same day to drag out the corpse of her child, a girl of about twelve, perfectly naked and leave her half covered with stones. In another house, within 500 yards of the cavalry station at Skibbereen, the dispensary doctor found seven wretches lying, unable to move, under the same cloak — one had been dead many hours, but the others were unable to move either themselves or the corpse.

To what purpose should I multiply such cases? If these be not sufficient, neither would they hear who have the power to send relief and do not, even 'though one came from the dead'.

Let them, however, believe and tremble that they shall one day hear the Judge of all the earth pronounce their tremendous doom, with the addition: 'I was hungered and ye gave Me no meat; thirsty and ye gave Me no drink; naked and ye clothed Me not.' But I forget to whom this is addressed. My Lord, you are an old and justly honoured man. It is yet in your power to add another honour to your age; to fix another star and that the brightest to your galaxy and glory. You have access to our young and gracious Queen — lay these things before her. She is a woman, she will not allow decency to be outraged. She has at her command the means of at least mitigating the sufferings of the wretched survivors of this tragedy. They will soon be few, indeed, in the district I speak of if help be longer withheld.

Once more, my Lord Duke, in the name of starving thousands, I implore you, break the frigid and flimsy chain of official etiquette and save the land of your birth — the kindred of that gallant Irish blood which you have so often seen lavished to support the honour of the British name — and let there be inscribed upon your tomb, *Servata Hibernia*.

I have the honour to be,

My Lord Duke,

Your Grace's obedient humble servant,

N.M. Cummins, J.P.

Ann Mount, Cork
December 17th, 1846.

Immediately following publication of this letter he journeyed to London, and with his uncle, James John Cummins, the banker, collected £10,000 for famine relief.

To the Editor, *Cork Constitution*: 'I have abounded satisfaction in being able to assure you that nine names alone in London have this day subscribed for the truly noble amount of £8,000. Surely her merchants are princes, and her traders the honourable of the earth. The names are as follows: Barings, Rothschilds, P.J. Smiths, Overends, Truman, Hanbury & Co., Duke of Devonshire, Jones Lloyd, a £1,000 each; Bruce Buxton, £500; Lord John Russell, £300; Roberts & Co., £200. Small sums, £200. — N.M.C.'

The Editor replied: 'We have seldom published a letter with more satisfaction than the above. The English do not want willingness — that they have proved a thousand times. All that they want is to be rightly called. They are ready to love, but must have the invitation. Let some recognised person lead and he won't lack followers. What is described in the letter has been done without meeting or appeal. It is the result of a mere consciousness that aid was needed, and it would be unjust to withhold from Mr Cummins the credit in having in no small degree contributed to create that consciousness. Indeed, we are persuaded that his single letter did more for it than anything else that has been said or written, and the blessings of thousands that are "ready to perish" will, we hope, reward him.'

N.M. Cummins was much criticised in the Press by people who stated that the conditions described by him were very much exaggerated. But these criticisms were refuted by Mr McCarthy Downing and Rev. Moloney, C.C., who visited the locality and made a most minute examination of the state of the inhabitants. The result was that the statement of N.M. Cummins was found to fall far short of giving the full and real state of wretchedness to which the people had been reduced. Later the following letter from a resident at Castletownshend was published: 'I have now to mention the lamentable fact that out of 60 houses and 320 inhabitants on the farm of South Reen, two years since, there now remain after the ravages of dysentery and starvation eight houses and about 50 persons. The houses were pulled down for firing and the people carried off by fever.' A man of superb physique, N.M. Cummins survived the famine years, but soon after 1847 he was compelled to leave the country a ruined and bankrupt man, having sacrificed his fortunes for the people when they were in dire need.

In 1847, 'The Jamestown', a man-of-war, was fitted out by the American Government and loaded with provisions and sent over to Cork for famine relief. She arrived in the outer harbour on 12th April, where Capt. Parker of the 'Sabrina', en route to Bristol, took her in tow and brought her alongside Haulbowline. A public meeting was held in the County Courthouse, and the following deputation, consisting of the High Sheriff, the Dean of Cork, M.J. Barry, Wm Fagan, T.R. Sarsfield, Rev. Theobald Mathew and Nicholas Cummins were appointed to express thanks to Captain Forbes and the American people for their kindness and sympathy. The gentlemen were severally introduced by Mr Nicholas Cummins, of the firm of Messrs Nicholas and Joseph Cummins of this city, who had started for Cove on the previous evening with dispatches for Mr Forbes on board 'The Jamestown', off the harbour, and accompanied him to Haulbowline. The following Committee, 'The American Relief Committee', was immediately formed to make arrangements for the distribution of the foodstuffs through Cork City and County: Lord Bernard, Chairman; Major N. Ludlow Beamish, Vice-Chairman;

The Dean and Archdeacon of Cork, R.C. Vicar Capitular; Collector Troy, Francis Lyons, M.D.; T. Jennings, R. Dowden, Rev. Father Mathew, J. Lyons, Acting Mayor; Wm Clear, J. Jennings, P. McSweeney, Sir Robert Lane, Caesar Otway. The Secretaries were the two cousins, Nicholas and Nicholas Marshall Cummins. In addition, Nicholas Cummins was Secretary to the British Relief Association in Cork. One hundred and fifty localities in the county, well-known to the Committee as possessing the strongest claims for relief, were selected for five tons of provisions apiece, the local distribution of which was left to the clergy of the various denominations rather than to the official relief committees. That Captain Forbes had ample evidence of how sadly needed were these provisions is shown by his description of the gruesome sights he witnessed during his brief stay in Cork:

'I went with Father Mathew only a few steps out of one of the principal streets of Cork into a lane — the valley of the shadow of death was it? Alas, no, it was the valley of death and pestilence itself. I saw enough in five minutes to horrify me: houses crowded with the sick and dying, without floors, without furniture, and with patches of dirty straw covered with still dirtier shreds and patches of humanity; some called for water to Father Mathew, and others for a dying blessing. From this very small sample of the prevailing destitution we proceeded to a public soup kitchen under a shed guarded by police officers. Here a long boiler containing rice, meal, etc., was at work, while hundreds of spectres stood without, begging for some of the soup which I can readily conceive would be refused by well-bred pigs in America. Every corner of the streets is filled with pale, careworn creatures, the weak leading the weaker; women assail you at every turn with famished babies imploring alms.'

Dr James McCormack wrote[5] from Crookhaven in January, 1847: 'Nothing can so truly depict our miserable condition as the deserted state of our religious houses of worship. Attendances a few months ago were about 400, last Sunday week about 50, and yesterday 20.' Skibbereen was described by one correspondent as 'one mass of famine, disease and death, the poor rapidly sinking under fever, dysentery and starvation. It was one of the longest to suffer and the slowest to recover.' Mr T.H. Marmion opened a soup kitchen which kept 600 persons alive and only supplied those who were most destitute.

On 13th February, 1847, Mr James Mahony, of Cork, wrote in the *London Illustrated News*: 'Neither pen nor pencil could ever portray the misery and horror witnessed in Skibbereen. I saw the dying, the living and the dead lying indiscriminately upon the same floor, without anything between them and the cold earth, save a few miserable rags upon them. Not a single house out of the 500 could boast of being free from death and fever, though several could be pointed out with the dead lying close to the living for the space of three, four and even six days, without any effort being made to remove the bodies to a last resting place.'

Dr O'Donovan continues the grim story: 'We next went to see the "hut". This shed is seven feet long and six feet in breadth. The hut is surrounded by a rampart of human bones which have accumulated to such a height that the threshold, which was originally on a level with the ground, is now two feet beneath it. In this horrible den, in the midst of a mass of human putrefaction, males and females with most malignant fever were huddled together as closely as were the dead in the graves around.' Before reaching Skibbereen, Mr Mahony visited Clonakilty. 'Here the horrors of poverty became visible in the vast number of famished poor who flocked around the coach to beg alms.'

In Bantry Workhouse, human beings were sleeping 4, 5 or even 6 in a narrow bed, and 'Medico' writes:[6] 'I visited fifty hovels, in every one of which there existed six or eight human beings, the greater part so reduced by emaciation from famine, fever and dysentery as scarcely to appear human. In one house, the first deserving the name that we visited, there were six families in six rooms, in all 35, the greater part dead or dying, the only distinguishing marks being the agonising shrieks of the latter for help to save them from starvation. If you can imagine an unconscious form in the agonies of death summon all the ebbing energies of life in one fearful scream and then relapsing back on the bed, dead, you can form a very slight idea of the most awful sound that ever met the ears or conscience of men, a sound that will ring in my memory till the oblivion of the grave overcomes it.'

In Bantry, 900 bodies were interred in a plot of ground only 40 ft square. 'Frightful and fearful', writes Rev. Dr Traill, Rector and Chairman of Schull Relief Committee, 'is the havoc around me. Our medical friend, Dr Sweetnam, informed me yesterday that if he stated the mortality in Schull at an average of 35 daily he would be within truth. The children in particular, he remarked,[7] were disappearing with awful rapidity. And to this I may add the aged, who with the young — neglected perhaps amidst the widespread destitution — are almost, without exception, swollen and ripening for the grave. Out of 18,000 persons in Schull, 5,000 have not a morsel more than charity supplies. My house is more like a beleaguered fortress besieged. Ere the day has dawned, the crowds are gathering; my family and I all are perfect slaves. Ourselves and our servants are worn out with attending to them. I would not wish, were it possible, for one starving creature to leave my doors without giving something to allay the cravings of hunger.' And later he wrote: 'I may say of a truth that the plague has begun. They could not count the bodies which were brought for interment yesterday. Every house is filled with fever and its attendants — dysentery, dropsy, death.'

Dr Traill died shortly afterwards, completely worn out from his exertions on behalf of the poor. He used his large fortune liberally for their relief.

A curious experience of a friend of the author is here recorded. I can vouch for this lady's absolute honesty and one must accept her story as she told it to me: 'I was motoring on a winter's evening on a lonely country road between Forrest and Nettleville and near Carrigadrohid, in Co. Cork, when coming down a hill I saw in the lights of the car about 50 yards ahead a tall gaunt figure standing motionless by the roadside. Drawing nearer, I beheld an emaciated woman with a death-like face. She was almost naked, except for a piece of greenish black cloth hanging from her shoulders. Her legs and arms were bare and thin as drumsticks. I was about to stop the car and offer her some assistance, when I suddenly became afraid and hurried home, intending to inform the Guards of her plight.

I, however, first of all asked the advice of my groom, who came from the locality. He exclaimed in an agitated voice: "Do nothing, ma'am; do nothing, ma'am! That road is a bad road, and many queer people have been seen there." I subsequently made further inquiries and discovered that a soup kitchen had been located near there in the great famine, and also that there had been much distress at that time and that many had died from starvation and typhus fever.'

Father Mathew wrote to Sir Charles Trevelyan, Assistant Secretary, on 16th December, 1846: 'I deeply regret the abandonment of the people to corn and flour dealers. They charge 50 per cent to 100 per cent profit. Cargoes of maize are purchased before their arrival and are sold like railway shares, passing through different hands before they are ground and sold to the poor.' Rev. Nicholas Martin wrote:[8] 'People are completely dependent for means of subsistence upon provisions which have been raised to an exorbitant price by merchants and speculators who take advantage of this trying emergency to enrich themselves at the expense of every humane and noble consideration.'

One firm alone in Cork made a profit of £80,000, another £40,000. In four days the price of Indian meal was raised by £3 5s. 0d. in speculations in the Cornmarket. Mrs Woodham Smith writes:[9] 'Flight or death was the choice. The people tramped to the ports and for as little as 2/6 were transported across the channel. 278,000 Irish poured into Liverpool; 90,000 into Glasgow. Mr Trevelyan gives the names of 19 relieving officers and 30 Catholic priests who caught the cholera and died. In Liverpool alone, 10,000 persons died of typhus in 1847. In 1847, 75,000 Irish emigrated to British North America, of whom nearly 10,000 died from fever either on the voyage or in the quarantine hospitals after arrival. Four ships from Cork and six from Liverpool had 804 deaths on the voyage and 876 on arrival.

No faintest apprehension of the fatal results crossed the minds of landlords, statesmen and philanthropists as the "coffin ships" made their slow voyage across the Atlantic, a voyage said by men who had experienced both to transcend in horror the dreaded middle passage of the slave trade, and bore with them a cargo of hatred. In that new world, which had been called into being to redress the balance of the old, there was to grow up a population among whom animosity to England was a creed; whose burning resentment could never be appeased, who, possessing the long memory of Ireland could never forget. The Irish Famine was to be paid for by England at a terrible price; out of it was born Irish America.'

Mrs Woodham Smith describes the utter ruthlessness of some of the Irish landlords in dealing with their tenants in Co. Mayo in her remarkable book, *The Reason Why*. As a contrast, we turn to A.M. Sullivan, who wrote: 'No adequate tribute has ever been paid to those Irish landlords — and they were of every party and creed — who perished, martyrs to duty, in that awful time; who did not fly from the plague-reeking workhouse, or fever-tainted court.' Amongst those he singled out for mention, Mr Martin of Ballinahinch, and Mr Nolan of Ballinderry (father of Col. Nolan, MP), the latter died of typhus caught in Tuam Workhouse. Mr Richard White, nephew of the Earl of Bantry, whose memory will be long cherished by the people of Bantry, died at Inchiclogh of fever. J.T. Collins continued:[10] 'Others who died at that time administering to the stricken people were Rev. J.R. Cotter of Innishannon, who died from fever. He was the second son of Sir James Cotter of Rockforest, near Mallow. At Bandon, of fever, caught in discharge of his duties as Poor Law Guardian, John Lovell, Esq., also Maskelyne Alcock, of Roughgrove, Bandon. At Ballindeasig House, near Minane Bridge, of fever caught in attendance on the poor of her neighbourhood, died Mrs Kenefick. At Robert's Cove, of fever contracted in discharge of his duties as Poor Law Guardian, Edward Galway, Esq. The Rev. Daniel Horgan, C.C., Donoughmore, caught the fever and died, aged 34 years. Also died, Mr Samuel Lane, of Frankfield House. He is said to have fed over 900 individuals who had neither food nor money to buy it. On June 1st, died of fever, Mr Richard Coppinger, of Camden Quay, Cork; on July 30th, at Clonakilty, of illness brought about by his exertions to relieve the poor, died John O'Hea, J.P., bank manager, leaving a widow and 10 children. On August 12th died Abraham Beale of fever. He was Secretary to the Friends' Committee in Cork and had travelled throughout the country distributing relief in money and food.'

A.M. Sullivan writes:[11] 'no pen nor tongue can trace nor relate the countless deeds of heroism and self-sacrifice which the dreadful visitation called forth on the part, pre-eminently, of two classes in this community, the Catholic clergy and Dispensary doctors'. The fatality amongst these two classes was lamentable. A very careful summary was made by Drs Stokes and Cusack: 'During the 25 years up to 1843, out of 1,220 medical practitioners in Ireland in charge of 406 medical institutions, 300 or nearly one-quarter died, and of these 132 died of typhus fever alone, while the remaining 168 deaths include cholera, scarlet and other fevers. One out of 2.29 deaths of doctors died from typhus fever. Dr John Popham, in his presidential address to the Cork Medical Society in 1861, states: 'We, in the famine years, became painfully accustomed to the mournful reiteration of the ill-boding words, "died of fever in the course of his medical duties".' And, he said, it was found in 1847 that one in fifteen of the whole medical community had been swept away. And that while the mortality from fever compared to deaths from all other causes for the whole community was 1 in 10, for the medical faculty it was 1 in 2¼; a mortality far exceeding that of army surgeons amidst the chances and privations of war.

'Christian heroes, martyrs for humanity, their names are blazoned on no courtly roll; yet shall they shine upon an eternal page, brighter than the stars.'

1. *Cork Constitution*, 13 April 1847.

2. *Cork Constitution*, 6 July 1847.

3. *Cork Evening Echo*, 10 November 1954.

4. *Cork Constitution*, 1 April 1847.

5. *Cork Constitution*, January 1847.

6. *Cork Constitution*, 1847.

7. *Cork Constitution*, 2 February 1847.

8. *Cork Constitution*, 2 February 1847.

9. *The Reason Why*, p. 126. [Cecil Woodham Smith (1896–1977), author of a history of the Famine entitled *The Great Hunger* (1962).]

10. *Cork Evening Echo*, 10 November 1954.

11. 'New Ireland', p. 137. [A.M. Sullivan (1830–84), editor of *The Nation*, lawyer and Home Rule MP.]

from *Some Chapters of Cork Medical History* (1957)

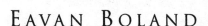

EAVAN BOLAND

Jail Journal *suggests that all relief work was the same, but in point of pedantic fact there were two phases of such work. The implementation of Sir Robert Peel's Relief Act of 1846 saw some productive work carried out, largely affecting roads, but also harbours. In 1847, however, Lord John Russell's administration took office; relief work was reorganised and the 'Poor-rate', referred to by Mitchel, was introduced. Later in 1847 both schemes were abandoned in favour of the provision of direct relief.*

Through the efforts of local history groups in recent years, much more has been unearthed about the contribution of the relief works to the landscape of rural Ireland.

That the Science of Cartography is Limited

— and not simply by the fact that this shading of
forest cannot show the fragrance of balsam,
the gloom of cypresses
is what I wish to prove.

When you and I were first in love we drove
to the borders of Connacht
and entered a wood there.

Look down you said: this was once a famine road.

I looked down at ivy and the scutch grass
rough-cast stone had
disappeared into as you told me
in the second winter of their ordeal, in

1847, when the crop had failed twice,
Relief Committees gave
the starving Irish such roads to build.

Where they died, there the road ended

and ends still and when I take down
the map of this island, it is never so
I can say here is
the masterful, the apt rendering of

the spherical as flat, nor
an ingenious design which persuades a curve
into a plane,
but to tell myself again that

the line which says woodland and cries hunger
and gives out among sweet pine and cypress,
and finds no horizon

will not be there.

from 'Writing in a Time of Violence', *Collected Poems* (1995)

CHARLES J. KICKHAM

'Security is the only thing to give a man courage', says a character in Knocknagow. *It is a thought that, understandably, recurs time and again in a great many aspects of post-Famine Irish life. Yet it is also a thought with which Kickham himself did not always agree. In 1848, he was a member of the Irish Confederation and was marginally involved in the one violent clash of the rebellion of that year — the so-called 'Battle of the Cabbage Patch', which took place at Ballingarry, Co. Tipperary, near his home. In 1865, as an editor of the Fenian newspaper, the* Irish People, *he was sentenced to fourteen years' imprisonment. He was released after four, on the grounds of ill-treatment.*

Set in the 1850s in Kickham's native landscape, Knocknagow, *or* The Homes of Tipperary, *is not only his best-known work but for many years was considered a classic depiction of a rural community, with its cast of largely idealised local characters such as Mat Donovan, the local blacksmith, and Barney Wattletoes, and its melodramatic sense of the social and economic changes that came into being in the wake of the Famine.*

Burglary and Robbery

Mr Sam Somerfield, J.P., with two policemen on his car, drove furiously up to Wellington Lodge. Other magistrates arrived soon after, and in the course of an hour or so quite a little army of police were on the spot. Mr Beresford Pender described, in a tremendous voice, the particulars of a most daring outrage which had occurred the night before. Wellington Lodge had been entered by a band of armed men. Two of them tied Mr Isaac Pender with ropes, and carried away all the money he had in the house. The robbers were so disguised, the old gentleman could not recognise them, but he had his suspicions, particularly of the tall man, who held a pistol to his head while another was breaking open the desk in which he kept his money. And most unfortunately he had a considerable sum just received from Maurice Kearney and other tenants of Sir Garrett Butler. The police were sent to scour the country in all directions; and by some chance the cover of a letter directed to Mr Pender was found on the brink of a deep, square hole in the bog. Beresford remembered immediately that he had met Mat Donovan near that place at an unseasonable hour the night before. The bog-hole was drained, and the box in which the money was kept was found at the bottom, empty and with the lock broken. The man who handed up the box, feeling something hard under his feet, thrust his hand down into the soft mould, and held up a long gun, to the great astonishment of Mr Beresford Pender and Darby Ruadh. It was at once recognised as Maurice Kearney's, for whom a policeman was immediately dispatched. Mr Kearney scratched his head, and in reply to questions put to him by the magistrates, said the gun usually hung in the kitchen, and was seldom taken down except to shoot crows; that his son the doctor broke the stock during the hard frost at Christmas, and that he gave the gun to Wattletoes to bring to Mat Donovan to be repaired, as he, Mat Donovan, could do it as well as a gunsmith. That's the last he saw of the gun.

'Where is Mat Donovan?' Mr Somerfield asked.

To the surprise of all present Hugh Kearney said he believed Mat Donovan was gone to America. He had been seen late the night before in the bog. The whole affair looked very suspicious, the magistrates said. Then it was asked where was the person called Wattletoes? He had gone with Mat Donovan as far as Waterford. The magistrates exchanged looks, and retired to consult as to what should be done. The country was in a very bad state.

from *Knocknagow* (1879)

FRIEDRICH ENGELS

Fenianism and its separatist outlook generally were in the air when this letter was written on 9 December 1869. The formation of an Amnesty Committee for the release of Fenian prisoners and the election of Jeremiah O'Donovan Rossa to parliament created talk of the suspension of Habeas Corpus. Engels's opening remarks are in reply to Marx's heavily ironic comments in a letter of 4 December: 'The "Irish" question must be treated as something quite separate, apart from the rest of the world, namely, it must be concealed, that English workers sympathise with the Irish. What a stupid beast! And this in respect of the International which has press organs all over Europe and the United States!'

The beast in question is Richard Pigott (1828–89), whose newspaper The Irishman *was. At that time, Pigott supported Fenianism. Later he was to become notorious for forgeries claiming that Parnell had endorsed the horrific Phoenix Park murders of 1882. Chartism was an English mass movement for social reform in the 1840s, the leader of which was an Irishman, Feargus O'Connor (1794–1855).*

Engels's common-law wife, Mary Burns, was Irish. When she died, he lived with her sister, Lizzie, and later married her. These relationships are the subject of a Frank McGuinness play, Mary and Lizzie *(1989).*

Engels to Marx

I half expected that about *The Irishman*. Ireland still remains the *sacra insula*, whose aspirations must on no account be mixed up with the profane class struggles of the rest of the sinful world. Partially, this is certainly honest madness on the part of these people, but it is equally certain that it is partially also a calculated policy of the leaders in order to maintain their domination over the peasant. Added to this, a nation of peasants always has to take its literary representatives from the bourgeoisie of the towns and their ideologists, and in this respect Dublin (I mean *Catholic* Dublin) is to Ireland much what Copenhagen is to Denmark. But to these gentry the whole labour movement is pure heresy and the Irish peasant must not on any account be allowed to know that the socialist workers are his sole allies in Europe.

In other respects, too, *The Irishman* is extremely lousy this week. If it is ready to retreat *in this way*, the minute it is threatened with a suspension of the Habeas Corpus Act, the former sabre-rattling was all the more out of place. And now even the fear that some more political prisoners may be elected! On the one hand, the Irish are warned, and quite rightly, not to let themselves be inveigled into unlawful action; on the other, they are to be prevented from doing the only lawful thing that is pertinent and revolutionary and alone able to break successfully with the established practice of electing place-hunting lawyers and to impress the English Liberals. It is obvious that Pigott is afraid that others might outstrip him.

You will remember, by the way, that O'Connell always incited the Irish against the Chartists although or, to be more exact, because they too had inscribed Repeal on their banner.

from *Ireland and the Irish Question: A Collection of Writings by Karl Marx and Frederick Engels* (1972)

W.B. YEATS

It is perhaps all too well known that Charles Stewart Parnell (1846–91) loved a lass, and a married lass at that, named Katharine O'Shea. Named as co-respondent in the O'Shea divorce case in 1890, Parnell was quickly dislodged from the leadership of the Irish Parliamentary Party by a combination of colleagues, clergy and the political realities facing his main English ally of that time, Prime Minister Gladstone.

As the poem indicates, Parnell was then at the height of his power and fame. Not only had he triumphed over imprisonment, and been instrumental in securing ameliorative legislation for the peasantry, he had also emerged victorious in the forgery case against Richard Pigott and his co-respondent, as it were, The Times. Not for nothing was he known as 'the uncrowned king of Ireland'. But his strenuous efforts to regain his eminence were unsuccessful.

'A husband that had sold his wife' refers to the belief that Captain O'Shea had been paid to allow his wife to do as she chose and then had reneged on the deal.

The poem was written in 1936, an unpropitious time for Parnellites.

Come Gather Round Me, Parnellites

Come gather round me, Parnellites,
And praise our chosen man;
Stand upright on your legs awhile,
Stand upright while you can,
For soon we lie where he is laid,
And he is underground;
Come fill up all those glasses
And pass the bottle round.

And here's a cogent reason,
And I have many more,
He fought the might of England
And saved the Irish poor,
Whatever good a farmer's got
He brought it all to pass;
And here's another reason,
That Parnell loved a lass.

And here's a final reason,
He was of such a kind
Every man that sings a song
Keeps Parnell in his mind,
For Parnell was a proud man,
No prouder trod the ground,
And a proud man's a lovely man,
So pass the bottle round.

The Bishops and the Party
That tragic story made,
A husband that had sold his wife
And after that betrayed;
But stories that live longest
Are sung above the glass,
And Parnell loved his country,
And Parnell loved his lass.

from *Last Poems* (1936–9)

ELIZABETH BOWEN

Bowen's Court, the author's family home, was situated in north County Cork, on the road from Mallow to Mitchelstown. The house had been in the family's hands since the first Bowen came soldiering in Ireland with Cromwell. Henry VI is the author's father — Henry Charles Cole Bowen — the last of the line, to whom Bowen's Court is dedicated.

As to the site of the 'gathering', Elizabeth Bowen noted earlier in the book: 'In 1823 the Lord Kingston called Big George once more rebuilt the Castle, at top speed and on a vast showy plan: his object was to entertain George IV, but the King after all never arrived.' There was an army camp at Kilworth and large army barracks at Fermoy and Buttevant.

The question 'Will this having happened stop Home Rule?' comes up because the Home Rule Bill of 1912 concluded its passage through the House of Commons in May 1914. It received the royal assent in September, but its implementation was suspended for the duration of the war. By 1918 the situation had changed utterly.

Bowen's Court survived the various wars. But Elizabeth Bowen sold it in 1959. Little more than a year later it was demolished.

August 1914

At the beginning of August 1914 Henry VI and I were at Bowen's Court. My cousin Audrey Fiennes was staying with us, and Aunt Sarah had come over from Mitchelstown, for that summer holiday, to keep house. She reassumed her born role with dignity. To signalise my beginning to grow up, or to comfort me on this return to the house, my father had had several rooms redecorated: my former nursery was now a stylish bedroom with light-grey walls and a lilac frieze. August having opened in heavy rain, my cousin and I spent the time indoors, constructing furniture for the dollshouse out of matchboxes and scraps of silk. I remember no concern but the dollshouse, also, the hope that the weather might clear up in time for the Mitchelstown Castle garden party, to be held on August 5th. Also, what hat was I to wear? What my father thought about I do not know: in breaks of the rain he walked up and down the avenues, hands behind his back, sometimes pausing to look reflectively at the house. Or, he talked to his sister Sarah — their voices pitched much on the same note, their very alike faces turned to each other. News in those days travelled slowly to Ireland: I do not even remember the word War.

August 4th passed: in the course of it the rain stopped. August 5th was a white-grey, lean, gritty day, with the trees dark. The newspaper did not come. A wind rose, and, as about eleven o'clock that morning we drove down the avenue in the large pony trap — the only conveyance Bowen's Court now had: but for the pony the carriage-stables were empty — my cousin and I held on the hats we had elected to wear. We were to go round by Rockmills, pick up the youngest Oliver — a girl, but christened Silver after her ancestor — then on to Mitchelstown, where we were to eat lunch at Aunt Sarah's house in King-square. Aunt Sarah remained at Bowen's Court: her friend Lady Kingston was now dead, and she did not care for Castle parties without her.

At Rockmills my father — whose manner, I do remember, had been growing graver with every minute — stopped the pony and went into the post office. There was a minute to wait, with the pony stamping, before I again saw him framed in the low dark door. He cleared his throat and said: 'England has declared war on Germany.' Getting back into the trap he added: 'I suppose it could not be helped.' All I could say was: 'Then can't we go to the garden party?' . . . We picked up Silver Oliver and drove on to Mitchelstown — Henry, with his whole mind, courteously answering a rattle of questions from us girls. If at ten or twelve I had been precocious, at fifteen I was virtually idiotic. The bye-roads had dried in the wind and were glaring white; the War already gave them an unreal look.

That afternoon we walked up the Castle avenue, greeted by the gusty sound of a band. The hosts of the party were the late Lady Kingston's second husband Mr Willie Webber and his companion Miss Minnie Fairholme. They were not young, and, owing to the extreme draughtiness everywhere, they received their guests indoors, at the far end of Big George's gallery. In virtue of this being a garden party, and of the fact that it was not actually raining, pressure was put on the guests to proceed outside — people only covertly made incursions into the chain of brocade saloons. Wind raced round the Castle terraces, naked under the Galtees; grit blew into the ices; the band clung with some trouble to its exposed place. The tremendous news certainly made that party, which might have been rather flat. Almost every one said they wondered if they really ought to have come, but they *had* come — rightly: this was a time to gather. This was an assemblage of Anglo-Irish people from all over north-east County Cork, from the counties of Limerick, Waterford, Tipperary. For miles round, each isolated big house had disgorged its talker, this first day of the war. The tension of months, of years — outlying tension of Europe, inner tension of Ireland — broke in a spate of words. Braced against the gale from the mountains, licking dust from their lips, these were the unmartialled loyalists of the South. Not a family had not put out, like Bowen's Court, its generations of military brothers — tablets in Protestant churches recorded deaths in remote battles; swords hung in halls. If the Anglo-Irish live on and for a myth, for that myth they constantly shed their blood. So, on this August 1914 day of grandeur and gravity, the Ascendancy rallied, renewed itself. The lack — it was marked — of one element at that party made us feel the immediate sternness of war: the officers from Kilworth, Fermoy and Buttevant had other things to do with the afternoon. They were already under orders, we heard. We few young people got together in groups — would the War prevent our return to England, to school?

My father's overcoat blew about; his head rose above the crowds on the terrace. I heard several people say, 'Let us ask Mr Bowen.' I have, now, some notion what he may have been asked. For through the grown-up talkers ran and recurred one question — Will *this* having happened stop Home Rule?

It was an afternoon when the simplest person begins to anticipate memory — this Mitchelstown garden party, it was agreed, would remain in every one's memory as historic. It was, also, a more final scene than we knew. Ten years hence, it was all to seem like a dream — and the Castle itself would be a few bleached stumps on the plateau. To-day, the terraces are obliterated, and grass grows where the saloons were. Many of those guests, those vehement talkers, would be scattered, houseless, sonless, or themselves dead. That war — or call it now that first phase of war — was to go far before it had done with us. After 1918 came the war in Ireland, with the burning down of many of the big houses — some already futureless, for they had lost their heirs. For Ireland, between 1918 and 1939, 'peace' contracted into a shorter space than people in England realise — in fact, perhaps one does not say of Ireland that war began again, but that war resumed. North of the Galtees, south of the Galtees, familiar military movement was to announce itself; and that landscape, known to so many generals, was soon mapped for other campaigns. Once more the old positions were fought for; once more, bridges were blown up; limestone valley walls rang with the old echoes, and flames were making people run through the night when, in their beds in the peaceful darkness of England, people dreamed that war would not occur again.

Even in the little area I have covered, the few miles of country between the Galtees and the Blackwater, even in the little society — Anglo-Irish settler society — whose evolution, being also that of the Bowens, I have tried to describe, the events and plans and passions of the years between 1914 and 1941 would make a book that should be as long again as the book that I have written by now. In the life of what we call the new Ireland — but is Ireland ever new? — the lives of my own people become a little thing; from 1914 they begin to be merged, already, into a chapter of different history. So, on the terrace of Big George's castle, I shall say goodbye to the society that he once so very fittingly led, and which, perhaps, in idea he continued to dominate — say goodbye at the start of one war that War as we now know it encloses in its immense To-day. The unseen descent of the sun behind the clouds sharpens the bleak light; the band, having throbbed out God Save the King, packs up its wind-torn music and goes home. From different points of the terrace, most of the landscape of which I have written is to be seen. So from here I say goodbye to the landscape too — for this book only, not for myself.

from *Bowen's Court* (1942)

JENNIFER JOHNSTON

The Dublin Fusiliers, the Royal Munsters, the Iniskilling Fusiliers, the Irish Guards ('the Micks'), the Connaught Rangers, the 36th (Ulster) Division. The names of these and other Irish regiments loom large in the annals of 'the war to end wars'. Some 100,000 Irishmen served in World War I.

Jennifer Johnston's novel is less about the actual action of the war than about the reactions of two Irishmen to it. The narrator, Alex Moore, a young Anglo-Irishman, is good friends with Jerry Crowe, a labourer on the Moore estate. The manner in which their experience at the front implicates each of them in the other's fate is in part a commentary on the kinds of moral challenge and shifting social landscape — the 'goodbye' of which Elizabeth Bowen wrote — that the Great War brought about. Major Glendinning is the villain of the piece.

Sailing to War

We were joined in Dublin by another hundred men and a couple of subalterns from the third battalion. They looked no great shakes. Poor Glendinning, I thought, how sad for you that we constitute no grave danger to the Hun. Grey crowds lined the grey streets. A few women called God bless you. We were soaked to the skin by the time we reached the boat. She backed, as she had done when I travelled with my mother, out of Kingstown harbour and then turned her stern towards the war.

Even under the low rain clouds the bay was beautiful, ringed by its hills and festooned with pale glittering lights, like jewels. The Bailey light flashed its warning and salutation. Kingstown answered. Gulls mewed above us and wheeled and skimmed the sky-grey sea. How many miles . . .? Some of the men went on waving until the city was no more than a soft green blur reflected in the clouds.

Our first casualty was some poor fool who cut his wrists before we even landed in England. Apart from that the journey was uneventful. Rules and yet more rules. Each of the men was given a copy of the following directive and told to keep it in his Pay Book and obviously read it in moments of temptation.

'You are ordered abroad as a soldier of the King to help our French comrades against the invasion of a common enemy. You have to perform a task which will need your courage, your energy, your patience. Remember that the honour of the British Army depends on your individual conduct. It will be your duty not only to set an example of discipline and perfect steadiness under fire but also to maintain the most friendly relations with those you are helping in this struggle. In this new experience you may find temptation in both wine and women. You must entirely resist both temptations, and, while treating all

women with perfect courtesy, you should avoid any intimacy. Do your duty
bravely. Fear God. Honour the King.'

Poor Jerry I thought, my heart bleeds for you.

from *How Many Miles to Babylon?* (1974)

T.M. KETTLE

Intellectual, politician, economist, poet, Kettle was a prominent member of the brilliant generation of Irish men and women which came to maturity during the teens of the century — not at all the 'M.T. Kettle' that George Moore sarcastically nicknamed him. Yet, despite his status and success, the end of Kettle's career is a graphic depiction of his generation's tensions and contradictions. An ardent nationalist, he nevertheless enlisted in the Dublin Fusiliers when war broke out in 1914. In 1916, disillusioned by the Easter Rising, he requested a transfer to France and was killed in September of that year at Ginchy in the Battle of the Somme. This sonnet to his three-year-old daughter was written in the week of his death. The last three lines of it are reproduced on Kettle's memorial in St Stephen's Green, Dublin.

To My Daughter Betty, the Gift of God

(Elizabeth Dorothy)

In wiser days, my darling rosebud, blown
To beauty proud as was your mother's prime,
In that desired, delayed, incredible time,
You'll ask why I abandoned you, my own,
And the dear heart that was your baby throne,
To dice with death. And oh! they'll give you rhyme
And reason: some will call the thing sublime,
And some decry it in a knowing tone.

So here, while the mad guns curse overhead,
And tired men sigh with mud for couch and floor,
Know that we fools, now with the foolish dead,
Died not for flag, nor King, nor Emperor,
But for a dream, born in a herdsman's shed,
And for the secret Scripture of the poor.

from *Poems & Parodies* (1916)

JAMES CONNOLLY

James Connolly started work at the age of ten in the print shop of the Edinburgh Evening News, and though he was soon dismissed through the intervention of a factory inspector, the sound of the print shop accompanied him throughout his career in Scotland, America and Ireland as a trade unionist and theorist. In addition to his numerous books and pamphlets, he edited six newspapers, from the Workers' Republic *of 1898–1903 to the* Workers' Republic *of 1915–16.*

Socialism and Catholicism were by no means incompatible in Connolly's mind, partly on the grounds that 'the Catholic Church is theoretically a community in which the clergy are but the officers serving the laity in a common worship and service of God'. While sternly critical of the hierarchy, Connolly's views on this subject are also noteworthy for their lack of sectarian spirit.

Connolly's consistent focus was on 'the daily and hourly struggles in the workshop'. But he was also opposed to 'doctrinaire socialists' who viewed questions of nationality and the national language as irrelevant. 'Therefore, in this, we can wish the Sinn Féiners, good luck.'

Nationalism and Religion

Church and Religion

Socialism, according to Connolly, far from being anti-Christian was consistent with the real Christian ethic. He was horrified at the debasement of true religion in the interests of capitalism.

Is not this attitude symbolic of the attitude of the Church for hundreds of years? Ever counselling humility, but sitting in the seats of the mighty; ever patching up the diseased and broken wrecks of an unjust social system, but blessing the system which made the wrecks and spread the disease; ever running divine discontent and pity into the ground as the lightning rod runs and dissipates lightning, instead of gathering it and directing it for social righteousness as the electric battery generates and directs electricity for social use.

Labour, Nationality and Religion (1910)

It is not Socialism but capitalism that is opposed to religion; capitalism is social cannibalism, the devouring of man by man, and under capitalism those who have the most of the pious attributes which are required for a truly deeply religious nature are the greatest failures and the heaviest sufferers.

Religion, I hope, is not bound up with a system founded on buying human labour in the cheapest market, and selling its product in the dearest; when the organised Socialist working class tramples upon the capitalist class it will not be trampling upon a pillar of God's Church but upon a blasphemous defiler of the Sanctuary, it will be rescuing the Faith from the impious vermin who made it noisome to the really religious men and women.

The Harp (January 1909)

Irish Language and Culture

Connolly was writing at the time of the Gaelic cultural and language revival, and he called on its supporters to recognise Socialists as 'your natural allies'. Addressing the Gaelic Leaguers he said:

Help us to secure to all our fellow-countrymen, a free, full and happy life; secure in possession of a rational, human existence, neither brutalised by toil nor debilitated by hunger, and then all the noble characteristics of our race will have full opportunity to expand and develop. And when all that is good in literature, art and science is recognised as the property of all — and not the heritage of the few — your ideals will receive the unquestioned adhesion of all true Irishmen.

Workers' Republic (1 October 1898)

. . . those who drop Irish in favour of English are generally actuated by the meanest of motives, are lickspittles desirous of aping the gentry, whereas the rank and file of the Gaelic movement are for the most part thoroughly democratic in spirit.

Workers' Republic (March 1903)

No revolutionary movement is complete without its poetical expression. If such a movement has caught hold of the imagination of the masses, they will seek a vent in song for the aspirations, the fears and hopes, the loves and hatreds engendered by the struggle. Until the movement is marked by the joyous, defiant, singing of revolutionary songs, it lacks one of the most distinct marks of a popular revolutionary movement; it is a dogma of a few, and not the faith of the multitude.

from *Introduction to Songs of Freedom* (1907)

Freedom and the State

During the First World War, under the guise of 'law and order', state emergency powers were considerable. Newspapers were censored, the 'Irish Worker' suppressed, and Conscription introduced. Connolly's comment was:

Magistrates and soldiers and policemen and Coalition Cabinets must be made to understand that they all exist in theory for the sake of serving the civilian.

If the contrary obtains, if, as seems to be the danger in Ireland, the civilian is subordinate to the soldier and the policeman and becomes a dog for all those we have named to kick and abuse, then it will become very difficult indeed to understand wherein lies the constitutional freedom we have lately heard so much about.

Workers' Republic (5 June 1915)

from *James Connolly Wrote for Today* (1978)

PROCLAMATION OF THE REPUBLIC (1916)

What happened in Dublin on Easter Monday, 24 April 1916, was not supposed to happen. An order issued the previous Saturday by Eoin MacNeill (1867–1965), Chief of Staff of the Irish Volunteers, and published in the Sunday papers, countermanded the manoeuvres planned for Easter Sunday. Nevertheless, elements of the Volunteers under Patrick Pearse, together with Connolly and the Irish Citizen Army, went ahead as planned on the Monday.

A number of sites around Dublin were occupied by detachments of Volunteers. The chief of these was the General Post Office. Operations began at noon. Easter Monday was a public holiday, and the races at Fairyhouse in north County Dublin were the day's main attraction. Hostilities commenced in earnest when a troop of cavalry returning from the races was fired upon. The Rising lasted a week, at which point Pearse surrendered, 'to prevent', as he said, 'further slaughter of Dublin citizens'. From mid-week the centre of Dublin had been subjected to a barrage from the gunboat Helga in the Liffey and other artillery.

All the signatories of the Proclamation of the Republic were executed, as were many other participants. The Republic of Ireland officially came into being in April 1949.

Poblacht na hÉireann

The Provisional Government of the Irish Republic to the People of Ireland.

IRISHMEN AND IRISHWOMEN: In the name of God and of the dead generations from which she receives her old tradition of nationhood, Ireland, through us, summons her children to her flag and strikes for her freedom.

Having organised and trained her manhood through her secret revolutionary organisation, the Irish Republican Brotherhood, and through her open military organisations, the Irish Volunteers and the Irish Citizen Army, having patiently perfected her discipline, having resolutely waited for the right moment to reveal itself, she now seizes that moment, and, supported by her exiled children in America and by gallant allies in Europe, but relying in the first on her own strength, she strikes in full confidence of victory.

We declare the right of the people of Ireland to the ownership of Ireland, and to the unfettered control of Irish destinies, to be sovereign and indefeasible. The long usurpation of that right by a foreign people and government has not extinguished the right, nor can it ever be extinguished except by the destruction of the Irish people. In every generation the Irish people have asserted their right to national freedom and sovereignty; six times during the past three hundred years they have asserted it in arms. Standing on that fundamental right and again asserting it in arms in the face of the world, we hereby proclaim the Irish Republic as a Sovereign Independent State, and we pledge our lives and the lives of our comrades-in-arms to the cause of its freedom, of its welfare, and of its exaltation among the nations.

The Irish Republic is entitled to, and hereby claims, the allegiance of every Irishman and Irishwoman. The Republic guarantees religious and civil liberty, equal rights and equal opportunities to all its citizens, and declares its resolve to pursue the happiness and prosperity of the whole nation and of all its parts, cherishing all the children of the nation equally, and oblivious of the differences carefully fostered by an alien government, which have divided a minority from the majority in the past.

Until our arms have brought the opportune moment for the establishment of a permanent National Government, representative of the whole people of Ireland and elected by the suffrages of all her men and women, the Provisional Government, hereby constituted, will administer the civil and military affairs of the Republic in trust for the people.

We place the cause of the Irish Republic under the protection of the Most High God, Whose blessing we invoke upon our arms, and we pray that no one who serves that cause will dishonour it by cowardice, inhumanity, or rapine. In this supreme hour the Irish nation must, by its valour and discipline and by the readiness of its children to sacrifice themselves for the common good, prove itself worthy of the august destiny to which it is called.

Signed on Behalf of the Provisional Government,

Thomas J. Clarke, Sean Mac Diarmada, Thomas MacDonagh, P.H. Pearse, Eamonn Ceannt, James Connolly, Joseph Plunkett.

SEAN O'CASEY

One of the features of Easter 1916 that The Plough and the Stars dramatises is the gap between the militants and the people in whose name the Rising was commissioned. The play portrays a generous selection of ordinary citizens, including the carpenter Fluther Good; the Covey, a would-be Marxist labourer; and Rosie Redmond, a prostitute. The portrayal of a prostitute cheek-by-jowl, as it were, with republican ardour caused ructions when the play opened at the Abbey Theatre in 1926. The speaker's lines are from Patrick Pearse's 1915 graveside oration at the funeral of the old Fenian O'Donovan Rossa.

O'Casey's work is to some extent indebted to his political background. An admirer of James Connolly, he was secretary of the Irish Citizen Army, a workers' defence force; his The Story of the Irish Citizen Army was published in 1919. His socialism made him somewhat sceptical of the nationalism being advanced here — the armed trio's toasts go on to conclude in 'Death for th' Independence of Ireland!' — particularly as Brennan, Langon and Clitheroe, all members of the Irish Citizen Army, seemed intoxicated by it.

The Plough and the Stars, the seven stars of the astral plough on a blue ground, was the Citizen Army flag.

Spirit and Flesh

Fluther [to the Barman]. Let him go, let him go, Tom: let him open th' door to sudden death if he wants to!

Barman [to the Covey]. Go on, out you go an' do th' bowsey somewhere else. [He pushes the Covey out and comes back.

Rosie [getting Fluther's hat as he is putting on his coat]. Be God, you put th' fear o' God in his heart that time! I thought you'd have to be dug out of him. . . . Th' way you lepped out without any of your fancy side-steppin'! 'Men like Fluther,' say I to meself, 'is gettin' scarce nowadays.'

Fluther [with proud complacency]. I wasn't goin' to let meself be malignified by a chancer. . . . He got a little bit too derogatory for Fluther. . . . Be God, to think of a cur like that comin' to talk to a man like me!

Rosie [fixing on his hat]. Did j'ever!

Fluther. He's lucky he got off safe. I hit a man last week, Rosie, an' he's fallin' yet!

Rosie. Sure, you'd ha' broken him in two if you'd ha' hitten him one clatther!

Fluther [amorously, putting his arm around Rosie]. Come on into th' snug, me little darlin', an' we'll have a few dhrinks before I see you home.

Rosie. Oh Fluther, I'm afraid you're a terrible man for th' women.

[*They go into the snug as Clitheroe, Captain Brennan, and Lieut. Langon of the Irish Volunteers enter hurriedly. Captain Brennan carries the banner of The Plough and the Stars, and Lieut. Langon a green, white, and orange Tri-colour. They are in a state of emotional excitement. Their faces are flushed and their eyes sparkle; they speak rapidly, as if unaware of the meaning of what they said. They have been mesmerised by the fervency of the speeches.*

Clitheroe [*almost pantingly*]. Three glasses o' port!

[*The Barman brings the drinks.*

Capt. Brennan. We won't have long to wait now.

Lieut. Langon. Th' time is rotten ripe for revolution.

Clitheroe. You have a mother, Langon.

Lieut. Langon. Ireland is greater than a mother.

Capt. Brennan. You have a wife, Clitheroe.

Clitheroe. Ireland is greater than a wife.

Lieut. Langon. Th' time for Ireland's battle is now — th' place for Ireland's battle is here.

[*The tall, dark figure again is silhouetted against the window. The three men pause and listen.*

Voice of the Man. Our foes are strong, but strong as they are, they cannot undo the miracles of God, who ripens in the heart of young men the seeds sown by the young men of a former generation. They think they have pacified Ireland; think they have foreseen everything; think they have provided against everything; but the fools, the fools, the fools! — they have left us our Fenian dead, and, while Ireland holds these graves, Ireland, unfree, shall never be at peace!

Capt. Brennan [*catching up The Plough and the Stars*]. Imprisonment for th' Independence of Ireland!

from *The Plough and the Stars* (1926)

HANNA SHEEHY SKEFFINGTON

Francis Sheehy Skeffington — pacifist, feminist, humanist — was one of the leading intellectual lights of his generation, and his cruel and untimely end during the 1916 Rising was a major scandal.

On the Tuesday of Easter Week, Sheehy Skeffington was taken prisoner by the military authorities, murdered in custody and secretly buried. No charge had been preferred against him. Though she had been making enquiries, his wife was still unaware of what had happened by the Friday of that week, which is when the first raid took place.

Captain Colthurst, the officer in charge of the raid, subsequently proved to be the murderer. Pleading insanity at his trial, Colthurst served less than two years in Broadmoor before emigrating to Canada. His actual name was John Bowen-Colthurst and he was a distant cousin of Elizabeth Bowen. A full account of the events is in Hanna Sheehy Skeffington's British Militarism as I Have Known It.

The young Sheehy Skeffington is the basis for McCann in A Portrait of the Artist as a Young Man *by his fellow-student and friend, James Joyce.*

The First Raid

I went home shortly after six, and before seven was putting my little boy to bed, when the maid noticed soldiers lining around the house. She got terrified and dashed out with Owen by the back door. I went to call her back, for I knew that the house would be guarded back and front, and feared the boy, especially, might be shot if seen running. When I got to the foot of the stairs a volley was fired in front of the house at the windows followed almost directly by a crash of glass which the soldiers shattered with the butt-ends of their rifles.

They broke in simultaneously all over the house — some went on the roof — and Capt. Colthurst rushed upon us — the maid, Owen and myself — with a squad with fixed bayonets, shouting, 'Hands up!' to the boy and me. The boy gave a cry at the sight of the naked steel, and I put my arms around him and said, 'These are the defenders of women and children.' That steadied them a little. The party consisted of about forty men and was in charge of Col. Allett (an officer of 29 years' service), Capt. Colthurst (16 years' service) and a junior officer, Lieut. Brown.

We were ordered all three to be removed 'under guard' to the front room and to be shot if we stirred while they searched the house. This was done. Soldiers with levelled rifles knelt outside the house ready to fire upon us, and inside we were closely guarded by men with drawn bayonets. This lasted over three hours. The house was completely sacked and everything of any value removed — books, pictures, souvenirs, toys, linen and household goods. I could hear the officers jeering as they turned over my private possessions. One of the soldiers (a Belfast man) seemed ashamed, and said, 'I didn't enlist for this. They are taking the whole bloomin' house with them.' They commandeered a motor car in which were women, and made them drive to the Barracks with the stuff — ordering the men to keep at a safe distance 'in case of firing'. They left an armed guard on the house all night. Colthurst brought my husband's keys, stolen from his dead body, and opened his study (which he always kept locked). All my private letters, letters from my husband to me before our marriage, his articles, a manuscript play, the labour of a lifetime, were taken. After endless application, I received back a small part of these, but most of my most cherished possessions have never been returned, or any attempt made to find them.

The regiment took with them to Belfast as a 'souvenir', my husband's stick, and an officer stole from his dead body, my husband's 'Votes for Women' badge. For days my house was open to any marauder, as none dared even to come to board up my windows. Capt. Colthurst later falsely endorsed certain papers as found on my husband's body.

from 'A Pacifist Dies', reprinted in Roger McHugh (ed.), *Dublin 1916* (1966)

KATHERINE MANSFIELD

'I have been wanting to write to you but felt that Ireland wouldn't permit' began an earlier 1916 letter from Katherine Mansfield to her friend Beatrice Campbell (née Elvery; 1885–1970). Like pretty much everyone else, including the people of Ireland, Katherine Mansfield was very much taken by surprise by the Easter Rising. Execution of the leaders began on 3 May 1916 and ended on 12 May, two days before this letter was written.

Charles Campbell (1885–1963), second Baron Glenavy, was a friend of Katherine Mansfield's husband, John Middleton Murry, which was how she came to know Beatrice Campbell. Lady Glenavy's account of the friendship is given in Today We Will Only Gossip *(1964).*

'George-out-of-Wells' means that Katherine Mansfield considered that the novels of W.L. George closely resembled those of H.G. Wells.

After the Rising

It is still awfully difficult to credit what has happened and what is happening in Ireland. One can't get round it. This shooting, Beatrice, this incredible shooting of people! I keep wondering if Ireland really minds. I mean really won't be pacified and cajoled and content with a few fresh martyrs and heroes. I can understand how it must fill your thoughts, for if Ireland were New Zealand and such a thing had happened there . . . it would mean the same for me. It would really (as *unfortunately* George-out-of-Wells would say) Matter Tremendously . . . Dear woman, I am a little afraid of jarring you by writing about the whole affair, for I know so little (except what you've told me) and I've heard no discussion or talk . . .

from *The Letters and Journals of Katherine Mansfield* (1928)

W.B. YEATS

Yeats, too, was taken aback by the Rising. 'I had no idea that any public event could so deeply move me', he said in a letter to Lady Gregory, going on: 'and I am very despondent about the future. At the moment I feel that all the work of years has been overturned, all the bringing together of classes, all the freeing of Irish literature and criticism from politics.' And, as the poem's opening stanza states, it had seemed as if the executed leaders were little more than lower-middle-class non-entities.

The second stanza characterises a cross-section of those involved. 'That woman' is Constance Markievicz (1868–1927), née Gore-Booth; 'This man' is Patrick Pearse (1879–1916) and 'This other' Thomas MacDonagh (1878–1916). 'This other man' is Major John MacBride (1865–1916), whom Maud Gonne married in 1903. Yeats was visiting Maud Gonne in France when he wrote 'Easter 1916'.

In his letter to Lady Gregory he said, 'If the English Conservative Party had made a declaration that they did not intend to rescind the Home Rule Bill there would have been no Rebellion.' This is the basis of the line 'For England may keep faith'.

Easter 1916

I have met them at close of day
Coming with vivid faces
From counter or desk among grey
Eighteenth-century houses.
I have passed with a nod of the head
Or polite meaningless words,
Or have lingered awhile and said
Polite meaningless words,
And thought before I had done
Of a mocking tale or a gibe
To please a companion
Around the fire at the club,

Being certain that they and I
But lived where motley is worn:
All changed, changed utterly:
A terrible beauty is born.

That woman's days were spent
In ignorant good-will,
Her nights in argument
Until her voice grew shrill.
What voice more sweet than hers
When, young and beautiful,
She rode to harriers?

This man had kept a school
And rode our wingèd horse;
This other his helper and friend
Was coming into his force;
He might have won fame in the end,
So sensitive his nature seemed,
So daring and sweet his thought.
This other man I had dreamed
A drunken, vainglorious lout.
He had done most bitter wrong
To some who are near my heart,
Yet I number him in the song;
He, too, has resigned his part
In the casual comedy;
He, too, has been changed in his turn,
Transformed utterly:
A terrible beauty is born.

Hearts with one purpose alone
Through summer and winter seem
Enchanted to a stone
To trouble the living stream.
The horse that comes from the road,
The rider, the birds that range
From cloud to tumbling cloud,
Minute by minute they change;
A shadow of cloud on the stream
Changes minute by minute;
A horse-hoof slides on the brim,
And a horse plashes within it;
The long-legged moor-hens dive,

And hens to moor-cocks call;
Minute by minute they live:
The stone's in the midst of all.

Too long a sacrifice
Can make a stone of the heart.
O when may it suffice?
That is Heaven's part, our part
To murmur name upon name,
As a mother names her child
When sleep at last has come
On limbs that had run wild.
What is it but nightfall?
No, no, not night but death;
Was it needless death after all?
For England may keep faith
For all that is done and said.
We know their dream; enough
To know they dreamed and are dead;
And what if excess of love
Bewildered them till they died?
I write it out in a verse —
MacDonagh and MacBride
And Connolly and Pearse
Now and in time to be,
Wherever green is worn,
Are changed, changed utterly:
A terrible beauty is born.

September 25, 1916

privately published (1916); republished in *Michael Robartes and the Dancer*
(1921)

ERNIE O'MALLEY

The countryside is probably more closely identified with the War of Independence than is the town. Unlike earlier conflicts, the 'Troubles', as the War of Independence was known, reached all parts of the country. Every so often, at seemingly innocuous points on Irish roads, crosses and other memorabilia mark where men fell in some engagement.

During the War of Independence, O'Malley was in military intelligence, working closely with Michael Collins. He was also Officer Commanding the 2nd Southern Division of the IRA. The scene of the action here, however, is southern County Mayo on the County Galway border.

The make-up of the two sides in the War of Independence was complicated. The IRA was the 'standing army of the republic' with an elaborate command structure and intelligence system. As a fighting force, however, it relied on the so-called 'flying columns', such as the one described here. These consisted of groups of activists continually on the run who carried out hit-and-run attacks on crown forces with the assistance of sympathetic locals. As O'Malley wrote elsewhere, 'a stand-up fight would not suit our country'. Crown forces comprised the British army, the Royal Irish Constabulary, and two paramilitary forces attached to the RIC, the Black and Tans, consisting of some ten thousand British ex-servicemen, and the Auxiliaries, two thousand British officers.

Moore Hall, birthplace of the writer George Moore, was burned during the Civil War.

Ambush and Aftermath

I n Ballinrobe, scouts watched both the RIC and the military barracks. When the police in a car and a Crossley tender had drawn up at Birmingham's to buy provisions for the Derrypark garrison, in keeping with the recently-established routine, Pádraic Feeney set out by bicycle to bring his information but he did not reach the Brigadier in time. Another scout was able to get through and take a despatch to the IRA in the village just ahead of the enemy convoy. It was then decided that the first vehicle, lorry or car, was to be allowed to pass through as far as Drumbane gateway over five hundred yards on, where Paddy May and his men lay waiting. The car was first and the driver was killed immediately by a rifleman who occupied a position behind a wall nearly opposite the entrance to Drumbane House. The vehicle crashed through the gateway, but the other police got out on the road and from there they engaged May's men.

At the sound of the firing the Crossley halted between the first and second IRA positions and was fired on by the unit led by Michael O'Brien to whose assistance the Column Commander sent half of his own men. Then, with the remainder of his section, the Commander advanced down the road to join in the fight against the first police car, and after a short exchange of shots this group of RIC were out of action, all of them being dead. Arms and ammunition were stripped quickly from the outstretched bodies, but as a noise of rifle fire was coming from the village the Commander was anxious to move in that direction so that he could find out exactly what was happening.

The remaining police from the Crossley were under the charge of a head constable who directed them while they carried their wounded and held off their attackers until they reached a hotel a little in from the roadside, beside a crossroads. They were then secure enough in a well-built house and they knew that if they were able to maintain their position the RIC in Derrypark, who had probably heard the firing, would be able to get a message through to Ballinrobe for reinforcements. There was a small plantation nearby from which the two rifles in O'Brien's command were being used. As soon as the RIC located the sound they used rifle grenades against their hidden attackers, and the bursting metal splinters made the shelter of the young trees a lesser security. O'Brien felt he could not achieve anything from his position and withdrew his men.

Tom Maguire had no immediate plan for attacking the hotel, and to organise even an impromptu attempt on the building would take some time. There had been no preparations made to cut roads, fell trees or destroy culverts so as to delay reinforcements, as it had been thought that the police would be forced to surrender soon after the action had begun. It was essential to move the Column away into the mountains and to disband the local Volunteers.

Soon after the IRA had left the village the RIC were able to venture out. They made use of the telegraph in the post office, but a wireless transmitter in the barracks at Derrypark had already sent information to Ballinrobe about the attack on the convoy.

Tourmakeady lies under the Partry mountains, but to the west and south-west are steeper heights: Buckaun, the great mass of Maumtrasna, and the Devil's Mother. The only cover is given by gullies which tear the denuded flanks of the mountainside, or that provided by river beds, cliff edges and dips in the ground. South-west from the village a road borders Lough Mask and continues along by Lough Nafooey over a pass to the Maum valley fourteen miles away. To the west of the village a rugged road crosses the mountains and drops down the far side towards Westport. The road from Castlebar to Ballinrobe borders the north-eastern mountain edges, and another road on the western mountain slopes connects the Castlebar road with the mountain road running across the heights from Tourmakeady.

Maguire intended to cross the road from Castlebar to Ballinrobe as he knew there was insufficient cover in the hills. When he reached a point two miles above Srah he rested his men. Most of the local lads had already been dismissed and had made for the hills, but Maguire kept a few of them to act as guides. While the men were resting he used his field-glasses to search for enemy reinforcements and as he looked towards Partry across Lough Mask he saw swirls of dust. Very few roads were then macadamised and in dry weather a lorry's path lay through several inches of dust, but a depth of mud whenever rain fell. As he counted those dust clouds Maguire knew that they signified enemy reinforcements which were already making for Tourmakeady. He counted twenty-four dust storms. That meant, he surmised, that Galway, a brigade headquarters, and possibly Claremorris, had sent on troops.

The lorries passed on towards the village while the Column men took cover, but evidently the soldiers knew where to seek their quarry. Lorries halted at intervals along the lake shore, soldiers and bottle-green police jumped out and were soon slowly making their way up in extended order towards the hills. Some of the lorries passed on to Tourmakeady and the Column Commander guessed that they would cross by the mountain road to Westport, and when they reached the far slopes they would steadily help to encircle his Column.

The Column now moved northwards. With it were some Srah men who knew the lines of the hills as they knew the creases in the palms of their hands, but the Column itself consisted mostly of men from the Ballinrobe battalion and they were not so limber as the Srah men.

The direction of the Column was changed again, further to the north, for that point would bring it across the hills which were about 1,200 feet high, topped by a plateau, but as soon as the men commenced to climb, the British followed them up. The men scattered out along the hillside and used their few rifles, but the British picked out the direction in which they were moving by the sound of their rifle shots and tended to close in on them. The Column hurried up the hills towards the road from Westport to Ballinrobe but, as the men climbed, their scouts found that military and constabulary who had come on from Westport and Castlebar were now stretched across the eastern slopes, barring their way to safety. These fresh reinforcements were still at a distance but they used their machine-guns at long range, prior to moving close.

The Column men looked about them for a position which might give them cover and which they could hold when the ring tightened around them. By this time they were high above Tournawoad village. The Commander with his officers picked a fold in the ground formed by a table of stone with a steep drop to the south and behind it a rise of ground. In Irish the place is known as 'Rock of the Sally Trees', but there are no sally trees there any longer.

It was now one o'clock and the men extended lines and settled down for a long fight. Below them they could see the shores of Lough Carra with the light green sheen on its waters, the oak trees around Moore Hall and the tiny islands of Lough Mask standing away from serrated lake edges. The peninsula between the two waters stood out clearly with its steep western end, and below it were the many islands in the Corrib until it narrowed on the way to Galway. Men could pick out their homes far below or guess at their location with the aid of well-known landmarks. Around them on the mountains were the British forces together with that old historical tradition of Irish mercenaries who now in their bottle-green uniforms helped to guide the troops and later would identify the prisoners and the dead.

from *Raids and Rallies* (1982)

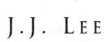

J.J. LEE

Eamon de Valera was a commander of Boland's Mills, one of the outposts around Dublin seized by the insurgents in Easter 1916. For this, he was court-martialled and sentenced to death. It used to be thought that he was not executed because he had been born in New York and the American authorities had intervened to save him. But recent scholarship indicates that he was saved by the British decision to stop executions.

De Valera was in the United States from June 1919 to December 1920. As well as raising funds — six million dollars — the visit was intended to secure official American recognition for the fledgling Irish Republic. In this it failed. Political disagreements arose between de Valera and Irish-American leaders.

One of the numerous areas of controversy in de Valera's career is his attitude to both the negotiation and implementation of the Anglo-Irish Treaty. One expression of that attitude was his founding in 1926 of Fianna Fáil, which remains the largest party in Irish politics.

The Treaty

De Valera had returned in December 1920 from his financially successful, if politically controversial, tour of America, where he 'had been a magnificent publicist for Ireland'.[1] He found the military situation transformed during his eighteen-month absence. In 1920–21 the crown forces suffered 525 dead, and almost 1,000 wounded. At least 707 civilians were to die between January and July 1921.[2] By Irish standards these were horrific figures. De Valera was humane enough to be disturbed. He also found Collins very much in the ascendant. He was human enough to be disturbed.[3] De Valera genuinely desired peace. He also realised that negotiations were inevitable, unless the IRA were crushed before Britain could be brought to the conference table.[4] It came as a relief when Lloyd George followed up the favourable response of British public opinion to the dramatic appeal for conciliation by George V on the opening of the Northern Irish parliament by proposing a truce, which came into effect on 11 July.[5]

Lloyd George succeeded in establishing, during a protracted bout of sparring with de Valera following the truce, that the achievement of a republic through negotiation was impossible. Nevertheless, de Valera eventually accepted Lloyd George's invitation to a conference in London 'where we can meet your delegates as spokesmen of the people whom you represent, with a view to ascertaining how the association of Ireland with the community of nations known as the British empire may be reconciled with Irish national aspirations'. So scholastic a scrutineer of texts as de Valera can hardly have overlooked the significance of 'how' rather than 'whether' in this formula, which already contained the seeds of compromise, as Collins correctly observed in the Treaty debate.[6]

Once the Sinn Féin cabinet accepted this invitation, it had to recommend the delegates to the Dáil. Ominous splits occurred immediately. The cabinet had seven members, de Valera, Collins, [Arthur] Griffith, [Cathal] Brugha, Austin Stack, Robert Barton and W.T. Cosgrave. Brugha and Stack refused to go to London at all. Neither one was regarded as serious negotiating material, however, and it is de Valera's refusal to go, decided by his own casting vote in the cabinet, that has aroused most controversy.

De Valera realised that the republic was unattainable in the short term. Compromise was inevitable. The crude realities of power politics made some form of association with the British empire unavoidable. He was already working on a constitutionally brilliant concept of 'external association'. According to this idea, Irish sovereignty in internal matters would be recognised, but Ireland would associate with the Commonwealth in external affairs and would guarantee her neutrality in wartime. Irish and British citizens would enjoy reciprocal, as distinct from common, citizenship. This would avoid the humiliations of the direct imperial link while simultaneously providing for British security, which de Valera acknowledged to be a legitimate concern of Westminster.[7] De Valera warned the Dáil in August 1921 as bluntly as was politically possible that compromise was inevitable. He stressed that he took office again as president only on condition that the Dáil recognised that

> I have one allegiance only to the people of Ireland, and that is to do the best we can for the people of Ireland as we conceive it . . . I would not like, therefore, that anyone should propose me for election as president who would think I had my mind definitely made up on any situation that may arise. I keep myself free to consider each question as it arises — I never bind myself in any other way.[8]

This came as close as de Valera could safely go in implying that the oath to the Republic taken by members should be considered more a means to an end than an end in itself. This was the antithesis of the doctrinaire mentality, and de Valera rightly feared that doctrinaire republicans would reject any compromise.

No analysis of de Valera's motives can be definitive, for 'it was never quite clear what de Valera stood for; or with whom he stood, at least from December 1920 until June 1922'.[9] Nevertheless, there seems no reason to reject the claim of his authorised biographers that 'unity on his side was his over-riding objective'.[10] He had acted as the unifier of the Sinn Féin since 1916,[11] and continued to see himself in that role. His preoccupation with unity confirms that he realised the inevitability of compromise. Indeed, so intent was he on negotiation that between July and October 1921 he took care to provide Lloyd George with no excuse for calling off the truce.[12] Realising that bitter controversy was likely to arise over the terms of any possible agreement, he apparently hoped that if he were not involved in the negotiations himself, he could wean the doctrinaires into accepting 'external association' as an honourable solution. He argued, in addition, from a more procedural perspective, that by remaining at home he would provide the delegates with the tactical excuse that they had to refer proposals to him, which would gain them valuable respite from the immediate pressures of the negotiation table.[13]

For all the weight that should be attached to any de Valera calculation, or even rationalisation, it really did not make sense for 'the best player', as W.T. Cosgrave rightly called him, to remain a non-playing captain in the biggest match his team was ever likely to play. James Craig always tried to present Northern Ireland's case himself in negotiations with the British. Lloyd George, with a far busier schedule, and also presiding over a potentially awkward cabinet, made sure to lead his team. De Valera did sometimes advance the argument that he should not involve himself in negotiations because, as president, he was the symbol of the Republic, and symbols should not negotiate. This sounds suspiciously like an anti-Collins rationalisation. The one thing de Valera was, and that Collins was not, was president! And there would seem to have been little point remaining as symbol if there was a danger that one's absence might lead to the sacrifice of the symbol in the negotiations. De Valera would have gained a more acute appreciation of the negotiating possibilities in London, where he could also presumably have exerted greater influence on the Irish delegates.

1. A.J. Ward, *Ireland and Anglo-American Relations 1899–1921* (London, 1969), p. 235. On the significance of the tour, see D. McCartney, 'De Valera's Mission to the United States, 1919–20', in A. Cosgrove and D. McCartney (eds.), *Studies in Irish History* (Dublin, 1979), pp. 304–33.

2. Kee, *Green Flag*, p. 699. See also Fitzpatrick, *Politics*, pp. 10, 27. [The two books referred to are Robert Kee, *The Green Flag* (London, 1972) and David Fitzpatrick, *Politics and Irish Life 1913–21* (Dublin, 1977).]

3. Miller, *Church, State and Nation*, pp. 477–8; Earl of Longford and T.P. O'Neill, *Eamon de Valera* (Dublin, 1970), p. 148. [Miller is D.W. Miller, *Church, State and Nation in Ireland, 1898–1921* (Pittsburgh, 1973).]

4. Townshend, *British Campaign*, pp. 179–96, discusses the balance of military strength in the early summer of 1921, as well as longer term prospects. [Townshend is Charles Townshend, *The British Campaign in Ireland 1919–1921* (Oxford, 1978).]

5. ibid., p. 191.

6. D.H. Akenson, *The United States and Ireland* (Cambridge, Mass., 1973), pp. 53ff; D.H. Akenson, 'Was de Valera a Republican?', *Review of Politics*, 33, 2 (1971), pp. 244–7.

7. Longford and O'Neill, *De Valera*, pp. 147–8.

8. M. Moynihan (ed.), *Speeches and Statements by Eamon de Valera 1917–73* (Dublin and New York, 1980), p. 70.

9. S.M. Lawlor, *Britain and Ireland 1914–23* (Dublin, 1983), p. xi.

10. Longford and O'Neill, *De Valera*, p. 147.

11. T. Ryle Dwyer, *Eamon de Valera* (Dublin, 1980), p. 11.

12. S.M. Lawlor, 'Ireland from Truce to Treaty: War or Peace? July–October 1921', *IHS*, 22, 85 (March 1980), pp. 63–4. [*IHS* is *Irish Historical Studies*, the foremost scholarly journal of Irish historiography.]

13. Longford and O'Neill, *De Valera*, pp. 147–8.

from *Ireland 1912–1985* (1989)

MICHAEL COLLINS

Michael Collins met Kitty Kiernan while campaigning during the Longford by-election of 1917. Her family owned the Greville Arms in Mullingar, Co. Westmeath. By this time he had taken part in the 1916 Rising and had been jailed at Frongoch camp in Wales as a result. Among his subsequent roles were his appointment as Minister for Finance by the first Dáil, President of the Supreme Council of the Irish Republican Brotherhood, Director of Intelligence during the War of Independence and Chairman of the Provisional Government set up under the Treaty. Often portrayed as a dashing military leader, the prominent positions he held argue for his administrative ability and his shrewd political intelligence.

Collins wrote this letter on 30 November 1921 while he was in London as a reluctant member of the team negotiating the Treaty. At this point he and Kitty Kiernan were engaged to be married. By signing the Treaty, Collins said, 'I signed my death warrant.'

Letter to Kitty Kiernan

Kitty dearest,

I read over all your letters again last night and I started writing to you sitting up in bed but I had to give it up. Positively I was too worn out to write legibly.

It was much worse than the production I turned out one night very late in Dublin. Do you recall that one? Even so I was up at 7.30 and am feeling as well and as vigorous as it is possible to feel. Don't worry about my rest. It's really all right. You know my maxim: 'It's better to wear out than to rust out.' That's really the important essential point, isn't it? Am writing this early before any one has started here. I went to St Mary's, lit a candle for you, came back, had breakfast and started this before 9! What do you think of that?

Here's a thing! I really and truly loved that suit of yours, but I was not in just the proper form on Sunday night to express my liking for it or indeed to appreciate it fully. I'd like you to know this. Do you like it? I mean this note.

Believe me I can understand your feelings about that week end, and I know how miserable the stress of my appointments must make the time for you. But how can I help it? I didn't have a minute more than you know of. If you can realise this, what does it matter if people do make suggestions like you say they did? I don't find it very agreeable sometimes, I assure you, and I don't find the forced absence very pleasant, but then it has to be seen through.

You scarcely understand my way of thinking and of doing things. I am not demonstrative (expect [sic] in showing my temper sometimes) and I hate demonstrative indications of feeling — I mean before people. They stand somehow in my mind for a kind of insincerity. That always makes me say that 'm'yes' of mine when I hear people at it. It may not be a pleasant way and it may not appeal to people, but there you are. It's there and I'm afraid there it will remain. It really means that I'm on the side of those who do things, not on the side of those who say things. And that's that!

That's enough, I think. You won't find this letter interesting, I'm greatly afraid, but I'm in a very troubled state of mind this morning. Troubled about many things. About you among them — first among them in my own personal mind. Do you grasp that? I'd never forgive myself if I made your life unhappy. Little wrongs I may have done people never cease coming back to my mind, let alone a matter of that kind. This is a side that perhaps you could not regard as being there, but it is there.

I was expecting a letter last night. Called to my sister's place. Nothing there. However I don't intend putting the two day rule into operation until tomorrow (*at earliest*).

Slán leat for today,
Fondest love,
Mícheál.

from León Ó Broin (ed.), *In Great Haste: The Letters of Michael Collins and Kitty Kiernan* (1983)

EILÉAN NÍ CHUILLEANÁIN

The ratification of the Treaty bringing about the Irish Free State in 1922 was followed immediately by the threat, and then the reality, of civil war. Armed hostilities broke out in June of that year and lasted until the following April.

Michael Collins was killed in an ambush at a place called Béal na mBláth in rural County Cork in August 1922; he was thirty-one years old. The name means 'mouth of flowers' and is an evocative instance of how jarringly an ugly historical event can collide with its natural surroundings. Still, the landscape maintains its timeless appearance even in the face of other, perhaps unnatural, factors influencing our perception of it.

from *Site of Ambush*

1. *Reflection*

You are not the sun or the moon
But the wolf that will swallow down both sun and moon.

They dance around but they must go down
You will devour them all.

The houses, flowers, the salt and ships
Streams that flow down mountains, flames that burn up trees.

You are the twining gulf Charybdis
Whose currents yield return to none.

2. *Narration*

At alarming bell daybreak, before
Scraping of cats or windows creaking over the street,
Eleven miles of road between them,
The enemy commanders synchronised their heartbeats:
Seven forty-five by the sun.
At ten the soldiers were climbing into lorries
Asthmatic engines drawing breath in even shifts.
The others were fretting over guns
Counting up ammunition and money.
At eleven they lay in wait at the cross
With over an hour to go.
The pine trees looked up stiff;
At the angle of the road, polished stones
Forming a stile, a knowing path
Twisting away; the rough grass
Gripped the fragments of the wall.

A small deep stream glassily descended:
Ten minutes to the hour.
The clouds grew grey, the road grey as iron,
The hills dark, the trees deep,
The fields faded; like white mushrooms
Sheep remote under the wind.
The stream ticked and throbbed
Nearer; a boy carried a can to the well
Nearer on the dark road.
The driver saw the child's back,
Nearer; the birds shoaled off the branches in fright.

Deafly rusting in the stream
The lorry now is soft as a last night's dream.
The soldiers and the deaf child
Landed gently in the water
They were light between long weeds
Settled and lay quiet, nobody
To listen to them now.
They all looked the same face down there:
Water too thick and deep to see.
They were separated for good.
It was cold, their teeth shrilling.
They slept like falling hay in waves.
Shells candied their skin; the water
Lay heavy and they could not rise but coiled
By scythefuls limply in ranks.
A long winter stacks their bodies
And words above their stillness hang from hooks
In skeins, like dark nets drying,
Flapping against the stream.
A watch vibrates alone in the filtering light;
Flitters of hair wave at the sun.

from *Site of Ambush* (1975)

P. F. QUINLAN

During the Civil War the diarist was a lieutenant in the pro-Treaty forces. The scene of
the action, the 'stunt', is in southern County Tipperary, near where Liam Lynch, one of
the commanders of the anti-Treaty forces, was killed in April 1923, an event that

brought an end to the military phase of the war. The author's friend Seán O'Donoghue was on the anti-Treaty side. He was killed in Cork city in 1922.

Remembering Seán

FRIDAY 26TH. Rose pretty early and had breakfast. Great hubbub over Doc. not visiting post. Bad cases sent away and Red Cross came up. Crossley going with Corporal G when stunt came on then off for we knew not where terrible secrecy. Got to Mtown [Mitchelstown]. Knocked up digs. Sgt Mc falling out exhausted on the way. Went into POBs had a few drinks and to bed.

SAT. 27TH. Up again with scarcely a doze in bed and on for Ballyp. [Ballyporeen] met several neighbours and lots of suspicious 'good days'. Spread out at [Meany's] and on for the open country. Got nothing so swung on for village. Had row with some of the boys. Called into Kennedys and had some chat on again for the village. Into MOBs and had some grub called down to Aunties with Jim Finn. Had tea and out at dark for the night on B-C. [Ballyporeen–Clogheen] road. Called into J. Ph's and got on fine had some tea etc. again in the morning — off again after great talk and horse lore.

SUN. 28TH. Through Bally. [Ballyporeen] spread out and on for the 'home of the irregulars' as it has come to be known not much of an appearance of irregulars about it as we moved on for the first hour. But hark a little shot. A pause. Another shot. Three almost together. How the sound of those death messages makes a chap's blood boil. What queer characteristics they bring to light in a bloke. How a man longs for blood at the sound of firing. What totally savage beings so called civilised men are. How near the polished surface is the bald proof of sheer savagery I have often seen proved on such occasions. Then on for our stunt. Stealth of movement passing along orders punctuated by the crack of skirmishing fire. *Nuf* said now. I shall not forget the rest of the scrap. But now that it is over I remembered I was near the burying place of Seán O'D. [Seán O'Donoghue] so I called in to see his grave. Heavens how small a little place we all can fit in some day but in that small place decorated by wreaths and tokens of sorrow from heartbroken friends lay my life-long friend poor Seán that I loved since I was so wee that I cannot remember and that everybody loved that ever met him. Ah how sorrowful. The bare bald tombstones seemed to fling scornful glances at me. The dove in the ivy-clad poplar which spread its apron of branches over that lonely grave cooed in such a manner as to mock my prayers for my poor friend as if he needed them for where else could he be but with his God, poor saint and the poplar branches solemnly beckoning their bare branches as if to token my attention to his grave. All, each, and everything seemed to mourn for him but seemed as if by mutual consent to exclude me from the circle of mourners. How deep down in my heart (if indeed I have such a thing) I felt the irony of my behaviour. Coming in the green uniform to pray for him that was done to death by men wearing same. But I was alone with the dead and I wanted no more. As I prayed and thought over his life and our associations I showed the woman. Try how I might I could not stop. Circumstances are indeed cruel here am I praying for poor Seán with the uniform of those that murdered him and I still cannot throw it off. I explained to him my friend. Gallant. Shapely boy. Gay and buoyant in the bloom of his youth now lying stiff and cold several feet down in the damp cold clay by the hand of a cowardly drunken parasite who would not dare to face him on equal terms. Yes, Seán, my old friend you told me long ago you would be shot but in that manner why who should have thought it possible? Very well I have made thee a promise. Seán death has made it impossible for us to shake hands upon it. But your ideals I shall strive to attain. Your death I shall revenge aye if I shall suffer death a thousand times over for it that man shall fall whatever the cost. I will send him before his God to account for his deeds and to be judged on his merits and your ideal. 'A Republic' I will fight for by my method different to yours. But Seán if I had misgivings as to a republic once when the path to such is rendered sacred by the blood of brave and noble souls more especially by your blood, then it is *the* path for me.

from Seán Dunne (ed.), *The Cork Anthology* (1993)

BERNARD SHAW

Shaw begins his preface to John Bull's Other Island *by noting that it was written 'at the request of Mr William Butler Yeats, as a patriotic contribution to the repertory of the Irish Literary Theatre. Like most people who have asked me to write plays, Mr Yeats got rather more than he bargained for.' And the preface continues as a typically abrasive homily on the misfortunes of both nationalism and religious intolerance.*

The play takes up these concerns by doing its utmost to reverse prevailing stereotypes of Celt and Saxon. Broadbent's opposite number is Larry Doyle, whose mordant criticisms of his native country challenge Broadbent's gung-ho materialism. The criticisms also place in perspective the stagey carry-on of Tim Haffigan. The play features an unfrocked priest named Keegan. His thoughtful views are a corrective to Doyle's, while his sense of religion has far more to it than that of Father Dempsey, the local priest.

In an author's note for a 1926 London production, Shaw points out that the play depicts a 'state of innocence and false security' before, for instance, 'the sanguinary campaign in which the Black-and-Tans and Sinn Féin tried which could burn most houses until Michael Collins won'.

Celt and Saxon

Tim. Youre goin to Ireland, then, out o sympithy: is it?

Broadbent. I'm going to develop an estate there for the Land Development Syndicate, in which I am interested. I am convinced that all it needs to make it pay is to handle it properly, as estates are handled in England. You know the English plan, Mr Haffigan, don't you?

Tim. Bedad I do, sir. Take all you can out of Ireland and spend it in England: thats it.

Broadbent [*not quite liking this*]. My plan, sir, will be to take a little money out of England and spend it in Ireland.

Tim. More power to your elbow! an may your shadda never be less! for youre the broth of a boy intirely. An how can I help you? Command me to the last dhrop o me blood.

Broadbent. Have you ever heard of Garden City?

Tim [*doubtfully*]. D'ye mane Heavn?

Broadbent. Heaven! No: it's near Hitchin. If you can spare half an hour I'll go into it with you.

Tim. I tell you hwat. Gimme a prospectus. Lemme take it home and reflect on it.

Broadbent. Youre quite right: I will. [*He gives him a copy of Mr Ebenezer Howard's book, and several pamphlets.*] You understand that the map of the city — the circular construction — is only a suggestion.

Tim. I'll make a careful note o that [*looking dazedly at the map*].

Broadbent. What I say is, why not start a Garden City in Ireland?

Tim [*with enthusiasm*]. Thats just what was on the tip o me tongue to ask you. Why not? [*Defiantly*] Tell me why not.

from *John Bull's Other Island* (1904)

WINSTON CHURCHILL

The collapse of the Austro-Hungarian empire after World War I was one reason why the drawing and redrawing of borders was a contemporary preoccupation. Closer to home, the existence of the Boundary Commission was another reason. When Churchill made this speech at Westminster in 1922, it was not clear what the eventual border of Northern Ireland would be. A distinct possibility being mooted was that Tyrone and Fermanagh would be part of the Irish Free State.

Churchill spent three years between the ages of two and five in Ireland, where his father was secretary to the Lord Lieutenant, the Duke of Marlborough, Winston's grandfather. One of his recollections of being there was that, 'It nearly always rained.'

Dreary Steeples of Fermanagh and Tyrone

Then came the Great War. Every institution, almost, in the world was strained. Great empires had been overturned. The whole map of Europe has been changed. The position of countries has been violently altered. The modes of thought of men, the whole outlook on affairs, the grouping of parties, all have encountered violent and tremendous change in the deluge of the world, but as the deluge subsides and the waters fall short we see the dreary steeples of Fermanagh and Tyrone emerging once again. The integrity of their quarrel is one of the few institutions that have been unaltered in the cataclysm which has swept the world. That says a lot for the persistency with which Irishmen on the one side or on the other are able to pursue their controversies.

from The World Crisis (1957)

LOUIS MACNEICE

There were many complicated reasons for Ireland's neutrality during World War II. Among them were concerns about the viability of the state's sovereignty and independence. Implicit also in the policy was an assertion of the political will and a belief in the social resourcefulness necessary to take a different path from the one enjoined on Britain.

MacNeice's people came from the West of Ireland, but he was born in Belfast. His father was a bishop and a supporter of Home Rule. MacNeice was in Ireland when World War II broke out. He gives his impressions in his autobiography, The Strings Are False (1965): 'Dublin was hardly worried by the war; her old preoccupations were still preoccupations. The intelligentsia continued their parties, their mutual malice was as effervescent as ever . . . The potboy priests and the birds of prey were still the dominant caste; the petty bureaucracy continued powerful and petty.' As for the non-neutral North: 'Belfast, gloomy at all times, was gloomier now, full of patriotic placards and soldiers; at night the tramcars moved slowly along like catafalques, glimmers of spectral blue.'

MacNeice worked for the BBC during the war. 'Neutrality' was written in September 1942.

Neutrality

The neutral island facing the Atlantic,
The neutral island in the heart of man,
Are bitterly soft reminders of the beginnings
That ended before the end began.

Look into your heart, you will find a County Sligo,
A Knocknarea with for navel a cairn of stones,
You will find the shadow and sheen of a moleskin mountain
And a litter of chronicles and bones.

Look into your heart, you will find fermenting rivers,
Intricacies of gloom and glint,
You will find such ducats of dream and great doubloons of ceremony
As nobody today would mint.

But then look eastward from your heart, there bulks
A continent, close, dark, as archetypal sin,
While to the west off your own shores the mackerel
Are fat — on the flesh of your kin.

from *Selected Poems* (1966)

EAMON DE VALERA

One of the terms of the 1921 Anglo-Irish Treaty was that Britain had the right to use the naval bases at Berehaven and Cobh, Co. Cork, and at Lough Swilly, Co. Donegal. In 1938, Britain — under Neville Chamberlain — gave up that right, Churchill being one of the few British politicians to object. Then war broke out, and Britain requested use of the ports, only to be refused, since to agree would be to break Ireland's policy of strict neutrality during World War II.

Churchill's remarks were made in his victory speech of 13 May 1945, in the course
of which he said: 'with a restraint and poise to which, I say, history will find few
parallels, His Majesty's Government never laid a violent hand upon them [the ports],
though at times it would have been quite easy and quite natural, and we left the de
Valera government to frolic with the Germans and later with the Japanese to their
heart's content'. But if the country was neutral, the people were not. Churchill's speech
also mentions the 'thousands of Southern Irishmen who hastened to the battle-front'.

De Valera's reply was broadcast to national acclaim on 16 May 1945.

From the Reply to Mr Churchill

Certain newspapers have been very persistent in looking for my answer to Mr Churchill's recent broadcast. I know the kind of answer I am expected to make. I know the answer that first springs to the lips of every man of Irish blood who heard or read that speech, no matter in what circumstances or in what part of the world he found himself.

I know the reply I would have given a quarter of a century ago. But I have deliberately decided that that is not the reply I shall make tonight. I shall strive not to be guilty of adding any fuel to the flames of hatred and passion which, if continued to be fed, promise to burn up whatever is left by the war of decent human feeling in Europe.

Allowances can be made for Mr Churchill's statement, however unworthy, in the first flush of his victory. No such excuse could be found for me in this quieter atmosphere. There are, however, some things which it is my duty to say, some things which it is essential to say. I shall try to say them as dispassionately as I can.

Mr Churchill makes it clear that, in certain circumstances, he would have violated our neutrality and that he would justify his action by Britain's necessity. It seems strange to me that Mr Churchill does not see that this, if accepted, would mean that Britain's necessity would become a moral code and that when this necessity became sufficiently great, other people's rights were not to count.

It is quite true that other great powers believe in this same code — in their own regard — and have behaved in accordance with it. That is precisely why we have the disastrous succession of wars — World War No. 1 and World War No. 2 — and shall it be World War No. 3?

Surely Mr Churchill must see that, if his contention be admitted in our regard, a like justification can be framed for similar acts of aggression elsewhere and no small nation adjoining a great power could ever hope to be permitted to go its own way in peace.

It is, indeed, fortunate that Britain's necessity did not reach the point when Mr Churchill would have acted. All credit to him that he successfully resisted the temptation which, I have no doubt, many times assailed him in his difficulties and to which I freely admit many leaders might have easily succumbed. It is, indeed, hard for the strong to be just to the weak, but acting justly always has its rewards.

By resisting his temptation in this instance, Mr Churchill, instead of adding another horrid chapter to the already bloodstained record of the relations between England and this country, has advanced the cause of international morality an important step — one of the most important, indeed, that can be taken on the road to the establishment of any sure basis for peace.

As far as the peoples of these two islands are concerned, it may, perhaps, mark a fresh beginning towards the realisation of that mutual comprehension to which Mr Churchill has referred and for which he has prayed and for which, I hope, he will not merely pray but work, also, as did his predecessor [Neville Chamberlain] who will yet, I believe, find the honoured place in British history which is due to him, as certainly he will find it in any fair record of the relations between Britain and ourselves.

That Mr Churchill should be irritated when our neutrality stood in the way of what he thought he vitally needed, I understand, but that he or any thinking person in Britain or elsewhere should fail to see the reason for our neutrality, I find it hard to conceive.

I would like to put a hypothetical question — it is a question I have put to many Englishmen since the last war. Suppose Germany had won the war, had invaded and occupied England, and that after a long lapse of time and many bitter struggles she was finally brought to acquiesce in admitting England's right to freedom, and let England go, but not the whole of England, all but, let us say, the six southern counties.

These six southern counties, those, let us suppose, commanding the entrance to the narrow seas, Germany had singled out and insisted on holding herself with a view to weakening England as a whole and maintaining the security of her own communications through the Straits of Dover.

Let us suppose, further, that after all this had happened Germany was engaged in a great war in which she could show that she was on the side of the freedom of a number of small nations. Would Mr Churchill as an Englishman who believed that his own nation had as good a right to freedom as any other — not freedom for a part merely, but freedom for the whole — would he, whilst Germany still maintained the partition of his country and occupied six counties of it, would he lead this partitioned England to join with Germany in a crusade? I do not think Mr Churchill would.

Would he think the people of partitioned England an object of shame if they stood neutral in such circumstances? I do not think Mr Churchill would.

from Maurice Moynihan (ed.), *Speeches and Statements by Eamon de Valera 1917–73* (1980)

ANDRÉE SHEEHY SKEFFINGTON

Owen Sheehy Skeffington (1909–70) was the only son of Hanna and Francis Sheehy Skeffington, and very much lived up to their intellectual and moral example. He was a noted spokesman on topics that made mid-century conservative Ireland and its custodians uncomfortable, publicising not merely instances of cowardice and ineptitude at the official level but also cases of injustice and humiliation among citizens who had no hope of having their own voices heard. Conceived in terms of a belief that 'the social and economic revolution had been betrayed from 1922 on', his role as critic and voice of conscience was exemplary and unique — speaking out in public not being one of the distinguishing features of Irish civic life.

The Censorship of Publications Act 1929 is one of the most visible institutional instances of the kind of narrowness against which Sheehy Skeffington campaigned. In 1958, Archbishop John Charles McQuaid of Dublin objected to the Dublin Theatre Festival production of O'Casey's The Drums of Father Ned; *the play was withdrawn.*

Censorship and Discreet Silence

I rish society, ambivalent or tolerant regarding the use of force in the cause of nationalism, accepted control and intolerance regarding freedom of conscience and expression.

In April 1957, following a report of the Congress of the Christus Rex Society, Sean O'Casey had taken up the cudgels on behalf of Irish writers and attacked Irish censorship, both official and unofficial. He was backed up by Austin Clarke. On 20 May Dr G.A. Little, for the Censorship Board, published a reply strongly supporting the idea of censorship, which, he claimed, was restrictive because protective, and asserting, at the same time, 'the ancient principle of morality through the influence of free will'. Dr Little, Owen wrote, 'provides an excellent example of doublethink', since he praised the virtue of voluntary rejection of the freely accessible forbidden fruit, yet wanted to 'safeguard' men's minds by forcibly preventing them from using this much-lauded free will.

Meanwhile, the theatre producer Alan Simpson had been arrested at the Pike Theatre, where he had been producing Tennessee Williams's play *The Rose Tattoo*, as part of the first Dublin International Theatre Festival.[1] The same play had been praised by the *Sunday Times* for 'its artistic integrity and high moral purpose'. When the case opened in July, Simpson was charged with having produced for gain an indecent, profane and obscene play injurious to public morals, and creating a public nuisance. Censorship of plays on the stage was a matter for the police, not the Censorship Board.

The final verdict was delivered the following year, when the case was dismissed by District Justice O'Flynn. Owen had written to both Alan and his father, Canon Simpson, expressing indignation and support, and congratulated O'Flynn for his 'brilliant and courageous' judgment.

The censoring minds were also active in an incident of parochial sectarianism which received wide coverage in the press. The story concerned the boycott of a Church of Ireland school and Protestant-owned shops in Fethard-on-Sea, Co. Wexford, by the Catholic community, after the disappearance of the Protestant wife of a 'mixed marriage', with her two young children. It was rumoured locally that the Protestants had been in league to help the wife's desertion. This had been repeatedly denied by them, and by the husband. The one teacher of this small Church of Ireland school was a Catholic (a tolerance on both sides remarked upon by Owen), who, it was said, was advised by a group of Catholic women to withdraw her services. Owen raised the matter in the Senate on the Adjournment. His question was to the Minister for Education, since children were being deprived of regular teaching through this boycott.

Official reaction to the boycott was mixed. The Bishop of Galway described it as a 'peaceful and moderate protest', while the Taoiseach, de Valera, thought it sufficiently important to make a statement in the Dáil urging a speedy end to 'this deplorable affair'.

When Owen's motion came up in the Senate, neither the Minister for Education nor any other member of the government was available. Pointing out that children were being victimised, Owen asked what action the minister proposed to take. The Leader of the House, Senator Eamon Kissane, said that there was 'no issue', as far as they were concerned. It was solely a matter for the manager of the school, another example of the government's abdication in the realm of education. Only Senator Stanford backed Owen.

The good name of the Catholic laity had been saved by Donal Barrington, lecturer in Public Administration and Constitutional Law at University College, Dublin. In a speech to the Catholic Social Study Conference in Dublin, he condemned the boycott as 'the most terrible thing that has happened in this part of the country since the Civil War'. He considered it his duty to speak up, saying, 'There is a time in the affairs of people when nothing is necessary for the triumph of evil but that good men should maintain what is called a discreet silence.' Owen was delighted and wrote at once to congratulate him.

Eventually the estranged wife returned home, and no more was heard on the subject. Owen believed that the *Ne Temere* decree had been the cause of the trouble and should be exposed and abolished. He saw it as a source of tragic division.

At about the same time, Owen supported another protest involving the Catholic Church. Under the patronage of Eamon de Valera, public subscriptions were being sought for a Terence MacSwiney Memorial Fund, to build a chapel in St George's Cathedral, Southwark.[2] Terence MacSwiney's widow, Muriel, was not consulted or informed. When he heard this, Owen promptly wrote to the *Dublin Evening Mail* saying that the whole project was exclusively sectarian, and strange, given that the Catholic Church condemned hunger-strikes. It was also discourteous to the widow. 'I realise that the fact that she is not a Catholic will have made officialdom, lay and clerical, regard her as not worth consulting', he added. He agreed with her publicly stated opinion that Ireland was the place for Terence MacSwiney's memorial, and that it should be something of non-sectarian benefit to people of all beliefs in his own land, beset as it still was by poverty, ignorance and disease.

Owen was never one to keep 'a discreet silence'. He ignored the minefields surrounding issues such as education or national unity. Senators or ministers often took refuge in silence after his hard-hitting speeches, or simply found it more convenient to be absent. 'I am getting used to raising matters here in the absence of Ministers', he remarked on one occasion, deploring this contempt for the Senate, and the resultant stifling of parliamentary debate.

1. Carolyn Swift, who was co-director of the Pike with Alan Simpson, recounted the event in *The Irish Times* many years later (*The Irish Times*, 7 December 1985).

2. Terence MacSwiney, Lord Mayor of Cork, died in England in Brixton Prison (1920) after 74 days on hunger-strike. Bishop Amigo of Southwark, who had never visited MacSwiney in prison, had allowed his dead body to lie in his church, defying the British authorities. Hence the suggestion, when Southwark Cathedral was being rebuilt long after Bishop Amigo's death, that a £10,000 Fund Appeal would get the backing of Irish people at home and in Britain to sponsor a chapel in MacSwiney's name. MacSwiney's widow, Muriel, had publicly left the Catholic Church before 1922 and had lived abroad, mostly in Germany, up to World War II. She alleged that in 1932 their daughter, aged fourteen, had been 'kidnapped' with de Valera's knowledge and connivance, to be brought up as a Catholic in Ireland by Terence's sister, Mary MacSwiney, and that her appeals to the government and the courts had been in vain. Her protest at the form of memorial to her husband and the insulting manner (to her) of its sponsorship was made public in *The Manchester Guardian* and *The Scotsman*, as well as in the *Dublin Evening Mail* and the *Sunday Review*. She died in 1984.

from *Skeff* (1991)

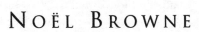

NOËL BROWNE

The coalition, or 'inter-party', government that came to power in 1948 was made up of conservative Fine Gael, Labour and National Labour, the left-tending-cum-republican Clann na Poblachta (the Republican Party), and the small-farmer Clann na Talmhan (the Land Party). Noël Browne was a member of Clann na Poblachta.

Seán MacBride (1904–88), son of Maud Gonne and Major John MacBride, was the leader of Clann na Poblachta, which he founded in 1946. Seán MacEntee was a prominent member of Fianna Fáil. Jim Larkin was the son of James Larkin (1876–1947), the noted trade unionist. Noel Hartnett was a member of Clann na Poblachta and for a time one of MacBride's close advisers.

Noël Browne is remembered less for his war on tuberculosis than for the so-called 'Mother and Child' controversy. He had proposed that free health care be provided to pregnant women together with appropriate post-natal care for the mothers and children. The proposal failed from lack of political will and from the objections of the Catholic hierarchy, who made it known that such a scheme was not in accord with church teaching.

The inter-party government fell in 1951 in an election which marked the start of the rapid decline of Clann na Poblachta.

Levers of Power

From the moment he assumed leadership of the ten deputies after the election, MacBride's policies were hard to rationalise. It has been said that he appointed me to Health instead of Con Lehane, the obvious choice, since in his opinion, I was an unknown nonentity appointed to an unimportant department. Con, a well-known solicitor, a rugged, opinionated republican, and well-liked, might have questioned the doubtful compromises to be made on republican issues in a Fine Gael coalition. There is also the possibility that the promise given by Hartnett to Harry Kennedy that the party would introduce an efficient TB service had had some influence.

Even to a seasoned experienced politician, the problems of coalition government are formidable. A succession of minority party leaders during the last forty years has failed to reconcile their membership of a coalition with their responsibilities to their own electorate. MacBride's problem was that he did not even appreciate the size of the dilemma. The Fine Gael leadership never fully trusted him, even though he believed he had captivated and out-foxed them. It is a grim statistic that of the five parties that formed the first coalition three, Clann na Talmhan, Clann na Poblachta, and National Labour, have not been heard of since and a fourth, Connolly's Labour Party, has declined continuously and no longer matters as a serious political entity.

Throughout the 1948 election, and especially after Seán MacEntee's revealing and unrefuted attack on MacBride, there was a feeling among some of us that we were working with people with whom we had little in common. Those of us who were non-army accepted the proposed coalition with Fine Gael because we had entered public life in hopes that we would see the end of the damaging and meaningless political alignments of the civil war. The proposed coalition would end the monopoly of office of Fianna Fáil. Since there was no precedent from which we could gain experience or warning of the possible insoluble contradictions in a coalition, we welcomed the innovation, with its possibility of breakthrough to conventional European-style left-right politics.

As it later transpired, the ex-IRA group, led by Seán MacBride particularly on the issue of the primacy of the Catholic Church over parliament, had no serious policy differences with Fine Gael. As Mr de Valera was to show later, neither had he nor his party.

I was powerfully motivated by my hope that we might make progress on general health needs in our hospitals, and especially to curb tuberculosis. In a discussion before the formation of the Cabinet about possible ideological conflicts with Fine Gael, as I even then envisaged them, Seán MacBride and I made a pact designed, in effect, to achieve limited objectives. This was certainly my understanding of it. MacBride went on to summarise it succinctly: 'When your health service objectives are fulfilled, tuberculosis controlled, your hospital buildings that high, Noël, we will go to the country, and ask for an increased mandate.'

With a mixture of innocence and naïveté I accepted this assurance. A little thought, and more of the scepticism which I later developed about such promises, would have shown me that whatever about Seán MacBride's good faith and the sincerity with which it was offered, such an assurance would cut no ice with his ex-IRA comrades. Had he indeed gone back to tell them that since I had now achieved our main objectives in the Department of Health, he intended to call an election for a larger mandate, his comrades would have been astounded.

In the negotiations leading to the formation of the coalition, an interesting piece of black propaganda appeared in de Valera's *Irish Press*. The paper issued a list of probable ministerial candidates for office were a Labour-Fine Gael coalition to be formed. The black propaganda element was the inclusion in the list of young Jim Larkin as Minister for Education. Larkin, many years previously, had returned to Dublin following a spell at universities and colleges in Moscow, and had stood for election as a member of the Communist Party. He backed his election campaign by putting out lurid anti-Catholic propaganda and called for the virtual suppression of the power of the church as the influential institution it then was in Irish public life. Not surprisingly he was defeated. Having become a respected member of the Labour Party, Larkin was elected to a Dublin constituency in the 1948 election. What the writer of the *Irish Press* article well knew was that the proposal of Larkin as Minister for Education would almost certainly scupper any possibility of the formation of a coalition government. A Communist in the Department of Education, even today, is unthinkable. That fine liberal politician, Owen Sheehy Skeffington, had been expelled from the Labour Party merely for being a liberal.

To give some idea about the attitudes to Communism at that time, even in Labour circles, I recall asking Jim Everett, leader of the National Labour Party, how it was that the very experienced, widely acknowledged and talented

Larkin had not been nominated by William Norton or elected by the party for a Cabinet post, even the most innocuous. Everett's reply was brief and instructive. There was no possibility of Larkin being brought into Cabinet because of his Communist background: 'If Larkin politically ever shows the whites of his eyes, we'll blow the top of his head off.'

With a mixture of bewilderment, unbelief, and delight at my new access to power and authority from a subordinate medical post in an obscure small country sanatorium, I took over the Department of Health determined to revolutionise the quality of the health service. In a small way we were to show just how much could be gained through the existing state bureaucracy, in spite of its inherent inefficiency and defects.

Easily the most important immediate need was the elimination of tuberculosis. We had promised to do this, if given power by the people. The response to my call for help from the much maligned 'intransigent' civil servant bureaucrats began my own re-education about the true potential of our civil service. There was no need for a Commission of Inquiry into what needed to be done. Tuberculosis control had been a special study of mine since I had qualified as a doctor.

The Department of Health was transformed into a battle headquarters. Since I had considered the need for an efficient tuberculosis service for many years a clear plan of action was quickly outlined. The first essential was the limitation of the disease by the isolation of existing known possible sources of infection. The nearly pandemic nature of the disease stemmed from the failure to establish a disease control organisation in which diagnosis, followed by isolation of the index case, was the most immediate need. Denmark, a small country, had already shown what could be done simply by efficient diagnostic isolation and treatment facilities. They had succeeded in containing the disease as a first step towards its control, long before the introduction of the miracle anti-tuberculosis drugs.

Although we were fully engaged in the anti-tuberculosis drive, we also established a badly-needed diagnostic and cancer hospital treatment service based on an entirely new, superbly equipped hospital, built on a new site on the outskirts of the city. This became known as St Luke's Cancer Hospital. A group of provincial centres was also established. These proposals had been recommended by the Cancer Council which we had established in April 1948, some two months after taking up office. We also set out to build anew or reconstruct some seven thousand hospital beds all over Ireland. We reconstructed and re-equipped our county homes. We launched a new 'clean food' code, backed with a press, radio and film campaign directed to educate the public in methods of hygienic food preparation, sale and usage.

We established new regional hospitals in Cork, Limerick, and Galway in addition to St Vincent's Hospital, Crumlin Children's Hospital, St Loman's in Dublin, Ardkeen in Waterford, County Hospital in Manorhamilton, Kilkreene

Hospital in Kilkenny, Gurranebraher Hospital in Cork, Foynes Children's Hostel. There were St Mary's Hospital in the Phoenix Park, the James Connolly Memorial Hospital, the St James's Municipal Hospital in Dublin and many more. We established a new National Rehabilitation Organisation in Dublin; it is now a great multi-million pound national institution. There was a BCG inoculation service, a diphtheria vaccination scheme, a mass radiography scheme.

from *Against the Tide* (1986)

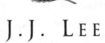

J.J. LEE

In 1959, Eamon de Valera was elected President of Ireland for the first time. His successor as Taoiseach was Seán Lemass (1899–1971), a 1916 veteran, who had been Minister for Industry and Commerce in the numerous Fianna Fáil administrations that had held office since 1932. Lemass did not share his predecessor's predilection for things rural and traditional, and was instrumental in the concerted effort during the 1960s to put Ireland on a more modern footing, particularly in the economic sphere.

The main basis for overdue change was a report entitled Economic Development *(1958) written by T.K. Whitaker, Secretary of the Department of Finance. Lemass saw to it that the report's recommendations were put into action. As a result, the state became much more involved in the country's economic life. The investment of foreign capital was actively and successfully sought. Free trade with Britain was reinstated. In various ways, these developments led to Ireland becoming a member of the European Economic Community in 1973 and, though the road has been decidedly rocky at times, to the kind of society the country now enjoys.*

Educational Revolution

The route sketched out in *Economic Development* pointed in the direction of efficiency, competitiveness, and quality — quality of administration, quality of management, quality of labour. Few of these goals could be achieved without a transformation of the quality and quantity of education. This in turn had fundamental implications for the nature of society. Lemass subsequently claimed that as late as 1956, when the government reduced the secondary school per capita grant by 10 per cent without serious public protest, 'There was no realisation of the importance of education in the modern world and there was certainly no evidence of this outburst of enthusiasm for education which is so characteristic now.'[1] Lemass appointed three of his best ministers, Patrick Hillery, George Colley and Donogh O'Malley, to Education. All were young, and anxious to make their mark by injecting some life into a traditionally moribund department.

Primary education experienced growing pressure on resources as numbers enrolled rose from 496,000 in 1960 to 544,000 in 1973. Teacher/pupil ratios nevertheless improved, if only slightly. The main advances came through reducing the sizes of appallingly large classes. The proportion of children in classes of more than forty-five pupils fell from 45 per cent in 1963 to 13.5 per cent in 1973. Facilities also improved as more than 1,000 small one- and two-teacher schools were closed. The proportion of schools with piped drinking water, for instance, rose from 47 per cent to 76 per cent between 1963 and 1974, and the proportion with flush toilets from 46 per cent to 93 per cent. Free school transport services helped compensate after 1967/8 for the closures.[2]

The situation was particularly serious at second level. The key contribution here came from *Investment in education*, the report of an OECD survey team under the chairmanship of Patrick Lynch.[3] The report collected important statistical data for the first time, intended to indicate the resources available, and the efficiency with which they were used. It provided striking evidence of the lack of opportunity for poorer children to proceed to secondary and higher education. After its exposure of the waste of talent fostered by an educational system based on low intellectual and relatively high financial entry requirements to advanced levels, it was no longer possible to sustain fond illusions about the wonderful educational performance.

Hillery announced in May 1963 that comprehensive schools would be established, under the control of the Department of Education, to provide a broader range of subjects than hitherto available and to improve the regional distribution of educational opportunities. He also announced that regional technical colleges would be established. Building grants for secondary schools were introduced in 1964. Policies initiated by Hillery, and continued by his successor, George Colley, laid much of the ground work for improving access to education. They also began to shift the balance of power in the administration of education between the traditionally hegemonic Catholic Church and the state. But it was during the tenure of the rumbustious Donogh O'Malley from 1965 to 1967 that education achieved a breakthrough in public consciousness.

O'Malley was to die suddenly at the age of forty-seven in 1968, at a moment when he had caught the public imagination to an exceptional degree. Many of his schemes were destined to remain stillborn, or to be buried beneath the crushing weight of vested interest (some of which may have chanced to coincide with the public interest). His best known initiative was the introduction of free secondary education. The 1923 Local Government Act had authorised local authorities to provide scholarships, financed from the rates, for secondary school pupils. The authorities, largely representing rate payer interests, naturally did relatively little under this provision for poor but able children. The amounts awarded were small, and as late as 1961 only 621 scholarships of this type were offered. An Amendment Act then proposed that the state should meet at least half the costs of these scholarships, and the number nearly trebled to 1,775 in 1963.⁴ But this still represented less than 2 per cent of the student body.

When O'Malley announced his free education scheme, reputedly with the prior approval of Lemass but without having consulted the cabinet or Finance, the government was swept along on the tide of public enthusiasm. The thinking of O'Malley and Lemass ran ahead of that even of the supportive Secretary of Education, Seán O'Connor.⁵ Between 1966 and 1969 the number of secondary school pupils rose from 104,000 to 144,000, or as much as in the previous ten years. Recognising the extra pressure that would be placed on schools, the state now began to provide support for capital expenditure in this area. Free secondary education opened up many doors that were previously shut to children born into the wrong families. Seán O'Connor's judgement, however, is that the initiative was not followed up with adequate resources for the schools, and that the impetus went out of the commitment to education with the resignation of Lemass and the death of O'Malley.⁶

1. 'Seán Lemass looks back', *Irish Press*, 4 February 1969.

2. NESC, *Educational Expenditure in Ireland* (Dublin, 1975), summarises the main developments between 1963 and 1974. [NESC is the National Economic and Social Council.]

3. *Investment in Education. Report of a Survey Team Appointed by the Minister for Education in Conjunction with the OECD* (2 vols., Dublin, 1965, 1966).

4. Lyons, *Ireland*, p. 635. [The work referred to is F.S.L. Lyons, *Ireland Since the Famine* (London, 1971).]

5. Seán O'Connor's interview with Christina Murphy, 'How O'Malley launched free scheme', *Irish Times*, 10 September 1986.

6. ibid.

from *Ireland 1912–1985* (1989)

NUALA NÍ DHOMHNAILL

One of the most complicated and unresolved issues in modern Irish culture is the language question. This has been so particularly since what has been termed 'the great silence', a verbal clearing and scattering that coincides with, and is thought of as, the linguistic replica of, the Great Famine. By the end of the nineteenth century, however, the Gaelic League — founded in 1893 by Douglas Hyde (1860–1949), later the first President of Ireland — was making an influential case for a connection between the Irish language and Irish identity, and there was a resurgence of interest in the language as a spoken and written medium. The Free State, in turn, undertook a major policy initiative to 'coordinate, democratise and Gaelicise our education'. But the language did not enter the lives of the people as a living presence, though it did continue to be a vital medium of cultural commentary and literary expression.

The present generation of Irish-language poets, of whom Nuala Ní Dhomhnaill is the best known, has attracted wider critical interest and, through translation into English, larger audiences than its predecessors. There seems to be a generally more relaxed acknowledgment of Irish as one of the country's languages.

The Corpse That Sits Up and Talks Back

Not so long ago I telephoned my mother about some family matter. 'So what are you writing these days?' she asked, more for the sake of conversation than anything else. 'Oh, an essay for *The New York Times*,' I said, as casually as possible. 'What is it about?' she asked. 'About what it is like to write in Irish,' I replied. There was a good few seconds' pause on the other end of the line; then, 'Well, I hope you'll tell them that it is mad.' End of conversation. I had got my comeuppance. And from my mother, who was the native speaker of Irish in our family, never having encountered a single word of English until she went to school at the age of six, and well up in her teens before she realised that the name they had at home for a most useful item was actually two words — 'safety pin' — and that they were English. Typical.

But really not so strange. Some time later I was at a reception at the American Embassy in Dublin for two of their writers, Toni Morrison and Richard Wilbur. We stood in line and took our buffet suppers along to the nearest available table. An Irishwoman across from me asked what I did. Before I had time to open my mouth her partner butted in: 'Oh, Nuala writes poetry in Irish.' And what did I write about? she asked. Again before I had time to reply he did so for me: 'She writes poems of love and loss, and I could quote you most of them by heart.' This was beginning to get up my nose, and so I attempted simultaneously to deflate him and to go him one better. 'Actually,' I announced, 'I think the only thing worth writing about are the biggies: birth, death and the most important thing in between, which is sex.' 'Oh,' his friend said to me archly, 'and is there a word for sex in Irish?'

I looked over at the next table, where Toni Morrison was sitting, and I wondered if a black writer in America had to put up with the likes of that, or its equivalent. Here I was in my own country, having to defend the official language of the state from a compatriot who obviously thought it was an accomplishment to be ignorant of it. Typical, and yet maybe not so strange.

Let me explain. Irish (as it is called in the Irish Constitution, to call it Gaelic is not PC at the moment, but seen as marginalising) is the Celtic language spoken by a small minority of native speakers principally found in rural pockets on the western seaboard. These Irish-speaking communities are known as the 'Gaeltacht', and are the last remnants of an earlier historical time when the whole island was Irish-speaking, or one huge 'Gaeltacht'. The number of Irish speakers left in these areas who use the language in most of their daily affairs is a hotly debated point, and varies from 100,000 at the most optimistic estimate to 20,000 at the most conservative. For the sake of a round number let us take it to be 60,000, or about 2 per cent of the population of the Republic of Ireland.

Because of the effort of the Irish Revival movement, and of the teaching of Irish in the school system, however, the language is also spoken with varying degrees of frequency and fluency by a considerably larger number of people who have learned it as a second language. So much so that census figures over the last few decades have consistently indicated that up to one million people, or 30 per cent of the population of the Republic, claim to be speakers of Irish. To this can be added the 146,000 people in the Six Counties of Northern Ireland who also are competent in Irish. This figure of one million speakers is, of course, grossly misleading and in no way reflects a widespread use of the language in everyday life. Rather it can be seen as a reflection of general good will toward the language, as a kind of wishful thinking. Nevertheless that good will is important.

The fact that the Irish language, and by extension its literature, has a precarious status in Ireland at the moment is a development in marked contrast to its long and august history. I believe writing in Irish is the oldest continuous literary activity in Western Europe, starting in the fifth century and flourishing in a rich and varied manuscript tradition right down through the Middle Ages. During this time the speakers of any invading language, such as Norse, Anglo-Norman and English, were assimilated, becoming 'more Irish than the Irish themselves'. But the Battle of Kinsale in 1601, in which the British routed the last independent Irish princes, and the ensuing catastrophes of the turbulent seventeenth century, including forced population transfers, destroyed the social underpinning of the language. Its decline was much accelerated by the great famine of the mid-nineteenth century; most of the one million who died of starvation and the millions who left on coffin ships for America were Irish speakers. The fact that the fate of emigration stared most of the survivors in the eye further speeded up the language change to English — after all, 'What use was Irish to you over in Boston?'

The indigenous high culture became the stuff of the speech of fishermen and small farmers, and this is the language that I learned in West Kerry in the 1950s at the age of 5 in a situation of total immersion, when I was literally and figuratively farmed out to my aunt in the parish of Ventry. Irish is a language of enormous elasticity and emotional sensitivity; of quick and hilarious banter and a welter of references both historical and mythological; it is an instrument of imaginative depth and scope, which has been tempered by the community for generations until it can pick up and sing out every hint of emotional modulation that can occur between people. Many international scholars rhapsodise that this speech of ragged peasants seems always on the point of bursting into poetry. The pedagogical accident that had me learn this language at an early age can only be called a creative one.

from *The New York Times Book Review* (8 January 1995)

PAUL MULDOON

Article 8, Clause 1 of the Irish constitution states: 'The Irish language as the national language is the first official language.' As such, however, Irish has often been used as a pretext for extreme cultural and political positions. Even official efforts to keep the language alive had their punitive aspect in the educational practice known as 'compulsory Irish'.

The name Joseph Mary Plunkett Ward invokes that of the poet and revolutionary Joseph Mary Plunkett (1887–1916), one of the signatories of the 1916 Proclamation who was executed for his part in the Easter Rising.

In addition to being one of the most original poets of his generation, Paul Muldoon is a noted translator of the poetry of Nuala Ní Dhomhnaill. He has also written poems in Irish.

Anseo

When the Master was calling the roll
At the primary school in Collegelands,
You were meant to call back *Anseo*
And raise your hand
As your name occurred.
Anseo, meaning here, here and now,
All present and correct,
Was the first word of Irish I spoke.
The last name on the ledger
Belonged to Joseph Mary Plunkett Ward
And was followed, as often as not,
By silence, knowing looks,
A nod and a wink, the Master's droll
'And where's our little Ward-of-court?'

I remember the first time he came back
The Master had sent him out
Along the hedges
To weigh up for himself and cut
A stick with which he would be beaten.
After a while, nothing was spoken;
He would arrive as a matter of course
With an ash-plant, a salley-rod.
Or, finally, the hazel-wand
He had whittled down to a whip-lash,
Its twist of red and yellow lacquers
Sanded and polished,
And altogether so delicately wrought
That he had engraved his initials on it.

I last met Joseph Mary Plunkett Ward
In a pub just over the Irish border.
He was living in the open,
In a secret camp
On the other side of the mountain.
He was fighting for Ireland,
Making things happen.
And he told me, Joe Ward,
Of how he had risen through the ranks
To Quartermaster, Commandant:
How every morning at parade
His volunteers would call back *Anseo*
And raise their hands
As their names occurred.

from *Why Brownlee Left* (1980)

MICHAEL HARTNETT

On 25 November 1892, Douglas Hyde gave a speech in Dublin entitled 'The Necessity for De-Anglicising Ireland', in which he said: 'What we must endeavour to never forget is this, that the Ireland of today is the descendant of the Ireland of the seventh century, then the school of Europe and the torch of learning.' But later poets, Michael Hartnett included, imagined contemporary Ireland not in terms of past glory and continuity, but in terms of darkness and rupture. Hartnett's gesture of turning away from English —

or, more particularly, of rejecting what he calls 'the celebrated Anglo-Irish stew' of derivative and inauthentic verse — is an expression of solidarity with late seventeenth-century poets like Aodhaghán Ó Rathaille and Daibhí Ó Bruadair. Hartnett has translated the latter's verse — Ó Bruadair *(1985). Many of these poets were associated with the court of poetry centred on Hartnett's native Croom, Co. Limerick, the Court of the Maigue, named for the river there.*

A bilingual poet, rather than one who writes exclusively in English or Irish, Hartnett published a number of books in Irish between A Farewell to English *(1975) and* Inchicore Haiku *(1985).*

from *A Farewell to English*

5

I say farewell to English verse,
to those I found in English nets:
my Lorca holding out his arms
to love the beauty of his bullets,
Pasternak who outlived Stalin
and died because of lesser beasts;
to all the poets I have loved
from Wyatt to Robert Browning;
to Father Hopkins in his crowded grave
and to our bugbear Mr Yeats
who forced us into exile
on islands of bad verse.

Among my living friends
there is no poet I do not love
although some write
with bitterness in their hearts;
they are one art, our many arts.

Poets with progress
make no peace or pact.
The act of poetry
is a rebel act.

7

This road is not new.
I am not a maker of new things.
I cannot hew
out of the vacuum-cleaner minds
the sense of serving dead kings.

I am nothing new.
I am not a lonely mouth
trying to chew
a niche for culture
in the clergy-cluttered south.

But I will not see
great men go down
who walked in rags
from town to town
finding English a necessary sin,
the perfect language to sell pigs in.

I have made my choice
and leave with little weeping.
I have come with meagre voice
to court the language of my people.

from *Selected and New Poems* (1994)

MICHAEL LONGLEY

Flax dams and bleaching greens and the weaving of coarse linen for domestic use were familiar in Ulster long before there was a linen industry. But that industry is the basis of Belfast's development as a nineteenth-century manufacturing powerhouse. By the 1840s there were nineteen plants in Belfast making linen.

Linen with its mills and chimneys and its labour-intensive methods changed the landscape. Linen drew people to the city from the Ulster countryside to work as doffers and hacklers and rovers and in the other highly specialised jobs created by the industrial process. Not only did large numbers of people come to Belfast, but they brought their faiths, their fears and their cultures with them. Linen produced not only material but the fabric of a new way of life. It changed everything.

The Linen Industry

Pulling up flax after the blue flowers have fallen
And laying our handfuls in the peaty water
To rot those grasses to the bone, or building stooks
That recall the skirts of an invisible dancer,

We become a part of the linen industry
And follow its processes to the grubby town
Where fields are compacted into window-boxes
And there is little room among the big machines.

But even in our attic under the skylight
We make love on a bleach green, the whole meadow
Draped with material turning white in the sun
As though snow reluctant to melt were our attire.

What's passion but a battering of stubborn stalks,
Then a gentle combing out of fibres like hair
And a weaving of these into christening robes,
Into garments for a marriage or funeral?

Since it's like a bereavement once the labour's done
To find ourselves last workers in a dying trade,
Let flax be our matchmaker, our undertaker,
The provider of sheets for whatever the bed —

And be shy of your breasts in the presence of death,
Say that you look more beautiful in linen
Wearing white petticoats, the bow on your bodice
A butterfly attending the embroidered flowers.

from *The Echo Gate* (1979)

TOM PAULIN

When the Northern Ireland parliament convened for the first time in 1921, nationalists refused to participate in it. When the first Prime Minister of Northern Ireland, James Craig, spoke of 'a Protestant Parliament for a Protestant people', the spiritual leader of Ireland's Catholics, Cardinal Joseph McRory, opined that the Protestant churches were beyond the pale of Christianity. Whatever the social, economic, cultural and historical differences between the communities in the North were, the alienating circumstances which prevailed under the fifty-year duration of the Northern Ireland parliament did little to address them, succeeding merely in conferring on them ostensibly permanent and effectively juridical form. No outspoken critical voice can be recalled.

The Northern Ireland parliament was supplanted by direct rule from Westminster in 1972.

Of Difference Does it Make

During the 51-year existence of the Northern Ireland Parliament only one Bill sponsored by a non-Unionist member was ever passed.

Among the plovers and the stonechats
protected by the Wild Birds Act
of nineteen-hundred-and-thirty-one,
there is a rare stint called the notawhit
that has a schisty flight-call, like the chough's.
Notawhit notawhit notawhit
— it raps out a sharp code-sign
like a mild and patient prisoner
pecking through granite with a teaspoon.

from *Selected Poems 1972–1990* (1993)

VINCENT BUCKLEY

In Northern Ireland, the removal of 'special category' status for those imprisoned for terrorist offences in 1976 led, first, to the refusal of prisoners newly jailed to wear prison uniforms. Instead they wore blankets. They were refused permission to leave their cells without wearing prison uniforms, so they opted to live in their own filth rather than comply. This was the dirty protest. The authorities did not budge, so a number of prisoners went on a hunger-strike that lasted from October to December 1980. The issue was not resolved and the hunger-strike began again, ending in October 1981. 'H-Block' is a term often associated with these events. It refers to the shape of the cell blocks at Long Kesh prison.

Ten prisoners died during the hunger-strike. Bobby Sands is the best known. The others are Mickey Devine, Kieran Doherty, Frank Hughes, Martin Hurson, Kevin Lynch, Raymond McCreesh, Joe McDonnell, Tom McElwee and Patsy O'Hara.

Le dur desir de durer — 'the firm resolve to last' — recalls the words of another hunger-striker, Terence MacSwiney: 'It is not those who can inflict the most, but those that can suffer the most who will conquer.' The French phrase is the title of one of the sections of Derniers poèmes d'amour, Last Love Poems, *by Paul Éluard (1865–1952).*

Hunger-strike

> **Warrior**: 1. One whose occupation is warfare; a fighting man; in eulogistic sense, a valiant or an experienced man of war. Now chiefly *poet.* and *rhet.*, exc. as applied to the fighting men and heroes of past ages and of uncivilized peoples.
>
>   *Shorter O.E.D.*

To Redefine 'Warrior'

Through this season
of hot clouds, you have needed
to redefine 'Warrior'; One
who makes war, with no weapons
but the sticks of his forearms,
the electric pain of his body
in his cell, away from the air
his family breathes, drenched with sweat
of armed men, with machines,
robots, automatics, clockbombs,
hijacked milk-lorries,
sprayguns and knapsacks of gas,
plastic bullets, shields, visors:
For the armed man is known by his tools,
but a warrior by the death of his terrors

and of their monstrous dream prototypes:
tortured heads, with holes large as faces
opened in them; a corpse hung at the ford;
a serf enduring the thousand lashes;
statues fighting; a masked man
beckoning between the armies;
a comrade lasting into his sixtieth day;
a lark, as he said to himself, at the window
but caught, crying, by the foot, in black wire.

Bobby Sands: One

Now he is laid on the sheepskin rug
so that his bones will not burn him,
pads are put on his heels

against the bedsores. He is blind
and deaf. The pain they told him of
jolts its thin current
into every movement. His teeth
protrude like the bones of a dead man.
He is dying for his word. *Geronimo.*

They would not let him alone.
Day and night they came and went
stirring his pallid shadow,
interpreters of his dying.
Day and night he hung on the wire,
his curled body outlasting them
till they fell silent; 'he was the piper
walking in the front of battle'.

Then, he died in a clean place,
crooked, on the waterbed, the Pope's
crucifix proudly beside him, his mind
open as a galaxy.
Le dur desir de durer
saw him buried as Geronimo.

Sands: Two

But, before that, he was lowered
into the deep trough
of others' wills, his wire thin bones
buzzing with speeches, lights
thick on his shrinking face,
died badgered with help,
not hearing
the faraway words his mother
spoke to the microphone.

For her the hard thing
must have been keeping her eyes down,
her lips steady, while blurting out
what they had said to each other: 'We talked
about old times . . . when he was at school
. . . and in the youth club . . .'

This was the time when
everyone came to talk at him
and to come out and tell the world
what he wanted, and why
he should/should not want it
                    [But he wanted not to give up,
                    and not to die either. Geronimo.]

The sky was full of mouths: except the father,
who said nothing, the brother,
who was an arm to lean on
for the sister, who could not hide her eyes,
and the mother, all large
unweeping features, and going in,
and coming out, and going
only to come back next day
to the reporters husking like bees:
'How is he today?' 'He's dyun.'

Francis Hughes

Colonel, press your cap down hard
or keep your fingers in your belt,
searchlights and men in every yard,
the tree beside you red with haws,
Saracens in the windgreen lanes,
the day they bury Francis Hughes.

Is this the corpse you hate so much,
that awesome boy, going to Mass
on a weekday morning in Bellaghy,
loitering so the late dews pass
along his footstep to the door,
thinking the land's his own, perhaps?

Go to your tea, sergeant, trooper,
his shadow follows you with scorn
now that you've lowered his starved face
deep in the ground where he was born:
the long-eyed kinsman drumming on it
tunes you will never learn or bear.

Raymond McCreesh

> Weeks later, it was his face
> that loomed on the hourly news,
> tilted back, fragile, laughing.
> To whom someone said, on the 58th day,
> do you want a drink of milk?
> He was blind now. He said, I don't know.
> Batlike his brain in and out
> of his body-shape, the mind's landscape
> entering and leaving sun and shade.
> For days, on the wire services,
> in press statements, they took his name:
> *Do you want a drink of milk? I don't know.*
>
> And they talked of his family
> as if he were straining
> to leave some mad priesthood, or to break
> some taboo of the townland,
> and the people he loved would not let him.
>> Eloquent assassins,
>> Oxbridge men, Sandhurst men,
>> I am almost too ashamed
>> to mention your shame.

from *Last Poems* (1991)

JOHN HUME

The New Ireland Forum was established by the Garret FitzGerald government in 1983. Invitations were extended to political parties North and South with a view to finding some way forward for Northern Ireland, recently traumatised by hunger-strikes and H-Blocks — not that the trauma was confined to that part of the world. All the main parties in the South participated in the New Ireland Forum, as did the Social Democratic and Labour Party from the North. Unionists, however, said no.

In the course of the following year, the Forum heard submissions from individuals, churches, trade unions, women's groups, business organisations and so on. A report was issued in May 1984 outlining three possible resolutions of the Northern impasse: a single Irish state, a federal or confederate arrangement in which the North would take on some form of regional autonomy, or joint British–Irish sovereignty over the North. The report was rejected out of hand by British Prime Minister Margaret Thatcher.

This extract is from the opening speech of John Hume, leader of the SDLP.

Reconciliation of the Irreconcilable

How can we reconcile the profound contradictions of Dublin Castle on this day? To the tradition gathered in this room, Dublin Castle spells *our* historic triumph: we finally reduced and took this bastion of oppression, this seat of an alien, arbitrary and cruel power. To Unionists, it is a souvenir of an older and more congenial order, a Mecca now tragically appropriated by infidels, a fortress whose very loss to the enemy has for sixty unhappy years been the cause of uncertainty and the source of a harsh and seemingly necessary intransigence. Yet it is our declared task here today to reconcile these contradictions — somehow.

I suggest that we begin by humbly admitting that no more difficult task ever confronted the Irish people. I suggest that we also understand clearly *why* we are attempting it — not because it would be gratifying to succeed, not because it would be interesting to attempt, not because it would be to our political advantage — only because it would be dangerously irresponsible not to do this now. We are condemned to try and to succeed because each one of us, if we fail or if we shirk this challenge, will be condemned by this and future generations of Irish men, women and children as uncaring, unworthy and selfish politicians. Unworthy, not just of Ireland but of the human cause itself.

from *Field Day Anthology of Irish Writing* (1991)

PAUL MULDOON

So much of the violence of the Northern Ireland conflict has been of a local, communal, intimate character, both in method and in target. In those circumstances, the mundane loses its ordinariness, the familiar cannot quite be taken for granted. Everything comes under suspicion, needs a second look, borders on uncertainty and instability. It becomes uncertain whether the landscape is one in which love is being made or war. Even simply 'ticking over' has an ominous connotation.

Ireland

The Volkswagen parked in the gap,
But gently ticking over.
You wonder if it's lovers
And not men hurrying back
Across two fields and a river.

from *Why Brownlee Left* (1980)

BENEDICT KIELY

In Proxopera, *the Binchey household is invaded by members of the IRA, who command elderly Mr Binchey, a retired Latin teacher, to drive a proxy bomb to the local town. As he drives he thinks: 'Not even the Mafia thought of the proxy bomb, operation proxy, proxopera for gallant Irish patriots fighting imaginary empires by murdering the neighbours.' The book is dedicated 'In Memory of the Innocent Dead'.*

The author explained in an afterword to the American edition that Mr Binchey was based on a beloved teacher, M.J. Curry. Dan Breen (1894–1969) took part in the 1919 ambush at Soloheadbeg, Co. Tipperary, that marked the beginning of the War of Independence. The lake is mentioned because Mr Binchey's present horror evokes memories of a body being taken from a nearby lake where he used to fish and where he used to admire the white house. This house is where he is living with his son and his son's family when the three IRA men arrive. They burn the house when they leave. The last words of Proxopera *are: 'To have your own stream on your own lawn is the height of everything.'*

Afterword

I t may have been my reading, in a newspaper sent out from Ireland, about the man near the village of Kesh, County Fermanagh, who saw red and turned his bomb-burdened auto on the gunmen who had so burdened it, and set them scarpering all the way to Bundoran, County Donegal, that provided my initial impulse for the writing of this story. Humour had thrown an odd Keystone-ish light on a particularly mean and cowardly type of intrusion and atrocity. But I was also remembering a day in class in the 1930s when M.J. turned from Livy XXII to ask me had I read Dan Breen's book, *My Fight for Irish Freedom*, and if I had so read it, what did I think of it.

Happened I had read it for it was, about that time, almost compulsory nationalist reading. But even though Dan Breen had to be accepted as a Tipperary hero battling, in the 1920s, the pretty atrocious Black-and-Tans, my sophisticated, high-school taste didn't rate his book too highly: not for political but for literary reasons. Don't remember now, if I ever did know, whether Dan Breen wrote the book himself or had somebody do it for him. But it was a crude enough story and not too well told.

M.J.'s objections were more than literary. He held it no heroic thing to hide behind a hedge and shoot men in the back. His was an outdated standard of behaviour even then and one that would have imposed an overrigorous discipline on the earnest guerrilla. Yet when, in later years, I met Dan Breen and found him to be a charming, humorous, and humane man, it occurred to me from the hints I gathered from his talk that his standards did not much differ from those of M.J. Curry. Deeds done in the heat of youth, and not only deeds of blood, seem different to the backward view of age. Naturally I did not raise the delicate topic with Dan Breen, to whom I was introduced by a celebrated Capuchin friar. But in the conversation that followed he spoke broodingly of bad times and of things then done that in the time and place he was talking in (Dublin in the late 1940s) would be difficult to justify. He was not speaking only of or for himself. We have lived, some of us, to see better times and more abominable deeds.

So that it seemed to me an obvious, perhaps too obvious, ploy, to place M.J. Curry in the middle of one of our happy contemporary situations and try to imagine how he might react. For the sake of the story I did give him what you might call a false or another identity and background: an ancestry in the town, a son and grandchildren, a white house by a lake.

The lake in which the body was found is somewhere in the county Fermanagh. The man whose body was found in it I once met in a pub in the village of Trillick. The lake I describe is close to my own hometown in the county Tyrone and the comic ballad about it was written by my relative Frank McCrory. The white house was there by the lakeshore and may still be there. But the stream at the end of the garden is to be found on the fringe of Sligo town and in front of a long house once inhabited by a relative of the poet Yeats.

You pick a bit here and a bit from there.

from *Proxopera: A Tale of Modern Ireland* (1977)

FRANK McGUINNESS

On Sunday 8 November 1987 an IRA bomb exploded during a Remembrance Day commemoration at the War Memorial in Enniskillen, Co. Fermanagh. Eleven people were killed. Of these Marie Wilson stands out because of the courage and nous of her father, Gordon Wilson, in whose arms she died. Gordon Wilson went on to become an important voice for peace. He was a member of the Irish senate before his death in 1995.

Frank McGuinness, a native of County Donegal, is one of the leading playwrights of his generation. His best-known work is Observe the Sons of Ulster Marching Towards the Somme *(1985), at which battle, among others in World War I, the Inniskilling Fusiliers distinguished themselves. Abortive attempts to interest the Nazi regime in Ireland's cause were made by elements of the IRA in the early years of World War II.*

Enniskillen

Passing through Cavan, I hear Gay Byrne castigate the *Irish Independent*. The paper has published a photograph of a child, dressed in her First Communion frock, branding her the daughter of the Fox. Byrne wonders if we have not gone beyond visiting the sins of the fathers upon the heads of children.

On the narrow streets of Cavan three shopfronts catch my eye. Monarch Fireplaces. The Gaelic Bar. Bier travel agency. Between king's men and Celts moves a path of fire. I bought white carnations in an undertakers called Flood. As we leave the county, the most southerly of my province, Ulster, I see to my right one magpie rising. Its wings are silver. As the road continues more birds seem to crowd it. I count at least thirty, scattering before the car as if it were a stone.

There are stone carvings on the islands of Lough Erne. These faces have never released their secrets. I look on the face of the friend who is driving. It is among the most beautiful I've ever set eyes on. Today it is different for it is set in stone. This is his first visit northward since the day of Bloody Sunday. There is silence between us, as there always is on long journeys, and in the silence I find my fear. For the first time am I afraid in my own country, now that it seems to be out of control?

I switch off the radio as a woman talks of friendship, our need to forgive. I am being driven to Enniskillen, the town I love most on this island, where something happened to me as a writer. Here I wrote my first ever poem. Here I once stood beneath a monument. The word Somme entered my head, for this was a monument to a warrior, image of youth lost, dead in a war. We are driving to Enniskillen for the burial of its dead.

The burial of the dead requires preparation. At home in Buncrana a woman washed them. At birth and at death we require cleansing. It is through respect that ritual evolves. What ritual came to the dead of Enniskillen? What respect was shown to young and old? I remember the ages of the married couples. Did they live their lives together for seventy years to lead to this end?

My head is wandering and for some crazy reason I have momentarily imagined that I am going to a wedding in Enniskillen. I shake myself from fantasy by giving precise directions. The car park beside the bus station is full, turn around, get to the one across the bridge. In the back seat the flowers I bought in Cavan lie waiting to be placed wherever I will put them. I planned it to be the War Monument.

The whole of Enniskillen has turned into a war monument. At the Presbyterian church they have gathered to pray for Ted Armstrong. Inside the Methodist chapel they congregate for Marie Wilson. Outside the Church of Ireland cathedral they wait for the body of Samuel Gault. Within the space of fifty yards or so, three commemorations of the dead take place.

I gather with people outside the Methodist church. The sky is blue. There's a chill in the air. If they talk, it's of weather. I ask a man beside me has the service started. I nearly said Mass. The coffin's inside, but we're waiting for the service. Another voice asks the same man about his child. A few scratches, but all right now, grand, in a state of shock, of course.

I see no children in the crowd. In the beautiful dialect of this town they call boys cubs and girls lassies. 'She was a good lassie', Gordon Wilson said of his daughter, 'She loved her profession, she was a pet. And she's dead.' When he spoke I heard in his voice the accent of David Craig, the most loved character of all I've created, who met his death at the Somme.

But what is a character compared to a child? And Marie Wilson is in her church for the last time. Here she was baptised, came to Sunday School, was loved, deeply loved. She played sports, she was proud, she won the Duke of Edinburgh's gold award, she went to receive it with her mother in St James's Palace.

The thoughts of a wedding flood back into my head. A kind girl, a good daughter, my country gave her in marriage to a coffin. Her father, who was not asked, forgave. His was the hand which raised us to our feet when we should have been on our knees with shame and grief. What hand can we give him now? As a family they know of their loss, but what have we as a people lost in the child of such a man? What have you done who has done this to her?

She was a nurse. The preacher thanks her profession. They did all they could for fragile flesh and bone. Heedless of such fragility, the bomb did not discriminate in its explosion against flesh and bone. Male and female, child and parent, young and old. I climb over the rubble of the building, St Michael's Community and Youth Centre. I threw the carnations into the ruins of concrete and plaster, wood and rusted nails.

We were told at school that it was St Michael who guarded the gates of the Garden of Eden after the Fall. His weapon was a burning sword. It was not an avenging angel who planted this sword. They hadn't a hope as they stood here that Sunday, in their home town, to honour the dead.

In the first World War they fought with such courage even the enemy never forgot. In the second World War they went against Hitler, fighting Nazism — let no one forget. Eleven are dead at the hands of a movement who willed Hitler to victory in that same war. Let no one forget. Let no one excuse. Sixty years of discrimination? I repeat, the bomb did not discriminate.

For the sins of the fathers revenge has been taken against the children of Enniskillen. From the day of this bombing they will date their lives. That is the legacy bestowed upon them. They in turn will bestow theirs on us, making us all children of Enniskillen, stumbling together through this island, crawling forward through the mess of our history, living and dying in a house that is now forever divided. All is changed after Enniskillen.

from *The Irish Times* (13 November 1987)

MARY ROBINSON

Mary Robinson was declared President of Ireland on 9 November 1990 — elected, as she said, 'by men and women of all parties and none, by many with great moral courage who stepped out from the faded flags of the Civil War and voted for a new Ireland. And above all by the women of Ireland — Mná na hÉireann! — who instead of rocking the cradle rocked the system, and who came out massively to make their mark on the ballot paper, and on a new Ireland.'

She undoubtedly won the election against all early expectations, and during her time as President the country saw marked social and economic changes. Her inauguration speech concluded: 'May I have the fortune to preside over an Ireland at a time of exciting transformation when we enter a new Europe where old wounds can be healed, a time when, in the words of Seamus Heaney, "hope and history rhyme". May it be a Presidency where I, the President, can sing to you, citizens of Ireland, the joyous refrain of the fourteenth-century Irish poet as recalled by W.B. Yeats: "I am of Ireland . . . come dance with me in Ireland." Go raibh míle maith agaibh go léir [Thank you all very much].'

A New Ireland

The Ireland I will be representing is a new Ireland, open, tolerant, inclusive. Many of you who voted for me did so without sharing all of my views. This, I believe, is a significant signal of change, a sign, however modest, that we have already passed the threshold to a new pluralist Ireland.

The recent revival of the old concept of the fifth province expresses this emerging Ireland of tolerance and empathy. The old Irish term for province is coicead, meaning a 'fifth'; and yet, as everyone knows, there are only four geographical provinces on this island.

So where is the fifth? The fifth province is not anywhere here or there, north or south, east or west. It is a place within each one of us — that place that is open to the other, that swinging door which allows us to venture out and others to venture in. Ancient legends divided Ireland into four quarters and a 'middle', although they differed about the location of this middle or fifth province. While Tara was the political centre of Ireland, tradition has it that this fifth province acted as a second centre, a necessary balance. If I am a symbol of anything I would like to be a symbol of this reconciling and healing fifth province.

My primary role as President will be to represent this State. But the State is not the only model of community with which Irish people can and do identify. Beyond our State there is a vast community of Irish emigrants extending not only across our neighbouring island — which has provided a home away from home for several Irish generations — but also throughout the continents of North America, Australia and, of course, Europe itself.

There are over 70 million people living on this globe who claim Irish descent. I will be proud to represent them. And I would like to see Áras an Uachtaráin serve — on something of an annual basis — as a place where our emigrant communities could send representatives for a get-together of the extended Irish family abroad.

There is yet another level of community which I will represent. Not just the national, not just the global, but the local community. Within our State there are a growing number of local and regional communities determined to express their own creativity, identity, heritage and initiative in new and exciting ways. In my travels throughout Ireland I have found local community groups thriving on a new sense of self-confidence and self-empowerment. Whether it was groups concerned with adult education, employment initiative, women's support, local history and heritage, environmental concern or community culture, one of the most enriching discoveries was to witness the extent of this local empowerment at work.

As President I will seek to the best of my abilities to promote this growing sense of local participatory democracy, this energising movement of self-development and self-expression which is surfacing more and more at grassroots level. This is the face of modern Ireland.

from President Robinson's inauguration speech (3 December 1990)

RELIGION

St Patrick

Patrick, the patron saint of Ireland, came to the country first as a prisoner, taken in a raiding party from his west of England home. A Roman citizen, he was enslaved for six years. Slemish, a mountain in County Antrim, and County Mayo are places associated with this period. Then Patrick escaped to the Continent where he studied for the priesthood. After his ordination, he had a vision in which he heard the voice of the Irish calling him back to them. His return resulted in the conversion of the country to Christianity. Though there is some scholarly dispute about them, the dates of his mission are commonly assumed to be 432 to 461.

St Patrick left two pieces of writing after him. One is the Letter to the Soldiers of Coroticus, a north British chieftain, and a Roman in the sense that Patrick himself was. Coroticus had captured some of Patrick's converts. Among the repercussions of this letter was Patrick's Confessio, in which among other things he gives an account of himself and his Irish mission.

Confessio

I, Patrick, a sinner, untaught, to be sure, established in Ireland, profess myself
    to be a bishop.
Most certainly I consider that I have received from God that which I am.
Consequently I dwell among barbarian gentiles
as a sojourner and a refugee because of the love of God.
He is the testifier whether that is so.
Not that I preferred to pour out from my mouth anything so harshly and so
    savagely,
but I am compelled by the zeal of God, and the truth of Christ has roused [me]
    up
for the love of [my] nearest neighbours and sons,
for whom I have handed over my fatherland and parents and my soul up to the
    point of death.
If I am worthy I live for my God to teach gentiles,
even if I am despised by some.
With my own hand I have written and composed these words,
to be given and handed over, dispatched to the soldiers of Coroticus,
I do not say to my fellow citizens, nor to fellow citizens of the holy Romans,
but to fellow citizens of demons because of their evil works.
By hostile behaviour they live in death,
comrades of Scots and Picts and apostates,
bloody men who are bloody with the blood of innocent Christians,
whom I have begotten for God, an innumerable number, and confirmed in
    Christ.

On the day after that on which the new converts in white clothing were
anointed with chrism,
it was shining on their brow while they were relentlessly slaughtered and slain
with the sword by the abovesaid men,
I dispatched an epistle with a holy presbyter,
whom I have taught from infancy, with clerics,
so that they might concede something to us from the loot or from the baptised
captives whom they captured.
They made guffaws about them.
Because of that I do not know what I should lament more,
whether those who were killed, or those whom they captured,
or those whom the devil has oppressively ensnared.
In everlasting punishment they will subject [themselves] to hell equally with
him,
because indeed he who commits sin is a slave,
and he is named a son of the devil.
On which account let every man fearing God get to know
that they are estranged from me
and from Christ my God,
for whom I perform an embassy.
Parricide, fratricide, rapacious wolves devouring the folk of the Lord as a meal
[lit. 'food'] of bread.
Just as it declares, The unjust have utterly destroyed Your Law, Lord,
which in these last times He had propagated in Ireland most excellently, kindly,
and it had been built up [also 'instructed, taught'] with God favouring it.

from *The Book of Letters of Saint Patrick the Bishop* (1952)

ANONYMOUS

Laoghaire (d. 461) was High King of Ireland in St Patrick's time. As such, it was part of his duties to light a fire at Easter — presumably around the time of the equinox — and he alone was allowed to light a fire then. But St Patrick lit his paschal fire on the Hill of Slane, Co. Meath, within sight of Tara, so Laoghaire set out with troops to arrest him. Legend is not entirely of one mind that Laoghaire bowed to the saint's power and became a Christian, though the consensus seems to be that that is what happened.

The Irish word for deer is 'fia' and the Irish word for God is 'Dia'. St Patrick has a serving-boy named Benignus — Benen.

The Deer's Cry

Patrick sang this hymn when the ambuscades were laid against him by King Loeguire (Leary) that he might not go to Tara to sow the faith. Then it seemed to those lying in ambush that he and his monks were wild deer with a fawn, even Benen, following them. And its name is 'Deer's Cry'.

I arise to-day
Through a mighty strength, the invocation of the Trinity,
Through belief in the threeness,
Through confession of the oneness
Of the Creator of Creation.

I arise to-day
Through the strength of Christ's birth with His baptism,
Through the strength of His crucifixion with His burial,
Through the strength of His resurrection with His ascension,
Through the strength of His descent for the judgment of Doom.

I arise to-day
Through the strength of the love of Cherubim,
In obedience of angels,
In the service of archangels,
In hope of resurrection to meet with reward,
In prayers of patriarchs,
In predictions of prophets,
In preachings of apostles,
In faiths of confessors,
In innocence of holy virgins,
In deeds of righteous men.

I arise to-day
Through the strength of heaven:
Light of sun,
Radiance of moon,
Splendour of fire,
Speed of lightning,
Swiftness of wind,
Depth of sea,
Stability of earth,
Firmness of rock.

I arise to-day
Through God's strength to pilot me:

God's might to uphold me,
God's wisdom to guide me,
God's eye to look before me,
God's ear to hear me,
God's word to speak for me,
God's hand to guard me,
God's way to lie before me,
God's shield to protect me,
God's host to save me
From snares of devils,
From temptations of vices,
From every one who shall wish me ill,
Afar and anear,
Alone and in a multitude.

I summon to-day all these powers between me and those evils,
Against every cruel merciless power that may oppose my body
    and soul,
Against incantations of false prophets,
Against black laws of pagandom,
Against false laws of heretics,
Against craft of idolatry,
Against spells of women and smiths and wizards,
Against every knowledge that corrupts man's body and soul.

Christ to shield me to-day
Against poison, against burning,
Against drowning, against wounding,
So that there may come to me abundance of reward.
Christ with me, Christ before me, Christ behind me,
Christ in me, Christ beneath me, Christ above me,
Christ on my right, Christ on my left,
Christ when I lie down, Christ when I sit down, Christ when I arise,
Christ in the heart of every man who thinks of me,
Christ in the mouth of every one who speaks of me,
Christ in every eye that sees me,
Christ in every ear that hears me.

I arise to-day
Through a mighty strength, the invocation of the Trinity,
Through belief in the threeness,
Through confession of the oneness
Of the Creator of Creation.

translated by Kuno Meyer, from *Selections from Ancient Irish Poetry* (1911)

LADY GREGORY

Second only to St Patrick in terms of significance to the early Irish church, St Brigit is best known for the monastery she founded in Kildare in the fifth century. But this Brigit had a pre-Christian namesake, who was the daughter of the goddess Dagda and a poet. It seems that she had two sisters, also called Brigit, one of whom was a doctor while the other was engaged in metalwork. Tradition seems to blur the distinction between these various figures. And the feast of St Brigit is 1 February, which coincides with Imbolc, an ancient festival of spring.

St Brigid's Cross, an angular-looking crucifix often woven from rushes or straw, was used in rural homes for protection and in farm-buildings to bless the beasts and harvest.

Brigit, the Mary of the Gael

Now as to Brigit she was born at sunrise on the first day of the spring of a bondwoman of Connacht. And it was angels that baptised her and that gave her the name of Brigit, that is a fiery arrow. She grew up to be a serving girl the same as her mother. And all the food she used was the milk of a white red-eared cow that was set apart for her by a druid. And everything she put her hand to used to increase, and it was she wove the first piece of cloth in Ireland, and she put the white threads in the loom that have a power of healing in them to this day. She bettered the sheep and she satisfied the birds and she fed the poor.

from *A Book of Saints and Wonders* (1906)

LADY GREGORY

Columcille's complicated lineage makes him out to be the descendant of Niall of the Nine Hostages, one of the high kings of Ireland. His family was of the Cenél Conaill, the kin of Conal, whose territorial lands were those of the modern counties of Tyrone and Donegal. The latter county used to be known as Tyrconnel. Ultimately, these people are O'Neills — that is, from Niall. Adomnán of Iona, in his seventh-century Life of St Columba, identifies Cruithnechan as Columba's foster-father. It was a common practice of the time for children to be fostered. One evening, says Adomnán, Cruithnechan saw a ball of fiery light over the head of the sleeping Columba. Cruithnechan took this as a manifestation of the Holy Ghost.

St Ciaran was the founder of the great monastic settlement of Clonmacnoise, on the Shannon, in County Offaly.

Columcille, Saint of the Gael

It is noble indeed was the race of Columcille as to this world; and he had a right through his blood to the kingship of Ireland but he put it from him for the sake of God. One time Fintain had a vision, and he saw in the vision two moons that rose up from Cluan Eraird, the one a silver moon and the other a golden moon. The golden moon went on towards the north till it lightened Scotland and the northern part of Ireland; and the silver moon went on till it stopped by the Sionnan and lightened the middle part of Ireland. Columcille now was the golden moon with his high race and his wisdom; and Ciaran was the silver moon with the brightness of his virtues and his pleasant ways. And the place where he was born was Gortan in the north; and it was on a Thursday he was born, that has from that time been a lucky day. And indeed it was a wonderful child was born that day, Columcille son of Fedilmid son of Fergus son of Connall Gulban son of Niall of the Nine Hostages. There was not a man of higher race or of greater name born of the Gael. And he was brought for baptism to Cruithnechan the noble priest; and it was he fostered him afterwards at the bidding of an angel; and it was angels gave him the name of Colum.

from *A Book of Saints and Wonders* (1906)

HELEN WADDELL

The animal emblems of the Four Evangelists are only the most familiar signs of the myriad symbolic ties between man and beast in the Christian imagination. So ancient and venerable is the tradition of such ties that it almost seems an aberration that St Patrick banished snakes from Ireland instead of involving them harmoniously in the scheme of things. But even before St Francis of Assisi, saints and animals combined to make stories of peace and goodwill.

Abbot Helenus was a Desert Father, a hermit; it was figures like him, of whom there were a large number in fourth-century Egypt, who indirectly influenced the idea of monastic rule in early Christian Ireland. The story of the Abbot and the crocodile was written in Greek by Palladius, 'a friendly, inquisitive, and much journeying monk', and is to be found in his Historia Lausiaca, *written in 420. Helen Waddell seems to have had such information at her fingertips.*

The Abbot Helenus and the Crocodile

He came at one time upon certain monks, upon a Sabbath day, and said to them, 'Why are ye not at Mass?' They made plain reply, 'Because the priest has not come.' Then said he, 'I shall go and call him.' Then they said that no one could cross the river, because of the depth of its channel. Also they said that there was a great beast in that place, namely a crocodile, who had eaten many men.

He, nevertheless, made no tarrying, but straightway getting up, made his way to the ford: and the crocodile at once took him upon its back and ferried him over to the opposite bank. He found the priest in the fields, and prayed him not to neglect the brotherhood. The priest, seeing him hung about with many patched rags, asked him where he got his coat, saying, 'Thou hast a most fair garment for thy soul, my brother,' and marvelling at his humility and frugality, followed him on his way to the river. And when they could find no skiff to ferry them across, the Abbot Helenus sent out a shout, to summon the crocodile. She at once obediently came up, and flattened her back: the Abbot invited the priest to mount along with him: but he, stricken with alarm at sight of the crocodile, retraced his steps. And great was his admiration, and that of the brethren on the further bank, when they saw the Abbot crossing the river upon a crocodile. Climbing up the bank he drew the crocodile after him, saying, 'Better is it for her that she should die, than suffer the penalty for the slaughter of souls.' And the crocodile fell down, and died on the spot.

from *Beasts and Saints* (1934)

ANONYMOUS

The monasteries that were established in every part of Ireland in the wake of St Patrick were usually the inspiration of one man — Kevin in Glendalough, for example, or Declan in Ardmore. Abandoning the places of power and intrigue in order to dedicate themselves to God, these men gained a following from which their impressive monastic sites developed. The founders' sanctity and self-sacrifice earned them the reputation of saintliness.

Each of the monasteries had its own rule, which varied in the degree of its severity. At the time, all these communities were in very remote parts of the country, and even now the whereabouts of some of them is somewhat inaccessible, particularly the island communities, whether on lake islands such as Devenish in County Fermanagh and Scattery in the Shannon estuary, on Skellig Michael off the coast of Kerry, or on Aran. The monastic model, which was heavily influenced by the church in England and Wales, was also brought to Europe, where it came into conflict with the episcopal and diocesan forms of church organisation.

The Hermit's Song

I wish, O Son of the living God, O ancient, eternal King,
For a hidden little hut in the wilderness that it may be my dwelling.

An all-grey lithe little lark to be by its side,
A clear pool to wash away sins through the grace of the Holy Spirit.

Quite near, a beautiful wood around it on every side,
To nurse many-voiced birds, hiding it with its shelter.

A southern aspect for warmth, a little brook across its floor,
A choice land with many gracious gifts such as be good for every plant.

A few men of sense — we will tell their number —
Humble and obedient, to pray to the King:—

Four times three, three times four, fit for every need,
Twice six in the church, both north and south:—

Six pairs besides myself,
Praying for ever the King who makes the sun shine.

A pleasant church and with the linen altar-cloth, a dwelling for God from
   Heaven;
Then, shining candles above the pure white Scriptures.

One house for all to go to for the care of the body,
Without ribaldry, without boasting, without thought of evil.

This is the husbandry I would take, I would choose, and will not hide it:
Fragrant leek, hens, salmon, trout, bees.

Raiment and food enough for me from the King of fair fame,
And I to be sitting for a while praying God in every place.

   translated by Kuno Meyer, from *Selections from Ancient Irish Poetry* (1911)

ANONYMOUS

*It remains unclear how many Irish people would have made a trip to Rome in the ninth
century. On the other hand, by that time Europe had seen some of the extraordinary*

missionary efforts of Irish pilgrim clerics. Monasteries associated with these men covered Europe from Geel in Belgium in the north to Bobbio and Fiesole in the south, and from Poitiers in the west to Salzburg and Vienna in the east. Not that relations between Ireland and the papacy ran smoothly. Indeed, there were periods of controversy during which it appeared that Christianity in Ireland might go its own way. But such periods do not appear to have seriously impinged on the fidelity of the typical – and, as here, typically anonymous – Irish communicant.

The Trip To Rome

Traveller, don't waste your trip,
A useless journey with every step,
The King you'll find in Rome, they say,
But only if he goes with you, anyway.

translated by Seán Dunne, from the ninth-century Irish

PETER FALLON

Remnants of legends, beliefs and properties connected with certain trees, wells and stones are considered 'pishogues' or mere superstitions in modern Ireland. But at the same time awareness of them has not altogether died out, and the persistence of these sacred natural presences from time immemorial is certainly remarkable. What the three items have in common is that they are all natural features of the landscape. The tree is not one that was planted, the well hasn't been dug, the stone is adjacent to the well.

Among the trees singled out by the old belief system were the rowan, the holly and the whitethorn. The so-called fairy thorn, that is a thorn tree growing in isolation or near a cairn, is of particular significance. Inevitably, the well-water was a byword for purity and curative powers — it made warts wither away at once. To benefit, a circuit of the well was made and, after a drink of well-water, a rag was hung on a nearby bush.

The Rag-tree, Boherard

They might have come on the wind,
these rags and tatters, or drifted down
the current of the ditch to dangle there
like seaweed. They were the bright hand-me-down

foliage of that thorn tree in winter.
Poor sinners came, warts and all,
for the holy water of that holy well.
They left loose tokens of a patchwork shawl,

prayed, and promised to return.
They say it stood since God was a boy,
a twisted stick of offerings
no weather could destroy.

It fell in our time. This was told to me
by one of a lost community
at the crossroads of Knocklough,
that lived from hand to mouth, past pity,

and held the rest of the world
long in the gaze of its one eye.
It will pass like their names,
Snows, Laws, into the legends of incubi.

Well they might have hung their coat
on that hawthorn bush at Boherard
or come to kneel near the church
where, late one night, at the graveyard

gate, a big tree moved. We heard it stood
three hundred years, heard tell of the way
it simply took up roots and walked.
Anyway it moved. Or so they say.

from *The News and Weather* (1987)

ANONYMOUS

Little poems like this tend to date from the eighteenth century, when major poets in Irish were few and far between. This was a period too when the Catholic population was facing important social and confessional challenges in the wake of the Battle of the Boyne, the Flight of the Wild Geese and the imposition of the Penal Laws. But these poems have a relation to the immensities of history similar to that which the marginal verses written by the anonymous scribes of early Christian Ireland have to their illuminated manuscripts. And they convey some sort of unforsaken and unexamined faith in, to use Thomas Kinsella's words, 'poetry as a useful and necessary art'.

To Christ the Seed

To Christ the seed, to Christ the crop,
   in barn of Christ may we be brought.

To Christ the sea, to Christ the fish,
   in nets of Christ may we be caught.

From growth to age, from age to death,
   Thy two arms here, O Christ, about us.

From death to end — not end but growth —
   in blessed Paradise may we be.

translated by Thomas Kinsella, from Thomas Kinsella and Seán Ó Tuama
(eds.), *An Duanaire: Poems of the Dispossessed 1600–1900* (1981)

ANONYMOUS

*Folk poems like this and 'To Christ the Seed' came in the form of riddles and curses too,
but mainly they were prayers. Issues of survival, continuity, security and fertility are
again to the fore, suggesting the need for care and protection. At the same time, the hope
that the natural is in the keeping of the supernatural does not diminish the value of
down-to-earth properties like fields, cattle and dairies. Faith in the here and now, and
in life's unassuming sustenances, is also to be prized.*

A Charm for Love and Lasting Affection

The charm Mary put on the butter
is the charm for love and lasting affection:
May your body not cease
to pay me attention
may your love follow my face
as the cow follows her calf
from today till the day I die.

translated by Thomas Kinsella, from *The New Oxford Book of Irish Verse*
(1986)

WILLIAM MAKEPEACE THACKERAY

Croagh Patrick is Ireland's holy mountain. It is said that St Patrick fasted here for forty days, and at the foot of it are two lakes into which the saint is said to have driven demons. Croagh Patrick is situated six miles to the south-west of Westport, Co. Mayo, and rises to a height of over 2,500 feet above Clew Bay. The appointed day for climbing the mountain is the last Sunday in July, and some pilgrims still make the climb in bare feet. Weather such as Thackeray experienced is not uncommon.

Patterns were festivals associated with the feast days of local patron saints — perhaps the word itself comes from a modulated pronunciation of 'patron'. Nineteenth-century accounts of them suggest that they had a distinctly bacchanalian aspect. Many Irish saints' days are in summer. Patterns still take place, though they tend to be much more sedate. Thackeray is writing about Ireland before the Famine, when Irish Catholicism was a very different entity from its post-Famine, and twentieth-century, successor.

The Pattern at Croaghpatrick

On the Pattern day, however, the washerwomen and children had all disappeared — nay, the stream, too, seemed to be gone out of town. There was a report current, also, that on the occasion of the Pattern, six hundred teetotallers had sworn to revolt; and I fear that it was the hope of witnessing this awful rebellion which induced me to stay a couple of days at Westport. The Pattern was commenced on the Sunday, and the priests going up to the mountain took care that there should be no sports nor dancing on that day; but that the people should only content themselves with the performance of what are called religious duties. Religious duties! Heaven help us! If these reverend gentlemen were worshippers of Moloch or Baal, or any deity whose honour demanded bloodshed, and savage rites, and degradation, and torture, one might fancy them encouraging the people to the disgusting penances the poor things here perform. But it's too hard to think that in our days any priests of any religion should be found superintending such a hideous series of self-sacrifices as are, it appears, performed on this hill.

A friend who ascended the hill brought down the following account of it. The ascent is a very steep and hard one, he says; but it was performed in company of thousands of people who were making their way barefoot to the several 'stations' upon the hill.

'The first station consists of one heap of stones, round which they must walk seven times, casting a stone on the heap each time, and before and after every stone's throw saying a prayer.

'The second station is on the top of the mountain. Here there is a great altar — a shapeless heap of stones. The poor wretches crawl *on their knees* into this place, say fifteen prayers, and after going round the entire top of the mountain fifteen times, say fifteen prayers again.

'The third station is near the bottom of the mountain at the further side from Westport. It consists of three heaps. The penitents must go seven times round these collectively, and seven times afterwards round each individually, saying a prayer before and after each progress.'

My informant describes the people as coming away from this 'frightful exhibition suffering severe pain, wounded and bleeding in the knees and feet, and some of the women shrieking with the pain of their wounds'. Fancy thousands of these bent upon their work, and priests standing by to encourage them! — For shame, for shame. If all the popes, cardinals, bishops, hermits, priests, and deacons that ever lived were to come forward and preach this as a truth — that to please God you must macerate your body, that the sight of your agonies is welcome to Him, and that your blood, groans, and degradation find favour in His eyes, I would not believe them. Better have over a company of Fakeers at once, and set the Suttee going.

Of these tortures, however, I had not the fortune to witness a sight; for going towards the mountain for the first four miles, the only conveyance I could find was half the pony of an honest sailor, who said, when applied to, 'I tell you what I do wid you: I give you a spell about.' But, as it turned out we were going different ways, this help was but a small one. A car with a spare seat, however, (there were hundreds of others quite full, and scores of rattling country-carts covered with people, and thousands of bare legs trudging along the road,) — a car with a spare seat passed by at two miles from the Pattern, and that just in time to get comfortably wet through on arriving there. The whole mountain was enveloped in mist; and we could nowhere see thirty yards before us. The women walked forward, with their gowns over their heads: the men sauntered on in the rain, with the utmost indifference to it. The car presently came to a cottage, the court in front of which was black with two hundred horses, and where as many drivers were jangling and bawling; and here we were told to descend. You had to go over a wall and across a brook, and behold the Pattern.

The pleasures of the poor people — for after the business on the mountain came the dancing and love-making at its foot — were wofully spoiled by the rain, which rendered dancing on the grass impossible; nor were the tents big enough for that exercise. Indeed, the whole sight was as dismal and half-savage a one as I have seen. There may have been fifty of these tents squatted round a plain of the most brilliant green grass, behind which the mist-curtains seemed to rise immediately; for you could not even see the mountain-side beyond them. Here was a great crowd of men and women, all ugly, as the fortune of the day would have it (for the sagacious reader has, no doubt, remarked that there are ugly and pretty days in life). Stalls were spread about, whereof the owners were shrieking out the praises of their wares — great coarse damp-looking bannocks of bread for the most part, or, mayhap, a dirty collection of pigsfeet and such refreshments. Several of the booths professed to belong to 'confectioners' from Westport or Castlebar, the confectionery consisting of huge biscuits and doubtful-looking ginger-beer — ginger-ale or gingeretta it is called in this country, by a fanciful people who love the finest titles. Add to these, caldrons containing water for 'tay' at the doors of the booths, other pots full of masses of pale legs of mutton (the owner 'prodding', every now and then, for a bit, and holding it up and asking the passenger to buy). In the booths it was impossible to stand upright, or to see much, on account of smoke. Men and women were crowded in these rude tents, huddled together, and disappearing in the darkness. Owners came bustling out to replenish the empty water-jugs: and landladies stood outside in the rain calling strenuously upon all passers-by to enter. . . .

Meanwhile, high up on the invisible mountain, the people were dragging their bleeding knees from altar to altar, flinging stones, and muttering some endless litanies, with the priests standing by. I think I was not sorry that the rain, and the care of my precious health, prevented me from mounting a severe hill to witness a sight that could only have caused one to be shocked and ashamed that servants of God should encourage it. The road home was very pleasant; everybody was wet through, but everybody was happy, and by some miracle we were seven on the car. There was the honest Englishman in the military cap, who sang 'The sea, the hopen sea's my 'ome', although not any one of the company called upon him for that air. Then the music was taken up by a good-natured lass from Castlebar; then the Englishman again, 'With burnished brand and musketoon'; and there was no end of pushing, pinching, squeezing, and laughing. The Englishman, especially, had a favourite yell, with which he saluted and astonished all cottagers, passengers, cars, that we met or overtook. Presently came prancing by two dandies, who were especially frightened by the noise. 'Thim's two tailors from Westport', said the carman, grinning with all his might. 'Come, gat out of the way there, gat along!' piped a small English voice from above somewhere. I looked up, and saw a little creature perched on the top of a tandem, which he was driving with the most knowing air — a dreadful young hero, with a white hat, and a white face, and a blue bird's-eye neckcloth. He was five feet high, if an inch, an ensign, and sixteen; and it was a great comfort to think, in case of danger or riot, that one of his years and personal strength was at hand to give help.

'Thim's the afficers', said the carman, as the tandem wheeled by, a small groom quivering on behind — and the carman spoke with the greatest respect this time. Two days before, on arriving at Westport, I had seen the same equipage at the door of the inn — where for a moment there happened to be no waiter to receive me. So, shouldering a carpet-bag, I walked into the inn-hall, and asked a gentleman standing there where was the coffee-room? It was the military tandem-driving youth, who with much grace looked up in my face, and said calmly, '*I dawn't knaw.*' I believe the little creature had just been dining in the very room — and so present my best compliments to him.

The Guide-book will inform the traveller of many a beautiful spot which lies in the neighbourhood of Westport, and which I had not the time to visit; but I must not take leave of the excellent little inn without speaking once more of its extreme comfort; nor of the place itself, without another parting word regarding its beauty. It forms an event in one's life to have seen that place, so beautiful is it, and so unlike all other beauties that I know of. Were such beauties lying upon English shores it would be a world's wonder: perhaps, if it were on the Mediterranean, or the Baltic, English travellers would flock to it by hundreds; why not come and see it in Ireland? Remote as the spot is, Westport is only two days' journey from London now, and lies in a country far more strange to most travellers than France or Germany can be.

from *The Irish Sketch Book* (1843)

ALEXIS DE TOCQUEVILLE

The date of the first note in Tocqueville's account of his Irish visit is 6 July 1835, and that of the last, 8 August. He was accompanied by a friend of his, Gustave de Beaumont, who found the country interesting enough to return two years later and to publish, in 1839, Ireland: Social, Political and Religious.

The brevity of the visit did not yield anything more systematic than notes — sketches of the passing scene and reconstructions of conversations. The journey began in Dublin, and was confined largely to the south-east — Kilkenny and Waterford — and the west, culminating in County Mayo where famine conditions were reported.

Throughout, there are indications that 'There exists an unbelievable union between the Irish clergy and the Catholic population. But that is not only because the clergy are paid by the people, but also because . . . [t]he clergy, rebuffed by high society, leans entirely towards the lower classes.' A burning issue of the day was a proposal that the Catholic clergy be paid a government stipend. Tocqueville learns that 'A parish yields generally about £300 sterling, but this sum is divided in general in three. The parish priest has about £120, the two curates the rest.'

Interview with the Parish Priest at Tuam

You have seen, Sir, how I am looked upon in this village. The people love me, Sir, and they have reason to love me, for I myself love them. They have confidence in me, and I in them. Every man considers me in some way as one of his brothers, the eldest in the family. How does this happen, Sir? It is that the people and I every day have need of each other. The people share liberally with me the fruit of their labours, and I give them my time, my care, my whole soul. I am nothing without them, and without me they would succumb under the weight of their sorrows. Between us there is a ceaseless exchange of affectionate feelings.

from Emmet Larkin (ed.), *Alexis de Tocqueville's Journey in Ireland* (1990)

WILLIAM CARLETON

Patrick Kavanagh considered William Carleton a good example of a parochial writer: 'he recorded the lives of his own people with a fidelity that preserves for us the culture of pre-Famine Ireland'. The crowded, animated landscape here is certainly a pre-Famine scene. But Carleton was not exactly the faithful chronicler of his own background. His works are filtered through complicated and largely unexamined layers of guilt, impatience, estrangement, attachment and various other ingredients of internal exile. And, obliged to earn his living by his pen, he was not always able to choose his audience. Carleton, in Yeats's phrase, 'lived between two worlds'.

Apart from the intrinsic fascination of his novels and stories, Carleton is an intriguing phenomenon, emerging as he did in the 1820s from Irish-speaking County Tyrone, without formal education, to become an internationally known author. His conversion to Protestantism has sometimes been cited as a reason for his success. But this view rather belittles his undoubted drive and courage and the life of debt he lived in the narrow world of nineteenth-century literary Dublin.

Midnight Mass

The parish in which the scene of this story is laid was large, consequently the attendance of the people was proportionably great. On Christmas Day a Roman Catholic priest has, or is said to have, the privilege of saying three masses, though on every other day in the year he can celebrate but two. Each priest, then, said one at midnight, and two on the following day.

Accordingly, about twenty or thirty years ago the performance of the Midnight Mass was looked upon as an ordinance highly important and interesting. The preparations for it were general and fervent; so much so, that not a Roman Catholic family slept till they heard it. It is true it only occurred once a year; but had any person who saw it once been called upon to describe it, he would say that religion could scarcely present a scene so wild and striking.

The night in question was very dark, for the moon had long disappeared, and as the inhabitants of the whole parish were to meet in one spot, it may be supposed that the difficulty was very great of traversing, in the darkness of midnight, the space between their respective residences and the place appointed by the priest for the celebration of mass. This difficulty they contrived to surmount. From about eleven at night till twelve or one o'clock the parish presented a scene singularly picturesque, and, to a person unacquainted with its causes, altogether mysterious. Over the surface of the surrounding country were scattered myriads of blazing torches, all converging to one point; whilst at a distance in the central part of the parish, which lay in a valley, might be seen a broad focus of red light, quite stationary, with which one or more of the torches that moved across the fields mingled every moment. These torches were of bog-fir, dried and split for the occasion. All persons were accordingly furnished with them, and by their blaze contrived to make way across the country with comparative ease. This mass, having been especially associated with festivity and enjoyment, was always attended by such excessive numbers that the ceremony was in most parishes celebrated in the open air, if the weather were at all favourable. Altogether, as we have said, the appearance of the country at this dead hour of the night was wild and impressive. Being Christmas, every heart was up, and every pocket replenished with money, if it could at all be procured. This general elevation of spirits was nowhere more remarkable than in contemplating the thousands of both sexes, old and young, each furnished, as before said, with a blazing flambeau of bog-fir, all streaming down the mountain-sides, along the roads, or across the fields, and settling at last into one broad sheet of fire. Many a loud laugh might then be heard ringing the night echo into reverberation; mirthful was the gabble in hard, guttural Irish; and now and then a song from some one whose potations had been rather copious would rise on the night breeze, to which a chorus was subjoined by a dozen voices from the neighbouring groups.

On passing the *shebeen* and public-houses, the din of mingled voices that issued from them was highly amusing, made up, as it was, of songs, loud talk, rioting, and laughter, with an occasional sound of weeping from some one who had become penitent in his drink. In the larger public-houses (for in Ireland there usually are one or two of these in the immediate vicinity of each chapel) family parties were assembled, who set in to carouse both before and after mass. Those, however, who had any love affairs on hand generally selected the shebeen house, as being private, and less calculated to expose them to general observation. As a matter of course, these jovial orgies frequently produced such disastrous consequences both to human life and female reputation, that the intrigues between the sexes, the quarrels, and violent deaths resulting from them ultimately occasioned the discontinuance of a ceremony which was only productive of evil. To this day it is an opinion among the peasantry in many parts of Ireland that there is something unfortunate connected with all drinking bouts held upon Christmas Eve. Such a prejudice naturally arises from a recollection of the calamities which so frequently befell many individuals while Midnight Masses were in the habit of being celebrated.

from *Traits & Stories of the Irish Peasantry*, 2nd series (1833)

MRS CECIL FRANCES ALEXANDER

As a clergyman's wife, Mrs Alexander made a round of parsonages in the north-west of Ireland — Tyrone and Donegal — before settling in Derry when her husband became Bishop of Derry and Raphoe. The landscape of the Lough Swilly area of County Donegal in particular inspired her to verse of the picturesque and conventional kind prevalent in her day.

Her most celebrated verses, however, were written when she was Miss Fanny Humphreys and living in Strabane, Co. Tyrone, where her father was the Duke of Abercorn's agent. Many of her hymns were initially written for the Sunday School class she had there. In addition to 'All Things Bright and Beautiful', which became popular after coming to the attention of John Keble (1792–1866), the prominent nineteenth-century English clergyman and hymnist, she wrote 'Once in David's Royal City' and 'There is a Green Hill Far Away'. The latter was set to music by Gounod.

All Things Bright and Beautiful

God saw every thing that he had made, and, behold,
it was very good. — Gen. 1.31.

All things bright and beautiful,
  All creatures great and small,
All things wise and wonderful,
  The Lord God made them all.

Each little flower that opens,
  Each little bird that sings,

He made their glowing colours,
　　He made their tiny wings:

The purpled-headed mountain,
　　The river running by,
The sunset, and the morning
　　That brightens up the sky:

The cold wind in the winter,
　　The pleasant summer sun,
The ripe fruits in the garden,
　　He made them every one:

The tall trees in the greenwood,
　　The meadows where we play
The rushes, by the water,
　　We gather every day:

He gave us eyes to see them,
　　And lips that we might tell
How great is God almighty,
　　Who has made all things well:

Amen.

from *Hymns, Descriptive and Devotional* (1858)

JOHN BETJEMAN

The decline of Protestant Ireland, in population and in social status, has gone on steadily since the establishment of the Free State. Estates have been sold, Big Houses have been torn down, the young generation has emigrated, churches have been converted to sites of light industry and the like. And the decline has been the subject of numerous novels and plays. Misleadingly, 'Protestant' in Ireland is a virtual synonym for Church of Ireland, and still carries with it overtones of class consciousness, snobbery and sectarianism.

John Betjeman first visited Ireland in 1926. He later recalled: 'Really what I liked was the Ireland of the Ascendancy, and I liked particularly people who'd gone rather to seed.' From 1941 to 1943 Betjeman was press attaché at the British Embassy in Dublin. During this period he became friends with Emily, Lady Hemphill, with whom he went on bicycle rides. She was an American who lived at Tulira Castle, Co. Galway, not far from Coole Park. It was the former home of Edward Martyn, an Abbey Theatre playwright in the early days of that venue.

Ireland with Emily

Bells are booming down the bohreens,
    White the mist along the grass.
Now the Julias, Maeves and Maureens
    Move between the fields to Mass.
Twisted trees of small green apple
Guard the decent whitewashed chapel,
Gilded gates and doorway grained
Pointed windows richly stained
    With many-coloured Munich glass.

See the black-shawled congregations
    On the broidered vestment gaze
Murmur past the painted stations
    As Thy Sacred Heart displays
Lush Kildare of scented meadows,
Roscommon, thin in ash-tree shadows,
And Westmeath the lake-reflected,
Spreading Leix the hill-protected,
    Kneeling all in silver haze?

In yews and woodbine, walls and guelder,
    Nettle-deep the faithful rest,
Winding leagues of flowering elder,
    Sycamore with ivy dressed,
Ruins in demesnes deserted,
Bog-surrounded bramble-skirted —
Townlands rich or townlands mean as
These, oh, counties of them screen us
    In the Kingdom of the West.

Stony seaboard, far and foreign,
    Stony hills poured over space,
Stony outcrop of the Burren,
    Stones in every fertile place,
Little fields with boulders dotted,
Grey-stone shoulders saffron-spotted,
Stone-walled cabins thatched with reeds,
Where a Stone Age people breeds
    The last of Europe's stone age race.

Has it held, the warm June weather?
    Draining shallow sea-pools dry,
When we bicycled together
    Down the bohreens fuchsia-high.
Till there rose, abrupt and lonely,
A ruined abbey, chancel only,
Lichen-crusted, time-befriended,
Soared the arches, splayed and splendid,
    Romanesque against the sky.

There in pinnacled protection,
    One extinguished family waits
A Church of Ireland resurrection
    By the broken, rusty gates.
Sheepswool, straw and droppings cover,
Graves of spinster, rake and lover,
Whose fantastic mausoleum
Sings its own seablown Te Deum,
    In and out the slipping slates.

from *Collected Poems* (1958)

SEÁN DUNNE

Dunmore East, Co. Waterford, where Seán Dunne was a frequent visitor as a boy, is a picturesque fishing village some ten miles south of his native Waterford city. Like many other Protestant churches in Irish towns and villages, St Andrew's has a highly visible presence, spacious grounds, a detached and settled air. It also commands a fine view of Waterford harbour.

Quite apart from family lore about the gentry, and Catholic prohibition on pain of sin against entry, the very physical location of this church and many like it could understandably create a sense of trespass, of a border crossed into terra incognita. *The ecumenical overtures of the Second Vatican Council, even supposing they were audible at the time of the experience recorded here, could hardly be expected to dispel the Catholic triumphalism, in whose glow the author, together with the vast majority of his fellow-citizens, grew up.*

The Protestant Church

Half-heartedly and with vague curiosity, I dipped into other faiths. I attended a service in a dreary Baptist hall in Waterford, but lost interest when the preacher said that Padre Pio, the Italian stigmatist, might well be an agent of the Devil. This seemed the replacement of doubt by absurdity.

The way in which such exploration was tied in with rebellion became particularly clear when, in what appeared to be one of the most anti-authoritarian acts of my adolescence, I entered a Protestant church in Dunmore East. The village was the home of my family on my father's side. In summer it teemed with visitors. In winter, it was a quiet place when the hotel closed and rain beat against pub windows.

My grandmother had told me that when she was a girl she lived in fear of what she called 'the gentry'. In one sense, this meant the Anglo-Irish families who lived in some of the large houses in the village or in the countryside around it. More crudely, it meant Protestants. When walking through the village in her girlhood, she sometimes had to step aside to let a member of the gentry pass. In certain instances, refusal to move aside would have meant a blow from a walking-stick or cane. My grand-uncle told me that there were men in the village from whose caps the peak had worn away as a result of being touched when the gentry passed. This all seemed to have happened a long time ago. Nonetheless, it was part of the atmosphere with which, for me, the Protestant church was imbued.

That church, as is sometimes the case in Ireland, stands in the centre of the village, while the Catholic church is situated on a hill at Killea, a mile or so outside. My grandparents are buried in the grounds of the Catholic church and when I walk among the headstones I am startled to see so many names that are familiar to me. These were simply names that I heard around me in my childhood. They are the names of Catholic farmers and fishermen, shopkeepers and women who once waved to me from doorways as I walked to coves.

The names of those who lie in the Protestant churchyard were almost entirely the names of strangers. They carried the vocables of another culture, while the names on the Catholic headstones were more comfortably my own. As a child, the only two things I knew about the Protestant church were its name and the fact that a friend of my grandfather's worked there. It was called Saint Andrew's. The man who worked there was Tommy Ivory, a low-sized fellow who cut the grass with a long scythe. Every now and then he would stop and lean on the handle as he lit a cigarette and regarded the world from beneath the curve of an old cap.

At some point, I was told that it was a sin to enter a Protestant church. This made the exterior of Saint Andrew's seem darker still. The church had a forbidden, if lyric, Englishness about it.

I thought of those who attended that church as people with names like Hilda, Cecil and Algernon, while those who attended 'our' church on the hill had plainer names like Michael, Mary and Ann. By the time I reached my teens, the Protestant church was simply the sum of these facts. When I passed it on the bus from Waterford, I would look through the window and see Tommy Ivory working behind the old wall. I had no desire to enter it — there was no point, after all, in pushing myself to the front of the queue at the gates of Hell.

And yet the day came when I went past Tommy Ivory and past the neat headstones. There was a singer in the village with the alliterative name of Willie Watt and in the early 1970s it was announced that he was to sing at a special harvest recital in Saint Andrew's. I had heard old records of his singing and I had liked it, and I was anxious to hear him in person.

I was no longer a child but neither was I a man, and the desire to see the inside of the Protestant church, and to hear the singing of Willie Watt, became as significant for my intellectual development as the appearance of hairs on my chin became for my physical growth. Accordingly, I entered the church and made my way to a pew. I felt self-conscious in the dark blazer of my Catholic school. I also felt a blend of unease and excitement. My grandmother's strictures on sin were becoming less meaningful by the second.

Like someone who has entered the house of a neighbour who has previously been scrutinised only from behind the twitching corner of a curtain, I had a good look around immediately. I noticed the minister and his strange rigout, to use one of my grandmother's words. I noticed the cushions and the soft kneelers. I noticed the way men and women bowed their heads deeply in prayer. Try as I might, I could not find a single horn growing from any of the heads, and every foot seemed sensibly shod, with not a cloven hoof in sight. There was a damp smell that was not so much a smell in itself but was the absence of other smells, like wax and incense.

The walls were free of statues but they were not free of memorials. These were a revelation. They commemorated the dead of certain wars that up to then had meant very little to me. Marble and limestone carried the names of local men, many of whom were members of the 'gentry', who had fought in the British army and had been in the Boer War or on French battlefields far from that seaside village. Up to then, I had known of these conflicts from my weekly reading of imported comics such as the *Hotspur* and *Victor*. Now, like the surnames and the accent of the minister, they assumed a visceral immediacy that complicated everything.

Irish nationalism ran deep in my family. My grandfather had fought with the IRA in the early 1920s and, like most Irish schoolchildren in the 1960s, I was familiar with the predictable course of Irish history. The world of Gallipoli and the Somme meant little, while the worlds of Aughrim and Clontarf meant a great deal more. As I stood in that small church, I felt that I was in the presence of something that was more than a religious difference. It was social, political, colonial. It was two pairs of eyes that looked in opposite directions and never met. I was too young to put all this into words. I found myself inhabiting the other side of a question, whereas before I had lived with a cosy answer.

Now, I often think of that first visit when I come on a broken Protestant church in a street or on some country road. Sometimes, such churches are transformed into offices or halls. Some seem to collapse in the countryside, beams sagging from ceilings and rooks flying around panes emptied of coloured glass. A few still thrive with busy congregations. Some continue to exist as churches from which a small congregation leaks on Sunday mornings.

Taking this aspect of religion into account, I think of how sectarian I was in a country where sectarianism kills and of how, with the easy collusion of community, I made ogres of those whose ancestors had fought with my own but with whom I had no need to quarrel. The way in which I saw Protestants was also a reflection of the way in which the very laws of my country saw them. On the day I entered Saint Andrew's church, a gap in me opened and a great deal of light was let in. In religious terms, I was confused. In social terms, that light removed a threat and offered an illumination.

from *The Road to Silence* (1994)

IAN PAISLEY

Ian Paisley is the co-founder and Moderator of the Free Presbyterian Church of Ulster, established in 1951. This piece of information might well strike people in the Irish Republic as a fundamentally Northern if not entirely alien fact of life. Pastors who have not only their own congregations but their own churches, in the sense of a network of affiliated clergy and worshippers, are very much against the grain of religion as it is organised in the South, where its structures are unwieldy and hierarchical. The fact that there are some Free Presbyterian chapels south of the border seems to be neither here nor there.

The tradition of personal witness which Paisley espouses is, in addition to its religious significance, an important one in Northern Irish culture and history. Street-corner preachers are still to be seen in Belfast, as are the statues of their nineteenth-century forefathers, such as Henry Cooke (1788–1868) and Hugh Hanna (1824–92), nicknamed 'Roaring'.

Of course Dr Paisley is best known as a founder and leader of the Democratic Unionist Party, the fundamentalist voice of Ulster unionism.

Ian Paisley was educated at the Barry School of Evangelism, in Barry, South Wales and the Theological Hall of the Reformed Presbyterian Church of Ireland, Belfast.

Open-air Preaching

I served my apprenticeship in preaching in the open air. I had a great tutor. My tutor in open-air preaching was a man that had been saved from the very depths of sin and from the dark dungeons of evil habit and polluting vice. His name was Teddy Sherwood. Once he was the champion welterweight boxer of Southern England. He had his prize gold belt always at the gospel meetings. He used to swing that great gold belt, which he won as the welterweight for the South of England, around his head and shout as only Ted Sherwood could shout. He had a voice like a trumpet. People had to heed and listen to him. When he got tired and husky, he used to say, 'Go on Ian, you have a go.' So he drew the crowd, and so I served my apprenticeship, preaching when his voice was gone, his throat husky and his powerful frame exhausted.

I remember very well, one Lord's Day afternoon during the war on Barry Island in South Wales. There was a tremendous gathering of servicemen and women at the amusements in that great amusement centre. I remember Teddy taking his gold belt and swinging it round his head as hard as he could, and shouting for the crowd to come. They gathered in their hundreds to hear that man preach. He threw down the belt, pulled off his coat, and rolled up his sleeves. When Teddy preached, you would have thought he was back in the boxing ring. I used to say, 'Teddy, you are taking on the devil.' He used to reply, 'Hallelujah! brother, I will give him a cauliflower ear tonight.' He would set about preaching like an old boxer would set about boxing in the ring.

After he had finished preaching one evening he said 'Ian, come on, get into the ring.' I was only a stripling lad of sixteen. I stood there with a Bible in my hand. As best as I could I followed that great open-air preacher. The crowd stayed, and a young woman started to heckle me. Of course, in those days I was a foolish young man. I thought that I could talk a woman down. I have more sense now. I know you could not talk any woman down. I talked on, and the crowd cried out, 'Come on and answer her question. Come on, answer her question.' I stopped and I said, 'What is your question?' She said 'How do you know there is a Jesus Christ? How do you know there is a Jesus Christ?' And oh, a great shout of derision went up from the ungodly in that crowd.

Here was I, a mere stripling with little experience, faced with a hostile crowd. I sent a prayer to Heaven. I said, 'Lord, give me an answer. Turn this weapon as a boomerang in the face of the devil.' God gave me the answer. I said, 'Young woman, I come from Ireland, and an Irishman always answers a question by asking another. I will answer your question, if you will answer me a question?' 'What is your question?' she replied. I said, 'Could you tell me what day it is?' The crowd laughed. She said, 'It is Sunday.' I said, 'Could you tell me what *month* it is?' She said, 'It is the month of August.' I said, 'Now I have only one more question. Could you tell me what *year* it is?' The crowd saw what I was getting at now. They started to laugh and sneer at her. She said, 'It is nineteen hundred and forty-two.' I cried. 'Where did you get that from? Nineteen hundred and forty-two years from where?' She mumbled and stuttered. I said, 'I will help you out. It is A.D. it is the year of our Lord, after the death of Christ. There is a Christ and young woman, when you take your Diary out and look at the year, that number stands as a living testimony that there is a Christ.'

Oh, friend, the best established fact in history is the Person of Jesus Christ. Let me talk about that Person tonight. Who would deny the Person of Jesus? Only a fool would shut his eyes to the reality of Christ. Christ divides men. Christ divides people. Christ divides history. Jesus Christ!

from *What Think Ye of Christ?* (1976)

FRANK ORMSBY

According to The Book of Invasions, *the first Jews came to Ireland at the time of the Flood. According to Mr Deasy in* Ulysses, *'We never let them in.' The historical evidence indicates that Jews and Ireland go back to medieval times, though the development of an Irish Jewry came rather later.*

This pattern of presence and development applies to Belfast, whose Jewish community became an identifiable presence in the mid-nineteenth century. Among the leaders of that emerging community were Daniel Jaffé, who built the Great Victoria Street synagogue; Gustav Wilhelm Wolff, co-founder of the Harland and Wolff shipyard; and Isaac Julian Weinberg, a prominent linen factor.

Chaim Herzog was President of Israel from 1983 to 1993. Solly Lipsitz owned Atlantic Records in Belfast's High Street, specialising in jazz, many famous exponents of which Mr Lipsitz brought to Belfast to perform.

At the Jaffé Memorial Fountain, Botanic Gardens

1

Lipman and Cohen, butchers, Hercules Lane,
Manuel Lightfoot, Smithfield, 'taylor and Jew'.
Names in the old leases, gone to ground
since the year the first sailing ships from Europe
breezed up the lough.

Wolff, Jaffé, Weinberg, purposeful merchant Jews
of Hamburg and Jessnitz. Later the refugees

on sleepless treks from places where they had grown
and spoke the language,
who improvised a style of making do
from trunks and travelling bags and the will to prosper.

2

What might they leave their children,
the dead Jews of Lübeck, Lublin,
packed in Antrim clay?
Faith and unhappy memories?
The desert flower that blooms after loss,
its red heart colouring obstinately against the urge,
insistent, inward, of the petals' bordering dark:
griefs not to be assuaged, the carrier blood's
murmur of vengeance?

3

A wind off the Lagan strays across open ground
at the Jaffé Memorial Fountain.
Half summerhouse, half temple, a room without walls,
its tenants river-smells, in-transit birds,
the dung-and-sawdust ghost of the Circus Hofmann
on a European Tour,
it stands for the ones who earned their monuments
and the ones whose lives were quiet streams hidden
for centuries in the foundations.
I think of dispersals, settlings, the random inheritors
of dispossession who kept an image of home;
of Solly Lipsitz walking his labrador
in the streets of South Belfast,
Chaim Herzog's birthplace on the Cliftonville Road.

from *A Northern Spring* (1986)

POPE JOHN PAUL II

The union of which the Pope speaks is the 'union of charity between Ireland and the Holy Roman Church', which 'has remained inviolable and unbreakable down all the centuries. You Irish Catholics have kept and loved the unity and peace of the Catholic Church, treasuring it above all earthly treasure.'

'Mass rocks' were slabs of stone which served as altars for clandestine masses celebrated by priests proscribed by the Penal Laws. Mass for the dead would be celebrated in 'wake-houses', while 'stations' were masses celebrated in homes in remote areas which people in the area would attend.

Much of Ireland's contribution to the church over the past one hundred years or so has been made by the many members of its numerous missionary orders.

Pope John Paul II visited Ireland between 29 September and 1 October 1979. In addition to this address to, as he said, 'A phobail dhílis na hÉireann' — 'Dear faithful of Ireland' — in the Phoenix Park, Dublin, he also spoke at Knock, Galway, Limerick and Drogheda.

Address in Dublin

I have come to you as Bishop of Rome and pastor of the whole Church in order to celebrate this union with you in the sacrifice of the Eucharist, here in Ireland's capital city of Dublin, for the first time in Irish history. As I stand at this moment, a pilgrim for Christ to the land from which so many pilgrims for Christ, *peregrini pro Christo*, went out over Europe, the Americas, Australia, Africa, Asia, I am living a moment of intense emotion. As I stand here, in the company of so many hundreds of thousands of Irish men and women, I am thinking of how many times, across how many centuries, the Eucharist has been celebrated in this land. How many and how varied the places where Mass has been offered — in stately medieval and in splendid modern cathedrals; in early monastic and in modern churches; at Mass rocks in the glens and forests by 'hunted priests' and in poor thatch-covered chapels, for a people poor in worldly goods but rich in the things of the spirit; in 'wake-houses' or 'station houses', or at great open-air hostings of the faithful — on the top of Croagh Patrick and at Lough Derg. Small matter where the Mass was offered. For the Irish, it was always the Mass that mattered. How many have found in it the spiritual strength to live, even through the times of greatest hardship and poverty, through days of persecutions and vexations — dear brothers and sisters, dear sons and daughters of Ireland, permit me, together with you, to glance back over your history, in the light of the Eucharist celebrated here for so many centuries.

From the upper room in Jerusalem, from the last supper, in a certain sense, the Eucharist writes the history of human hearts and of human communities. Let us reflect on all those, who, being nourished on the body and blood of the Lord, have lived and died on this island, bearing in themselves, because of the Eucharist, the pledge of eternal life. Let us think of so many generations of sons and daughters of this country, and at the same time, sons and daughters of the Church. May this Eucharist of ours be celebrated in the atmosphere of the great communion of the saints. We form a spiritual union in this Mass with all the generations who have done God's will throughout the ages up to the present day. We are one in faith and spirit with the vast throng which filled this Phoenix Park on the occasion of the last great Eucharistic hosting held on this spot, at the Eucharistic Congress in 1932.

Faith in Christ has profoundly penetrated into the consciousness and life of your ancestors. The Eucharist transformed their souls for eternal life, in union with the living God. May this exceptional Eucharistic encounter of today be at the same time a prayer for the dead, for your ancestors and forebears. With their help, may it become more fruitfully a prayer for the living, for the present generation of sons and daughters of today's Ireland, preparing for the end of the twentieth century, so that they can meet the challenges that will be put before them.

from *The Pope in Ireland: Addresses and Homilies* (1979)

PAULA MEEHAN

On the night of 31 January 1984, a fifteen-year-old schoolgirl, Ann Lovett, died in childbirth near the statue of the Blessed Virgin in the grounds of the Catholic church at Granard, Co. Longford. This traumatic case sent shock-waves through the country, particularly since it occurred so closely after the highly contentious 'pro-life' referendum of the previous September. And it has not been the only case concerning pregnant teenagers which has caused deep moral unrest in Ireland in the recent past.

All Souls' Night is near enough to the ancient Irish festival of Samhain, which ushered in winter, a season of darkness and nature's death. Samhain was actually All Hallows' Eve.

The dogma of the Immaculate Conception of the Blessed Virgin Mary, which states that Mary the mother of God conceived Jesus without losing her virginity, was promulgated as an article of faith — and thus became incumbent on Catholics to believe — in 1854.

The Statue of the Virgin at Granard Speaks

It can be bitter here at times like this,
November wind sweeping across the border.
Its seeds of ice would cut you to the quick.
The whole town tucked up safe and dreaming,
even wild things gone to earth, and I
stuck up here in this grotto, without as much as
star or planet to ease my vigil.

The howling won't let up. Trees
cavort in agony as if they would be free
and take off — ghost voyagers
on the wind that carries intimations
of garrison towns, walled cities, ghetto lanes
where men hunt each other and invoke
the various names of God as blessing
on their death tactics, their night manoeuvres.
Closer to home the wind sails over
dying lakes. I hear fish drowning.
I taste the stagnant water mingled
with turf smoke from outlying farms.

They call me Mary — Blessed, Holy, Virgin.
They fit me to a myth of a man crucified:
the scourging and the falling, and the falling again,
the thorny crown, the hammer blow of iron
into wrist and ankle, the sacred bleeding heart.
They name me Mother of all this grief
though mated to no mortal man.
They kneel before me and their prayers
fly up like sparks from a bonfire
that blaze a moment, then wink out.

It can be lovely here at times. Springtime,
early summer. Girls in Communion frocks
pale rivals to the riot in the hedgerows
of cow parsley and haw blossom, the perfume
from every rushy acre that's left for hay
when the light swings longer with the sun's push north.

Or the grace of a midsummer wedding
when the earth herself calls out for coupling
and I would break loose of my stony robes,
pure blue, pure white, as if they had robbed
a child's sky for their colour. My being
cries out to be incarnate, incarnate,
maculate and tousled in a honeyed bed.

Even an autumn burial can work its own pageantry.
The hedges heavy with the burden of fruiting
crab, sloe, berry, hip; clouds scud east
pear scented, windfalls secret in long

orchard grasses, and some old soul is lowered
to his kin. Death is just another harvest
scripted to the season's play.

But on this All Souls' Night there is
no respite from the keening of the wind.
I would not be amazed if every corpse came risen
from the graveyard to join in exaltation with the gale,
a cacophony of bone imploring sky for judgement
and release from being the conscience of the town.

On a night like this I remember the child
who came with fifteen summers to her name,
and she lay down alone at my feet
without midwife or doctor or friend to hold her hand
and she pushed her secret out into the night,
far from the town tucked up in little scandals,
bargains struck, words broken, prayers, promises,
and though she cried out to me in extremis
I did not move,
I didn't lift a finger to help her,
I didn't intercede with heaven,
nor whisper the charmed word in God's ear.

On a night like this I number the days to the solstice
and the turn back to the light.
                              O sun,
centre of our foolish dance,
burning heart of stone,
molten mother of us all,
hear me and have pity.

from *The Man who was Marked by Winter* (1991)

PATRICK KAVANAGH

Lough Derg, in southern County Donegal, not far from Pettigo and the Fermanagh border, is another place with strong connections with St Patrick. Here he is said to have fasted for forty days, and to have had visions of purgatory and hell. An island in the lake is known as St Patrick's Purgatory, a name that has been attached to the place as a whole.

Famed throughout medieval Europe as a place of pilgrimage, Lough Derg has continued to attract Irish pilgrims, who observe a strict penitential regime of fasting and keeping vigil and walking barefoot on rough ground. These and other spiritual exercises connected to the basilica and to the six 'stations' or 'beds', which are the sites of ancient monastic cells, are carried out on another island in the lake, Station Island. The island also has a St Brigid's and a St Patrick's Cross. Pilgrimages last for three days and two nights.

Patrick Kavanagh's long poem is one of a number of works in Irish literature devoted to Lough Derg. Other authors to have made imaginative use of the place include William Carleton and Seamus Heaney, the title sequence of whose Station Island *(1984) is set here.*

Castleblaney is one of the smaller market towns in Kavanagh's native County Monaghan.

from *Lough Derg*

Over the black waves of the lake trip the last echoes
Of the bell that has shooed through the chapel door
The last pilgrims, like hens to roost.
The sun through Fermanagh's furze fingers
Looks now on the deserted penance rings of stone
Where only John Flood on St Kevin's Bed lingers
With the sexton's heaven-sure stance, the man who knows
The ins and outs of religion. . . .
'Hail glorious St Patrick' a girl sings above
The old-man drone of the harmonium.
The rosary is said and Benediction.
The Sacramental sun turns round and 'Holy, Holy, Holy'
The pilgrims cry, striking their breasts in Purgatory.
The same routine and ritual now
As serves for street processions or congresses
That take all shapes of souls as a living theme
In a novel refuses nothing. No truth oppresses.

Women and men in bare feet turn again
To the iron crosses and the rutted Beds,
Their feet are swollen and their bellies empty —
But something that is Ireland's secret leads
These petty mean people
For here's the day of a poor soul freed
To a marvellous beauty above its head.
The Castleblaney grocer trapped in the moment's need
Puts out a hand and writes what he cannot read,
A wisdom astonished at every turn

By some angel that writes in the oddest words.
When he will walk again in Muckno street
He'll hear from the kitchens of fair-day eating houses
In the after-bargain carouses
News from a country beyond the range of birds.

The lake waves caught the concrete stilts of the Basilica
That spread like a bulldog's hind paws. A Leitrim man
With a face as sad as a flooded hay-field,
Leaned in an angle of the walls with his rosary beads in his hands.
Beside St Brigid's Cross — an ancient relic
A fragment of the Middle Ages set
Into the modern masonry of the conventional Basilica
Where everything is ordered and correct —
A queue of pilgrims waiting to renounce
The World, the Flesh, the Devil and all his house.

from *The Complete Poems* (1964)

SEAMUS HEANEY

The ancient church known as Gallarus Oratory stands in a field near the village of Ballyferriter, Co. Kerry. As unassuming as a beehive and as unexpected as a spacecraft, this national monument is in a remarkable state of preservation. Shaped like an upside-down boat, and as the poet himself has remarked, 'about the size of a large turfstack' (actual interior measurements are roughly 15 feet by 10 feet), it is an eye-opening feat of architecture and engineering. Who brought the stones here? How were they carried? How was the curve of the walls calibrated and maintained? Not even its age is known for certain, though it may date from as early as the eighth century. A barrow is an ancient grave-mound or tumulus.

In Gallarus Oratory

You can still feel the community pack
This place: it's like going into a turfstack,
A core of old dark walled up with stone
A yard thick. When you're in it alone
You might have dropped, a reduced creature
To the heart of the globe. No worshipper
Would leap up to his God off this floor.

Founded there like heroes in a barrow
They sought themselves in the eye of their King
Under the black weight of their own breathing.
And how he smiled on them as out they came,
The sea a censer, and the grass a flame.

from *Door into the Dark* (1969)

PATRICK KAVANAGH

This poem first appeared in the closing issue of Kavanagh's Weekly, *a newspaper that
the poet and his brother Peter set up in Dublin in 1952. Filled with tendentious and
satirical commentary written by the two proprietors, it caused quite a stir in the tepid
Dublin of the early 1950s. As Peter Kavanagh later reported: 'Our paper with its intense
point of view startled as well as amused. We received enthusiasm, congratulations and
advice but no supporting cash.' The paper closed down after thirteen issues.*

*The note that it closed on anticipates the way Kavanagh's verse was to develop
during the final phase of his career — away from the hurly-burly of the metropolis
towards composure and the confessional. As the poet wrote in his* Self-Portrait *(1962):
'Curious this, how I started off with the right simplicity, indifferent to crude reason and
then ploughed my way through complexities and anger, hatred and ill-will towards the
faults of man, and came back to where I started.'*

Having Confessed

Having confessed he feels
That he should go down on his knees and pray
For forgiveness for his pride, for having
Dared to view his soul from the outside.
Lie at the heart of the emotion, time
Has its own work to do. We must not anticipate
Or awaken for a moment. God cannot catch us
Unless we stay in the unconscious room
Of our hearts. We must be nothing,
Nothing that God may make us something.
We must not touch the immortal material
We must not daydream to-morrow's judgement —
God must be allowed to surprise us.
We have sinned, sinned like Lucifer

By this anticipation. Let us lie down again
Deep in anonymous humility and God
May find us worthy material for His hand.

from *The Complete Poems* (1964)

THE IMAGINED COUNTRY

ANONYMOUS

Although this story is set in pre-Christian Ireland, it seems to date from late medieval times. So it is not clear if the Lir here is the same one whose son was Manannán, the Irish Proteus. The children were two sets of twins, Aodh and Fionnuala first, then Fiachra and Conn.

The Lake of the Oaks is Lake Derravarragh, Co. Westmeath. The second site of banishment is the North Channel, between County Antrim and Scotland. Finally we find them in Erris, Co. Mayo; Inis Gluaire is Inishglory in Erris Bay. It is said that they are buried in Erris.

'The Children of Lir' is one of the most popular and best-known old Irish stories, its themes of dispossession, lovelessness, family trouble and exile evidently striking a chord. It has been retold many times in children's story-books. In the Garden of Remembrance in Parnell Square, Dublin, commemorating those who died for Ireland, there is a dramatic sculpture of the children of Lir by Oisín Kelly.

The Fate of the Children of Lir

Before the Gaels came to Ireland, the Tuatha de Danaan were kings there. They were tall and fair like the Gaels who conquered them; some knowledgeable scholars are of the opinion that the Tuatha de Danaan were the same people who now live in Denmark. This may be true, for there are many people in Ireland with the appearance of Swedes, Danes and Norwegians.

However it may be, after they were conquered by the Gaels, the Tuatha de Danaan went to live on their own in another part of Ireland. There they elected a king, Bov Deareg. His rival for the throne was Lir. When Lir lost the kingship, he went to live apart from the rest of the Tuatha de Danaan. Later he married Aev, one of three foster children of Bov Deareg. She bore Lir four children, three boys, Fiachra, Aodh and Conn, and one daughter, Fionnuala.

Shortly after the birth of Conn, Aev died; and because he needed a mother for his children, Lir married Aev's sister Aoife. The children were the most beautiful ever seen in Ireland. They had bright red lips, snow white skin, and eyes that were green when they gazed upon the sea, blue when they looked at the sky. So handsome were they that King Bov Deareg himself used to come over just to look at them in joy and delight.

This made Aoife madly jealous. One day, she yoked a chariot and put the four children in it and set out for Bov Deareg's palace. On the way, they stopped at the Lake of the Oaks, and she sent the children in for a bathe. While they were in the water, she touched them with a magic wand, and they were turned into four swans.

'It is with flocks of birds now your cries will be heard forever,' she cried triumphantly to the four children.

The children were terrified to have this magic trick played on them; and they begged her to undo her magic and give them back their human forms. She would not. Finally, Fionnuala, who was the eldest of the four and the wisest said:

'You have done a wicked thing on us, but at least will you not put some boundary to the enchantment, so that one day we will be human beings again?'

'I will,' said Aoife. 'But it would be better for you if you had not asked me. For three hundred years, you will remain on the Lake of the Oaks: for three hundred years after you will go to the Isle of Maoile, between Ireland and Scotland; and for three hundred years more you will remain at Innis Gluaire, on the wild North Coast of Ireland. You will not get human form again until on this Lake you will hear a bell chiming in honour of God, three times each day.'

With that, her face hardened and she ordered her step-children out of her sight. But as she turned away, her heart was touched for a second, and she said to the four swan children:

'You may keep your own human voices and sing the sweet music of the fairies. And your own sense of nobility will stay with you, that way it will not weigh so heavy on you to be in the shape of birds.'

When Lir heard of the fate of his children, he rushed to the side of the lake. He saw the four swans and asked them what had happened. Fionnuala told him what Aoife had done.

'We have not the power,' said Fionnuala, 'to live with any person at all from this time; but we have our own language, the Irish, and we have the power to sing sweet music, and it is enough to satisfy the whole race of men to be listening to that music. Let you stop here tonight,' she said, 'and we will be making music for you.'

Lir waited with his retinue that night by the lake and they were delighted with the music they heard. Then he went in anger to King Bov Deareg and told him what Aoife had done. And the king struck Aoife with the druid wand and she turned into a witch of the air and she went away in that shape, and she is in it yet.

Meanwhile on the lake, there gathered each day thousands of the nobles and peoples of Ireland to listen to the wonderful music of the swan children. There never was any music or any delight heard in Ireland compared with that music of the swans. And they used to be telling stories, to be talking with the men of Ireland every day and with their teachers and their fellow-pupils and their friends. And every night they used to sing the sweet music of the fairies, and everyone that heard that music would sleep soundly and quiet, whatever trouble or long sickness might be on him; for everyone that heard the music of the birds, it is happy and contented he would be after it.

At the end of three hundred years on the lake, Fionnuala said:

'Now we must leave the Lake of the Oaks and go to the Isle of Maoile.'

Her brothers were sad when they heard this, because in their own way they had been happy on the Lake of the Oaks, talking and singing with the Gaels and the Tuatha de Danaan.

They took flight to Maoile, and it was three hundred years they spent on that island. Often their feathers were frozen from the ice and their wings were heavy and wet from the cold sea spray. There was one time in a furious storm the children of Lir almost lost one another. What would have happened to them then? They were neither swans nor human beings, and had they been apart from one another, who in the world could they have turned to for companionship? A fierce burst of wind tore them apart. As they were swept away from one another, Fionnuala, who was the wisest of the four, shouted that they should meet again on the island of Seals. After three days being buffeted around by the winds and the sea, Fionnuala reached the island of Seals where she waited for her brothers to turn up. She waited two days and there was no sign of them. Now she was sad because she felt she might not see her brothers again. But there against the setting sun was Conn, the youngest of her brothers, flying towards her, his head hanging and feathers wet through, and after him presently came Fiachra, wet and perished with the cold. She spread both of them under her wings to dry, and they lay there on the Seal island, the three swan children waiting for their brother to come. At last he came, too, with his feathers beautiful, because he had been flying in a region where there was sun and comfort. On that lonely island in the Irish sea, the four swan children made music and sang songs together. And it is a great pity there was no one to hear them except the seals on that cruel island.

It is little chance they had of singing or making music or telling tales in the next hundred years. For the sound of the wind drowned their music, and they were too cold by far on that awful island of Maoile to tell tales to one another. Three hundred years they spent on the island of Maoile, and then three hundred more on Innis Gluaire. And finally they decided that they could return to their own country of Lir. So they set off one day, flying along and singing songs the while. But when they returned, there was no one left of all those they had known in their lifetime. The castle was empty and nothing in it but green hillocks and thickets of nettles. Neither was there a fire or a hearthstone. They stopped near the ruins of their own home that night. Next day they went back to Innis Gluaire and all the birds of the country gathered near them on Loc na n-Ean, the lake of the birds. And they used to go out to feed everyday to the far parts of the country and to all the western islands of Connaught.

About this time in history, St Patrick arrived in Ireland, to convert the Irish to Christianity. His missionaries and priests travelled all over Ireland. One of them, St Mackevig, came to Innis Gluaire. On the island, he built a little chapel. One day he was putting on his vestments to say Mass when he heard the song of the swan children coming across the water to him:

'That is most beautiful music,' he said to himself. 'I must go and find it, because people who sing as beautifully as this could be singing hymns in my church to the praise of God.'

He went out and searched around. After some time when he had questioned many people as to the source of the music, he discovered to his astonishment that the music came not from human beings, but from four swans. St Mackevig was a very kind man and his heart was touched with the predicament of the children of Lir who were neither swans nor human. He asked them would they come to his church each day, because he thought they might take comfort from the Mass and the praises that were offered to God. They told him they would come, and before he left, he made them a little chain of silver, one between Fionnuala and Conn, and another between Aodh and Fiachra.

They arrived along at his church next morning. There was quite a lot of trouble about this, as the holy men from other islands near Innis Gluaire heard about it, and they said it was not right to bring swans into Holy Mass. The people of Innis Gluaire too said that it was not right to let swans into church. But St Mackevig was not only a saint, he was a holy man as well; and since, from time to time, he had quite intimate conversations with God, he was perfectly certain that the Almighty would be very pleased with the beautiful music which would come from the side of the altar when the children of Lir would sing there.

So it happened, at Mass one morning in Innis Gluaire, that the children of Lir were beside the priest on the altar. Three bells were rung for the Elevation of the Host when an astonishing thing happened. The feathers fell from the bodies of the children of Lir and in half a second they had got back their human forms again. This was the prophecy of their step-mother; that her curse would go from them when they would hear a bell rung in Ireland three times each day in honour of God.

But now we come to the saddest part of the story. What St Mackevig and the other people at Mass saw was not three handsome young men and a fair young girl, but one lean old woman and three withered men. For it was nine hundred years since the curse was put on them. St Mackevig was touched at this sad sight:

'It is a pity for you, O Children of Lir, to become human beings again, and at the end of all to find yourselves like this.'

He hurried away for a few minutes and came back with the Holy Water. He gave them God's blessing and baptised them. Shortly afterwards they died. Their time on earth was a sad one. It would not be so in eternity.

THE TÁIN

Táin Bó Cuailnge — Cattle Raid of Cooley, *a place in County Louth* — *is the most elaborate of the ancient Irish sagas and the closest thing to an Irish epic. A centrepiece of the Ulster cycle of narratives, it features at the height of their powers the best-known characters of ancient Irish prehistory — particularly Medb, or Maeve, the scheming, sexy queen of Connacht, and Cúchullain, the warrior-hero of the Ulster cycle, whose energy and exploits made such a striking impact on the imaginations of W.B. Yeats and Patrick Pearse in the years leading up to Easter 1916.*

The story of the Táin presents Medb as the aggressor. Annoyed that her husband, Ailill, has a prize bull, she wants one for herself and goes about getting the renowned brown bull of Cooley. Failing to acquire the beast peacefully, she gathers her army to fight the men of Ulster for it. Her adviser, Fergus, is an Ulsterman, an enemy for reasons of his own of Conchobor, king of Ulster. Slaughter and magic are the order of the day as the sides clash. The story ends with a fight between the two bulls, in which the brown bull of Cooley defeats the white bull of Connacht.

Much of the action is set in County Meath. The 'ford of the forked branch' is in the Boyne, near Drogheda, Co. Louth.

Cúchulainn

Cúchulainn went around the armies until he reached Ath Gabla. There he cut out a tree-fork with a single stroke of his sword and stuck it in the middle of the stream, so that a chariot would have no room to pass it on either side. The warriors Err and Innel, and their two charioteers Foich and Fochlam, came upon him. He cut off their four heads and tossed them onto the four points of the tree-fork. (It is from this that the name Ath Gabla comes, the ford of the forked branch.)

The horses of the four men went back toward the army with their coverings all crimson. Everyone thought there was a battle-force waiting for them at the ford. A troop of them went to inspect the ford, but they saw nothing there except the track of a single chariot, and the fork with the four heads and the words in ogam cut into its side. Then the whole army came up.

'Do these heads belong to our people?' Medb said.

'Yes they do, and to the very best among them,' Ailill said.

One of their men read out the ogam on the side of the fork: that it was a single man who had thrown the fork, using one hand, and that they mustn't go past until one of them — not Fergus — did the same, single-handed.

'I am surprised,' Ailill said, 'how swiftly these four were killed.'

'That isn't what should surprise you,' Fergus said, 'but that the fork was struck from its trunk by a single stroke; that though its base is only a single cut this makes it better; and that it is driven in the way it is — for no hole was dug to receive it, and it was thrown one-handed from the back of a chariot.'

'Get rid of the obstruction for us, Fergus,' Medb said.

'Give me a chariot, then,' Fergus said. 'I'll take it out and make sure the base was made with only one cut.'

Fourteen of their chariots broke up under Fergus. Finally he brought the fork on to dry land with his own chariot and they could see that its base was a single cut.

'We should turn our minds,' Ailill said, 'to the sort of people we are approaching. Let each of you get your food ready — it wasn't easy for you last night with the snow — and then let us hear some of the doings and stories of the sort of people we are approaching.'

It was here that they heard for the first time about the exploits of Cúchulainn.

Ailill said:

'Was it Conchobor who did this?'

'No,' Fergus said. 'He never comes to the border country without a full battle-force around him.'

'Was it Celtchar mac Uthidir, then?'

'No. He never comes to the border country, either, without a full battle-force around him.'

'Well, was it Eogan mac Durthacht?'

'No,' Fergus said. 'He would never cross the border without a troop of three thousand bristling chariots around him. The man who did this deed,' Fergus said, 'is Cúchulainn. It is he who struck the branch from its base with a single stroke, and killed the four as swiftly as they were killed, and who came to the border with only his charioteer.'

'What sort of man,' Ailill said, 'is this Hound of Ulster we hear tell of? How old is this remarkable person?'

'It is soon told,' Fergus said. 'In his fifth year he went in quest of arms to the boy-troop in Emain Macha. In his seventh year he went to study the arts and crafts of war with Scáthach, and courted Emer. In his eighth year he took up arms. At present he is in his seventeenth year.'

'Is he the toughest they have in Ulster?' Medb said.

'Yes, the toughest of all,' Fergus said. 'You'll find no harder warrior against you — no point more sharp, more swift, more slashing; no raven more flesh-ravenous, no hand more deft, no fighter more fierce, no one of his own age one third as good, no lion more ferocious; no barrier in battle, no hard hammer, no gate of battle, no soldiers' doom, no hinderer of hosts, more fine. You will find no one there to measure against him — for youth or vigour; for apparel, horror or eloquence; for splendour, fame or form; for voice or strength or sternness; for cleverness, courage or blows in battle; for fire or fury, victory, doom or turmoil; for stalking, scheming or slaughter in the hunt; for swiftness, alertness or wildness; and no one with the battle-feat "nine men on each point" — none like Cúchulainn.'

'Let us not make too much of it,' Medb said. 'He has only one body. He can suffer wounding. He is not beyond being taken. Besides he is only in his early youth, and his manly deeds are yet to come.'

'By no means,' Fergus said. 'It would be nothing strange for him to do mighty deeds at this point. When he was younger his acts were already manly.'

from *The Táin* (1985), translated by Thomas Kinsella from the Irish
Táin Bó Cuailnge

W.B. Yeats

'When we remember the majesty of Cuchullin and the beauty of sorrowing Deirdre', Yeats wrote in a letter in 1892, 'we should not forget that it is that majesty and beauty which are immortal, and not the perishing tongue that first told of them.' Captivated by old Irish lore and legend in his early poetry and plays, Yeats seemed to grow out of them as he found themes in personal and contemporary history and Anglo-Irish history.

But in the works written when he was at the very end of his life, he returns to the site of youthful inspiration. His last play is The Death of Cuchulain, *and this poem envisaged his hero's arrival in, as he said, 'a valley in the Country of the Dead'.*

'Cuchulain Comforted' is dated 13 January 1939. Yeats died fifteen days later.

Cuchulain Comforted

A man that had six mortal wounds, a man
Violent and famous, strode among the dead;
Eyes stared out of the branches and were gone.

Then certain Shrouds that muttered head to head
Came and were gone. He leant upon a tree
As though to meditate on wounds and blood.

A Shroud that seemed to have authority
Among those bird-like things came, and let fall
A bundle of linen. Shrouds by two and three

Came creeping up because the man was still.
And thereupon that linen-carrier said:
'Your life can grow much sweeter if you will

'Obey our ancient rule and make a shroud;
Mainly because of what we only know
The rattle of those arms makes us afraid.

'We thread the needles' eyes and all we do
All must together do.' That done, the man
Took up the nearest and began to sew.

'Now must we sing and sing the best we can
But first you must be told our character:
Convicted cowards all by kindred slain

'Or driven from home and left to die in fear.'
They sang, but had nor human tunes nor words,
Though all was done in common as before,

They had changed their throats and had the throats of birds.

from *Last Poems* (1936–9)

STANDISH JAMES O'GRADY

The stag's belling and the hound's howl were, to Fionn Mac Cumhail, leader of the Fianna, the best music in the world. And it does not take much imagination to realise that for a band of ancient warriors like the Fianna, hunting was important. It was a form of training, requiring endurance and alertness, and it helped to keep the warriors' woodcraft up to the mark. As the Fianna were an elite, it comes as no surprise to find that they had their own deerparks, though of course prehistoric ideas of property were not the same as modern ones.

A revealing feature of the Ireland of the legends is how abundant the country was. Other tales echo the proliferation of game here with great harvests of berries and heavy downpours of nuts. Later Irish poetry reproduces such conceits. But the legends do not contain much evidence of 'husbandmen', and the prominence of cattle in them suggests an emphasis on pasture rather than on tillage.

Aongus Óg, the god of love, was the foster-father of Diarmaid of Diarmaid and Gráinne fame.

Fionn goes Hunting

Fionn and his men went hunting to one of his great forests in Leinster, for the Fianna had forests in all parts of Ireland, and no one dared to hunt in them or kill any game there without Fionn's permission. Early in the morning, before the sun had yet risen, they entered the forest. Each huntsman held back a straining hound by a leash which passed through a ring in the hound's collar. He held in his hands the two ends of the leash; when he wished to let the hound slip, he loosed one of the ends of the leash. Before them went the beaters with long sticks, beating the bushes and rousing the game. Between the places that gave cover for the game there was much open and smooth ground. Fionn himself was on the right of the line of huntsmen, leading his favourite hound Bran.

The first animal that they started was a wild boar. He could not be seen from the place where Fionn stood, but the sound of the horn on the left gave notice that some great game had been roused, and the cries of the hunters and the loud baying of the hounds showed that it was some great beast. 'That is a boar,' said Fionn to the hunter who was next him. 'He is charging down our way and killing or injuring every dog which is loosed upon him.' Presently the boar broke through a coppice; his eyes were like fire and his white tusks red with blood; the bristles on his neck stood up like rods, and the froth flew from his mouth like snow. Some of the huntsmen refused to slip their hounds against such a beast. Three were loosed upon him after he passed the coppice: one he tossed over his head, the second he trampled and injured, and the third only stood at a distance and howled. Then Fionn slipped Bran. So swiftly flew Bran upon the boar that her track was like a black and yellow flash over the green turf, and at her baying as she was let loose the hollows of the distant mountains rang, and far away husbandmen labouring in fields said: 'Hark! that is the voice of Bran. The Fianna are hunting today.' Bran seized the huge boar by the throat and shook him to and fro as a puppy-dog shakes a rag.

Then, leaving the boar dead, she returned to be petted and made much of by her master, who said: 'My brave Bran, you have not done such a deed since the son of the great enchanter Aongus Óg, having taken a boar's form, was dragged down by you.'

So while the red sun climbed the sky, Fionn's men advanced through the forest. The horns continually sounded, and the mingled baying of the hounds and the cries of the hunters cheering on their dogs made a sweet music. Many of the poor people of the country, who lived in the borders of that forest, stood on the neighbouring hills and watched the scene with great joy. Before noon there were killed many boars and badgers, many an antlered stag, many wolves; and as for hares and such-like small game, it would have been hard to count them. So eager were the huntsmen that they did not feel hunger till the sun was near setting.

from *Legends of the Fianna* (1921)

ANONYMOUS

Fionn Mac Cumhail has seen his best years by the time of this story. Recently widowed, he is promised youthful Gráinne in marriage. At a feast in Tara, Gráinne drugs the drinks of all the guests except those she finds attractive, and obliges Diarmaid to go away with her. Aonghus, Diarmaid's foster-father, helps them elope. But their relationship remains chaste, while Fionn pursues them throughout the country. At length, Aonghus sees to it that the couple are left to themselves, and Gráinne bears Diarmaid a family. The end comes many years later when Fionn and Diarmaid go hunting, although it is taboo for Diarmaid to hunt the boar.

'The Pursuit of Diarmaid and Gráinne' is one of the best-known tales from the Fenian cycle of ancient Irish stories. The hunt takes place on the slopes of Ben Bulben in County Sligo.

The Pursuit of Diarmaid and Gráinne

After that the boar came up the Beann with the Fiana after it, and Diarmaid slipped Mac an Chuill from its leash against it, and that did not profit him for he did not wait for the boar but fled before it. Diarmaid said:

'Woe to him who does not follow the counsel of a good wife, for Gráinne told me at dawn to take the Móraltach and the Ga Dearg with me.'[1]

With that he put a finger in the silken loop of the Ga Buidhe an Lámhaigh which he had in his hand and he aimed a most successful cast at the pig so that he struck it right in the middle of its face and of its forehead, and he did not cut a single bristle on it and not even did he wound it. With that he took out his sword, namely, the Beagaltach, and he struck it on the back and he did not cut a single bristle on it, and his sword broke in two.

With that the boar made a venomous fearless spring on Diarmaid and it tripped him and he fell headlong.

And when he was rising up it happened that one leg was on either side of the boar and his face looking backward and it went down the slope of the hill without being able to put Diarmaid off [from its back]. And off it went from there until it reached Eas Ruaidh mhic Bhadhoirn, and when it reached the waterfall it gave three swift leaps across the fall hither and thither and it could not put Diarmaid off during that time. It came back the same way and uphill to the Beann again, and when it reached the top of the hill it put Diarmaid off, and when he was falling to the ground it gave a fearless spring on him and it let out his bowels and his entrails about him. And as it was leaving the mound Diarmaid aimed a successful cast at it with the stump of the sword which was in his hand, so that he struck it in the middle of the navel letting out its bowels and its entrails about it, so that he left it without life. Therefore Ráithín na hAbarnaigh is the name of the rath which is on top of that Beann since then.

With that Fionn and the Fiana of Ireland came to the place, and the signs of death and of lasting extinction were coming on Diarmaid. It was then Fionn said:

'I like to see you like that, Diarmaid,' said he, 'and I regret that all the women of Ireland are not looking at you now, for your beauty is turned to ugliness and your good form to deformity.'

'It is in your power to heal me from those,' said Diarmaid, 'if you yourself wish it.'

'How should I heal you?' said Fionn.

'Well indeed,' said Diarmaid, 'for you handled the salmon of knowledge which was on the Boyne, and to whomsoever you should give a drink from your palms would be perfectly sound from all diseases after that.'

'You have not deserved of me that I should give you that drink,' said Fionn.

'That is not true,' said Diarmaid, 'for well I earned it from you the night you went to the house of Dearg son of Dionnarthach,[2] and the chiefs and great nobles of the Fiana of Ireland with you, to partake of a banquet. And Cairbre Lifeachair son of Cormac and the men of Breagha and Meath and Cearmna, and the strong Pillars of Tara came around the hostel against you, and they uttered three mighty shouts out loud around it and they put fires and flames into it, and you rose up, Fionn, and it was your wish to go out and I told you to stay inside where you were drinking and enjoying yourself and that I myself would go out and that I would stop those. And I went out and quenched the fires and made three fierce attacks around the house and I killed a hundred in every attack of them, and I myself went in safe from them without loss of blood, without a wound on me. And you were joyous fill-spirited before me that night, Fionn, and you gave me a drink that night, and it was not more proper for you to give it to me that time than now.'

'That is not true,' said Fionn, 'for you ill deserved of me to give you a drink or to do any other goodness for you the night you came to Tara with me and took Gráinne with you from me out at Tara in the presence of the men of Ireland, and [considering] that you were my body-guard that night in Tara.'

'That is not true,' said Diarmaid, 'for I was not guilty of that, but Gráinne put injunctions on me and I would not violate my injunctions for the gold of the world. I have well deserved of you that you should give me a drink if you may remember when Míodhach son of Colgán made the feast of Bruidhean Chaorthainn for you.[3] And he had a hostel on land and a hostel on sea, and he brought the King of the World and the three kings of Inis Tíle to the hostel which he had on sea in order to take your head off. And the feast was being given in the hostel which he had on land, and you went and a number of the chiefs of the Fiana of Ireland with you to Bruidhean an Chaorthainn to partake of that feast, and Míodhach put [some of] the soil of Inis Tíle under you so that your feet and your hands stuck to the ground at the same time. And when the King of the World heard that you and your people were tied and hard-bound like that he sent a chief of a hundred [men] of his own people to seek your head. And you put your thumb under your tooth of knowledge, and knowledge and information were revealed to you.

And that was the occasion and time that I came myself after you to Bruidhean an Chaorthainn and you recognised me as I was coming towards the hostel, and you revealed to me that Míodhach son of Colgán and the King of the World and the three kings of Inis Tile were in Bruidhean an Oileáin on the Shannon, and that it would not be long before some of them would come to seek your own head and to bring it to the King of the World. And when I heard that I took the protection of your life and your body on myself till daybreak on the morrow.

And I went to the ford which was by the hostel to defend it. I had not been long there when that chief of a hundred [men] of the people of the King of the World came to me, and we fought with each other and I cut his head off himself and made slaughter of his people, and I followed them to Bruidhean an Oileáin, and I found the King of the World occupied in drinking and pleasure there, and the three kings of Inis Tile with him. And I took my sword out and I cut the head off the King of the World with the first stroke, and I cut their three heads off those three other kings who were with him and I put them into the boss of my shield. And I took the golden-jewelled ornate goblet, being full of old mead pleasant to drink, which was before the King of the World in my left hand and I made an edge-feat[4] with my sword around me, and I came, as a result of my heroism and of my valour, to Bruidhean an Chaorthainn. And I gave those heads and those goblets to you, Fionn, as a sign of victory and triumph, and I rubbed the blood of the necks of those three kings on you and on that company of the Fiana of Ireland who were bound along with you, so that I restored to them the use of their hands and the movement of their feet. And had I asked a drink of you that night, Fionn, I would have got it.'

It was then Osgar son of Oisín said:

'Fionn,' said he, 'do you know that I am closer akin to Diarmaid ó Duibhne than to you, and that I would not allow you not to give him a drink.'

'I do not know of a well on this Beann,' said Fionn.

'That is not true,' said Diarmaid, 'for but only nine paces from you is the most truly beautiful, pure-watered well in the whole world.'

After that Fionn went towards the well and he took the full of his two palms with him, and he had not reached more than half-way when he let the water run down through his palms, and he said that he could not bring the water with him.

'I give my word,' said Diarmaid, 'that you are doing that purposely.'

Fionn went for the water again, and he had not brought it more than the same distance when he let it down through his palms.

'I swear before my arms,' said Osgar, 'that if you do not bring the water with you quickly, Fionn, there shall not leave this place of the two of us but he who is strongest.'

Fionn returned for the water the third time for Diarmaid because of that speech, and he brought with him the full of his two palms of water. And as he was coming to the place the life parted from the body of Diarmaid. And the company of the Fiana of Ireland that was at that place raised three mighty exceedingly great mournful shouts out loud mourning Diarmaid ó Duibhne. And Osgar rose up in a fierce attack of great anger and was about to cut his head off Fionn on that spot but that Oisín said:

'Son,' said he, 'it is true that he has deserved that of you and of all the Fiana of Ireland through not helping Diarmaid, but do not cause the two sorrows in one day for us, and let us leave this mound now for fear that Aonghus might come to us and that he would not believe from us that it was not we who brought death to Diarmaid although Fionn is guilty of his death.'

1. It was common for the chief warriors of the Fiana to have special weapons with their own particular names.

2. A reference to another story about the Fiana.

3. This refers to another Fenian tale, 'Bruidheann Chaorthainn' (The Rowantree Fort), in which the Fiana are enticed to a fort from which they cannot escape.

4. The Fiana were renowned for their martial prowess. This is obviously a feat of dexterity with a sword, but we have no exact description of it.

translated by Nessa Ní Sheaghdha, from *Field Day Anthology of Irish Writing* (1991)

MICHAEL HARTNETT

The ancient figure at the centre of this poem is thought by scholars to have her origin in the Celtic goddess Buí, or Boí, the old Irish word for cow. And, since the Celts were an Indo-European people, and the cow is a holy animal in India, there has been a suggestion that this old woman is something of a sacred cow. In any case, her name provides the origins of the river Boyne, and she evidently presided over a tribe who lived around the Beara peninsula, at the westernmost end of western County Cork. The idea of her sanctity is preserved in the Irish original of this poem, which dates from the ninth or tenth century. Once upon a time, 'cailleach' — the modern translation of which is hag — could have meant nun, or possibly female hermit.

Many Irish readers of a certain age will recall learning a condensed and revised version of this poem by the Easter 1916 leader, Patrick Pearse, in which the ancient figure is yet another female embodiment of Ireland. The name of that poem is 'Mise Éire', which means 'I am Ireland'.

The Hag of Beare (1969)

The woman of Beare sang this when old:

as to the sea laps low tide
    to me falls fading of age:
grief for myself at fading,
    greed in the teeth of my days.

I am Buí, the hag of Beare,
    I wore an eternal gown:
but I am naked today
    of even a cast-off shroud.

money was
all you loved, and not people.
    but we, while we were alive
    our love was for the people.

for we loved the peopled plains
    we rode, and we loved our hosts,
hospitable, good, they made
    of no giving a long boast.

today you claim all, yet you
    grant none nothing: if you give
you shame the given, with great
    boasting of a little gift.

now my body, bitter, finds
    the corridors of final
recognition, the gaze of
    God in his own possession.

now my hands, wrinkled to long
    bones, hang down dead, hands that locked
kings of this land in loving,
    in the old days, my lost days.

o hands wrinkled to long bones
    even at my odd hours of lust
I must tell young men begone
    should they come. I have no love.

the bodies of young women
   bound as rabbits in spring-time.
I only regret. *I* am
   a barren unloved woman

for my tongue hides no honey
   and I look to no wedlock:
white that is left of my hair
   hidden under a hag's cloak.

not the old
I envy: they die: but youth
   and monuments, both assailed
   as I am, and they still hold.

winter makes war with the waves:
   today no king will come here:
nor the lowest road-walker.
   I expect no one today.

I know what they are doing,
   liquid horses of the sea:
spaced far in their manéd groups
   they gallop away from me.

by loving
I wasted my self to age,
   but beauty leaves me alone:
   I am told, and no lust stays.

when the sun
beats a haze of hotness from
   the sea, so yet I must go
   clothed. I am spent, and old.

and yet to waste by loving
   is no waste: for I am glad
I was made old by pleasure:
   I am glad my flesh was glad.

green to grass comes back each spring:
   I am eternally old.
each acorn gives way to earth,
   bright tables fall to bare boards.

past, in my days of firm breasts,
   wine was my drink and sweet words
my food, tall men my lovers:
   now, curds, sour as my own milk.

beneath my cloak my skin hides
   grained with age and unlovely:
a white hair covers my skin
   like fungus on a dead tree.

robbed of me my blue right eye,
   lent for land I own forever:
and robbed of me, my left eye
   secures it, mine forever.

the three floods
in which I would dream to drown:
   a flood of loves, of horses
   and of gentle slim grey hounds.

o birth-wave,
death-wave, you bore, you broke me:
   you, last, I will know your face
   when you must come to take me.

o death-wave,
though great, my friends in darkness
   are — yet come and make your use
   of me. I never refuse.

well for the islands to which
   again the flood-waves come: now
   I, alone on my ebbed beach
I know no face nor no house.

from *Collected Poems*, Vol. II (1985)

ST BRENDAN

St Brendan flourished in the sixth century, founding monasteries in County Galway and in County Kerry, his native county. Among the many places associated with him is

Mount Brandon, on the Dingle peninsula. He was known in parts of Celtic Europe also — in Wales and in Brittany, for instance.

His greatest claim to fame, however, is that he discovered America. The basis of this claim is the Navigatio Sancti Brendani, which dates from the ninth century. It is the kind of story known in Irish as 'imramm'. These are tales of voyages, often fantastic, and frequently relating trips to the next world.

In 1978, the English explorer Tim Severin published The Brendan Voyage, an account of how he sailed in a leather boat from the coast of Kerry to America, via the Shetland Islands, the Orkneys, the Faroes and Iceland.

Jasconius

W hen they approached the other island, the boat began to ground before they could reach its landing-place. Saint Brendan ordered the brothers to disembark from the boat into the sea, which they did. They held the boat on both sides with ropes until they came to the landing-place. The island was stony and without grass. There were a few pieces of driftwood on it, but no sand on its shore. While the brothers spent the night outside in prayers and vigils, the man of God remained sitting inside in the boat. For he knew the kind of island it was, but he did not want to tell them, lest they be terrified.

When morning came he ordered each of the priests to sing his Mass, which they did. While Saint Brendan was himself singing his Mass in the boat, the brothers began to carry the raw meat out of the boat to preserve it with salt, and also the flesh which they had brought from the other island. When they had done this they put a pot over a fire. When, however, they were plying the fire with wood and the pot began to boil, the island began to be in motion like a wave. The brothers rushed to the boat, crying out for protection to the holy father. He drew each one of them into the boat by his hand. Having left everything they had had on the island behind, they began to sail. Then the island moved out to sea. The lighted fire could be seen over two miles away. Saint Brendan told the brothers what it really was, saying:

'Brothers, are you surprised at what this island has done?'

They said:

'We are very surprised and indeed terror-stricken.'

He said to them:

'My sons, do not be afraid. God revealed to me during the night in a vision the secret of this affair. Where we were was not an island, but a fish — the foremost of all that swim in the ocean. He is always trying to bring his tail to meet his head, but he cannot because of his length. His name is Jasconius.'

from The Voyage of Saint Brendan: Journey to the Promised Land (1991),
translated from the Latin by John J. O'Meara

ANONYMOUS

Liadan and Cuirithir is a tragic love-story written in the ninth or tenth century, but dealing with events that supposedly took place three hundred years earlier.

Liadan was a nun and Cuirithir a poet. They fell for each other, but Liadan's superior at the monastery of Clonfert — founded by St Brendan — would not allow them to live together, which, the story seems to suggest, they thought they could. So they part, and Cuirithir becomes a monk and sets off for County Waterford. Liadan follows him, but he moves on again, this time across the sea. Liadan stays in the place Cuirithir has left. She mourns his absence, goes into a decline and dies.

Lament of Liadan

No pleasure
that deed I did, tormenting him,
tormenting what I treasure.

Joyfully
but that God had come between us then
had I granted what he begged of me.

Not unwise
is the way that he is taking now,
enduring pain and gaining Paradise.

Great folly
where once I showed such gentleness
to set Cuirithir against me!

Liadan I;
they say that I loved Cuirithir,
nor would I, if I could, deny.

The while I bless
that I was in his company
and was treating him with tenderness.

A woodland breeze
was my melody with Cuirithir,
sounding harmony of reddening seas.

It seemed thus:
the last thing I would ever do
was a deed to come between us.

Cry clearly:
if any lovers this heart cherishes,
he its darling, loved most dearly.

A cry of pain
and the heart within was rent in two,
without him never beats again.

translated by Kuno Meyer, from James Carney (ed.), *Early Irish Poetry* (1965)

ANONYMOUS

*The setting of this fourteenth-century poem has been discovered to be a Cistercian
monastery and convent near Clonmel, Co. Tipperary — whose name in Irish means
'meadow of honey'. The material perks of monastic life as presented here seem a far
cry from the poor mouth and puritan outlook inextricably connected with the Irish
Catholicism of later times. The poem frankly avows the pleasures of 'gees irostid on
the spitte' (roast goose), and even more frankly the pleasures enjoyed by monks and
nuns together.*

Of Cockaigne, the Oxford English Dictionary *says: 'The Romanic word must have
originated in some fabulous geographical notion. Its derivation has been much
discussed, but has remained obscure.' It goes on to cite the Old French phrase,* trouver
cocaigne, *'to find the country where good things drop of themselves into the mouth'.
London has also been called Cockaigne, in the affectionate sense of 'cockney-land',
rather than in the sense of earthly, or, as some would have it, fools' paradise.*

The glosses are from the source.

from *The Land of Cockaygne*

In Cokaigne is met and drink
Withvte care, how and swink;
The met is trie, the drink is clere
To none, russin and sopper.
I sigge for soth, boute were,
Ther nis lond on erthe is pere,
Vnder heuen nis lond iwisse
Of so mochil ioi and blisse.
Ther is mani swete sighte,
Al is dai, nis ther no nighte.

Ther nis baret nother strif,
Nis ther no, ac euer lif,
Ther nis lac of met no cloth,
Ther nis man no womman wroth,
Ther nis serpent, wolf no fox,
Hors no capil, kowe no ox,
Ther nis schepe no swine no gote
No non horwgh la, god it wote,
Nother harace, nother stode,
The lond is ful of other gode.

Nis ther flei, fle no lowse
In cloth, in toune, bed no house;
Ther nis dunnir, slete no hawle
No none vile worme no snawile
No non storme, rein no winde;
Ther nis man no womman blinde,
Ok al is game, ioi and gle,
Wel is him that ther mai be.
Ther beth rivers gret and fine
Of oile, melk, honi and wine,
Watir servith ther to no thing
Bot to sight and to waiissing,
Ther is al maner frute,
Al is solas and dedute.

Ther is a wel fair abbei
Of white monkes and of gre.
Ther beth bowris and halles
Al of pasteiis beth the walles,
Of fleis, of fisse and rich met,
The likfullist that man mai et.
Fluren cakes beth the schingles alle
Of cherche, cloister, boure and halle,

The pinnes beth fat podinges,
Rich met to princes and kinges.
Man mai tereof et inogh,
Al with right and noght with wogh,
Al is commune to yung and old,
To stoute and sterne, mek and bold.
Ther is a cloister fair and light,
Brod and lang, of sembli sight.
The pilers of that cloister alle
Beth iturned of cristale,
With har bas and capitale
Of grene Iaspe and rede corale.
In the praer is a tre
Swithe likful for to se,
The rote is gingeuir and galingale,
The siouns beth al sedwale,
Trie maces beth the flure,
The rind canel of swet odur,
The frute gilofre of gode smakke,
Of cucubes ther nis no lakke;
Ther beth rosis of rede ble
And lilie likful for to se.

how . . . anxiety
swink . . . toil
trie . . . choice
none . . . noon
russin . . . lunch
sopper . . . supper
I sigge for soth, boute were . . . I say for sooth, without a doubt
nis . . . is not
baret nother . . . quarrel or
lac . . . lack
capil . . . nag
horwgh . . . dirt
harace . . . stable
stode . . . stud
toune . . . farm
dunnir . . . thunder

hawle . . . hail
game, ioi and gle . . . sport, joy and glee
sight . . . seethe
waiissing . . . washing
solas . . . ease
dedute . . . delight
fleis . . . flesh
fisse . . . fish
likfullist . . . pleasantest
Fluren . . . flour
schingles . . . shingles
pinnes . . . pins (of the shingles)
Man . . . one
et inogh . . . eat enough
wogh . . . wrongdoing
sembli . . . seemly

praer . . . lawn
Swithe likful . . . very pleasant
rote . . . root
siouns . . . shoots
sedwale . . . zedoary [an aromatic root]
canel . . . cinnamon
gilofre . . . gillyflower
smakke . . . scent
cucubes . . . cubebs [a spicy fruit]
lakke . . . lack
ble . . . complexion

from Thomas Kinsella (ed.), *The New Oxford Verse* (1986)

HUBERT BUTLER

Slievenaman in south-eastern County Tipperary is famous in song and story. Not only is it a celebrated site in the Fenian cycle, as Butler mentions, it is also one of those places where Oisín and St Patrick conversed, as is pointed out later on in the essay. In addition, this is the mountain that presides over the highly domesticated landscape of Kickham's Knocknagow, with its unassuming and good-natured peasantry.

The rest of the essay goes on to tell how Bridget is burned to death, how the trial resulted in the defendants receiving 'a merciful sentence', and how the case got widespread press attention in Ireland and England. Butler also points out that 'All of the Clearys and their neighbours lived in that perilous region of half-belief which the sophisticated find charming because they are more acquainted with its tenderness than its cruelty. It is a no-man's land of the imagination, in which fantasy, running wild, easily turns into falsehood and ruthlessness. It has still in the twentieth century its appeal and highly civilised people, as well as simple ones, claim access to it.'

'Frochans' are whortleberries, pretty much the same as blueberries. A 'rath' is a fairy fort. 'The Eggman and the Fairies' was first published in 1960.

from *The Eggman and the Fairies*

You can see Slievenaman from my fields, though it is across the Tipperary border, a pale blue hump with the soft, rounded contours of ancient hills whose roughnesses have been smoothed away by time. Starting after lunch you can climb to the tip and be back by summer daylight, though it is over 2,000 feet high. It can be seen from five or six southern counties and is one of the three or four most famous of Irish hills. Finn MacCool lived there and so did Oisin and Oscar, and fifty beautiful maidens, who give it its name, 'The Mountain of Women', embroidered garments for them there, or so they say. The top of the mountain to within a couple of hundred feet of the cairn of stones is bare except for an odd patch of sphagnum moss and heather. Below it there is more heather, well grazed by sheep, and a few frochan clumps, but except for some piles of stones that might once have been a house and a rough track for carting turf, there is not much sign of human traffic. I had always supposed that the Clearys' house had been in one of these ruined stone heaps upon the mountain side, because I could not associate their uncanny story with the prosperous and populous plain below. But one day I went to look for Ballyvadlea, where they lived at the foot of the mountain. A hurling match was being broadcast from Dublin and the cottagers came reluctantly from their wireless sets to direct me to the 'fairy-house'. It was almost indistinguishable from their own, except that it was bare and without flowers or shrubs, an ugly cement building rather smaller than the county council houses of today but of the same type. It was only a couple of hundred yards from a main road and, though it suggested poverty, it did not suggest mystery, remoteness, primeval superstition. Farmers and gentry driving past the door to Fethard or Clonmel will in 1895 have been talking of Dreyfus and Cecil Rhodes and some of these, who took part in the Ballyvadlea tragedy, may be still alive. They belong to our age and clime. The fairies are, if not exactly at the bottom of the garden, at least only a few fields and a few years away.

It is not very easy to build up a consecutive story out of a court case, for the end is always told before the beginning, and the central episode, seen differently by different witnesses, is often blurred like a negative several times exposed. But roughly this is how it happened.

In the spring of 1895 the Clearys were living at Ballyvadlea below Slievenaman. Michael Cleary was a labourer and his young wife, Bridget, was the daughter of a neighbour, Patrick Boland. Michael and Bridget were fond of each other and never quarrelled. They were religious people believing in the mysteries of the Catholic Church. But they also believed in the fairies and Michael was persuaded that, many years before, his mother had changed her nature. A fairy had entered into her body and once she had disappeared for two nights and it was known that she had spent them on the fairy-haunted rath at Kilnagranagh. It lay above John Dunne's cottage on the low road, and when Bridget too began to talk, like his mother, of Kilnagranagh and often to walk towards it of an evening on the low road, the old dread took shape in Michael's twilit mind. And some contagion of his fears spread to all his neighbours and all his relations, the Kennedys, the Bolands, the Dunnes, the Ahearns and Burkes, paralysing their wills and dulling their sensibilities. A whole community seemed to be bound with the spells of fairyland and powerless to extricate themselves. They appealed to the priests and the peelers to save them from themselves, but no external power was stronger than their obsessions. 'It's not my wife I have,' Michael told John Dunne, 'she's too fine a woman for my wife. She's two inches taller than my wife.' And even Bridget Cleary herself talked to her cousin, Mary Kennedy, as though she were bound with spells. 'I've a pain in my head,' she said, 'he's making a fairy of me now and an emergency. He thought to burn me three months ago.' She began to suffer from nerves and her illness was to Michael yet stronger proof that she was possessed. Dr Creary, the local doctor, declared it was due to dyspepsia, but he carried no conviction, and Michael went to Denis Guiney, the herb doctor, who prescribed a decoction of herbs and milk to be cooked in a saucepan and fed to the possessed woman.

But Michael had not much faith, either, in this innocent herbal remedy. He was convinced that there was only one way in which his Bridget could be restored to him. The fairy must be burnt out of her and then he would go to Kilnagranagh, and he would find the real Bridget there. She'd come out of the rath, riding a white horse and bound by cords to the saddle. He'd have to cut the ropes and then, if he was able to keep her, she'd stay with him.

But I should have mentioned that Michael Cleary once casually told his cousin John that Bridget on her evening walks to the fairy rath sometimes met an eggman on the low road. He used to go the rounds of the Tipperary farmsteads with his cart, collecting eggs for a wholesale distributor in Clonmel. When the story was all told in the Clonmel Court House the eggman was only mentioned once and never again by judge, jury, witnesses or prisoners. For all the relevance he appeared to have to the story he and his cart might well have been swallowed up into the fairy mound. Yet these oblique and tender-hearted people had a habit of hiding their thoughts from themselves, and perhaps they sometimes thrust upon the fairies the guilt for desires and jealousies whose crudities they shrank from facing. It is possible that Michael suspected his wife of a tenderness for the eggman and just as a grain of grit will provoke an oyster to secrete a pearl, so the eggman from Clonmel unlocked the door to fairyland.

When Michael Cleary's father died he was waked in a house eleven miles from Ballyvadlea and on their way to the wake, the neighbours assembled the evening before in Michael's house. Patrick Boland, Bridget's father, was there and the Kennedy cousins including William, aged sixteen, and William Ahearn and several others. Bridget's cousin, Hannah Burke, was still washing some shirts that were needed for the wake and Mary Kennedy, young William's mother, went off to feed their hens, but when the others started to walk off for the wake, Michael Cleary stopped them. He said he would not leave his wife's sick-bed and that 'he did not care the devil about his father whether he was alive or dead'. 'No and ye won't go either,' he said to them, 'until I give her a little of the business I have to give her. Wait, boys, till you see her, till you see what I'll put out the door. I haven't Bridgie here these six weeks.'

So they did not leave for the wake, but stood about till midnight watching with mild exclamations while Michael tried to drive the fairy out of Bridget's body. Her father, Patrick Boland, raised some objections which Michael dealt with impatiently. 'Haven't you any faith?' he said. 'Don't you know it's with an old witch I'm sleeping.' 'You are not,' said Patrick Boland, 'you are sleeping with my daughter.' And telling about it later in the Clonmel courts, he, like the other witnesses, preserved a trance-like calm, as though he were watching a tragedy in which he was doomed to be a spectator, knowing the truth and yet powerless to intervene.

It is Johanna Burke who gives us the most coherent account of it all. She came back from washing the shirts about 7 p.m. on this first day of fairy exorcism, 14 March 1895. She found the Clearys' door locked and two neighbours called Simpson standing outside unable to get in. Through the window they could hear a voice saying, 'Take it, you witch or you bitch!' And when the three of them were at last let in she found the three Kennedys and John Dunne holding Bridget down on the bed, while Michael tried to give her herbs boiled in new milk from a spoon. Mary Kennedy, returned from feeding the hens, had brought some wine with her, and Michael threw it over Bridget's face and breast, exclaiming 'Are you Bridget Boland in the name of God?' while her father echoed, 'Are you Bridget Boland, in the name of God, the daughter of Patrick Boland?' But Bridget was exhausted and speechless and the liquid was pouring down her chemise. So, while the Rosary was recited, the men raised her out of the bed and put her onto the fire. It was John Dunne's suggestion. 'We raised her over it,' he explained to the courts, 'I thought it belonged to the cure.' Hannah had just been putting sticks on the fire to make them a cup of tea and when Bridget, in the men's arms, saw her, she exclaimed in a mournful voice 'Oh, Han, Han!' She was wearing, Hannah recollected, a red petticoat and navy-blue flannel dress, green stays and navy-blue cashmere jacket, and Hannah, a conscientious witness, said of her later: 'When she was taken out, she looked like one that was silly, she looked wild and deranged and had not her own appearance. She looked different. She looked worse when she was taken out of bed than when I went into the room.' She was just 'tipping the bars' and her father and Michael Cleary were questioning her urgently in the name of God. It was too much for Hannah, she shouted out, 'Burn her away, but let me out and I'll go for the peelers.' She got out, but she did not go for the peelers.

That was the first night of burning; though there had been thirteen people in the house, we do not know much else about the remaining five hours before the visitors walked off to the funeral, except for what Patrick Boland told the court. About the first night he was very reassuring. 'Indeed,' he said, 'the fire wouldn't do anything the first night, 'twas no fire I might say.' He had left with the others at midnight and returning with them from the wake the following day, he had found nothing to complain of in Bridget's condition. 'She was grand then when I came back from Michael's father's wake, and the next night after that she was grand and the night after that she was grand until we were all taking a cup of tea.' At this point the old man broke off in tears; he tried to tell what happened on the third night in a few disjointed phrases. It appeared that Michael had gone to his wife with the dish of herbs and milk and said: 'I'll make you take it, you old witch! I have herbs that there's nine cures in. It will be very hard to make her take these.' He struggled to explain what followed but failing to articulate, wound up: 'I had to run away from the smell. So 'tis all the way to make a long story short he burnt her.'

The witnesses all rambled incoherently backwards and forwards between the two nights of burning, lingering over what seems to us trivial, suppressing what appears to be relevant. They lived in a fairy-haunted world, whose thoughts and feelings can be measured by no ordinary rule. The poet is apt to overestimate its charm, the moralist its cruelty. The mere chronicler is exasperated by his powerlessness to sort out the events of the successive nights. Of all the witnesses Hannah Burke is the most easy to follow. The peelers to her were almost as real as the fairies, she had actually thought of going to fetch them, and her chronology is the same as ours. After Bridget had been on the fire the first night, Hannah Burke had returned and put on her a fresh nightdress, which she had been airing for her and she had examined her body. Like Patrick Boland, she agreed that Bridget was 'grand'. 'I saw no marks on her except the size of a pin and a little blister on her hip not the size of sixpence, and a couple of little spots of burns on her chemise and a red spot under her chin. I thought it might be from the pin in her chemise so I put a safety pin there instead.' She stayed on with Bridget after the men had left for the wake and gave her some new milk, whey and claret wine, but when she left at 2 a.m. Bridget was still awake.

from *Escape from the Anthill* (1985)

Flann O'Brien

Shanahan is a member of a band of cowboys whose bailiwick is the Ringsend area of Dublin. This is only one of the myriad comic juxtapositions and language experiments in At Swim-Two-Birds, *an undoubted masterpiece of twentieth-century Irish literature. Shanahan also happens to be a character in a novel being written by a certain Trellis, himself a character in a novel being written by the nameless protagonist of* At Swim-Two-Birds. *Furriskey, Lamont and Finn MacCool are also characters in the Trellis novel. Shanahan is delighting them by reciting the verse of Jem Casey, 'the poet of the pick'.*

Finn's verses are the overture to King Sweeny on trees, the verses and narrative of Buile Suibhne — as translated by O'Brien — being one of the key texts used in At Swim-Two-Birds. *The title of* At Swim-Two-Birds *is taken from a noted section in* Buile Suibhne *where Sweeny visits a place, the name of which in translation could be rendered as 'Two Birds at Swim'.*

Casey and Sweeny

But wait till you hear the last verse, man, the last polish-off, said Shanahan. He frowned and waved his hand.

Oh it's good, it's good, said Furriskey.

> In time of trouble and lousy strife,
> You have still got a darlint plan,
> You still can turn to a brighter life —
> A PINT OF PLAIN IS YOUR ONLY MAN.

Did you ever hear anything like it in your life, said Furriskey. A pint of plain, by God, what! Oh I'm telling you, Casey was a man in twenty thousand, there's no doubt about that. He knew what he was at, too true he did. If he knew nothing else, he knew how to write a pome. A pint of plain is your only man.

Didn't I tell you he was good? said Shanahan. Oh by Gorrah you can't cod me.

There's one thing in that pome, *permanence*, if you know what I mean. That pome, I mean to say, is a pome that'll be heard wherever the Irish race is wont to gather, it'll live as long as there's a hard root of an Irishman left by the Almighty on this planet, mark my words. What do you think, Mr Shanahan?

It'll live, Mr Lamont, it'll live.

I'm bloody sure it will, said Lamont.

A pint of plain, by God, eh? said Furriskey.

Tell us, my Old Timer, said Lamont benignly, what do you think of it? Give the company the benefit of your scholarly pertinacious fastidious opinion, Sir Storybook. Eh, Mr Shanahan?

Conspirators' eyes were winked smartly in the dancing firelight. Furriskey rapped Finn about the knees.

Wake up!

And Sweeny continued, said corn-yellow Finn, at the recital of these staves.

> If I were to search alone
> the hills of the brown world,
> better would I like my sole hut
> in Glen Bolcain.
>
> Good its water greenish-green
> good its clean strong wind,
> good its cress-green cresses,
> best its branching brooklime.

from *At Swim-Two-Birds* (1939)

MICHAEL HARTNETT

Writing about his attempts to come to terms with Daibhí Ó Bruadair, Michael Hartnett notes of his 'idol': 'He would not have liked the Ireland of the 1980s.' But poets generally tend not to be at home in their own times. They want to go sailing to Byzantium, or to say farewell to English, or to find any other imaginatively persuasive way to ratify the world's need of their voices and values, practices and presumptions.

Is there a passing glance at Keats's 'Ode on a Grecian Urn' in those lines that ask a question here? Keats's poem has the famous ending: '"Beauty is truth, truth beauty", — that is all/Ye know on earth, and all ye need to know.'

There Will Be A Talking

There will be a talking of lovely things
there will be cognisance of the seasons,
there will be men who know the flights of birds,
in new days there will be love for women:
we will walk the balance of artistry.
And things will have a middle and an end,
and be loved because being beautiful.
Who in a walk will find a lasting vase
depicting dance and hold it in his hands
and sell it then? No man on the new earth
will barter with malice nor make of stone
a hollowed riddle: for art will be art,
the freak, the rare no longer commonplace:
there will be a going back to the laws.

from *Collected Poems,* Vol. I (1984)

ALL OF LIFE IS THERE

EAMON DUNPHY

When the Irish soccer team qualified for the World Cup finals in Italy in 1990, euphoria was the order of the day, and the team's early success in the tournament caused the country to close down and watch television at game time. This degree of popular success on the international stage temporarily eclipsed those already experienced in the mass markets of tourism and pop music, and has been regarded as an expression of a more outward-looking, competitive and self-confident Ireland.

The fact that the team was managed by Jack Charlton, an Englishman, and had many players of Irish descent rather than Irish birth, added piquancy to the occasion. These developments may have overshadowed Irish soccer as such, its working-class origins and its industrial affiliation in old clubs like Transport, St James's Gate and TEK, and its regular supply of promising teenagers to English clubs.

The Ireland soccer team is the one that represents the Republic of Ireland. A different league, with a different governing body and a different international team, represents Northern Ireland. This is not the case with other sports in which Ireland competes internationally.

Italia '90

A ll World Cups are special, this time our participation should ensure that the next few weeks are memorable, a time we will recall for our grandchildren, a Golden Age when we took our place among the nations of the world in the greatest of all international sporting festivals.

A cult has grown around Jack Charlton. We owe him much it's true, but things have got out of hand. Jack didn't invent Irish soccer, he has simply presided over its finest hours, guiding (or should I say *driving*) us to our destination.

When we take the field for our opening World Cup match against England the lump in my throat will have little to do with 'Big Jack'. I will be thinking of other men to whom we owe much more, whose lives were dedicated to soccer in Ireland long before it was fashionable to get pissed in the Berkeley Court after international matches.

There are too many names in my head right now, some who played, like Peter Farrell, Tommy Eglington and Joe Haverty, a couple, Mick Meagan and John Giles, who played and managed Ireland, and many many others . . . heroes of the League of Ireland when it was worth knowing . . . 'Bunny' Fullam, 'Kit' Lawlor, Paddy Coad, 'Rosy' Henderson, Shay Gibbons, and Ronnie Whelan senior.

I think too of Billy Behan, the great Irish talent scout who discovered so many fine players for Manchester United, from the late Billy Whelan who died at Munich to Kevin Moran who will, I hope, be on the pitch in Cagliari.

Nor should we forget amid the contemporary hype the anonymous heroes of the Dublin Schoolboy League without whom there would be no World Cup team, no Arnold O'Byrne; 'Jem' Kennedy, God rest him, riding on his old Gas Company bike up the steep hill to the 15 acres in the Phoenix Park. Fr 'Mac' at Stella Maris, all those snobby sods who ran teams at Home Farm, and Eddie Corcoran of Young Elms.

This World Cup is for them and all the others like them who helped create the wonder of this year. By a strange coincidental quirk Eddie Corcoran is now Jack Charlton's indispensable aide-de-camp, a link between aspiring past and glorious present. He's not allowed to talk to dissidents . . . but he winks at me occasionally, an acknowledgment of the Good Old Days.

from *Sunday Independent* (1990)

P.D. MEHIGAN (CARBERY)

One of the most powerful cultural institutions in Ireland is the GAA, the Gaelic Athletic Association. Founded in Hayes's Hotel, Thurles, in 1884, it codified, organised and supervised the playing of the four official Gaelic games — hurling, football, camogie and handball — throughout the island at the local, intercounty and interprovincial level. Its first and most important patron was Archbishop Croke of Cashel (1824–1902).

The main Gaelic games are hurling and football, and Cork has had outstanding success in both codes. The greatest Cork hurling legend is Christy Ring (1920–79), who played for the Glen Rovers club in Cork city. Hurleys, the sticks used to play the game, are made of ash and curve upwards into a somewhat broad flat bottom. This is the 'boss'.

Since the game is being played during the Emergency, when petrol was in short supply and rail travel unreliable, the size of the crowd is noteworthy.

Munster Final, 1944

A n hour after the drawn game of July 16th, I met John Quirke and Christy Ring. We thrashed out the pros and cons of a startling finish, and I told them of my friendly sporting bet with an old Limerick friend. 'Double it next time,' said John Quirke.

'Carbery boy,' says fair-haired Christy Ring of the beaming, ruddy face, 'Quirky and I won't let you down,' and the flashing Glen Rovers' winger shook my hand heartily.

Last Sunday, another glamorous day in Thurles town — same lighthearted, good tempered, 20,000 crowd. Same brisk air in the stately square. There seemed a smile of pride and triumph on the bronze face of Dr Croke as the glad throngs of young vigorous folk — and old men too! — trooped past for the Gaelic Park over the bridge. Our transport scheme worked out difficult and slow; we were late for the opening scenes of the game which will rank with the classic Munster finals of the past in its stern, naked grandeur; in its hearty, manly spirit where rival surging bloods swung ash with freedom and abandon; where scores were level three times in the hour; where Mick Mackey treated us all to his wizard artistry; where Malone (from the Hill of Fedamore) proved almost the equal of Scanlon himself in the Limerick goal; where Limerick's flag was in the ascendant through 55 pulsating minutes until they were sailing home five points in front with only broken time to play. Cork's desperate final rally, whilst the clock ticked its last fateful minutes — a rally which every man in the field from Mulcahy out seemed to share — a rally which the spearheads (Morrison and Quirke) clinched with balancing scores that sent the comparatively small but virile Cork contingent shouting hoarsely.

Then came as dramatic and brilliant a score as ever Thurles finals have recorded. Christy Ring (of the Glen) still bounding with life and energy, nosed a rolling ball to the 'boss' of his hurley, raced through on Cork's right wing and let fly a daisy-clipper — dead on the post. Five stout Limerick backs pulled and parried. That ball's pace deceived one and all. Malone shadowed in, made a despairing effort to arrest its flight, and all but succeeded. Young Kelly (the sheet-lightning boy-sprinter) sped to the ball's aid — 'twas over the line; the great game was lost and won!

John Lynch, playing confidently in his old, new and favourite place, broke away for a long-range point shortly after Mr Seamus Gardiner had led in Most Rev. Dr O'Dwyer, Superior General of Maynooth's Mission, an old All-Ireland and Tipperary hurler, to set the boys under way. In a crack Dick Stokes had balanced and McCarthy's score gave Limerick the lead. Cork were quickly down-field, and Morrison pulled hard and low for a ball to the net which gave Malone no chance.

Cork's lead was short-lived. McCarthy and Ryan were breasting the ball well and Mick Mackey was away on one of his specialities — a swerving, dodging solo run — he flashed the ball to his brother John close on the square: a deft tap and the ball was through. Limerick led now and played with abundant confidence.

Hurling on both sides was sweet and true. Sean Condon hit a beauty point, but Limerick were soon surging up and Mick Mackey was again on the job. The Ahane leader was in irresistible mood as he crashed a goal and a point home in effortless fashion — Limerick leading nine points to five and a third of the hour gone.

Alan Lotty (of 'Sars') was holding Stokes well, but Cork's tall centre-half was limping badly. That old knee had let him down again. Cork's sideline brain-trust now got busy. Mick Mackey must be held or the day was lost to the triple champions! And so the brain-wave brought a rapid switch — Din Joe Buckley down to mark Limerick's star attacker; Curly Murphy in Lotty's place and big Pat Donovan of the Glen at right-half. Stokes swung a glorious shot for a point but Condon and Lynch were dead on the mark with high drives above the bar leaving Limerick a goal clear after a gallant first half: 2–4 to 1–4.

Malone had brought down many hot shots and continued to play well. At the other net Mulcahy was watchful as a lynx between the branches of a tree. Dick Stokes, from accurate frees, put Limerick five points clear. When Lynch and Cottrell — both hurling well now — opened up Cork fireworks, Malone stopped one from 10 yards out. Ash clashed; strong men pulled hard and fierce — there was a brief flare-up by lusty bloods. 'Twas quelled at once and the great game swung on. Joe Kelly again streaked in from Cork's left wing and pulled hard and true to whip a Cork goal home. Once again the scene changed to the other goal. Mick Kennedy, brought back after several years, had been doing right well in front of Malone. He cleared again; Johnny Power helped the good work; Limerick were away in a Shannon flood; young Clohessy raced past, and John Mackey made no mistake with a glorious swerve and shot — net — Limerick still five points clear and time running on.

Another wave from the Cork brain-trust. John Quirke who saved the game last time came in to the 40 mark. He had a sweet point in a tick. Cork were now staging a most determined final assault. John Lynch and Con Cottrell were bringing down every ball and feeding their front lines. Power and Cregan swung long balls back. Limerick's big contingent roared in one voice as Mick Mackey got possession — fouled on the way as he netted after the whistle had gone. Dick Stokes missed the free for once. Young, Buckley, the Murphys, Lynch and Cottrell were all moving fast — Morrison on the ball, a lightning swing — net — Cork one point behind and broken time being played.

John Quirke's cool skill again to the aid. A lovely neat swing — ball sails over the bar for the equalizer. Referee looks at his watch — we make it one minute to go — Christy Ring gets the ball; it glues to his hurley as he sprints up the wing like a shadow — away she goes — dead straight, fast and true to the Limerick net for so sensational a win that we are silent until the whistle blows. The 1940 final, when Limerick won the replay, was reversed. Limerick had led for the bulk of the hour and may have had the rough end of the day's fortunes. But there is no mistaking Cork's determined final stand and rousing rally. Christy Ring had prophesied truly — his goal will live in hurling history.

from *Vintage Carbery* (1984)

BERNARD O'DONOGHUE

The game is Gaelic football, and in Munster two teams perennially contest the final of the provincial championship, those of the neighbouring counties of Cork and Kerry. So great is the rivalry between them that the Cork visitors have nothing to say about Killarney's scenic delights — the Gap of Dunloe, for instance — to view which sightseers are driven in traditional sidecars by 'jarveys'. Nor are they distracted by the bizarrely out of place strict-tempo Scottish dance music of Jimmy Shand and his band — extremely popular in the 1950s. Catching the ball in the air and kicking it — fielding and clearing — are what concentrate the mind.

Among the Cork stars of the 1970s was Tom Creedon of Macroom (1955–83).

Munster Final

in memory of Tom Creedon, died 28 August 1983

The jarveys to the west side of the town
Are robbers to a man, and if you tried
To drive through The Gap, they'd nearly strike you
With their whips. So we parked facing for home
And joined the long troop down the meadowsweet
And woodbine-scented road into the town.
By blue Killarney's lakes and glens to see
The white posts on the green! To be deafened
By the muzzy megaphone of Jimmy Shand
And the testy bray to keep the gangways clear.

As for Tom Creedon, I can see him still,
His back arching casually to field and clear.
'Glory Macroom! Good boy, Tom Creedon!'
We'd be back next year to try our luck in Cork.

We will be back next year, roaring ourselves
Hoarse, praying for better luck. After first Mass
We'll get there early; that's our only hope.
Keep clear of the carparks so we're not hemmed in,
And we'll be home, God willing, for the cows.

from *Poaching Rights* (1987)

BREANDÁN Ó HEITHIR

The 'brief flare-up by lusty bloods' mentioned by Carbery at the 1944 Munster Final is comparatively rare in intercounty championship games. Club games for county championships can be another matter. Rivalries are frequently intense, and often seem to have no greater basis than that familiarity breeds contempt. Every parish has at least one team. It becomes a matter of great pride and importance to assert difference. Political differences and family affiliations can enter into the volatile mix, but are not required for combustion to take place. According to some commentators, such hostilities derive from faction-fights, pitched battles between gangs that typically took place at fair days and similar public events in nineteenth-century rural Ireland. The political insults exchanged here make this a rather high-toned confrontation.

In their role of community leaders, priests were often managers of local clubs, and generally had a calming influence. Young members of the junior clergy sometimes played.

But times have changed. Now intercounty teams have commercial sponsors, there is a corps of professional team managers, and Gaelic games have to compete with television and other entertainment outlets.

Footballers

I t was in the company of my Uncle Tomás, who inherited the family farm, that I came to know various facets of life, including the GAA, at the most interesting human level. Football in west Clare was full of history and as with everything else in that most remarkable of Irish counties, countless hours were spent 'tracing' every detail of the politics, family history and social background of all participants. It was bubbling with life and fun and even scandal.

Once Tomás took me on the crossbar of his bike to a match at which a row started between two bands as to which of them would have place of honour in the pre-match parade — or something of that nature. It really was not about that at all. One band seemed to have stronger political views than the other, for its members and supporters referred loudly to the others as 'Free Staters', 'Blueshirts' and other low forms of Irish political life. At one stage the big drum was seized by a man who threatened to put it out of action with his boot.

This was great stuff, but when I tried to wriggle closer to the action I was hauled back by the scruff of the neck by Tomás.

'If you are trampled to death,' he wanted to know, 'how the hell am I going to explain it to your father and mother?'

Then a priest arrived and called everyone to order. He was very angry and said that the affair was an affront to his own authority, as a priest and an officer of the GAA. But he was clearly not neutral, for he addressed the leader of the republican band as a 'blackguard' who had come to make mischief.

As if we didn't have it in our own house, I thought to myself, the church triumphant rules here also. But no sooner had that thought lodged itself in my mind than up spoke a little piper in a green kilt who addressed the priest loudly, informing him that it was hard for them to take him seriously in either one of his two offices. Now, if he stopped drinking whiskey after hours, in a certain named public house, in the company of various named citizens — male and female — then he, the piper, might even listen to him with a little respect. When somebody in the background suggested that a blue shirt would look better on the priest than the black one he was wearing, my Uncle Tomás hauled me off out of earshot and refused point-blank to discuss the matter with me later as we headed for home after the match. But that night, when I was supposed to be asleep in bed, I crept down and listened at the kitchen door as Tomás gave my grandmother a richly-embellished version of the day's happenings with many illuminating footnotes.

Just after the outbreak of war one of the county footballers came to work in Inis Mór. He was Pat Mór Mac Donncha from Ros a' Mhíl who came to replace Seosamh Ó Flannagáin in Eoghnacht school until the eldest of Ó Flannagáin's family had come through the training college. Big Pat was really big. He played at full forward in the 1941 All-Ireland against Kerry and although I had not yet made the acquaintance of the Kerry full back, Joe Keohane, whenever I saw Big Pat cycle past our house on his racer, which looked like a child's bicycle beneath his great bulk, I imagined Joe Keohane as some sort of giant.

Also on that team in 1941 was another Pat McDonough, christened Small Pat to distinguish him from his Ros a' Mhíl namesake. Small Pat, who was from Tuam and played in the backs, was not small at all and he was also part of a Galway team that had many stars and very few All-Irelands to show for their considerable efforts.

The Kerry footballers were the bane of my youthful life. Apart from Joe Keohane, who now inhabited a special corner of my imagination, the rest of them seemed to inhabit the same world as the Cannonball Kid, or indeed, Fianna Éireann. Only when I saw some of them at close quarters, at half-time in a National League match against Galway in the Sportsground, taking swigs out of a brandy bottle to fortify them against the bitter March wind, did they assume human proportions.

from *Over the Bar* (1984)

JOHN WATERS

The Heaney reference is, the author explains, to his keynote address to the annual conference of the Ireland Fund in 1988, in which the poet 'makes a stab at defining the shifting ground underneath all Irish feet'. Among the quotations from that speech is the following: 'You are a secular, modern citizen of the world, with a sort of lacuna in your midriff . . . You are vaguely in exile from somewhere inside or outside yourself, but you don't quite know how or why. You are probably a professional, urban, Irish eighties success story . . . but whoever you are, you feel this vestigial capacity to focus around an old field of force that is neither marked on the map nor written into the schedule.'

U2 is Ireland's most successful rock band. Formed in 1977, its members are four Dubliners: Paul Hewson, known as Bono, vocalist; David Evans, known as The Edge, guitar; Adam Clayton, bass; and Larry Mullen, drums.

Lifting a Latch

In all of us, said Heaney, there is a supply of dammed-up energy to be released. There is a trigger somewhere that, if we could find and pull it, would release the floodgates. He told of one such experience he himself had, a visit to an old house, lifting a latch for the first time in years, feeling the cold of the metal on his hand and the harsh slap of the latch mechanism. 'My body awakened in its very capillaries to innumerable and unnameable rivulets of affection and energy.' In other words, he said, 'a connection is possible between your present self and your intuited previousness, between your inchoate dailiness and your imagined identity. Your Irishness, to put it in yet another way, constitutes a big unconscious voltage and all it needs is some transformer to make it current in a new and significant and renovative way.'

But Heaney knew, too, the pitfall he was heading for. In modern Ireland, to talk of a slap of a latch with such feeling and conviction is to invite irritation and dismissiveness. The thirst for modernity contaminates everything old or past with a coating of sentiment, which, like rust, has no neutral existence. Between prejudice and nostalgia there is no middle way. We reject the mention of the old as we mistrust the sentiment in ourselves. It is difficult to find reference points to which any two people will attach the same meaning. Most of us cannot see beneath the patina of the illustration to the meaning below. The task, as Heaney said, is to find *new* things, to create new points of recognition, on which to construct a meaning for ourselves.

We are already doing this, although frequently our efforts are all but futile on account of being mistaken for something else. Such a phenomenon is the music of U2. Their music is the expression of that unconscious voltage, the transformer that makes the meaning of one existence current in a renovative way. They are in the business of creating shapes to fill that lacuna in our midriff.

from *Race of Angels: Ireland and the Genesis of U2* (1994)

ANONYMOUS

This fourteenth-century poem is thought to be the oldest English dance song preserved in manuscript form. Dance songs were sung in public and at taverns. The conventions of such songs mean that the singer is a girl. Nowadays the poem is widely known and frequently quoted, and appears to be understood as an expression of hospitality and good fellowship. Yeats's version in Words for Music, Perhaps *(1932) introduced the poem to a wider audience.*

What with the success of Brian Friel's play Dancing at Lughnasa *(1990), John Waters's social commentary* Jiving at the Crossroads *(1991), and* Riverdance *(1995), tripping the light fantastic has quite a resonance in present-day Ireland.*

'Yloren' means lost; 'leven' means live.

Two Fragments

Icham of Irlaunde
Ant of the holy londe of irlonde
Gode sir pray ich ye
for of saynte charite,
come ant daunce wyt me,
in irlaunde.

Alas! How should I sing?
Yloren is my playing.
How should I with that old man
To leven, and leave my leman,
Sweetest of all thing?

LAURENCE WHYTE

Eighteenth-century Dublin was a show-place, in a number of senses of the term. The Viceroy and his court were obviously ostentatious presences. So were the townhouses of the Irish nobility. And, perhaps as a result, there was much greater interest in the performing arts. Theatres in Smock Alley, Crow Street and Aungier Street saw many noteworthy new plays and, particularly, players, not to mention packed audiences. Musical life was also thriving. Its high point was the première of Handel's Messiah, *in the Music Hall, Fishamble Street, in April 1742, with the composer conducting.*

The full title of Whyte's poem is A Dissertation on Italian and Irish Musick, With Some Panegyrick on Carrallan Our Late Irish Orpheus. Intriguingly, many of the landed gentry were patrons of indigenous music and musicians. The most famous case in point is that of Turlough Carolan (1670–1738), a blind, itinerant harper, whose compositions reveal a fascinating interplay between traditional and contemporary musical idioms.

Recitativo

Some *Solo's* Songs, and merry Lays,
These are which will for ever please,
When well perform'd or sung with Art,
With graces proper for each Part.
Some old ones we have oft reviv'd,
For modern Opera's contriv'd,
Instead of those *Italian* Airs,
So much in Vogue for many Years;
Poor *Ireland*, like *old England* doats
On Multiplicity of Notes,
And with few *Words* she can dispense,
Sometimes with little or no Sense,
And those spun out so very long,
A *Word* or two wou'd make a *Song*,
Thro' various *Bars* they rise and fall;
They might as well have none at all;
But to begin with ha, ha, ha,
And to conclude with fa, la, la,
The Words are vanish'd quite away,
Whilst they in such Meanders stray,
Or swell'd so high, so long and loud,
They burst like Thunder from a Cloud,
That from *Olympus* down is cast,
And at the Bottom breath their last.
    A *Word's* sufficient to the wise,
But *Words* exotick bear the Prize,
Whatever has a *Foreign* tone,
We like much better than our own,
'Tis often said, *few Words are best*,
To trace their meaning is a Jest,
And such as cannot well be scan'd,
What need have we to understand.

'Tis well the *Vulgar* now of late,
Can relish *Sounds* articulate,
There's scarce a *Forthman*[1] or *Fingallion*,[2]
But sings or whistles in *Italian*,
Instead of good old *Barley Mow*,[3]
With *Tamo tanto*[4] drive the Plow,
They o'er their Cups can sing, *Si caro*,[5]
And dare prophane it at the *Harrow*,
There's *Ariadne* cross'd the *Shannon*,
She sings in *Gallaway*, *Tuam*, and *Mannin*,
And in her Progress to and fro,
Expels a sweeter Song, *Speak Shoy*,[6]
She travels down to *Portaferry*,
To *Omy* and to *London-derry*,
Where People hears her with more Pleasure,
Than highland *Lilt*, or *Scottish Measure*,
She, of the *Truagh*,[7] has taken place,
And *Meu Vin Yall*,[8] of Irish Race.

    She flies to *Munster* for the Air,
To clear her pipes and warble there,
Poor *Cronaan*,[9] being turn'd out of Play,
With *Rinke Mueenagh*[10] flew away,
To the remotest part of *Kerry*,
He hopes to make the Vulgar merry,
But scarce one Cabbin in their Flight,
You'd give them Lodging for a Night,
So taken up with foreign Jingle,
Tralee despis'd them, likewise *Dingle*.

    But *Drimin duh*[11] is still in favour,
Once we from *Murphy*, beg, and crave her,
Of him alone we must require
To do her Justice on the Lyre,
She, and old *Eveleen a Rune*,
Are by the *Muses* kept in Tune,
Who many Centuries have thriv'd,
And doom'd by fate to be long liv'd,
With many others we know well,
Which do in harmony excel.
Dub — g improves them in our Days,
And never from the subject strays,
Nor by Extravagance perplext,
Will let them wander from the text.

Mac — n,[12] on the *Coal Black Joke*,
(To his great Credit be it spoke)
Has multiply'd upon that Strain,
To shew his vast extensive Vein.
　　Sweet *Bocchi*[13] thought it worth his while,
In doing honour to our *Isle*,
To build on *Carallan's*[14] Foundation,
Which he perform'd to Admiration,
On his Pheraca's[15] went to work,
With long Divisions on *O Rowrk*.[16]
　　A *Dean* the greatest Judge of Wit,
That ever wrote amongst us yet,
Gave us a Version of the Song,
Verbatim from the *Irish* Tongue.
　　Ta me ma choll,[17] and *Candun dilish*,[18]
For Ages have preserv'd their Relish,
Together with *Da mihi Manum*,[19]
Which we may reckon an *Arcanum*,
With all the *Planksty's*[20] and *Plenacca's*,
By *Carallan* in his Sonata's,
The greatest *Genius* in his way,
An *Orpheus*, who cou'd sing and play,
So great a *Bard* where can we find,
Like him illiterate, and blind.

1.　A man from Forth, a barony in the south-east of County Wexford, which was settled in the wake of the Norman invasion of 1169 by a mixture of Normans, Flemings, Welsh and English. Various forms of twelfth-century English, which survived until recently in Forth and the adjoining barony of Bargy, are now referred to as the dialect of Forth and Bargy.

2.　A man from Fingal, 'the land of the Norsemen, or foreigner', an area of very early settlement to the north of Dublin, where the dialect which survived until recently was similar to the dialect of Forth and Bargy. The term 'Fingallian' came to be used of the inhabitants of the Pale, the area of settlement extending from Dublin (Russell K. Alspach).

3.　An English folk song.

4.　Possibly an Italian aria.

5.　An Italian aria.

6.　In modern Irish 'Spéic Seoigheach', an Irish tune whose title is obscure and which has been variously translated as 'Joices' Tune', 'The Joyces' Cry' and 'The Humours of Joyces' Country'.

7.　A tune with the title 'Ye Trugh' appeared in John and William Neal's *A Collection of the Most Celebrated Irish Tunes* (1724). In modern Irish this title is 'An Triúch', 'a word denoting a cantred or district. Truagh is the most northerly barony of County

Monaghan, and the words of a poem in its praise to this tune survive' (Nicholas Carolan).

8. The title of an Irish tune; its meaning is obscure.

9. In modern Irish *crónán*, a word denoting humming or crooning, and therefore a song of that type.

10. In modern Irish 'Rince Muimhneach', a Munster dance.

11. In modern Irish 'Druimin dubh' (Black Cow), an ancient tune whose author and date are unknown. It is a lament for a drowned cow.

12. Possibly Aodh Mac Gabhráin or Hugh MacGauran, the Irish poet of the early eighteenth century who wrote the poem 'Pléaráca na Ruarcach', which Swift rendered as 'The Description of an *Irish-Feast*', and which inspired Turlogh Carolan, MacGauran's close friend, to compose the air 'The O'Rourke's Feast'.

13. Lorenzo Bocchi, the Italian musician, who was known in Dublin by 1724, when John and William Neal gave him special prominence on the title page of their *Collection of the Most Celebrated Irish Tunes*.

14. Carolan, who is also 'Carrollan', 'Carrallan' and 'Signor Carrollini' in the Neals' *Collection*.

15. The modern Irish 'Pheraca' is 'Pléaráca', a word of disputed meaning that has been derived from 'play-raking' and which here means tunes of revelry.

16. The central piece of the Neals' *Collection* was Bocchi's 'Plea Rarkeh na Rourkough or ye Irish weding improved with diferent divitions after ye Italian maner with A bass and Chorus'. In modern Irish 'Pléaráca na Ruarcach' means 'The revels of the O'Rourkes'. 'The English title here seems to arise from a misunderstanding of the subject. The simple unfigured bass may be for Bocchi's instrument, the cello, the instrumental chorus probably for violins' (Carolan).

17. The Neals' *Collection* included 'Ta me ma Chulla's na doushe me', which in modern Irish is 'Tá mé i mo chodladh is ná dúisigh mé' (I am asleep and don't waken me). 'The composer is unknown, but the tune here is probably a song air, and several later texts are found to versions of it' (Carolan).

18. The Neals' *Collection* included 'Can duh Dilish', which in modern Irish is 'Ceann dubh dílis' (Dear dark head). 'The composer is unknown, but the tune was evidently popular earlier in the century.' The version in the Neals' *Collection* 'is the air of a love song'. (Carolan).

19. Latin for 'Give me your hand'. The Neals' *Collection* included this tune, which is said to have been composed by Ruairí Dall Ó Catháin (Blind Rory O'Cahan or O'Kane) and which was probably written in the early seventeenth century. Ó Catháin wrote the tune for a Lady Eglinton in Scotland after she had apologised to him for not according him the status that he considered was his due (Carolan).

20. Celebratory tunes and lively instrumental airs. A planksty is not necessarily a dance.

from *Field Day Anthology of Irish Writing* (1991)

CHEVALIER DE LA TOCNAYE

There are two Rotundas, though only one of them is round. They stand side by side in Dublin's Parnell Square. The one that is not round is a maternity hospital. It was the brainchild of Dr Bartholomew Mosse (1712–59). He had already made a name for himself by opening the first maternity hospital in the British Isles in Dublin in 1745. Built to a design of Richard Cassels, the new hospital was opened in 1757.

Mosse's plan was that the hospital be supported by the public. The land behind it was laid out as a garden and there were various amenities in it to attract fashionable Dublin. The round Rotunda is an assembly room — 'the finest room in Ireland', according to Sir Jonah Barrington — and was one of these amenities. It opened in 1764, and its original design was improved by the celebrated architect James Gandon in the 1780s. Among the noteworthy events to have taken place here was the Volunteer Convention of 1783.

Dublin Promenades

They have devised in Dublin a rather singular form of entertainment, the proceeds of which are applied to the maintenance of a Maternity Hospital. It is called a Promenade, and the name made me wish to go and see one. The visitors walk in a circular hall called the Rotunda, and while there is somewhat more freedom than that which obtains at private entertainments, people only mix with, and speak to, members of their own circle. After a certain time a bell sounded, and the company hurried through a door just opened, and groups of friends settled round tea-tables. My society consisted of myself, and being unable to join any party I had opportunity to scan the various groups: everywhere there reigned a kind of quiet enjoyment which gave me much more pleasure than I had expected to find. The good mammas were not very numerous, and those who were present appeared to be absent-minded. The young folk, on the other hand, were very numerous and making good use of their time — I think, perhaps, the Promenade attained its object along more lines than one. The cash result is nearly all the hospital has to depend on for maintenance; balls are given sometimes, and for these the hall seems to be better suited than for Promenades.

from *A Frenchman's Walk Through Ireland* (1797)

CHEVALIER DE LA TOCNAYE

As all the world knows, Dublin is the home of Guinness's brewery and Jameson's and Power's distilleries. Arthur Guinness began brewing in 1759. Jameson's dates from 1780, and Power's from 1791. There seems to be a good chance that their products are among those sampled by the belligerent toper depicted here. It need hardly be said that drinking in Dublin and every other part of Ireland did not begin when those firms came on stream.

The bibulous character of eighteenth-century Irish high society is also very well known. This was an age when a gentleman's social stature grew in direct proportion to the amount of claret he could hold. If you didn't drink you were nobody, even if your land and title said you were somebody. The surprise that the Chevalier registers in his opening sentence here is hardly less great than that of the modern reader.

Drinking in Dublin

They drink infinitely less in Dublin, and, indeed, all over Ireland, than I could have believed. Generally, in the principal houses, an hour, or perhaps only half an hour, after the ladies have quitted the dining-room, the master of the house pushes his glass to the middle of the table and rises. I am not going to deny that there are such things as drinking parties where one may get straightforwardly drunk; I have indeed seen a somewhat original example of the outcome of one of these. Returning home one evening I saw a tipsy, rather, I should say, a drunk, man elbow a passer-by, and the latter standing the shock stiffly, the reaction carried the drunkard off his feet. In a fury the incapable arose, seized the man he had jostled by the collar, demanding his name, tendered his own, and insisted on fighting. The assaulted refused, and answered the challenger very coldly. 'I see you're not the man to fight like a gentleman,' said the aggressor. 'Well, I'll box you for sixpence.' The other appeared to consent, and then, as one must strip to box, the tipsy man let go his hold of the collar of his adversary, and the latter immediately slipped through the crowd and disappeared. When the warrior had stripped, he looked for his antagonist, and not finding him he began to swear and shout, 'Where is the lousy rascal? Where is the lousy rascal?' and he went through the crowd asking, 'Are you the lousy rascal?' Having exhausted his rage — no one deemed it his duty to answer such a discourteous question — he looked for his clothes and found the shirt had disappeared. For boxing in earnest to be in order bets must be deposited, otherwise the vanquisher must accept responsibility for consequences. But if a bet has been made, you may with safety, and with an easy conscience, punch out the eye or break the jaw of your opponent.

from *A Frenchman's Walk Through Ireland* (1797)

DAIBHÍ Ó BRUADAIR

In a letter of 1917, Stephens wrote: 'There is a man named O'Bruadair who lived and sang and was very hungry and exceedingly thirsty in the time of Cromwell, Crumwell as we call him and with whose name we inevitably link the worst of our curses. But O'Bruadair is gorgeous, a very learned man and a very poor one, a man who was devout and thirsty in equal and terrific extreme. I have never met such an avalanche of eloquence, poetry and rage under the one skin.'

The poem is also a reminder of the peculiar power of public speech in all forms which Irish poets traditionally believed was vested in them.

A Glass of Beer

The lanky hank of a she in the inn over there
Nearly killed me for asking the loan of a glass of beer:
May the devil grip the whey-faced slut by the hair,
And beat bad manners out of her skin for a year.

That parboiled imp, with the hardest jaw you will see
On virtue's path, and a voice that would rasp the dead,
Came roaring and raging the minute she looked at me,
And threw me out of the house on the back of my head!

If I asked her master he'd give me a cask a day;
But she, with the beer at hand, not a gill would arrange!
May she marry a ghost and bear him a kitten, and may
The High King of Glory permit her to get the mange.

translated by James Stephens, from *Collected Poems* (2nd edn, 1954)

PETER SOMERVILLE-LARGE

'Although Irish people as a whole are considered unconventional, it is the Anglo-Irish who generally make the records for eccentricity', writes the author in his book, Irish Eccentrics. There is a view of the Irish landed gentry which sees them as whimsical and vaguely seedy laws unto themselves. Where and how they lived either made the standards of their class irrelevant, creating a sense of 'anything goes', or were adhered to with such rigidity that nothing went. In either case, it is thought that theirs is the story of the class that imploded. Of course many individual members of the gentry made

sizeable contributions to Irish public life and to the British empire. Those of their homes that remain, the Big Houses of Ireland, are architectural and historical sites of great importance. Their preservation has frequently caused controversy.

The admiral is Boyle Somerville, brother of the novelist Edith Somerville; the IRA shot him to death in 1936 at his home in County Cork. Wapiti are large North American deer. Estates often featured deer parks.

The Anglo-Irish

S ome big houses had more exotic pets, like Lord Gormanston's eagle or George Robert Fitzgerald's bear or those belonging to Mary Hamilton's neighbour in Co. Meath — half a dozen old deer, a fox kept in a dog box on the lawn, a zebra called Stripes which kicked the spring cart to pieces when they tried to make him pull it. There was also a large brown bear whose skin was made into a covering for an ottoman after it died. Bears were a popular exotic; Lord Caledon kept small black bears from Canada as well as a herd of wapiti, a change from the deer park.

Somerville and Ross were hard on their own kind. *The Real Charlotte* is an examination of the nuances of Protestant class structures. Their letters reveal similar degrees of snobbery. They looked down on my family at Newcourt, deriding old Mrs Fleming's accent; she said 'pairfectly' and 'pork' instead of 'Park' — hence 'Pork cottage'; she pronounced girl 'gay-erl' and talked of 'gay-erlies'. In that society it made no difference that the Flemings lived in a house as big as Drishane. Probably it did not help that Newcourt was full of girls.

Accents were ephemeral. Anita Leslie recalled meeting the six spinster Ladies Lowry-Corry, all born after 1861, who 'talked with a curious hissing intake of breath . . . and my grandmother told me that was how genteel people talked in early Victorian times'.

In *The Rising Tide*, published in 1937, Molly Keane has a couple of old ladies talking 'like so many Irish ladies of their generation with rather plummy brogues which, however, detracted nothing from the brisk and distinguished pronunciation of each word'. Anything but the brogue.

Opposition to Edith Somerville's writing came from her mother, undoubtedly for social reasons; writing was not a ladylike occupation, nor did it find a place in a society that had little regard for reading. Molly Keane encountered a similar prejudice when she chose a publican's pseudonym for her books. Autobiography did not arouse similar misgivings; soon scores of literate big-house exiles would recall times past and things gone.

Much of the plot of *The Real Charlotte* turns on the *de haut en bas* attitude of the Dysarts towards the socially inferior Francie Fitzpatrick. When Francie comes to visit Bruff, Somerville and Ross describe with relish the ceremony of a summer's day at the big house. Long hours are spent cutting out clothes for charity and gardening interspersed by very formal meals — luncheon, the full tea with cream poured from a brilliant silver jug, and dinner. The painful Victorian evening concludes 'in the dim pink light' of the 'shaded' drawing room with photograph albums examined and Grieg played on the piano to signal what a civilised lot the Dysarts are.

At Bruff, dinner, served to two female house guests, consists of eight courses. The men would have worn evening clothes, a custom that continued as long as the big house lasted. Lionel Fleming got into trouble for insensitivity when he observed how Admiral Somerville, dining with his sister on the evening he was shot, wore a dinner jacket; that was in 1936. Every evening, even when no guests were present, wine would be served. After dinner at Bruff the butler 'Gorman was regaling his fellows in the servants' hall with an account of how Miss Fitzpatrick had accepted every variety of wine he had offered her and taken only a mouthful of each, an eccentricity of which William was even now reaping the benefit in the pantry'. But Francie's behaviour would have been acceptable at other houses. Patricia Cockburn refers to an eighteenth-century Irish tradition still observed in the Arbuthnot household in the 1930s whereby the wine footmen kept filling up a diner's glass as he drank so that at the end of the meal the diner had four full glasses of wine beside him. This wine was the perquisite of the footman to drink or bottle and sell.

The Anglo-Irish adapted and exaggerated the full panoply of English Victorian custom. Maria La Touche, who had been brought up in Desart Court and then lived at Harristown, was critical of the long stuffy dinner parties with their solemn procession downstairs and endless steamed dishes with stilted conversation, 'all toil and trouble, ostentation, expense and discomfort'. But Mrs La Touche was eccentric enough to dislike the social round — the Dublin season with its viceregal balls from February to March, followed by a sojourn in London from May to July, when wealthy Irish families took their plate and their servants across the water. She was not even enthusiastic about dogs. 'No I won't have a little dog. Dogs interfere too much with one's personal freedom. They are inquisitive about one's daily plans and express their own wishes on every subject in a manner no one can stand from a Christian child.'

Life went on as before. There were the old summer pastimes like archery and cricket and new ones like tennis and even rounders. 'It is all the rage now,' Mrs La Touche wrote in 1888, 'and it amazes me to see British matrons racing round and round in a wet meadow, squires, barristers, Majors and lesser lights fling balls at them. Occasionally there are collisions and ladies of quality may be seen floundering on the grass with their shoes in the air. All this is accompanied by the wildest shrieks and yells.'

from *The Irish Country House* (1995)

MOLLY KEANE

The 'great big girl' telling the story is Iris Aroon St Charles of Temple Alice. The Major is her father, who is on his last legs, and so is the house. Richard, with whom Aroon rather impractically falls in love, is the son of an impossibly toplofty neighbour, Lady Grizel Massingham. The name of her house is Stoke Charity. Such names and places situate us in that absorbing, odd-ball, ruritanian milieu of the Irish Big House novel.

Aroon says at the outset, 'I like things to be right.' But as Good Behaviour *unfolds and Aroon embarks on her trawl through her early years, the unlovely conduct of everybody connected with the Temple Alice household, including Aroon, becomes plain to see. As in* Castle Rackrent *and many other Big House novels, moral delinquency and economic mismanagement go hand in hand. There is hardly a Big House novel that doesn't have decline for a theme. But Aroon can't see it. Her preoccupation with correctness and* comme il faut *reveals her as the biggest misfit of all.*

A Massive Statue

I leaned my bicycle against the wall of Mrs Harty's house. A winter jasmine grew at the door. Flowerless, only its tight, fish-shaped buds had survived the frost. As I knocked I could hear her lurching across the kitchen floor, and I shared her pause at the thick net curtains before she let me in. After my morning in the starved spaces of Temple Alice, Mrs Harty and her warm house pleased me as though she and her kitchen were a refuge and safety from wolves.

'Well, and how are you?' Mrs Harty took the box from me as if it were a Christmas present. 'And the Major, poor man? A little better . . . ah, please God.'

I stood with my back to the dirty blazing stove; the warmth of the room was sublime.

Mrs Harty put the parcel of my dresses down on top of a stuffed fox in his glass-fronted box. Fashion magazines cascaded past his improbable glass button eyes. It was a doll-like fox and I suppose it was company for her. So was the stuffed badger, curled and nailed on a board where she rested her club foot while the other worked the treadle of her magnificent Singer sewing-machine. Now, shaking out my dresses, she handled them preciously, pinching back their waists so that the skirts were blowing outwards, like those in an advertisement. I was glad to think that that was once how I must have looked to Richard.

Mrs Harty wore a stuffed satin heart hung on a corset lace. It swung, full of pins, between her breasts. I felt some connection between it and the sacred heart of Jesus flaming away in its holy picture, the constant small light burning below. Mrs Harty plucked pins out of hers and lurched about on her club foot, standing back to survey her work, or pouncing forward to remedy a fault. While the light shrank from her windows she swooped on me and round me with her scissors, and mumbled at me as she changed pins from her heart to her lips, and then to the seams of my dress; at last she staggered away. . . . I could feel her dissatisfaction, and through it my bulk loomed to me — a battleship through fog. 'The wholly all about it is,' she said, 'there's not enough of it in it.'

I could imagine the wedge-shaped gaps to be filled, and the strains that the pink chiffon would not take. I knew better than to look into the narrow slit of mirror. 'Do you know what we'll do — how would it work, I wonder, if we used our gold to drape our troubles?'

I demurred — then I agreed. Panels of gold lace swept from my hips to the ground, chiffon clouded my bosom.

'And a big rose in gold and pink — imagine — on one shoulder.' The rose was not there. She sketched it on the air, and pinned the air down my left bosom. I moistened my lips and nodded agreement. In the wintry light, between the fox, the badger, and the sacred heart of Jesus, I began to feel a storybook little-princess character taking me over — possessing me.

'Now. Look at yourself.' She turned me about like a child or a dummy to face my reflection. I spun willingly round on my Louis heels. I closed my eyes, I spread my hand like a fan across my chest. I decided how I should smile — I smiled. I opened my eyes, I pulled in my stomach, and I leaned a little forwards to my reflection. Gold lace fell in points and godets to the floor. Flesh and chiffon were indistinguishable in the sweetheart neckline. I caught my breath, and for a moment I was standing alone with the beautiful doll that was me.

Mrs Harty broke the silence. She too was looking enchantedly from me to my reflection. 'Well, Miss Aroon,' I could feel her searching for the absolute word, 'wouldn't you make a massive statue?'

Statue? I knew just what that meant. And I had been feeling so mignonne and cherished. I was Aroon again — a big girl, even a great big girl. She turned away from me. 'I'll have to light the lamp,' she said, 'till I see how do it fall.'

But how could I face the statue she saw? I had to get away before she said 'statue' again. I dragged my dress over my head. I struggled in the slippery darkness of the lining. I tore my way out. When she came back, carrying the lighted lamp, I was walloping round, a great half-naked creature, searching for my winter clothes.

What panic had taken me over? I wondered, pedaling home with the frost on my cheeks, and the wheels of my bicycle sailing effortlessly under my weight. Assurance re-enfolded me as I remembered that 'massive' was Mrs Harty's word for beautiful. A rose could have a massive scent. Six yards of cobweb lace a massive quality. Statue was all right too. A nymph in a glade, perhaps.

from *Good Behaviour* (1981)

ALICE TAYLOR

Once upon a time in rural Ireland, goose was the dish of choice for Christmas dinner, so much so that there was a traditional rhyme that began, 'Christmas is coming, and the goose is getting fat'. Equally traditional was the Christmas candle. A white candle was favoured in County Cork, where the author grew up. In other parts of the country, candles could be red, green or even pink, and in Dublin blue candles were preferred.

In purely chronological terms, it is hardly more than a generation ago that Alice Taylor's traditional Christmases were common. Recent changes in Irish society are such, however, that those Christmases seem much further off, an impression reinforced by the noticeable presence of nostalgia in the current cultural air.

The Christmas Candle

With the goose out of the way, my mother turned her attention to the Christmas candle. There was no argument involved here because this was my mother's domain and we all bowed to her right to do it her way, following her instructions without question. My father brought in the big yellow turnip with an odd purple bulge which he had lifted from the turnip pit and scrubbed in the water barrel on his way in. He put it, still dripping, on the deep window-sill and proceeded to scoop out a hole with his penknife. He fitted and refitted the big white two-pound Christmas candle until it was rock-solid in position, making sure that it couldn't be overturned by his noisy brood whom he always considered capable of burning him out of house and home. With the candle standing pale and upright in its yellow bed, my mother wrapped a red, pleated paper skirt around the turnip. We had made the skirt the night before with crêpe paper and straight pins and with much ripping and patching. Now my mother stuck the best of the red-berry holly into the turnip, where it curved upwards around the candle and fell out over the frilled skirt. The dark green holly and the bright red berries contrasted vividly with the tall white candle. Then she put holly all around the window-sill and shutters. We stood back, silenced by her serenity, and were impressed by the lovely effect she could achieve with the minimum of fuss.

Then she brought what she called her 'Christmas mottoes', brightly coloured, unframed pictures, and hung them in their usual places. One depicted a fat Santa with an overflowing bag of toys and she placed it above the new oilcloth over the fireplace; another, of Mary and Joseph and the donkey, she put on the wall beside the oil lamp. Finally she positioned a little battered cardboard crib under the tree, and now we were ready for Santa.

from *The Night Before Christmas* (1994)

JONATHAN SWIFT

Legend has it that this poem recounts a great feast given by the O'Rourke, one of the Ulster chieftains to take part in the Elizabethan wars in the late sixteenth century. But, as Harold Williams, editor of Swift's poems, points out, the poem's Irish original, Pléaraca na Ruarcach, dates from the early eighteenth century. Williams says that its author was Hugh MacGuaran, and that he gave Swift 'a literal translation' of the poem when Swift was 'staying at a country house near Cavan'. This is a part of the country that Swift is known to have visited. It is also the country of Breffni O'Rourke.

The original poem contains ninety-six lines, of which Swift translated sixty-seven, up to line 72. There is a translation of the final twenty-four lines of the poem by Sir Walter Scott in his edition of Swift's works.

O'Rourk's Noble Fare

Translated in the year 1720

O Rourk's noble fare
   Will ne'er be forgot,
By those who were there,
   Or those who were not.
His revels to keep,
   We sup and we dine,
On seven score sheep,
   Fat bullocks and swine.
Usquebagh[1] to our feast
   In pails was brought up,
An hundred at least,
   And a madder[2] our cup.
O there is the sport,
   We rise with the light,
In disorderly sort,
   From snoring all night.
O how was I trick'd,
   My pipe it was broke,
My pocket was pick'd,
   I lost my new cloak.
I'm rifled, quoth Nell,
   Of mantle and kercher,
Why then fare them well,
   The De'il take the searcher.
Come, harper, strike up,

But first by your favour,
   Boy, give us a cup;
Ay, this has some savour:
   O Rourk's jolly boys
Ne'er dreamt of the matter,
   Till rous'd by the noise,
And musical clatter,
   They bounce from their nest,
No longer will tarry,
   They rise ready dressed,
Without one *Ave Mary*.
   They dance in a round,
Cutting capers and ramping,
   A mercy the ground
Did not burst with their stamping.
   The floor is all wet
With leaps and with jumps,
   While the water and sweat,
Splish, splash in their pumps.
   Bless you late and early,
Laughlin O Enagin,
   By my hand, you dance rarely,
Margery Grinagin.
   Bring straw for our bed,
Shake it down to the feet,

Then over us spread,
   The winnowing sheet.
To show, I don't flinch,
   Fill the bowl up again,
Then give us a pinch
   Of your sneezing; *a Yean*.[3]
Good Lord, what a sight,
   After all their good cheer,
For people to fight
   In the midst of their beer:
They rise from their feast,
   And hot are their brains,
A cubit at least
   The length of their skeans.[4]
What stabs and what cuts,
   What clatt'ring of sticks,
What strokes on the guts,
   What bastings and kicks!
With cudgels of oak,

Well harden'd in flame,
An hundred heads broke,
   An hundred struck lame.
You churl, I'll maintain
   My father built Lusk,
The castle of Slane,
   And Carrickdrumrusk:
The Earl of Kildare,
   And Moynalta, his brother,
As great as they are,
   I was nurs'd by their mother.
Ask that of old Madam,
   She'll tell you who's who,
As far up as Adam,
   She knows it is true,
Come down with that beam,
   If cudgels are scarce,
A blow on the weam,
   Or a kick on the arse.

1. whiskey

2. wooden vessel

3. (*recte: A bhean*) woman

4. (*recte: scian*) knives, or daggers

from Harold Williams (ed.), *The Poems of Jonathan Swift*
(2nd edn, 1958)

MYRTLE ALLEN

As a cookery school and restaurant, Ballymaloe in south-eastern County Cork is one of the Big Houses that have survived and prospered. Its recipes and reputation are among the factors that have initiated the notion of an Irish cuisine, based on the fresh, indigenous products of the country. Local cheesemakers, fisheries and vegetable-growers have greatly increased in number. Modern methods and a European market have stimulated exports. There is a greater range of places to eat out, and more people going to them.

Ballymaloe Brown Bread

When making this bread, remember that yeast is a living fungus. In order to grow, it requires warmth, moisture and nourishment. The growing process produces carbon dioxide which makes the bread rise. Hot water will kill yeast. Have the ingredients and equipment at blood heat. The yeast will rise on sugar or treacle. We use treacle. The dough rises more rapidly with 110 g/4 oz yeast than with only 55 g/2 oz. The flour we use is wholemeal, stone ground. Different flours produce breads of different textures. The amount of natural moisture in flour varies according to atmospheric conditions. The quantity of water should be altered accordingly. The dough should be just too wet to knead. In fact it does not require kneading. The main ingredients, wholemeal flour, treacle and yeast, are highly nutritious.

Mix flour with salt and warm it (in the cool oven of an Aga or Esse or in the electric or gas oven when starting to heat). Mix treacle with some of the water in a small bowl and crumble in the yeast. Put the bowl in a warm position such as the back of the cooker. Grease bread tins and put them to warm, also warm a clean tea-towel. Look to see if the yeast is rising. It will take 5 minutes approx. to do so and will have a frothy appearance on top. Stir it well and pour it with remaining water into the flour to make a wettish dough. Put the mixture into the greased, warmed tins and put the tins back in the same position as used previously to raise the yeast. Put the tea-towel over the tins. In 20 minutes approx. the loaves will have risen by twice their original size. Now bake them in a hot oven, 230°C/470°F/Regulo 8, for 45–50 minutes or until they look nicely browned and sound hollow when tapped. Dried yeast may be used instead of baker's yeast. Follow the same method but use only half the weight as given for fresh yeast. Allow longer to rise.

This is our version of 'The Grant Loaf' (Doris Grant, *Our Daily Bread*, Faber and Faber). American measures as given by James Beard.

For four loaves
(13 cm x 20 cm/5 in x 8 in approx.)
1½ kg/3½ lb wholemeal flour
1¼ litres/2¼ pints water at blood heat
1 tablesp. salt
1–2 well-rounded teasp. black treacle
2–4 oz yeast

For one loaf
(13 cm x 20 cm/5 in x 8 in approx.)
450 g/1 lb wholemeal flour
350 ml/12 oz water at blood heat

1 teasp. black treacle
2 teasp. salt
30 g/1 oz yeast

For one loaf (American measures)
(13 cm x 20 cm/5 in x 8 in approx.)
3¾ cups whole wheat flour
1½ cups (or more) warm water
1½ packages granular yeast
2 tablesp. molasses
salt

from *The Ballymaloe Cookbook* (1984)

MRS DELANY

John Boyle (1707–62), fifth Earl of Orrery, was a descendant of the Earls of Cork. He became fifth Earl in 1753. Caledon became his property through his second wife, Margaret Hamilton. Caledon House, Co. Tyrone, one of the most impressive houses in Northern Ireland, was built in 1779. Lord Orrery's claim to fame is his book, Remarks on Swift *(1751), which did not speak all that well of his lordship's recently deceased friend. Mrs Delany's husband, Patrick, took exception to this work in his* Observations upon Lord Orrery's Remarks on the Life and Writings of Dr Jonathan Swift *(1754). The noted World War II commander Field Marshal Viscount Alexander of Tunis was born at Caledon House in 1891.*

As in England, the eighteenth century saw great interest in gardening, though kitchen garden, orchard and 'physick garden' existed in Elizabethan times. A physick garden was where medicinal herbs were grown.

Caledon House

U pon inquiry we found it would not be greatly out of our way to return back by my Lord Orrery's so we chose to make him a visit and return back to this place, which we did. We went on Friday, and got there by one. Lord Orrery is *more agreeable* than he used to be; he has laid aside the ceremonious stiffness that was a great disadvantage to him. He is very well-bred and entertaining; his lady (whose fortune is near 3000 pounds a year) is very plain in her person and manner, but to make amends for that she is very sensible, unaffected, good-humoured and obliging. I spent the day very pleasantly; it is a fine place by nature, and they are both fond of the country; *she delights in farming* and *he in building and gardening* and he has very good taste.

They have a lodge about a mile from their house, where they spend most of their time; it has all the advantages of water, wood and diversified grounds; and there the new house is to be built. Nothing is completed yet but an *hermitage* which is about an acre of ground, an island, planted with all the variety of trees, shrubs and flowers that will grow in this country, abundance of little winding walks, differently embellished with little seats and banks: in the midst is placed an hermit's cell, made of the roots of trees, the floor is paved with pebbles, there is a couch made of matting and little wooden stools, a table with a manuscript on it, a pair of spectacles, a leathern bottle: and hung up in different parts, an hourglass, a weather glass and several mathematical instruments, a shelf of books, another of wooden platters and bowls, another of earthen ones, in short everything that you might imagine necessary for a recluse. *Four little gardens surround his house* — an orchard, a flower-garden, a physick garden and a kitchen garden with a kitchen to boil a teakettle or so: I never saw so pretty *a whim* so *thoroughly well* executed.

from Angelique Day (ed.), *Letters from Georgian Ireland: The Correspondence of Mary Delany 1731–68* (1992)

FRANCIS LEDWIDGE

Francis Ledwidge was a County Meath road-mender. Through the good offices of AE — George Russell — one of the leading lights in the Irish Literary Revival, Ledwidge was introduced to the author Lord Dunsany, who lived near the poet's native Slane and from whom he received encouragement and assistance. Dunsany assessed his protégé as follows: 'Of pure poetry there are two kinds, that which mirrors the beauty of the world in which our bodies are, and that which builds the more mysterious kingdoms where geography ends and fairyland begins . . . Mr Ledwidge gives us the first kind.' His lordship's work was of the second. Ledwidge joined the Royal Inniskilling Fusiliers at the beginning of World War I. He was killed at the Battle of Ypres in 1917 when a road-building party he was in was hit by a shell.

St Elmo's fire is superstitiously associated with bad weather. The name Noah comes from the Hebrew for 'to rest'. After the Flood, Noah 'planted a vineyard. And he drank of the wine and was drunken. . . .' And what happened then is recorded in chapter 9 of the Book of Genesis.

June

Broom out the floor now, lay the fender by,
And plant this bee-sucked bough of woodbine there,
And let the window down. The butterfly
Floats in upon the sunbeam, and the fair
Tanned face of June, the nomad gipsy, laughs
Above her widespread wares, the while she tells
The farmers' fortunes in the fields, and quaffs
The water from the spider-peopled wells.

The hedges are all drowned in green grass seas,
And bobbing poppies flare like Elmo's light,
While siren-like the pollen-stainéd bees
Drone in the clover depths. And up the height
The cuckoo's voice is hoarse and broke with joy.
And on the lowland crops the crows make raid,
Nor fear the clappers of the farmer's boy,
Who sleeps, like drunken Noah, in the shade.

And loop this red rose in that hazel ring
That snares your little ear, for June is short
And we must joy in it and dance and sing,
And from her bounty draw her rosy worth.
Ay! soon the swallows will be flying south,
The wind wheel north to gather in the snow,
Even the roses spilt on youth's red mouth
Will soon blow down the road all roses go.

from Alice Curtayne (ed.), *The Complete Poems of Francis Ledwidge* (1974)

BRIAN MERRIMAN

Bawdy, bouncy, brazen, there is nothing quite like The Midnight Court *in Irish literature. Written towards the end of the eighteenth century, it remains as fresh now as it was then, not only because of its jaunty metre but because of the way it portrays sexual politics. And not only does* The Midnight Court *strike an earthy note in Irish poetry — a note not often heard in seventeenth- and eighteenth-century poetry of loss and lamentation — it does so by playing with the conventions of the 'aisling', or dream poem, in which loss is often sublimated in a vision of Ireland as a 'spéirbhean' (literally* a 'sky-woman'). At the end of the poem, Aoibheall decrees that bachelors aged twenty-one and older are to be tied to a tree in the local graveyard and soundly whipped, while impotent husbands should assist in procuring young lovers for their lusty wives.

In view of what Seamus Heaney has called 'the poem's overall drive to celebrate the creaturely over the ethereal in human beings', The Midnight Court proved controversial in modern Ireland when made widely available through translation. Frank O'Connor's 1945 version was banned by the Censorship Board.

The poem opens on the shore of Lough Graney in eastern County Clare, the writer Edna O'Brien's home ground.

from *The Midnight Court*

The poet goes for a walk on a summer morning. After a while he falls asleep and a vision of a 'spéirbhean' comes to him. She obliges him to attend a court presided over by women.

> Beside the water I often walk
> Through fields where the dew is as thick as chalk;
> With the woods and the mountains just in sight
> I hang around for the dawn to light.
> Loch Gréine lifts my soul with joy —
> Such land! Such country! What a sky!
> How silently the mountains rest
> Their heads upon each other's breast.
>
> Brief was my rest when, it appeared,
> With shocks and shakes the mountains reared,
> The north was numbed with thunder-crash,
> The waves were laced with lightning-flash;
> Whatever look I chanced to take
> I saw, approaching by the lake,
> A hellish, hairy, haggard hank,
> Bearded, bony, long and lank;
> Her height I'd estimate for sure
> At twenty feet, and maybe more,
> For yards behind she dragged her coat
> Through all the muck and mire and mud;
> It took some nerve merely to glance
> Upon that ghoulish countenance
> For with her ghastly, toothless grin
> She'd frighten the life out of anyone.
> To top it all, in a mighty paw
> Was the biggest staff I ever saw,

And in letters of brass the information
That she had a bailiff's qualification.

Then, with a gruff and angry shout,
'Get up,' she snarled, 'you lazy lout!
A nice, bloody thing: you're stretched in state
While the Court's convened and thousands wait.
And this is no court where the law is bent
Like the courts of graft that you frequent,
But one that is run by the pure in heart
Where Virtue, Justice, Right take part.'

A young woman speaks before the court. She complains that the young men are unwilling to marry.

'The reason I'm senseless and almost insane,
The thing that has taken and torn me in twain
And has pricked me with pangs and has plagued me with pain —
Is the number of women, old and young,
For whom no wedding bells have rung,
Who become in time mere hags and crones
Without man or money to warm their bones.
Thousands will back my evidence,
And I speak, alas, from experience;
Like me, I can swear, there's many another
Aching to be a wife and mother,
But the way we're ignored you'd think we're wrecks
Possessed of gender but not of sex;
At night with longing I'm lacerated,
Alone in bed I lie frustrated
And damned with dreams of desire denied
My hunger goes unsatisfied.
O Aeval, you must find a way
To save our women without delay,
For if the men are allowed to shirk
We'll have to force them to do their work.
By the time they're ready to take a wife
They're not worth taking to save their life,
They're stiff and shrunken and worn and weak
And when they mount you they wheeze and creak.
Then if, by chance, some lusty beau
Whose beard has hardly begun to grow
Decides to marry, whom does he wed —

Not a girl who is finely-bred,
With fawn-like figure and fetching face,
Who knows how to carry herself with grace,
But a wicked witch or a female Scrooge
Who gathered her dowry by subterfuge!'

Aoibheall, queen of the fairies, gives judgement and the poet, as a bachelor, is sentenced to be the first male to receive punishment. The 'spéirbhean' or bailiff arrives to administer it but the poet wakes up just in time.

'Now, my hearties, be prepared,
No endeavour must be spared;
Recall the times when we were spurned,
But here, at last, the worm has turned.
All hands now! Help! Hold down the pup!
Run, Una! Rope him! Tie him up!
Push Anne! You can do better surely!
Mary, tie his hands securely!
Sheila, Sal, don't stand and stare,
Hurry now and do your share,
You heard his punishment announced
So see he's well and truly trounced,
Lay into him each time you hit,
His bottom's broad enough for it;
Just keep on striking where he bends,
You'll soon reduce his fat, my friends,
Don't weaken, don't be faint of heart,
You're not to miss a single part.
Beat hard so that his screams and cries
Will freeze the other nancy-boys.
No better day than this could be,
It should go down in history,
So write it out, and don't forget
We may be all quite famous yet —'
She took her pen; I gave a moan;
Her threats had chilled me to the bone;
And as she scribbled in a book
And eyed me with a dreadful look,
I took a breath that was long and deep,
And opened my eyes — I had been asleep.

translated by David Marcus, from Sean McMahon and Jo O'Donoghue (eds.),
Taisce Duan: A Treasury of Irish Poems with Translations in English (1992)

ANONYMOUS

'*The consciousness of the warm sunny city outside his window and the tender tremors with which his father's voice festooned the strange sad happy air, drove all the mists of the night's ill humour from Stephen's brain' in James Joyce's* A Portrait of the Artist as a Young Man. *'Love is Teasing' is the song in question, and Stephen's father agrees with his son that, 'It's a pretty old air.' He sings the male version of it, with somewhat different words and the addition of one more verse.*

The thought in the final verse here of a young woman setting sail by herself for America is rather arresting and sheds an unusually personal and intimate light on emigration.

Love is Teasing

I wish, I wish, I wish in vain
I wish I was a maid again
But a maid again I ne'er will be
'Til cherries grow on an apple tree.

Ah love is teasing and love is pleasing
And love is a treasure when first it's new
But as love grows older and love grows colder
It fades away like the morning dew.

There is an ale house in the town
And 'tis there my love he sits him down
And he takes a strange girl on his knee
And he tells her things that he once told me.

Ah love and porter make young men older
And love and whiskey makes them old and grey
But what cannot be cured love must be endured love
And so I am bound for America.

EDNA O'BRIEN

'*I then hoofed off to another part of Scotland, said my work took me there, to a castle. My work was to restore pictures. Galling. To think that I could bring a cheek back to life, give it its due of paint or turpentine, rub life-likeness into it, make it seem to*

breathe again, to think that I could take a ravelled sleeve and make it whole again . . .
I find it bizarre. As he died the colour in his cheeks came and went like dye.' As the old
marching song goes: 'Darling, dear, you look so queer./Johnny, I hardly knew you.'

It is the eve of the opening of her trial for the murder of her lover, who also happens
to be her son's best friend, and Nora in her dark night of the soul relives her love and
loss.

I Brought It On Myself

So the castle was a stronghold where I could hide. It was built of stone, a pretty stone of soft pink, and a horse-shoe stairs led the way to the studded oak door. As I stepped into the entrance hall I felt that I had stepped into immunity. No one could dare follow me there, not even his ghost, since castles have their own ghosts, their own watchers. I was told 'Her Grace' was waiting in the Morning Room and passing through the inner hall, just scanning the ancestral portraits and the great dazzle of sword metal, I felt that I was resuming my former life. Work and etiquette would rescue me. Yet a peculiar thing happened. The handle of my teacup came away on my finger. I had not wrenched it, not wrested it. It simply adhered to me and I wore it like a ring, while my hostess first flinched and then most graciously laughed. We put it into a denture box so as to send it to the china menders and then she suggested that I take a rest. Perhaps she sensed my unease.

My bedroom was a bower. It faced the woods. Autumn, this self-same autumn was just beginning and so the pines and the spruces seemed more proudly green as the rest of the wood was a blur of red and bronze, that by degrees, as I pre-imagined, would become more of a red and more of a bronze until the whole landscape was drenched in those colours. There was a donkey outside. The very epitome of unedifying melancholy. It brayed. The lady-in-waiting warned me that the owls would snore at night. They might even scream I thought. Did anyone guess that I had come almost immediately from a deathbed. Outside a swarm of birds were preparing to leave. It was an amazement the way they wheeled and darted about, the way they assembled and scattered again as if they were testing their powers, their convening, and their might. The lady-in-waiting said they were heading for Africa. She had unpacked for me. I said that would be all. She did the brasses while inside I paced the room and tried doing little doodles to see if I would get away with it. Everything was an omen, for good or bad, the birds, their convening, the miserable donkey, the overhanging rocks and boulders that guarded the woodland path. I must walk there, I must risk being struck by a boulder. Suddenly I dragged on a trench coat and hurried out even though I knew the lady-in-waiting had run my bath.

In the woods, helped somewhat by the air, the drip of trees, and the peacefulness I resolved to ring the chemist's. Once I had rung the chemist everything would be better.

During dinner I got a bit pompous. I talked about the drapes, the furnishings, the different designs in fabrics; I talked about the pictures throughout the house and said how I was looking forward to my work to restoring their old lady, their Rembrandt, with the brown gnarled hands. I even told them about my previous job, about how I'd gone to Tuscany to restore a picture for a millionaire and how I had never seen him, I had only heard his peacocks cry. They said how amusing, what fun. The only thing that jolted me was any sudden sound. Any little thud or bell made me jump like a yo-yo. I thought that if I got through a month they would not find me.

Then I would remember where after years, even decades, how a particular murder was traced, and then whatever room I was in and its contents would swim and clatter before my eyes, and my heart would spring as if trying to get up my windpipe and out of my mouth. After dinner I rang the chemist and said that I'd given their name by mistake for getting tablets. They seemed to attach no importance to what I said. Then I rang my son and he said the remains had been sent down. I told him about the pictures, the duck we'd had for dinner, the size of my bath towel, all sorts of gibberish. I think he thought that I was distracted out of grief. It might have rested there but for that one mistake in ringing the chemist's. I believe it is a common lapse. I have heard of a criminal — not one in my class — just a petty thief, who checked into a country hotel and quickly incurred the suspicion of the manager by ordering exotic drinks, highballs and things. He was a labouring man and the madness of his taste brought suspicion to his bedroom door. You could say I brought it on myself.

from *Johnny I Hardly Knew You* (1977)

SAMUEL BECKETT

'I associate, rightly or wrongly, my marriage with the death of my father, in time. That other links exist, on other planes, between these two affairs, is not impossible. I have enough trouble as it is in trying to say what I think I know.' The opening words of First Love *introduce the reader to a nameless narrator for whom, as things turn out, love is as impossible to experience as death. The woman he marries is called Lulu, then later Anna, as if it makes a difference. They live off her street-walking, though our hero objects to the noise of the clients. Lulu becomes pregnant and disregards her husband's advice to 'Abort, abort.' Predictably, paternity proves to be too much. The father leaves as his child is born. Not that leaving accomplishes anything particularly, since he*

remains haunted by the infant's cries, just as earlier he could not rid himself of the siren sound of a woman singing.

One of the author's works in French, First Love was written in 1946. Beckett reluctantly published it in 1970.

No Bone to Pick with Graveyards

Personally I have no bone to pick with graveyards, I take the air there willingly, perhaps more willingly than elsewhere, when take the air I must. The smell of corpses, distinctly perceptible under those of grass and humus mingled, I do not find unpleasant, a trifle on the sweet side perhaps, a trifle heady, but how infinitely preferable to what the living emit, their feet, teeth, armpits, arses, sticky foreskins and frustrated ovules. And when my father's remains join in, however modestly, I can almost shed a tear. The living wash in vain, in vain perfume themselves, they stink. Yes, as a place for an outing, when out I must, leave me my graveyards and keep — you — to your public parks and beauty-spots. My sandwich, my banana, taste sweeter when I'm sitting on a tomb, and when the time comes to piss again, as it so often does, I have my pick. Or I wander, hands clasped behind my back, among the slabs, the flat, the leaning and the upright, culling the inscriptions. Of these I never weary, there are always three or four of such drollery that I have to hold on to the cross, or the stele, or the angel, so as not to fall.

from *First Love* (1970)

ANONYMOUS

Much has been written and said about the puritanical side of Irish life, its paralysing chastity, late marriages, and generally repressive air. While there is no denying that aspect of the country's social history, this little poem is a reminder that it is possible to exaggerate it. Pervasive as it may have been, it is not necessarily the whole story. Here is an almost modern voice so consumed by adulterous bliss that he implores his Lord and Saviour to help him acquire more of the same. It is very doubtful that what's being expressed here is all that exceptional or anomalous.

The poem is thought to date from the fifteenth or sixteenth century.

Keep Your Kiss To Yourself

Keep your kiss to yourself,
   young miss with the white teeth.
I can get no taste from it.
   Keep your mouth away from me.

I got a kiss more sweet than honey
   from a man's wife, for love,
and I'll get no taste from any kiss
   till doomsday, after that.

Until I see that same woman
   (grant it, gracious Son of God)
I'll love no woman young or old
   because her kiss is — what it is!

translated by Lord Longford, from Thomas Kinsella (ed.), *The New Oxford
Book of Irish Verse* (1986)

NUALA NÍ DHOMHNAILL

*Though not very audible at times, the voice of the love poet has made a distinctive
contribution to poetry in Irish. It comes in various shapes and sizes, among which is
the type of sensual hymn of which Nuala Ní Dhomhnaill has become a noted exponent
— not that her poetry is confined to any one type. These words in a woman's voice,
spoken for all to hear, are a new departure in writing in Ireland.*

*There is a place called Labasheeda in southern County Clare, on the Shannon
estuary; the name is Irish for 'silken bed'. Silk is a synonym for richness and
preciousness in Irish. One of Ireland's mythological names is 'the silk of the kine'.*

Labasheeda (The Silken Bed)

I'd make a bed for you
in Labysheedy
in the tall grass
under the wrestling trees
where your skin
would be silk upon silk

in the darkness
when the moths are coming down.

Skin which glistens
shining over your limbs
like milk being poured
from jugs at dinnertime;
your hair is a herd of goats
moving over rolling hills,
hills that have high cliffs
and two ravines.

And your damp lips
would be as sweet as sugar
at evening and we walking
by the riverside
with honeyed breezes
blowing over the Shannon
and the fuchsias bowing down to you
one by one.

The fuchsias bending low
their solemn heads in obeisance to the beauty
in front of them
I would pick a pair of flowers
as pendant earrings
to adorn you
like a bride in shining clothes.

O I'd made a bed for you
in Labasheeda,
in the twilight hour
with evening falling slow
and what a pleasure it would be
to have our limbs entwine
wrestling
while the moths are coming down.

from *Selected Poems* (1986), translated by Michael Hartnett

W.B. YEATS

When this poem was published in The Wind Among the Reeds *(1899), it was entitled 'Aedh wishes for the Cloths of Heaven', although the present title has been used in all subsequent selected and collected editions of Yeats's poems. Aedh, or Aodh, was one of the personages through whom Yeats wished his verse to speak in the book. As well as being the Irish equivalent of Hugh, it is also a word in Irish for 'fire'. Together, Aedh and the book's two other speakers, Michael Robartes and Red Hanrahan, were intended to represent, Yeats said, 'principles of mind', not 'actual personages'. Still, for all their mystique, the poems try to recapture, as the book's title suggests, the furtive and unnoticed eddies of nature, gusts of desire, tremors of anxiety. The volume also contains a poem entitled 'He wishes his Beloved were Dead'.*

The atmosphere of The Wind Among the Reeds *is, to some extent, redolent of the Celtic Twilight. However, while writing it, Yeats was heavily committed to matters mystical and the Order of the Golden Dawn. He was also suffering in his relationship with Maud Gonne, who shortly before the book's publication had again turned down his proposal of marriage.*

'In dreams begin responsibilities' is the epigraph to a later book of Yeats's poems, Responsibilities *(1914).*

He wishes for the Cloths of Heaven

Had I the heavens' embroidered cloths,
Enwrought with golden and silver light,
The blue and the dim and the dark cloths
Of night and light and the half-light,
I would spread the cloths under your feet:
But I, being poor, have only my dreams;
I have spread my dreams under your feet;
Tread softly because you tread on my dreams.

from *The Wind Among the Reeds* (1899)

ANONYMOUS

Writing about his own translations from the Irish, Frank O'Connor said that in them he could 'emphasise what it was that impressed me in the originals'. It is not too difficult to see the emphasis here on the inviolability of love and the persistence of a certain kind of emotional weather.

The poem is also an example of how complicated tradition can be. In 1981, An Duanaire: Poems of the Dispossessed, 1600–1900 was published. A collaboration between two distinguished literary figures, Seán Ó Tuama and Thomas Kinsella, this important book contains a less well-known alternative version of this poem which includes an extra verse beginning, 'Give my curse to your mother/and the same to your father' for having 'hindered our marriage'. There is also a note saying, 'This song is a standard international ballad type (The Unquiet Grave).' The note continues, 'There are very few standard ballads to be found in Irish.'

I Am Stretched On Your Grave

I am stretched on your grave
   And would lie there forever;
If your hands were in mine
   I'd be sure we'd not sever.
My apple tree, my brightness,
   'Tis time we were together
For I smell of the earth
   And am stained by the weather.

When my family thinks
   That I'm safe in my bed
From night until morning
   I am stretched at your head,
Calling out to the air
   With tears hot and wild
My grief for the girl
   That I loved as a child.

Do you remember
   The night we were lost
In the shade of the blackthorn
   And the chill of the frost?
Thanks be to Jesus
   We did what was right,
And your maidenhead still
   Is your pillar of light.

The priests and the friars
   Approach me in dread
Because I still love you
   My love and you dead,
And would still be your shelter
   From rain and from storm,
And with you in the cold grave
   I cannot sleep warm.

translated by Frank O'Connor, from *Kings, Lords & Commons* (1959)

SAMUEL BECKETT

Beckett's poems are the least well-known of his works. Still, his first important publication was a poem, 'Whoroscope'. He won a £10 prize for it in 1930, and most of his most notable verse was written in the ensuing decade. These are significant expressions of Beckett's troubled efforts to find himself artistically. And he resorted to verse intermittently throughout his career.

This poem was written in 1948. Stripped of colour and romance, Yeats's 'He wishes his Beloved were Dead' could look something like this. And in Beckett's major works, making an end of colour and romance beset his imagination. Within the Irish literary tradition Beckett may be seen as a fascinating — and fascinated — critic of Yeats.

[I would like my love to die]

I would like my love to die
and the rain to be falling on the graveyard
and on me walking the streets
mourning the first and last to love me

translated from the French by the author, from *Collected Poems in English and French* (1977)

GEOFFREY KEATING

Much less well known than his massive history of Ireland, or even than his poems, Keating's The Three Shafts of Death *— Trí Biorghaoithe an Bháis — is nevertheless a reminder of the extent of the author's education and learning. Drawing on such noted fathers of the church as Augustine, Jerome and Gregory, together with a large number of other minor theologians, Keating provides a series of elaborately structured meditations on death.*

The three kinds of death he identifies are corporeal death, spiritual death, and the death that is eternal suffering (the work contains a section on hell). As Osborn Bergin, the work's modern editor, said, however: 'Keating will be studied, not as a theologian . . . but as a writer of Irish.' There is no translation of The Three Shafts of Death *in its entirety.*

from *The Three Shafts of Death*

From this it is to be understood that we are only guests lodging in this life. And so I think it is for everyone before they leave this world just as it was for the wild ignorant outlaw[1] from west Munster who went in a warship on the sea, seeking booty. And they put in to land in England; and at the first town they came to, the people made a great fuss of them, bringing them to their houses and giving them hospitality; this was because the people who lived in that town were innkeepers. And the outlaw was surprised at his welcome, seeing that none of them knew him. Now the people of the household were very good to them, so that the outlaw was happy with the situation he was in; the house he was in was clean, the beds, food and drink were excellent. However, when he and his company were taking their leave, the innkeeper called in the accountant saying to him *make reckoning*[2] i.e. make up the bill. With that the accountant came and began to take from[3] the outlaw and his companions, so that they had to make full payment for everything they had had in the house while they were there, and they went away destitute. And because of that, their great grief because of their poverty was equal in proportion to their happiness and joy while they lived comfortably in the inn. The outlaw wondered why he and the others had been fleeced; because he had not been used to buying food and drink ever before that. When he arrived in Ireland, his friends began asking him to give an account of England. He began his tale and said that he never saw a land better for food and drink, material for heating and beds and with the pleasantest people. 'And I can discern no fault there, except when strangers are saying goodbye to those who have given them hospitality a boorish diabolic wretch comes; his name is Mac Raicín[4] and he manhandles strangers and attacks and fleeces them.'

1. *ceithearnach* = footsoldier, outlaw. Anglicised as *kern*.
2. These words are in English script in the text.
3. *feannadh* = flay; figuratively: criticise, take from, fleece.
4. In English this means 'make reckoning'.

translated by Alan Harrison, from *Field Day Anthology of Irish Writing* (1991)

JOHN BANVILLE

The narrator of The Book of Evidence *is Freddie Montgomery, who early on in the story drifts away from his promising career as a mathematician and becomes a ne'er-do-well. Living on a Mediterranean island, he gets mixed up with drug dealers. Money problems ensue. He returns to the family Big House in Ireland where he hopes his mother will meet his financial needs. She can not. The cost of keeping up the house has obliged her to sell the family paintings to a neighbour. Visiting this neighbour, Freddie falls for an anonymous seventeenth-century Dutch picture. But when he returns to steal it, a servant, Josie Bell, catches him in the act. This is who he takes with him and murders. Afterwards he jettisons the painting and hides out in Dublin until he is arrested.*

The novel takes the form of Freddie's prison journal, in which he acknowledges his numerous failings, including the inability to give due respect to the reality of Josie Bell. The Book of Evidence *won the 1989 GPA award.*

A Murder

I caught her wrist in an iron claw and, wrenching open the car door, fairly flung her into the back seat. Oh, why did she not run away! When I got behind the wheel, fumbling and snarling, I caught a whiff of something, a faint, sharp, metallic smell, like the smell of worn pennies. I could see her in the mirror, crouched behind me as in a deep glass box, braced between the door and the back of the seat, with her elbows stuck out and fingers splayed and her face thrust forward, like the cornered heroine in a melodrama. A fierce, choking gust of impatience surged up inside me. Impatience, yes, that was what I felt most strongly — that, and a grievous sense of embarrassment. I was mortified. I had never been so exposed in all my life. People were looking at me — she in the back seat, and the tourists up there jostling at the window, but also, it seemed, a host of others, of phantom spectators, who must have been, I suppose, an intimation of all that horde who would soon be crowding around me in fascination and horror. I started the engine. The gears shrieked. In my agitation I kept getting ahead of myself and having to go back and repeat the simplest actions. When I had got the car off the grass and on to the drive I let the clutch out too quickly, and the machine sprang forward in a series of bone-shaking lurches, the bonnet going up and down like the prow of a boat caught in a wash and the shock absorbers grunting. The watchers at the window must have been in fits by now. A bead of sweat ran down my cheek. The sun had made the steering-wheel almost too hot to hold, and there was a blinding glare on the windscreen. The maid was scrabbling at the door handle, I roared at her and she stopped at once, and looked at me wide-eyed, like a rebuked child. Outside the gate the bus driver was still sitting in the sun. When she saw him she tried to get the window open, but in vain, the mechanism must have been broken. She pounded on the glass with her fists. I spun the wheel and the car lumbered out into the road, the tyres squealing. We were shouting at each other now, like a married couple having a fight. She pummelled me on the shoulder, got a hand around in front of my face and tried to claw my eyes. Her thumb went up my nose, I thought she would tear off the nostril. The car was going all over the road. I trod with both feet on the brake pedal, and we sailed in a slow, dragging curve into the hedge. She fell back. I turned to her. I had the hammer in my hand. I looked at it, startled. The silence rose around us like water. Don't, she said. She was crouched as before, with her arms bent and her back pressed into the corner. I could not speak, I was filled with a kind of wonder. I had never felt another's presence so immediately and with such raw force. I saw her now, really saw her, for the first time, her mousey hair and bad skin, that bruised look around her eyes. She was quite ordinary, and yet, somehow, I don't know — somehow radiant. She cleared her throat and sat up, and detached a strand of hair that had caught at the corner of her mouth.

You must let me go, she said, or you will be in trouble.

It's not easy to wield a hammer in a motor car. When I struck her the first time I expected to feel the sharp, clean smack of steel on bone, but it was more like hitting clay, or hard putty. The word *fontanel* sprang into my mind. I thought one good bash would do it, but, as the autopsy would show, she had a remarkably strong skull — even in that, you see, she was unlucky. The first blow fell just at the hairline, above her left eye. There was not much blood, only a dark-red glistening dent with hair matted in it. She shuddered, but remained sitting upright, swaying a little, looking at me with eyes that would not focus properly. Perhaps I would have stopped then, if she had not suddenly launched herself at me across the back of the seat, flailing and screaming. I was dismayed. How could this be happening to me — it was all so *unfair*. Bitter tears of self-pity squeezed into my eyes. I pushed her away from me and swung the hammer in a wide, backhand sweep. The force of the blow flung her against the door, and her head struck the window, and a fine thread of blood ran out of her nostril and across her cheek. There was blood on the window, too, a fan-shaped spray of tiny drops. She closed her eyes and turned her face away from me, making a low, guttural noise at the back of her throat. She put a hand up to her head just as I was swinging at her again, and when the blow landed on her temple her fingers were in the way, and I heard one of them crack, and I winced, and almost apologised. Oh! she said, and suddenly, as if everything inside her had collapsed, she slithered down the seat on to the floor.

There was silence again, clear and startling. I got out of the car and stood a moment, breathing. I was dizzy. Something seemed to have happened to the sunlight, everywhere I looked there was an underwater gloom. I thought I had driven only a little way, and expected to see the gates of Whitewater, and the tour bus, and the driver running towards me, but to my astonishment the road in both directions was empty, and I had no idea where I was. On one side a hill rose steeply, and on the other I could see over the tops of pine trees to far-off, rolling downs. It all looked distinctly improbable. It was like a hastily painted backdrop, especially that smudged, shimmering distance, and the road winding innocently away. I found I was still clutching the hammer. With a grand sweep of my arm I flung it from me, and watched it as it flew, tumbling slowly end over end, in a long, thrilling arc, far, far out over the blue pine-tops. Then abruptly I bent forward and vomited up the glutinous remains of the breakfast I had consumed an age ago, in another life.

from *The Book of Evidence* (1989)

ANONYMOUS

Writer, teacher, soldier, Patrick Pearse's life and work are often thought to crystallise the idealising energy and impractical, though uplifting, heroics of the generation of 1916. Pearse's initial engagement with Irishness came through the Gaelic League and from inspirational visits to Aran and Connemara. Most of his stories and poems are set in the West of Ireland, a landscape that Pearse was not alone in viewing as a sanctuary of Gaeldom. Pearse's favourite writer in Irish, however, is reported to have been Geoffrey Keating. Pearse also gave Irish language classes, in one of which James Joyce was briefly a student, dropping out because of what he considered ideological narrowness.

This poem is one of a number of translations made by Pearse during his Gaelic League days. They appear in his Collected Works *under the heading 'Specimens from an Irish Anthology'. The image of the vulnerable little boy is one that recurs throughout Pearse's poetry and fiction.*

Although keening is generally associated with women, men were also known to do it.

A Father Keens His Drowned Child

Ochón, O Donough! my thousand whispers stretched under this sod,
The sod of sorrow on your little body, my utter anguish!
If this sleep were on you in Cill na Dromad, or some grave in the West,
'Twould soften my suffering, though great my hurt, and I would not repine
    for you!

Withered and wasted are the flowers they scattered on your narrow bed,
They were lovely for a little time, but their radiance is gone, they have no
    comeliness or life;
And the flower I held brightest of all that grew in soil or shall ever grow
Is rotting in the ground, and will spring no more to lift up my heart.

Alas, beloved! was it not a great pity, the water rocking you,
With no strength in your pulses nor anyone near you that might save:
No news was brought to me of the peril of my child or the extremity of his
    need —
Ah, though I'd gladly go to Hell's deep flag to rescue you!

The moon is dark, I cannot sleep, all joy has left me:
Rough and rude to me the open Gaelic ('tis an ill sign);
I hate a while in the company of friends, their merriment tortures me;
From the day I saw you dead on the sand, the sun has not shone for me.

Alas, my grief! what shall I do henceforth, the world wearing me,

Without your chalk-white little hand like a breath through trees on my
    sombre brow,
Your little mouth of honey like angels' music sweet in my ears
Saying to me gently, 'dear heart, poor father, be not troubled!'

translated by Patrick Pearse, from Collected Works (1917)

JOHN MILLINGTON SYNGE

The word 'keen' is from the Irish word 'caoin' — pronounced more like 'queen' — meaning 'to mourn, to lament'. The practice is among the more noted features of island life, one of the ways in which the natives seemed to be still connected with rites and rituals that had long become extinct on the mainland. From Synge's account here, it seems as if it is the neighbours who are doing the keening. It was also common for official — as it were, professional — keeners to be asked to funerals where, in addition to the 'profound ecstasy of grief', they extemporised poetry in praise of the deceased.

Although the keen's note of lamentation comes first and foremost, grief is not expressed with abandon. As Synge notices, rhythm is also a fundamental component. It intensifies the cries by making them seem repetitive, while at the same time rhythm contains the cries by making them appear ritualised. The artful structure of rhythm in the keen is one of the ways in which this ostensibly 'primitive' event can be appreciated as an organised, complex act of social witness.

Keening

After Mass this morning an old woman was buried. She lived in the cottage next mine, and more than once before noon I heard a faint echo of the keen. I did not go to the wake for fear my presence might jar upon the mourners, but all last evening I could hear the strokes of a hammer in the yard, where, in the middle of a little crowd of idlers, the next of kin laboured slowly at the coffin. To-day, before the hour for the funeral, poteen was served to a number of men who stood about upon the road, and a portion was brought to me in my room. Then the coffin was carried out, sewn loosely in sailcloth, and held near the ground by three cross-poles lashed upon the top. As we moved down to the low eastern portion of the island, nearly all the men, and all the oldest women, wearing petticoats over their heads, came out and joined in the procession.

While the grave was being opened the women sat down among the flat tombstones, bordered with a pale fringe of early bracken, and began the wild keen, or crying for the dead. Each old woman, as she took her turn in the leading recitative, seemed possessed for the moment with a profound ecstasy of grief, swaying to and fro, and bending her forehead to the stone before her, while she called out to the dead with a perpetually recurring chant of sobs.

All round the graveyard other wrinkled women, looking out from under the deep red petticoats that cloaked them, rocked themselves with the same rhythm, and intoned the inarticulate chant that is sustained by all as an accompaniment.

The morning had been beautifully fine, but as they lowered the coffin into the grave, thunder rumbled overhead and hailstones hissed among the bracken.

from *The Aran Islands* (1907)

St Columcille

St Patrick, St Brigid and St Columcille, or Columba, are the three patron saints of Ireland. Columcille's name means 'dove of the church', and he is the patron saint of Derry. The Irish name for the city — Doire Columcille — bears his name. 'Doire' means 'oak wood'; the saint founded a monastery in one around the middle of the sixth century.

Columcille is even more famously associated with the island of Iona, off the west coast of Scotland. This is where he spent the most illustrious part of his life, as a result either of being exiled or of imposing exile on himself after his involvement in a brief but violent challenge to the authorities regarding a copy of a psalter which he supposedly had made without permission. He founded a celebrated monastery on Iona. From here, he and his companions — twelve in number, as tradition has it — carried out prodigious feats of missionary work, establishing many monasteries in Scotland and the north of England. Among the various legends ascribed to him is one which makes his name synonymous with the heartbreak of exile. He is also said to have been a noted poet, a miracle-worker and a prophet.

The Sea-Blue Eye

There's a sea-blue eye that stares
At Ireland drawing away.

It will never look again
On the women of Ireland, or its men.

translated by Seán Dunne, from *An Introduction to Irish Poetry* (1991)

SHANE MacGOWAN

Shane MacGowan was the lead singer and songwriter for The Pogues, a group of Irish and English-of-Irish-extraction musicians formed in London in 1982. An eight-piece band — most unusual nowadays — their sound came basically from acoustic instruments such as banjo, flute and accordion, as befitted their folk-music material. Nevertheless, they made many listeners uncomfortable. Their sound and songs were generally ruder, more driven, and gave the impression of being more desperate than folk-music does. And Shane MacGowan's lyrics, while focusing on such standard folk-song themes as lost love, exile and drinking, did so in ways that sometimes emphasised the darkness lurking in those themes — alcoholism, homelessness and isolation — and sometimes frankly mocked them.

'Spanish wine', a staple of smugglers on the south-west coast of Ireland for generations, was also code for Spanish military assistance, so much so that it became pretty much a cliché, like other catch-phrases — 'Erin go bragh', for instance.

An interesting development in English popular music is the number of personalities of Irish ancestry who have come to the fore in it since the 1970s.

The Body of an American

The cadillac stood by the house
And the yanks they were within
And the tinker boys they hissed advice
'Hot wire her with a pin'
We turned and shook as we had a look
In the room where the dead man lay
So big Jim Dwyer made his last trip
To the home where his fathers laid

Fifteen minutes later
We had our first taste of whiskey
There was uncles giving lectures
On ancient Irish history
The men all started telling jokes
And the women they got frisky
At five o'clock in the evening
Every bastard there was pisskey

Fare thee well going away
There's nothing left to say
Farewell to New York City boys
To Boston and PA

He took them out
With a well-aimed clout
He was often heard to say
I'm a free born man of the USA

He fought the champ in Pittsburgh
And he slashed him to the ground
He took on Tiny Tartanella
And it only went one round
He never had no time for reds
For drink or dice or whores
And he never threw a fight
Unless the fight was right
So they sent him to the war

Fare thee well gone away
There's nothing left to say
With a slainte Joe and Erin go
My love's in Amerikay
The calling of the rosary
Spanish wine from far away
I'm a free born man of the USA

This morning on the harbour
When I said goodbye to you
I remember how I swore
That I'd come back to you one day
And as the sunset came to meet
The evening on a hill
I told you I'd always love you
I always did and I always will

Fare thee well gone away
There's nothing left to say
'cept to say adieu
To your eyes as blue
As the water in the bay
And to big Jim Dwyer
The man of wire
Who was often heard to say
I'm a free born man of the USA

from *Poguetry: The Lyrics of Shane MacGowan* (1989)

INDEX OF CONTRIBUTORS
AND ACKNOWLEDGMENTS

The numbers set in bold in square brackets represent page references for the author's work.

ALEXANDER, Mrs Cecil Frances, *née* Humphreys [336], was born in Dublin in 1818 and brought up in County Wicklow. Her *Hymns for Little Children* was published in 1848 and her *Poems* in 1896. She died in Derry in 1895.

ALLEN, Myrtle [409] was born in Cork in 1924 and was educated in England and Ireland. Ballymaloe House in County Cork, her restaurant and hotel, has an international reputation. She is the author of *The Ballymaloe Cookbook* (1977, 1984, 1987).

Extract from *The Ballymaloe Cookbook* by Myrtle Allen. Reproduced by permission of the publishers, Gill & Macmillan.

ALLINGHAM, William [182] was born in Ballyshannon, Co. Donegal in 1824. Before turning to literature, he served as a customs officer in various parts of Ireland and England. Settling in London, he became acquainted with many Victorian literary figures, as is recollected in his *Diary* (1907). His major work is a novel in verse, *Lawrence Bloomfield in Ireland* (1864). He died in London in 1889.

BANVILLE, John [426] was born in Wexford town in 1945 and educated locally. Widely considered to be the most original Irish novelist of his generation, his work reveals a distinctly European cast of mind. Among his novels are *Doctor Copernicus* (1976), *The Newton Letter* (1982), *The Book of Evidence* (1989) and *The Untouchable* (1997). He is literary editor of *The Irish Times*.

Extract from *The Book of Evidence* by John Banville. Reproduced by kind permission of the author.

BARKER, George [138] was born in Essex in 1913 and attended Regent Street Polytechnic, London. He wrote novels and plays, but his main works are the long poem, *The True Confessions of George Barker* (1950) and *Collected Poems* (1987). He died in Norfolk in 1991.

'Galway Bay' from *Selected Poems* by George Barker. Reproduced by kind permission of Faber and Faber.

BARRINGTON, Sir Jonah [112] was born in Abbeyleix, Co. Laois in 1760. A member of the Irish Parliament during the passage of the Act of Union, his subsequent career was largely devoted to writing, most notably the three-volume memoir, *Personal Sketches of His Own Time* (1827–32). He died in Versailles in 1834.

BECKETT, Samuel [419, 424] was born in Foxrock, Co. Dublin in 1906 and educated at Portora Royal School, Enniskillen and Trinity College Dublin. He settled in Paris in 1937, and was a member of the Resistance during World War II. A productive writer of prose and verse during the 1930s, his most famous works were written after World War II. Among these is the play *Waiting for Godot* (1948) and a trilogy of novels, *Molloy* (1951), *Malone Dies* (1951) and *The Unnameable* (1953). He was awarded the Nobel Prize for Literature in 1969. He died in Paris in 1989.

Extracts from *First Love* and *Collected Poems in English and French* by Samuel Beckett. Reproduced by kind permission of Calder Publications Ltd.

BEHAN, Brendan [48] was born in Dublin in 1923. Youthful membership of the IRA and subsequent imprisonment led to the autobiographical *Borstal Boy* (1958). His literary reputation is based on two plays, *The Quare Fellow* (1954) and *The Hostage* (1959), but he also published a number of volumes of anecdotal journalism. He died in Dublin in 1964.

Extract from *Brendan Behan's Island* by Brendan Behan, published by Hutchinson & Bernard Geis. Reproduced by kind permission of Random House UK Ltd.

BETJEMAN, John [337] was born in London in 1906. He was educated at Marlborough College and at Magdalen College, Oxford. His most popular books of poetry are *Collected Poems* (1958) and *Summoned by Bells* (1960). He was also an expert on Victoriana. Among his many honours were a knighthood in 1969 and appointment as poet laureate in 1972. He died in Cornwall in 1984.

'Ireland with Emily' from *Collected Poems* by John Betjeman. Reproduced by kind permission of John Murray (Publishers) Ltd.

BOLAND, Eavan [251] was born in Dublin in 1944 and educated at Trinity College Dublin. She has published numerous volumes of poetry, including *Outside History: Selected Poems 1980–1990* (1990) and *An Origin Like Water: Collected Poems* (1996). *Object Lessons* (1995) is a collection of essays. She is a visiting professor at Stanford University, California.

Extract from 'Writing in a Time of Violence' in *Collected Poems*. Reproduced by kind permission of Carcanet Press Limited.

BOLGER, Dermot [42] was born in Dublin in 1959. He began his prolific career as a poet, but is also a successful playwright — *The Lament for Arthur Cleary* (1989) — and novelist — *The Journey Home* (1990). A leading figure in the revival of Dublin writing in the 1980s, he is the founder of Raven Arts Press and New Island Books.

Extract from *The Woman's Daughter* by Dermot Bolger, first published 1987, revised and expanded edition published by Penguin Books, London (1992). Reprinted by kind permission of the author.

BOWEN, Elizabeth [45, 257] was born in Dublin in 1899 and educated at Trinity College Dublin and Oxford University. A major figure in Anglo-Irish literary history, her works include the novels *The Last September* (1929), *The Death of the Heart* (1938) and *The Heat of the Day* (1949). Her *Collected Stories* was published in 1980. In addition to *Bowen's Court* (1942), her non-fiction includes essays and autobiographies. She died in London in 1973.

Extract from *Seven Winters* © 1943 by Elizabeth Bowen, reproduced by kind permission of Curtis Brown, London; and from *Bowen's Court* © 1942, 1964 by Elizabeth Bowen, reproduced by kind permission of Curtis Brown, London and New York.

BROWNE, Noël [291] was born in Waterford in 1915 and educated at Trinity College Dublin. A doctor by training, he was appointed Minister for Health in the inter-party government of 1948. His policies were largely responsible for the eradication of tuberculosis in Ireland, but the opposition of the Catholic hierarchy to his 'Mother and Child' scheme led to his resignation in 1951. He is the author of *Against the Tide* (1986). He died in Connemara in 1997.

Extract from *Against the Tide* by Noël Browne. Reproduced by permission of the publishers, Gill & Macmillan.

BUCKLEY, Vincent [305] was born in 1925 in Romsey, Victoria, Australia and educated at the University of Melbourne. A poet and critic, his *Selected Poems* was published in 1981.

His memoir *Memory Ireland* appeared in 1985. He died in Melbourne in 1988.

BUTLER, Hubert [377] was born in Kilkenny in 1900 and educated at Oxford University. Renowned as an essayist, his writings cover his experiences in Eastern Europe during the 1930s, in wartime Yugoslavia, and as a public-spirited Anglo-Irishman. Four volumes of his essays have been published, and a selection: *The Sub-Prefect Should Have Held His Tongue and other essays* (1990). He died in Bennetsbridge, Co. Kilkenny in 1991.

Extract from 'The Eggman and the Fairies' in *Escape from the Anthill* by Hubert Butler. Reproduced by kind permission of The Lilliput Press.

CAMBRENSIS, Giraldus [1] was born in Pembrokeshire c. 1146 to a high-ranking Norman family. Ordained a priest, he became a noted churchman and served as Archdeacon of Brecon. As well as the *Topography*, his seventeen books include the *Conquest of Ireland*. He failed to realise his clerical ambitions and died in obscurity in 1223.

CARBERY. See Mehigan, P.D.

CARLETON, William [334] was born in Prillisk, Co. Tyrone in 1794. Informally educated, he achieved literary notoriety during the 1830s with his *Traits and Stories of the Irish Peasantry* (1830, 1833). A number of novels followed, among them *The Black Prophet* (1847). He died in Dublin in 1869.

CASEY, John Keegan [223] was born in Mullingar, Co. Westmeath in 1846. Writing under the pseudonym Leo, he produced poems and short stories. His books include *A Wreath of Shamrocks* (1866). He was jailed for membership of the Fenians. He died in Dublin in 1870.

CHESSON, Nora Hopper [180] was born in Exeter, Devonshire in 1871. A student of folklore, she contributed to the cultural ambience of the Celtic Twilight with such books as *Ballads in Prose* (1894) and *Under Quicken Boughs* (1896). She died in London in 1906.

CHURCHILL, Winston [285] was born in Woodstock, Oxfordshire in 1874. His political career included a number of terms as British Prime Minister. A prolific author, among his works are *The Second World War* (6 vols, 1948–53) and *A History of the English-Speaking Peoples* (4 vols, 1956–8). He was awarded the Nobel Prize for Literature in 1953. He died in London in 1965.

COADY, Michael [87] was born in Carrick-on-Suir, Co. Tipperary in 1939 and educated at University College Cork and University College Galway. His volumes of poetry include *Oven Lane* (1987).

'Stopping by a Clare Graveyard After Hours' in *Oven Lane* by Michael Coady. Reproduced by kind permission of the author and The Gallery Press.

COCKBURN, Claud [57] was born in Peking in 1904. Educated at Berkhampstead School and Keble College, Oxford, he worked as a journalist for *The Times* and *The Daily Worker*. He also ran a newspaper of his own, *The Week*. His works include the novel *Beat the Devil* (1953) and *I Claud* (1967), an autobiography. He died in Cork city in 1981.

Extract from *I Claud* by Claud Cockburn. Reproduced by kind permission of the Estate of the late Claud Cockburn.

COLLINS, Michael [278] was born near Clonakilty, Co. Cork in 1890. As an emigrant in London, he joined the Irish Republican Brotherhood and fought in the Easter Rebellion of 1916. He became a central figure in the War of Independence (1919–21), and was a member of the team which negotiated the Treaty of 1921 that established the Irish Free State.

Commander-in-Chief of Free State forces in the Civil War, he was killed in an ambush at Béal na mBláth, Co. Cork in 1922.

Extract from *In Great Haste: The Letters of Michael Collins and Kitty Kiernan*, edited by León Ó Broin. Reproduced by permission of the publishers, Gill & Macmillan.

CONNOLLY, James [262] was born in Glasgow in 1868 and was self-educated. The founder of Irish trade unionism, he is an important figure in the history of world socialism. In 1914 he organised the Irish Citizen Army, a workers' militia which participated in the Easter Rebellion of 1916. A prolific writer, his theoretical works include *Labour in Irish History* (1910) and *The Reconquest of Ireland* (1915). Connolly was executed for his part in the 1916 Rising.

CORKERY, Daniel [18] was born in Cork in 1878 and educated at University College Cork, subsequently becoming Professor of English there. In addition to writing fiction, he was also a playwright, though he is mainly remembered for such works of criticism as *The Hidden Ireland* (1925) and *Synge and Anglo-Irish Literature* (1947). Corkery died in Cork in 1964.

CRAIG, Maurice [33, 163] was born in Belfast in 1919 and educated at Magdalene College, Cambridge and Trinity College Dublin. Author of numerous major works of architectural history, he has also published two volumes of poetry and an autobiography, *The Elephant and the Polish Question* (1990). His major work is *Dublin 1660–1860* (1952).

Extract from *Dublin 1660–1860* and 'Ballad to a Traditional Refrain' by Maurice Craig. Reproduced by kind permission of the author.

CRONIN, Anthony [230] was born in Enniscorthy, Co. Wexford in 1926. A well-known poet — *New and Selected Poems* (1982) — he has written criticism, novels, a memoir — *Dead as Doornails* (1976) — and biographies of Flann O'Brien and Samuel Beckett. From 1980 to 1983 he was artistic and cultural adviser to the Taoiseach.

Extract from *An Irish Eye: Viewpoints* by Anthony Cronin. Reproduced by kind permission of the author.

CURRAN, John Philpot [218] was born in Newmarket, Co. Cork in 1750 and was educated at Trinity College Dublin and at the Middle Temple. A member of the Irish Parliament, he was a leading wit and orator in the heyday of Georgian Dublin. He defended Wolfe Tone after the Rebellion of 1798. He died near London in 1817.

DEANE, Seamus [170] was born in Derry in 1940 and was educated at Queen's University, Belfast and at Cambridge University. A poet, critic and academic, he is the general editor of the three-volume *Field Day Anthology of Irish Writing* (1991). He has published four books of poetry, including *Selected Poems* (1988), and a novel, *Reading in the Dark* (1996). He holds the Donald and Marilyn Keough Chair of English at the University of Notre Dame, Indiana.

'Fair Churchyard of Cregan' translated by Seamus Deane. Reproduced by kind permission of the translator.

DELANY, Mrs, *née* Mary Granville [411], was born in Wiltshire in 1700. She visited Ireland between 1731 and 1733, where she met Patrick Delany. They married in 1743. Her six-volume *Autobiography and Correspondence* (1861–2) contains anecdotes of the leading figures of her day, including Swift. She died in Windsor in 1788.

DE LA TOCNAYE, Chevalier [40, 81, 400, 401]. Jacques Louis de Bougrenet, Chevalier de La Tocnaye, was born in Brittany in 1767. As an officer in the Royal army of France, he was forced to flee the French Revolution in 1792. His *Promenade d'un Français en l'Irlande* appeared in 1797, and in translation a year later. Little is known of his later years.

DE TOCQUEVILLE, Alexis [333] was born in 1805. A year's stay in the United States (1831–2) was the basis of his two-volume work *De la Democratie en Amérique* (1835–40). His other major work is *L'Ancien Régime et la Révolution* (1856). He died in Nice in 1859.

DE VALERA, Eamon [286] was born in New York city in 1882 and reared in Bruree, Co. Limerick. He was educated at Blackrock College and the Royal University of Ireland. A participant in the 1916 Rising, he rejected the 1921 Treaty. In 1926 he founded Fianna Fáil and led it to power in the 1932 election; with de Valera as Taoiseach, the party remained in power until 1948. Two briefer periods as Taoiseach followed in the 1950s. He was elected President for two terms (1959–73). He died in Dublin in 1975.

Extract from *Speeches and Statements by Eamon de Valera 1917–73* edited by Maurice Moynihan. Reproduced by permission of the publishers, Gill & Macmillan

DEVLIN, Polly [175] was born in 1944 in Ardboe, Co. Tyrone. A journalist based in England, she has written for such publications as *Vogue* and *The Sunday Times Magazine*. Her books include *The Vogue History of Photography* (1979) and a novel, *Dora* (1990).

Extract from *All of Us There* by Polly Devlin. Reproduced by kind permission of The Blackstaff Press.

DILLON, Eilís [207] was born in Galway in 1920. A writer of prize-winning children's books and a dramatist, she also wrote a number of historical novels, among which are *Across the Bitter Sea* (1973) and its sequel *Blood Relations* (1977). She died in Dublin in 1994.

'The Lament for Arthur O'Leary' translated by Eilís Dillon. Reproduced by kind permission of Eiléan Ní Chuilleanáin on behalf of the Estate of the late Eilís Dillon.

DUNNE, Seán [62, 326, 339, 431] was born in Waterford city in 1956 and educated at University College Cork. His three volumes of poetry include *The Sheltered Nest* (1991) and *Time and the Island* (1996). The author of two volumes of autobiography, he edited — among other works — *The Cork Anthology* (1993). He also chose the material for the present volume. Seán Dunne died in Cork in 1995.

Extract from *In My Father's House*, 'The Trip To Rome' (translation), extract from *The Road to Silence* and 'The Sea-Blue Eye' (translation) by Seán Dunne. Reproduced by kind permission of the Estate of the late Seán Dunne.

DUNPHY, Eamon [387] was born in Dublin in 1943. After a career as a professional soccer player in England, he became a journalist. His books include *Only A Game?* (1976), *Unforgettable Fire: The Story of U2* (1987) and *A Strange Kind of Glory: Sir Matt Busby and Manchester United* (1991).

Article by Eamon Dunphy in the *Sunday Independent*. Reproduced by kind permission of the author.

DURCAN, Paul [136] was born in Dublin in 1944 and educated at University College Cork. One of the most distinctive poetic voices of his generation, his books include *Teresa's Bar* (1976), *Jesus, Break His Fall* (1980) and *Going Home to Russia* (1987). *A Snail in My Prime: New and Selected Poems* was published in 1993.

'Going Home to Mayo, Winter, 1949' by Paul Durcan. Reproduced by kind permission of the author.

EDGEWORTH, Maria [214] was born in Oxfordshire in 1767, but from an early age lived on her father's estate at Edgeworthstown (now Mostrim), Co. Longford. The author of pioneering works on education and books for children, her fame rests on her novels. In addition to *Castle Rackrent* (1800), these include *Belinda* (1801), *The Absentee* (1812), *Patronage* (1813) and *Ormond* (1817). She died in Edgeworthstown in 1849.

EMMET, Robert [227] was born in Dublin in 1778 and educated at Trinity College Dublin. He joined the United Irishmen while at university. His revolutionary activity culminated with an abortive uprising in 1803. He is remembered less for his politics than for his romantic attachment to Sarah, daughter of John Philpot Curran, and his famous speech from the dock. He was executed in Dublin in 1803.

ENGELS, Friedrich [254] was born in Barmen, Germany in 1820. Through his involvement with the radical group known as the Young Hegelians, he met Karl Marx, with whom he collaborated on *The German Ideology* (1845) and *The Communist Manifesto* (1848). Among his numerous other writings is *The Origins of the Family, Private Property and the State* (1884). He died in London in 1895.

EVANS, Emer Estyn [14] was born in Shrewsbury and educated at the University of Wales, Aberystwyth. Appointed to a lectureship in geography at Queen's University, Belfast in 1928, he produced a series of influential studies on social and environmental issues in Ireland, including *Irish Heritage* (1942), *The Personality of Ireland* (1973, 1981) and *Ireland and the Atlantic Heritage: Selected Writings* (1996). He died in Belfast in 1989.

Extract from *The Personality of Ireland* by E. Estyn Evans. Reproduced by kind permission of Mrs Gwyneth Evans and The Lilliput Press.

FAHY, A. Francis [137] was born in Kinvara, Co. Galway in 1854. A civil servant, he was involved in the Irish Literary Revival in London. A songwriter, his best-known work is 'The Ould Plaid Shawl'. He died in London in 1935.

FALLON, Peter [327] was born in Osnabrück, Germany in 1951 and educated at Trinity College Dublin. In 1970 he founded The Gallery Press, which has published works by many of Ireland's leading poets and playwrights. He has also written a number of volumes of poetry, including *Winter Work* (1983) and *News of the World: Selected Poems* (1993).

'The Rag-tree, Boherard' by Peter Fallon. Reproduced by kind permission of The Gallery Press.

FENNELL, Desmond [121] was born in Belfast in 1929 and educated at University College Dublin and the University of Bonn. A journalist and academic, his often controversial views on modern Irish culture are contained in, among other works, *The State of the Nation: Ireland since the Sixties* (1983) and *Heresy: The Battle for Ideas in Modern Ireland* (1993).

Extract from *A Connacht Journey* by Desmond Fennell. Reproduced by kind permission of the author and Gill & Macmillan.

FERGUSON, Sir Samuel [80] was born in Belfast in 1810 and educated at Trinity College Dublin. His work as an antiquarian and translator of poetry from Irish contributed much to the cultural climate of his day. *The Poems of Samuel Ferguson* (1880) contains most of his verse. He died in Howth, Co. Dublin in 1886.

FOLEY, Donal [98] was born in Ring, Co. Waterford in 1922. After a period working in England, he became news editor of *The Irish Times* in 1963. His satirical column, 'Man Bites Dog', was a popular feature in that newspaper during the 1970s. Several collections of the column were published from 1972. He died in Dublin in 1981.

Extract from *Three Villages* by Donal Foley. Reproduced by kind permission of Patricia Foley.

FRENCH, Percy [168] was born in County Roscommon in 1854 and educated at Trinity College Dublin. His comic songs draw on scenes and characters from the rural Ireland of his day and have been popular ever since. Among his songs are 'The Mountains of Mourne' and 'Phil the Fluter's Ball'. He died in Formby, Lancashire in 1920.

GOGARTY, Oliver St John [44] was born in Dublin in 1878 and educated at Clongowes Wood College and Trinity College Dublin. A noted ear, nose and throat surgeon, he was also associated with the Irish Literary Revival. His *Collected Poems* was published in 1951. He also wrote a number of autobiographical works, including *As I Was Going Down Sackville Street* (1937). He died in New York in 1957.

'An Offering of Swans' in *Collected Poems* by Oliver St John Gogarty. Reproduced by kind permission of Colin Smythe Limited.

GOLDSMITH, Oliver [109] was born in Pallas, Co. Longford in 1728 and educated at Trinity College Dublin. Widely travelled in Europe, he became a much-loved member of Samuel Johnson's celebrated London club. The author of much miscellaneous work, including some notable essays, he also wrote *The Vicar of Wakefield* (1766), a novel, and the play *She Stoops to Conquer* (1773). He died in London in 1774.

GREGORY, Augusta Lady, *née* Persse [147, 323, 324], was born in Roxborough, Co. Galway in 1852. In 1880 she married Sir William Gregory of Coole Park, Co. Galway. After she was widowed in 1892, Coole became one of the nerve-centres of the Irish Literary Revival, to which she contributed, inspired by W.B. Yeats, with translations such as *Gods and Fighting Men* (1904), plays like *The Rising of the Moon* (1907) and her directorship of the Abbey Theatre. She died at Coole in 1932.

Extract from *The Journals*, Vol. 2, edited by Daniel J. Murphy; and extracts from *A Book of Saints and Wonders* by Lady Gregory. Reproduced by kind permission of Colin Smythe Limited, on behalf of Anne de Winton and Catherine Kennedy.

HALL, Anna Maria, *née* Fielding [37], was born in Dublin in 1800 and brought up in County Wexford, the setting for many of her tales. She married Samuel Carter Hall in 1824. Mrs Hall wrote some fifty books, among them *Tales of the Irish Peasantry* (1840) and, with her husband, the three-volume *Ireland, its Scenery, Character, &c* (1841–3). She died in Surrey in 1881.

HALL, Samuel Carter [37] was born near Waterford in 1800. He emigrated to England in 1821 where he had an extensive career as a journalist. Less prolific than his wife, his works include a two-volume autobiography, *Retrospect of a Long Life* (1883). He died in London in 1889.

HARTNETT, Michael [301, 369, 384, 421] was born in Croom, Co. Limerick in 1941. His poems were first published while he was in his teens. Among his early volumes is *Anatomy of a Cliché* (1968). *A Farewell to English* (1975) began a period when he published only in Irish. Two volumes of his *Collected Poems* have appeared (1984; 1989). *New & Selected Poems* was published in 1994.

Extract from 'A Farewell to English', 'The Hag of Beare (1969)', 'There Will Be A Talking', and 'Labasheeda (The Silken Bed)' (translation) by Michael Hartnett. Reproduced by kind permission of the author/translator.

HEALY, Dermot [115] was born in Finea, Co. Westmeath in 1947. Author of a volume of poetry, plays and a memoir, *The Bend for Home* (1996), he is best known for his fiction, in particular *A Goat's Song* (1994). He has worked extensively with local drama groups, and has edited *The Drumlin* and *Force 10*, two succesful periodicals devoted to local artistic and cultural endeavours.

Extract from *A Goat's Song* by Dermot Healy. Reproduced by kind permission of the author.

HEALY, John [157] was born in Charlestown, Co. Mayo in 1930 and became one of Ireland's leading journalists, particularly for his Backbencher column in *The Irish Times*. In addition to *Nobody Shouted Stop!*, he wrote *Nineteen Acres* (1978). He died in Dublin in 1991.

Extract from *Nobody Shouted Stop!* by John Healy. Reproduced by kind permission of the Estate of the late John Healy.

HEANEY, Seamus [21, 185, 351] was born in Mossbawn, Co. Derry in 1939. He was educated at Queen's University, Belfast and trained as a teacher. He is the author of ten books of poetry, including *The Spirit Level* (1996), three volumes of essays, and an adaptation of Philoctetes, *The Cure at Troy* (1990). Among his numerous academic appointments are Professor of Poetry at Oxford University (1989–94) and Boylston Professor of Rhetoric and Oratory at Harvard University. He was the 1995 recipient of the Nobel Prize for Literature.

Extract from 'Sweeney Praises the Trees' in *Sweeney Astray*, 'The Strand at Lough Beg' in *Field Work*, and 'Gallarus Oratory' in *Door into the Dark* by Seamus Heaney. Reproduced by kind permission of Faber and Faber and Farrar Straus & Giroux.

HEWITT, John [186] was born in Belfast in 1907 and educated at Queen's University, Belfast. A leading figure in Northern Irish artistic and cultural circles, he was curator of the Ulster Museum, Belfast and subsequently director of the Herbert Art Gallery, Coventry. A selection of his prose, *Ancestral Voices*, appeared in 1987. His *Complete Poems* was published in 1991. He died in Belfast in 1987.

'Ulster Names' and 'Postscript 1984' by John Hewitt in *The Collected Poems of John Hewitt*, edited by Frank Ormsby. Reproduced by kind permission of the Estate of the late John Hewitt and The Blackstaff Press.

HIGGINS, Aidan [107] was born near Celbridge, Co. Kildare in 1927 and was educated at Clongowes Wood College. He has spent considerable time in England, South Africa, Spain and Berlin. Among his novels are *Langrishe, Go Down* (1966) and *Balcony of Europe* (1967). A memoir, *Donkey's Years*, was published in 1995.

Extract from *Donkey's Years* by Aidan Higgins. Reproduced by kind permission of the author.

HUME, John [309] was born in Derry in 1937 and has lived there all his life. He was an active member of the Northern Ireland Civil Rights Association in the 1960s. First elected to the old devolved Northern Ireland Parliament in 1969, he was a founder member of the Social Democratic and Labour Party the following year. He was a member of the short-lived power-sharing executive of 1974 and since 1979 has been leader of the SDLP. He is also a Westminster MP and a Member of the European Parliament. He is the outstanding constitutional nationalist in Northern Ireland politics, a courageous opponent of all political violence, one who combines a tough-minded intellect with a refusal to despair.

Extract by John Hume from *Field Day Anthology of Irish Writing* (1991). Reproduced by kind permission of the author.

JOHN PAUL II, *né* Karol Wojytola [345], was born in Wadowice, Poland in 1920 and educated at the Jagiellonian University, Kraków and the Angelicum University, Rome. During World War II, he did hard labour under the Nazi occupation. Ordained a priest in

1946, he was consecrated a bishop in 1958, and cardinal in 1967. He was elected Pope in 1978. Among his many publications are plays, poems and a philosophical work, *Osoba i czyn* (1969; *The Acting Person*, 1979).

JOHNSTON, Jennifer [260] was born in Dublin in 1930 and educated at Trinity College Dublin. Daughter of dramatist Denis Johnston (1901–84), she has written a number of plays, but is known mainly for her novels. These include *The Captains and the Kings* (1972), *How Many Miles to Babylon?* (1974) and *The Invisible Worm* (1992).

Extract from *How Many Miles to Babylon?* by Jennifer Johnston. Reproduced by kind permission of the author.

KAVANAGH, Patrick [162, 349, 352] was born in Inniskeen, Co. Monaghan in 1904 but spent his writing life in Dublin. Best known as a poet, he also wrote a number of prose works — *The Green Fool* (1938), an autobiography, and *Tarry Flynn* (1948), a novel. His *Collected Poems* was published in 1964. *Collected Pruse* (1967) is a selection of his literary journalism. He died in Dublin in 1967.

'Shancoduff', extract from 'Lough Derg', and 'Having Confessed' by Patrick Kavanagh. Reproduced by kind permission of the Trustees of the Estate of Patrick Kavanagh, c/o Peter Fallon, Literary Agent, Loughcrew, Oldcastle, Co. Meath.

KEANE, Molly, *née* Skrine [405], was born in County Kildare in 1904. An author with two careers, she was a successful novelist and playwright during the 1930s, writing under the pseudonym M.J. Farrell. Her career lapsed until the publication of the novel *Good Behaviour* in 1981 under her own name. A number of other novels followed. She died in Ardmore, Co. Waterford in 1996.

Extract from *Good Behaviour* by Molly Keane. Reproduced by kind permission of Andre Deutsch Ltd and David Higham Associates.

KEATING, Geoffrey [194, 425] was born in Burgess, near Cahir, Co. Tipperary around 1570. Ordained a priest in Bordeaux, he returned to Ireland where he won fame as a preacher. His reputation now rests on his *History of Ireland*, dating from the 1620s. He also wrote a theological study, *The Three Shafts of Death*, and some poetry. He died in the early 1640s and is buried at Tubrid, Co. Tipperary.

KENNELLY, Brendan [26] was born in Ballylongford, Co. Kerry in 1936 and was educated at Trinity College Dublin and the University of Leeds. The author of two novels, he is known primarily as a poet. His works include *Dream of a Black Fox* (1968), *Cromwell* (1983) and *Judas* (1991). *Journey into Joy: Selected Prose* appeared in 1994. He is Professor of Modern Literature at Trinity College Dublin.

'Sea' by Brendan Kennelly. Reproduced by kind permission of the author.

KETTLE, Thomas M. [261] was born in Dublin in 1880. A classmate of James Joyce at the Royal University of Ireland, he became that institution's first Professor of Economics. He was MP for East Tyrone from 1906 to 1910, though later his nationalism briefly took a more militant turn. Among his writings is a collection of essays, *The Day's Burden* (1918). He died at the Battle of the Somme in 1916.

KICKHAM, Charles J. [253] was born in Mullinahone, Co. Tipperary in 1828. His career as an active republican culminated in his membership of the supreme executive of the Fenian Brotherhood. Having written the novel *Sally Kavanagh* in jail, he devoted himself to literature on his release. *Knocknagow* appeared in 1879. He died in Blackrock, Co. Dublin in 1882.

KIELY, Benedict [311] was born in Dromore, Co. Tyrone in 1919 and educated at University College Dublin. He was literary editor of the *Irish Press* from 1945 to 1964 and has held a number of academic appointments in the United States. His novels include *In a Harbour Green* (1949), *The Cards of the Gambler* (1953) and *Nothing Happens in Carmincross* (1985), and his short stories have been collected in *States of Ireland* (1980).

Extract from *Proxopera: A Tale of Modern Ireland* by Benedict Kiely. Reproduced by kind permission of the author.

KINSELLA, Thomas [328, 329, 361, 376, 421] was born in Dublin in 1928. His work as a poet includes a substantial number of translations from the Irish, notably *The Táin* (1969), and he edited, with Seán Ó Tuama, *An Duanaire: Poems of the Dispossessed 1600–1900* (1981). Many of his poems were collected in *Poems 1956–1973* (1979) and *Peppercannister Poems 1972–1978* (1979). Later work from his Peppercannister Press were collected in *Blood and Family* (1988) and *From Centre City* (1994). His *Collected Poems* was published in 1996.

'To Christ the Seed', 'A Charm for Love and Lasting Affection' and an extract from *The Táin* (all translations) by Thomas Kinsella. Reproduced by kind permission of the translator.

LEDWIDGE, Francis [412] was born in Slane, Co. Meath in 1887 and received little formal education. He worked locally as a labourer and also in Dubin, where he was involved with the cultural and political movements of the day. His *Complete Poems* was published in 1919 and *Selected Poems*, with an introduction by Seamus Heaney, was published in 1992. He was killed in the Great War in 1917.

LEE, J.J. [275, 295] was born in Tralee, Co. Kerry in 1942 and educated at University College Dublin and at Peterhouse, Cambridge. Since 1974 he has been Professor of Modern History (now History) at University College Cork. He was a member of the Irish Senate from 1992 to 1997. His books include *The Modernisation of Irish Society 1848–1914* (1973) and *Ireland 1912–1985: Politics and Society* (1989).

Extracts from *Ireland 1912–1985* by J.J. Lee. Reproduced by kind permission of the author.

LEWIS, Samuel [1, 236] was born in London. A publisher and cartographer, he produced numerous topographical dictionaries and maps of England, Scotland and Wales as well as his *Topographical Dictionary of Ireland* (1837). He died in London in 1865.

LONGLEY, Michael [145, 303] was born in Belfast in 1939 and educated at Royal Belfast Academical Institution and Trinity College Dublin. He worked for the Arts Council of Northern Ireland from 1970 to 1991. His volumes of poetry include *Poems 1963–1983* (1985) and *Gorse Fires* (1991). He has also published *Tuppeny Stung: Autobiographical Chapters* (1994).

'On Mweelrea' and 'The Linen Industry' by Michael Longley. Reproduced by kind permission of the author.

McAUGHTRY, Sam [172] was born in Belfast in 1923. He served in the Royal Air Force in World War II, and worked for many years in the Northern Ireland Civil Service. His books include *Blind Spot* (1979), short stories; a travel book, *Down in the Free State* (1987); and a novel, *Touch and Go* (1993). He was a member of the Irish Senate from 1996 to 1997.

'Funerals Have Lost Their Style' in *Belfast Stories* by Sam McAughtry. Reproduced by kind permission of the author.

McCAFFERTY, Nell [164] was born in Derry in 1944 and educated at Queen's University, Belfast. A noted print and radio journalist, her books include *The Best of Nell* (1984) and *A*

Woman to Blame: The Kerry Baby Story (1985).

Extract from *Peggy Deery* by Nell McCafferty, published by Attic Press, 29 Upper Mount Street, Dublin 2 and by Cleis Press, Publishers Group West, Box 8933, Pittsburgh, PA 15221. Reproduced by kind permission of the author.

McCALL, P.J. [222] was born in Dublin in 1861. Among his well-known ballads are 'Follow Me Up to Carlow' and 'Kelly the Boy from Killann'. His books include *The Shadow of St Patrick* (1894) and *The Fenian Nights' Entertainment* (1897). He died in Dublin in 1919.

McCANN, Eamonn [166] was born in Derry in 1943 and attended Queen's University, Belfast. Actively involved in politics, he has stood in Westminster elections a number of times. His books include *War and an Irish Town* (1974) and *Bloody Sunday in Derry* (1992).

Extract from *War and an Irish Town* by Eamonn McCann. Reproduced by kind permission of the author.

McGAHERN, John [150] was born in Dublin in 1934 and grew up in County Roscommon. He was educated at St Patrick's Training College, Dublin and University College Dublin. Best known for his fiction, particularly the novel *Amongst Women* (1990), he has also written a play, *The Powers of Darkness* (1991). His *Collected Stories* appeared in 1992.

'Why We're Here' in *The Collected Stories* by John McGahern. Reproduced by kind permission of the author.

MacGILL, Patrick [181] was born near Glenties, Co. Donegal in 1891. His early life as an itinerant labourer is the basis for his best-known work, the novels *Children of the Dead End* (1914) and *Moleskin Joe* (1923). He also published several books of poetry, including *Songs of the Dead End* (1912). He died in Fall River, Massachusetts, in 1963.

MacGOWAN, Shane [432], born in London in 1957, is the main singer/song-writer for The Pogues, a folk-rock group. His lyrics, including the famous 'Fairytale of New York', have been published in *Poguetry: The Illustrated Pogues Songbook* (1989).

McGUINNESS, Frank [312] was born in Buncrana, Co. Donegal in 1953 and educated at University College Dublin. A prolific dramatist, his works include *Observe the Sons of Ulster Marching Towards the Somme* (1985), *Innocence* (1986) and *Someone Who'll Watch Over Me* (1992). He has translated plays by Ibsen, Chekhov, Lorca and Brecht.

Article by Frank McGuinness from *The Irish Times*. Reproduced by kind permission of the author.

MacNEICE, Louis [285] was born in Belfast in 1907 and brought up in Carrickfergus, Co. Antrim. He was educated at Marlborough and at Merton College, Oxford. One of the generation of poets who made their names in the 1930s, his best-known volume is *Autumn Journal* (1939). A distinguished critic, he also was a noted radio dramatist. His *Collected Poems* was published in 1966 and his *Selected Plays* in 1993. He died in London in 1963.

'Neutrality' in *Selected Poems* by Louis MacNeice, published by Faber and Faber. Reproduced by kind permission of David Higham Associates.

McWILLIAMS, Brendan [17] was born in Dublin in 1944 and educated at University College Dublin. He is assistant director of Met Éireann, Ireland's meteorological service. His daily 'Weather Eye' column has been appearing in *The Irish Times* since 1988. As well as *Weather Eye* (1994), he has written *Weather Eye on Literature* (1996).

Extract from *Weather Eye* by Brendan McWilliams. Reproduced by kind permission of the author and The Lilliput Press.

MADDEN, Deirdre [20] was born in Belfast in 1960 and educated at Trinity College Dublin and at the University of East Anglia. Among her novels are *Remembering Light and Stone* (1992), *Nothing is Black* (1994) and *One by One in the Darkness* (1996).

Extract from *Nothing is Black* by Deirdre Madden. Reproduced by kind permission of the author.

MAHON, Derek [90] was born in Belfast in 1941 and educated at Royal Belfast Academical Institution and Trinity College Dublin. His volumes of poetry include *Selected Poems* (1992) and *The Hudson Letter* (1996). Among his translations from the French are *Phillippe Jaccottet: Selected Poems* (1987). His version of Racine's *Phèdre* premièred at the Gate Theatre, Dublin in 1996.

'A Disused Shed in Co. Wexford' by Derek Mahon. Reproduced by kind permission of the author.

MAHONY, Francis Sylvester [59] was born in Cork in 1804. He was educated at Clongowes Wood College and abroad. Ordained a priest in 1832, by 1834 he was a London journalist using the pseudonym 'Father Prout'. *The Reliques of Father Prout* (1837) is a collection of his humorous articles and verse. He died in Paris in 1866.

MANSFIELD, Katherine, *née* Beauchamp [269], was born in Wellington, New Zealand in 1888. Her noted short stories were published in two collections, *Bliss* (1920) and *The Garden Party* (1922). In 1918 she married the critic John Middleton Murry. She died in Fontainebleau in 1923.

MARCUS, David [413] was born in Cork in 1924 and educated at University College Cork and King's Inns, Dublin. The author of a number of historical novels, he is also renowned as an editor. He co-edited *Irish Writing* (1946–54) and edited *Poetry Ireland* (1948–54) and the 'New Irish Writing' page of the *Irish Press* (1968–86). He has also edited a number of anthologies of Irish short fiction.

Extract from *The Midnight Court* translated by David Marcus in *Taisce Duan: A Treasury of Irish Poems with Translations in English*. Reproduced by kind permission of the translator.

MEEHAN, Paula [347] was born in Dublin in 1955 and educated at Trinity College Dublin and at Eastern Washington University. Her volumes of poetry include *The Man who was Marked by Winter* (1991) and *Pillow Talk* (1994).

'The Statue of the Virgin at Granard Speaks' by Paula Meehan. Reproduced by kind permission of the author.

MEHIGAN, P.D. [388] was born in Ardfield, Co. Cork in 1884. After a career in the civil service, as 'Carbery' his name became synonymous with sport in Ireland, particularly hurling. His journalism appeared regularly in *The Irish Times* and *The Cork Weekly Examiner*. *Vintage Carbery* (1984) is a selection of his work. He died in Dublin in 1965.

Extract from *Vintage Carbery* by P.D. Mehigan. Reproduced by kind permission of Denis Mehigan and Seán Kilfeather.

MERRIMAN, Brian [413] was born around 1749 in Ennistymon, Co. Clare. A farmer and a hedge-schoolmaster, he is primarily known for his much-translated poem *The Midnight Court*, which is thought to date from 1780. He also taught mathemathics. He died in Limerick in 1805.

MEYER, Kuno [320, 325, 374] was born in Hamburg in 1858 and educated at Edinburgh and Leipzig universities. A major figure in the fields of Irish language, linguistics and textual scholarship, he founded the School of Irish Learning in Dublin in 1903. His *Selections from Ancient Irish Poetry* (1911) is a volume of translations. He died in Leipzig in 1919.

MILLIKEN, Richard [55] was born in Castlemartyr, Co. Cork in 1767. A poet and novelist, he is remembered only for 'The Groves of Blarney'. He died in Cork in 1815.

MITCHEL, John [237] was born in Dungiven, Co. Derry in 1815 and educated at Trinity College Dublin. A militant nationalist, he was a Young Irelander and edited *The Nation*. In 1848 he founded his own newspaper, *The United Irishman*. Its revolutionary rhetoric led to Mitchel's arrest and transportation to Australia. The latter experience is the basis of his best-known work, *Jail Journal* (1854). His escape eventually led to his return to Ireland, via the United States. He died in Newry in 1875.

MONTAGUE, John [4, 179, 193] was born in Brooklyn, New York in 1929, and grew up in Garvaghey, Co. Tyrone. He was educated at University College Dublin and Yale University. His numerous volumes of poetry include *A Chosen Light* (1967) and *The Rough Field* (1972). Among his other works are two collections of short stories, *Death of a Chieftain* (1964) and *A Love Present and other stories* (1997), and *The Figure in the Cave* (1989), essays. His *Collected Poems* was published in 1995.

'Windharp', 'Dancehall' and 'The First Invasion of Ireland' by John Montague from *Collected Poems* published by The Gallery Press. Reproduced by kind permission of the author and The Gallery Press.

MOORE, Thomas [114, 235] was born in Dublin in 1779 and was educated at Trinity College Dublin. He went to London in 1799. His *Irish Melodies* began appearing in 1807. Other volumes of poetry include *Lalla Rookh* (1817). Moore also wrote biographies of Richard Brinsley Sheridan, Lord Edward Fitzgerald and Lord Byron. He died in Wiltshire in 1852.

MULDOON, Paul [300, 310] was born in Portadown, Co. Armagh in 1951 and grew up in Collegelands, Co. Armagh. He was educated at Queen's University, Belfast. His books of poetry include *New Weather* (1973), *Meeting the British* (1987) and *The Annals of Chile* (1994). He teaches at Princeton University.

'Anseo' and 'Ireland' from *Why Brownlee Left* by Paul Muldoon. Reproduced by kind permission of Faber and Faber and Wake Forest University Press.

MURPHY, Dervla [67] was born in Lismore, Co. Waterford in 1931. She has written works of social commentary, but is noted mainly for her travel books. Among these are *Full Tilt* (1965), *Tibetan Foothold* (1966) and *A Place Apart* (1978), about Northern Ireland. *Wheels Within Wheels* (1979) is an autobiography.

Extract from *Wheels Within Wheels* by Dervla Murphy. Reproduced by kind permission of John Murray (Publishers) Ltd.

MURPHY, Richard [27, 203] was born in County Galway in 1927 and spent some of his childhood in Sri Lanka. He was educated at Wellington and Magdalen College, Oxford. Among his books of poetry are *Sailing to an Island* (1963) and *The Battle of Aughrim* (1968). Sri Lankan culture and art are used in *The Mirror Wall* (1989).

'Pat Cloherty's Version of *The Maisie*', and 'Planter' and 'Rapparees' from *The Battle of Aughrim* by Richard Murphy. Reproduced by kind permission of the author.

NELSON, E. Charles [22] was born in Northern Ireland and educated at the University College of Wales at Aberystwyth and the Australian National University. He has been on the staff of the National Botanic Gardens, Dublin and wrote its history, 'The Brightest Jewel': A History of the National Botanic Gardens (1987). His other books include The Shamrock: The Botany and History of an Irish Myth (1991) and, with Wendy Walsh, The Burren (1991).

Extract from The Trees of Ireland by E. Charles Nelson and Wendy Walsh. Reproduced by kind permission of the authors and The Lilliput Press.

NÍ CHUILLEANÁIN, Eiléan [280] was born in Cork in 1942 and educated at University College Cork and Oxford University. Her first collection of poems was Acts and Monuments (1972). Other books include Site of Ambush (1975) and The Magdalene Sermon (1989). She teaches English at Trinity College Dublin.

Extract from Site of Ambush by Eiléan Ní Chuilleanáin, published by The Gallery Press. Reproduced by kind permission of the author.

NÍ DHOMHNAILL, Nuala [297, 421] was born in St Helen's, Lancashire in 1952, grew up near Ventry, Co. Kerry and was educated at University College Cork. The most celebrated writer in Irish of her generation, her books of poems include An Dealg Droighin (1981), An Féar Suaithinseach (1984) and Feis (1991). Two selections of her works in English translation, Pharaoh's Daughter and The Astrakhan Cloak, appeared in 1991.

The Corpse That Sits Up and Talks Back and 'Labasheeda' by Nuala Ní Dhomhnaill. Reproduced by kind permission of the author.

Ó BRAONÁIN, Micheál [89]. Nothing is known of his origins or end. His only known work is Príomhshruth Éireann ('Ireland's Chief River'), about the Shannon, which he completed in 1794 while living near the town of Roscommon.

O'BRIEN, Edna [417] was born in Tuamgraney, Co. Clare in 1930. She has lived in London since 1959. Among her many novels are a trilogy, The Country Girls (1960), The Lonely Girl (1962) and Girls in their Married Bliss (1963); A Pagan Place (1971) and House of Splendid Isolation (1994). A Fanatic Heart (1982) is a selection of her short stories. Other works include Mother Ireland (1976).

Extract from Johnny I Hardly Knew You by Edna O'Brien. Reproduced by kind permission of The Wylie Agency.

O'BRIEN, Flann, né Brian O'Nolan [381], was born in Strabane, Co. Tyrone in 1911 and educated at University College Dublin. Working in the civil service, he published one unique novel, At Swim-Two-Birds (1939), and wrote another, The Third Policeman (1967). Under the pen-name Myles na gCopaleen, he wrote a celebrated satirical column for The Irish Times from 1940 until his death. Other novels include An Béal Bocht (1941; The Poor Mouth, 1964), The Hard Life (1961) and The Dalkey Archive (1964). He died in Dublin in 1966.

Extract from At Swim-Two-Birds by Flann O'Brien, Copyright © The Estate of the Late Brian O'Nolan. Reproduced by kind permission of A.M. Heath.

O'BRIEN, George [64] was born in Enniscorthy, Co. Wexford in 1945 and was reared in Lismore, Co. Waterford. Educated at Ruskin College, Oxford and the University of Warwick, he is Professor of English, Georgetown University, Washington D.C. He is the author of an autobiographical trilogy and of two books on Brian Friel. He has provided the introduction, head notes and original footnotes for this anthology.

Extract from *The Village of Longing* by George O'Brien. Reproduced by kind permission of the author.

O'BRIEN, Kate [83] was born in Limerick in 1897 and educated at University College Dublin. Her novels include *Without My Cloak* (1931), *The Land of Spices* (1941) and *That Lady* (1946). Other works include *Teresa of Avila* (1951), *Presentation Parlour* (1963) and *My Ireland* (1962). She died in Canterbury, Kent in 1974.

Extract from *The Land of Spices* by Kate O'Brien. Reproduced by kind permission of John O'Brien.

Ó BRUADAIR, Daibhí [402] was born c. 1625 near Carrigtwohill, Co. Cork. A good deal of his life was spent in County Limerick. His poetry deals forcefully with the ruinous historical events of his time. *Ó Bruadair* (1985) is a volume of his verse in translations by Michael Hartnett. Ó Bruadair died in 1698.

O'CASEY, Sean [266] was born in Dublin in 1880. A self-educated worker, he became active in trade union politics and in organising the Irish Citizen Army in 1913. His most famous works are the plays *The Shadow of a Gunman* (1923), *Juno and the Paycock* (1924) and *The Plough and the Stars* (1926). After the rejection of a World War I play, *The Silver Tassie* (1928), O'Casey settled in England. He wrote many other plays, and his other notable work is a six-volume autobiography, *Mirror in My House* (1939–54). He died in Torquay, Devon in 1964.

Extract from *The Plough and the Stars* by Sean O'Casey. Reproduced by kind permission of Macmillan General Books.

O'CONNOR, Frank, *né* Michael O'Donovan [24, 111, 196, 201, 423], was born in Cork in 1903. A participant and internee during the Civil War, he trained as a librarian and began to write his widely admired short stories. Among his works are *Collected Stories* (1981); the novel *Dutch Interior* (1940); translations from the Irish, *Kings, Lords & Commons* (1959); an autobiography, *An Only Child* (1961); and a study of the short story, *The Lonely Voice* (1962). He died in Dublin in 1966.

'The Blackbird by Belfast Lough', 'The Viking Terror', 'Last Lines' and 'I Am Stretched On Your Grave' (translations) and extract from *Irish Miles* by Frank O'Connor. Reproduced by kind permission of Harriet O'Donovan Sheehy.

Ó CRIOMHTHAIN, Tomás [70] was born on the Great Blasket Island, off County Kerry, in 1856. Encouraged by writers from the mainland, he began to write in 1917. In addition to *The Islandman* (1934), his two other works have also appeared in translation: *Lore from the Western Island* (1956) and *Island Cross-Talk* (1986). He died on the Great Blasket in 1937.

Extract from *The Islandman* by Tomás Ó Criomhthain translated by Robin Flower (1951). Reproduced by kind permission of Oxford University Press.

O'DONOGHUE, Bernard [391] was born in Cullen, Co. Cork in 1945 and educated at Oxford University. Among his books of poetry are *Poaching Rights* (1987) and *Gunpowder* (1995). His works of criticism include *Seamus Heaney and the Language of Poetry* (1994). He is a lecturer in medieval English language and Anglo-Irish literature at Wadham College, Oxford.

'Munster Final' in *Poaching Rights* by Bernard O'Donoghue published by The Gallery Press. Reproduced by kind permission of the author.

O'DRISCOLL, Dennis [78] was born in Thurles, Co. Tipperary in 1954 and educated at University College Dublin. A civil servant, his books of poetry are *Kist* (1982), *Hidden*

Extras (1987), *Long Story Short* (1993), *The Bottom Line* (1994) and *Quality Time* (1997). He has also written criticism.

'Thurles' from *Hidden Extras* by Dennis O'Driscoll, published by Anvil Press, London and Dedalus Press, Dublin, 1987. Reproduced by kind permission of the author.

O'FAOLAIN, Sean [58, 196] was born in Cork in 1900 and educated at University College Cork and Harvard University. Noted for his short stories — *Collected Stories* (3 vols, 1980–82) — his many other works include novels, foremost among them *Bird Alone* (1936); biographies of Daniel O'Connell, *King of the Beggars* (1938) and Hugh O'Neill, *The Great O'Neill* (1942); numerous works of criticism of which *The Irish* (1948) is the best known; and an autobiography, *Vive Moi!* (1964; 1993). His founding and editing of the periodical *The Bell* is a landmark in modern Irish cultural history. He died in Dún Laoghaire, Co. Dublin in 1991.

Extracts from *An Irish Journey* by Sean O'Faolain. Copyright © 1940 Sean O'Faolain; and from *The Great O'Neill, A Biography of Hugh O'Neill, Earl of Tyrone* by Sean O'Faolain. Copyright © 1942 Sean O'Faolain. Reproduced by kind permission of the Estate of Sean O'Faolain c/o Rogers, Coleridge & White Ltd, 20 Powis Mews, London W11 1JN.

O'FLAHERTY, Liam [132] was born on Inishmore, Aran Islands in 1896. He saw action and was wounded in World War I, and took part in the Irish Civil War. A prolific novelist and short-story writer, his works include the novels *The Informer* (1925), *Skerrett* (1932) and *Famine* (1937), and *The Stories of Liam O'Flaherty* (1956). Among his various other books are three volumes of autobiography. He died in Dublin in 1984.

'The Black Bullock' in *The Short Stories of Liam O'Flaherty*. Reproduced by kind permission of The Peters, Fraser and Dunlop Group Limited on behalf of: The Estate of Liam O'Flaherty. © Liam O'Flaherty 1937.

O'GRADY, Desmond [76] was born in Limerick in 1935. Educated at University College Dublin and Harvard University, he has spent long periods in Mediterranean countries. His many books include *Chords and Orchestrations* (1956), *The Dark Edge of Europe* (1967), *A Limerick Rake* (1978) and *Seven Arabic Odes* (1991).

'Tipperary' by Desmond O'Grady. Reproduced by kind permission of the author.

O'GRADY, Standish James [364] was born in Castletown Berehaven, Co. Cork in 1846 and educated at Trinity College Dublin. He was called to the Bar in 1872. His versions of ancient Irish legends — which include *History of Ireland: The Heroic Period* (1878) and *History of Ireland: Cuchulain and His Contemporaries* (1880) — influenced younger writers such as W.B. Yeats. Among his other works are *The Flight of the Eagle* (1897), a novel, and various retellings of the legends for children. A staunch Unionist, his political commentaries include *Toryism and Tory Democracy* (1886). He died on the Isle of Wight in 1928.

Ó HEITHIR, Breandán [392] was born on Inishmore, Aran Islands, in 1930 and was educated at University College Galway. His non-fiction books include *Over the Bar* (1984) and *The Begrudger's Guide to Irish Politics* (1986). He translated his first novel from the Irish: *Lead Us Into Temptation* (1978). He died in Dublin in 1990.

Extract from *Over the Bar* by Breandán Ó hEithir. Reproduced by kind permission of Poolbeg Group Services.

O'MALLEY, Ernie [272] was born in Castlebar, Co. Mayo in 1898 and grew up in Dublin. A participant in the Easter Rising, he played a prominent part in the War of Independence and in the Civil War. In addition to *On Another Man's Wound* (1936), his publications include two posthumous volumes, *The Singing Flame* (1978) and *Raids and Rallies* (1982). He died at Howth, Co. Dublin in 1957.

O'MALLEY, Tony [94] was born in Callan, Co. Kilkenny in 1913. His early working life was spent as a bank official, from which ill health obliged him to retire in 1958. Generally regarded as one of the most original and distinctive painters of his generation, in 1993 Aosdána elected him to the rank of Saoi.

Inscape — Life and Landscape in Callan and County Kilkenny by Tony O'Malley. Reproduced by kind permission of the author.

O'MEARA, John J. [372] was born in Eyrecourt, Co. Galway in 1915 and was educated at University College Dublin and Oxford University. He became Professor of Latin at University College Dublin in 1948. An international authority on the works of St Augustine, his works also include translations of *Navigatio Sancti Brendani* (1976) and of Giraldus Cambrensis's *The History and Topography of Ireland* (1951; 1982).

Ó RATHAILLE, Aodhaghán [201] was born in 1670 in rural County Kerry. Generally noted as the finest Irish language poet of his generation, his verse records with pained fervour the disruptive conditions of the Ireland of his day. He died in County Kerry in 1729.

ORMSBY, Frank [344] was born in Enniskillen, Co. Fermanagh in 1947 and was educated at Queen's University, Belfast. His books of poems include *A Store of Candles* (1977), *Northern Spring* (1986) and *The Ghost Train* (1995). He edited *The Honest Ulsterman* for many years and has edited numerous anthologies and *The Collected Poems of John Hewitt* (1991).

PAISLEY, Ian [342] was born in Armagh in 1926 and educated at South Wales Bible College and the Reformed Presbyterian Theological College, Belfast. Ordained in 1946, he is the leading cleric-politician in Northern Ireland, and has been elected to parliament on numerous occasions. His many books include *The Massacre of St Bartholomew* (1972), *Jonathan Edwards: The Theologian of Revival* (1987) and *The Revised English Bible: An Exposure* (1990).

Extract from *What Think Ye of Christ?* by Ian Paisley. Reproduced by kind permission of the author.

PAULIN, Tom [304] was born in Leeds in 1949 and brought up in Belfast. He was educated at the University of Hull and Oxford University. Among his volumes of poetry are *A State of Justice* (1977), *Liberty Tree* (1983) and *Walking a Line* (1994). His works of criticism include *Ireland and the English Question* (1984) and *Minotaur: Poetry and the Nation State* (1992). He is a director of the Field Day Company.

'Of Difference Does it Make' by Tom Paulin. Reproduced by kind permission of the author.

PEARSE, Patrick [429] was born in Dublin in 1879 and was educated at the Royal University of Ireland. He was editor of the newspaper *An Claidheamh Soluis* ('The Sword of Light') and in 1908 established the bilingual school, Scoil Eanna. An essayist, poet and dramatist, his collected works were published in 1917. He was Commander-in-Chief of the republican forces in the Easter Rising and was executed in May 1916.

PLUNKETT, James, *né* James Plunkett Kelly [105], was born in Dublin in 1920. As a young man he was an active trade unionist. The author of plays and short stories, he is known mainly as a novelist. His novels include *Strumpet City* (1969), *Farewell Companions* (1977) and *The Circus Animals* (1990).

Extract from *The Gems She Wore* by James Plunkett. Reproduced by kind permission of the author.

POCOCKE, Richard [127] was born in Southampton in 1704 and educated at Corpus Christi College, Oxford. Widely travelled in Europe and the Near East, he held numerous ministries in the Church of Ireland, eventually becoming Bishop of Meath. *Pococke's Tour of Ireland* is one of his many travel books. He died near Tullamore, Co. Offaly in 1765.

PRAEGER, Robert Lloyd [11] was born in Hollywood, Co. Down in 1865 and educated at Queen's College, Belfast. He worked as an engineer and a librarian, his botanical interests emerging fully only in retirement. His books include *The Botanist in Ireland* (1934), *The Way That I Went* (1937) and *The Natural Life of Ireland* (1950). He died in Belfast in 1953.

Extract from *The Way That I Went* by Robert Lloyd Praeger. Reproduced by kind permission of Allen Figgis.

PROUT, Father. See Mahony, Francis Sylvester.

QUINLAN, P.F. [281] (n.d.). His career was spent mainly in farmers' organisations, in particular Macra na Feirme (Sons of the Farm) and the Irish Agricultural Organisation, of which he became president. He was also agriculture columnist for *The Irish Times*.

ROBINSON, Mary, *née* Bourke [315], was born in Ballina, Co. Mayo in 1944. She was educated at Trinity College Dublin, King's Inns and Harvard University. She was a law lecturer at Trinity, and has served in the Irish Senate and as a member of Dublin City Council. She was President of Ireland 1990–97. She is the United Nations High Commissioner for Human Rights.

ROBINSON, Tim [123] was born in Yorkshire in 1935 and educated at Cambridge University. An artist and a cartographer as well as a writer, he moved to Ireland in 1972, living first on the Aran Islands, then in Connemara. His time there provided the basis for his two noted works, *Stones of Aran: Pilgrimage* (1986) and *Stones of Aran: Labyrinth* (1995).

Extract from *Stones of Aran: Pilgrimage* by Tim Robinson. Reproduced by kind permission of the author and The Lilliput Press.

ROSS, Martin. See Somerville and Ross.

SHAW, Bernard [283] was born in Dublin in 1856 and moved to London in 1876. Initially a novelist and journalist, he went on to become the most celebrated playwright of his day. Among his many well-known plays are *John Bull's Other Island* (1904), *Man and Superman* (1905), *Pygmalion* (1913) and *Heartbreak House* (1921). A noted controversialist and outspoken socialist, he published widely on issues of the day. He died in Hertfordshire in 1950.

Extract from *John Bull's Other Island* by Bernard Shaw. Reproduced by kind permission of The Society of Authors on behalf of the Bernard Shaw Estate.

SKEFFINGTON, Andrée Sheehy [289] was born in Amiens, France in 1910 and educated at the Sorbonne. She is the author of her husband's biography, *Skeff: A Life of Owen Sheehy Skeffington 1909–1970* (1991).

Extract from *Skeff* by Andrée Sheehy Skeffington. Reproduced by kind permission of the author and The Lilliput Press.

SKEFFINGTON, Hanna Sheehy [268] was born in Kanturk, Co. Cork in 1877 and educated at the Royal University of Ireland. A feminist and social activist, her many writings include *British Militarism as I Have Known It* (1918). She died in Dublin in 1946.

SOMERVILLE, Edith and Ross, Martin [129]. Edith Somerville was born on the island of Corfu, Greece in 1858. After studying art in London and Paris, she settled at Drishane, Skibbereen, Co. Cork. In 1886, she became friends and literary collaborators with her second cousin, 'Martin Ross', *née* Violet Martin, born in Ballinahinch, Co. Galway in 1862. Together they wrote a noted series of short stories detailing episodes in the life of a Resident Magistrate in rural Ireland, including *Some Experiences of an Irish RM* (1899) and *Further Experiences of an Irish RM* (1908). Among their other works is the novel *The Real Charlotte* (1894). The collaboration survived in name after Violet Martin's death in 1915. Among Edith Somerville's later works is the novel *The Big House at Inver* (1925). She died at Drishane in 1949.

Extract from *Through Connemara in a Governess Cart* by Somerville and Ross. Reproduced by kind permission of Little, Brown UK.

SOMERVILLE-LARGE, Peter [402] was born in 1928 and educated at Trinity College Dublin. A noted traveller, his books about Ireland include *From Bantry Bay to Leitrim* (1974), *Dublin* (1979) and *Cappaghglass* (1985).

Extract from *The Irish Country House* by Peter Somerville-Large. Reproduced by kind permission of the author.

SPENSER, Edmund [7] was born in London in 1552 and educated at Merchant Taylors' School and Pembroke Hall, Cambridge. One of the leading English poets of his day as well as an important imperial civil servant, Spenser was well acquainted with such poet-courtiers as Sir Philip Sidney and Sir Walter Raleigh. In addition to *The Faerie Queen*, his poems include *The Shepheardes Calendar* (1579), *Amoretti*, a sonnet sequence which was a prelude to the famous wedding song with which it was published, *Epithalamion* (1595). He died in London in 1599.

STEPHENS, James [402] was born in Dublin in 1882. Essayist, poet, editor and novelist, his most noted work is the novel *The Crock of Gold* (1912). His other fiction includes the novels *The Charwoman's Daughter* (1912) and *Deirdre* (1923), and the short-story collection *Etched in Moonlight* (1928). His *Collected Poems* appeared in 1926. He also wrote an eyewitness account of Easter 1916, *The Insurrection in Dublin* (1916). He died in London in 1950.

'A Glass of Beer', translation by James Stephens. Reproduced by kind permission of The Society of Authors as the Literary Representative of the Estate of James Stephens.

STUART, Francis [11] was born in Townsville, Queensland, Australia in 1902 and brought up in County Antrim. He was educated at Rugby. In 1920 he married Iseult Gonne. His early work drew praise from Yeats. Among his numerous pre-war books are the novels *The Coloured Dome* (1932), *Pigeon Irish* (1932) and *Try the Sky* (1933). After spending World War II in Berlin, he resumed his career as a novelist with *The Pillar of Cloud* (1948). Many other novels followed, notably *Black-List Section H* (1971). Aosdána elected him to the rank of Saoi in 1996.

'Ireland' by Francis Stuart. Reproduced by kind permission of New Island Books.

SWIFT, Jonathan [205, 408] was born in Dublin in 1667 and educated at Kilkenny School and Trinity College Dublin. He was a member of Sir William Temple's household at Moor Park, Surrey. There he wrote *A Tale of a Tub* and *The Battle of the Books*. His most famous work is *Gulliver's Travels* (1726), though his poems and political writings are also of great interest and importance. Swift is one of the handful of central figures in Anglo-Irish writing. He served as Dean of St Patrick's Cathedral, Dublin from 1713 until his death in 1745.

SYNGE, Alexander [126] was born in Dublin in 1821. An uncle of the playwright J.M. Synge, he served on Aran from 1851 to 1855. Later he was appointed rector of St Peter's, Ipswich. He died in Sussex in 1872.

SYNGE, John Millington [24, 25, 103, 430] was born in Rathfarnham, Co. Dublin in 1871 and was educated at Trinity College Dublin and at the Royal Irish Academy of Music. He was a proficient violinist. His career took shape when he began to write for the Irish National Theatre, and later the Abbey. His works include *Riders to the Sea* (1904), *The Well of the Saints* (1905) and one of the classics of modern Irish theatre, *The Playboy of the Western World* (1907). He died in Dublin in 1909.

TAYLOR, Alice [407] was born in 1938 in Newmarket, Co. Cork. Her books include the runaway bestseller, *To School through the Fields* (1988), *Quench the Lamp* (1990) and *The Village* (1992).

Extract from *The Night Before Christmas* by Alice Taylor. Reproduced by kind permission of Brandon Book Publishers Ltd.

THACKERAY, William Makepeace [74, 140, 330] was born in India in 1811 and educated at Charterhouse and at Trinity College, Cambridge. He trained as an artist in Paris, and then began to write under a number of pseudonyms for *Fraser's Magazine*. One of the pseudonyms was Michael Angelo Titmarsh, used for *The Irish Sketch Book* (1843). Among the most prominent novelists of the early Victorian period, Thackeray's works include *Vanity Fair* (1848), *Pendennis* (1851) and *The History of Henry Esmond* (1852). He died in London in 1863.

THOMSON, David [118] was born in India and grew up in England and Scotland. He was educated at Oxford and worked for the BBC and UNESCO. In addition to *Woodbrook*, his books include *In Camden Town* (1983) and *Nairn in Darkness and Light* (1987). He died in London in 1988.

TÓIBÍN, Colm [158] was born in Enniscorthy, Co. Wexford in 1955 and was educated at University College Dublin. A prolific journalist, his non-fiction books include *The Sign of the Cross* (1994). He has also written three novels, among them *The Heather Blazing* (1992) and *The Story of the Night* (1996).

Extract from *Walking Along the Border* by Colm Tóibín. Reproduced by kind permission of the author.

TREVOR, William [52] was born in Mitchelstown, Co. Cork in 1928 and was educated at Trinity College Dublin. Among his many prize-winning novels are *The Old Boys* (1964), *Fools of Fortune* (1983) and the novellas *Two Lives* (1991). His short-story collections include *The Ballroom of Romance* (1972) and *The Collected Stories* (1992). He has also edited *The Oxford Book of Irish Short Stories* (1989) and written *A Writer's Ireland* (1984).

Extract from *Excursions in the Real World* by William Trevor. Reproduced by kind permission of Random House UK Ltd and of Peters, Fraser and Dunlop.

WADDELL, Helen [324] was born in Tokyo in 1889 and educated at Queen's University, Belfast and Oxford University. A noted medieval scholar, her best-known work is *The Wandering Scholars* (1927). Among her other works is *Peter Abelard* (1933), a novel. She died in London in 1965.

Extract from *Beasts and Saints* by Helen Waddell. Reproduced by kind permission of Constable & Co. Ltd.

WALSH, Wendy [22] was born in Westmoreland, England. A noted botanical artist, her works include *An Irish Florilegium* (1983), *An Irish Florilegium II* (1988) and, with E. Charles Nelson, *The Burren* (1991).

Extract from *The Trees of Ireland* by E. Charles Nelson and Wendy Walsh. Reproduced by kind permission of the authors and The Lilliput Press.

WATERS, John [153, 394] was born in Castlerea, Co. Roscommon in 1955. One of Ireland's best-known journalists, his books include *Jiving at the Crossroads* (1991), *Race of Angels: Ireland and the Genesis of U2* (1994) and *An Intelligent Person's Guide to Modern Ireland* (1997).

Extract from *Jiving at the Crossroads* by John Waters, reproduced by kind permission of the author and The Blackstaff Press; and from *Race of Angels* by John Waters, reproduced by kind permission of the author and Fourth Estate Ltd.

WHYTE, Laurence [395] was born in County Westmeath around 1700. Little is known of his life, apart from the fact that he was a schoolmaster and published two volumes of poetry, including *Original Poems on Several Occasions* (1740). He died in Dublin in 1755.

YEATS, William Butler [146, 255, 270, 363, 423] was born in Dublin in 1865 and spent much of his childhood in Sligo. Early in his career as a poet he espoused many of the prominent political and cultural causes of the day, including theosophism and nationalism. He was also the inspiration of the activity that led to the creation of the Abbey Theatre in 1904. A prolific writer of poetry, prose and drama, his works include the plays *Cathleen ni Houlihan* (1902), *On Baile's Strand* (1904), *Purgatory* (1939) and *The Death of Cuchulain* (1939); *Autobiographies* (1955); and *Collected Poems* (1950). Yeats died at Roquebrune, France in 1939 and is buried in Drumcliff, Co. Sligo.

'The Wild Swans at Coole', 'Come Gather Round Me, Parnellites', 'Easter 1916', 'Cuchulain Comforted' and 'He wishes for the Cloths of Heaven' by W.B. Yeats. Reproduced by kind permission of A.P. Watt Ltd on behalf of Michael Yeats; and Simon & Schuster from *The Collected Works of W.B. Yeats*, Volume I: *The Poems*, revised and edited by Richard J. Finneran (New York: Macmillan, 1989).

YOUNG, Arthur [5] was born in Suffolk in 1741. Best known as a prolific and influential writer on agricultural matters, he was also a political commentator of note. His *Tour in Ireland* had less public impact than his *Travels in France* (1792). He died in London in 1820.

The Publishers have used their best efforts to trace all copyright-holders and have sought and received permission from each contributor in this anthology. However, they will make the usual and appropriate arrangements with any who may have been overlooked inadvertently and who contact them.